NORTH
A

San Francisco

Los Angeles

30°

Tropic of Cancer

20°

*A C I F I C*

CENTRAL
AMERICA

10°

PANAMA CANA

Equator                    0°

GALAPAGOS
ISLANDS

Guayaqu

MARQUESAS

10°

| O | 500 | 1000 | | 2000 |
Scale of Miles

TUAMOTU ARCHIPELAGO

AHITI

20°

Tropic of Capricorn

ISLANDS

PITCAIRN I.

EASTER I.

Valparai

30°

JUAN FERNÁNDEZ
IS.

Santia

Concepción

40°

*P A C I F I C*

*C E A N*

SOUTH

AMERICA

50°

140°        120°        100°        80°        Cape

*Samoa 1830 to 1900*

R. P. GILSON

# Samoa 1830 to 1900

## THE POLITICS OF
## A MULTI-CULTURAL COMMUNITY

*with an introduction and conclusion by*
J. W. DAVIDSON

MELBOURNE
OXFORD UNIVERSITY PRESS
LONDON WELLINGTON NEW YORK
1970

*Oxford University Press, Ely House, London, W.1*

GLASGOW NEW YORK TORONTO MELBOURNE WELLINGTON
CAPE TOWN SALISBURY IBADAN DAR ES SALAAM NAIROBI LUSAKA ADDIS ABABA
BOMBAY CALCUTTA MADRAS KARACHI LAHORE DACCA
KUALA LUMPUR SINGAPORE HONG KONG TOKYO

*Oxford University Press, 7 Bowen Crescent, Melbourne*

*This book has been published with the assistance
of the Republic of Nauru Fund of the Australian
National University.*

© Oxford University Press 1970

SBN 19 550301 5

134898.

Registered in Australia for transmission by post as a book
PRINTED IN AUSTRALIA BY HALSTEAD PRESS, SYDNEY

*For Helen and Michael*

# Introduction

GOOD GENERAL histories of Pacific island groups are still few in number. Among those that have been written only Ralph S. Kuykendall's *The Hawaiian Kingdom*, in three massive volumes, equals Gilson's *Samoa 1830 to 1900* in the exhaustiveness of the research upon which it is based. Gilson, like Kuykendall, ransacked the world for every scrap of evidence relevant to his subject before he began to write. Like Kuykendall, too, he developed an almost obsessive concern with ensuring that every nuance of his interpretation should be as true to the facts as he could make it. But there, except that they were both Americans, the comparison ceases. Kuykendall was born in the century that saw the rise and fall of the Hawaiian kingdom; and his conception of the historian's role remained, broadly, that which he had accepted as a young man. Gilson belonged to a later generation; he had been trained in political science and anthropology; and the country that he chose to study was one in which the indigenous people still constituted the vast majority of the population and where traditional patterns of thought and behaviour were still observable in the course of everyday life. He learnt the Samoan language. He spent much time following the debates in village *fono* and in perceptive questioning of his Samoan friends. As his work developed, it brought him a growing reputation among anthropologists, as well as among historians.

Kuykendall published the first volume of *The Hawaiian Kingdom* in 1938. The third was nearing completion when he died in May 1963. Fate dealt less kindly with Gilson. He had plans for many years of further work in Samoan history; but the present book was still unfinished when he died a month before Kuykendall.

RICHARD PHILLIP GILSON was born in Eugene, Oregon, in 1925. He graduated B.A. (*summa cum laude*) from the University of Southern California in 1947. Two years later he was awarded the M.A. degree of the same university, in Political Science, after presenting a thesis on the Gaullist movement in France.

In 1949 Gilson received a Fulbright scholarship for post-graduate study in New Zealand. This event determined the future shape of his life, both professionally and personally. He studied New Zealand's role in her Pacific dependencies at the Victoria University of Wellington (then Victoria University College) and visited the Cook Islands and Samoa. He became engaged to Miriam Baird, of Wellington.

In 1950 Dick Gilson moved to London, where he and Miriam were married in October. He had been awarded a second Fulbright scholarship for study at the London School of Economics and Political Science. Working under Professor Raymond Firth and Dr Lucy Mair, he wrote an administrative history of the Cook Islands and, in 1952, received the degree of M.Sc. (Econ.) of the University of London. When Gilson had returned from the Cook Islands to New Zealand two years earlier, he had been asked by the Department of Island Territories to submit a report on the current administrative situation in the islands. This report, which was highly critical, in parts, was regarded as useful and stimulating. Subsequently, his London thesis has been in constant use by both the New Zealand department and the Government of the Cook Islands. He used a small part of the material it contains in the writing of articles. He remained unwilling, however, to publish the whole work as a book till he had found time to revise it and reduce its length. This task is now being undertaken by his friend Dr R. G. Crocombe (see Bibliography of Richard Phillip Gilson, below, p. xiii).

I first met Dick Gilson when he visited Samoa in 1950. Though he was primarily a scholar, earnest in his pursuit of understanding of the history and politics of the islands, he was also a man of unusual sensitivity. He mixed easily with Samoans and with expatriates. Although his visit was a relatively short one, he made many firm friends. Moreover, he was becoming deeply conscious of the responsibility of the Western Powers towards developing countries. A year later, in a letter from London, he wrote:

> The other evening Miriam and I went to hear one of the prominent 'neo-New Deal' congressmen, Senator Humphrey. He was all fired up with the grave problems of unifying Europe for defensive purposes. . . . The basic question of doing something about the root causes of the spread of Communism in backward areas—where we are most vulnerable—was dismissed with scarcely any comment at all. It seems altogether fantastic how little understanding there is of the basic problems of nationalism, colonialism, and the like.

It was not surprising therefore that, on the completion of his research on the Cook Islands, he should think of tackling the tangled history of Samoa during its period of contact with the Western world. He already knew, and felt an affection for, the country and its people; and, since it was lack of understanding with which he was wont to charge the world's political leaders, perhaps work as a historian in a colonial society could satisfy his sense of obligation as a man, as well as his curiosity as a scholar.

Gilson was appointed a Research Fellow in Pacific History in the Australian National University in 1952. After collecting the material on nineteenth-century Samoa available in London, he came to Canberra in April 1953. From that time till his death, just ten years later, the completion of the present book remained his primary academic interest. Between January 1954 and May 1955, he was engaged on fieldwork in Samoa and New Zealand. During that period he worked through the official records in both countries and the private papers and other material in the custody of libraries, churches and other organizations. But he also sought, with great assiduity, for papers that might still be in private possession. His location, in New Zealand, of those of the late E. W. Gurr was perhaps his most important discovery.

Gilson never permitted himself to be entirely free, however, for the pursuit of his own research. While he was in Western Samoa, for example, he spent several months locating and collecting the surviving records of the former German administration and in arranging for their deposit in the National Archives of New Zealand. Similarly, in Canberra, he devoted much time to building up a detailed knowledge of Pacific historical sources that was as valuable to his colleagues as to him. A similar generosity made him the willing helper of academic 'lame dogs', so that incompetently constructed manuscripts would be passed to him and returned to their authors substantially rewritten. Moreover, his own academic interests were not confined to the nineteenth century or to Samoa. He kept himself closely informed on contemporary political, social and economic developments in the Pacific. In Western Samoa, for example, he gained an intimate understanding of the currents of opinion, and the interests, reflected in the proceedings of the Constitutional Convention of 1954, though, unfortunately, he failed to commit his conclusions to writing.

In 1956, while I was myself on study leave, Gilson was acting-head of the Department of Pacific History. He performed the duties that fell to him meticulously and with unfailing good sense. Indeed, my only reservation was regarding the amount of time he must have spent keeping me informed of developments, not only in the Department, but also in the University as a whole. He was an admirable colleague and a sensitive and warm-hearted friend.

Gilson's Research Fellowship terminated in November 1957. He continued to live in Canberra and to work on his book. He undertook a substantial amount of writing—more than is apparent from his Bibliography—for encyclopaedias. In 1960-1 he made a survey of manuscript material in New Zealand relating to the Pacific for the Department of Pacific History.

Early in 1962 Gilson took up an appointment as Assistant Professor of Anthropology at Los Angeles State College. He quickly established himself as a stimulating teacher of undergraduates. But on 29 April 1963, shortly after delivering a lecture, he collapsed and died.

In addition to his wife, Miriam, Dick Gilson left a son and a daughter. His valuable library of Pacific books was presented by Miriam Gilson to the library of Los Angeles State College, where it has been established as a special collection named in his memory. His equally valuable notes of Samoan source material—typed and indexed with quite extraordinary care—were presented to the Department of Pacific History. Already they have been of major use in our research programme, most particularly to me in my own work on Samoa.

THE sources on which *Samoa 1830 to 1900: The Politics of a Multi-cultural Community* is based are vast in quantity and complex in content. It is always difficult to use documents written by Europeans as a guide to the realities of a non-Western society. It is often equally difficult to interpret those written in a language like Samoan when they deal with the intricacies of law and politics in a period of profound social change. And Gilson did not find writing easy, since he aspired to a precision and clarity that taxed his abilities to the uttermost. Yet, in the earlier chapters particularly, he attained a level of analysis that, in my opinion, is superb. Unhappily, however, the task confronting him seemed to become more formidable, rather than more straightforward, as he proceeded. Eventually, he decided to deal with the period from 1876 to 1900 in a more summary way than he had with the events of earlier years—in three concluding chapters.

At the time of his death, Gilson had completed work on Chapters 1 to 13. No change has been made to them, apart from a simplification of the form (though not the content) of the footnotes. Chapters 14, 15 and 16 existed, however, only as preliminary drafts. Chapter 16, indeed, was still being written. From these drafts, and often exiguous indications of the intended documentation, Miriam Gilson constructed a text. This text of the final chapters has been checked against Gilson's notes, or the original sources, by members of the Department of Pacific History. In this work, I have had the help of Mrs Carol Dossor, Mrs Marney Dunn and Mrs Honore Forster. Mrs Dossor has also compiled the Bibliography to the book. To all of them, I express my warmest thanks. For any errors that may remain undetected in these chapters, the responsibility is mine.

Chapters 1 to 13 were typed by Mrs Aino Guenot, of Canberra. The care that she bestowed on the task owed as much to interest in the book and respect for its author as to the strict call of duty. I know that Dick Gilson and his wife fully reciprocated her regard.

*Australian National University*                          J. W. Davidson
*Canberra*

# Bibliography of
## RICHARD PHILLIP GILSON

'The South Pacific Commission: one aspect of regional security', *World Affairs Interpreter*, 1950, pp. 181-90.

'Some administrative problems in the Cook Islands', *South Pacific*, December 1950, pp. 213-15, 232.

'The background of New Zealand's early land policy in Rarotonga', *Journal of the Polynesian Society*, vol. 74, no. 3, September 1955, pp. 267-80.

'Negotiations leading to British intervention in Rarotonga (Cook Islands)', *Historical Studies: Australia and New Zealand*, vol. 7, no. 25, November 1955, pp. 62-80.

'The South Pacific area: its potentials for Fulbright grantees', *Institute of International Education News Bulletin*, March 1958, pp. 11-17.

'Samoan descent groups: a structural outline', *Journal of the Polynesian Society*, vol. 72, no. 4, 1963, pp. 372-7.

Articles published in *Encyclopaedia Britannica Book of the Year*:

'British Borneo', 1958, pp. 99-100.

'Fiji', 1959, p. 208.

'New Hebrides', 'Pacific Islands, British', 1960, p. 135.

'Papua-New Guinea', 1961, p. 388.

'Tonga', 1962, pp. 504-5.

'Western Samoa', 1962, pp. 542-3.

Articles published in the *Children's Britannica*:

'Pacific Islands', 1960, vol. 7, p. 203.

'Philippines', 1960, vol. 7, p. 344.

A book tentatively entitled *The Cook Islands. The mission and colonial eras 1821-1946*, edited by R. G. Crocombe, is being prepared for publication.

# Contents

# Abbreviations used in the Footnotes

All official publications, whether manuscript or printed, are referred to by an abbreviation. Private or mission manuscript sources are preceded by MS. for identification. Published works are referred to, on first appearance, by an abbreviated title following the author's surname and thereafter by name only, except when there are two works by the one author, in which case the abbreviated title is repeated. When a periodical article is referred to, the author and the name of the periodical are given, e.g. 'Smith in *South Pacific*'.

## Manuscript Sources

ASG     Records of the government of American Samoa [see under Samoa, American Administration]

Adm.    British Admiralty records [see under Great Britain, Admiralty]

BCS     Records of the British Consulate, Samoa [see under Great Britain, Consulate, Apia]

BCT     Records of the British Consulate, Tahiti [see under Great Britain, Consulate, Tahiti]

BDCS   Letterbooks of the Deputy Commissioner, Samoa [see under Great Britain, Deputy Commissioner]

BMG    Records of the British Military Government of Samoa [see under Samoa, British Military Administration, Native Department]

FO      British Foreign Office records [see under Great Britain, Foreign Office]

FSD     Despatches of the Secretary of State for Foreign Affairs [see under Great Britain, Secretary of State, Despatches]

GCA    Records of the German administration of Samoa [see under Samoa, German Administration]

GCS    Records of the German Consulate, Samoa [see under Germany, Consulate, Apia]

GFO    Documents relating to three-power negotiations in 1899 [see under Germany, Foreign Office]

HFO    Hawaiian Foreign Office records [see under Hawaii, Foreign Office]

MP     Malietoa Government Papers [see under Samoa, Malietoa Government]

RP      Reichstag Papers [see under Germany, Reichstag]

SLC     Records of the Samoan Land Commission and Supreme Court [see under Samoa, Native Administration, Land Commission and Supreme Court]

B

SP     Steinberger Papers [see under Samoa, Steinberger]
SSJ    London Missionary Society, South Seas Journals [see under Mission]
SSL    London Missionary Society, South Seas Letters [see under Mission]
TBP    Tamasese-Brandeis Papers [see under Samoa, Brandeis]
TFP    Taimua-Faipule Papers [see under Samoa, Taimua-Faipule Government]
USCD   United States Consular Despatches [see under United States]
USCI   United States Consular Instructions [see under United States]
USN   United States Navy [see under United States, Navy]
         Cmdr L.    Letters from Commanders to Secretary of Navy
         Pac. Sqd.   Letters from Commanding Officers of Squadrons to Secretary of Navy
         W.E.    Records relating to the exploring expedition under the command of Lt Charles Wilkes, 1836-42

*Printed Sources*

APF    *Annales de La Propagation de La Foi* [see under Newspapers and Periodicals Cited]
ASM    *Annales de La Société de Marie* [see under Newspapers and Periodicals Cited]
BCP    British Command Papers [see under Great Britain, Parliament]
CPIP    Central Pacific Islands Project [see under United States, Ward ed.]
FOCP   British Foreign Office Confidential Prints [see under Great Britain, Foreign Office]
GBPP   British Parliamentary Papers [see under Great Britain, Parliament]
HRA    *Historical Records of Australia* [see under Australia, Historical Records of Australia]
NZPP   New Zealand Parliamentary Papers [see under New Zealand, General Assembly]
USCP   United States Congressional Papers [see under United States, Congress]

Samoan terms are usually defined where they first occur in the text. These terms are therefore included in the index, with a reference to the page on which a definition or explanation may be found. In a few cases, where a Samoan term is not explained in the text, a brief definition has been added to the index entry.

# I

## SAMOA AND THE SAMOAN VILLAGE

THE SAMOAN or Navigators' archipelago lies in the central Pacific, near the western fringe of Polynesia, within an area bounded by latitudes 13° and 15° south and longitudes 168° and 173° west. Extending along the east-west axis of the archipelago, over a distance of about 225 miles, are nine main islands which were inhabited by Samoans at the time of their discovery by Europeans and which have remained under continuous habitation ever since. These islands are: Ta'ū, Olosega and Ofu (comprising the Manu'a group, 20 square miles in land area); Tutuila and Aunu'u (50 square miles); Upolu (430 square miles); Manono and Apolima (1.5 square miles); and Savai'i (700 square miles). Samoa's nearest neighbours are the Tongan group and Niue to the south, the northern Cooks to the north-east, the Tokelau group to the north, and the islands of Wallis and Futuna to the west. The shortest intervening distances between these other islands and Samoa vary from about 200 to 300 miles. Auckland (1,600 miles away), Suva (700 miles), Honolulu (2,300 miles) and Sydney (2,400 miles) are the closest major overseas ports.

All the inhabited islands of Samoa are of recent volcanic origin and lack deposits of valuable minerals. The mountains of Manu'a and Tutuila are steep and rugged, leaving only small areas of level or gently sloping land for cultivation. On Tutuila, the best agricultural land is found in the south-west, while the harbour of Pago Pago, farther to the east on the same coast, is ringed by mountains. Apolima is simply the exposed and partly broken-down cone of a subterranean peak, small in area, with little arable land. Aunu'u and Manono, also small, have more even surfaces and relatively larger cultivable areas; but unlike Tutuila and Manu'a, they have no permanently-flowing surface streams.

Upolu, next in size to Savai'i, is the richest of the islands. It, too, is mountainous, with a volcanic ridge extending the fifty-mile length of its longer axis; but there are strips of gently sloping arable land along a considerable length of its coastline. The more rugged and broken eastern half of Upolu—that in which volcanic activity subsided at an earlier date—possesses the island's principal streams. In most of the western half, which is also the widest (up to sixteen miles), slopes of porous lava descend gradually from a central ridge of extinct volcanoes. The surface rock is sufficiently decomposed, however, to permit cultiva-

tion in that part of the island, and it is there that Samoa's most
ambitious plantation development has occurred.

Savai'i is roughly the same length, on the east-west axis, as Upolu
but has a width of up to twenty-seven miles. The whole of the larger
island resembles western Upolu, for though its height ranges up to six
thousand feet—nearly twice the highest altitude of Upolu—its greater
width, combined with the effects of recent volcanic activity, still makes
for a moderate gradient of fairly even contour. Owing to volcanic
eruptions which took place early in the present century, there are large,
but now diminishing, areas of bare, unproductive scoria on the north
side of Savai'i.[1] Otherwise, the soil of the island is generally fertile, but
poor harbours and the almost complete lack of surface water, as well as
the stoniness of the land, discouraged European plantation development
in the nineteenth century.[2]

The quality and location of harbours have always influenced the
pattern of European activity and settlement in the South Seas. The
small but well-protected bay of Pago Pago, for example, was once a
popular whaling port, a resort where long periods could be safely spent
taking on provisions and making repairs. Until the advent of steamers,
however, it was of little value to cargo or naval ships; for in addition to
the ruggedness of the surrounding countryside, which limited the commercial potentialities of the harbour, its location in a deep inlet of the
south coast made brief calls there hazardous when the south-east trades
were blowing. Meanwhile, the poorer but still usable anchorage at
Leone, in Tutuila's richest agricultural region, became a more important
centre of trade. In most other parts of that island, iron-bound coasts and
reefs made it dangerous or impossible for European vessels to approach
the shore.

Upolu and Savai'i are almost entirely surrounded by reefs or rocky
cliffs, and in Savai'i the few reef passages are too shallow for ordinary
ocean-going vessels. Upolu has no natural deep-water harbours to com-
pare with Pago Pago, but there are openings in the off-shore reefs,
usually at river mouths, where ships can find shelter from the open sea.
Of such a mediocre character is the anchorage at Apia Bay. Having the

---

[1] There were bare lava fields in the A'opo region of Savai'i early in the nineteenth
century; but by the 1850s the land was covered again by vegetation (SSL, Pratt,
22 December 1853).

[2] Some early accounts greatly exaggerated the extent of Savai'i's surface water, e.g.
Sterndale's report of 1874, which stated that the island possessed 'innumerable
waterfalls for the turning of saw-mills, and streams for the floatage of logs'
(NZPP, A/4, 1884, Sess. 1, 26). Since the soil of Savai'i is so porous that water
filters rapidly through the surface, the only permanent flows above ground are
from the near-sea-level outlets of springs and underground rivers. Heavy rainfall
will produce some surface run-off but this flow is short-lived.

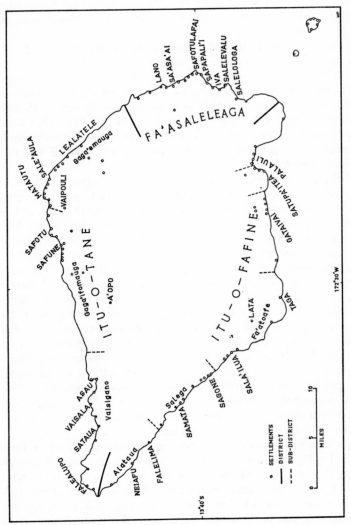

Savai'i

advantage, however, of being centrally and accessibly situated on the north coast, where the prevailing winds blow off-shore and large areas of land in the vicinity are highly productive and easily cultivated, Apia none the less became Samoa's chief seaport and the main centre of European settlement.

Samoa's climate is tropical, characterized by heavy rainfall, high relative humidity and a maximum temperature averaging, over the year, about 85°F. at sea-level. There are seasonal variations, the period December-March being hot, wet and windy as compared with the rest of the year; but generally the seasons are less sharply defined than in the higher latitudes, for example, or in the Asian monsoon belt. Samoa, unlike Fiji to the west and the Cook Islands to the east, is rarely struck by winds above gale force. Till the 1960s, its last hurricane was that which laid waste Manu'a in 1915.

Warm and well-watered, Samoa is capable of supporting a wide range of equatorial flora; and on its slopes, many temperate and sub-tropical forms of plant life will also thrive. Ringing the coasts, and extending inland for varying distances up to about four miles, is the 'coconut belt'. Within this zone grow, too, most of the other tropical flora which the Samoans require for their regular use: for example, breadfruit, taro, *ta'amū* or giant taro, yams and bananas (for food); sugar cane (for thatch); paper mulberry (for the making of bark-cloth or *siapo*); the kava plant, pandanus, hibiscus and many timbers. In addition to the above-listed food plants, which account for most of what the Samoans themselves cultivate, there are many others, growing wild, that may be used on special occasions or in time of shortage. Since Europeans first settled in Samoa, a great number of exotic plants have been introduced. Some of these have been used locally, such as the pineapple, maize and certain citrus fruits; but more important are those which have been, or now are, produced chiefly for export, for example, cocoa, cotton, rubber and coffee. A few exotics, notably the cavendish banana, have figured in both export trade and local diet.

For domesticated animals the Samoan environment is rather more restrictive. Pigs, fowls and dogs, seen in large numbers by early European voyagers, were presumably brought to the islands by aboriginal migrants or visitors from the south or east. Of the species which have been introduced at various times by Europeans, only horses, cattle and goats have adapted very well. In the bush, rats, pigeons and flying-foxes abound. At one time the pigeon was sacred and could not be eaten, while the consumption of the flying-fox was limited by certain prohibitions; but today, both are killed and used freely, especially on festive occasions. In the past, pigs and fowls were kept mainly for feasts, the Samoans' staple supply of protein coming, rather, from the lagoons, reefs and open sea,

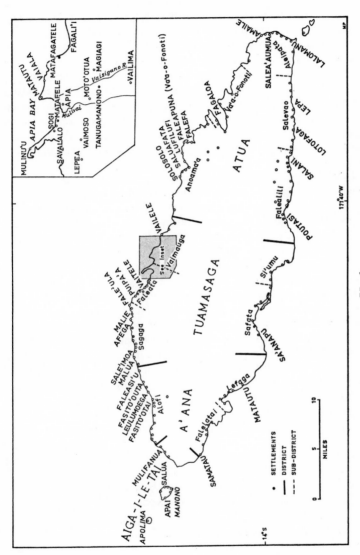

Upolu

where a great variety of edible marine life could be obtained. Now, fishing has become a much less essential occupation than it was in the nineteenth century, for the Samoans have acquired a taste for the preserved beef, salmon and pilchards stocked by the trade stores.

Outside the areas which have been cleared for cultivation or settlement, most of the land surface of the Samoan islands is covered by dense rain forest. Stands of massive hardwoods, with thick undergrowth of vines and creepers, extend to the tops of the peaks; and where inland clearings have been abandoned, the forest usually takes quick possession again. The almost consistently heavy ground cover, together with porous volcanic soil, has no doubt inhibited erosion, a salutary condition for the Samoans' maintenance of a settled agricultural subsistence economy.

If the Samoan pattern of life is considered, along with the size of the population, the physical environment seems indeed to have provided, in the past, an ideal basis for comfortable and convenient settlement. In the early nineteenth century the Samoans numbered approximately forty thousand, which population was distributed among small and, in many respects, independent villages that ranged in membership from about fifty to three hundred persons.[3] Most of the villages were permanently established, with the system of agriculture being based upon exploitation of fixed holdings.[4] Each of these communities was usually able to produce its own requirements of foodstuffs and of building and plaiting materials. There was some specialization of skills, in carpentry, carving and tattooing, for example, and uneven territorial distribution of natural resources needed for the practice of certain crafts, which occasioned some economic exchange between villages; but such trade, for the purpose of mere subsistence, was not extensive,[5] nor was there any tendency towards economic or any other form of 'urbanization'.

Given several hundred miles of coastline, it was possible for the villages to be sited on or near the shore, close to river-mouths or freshwater springs, with arable land readily accessible. There was, moreover, sufficient space to permit most Samoans to be settled where access by sea was relatively safe and easy. Rocky coasts unprotected by off-shore reefs were sparsely populated, even where the land was capable of development. Most villages were located on lagoons and on inlets and bays,

[3] A summary and analysis of Samoan population data for the nineteenth century may be found in McArthur, *Island Populations*. A geographer's treatment of Samoan population data, including that for the nineteenth century, will be found in MS., Pirie.

[4] Some land had to be fallowed periodically and crops rotated, but the Samoans were not shifting agriculturalists, burning, planting and moving on.

[5] There were, however, highly institutionalized forms of exchange which served social more than economic needs.

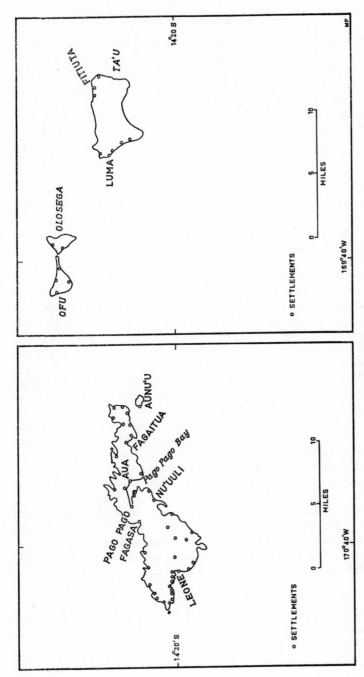

Tutuila and Manu'a

which facilitated communication by sea. This was most important to the Samoans; for their social and family relationships called for much visiting between villages, an activity for which, in view of the ease with which they earned their livelihood, they had a considerable amount of free time. When a long trip was to be made, they would usually take to their canoes, even if the entire distance could have been covered by land. For if rough tracks and the necessity of porting heavy loads of gear made overland travel difficult, the presence of mischievous spirits in the bush and often the risk of encountering enemies in villages along the shore also made it dangerous.

For as long as Europeans have known them, then, the Samoans have been predominantly a coast-dwelling people. In the last century there were a few inland villages, cut off from direct contact with the sea; but most of them were small and unimportant, and the total number of people concerned was negligible. Some of those villages are now abandoned, and in spite of rapid population growth in recent years, the proportion of Samoans who live permanently away from the sea is still quite small. In the nineteenth century there were only three conditions that would cause the Samoans to leave the coast in large numbers for protracted periods of time: crop-destroying droughts, storms or pestilences, which forced the people to scavenge deep in the bush for wild fruit and vegetables; war, which led to the destruction of villages and gardens and to the establishment of camps and temporary cultivations well away from the sea; and attack, or threat of attack, by foreign warships. Some of the first European visitors to Samoa assumed, without checking, that large areas of the interior were as thickly populated as the coast,[6] but closer observation subsequently corrected the impression. Years later, however, the existence of disused tracks and long-abandoned camp or village sites in the bush of Upolu and Savai'i was adduced by some Europeans as evidence that the islands had once had a far more numerous and industrious population.[7] This view often had a more subjective basis than the earlier accounts, being accompanied by the contention that the Samoans, allegedly in a 'state of decline', would never have any use for most of their land, which Europeans wanted for plantations and pasturage. The fact is that neither oral tradition nor, as yet, archaeological research has borne out the theory of a densely settled and more 'civilized' Samoa of a past age.

## The scale of Samoan society

Among Polynesian societies, that of Samoa was found by Europeans to be comparatively large in size or scale and complex in organization,

[6] e.g. MS., Williams, Journal 1836.
[7] e.g. NZPP, A/4, 1884, Sess. 1, 26; *Samoa Times*, 4 October 1879.

in which respects it rather resembled the societies of Tonga, Hawaii and New Zealand and differed from those of the Ellices, the Cook Islands and parts of French Oceania. Early settlers and visitors in the southern Cooks, for example, discovered that the inhabitants of each small island there were quite aware of the existence and location of other islands near by but that most of the people of that area were out of regular contact with their inter-island neighbours, in which circumstance the six or seven thousand people of Rarotonga comprised the largest exclusive social grouping or society. In Samoa, on the other hand, close cultural and social affinities extended to the outer boundaries of the geographical region, a fact which was plain to even the most superficial observers. From Manu'a to the west end of Savai'i the people all acknowledged having a common identity as Samoans.[8] With some local variations, they spoke the same Polynesian dialect; they dressed and housed themselves in similar ways; they built their canoes to similar designs; they intermarried widely, recognized far-flung family and political relationships, and maintained these relationships by paying each other frequent visits and joining in a variety of inter-village activities; they shared some of the same deities and creation myths; they organized and conducted their local political affairs in similar fashion; and they employed common agricultural techniques.

Samoan society, like most others of Polynesia, had no central political authority or government exercising control over all its members. Rather, political organization rested largely upon the ramified lineage and the local extended family, and also upon the village, in which members of several families joined in dealing with common local problems. The interaction and cross-cutting of principles of kinship and locality, among others of lesser importance, produced within Samoa's relatively large-scale society a complex pattern of associations, obligations and alliances, many of which conflicted, with the result that Samoans, in contemplating or undertaking political action, were often torn by opposing claims and loyalties. Such was the extent of this conflict pertaining in those Samoan affairs which most interested Europeans in the nineteenth century that exploration of the bases of it, in the very organization and structure of Samoan society, is an essential part of the study of the history of that period. This necessity is further enhanced by the fact that few, if any, Europeans of the time understood the intricacies of the Samoan social order or, in consequence, the nature of the system of conflict and choice which defined and limited the range of action open to the Samoans in the conduct of their relations with foreigners. That is not to say that a

---

[8] The Samoans had contacts with members of other Polynesian societies, e.g. Tongans and Wallis Islanders, whom they considered kindred but nevertheless separate people.

better understanding of the Samoans would have added greatly to the Europeans' capacity to predict the outcome of specific situations and events; even today such understanding has but slight predictive value. But a fuller appreciation of the causes and content of actual happenings, of the lessons of experience which seem in practice to have been highly elusive, might well have altered the long-term course of Samoan history, in so far as it lay within the power of Europeans to determine it.

What follows here represents an attempt to describe, without undue frills and abstractions, some of the values and dynamics characteristic of Samoan society in the nineteenth century. In the making of this effort, which is based upon recent fieldwork as well as documentary research, recognition is given the fact that many changes have occurred. It is contended, however, that these changes have been mainly in matters of incidental detail—that, overall, there was no radical break or reorientation in the constitution of Samoan society during the period covered by this study or by the research that preceded its presentation. Current trends in Samoa, which seem headed towards more individualistic economic enterprise, the progressive weakening or decentralization of traditional political authority and the development of an increasingly powerful central government, may soon produce quantitative social changes in which fundamental changes of quality are inherent; but that is a problem outside the scope of this work. What is stated here as applying in the present refers generally to the period of Samoan-European contact extending to the middle of the twentieth century, with relevant changes over that time being appropriately and, it is hoped, clearly noted in each case.

## The village environment

The typical Samoan village lies along a stretch of coast limited at either end by definite boundaries such as rivers, rocky promontories or man-made walls of stone. Each household within the village has its residential site upon which are erected one or more dwellings, cook houses, and possibly a special guest and meeting house. These sites are normally arranged around an axis running parallel to the beach, with the greatest concentration of dwelling and guest houses being at the *malae,* the village 'square' or centre where open-air feasts and meetings are held. The maintenance of a neat, attractive *malae*, bordered by shade trees and flowers and kept free of rubble, is a matter of considerable pride among the Samoans, one usually occasioning regulative action on the part of the village authorities.

The traditional Samoan house, which by design and construction is admirably suited to the tropical environment, consists basically of a roof of round bee-hive shape, or a long semi-ellipsoid, supported at the perimeter by upright posts. The round type of structure involves the use of central columns for key support of the roof, which may be steeper in pitch than the long roof. The long house, too, may be raised on internal columns, but these are distributed rectangularly under a box frame of horizontal beams. Either type of roof is made of an elaborate network of curved members, covered with sugar-cane thatch. The spaces between the outer supporting posts are open, allowing free circulation of air, but each space is fitted with a set of collapsible blinds of plaited coconut leaves which can be let down against the weather, enabling the entire house to be enclosed if necessary. The interior of the house is usually free of fixed partitions, though screens of cloth may be strung up to provide some measure of privacy. The round house is called the *fale tele* and is the type preferred for the accommodation of guests and the conduct of village council meetings, while the elliptical structure is the *fale afolau*, principally a dwelling house.

The finest houses are of a most intricate design and solid construction, the ultimate achievements of a skilled and honoured Samoan craft. A chief of high rank, sensible of the dignity of his position, would want to engage the most expert carpenter he could find when undertaking to build a new house, especially if it were to be a *fale tele*, which only a chief of high rank would build. Upon the generosity of the payment given the carpenter, as well as upon the excellence of the construction and finish of the house itself, would depend the chief's continued prestige. Yet another aspect of Samoan house building which figures in the system of rank is the sloping or terraced stone platform upon which the structure is based. The dampness of the climate requires that a house-floor should in any case be raised above ground level, but this need has been adapted by the Samoans so that the higher the rank of a chief, the greater the height of his house-platform or the number of terraced set-backs it incorporates.

Immediately behind the village, topography permitting, there will be gardens of taro, *ta'amū* and other food crops, some maintained by the entire village for ceremonial and other special purposes, and the remainder kept by individual households. Many gardens are also planted farther inland. All land near the village, and all cleared land to the interior, is distinguished by known boundaries marking the sub-divisions, most of which belong to individual descent groups and are used by their members and affinal connections in the various households in the village. This applies to fallowed land as well as to that under active cultivation.

The virgin bush land behind the village is usually regarded as belonging to the village, extending right to the top of the dividing range or to some comparable land mark. Boundaries separating one village from another, which are clearly set out near the coast, frequently run inland

for considerable distances, following rivers or ridges, or being marked
by stones or tracks. In a few places boundary walls are found trailing far
into the bush, their origins lost in antiquity. Customs relating to the
control and use of bush land vary a good deal, but as a rule, the people
of a village, and even outsiders, are free to hunt and scavenge there. In
the past, however, there were, in the interior, the abodes of spirits, the
pigeon-hunting grounds of chiefs and some other areas to which access
was restricted.

When new cultivation is necessary, bush land is available to people
of the village, but the permission of the village council may have to be
given before clearing can commence. An attempt by anyone to clear and
cultivate inside the inland boundaries of a village in which he has no
rights by virtue of kinship or established residence would lead to a
charge of encroachment, or 'land-eating', unless special permission had
first been given. Some villages are now short of land, but until recent
times, most had a surplus. No one would have thought of going very far
from his village to plant crops except when, as a war refugee, he had to
hide for long periods in the bush or seek protection in a friendly village
where virgin land might have to be cleared to meet the subsistence
requirements of himself and his fellow exiles. Otherwise, the question of
the immediate control of bush lands, when it arose at all, was related
chiefly to the problem of land sales to Europeans.

A notable feature of the Samoan village is the stone wall or fence
erected to keep pigs away from the *malae* and house sites and from the
gardens. Present-day health and sanitation regulations require that pigs
be kept away from the village centre, but at an earlier date they were
free to wander in the village and were only shut out of the gardens.
Each household had its own pigs, as it has now, and was responsible
for preventing them from damaging crops. It has long been the custom
that domestic animals found trespassing in gardens may be killed without payment of compensation to their owners.

Burial customs comprise another aspect of village life which has been
affected by modern legislation. It was common practice, formerly, to
bury the dead near the houses in which they had lived or where they
had kinsmen, graves often being marked with stone borders or, in the
case of important chiefs, by mounds of stone. In a few villages the
corpses of high chiefs were embalmed or mummified and kept stretched
out on frames in special houses,[9] a practice which was soon suppressed
by Christian missionaries. In recent years, for reasons of hygiene, burial
within residential areas has been proscribed by law, and one now finds

[9] e.g. Mata'afa's village of Amaile in Aleipata, where the frames resembled double
canoes (MS., Turner, Journal 1836).

single-community cemeteries attached to many villages, while some have several burial grounds, segregated by kinship but all situated well away from the *malae* and the house sites. Old graves still remain inside the village, however, and are clearly discernible on account of the mounds or borders of stone that mark them and the flowers and other objects that are commonly used to decorate them.

The village's supply of fresh water is, needless to say, of crucial importance. Economic development and Western technology have brought piped water and catchment tanks to many villages within the past few years; but as the typical Samoan settlement is established on a site that has been used for generations, one may assume that its original location was determined at least partly by the accessibility of a stream or spring. Care is taken to protect the water supply against pollution, and where possible, stretches of river or separate springs are set aside for different purposes. Where water is piped in, the maintenance and care of the system is a village responsibility. Access to the fresh water supply is also controlled by the village, but use by outsiders may be granted as a courtesy.

Its bordering lagoon or shallow water was a special preserve in which the village maintained rights of use and access in much the same way as it controlled its lands. These property rights have been altered considerably by colonial governments, for Europeans would not accept or enforce private restrictions upon the free use of Samoa's waters. This interference has influenced all aspects of the village's control of the sea, including fishing rights, so that it is now difficult to say just what forms that control originally took. It would appear, however, that the highest-ranking chief or chiefs of a village, or the village council, regulated fishing by boat and net and imposed conditions upon outsiders who wished to use, or traverse, the village's in-shore waters. Travellers were given access as a matter of courtesy, just as the track through the village was open to those who went in peace. The conditions required, further, that due respect be paid to the village on the way through. To stand up in a boat or to interrupt a ceremony or meeting with shouts and singing were insults and might lead to violence. When a chief died, traffic through the village by the lagoon, as well as by the track, was prohibited until the funeral rites had been performed, violation of which rule was an act of grave disrespect.

With the exception of scavenging off the reef and lagoon-floor at low tide, fishing was generally a communal effort led by the village's principal fisherman. In some places this expert was given the authority to restrict boat-fishing to parties which he either organized or sanctioned. In turn, he was bound to ensure that all catches were fairly divided among the households of the village and that species of fish reserved for

chiefs were given only to those who had a right to them. A village
without a safe fishing ground, or without any sea frontage, was greatly
handicapped, but in some cases its members might be permitted to use
the fishing-ground of a neighbouring village, for which privilege the
people of the latter place would expect to receive a portion of the catch.

The finest boats and canoes, like houses, are built by experts. The
small outriggers—bonito canoes or *va'aalo*—which are used for fishing
and short trips are the property of individuals or descent groups. Larger
craft, such as the present-day long-boat (*fautasi*) and the former double-
canoe (*'alia*), might be owned by the entire village, sometimes in the
name of its leading chief. At one time the Samoans took the greatest
pride in the appearance and condition of their vessels, regarding them as
signs of chiefly rank and village wealth. This is less true today, but in a
few places one may still see boats and canoes sheltered in special houses
where they will be noticed by travellers and visitors.

Finally, there is the church, which symbolizes one of the most substantial contributions of European civilization to the Samoan way of life.
The chapel and the house of the Samoan pastor are the most conspicuous
buildings in the village, one of each appearing in every centre and, if
there should be a division of sectarian affiliation, more than one. For
many years Samoan congregations have been building churches of
Western design, expending vast amounts of money, material and labour
in the process. Until recently, pastors' houses were of the traditional *fale
āfolau* type, but lately there has been a fad for building them of imported
materials in a style combining European and Samoan elements. These
are further distinguished by their large size and bright colours.

There were undoubtedly many ideological and organizational affinities
between Samoan religion and Samoan versions of Christianity, but it is
clear that the physical dominance of the village church, so like that of
the parish church of Europe, had no counterpart in pre-Christian times.
The Samoans had a few shrines, many sacred stones and trees, and spirit
beings incarnate in animal species. They had priests and ritual prohibitions, observances and sacrifices. But their religious practices were
not institutionalized in elaborate structures comparable to the *whare kura*
or sacred house of New Zealand or the *marae* and idols of Tahiti and
Rarotonga. Because of this difference, the pre-Christian Samoans were
often considered, quite erroneously, as less 'religious' than other Polynesian peoples. There are still the most striking visible differences between Samoan religion and that of many other Polynesian groups, but
these are of quite another order. For while the Samoans now surpass all
others in the number, size and grandeur of their religious structures,
they have been able to adopt Christianity, and adapt it, with greater
resilience, experiencing scarcely any disintegration of their traditional

social structure and way of life. There are historical as well as social reasons for this, but in general, the village church, however out of keeping with the island landscape, may be seen as a monument to the selectivity of the Samoan reaction to European contact.

## The domestic household

The basic economic work-unit in Samoan society is the domestic household, which generally comprises an extended rather than elementary family, a corporate group that would appear to have had, in the nineteenth century, an average membership of between eight and twelve persons.[10] There is no rule restricting a Samoan's residence to one particular household, but there is a strong preference for him to live most of the time where his father lives, or lived, and when marriage necessitates a choice of residence, for a woman to move from her father's household to that of her husband's father. Samoans are, however, a fairly mobile people; besides visiting each other a great deal, they may alternate their places of residence within their circles of kindred.

Each household has its chief, or *matai*, a man whose authority extends to all members in their performance of domestic tasks, in the maintenance of orderly relations among them, and in the regulation of their relations with other village households. The chief controls the recruitment of household members and may expel anyone who, by refusing to submit to his authority, threatens the unity of the group.[11] On the other hand, a member of a household—an adult member, at any rate—will nearly always have several alternative places in which he may reside; if conditions in one become unsatisfactory, he may choose to go elsewhere. Such a choice may entail great sacrifice—giving up friendships, opportunities for personal advancement, property rights—but the fact that it can be made at all is of great importance; for no Samoan must depend for his survival upon residence in one particular place, among a particular group of people.[12]

10 From data relating *matai* numbers to the total population of villages or larger areas (*Samoan Reporter*, January 1854; SSL, Pratt, 6 August 1852 and Powell, 14 August 1853; GCA, IV.5.a, Annual Report, 1900-1901, and III.11/1, *matai* list, 1903).

11 Colonial governments prohibited banishment by village authorities, but the practice has not been entirely wiped out. In any case, non-conformists may still be excluded from group activities and subjected to such criticism and ridicule that they ultimately choose voluntarily to leave the place where they have become unpopular.

12 Hence, a Samoan need not become 'detribalized' while living in his island group. This applies even to people who have had to leave their home villages on account of land shortages, e.g. in Vailele and Vaitele near Apia, where large-scale alienations occurred in the nineteenth century. There have been, in recent times,

C

The chief's authority, then, applies irrespective of the places from which the people of his household may have come, of the terms of their residence in his household, and of the authority to which they are, or have been, subject elsewhere. It also applies whatever the number of elementary family units within the household. But if the chief wishes to ensure harmony among his people, he will consult them and consider their separate interests, though he is ultimately responsible for decisions affecting the household as a corporate group.

In matters of subsistence, the household is expected to be almost self-supporting, there being few tasks that are beyond its capacity unless its membership is unusually small. It is the chief's duty to see that this standard of self-sufficiency is met, and the extent to which he succeeds is an important index of his reputation as a leader. He has the authority to organize and control his household in its use of land, whether it works as a single unit or is divided into two or more land-working groups, for example, on the basis of separate elementary families. The chief determines which crops are to be planted to supply food for the household, and he decides when and how they are to be planted. Since the coming of European traders, the Samoan household has also engaged in the production of cash crops, again under the direction of its chief.

The chief may supervise plantation work, and if he has the strength, he may join in the heavier physical labour, which is performed by the able-bodied men. The lighter work, such as weeding, is done by women and children.

Other tasks performed within the household include harvesting, cooking, hunting, some fishing, the plaiting of mats and the making of bark-cloth (*siapo*). The household may also build its own canoes and houses, or some of them. In most cases, labour is divided according to sex, age and individual skill, but the chief is still responsible for mobilizing and allocating the labour-power of his household.

Religious worship is another important aspect of household activity. It is commonly found that religious affiliation is related to descent-group membership, carrying over to Christian sectarianism a feature of the departmentalized system of 'family gods' and totems which prevailed at an earlier time. But as a household brings together people belonging to different descent groups, which are non-local, it may arise that the members of a household differ in their original church affiliations. When this happens, the chief may insist that all attend his church, in the same way as he might formerly have required them to join in the rites per-

several cases in which land shortage has led to the formal division of villages and the removal of entire sections to establish new villages elsewhere, as instanced by the division of the people of the island of Apolima, and also those of Lealatele, a Savai'i sub-district inundated by lava flows early in the present century.

taining to the deities of his own family and village;[13] for religious observances are a public affair in Samoa, entailing ceremonies that test the solidarity, energy and influence of the people under a chief's authority. The examination of children in the catechism, the sacraments of church membership, attendance at services, participation in a choir, the collection of church funds, the erection of church buildings and the rendering of material support for the pastor—all may reflect the quality of a chief's leadership in as much as all are vehicles of competition between households and between congregations. Therefore, a chief can scarcely afford to allow the people of his household, while living in his village, to participate in the affairs of other churches to the detriment of those of his own.

The household can undertake many essential activities, but it is far from being an independent local unit in the society. There are some economic tasks which necessitate relations with other groups in order to secure the assistance they can provide, either for direct payment or for a return of services. Beyond this, the household engages in social relations with others which, by their very nature, create tasks superfluous to subsistence requirements but otherwise fundamental to the Samoan way of life.

The former type of inter-group relationship is determined very largely by considerations of manpower and skills. Certain methods of fishing, for example, require more boats and crewmen than one household can ordinarily supply; they also require expert knowledge which members of the household may not possess. Boat- and house-building and the clearing of land may also create demands for assistance from outside the household and even from outside the village.

It does not necessarily follow that multi-household communities formed in Samoa for the purpose of undertaking large-scale and specialized tasks; but it must be plain that the existence of such communities facilitates their accomplishment and thereby contributes to the support and well-being of the individual household. It follows too that common problems arise when several domestic groups inhabit the same area and interact in certain spheres. In addition to the work they perform for each other, they are confronted with a need to co-ordinate and regulate the activities of individual groups and their members in matters of interest to them all. If one household allows its pigs to stray, all may suffer. If the nearest water supply is polluted, all will be inconvenienced. Like most people living in settled towns or villages, then, the Samoans must deal with problems of community order and responsibility. This

---

[13] Before the partition of Samoa it was common for villages to have rules restricting public worship to specific denominations. Missions and governments have attempted to overthrow these restrictions, but some persist even today.

means that there must be some unit of local control above the leader or head of the domestic household, which, in Samoa, is the formal village council.

Given a central authority, specialized community activities and functions are, of course, promoted. Some of these pertain directly to the actual work of government itself, for example, the provision and maintenance of meeting places. Further, though, centralized government provides means of mobilizing and utilizing surplus resources, just as it helps to increase the margin of surplus by facilitating the more efficient and sure execution of necessary tasks. In Samoa, nature yields an abundance in return for comparatively little work, and the Samoans, even without an advanced technology, command a large productive surplus. Until recently, little of this capacity was used by the Samoans to improve their material standard of living, their public works or their technology. At one time, it would seem, they also devoted relatively little of it to the making of ritual sacrifices or the creation of monuments and symbolic art, but there has been a change in that respect since the introduction of Christianity, competitive church-building and mission contributions having become powerful incentives to produce. The Samoans' strongest traditional incentive is, however, of great importance still, and that arises from the conduct of certain institutionalized social and political relations. Few of these relations are unique to Samoa; they cover the usual range, from marriage to the validation of rank, from the entertainment of guests to competition in sports. But Samoa *is* exceptional in the extent to which they are formalized and in the amount of resources consumed in feasts and exchanges, gifts and forfeits. The remarkable thing is that the Samoans are able to produce as much as they do and yet have sufficient leisure time for the functions in which their surplus goods are used.

The people who participate in these formal activities may be drawn together from several villages or from only one, but in either case, they use the facilities of a single village and consume goods supplied by some or all of its constituent households. Almost needless to say, part of a household's productive capacity must therefore be geared not only to the making of goods for ceremonial exchange, for example, *siapo* and fine mats (*'ie tōga*), but to providing for the entertainment of guests. Very often the village council also comes into the picture here, setting quotas of food and other items to be produced and supplied by each household and acting to develop and maintain village plantations for the provision of ceremonial requirements.

To sum up, the household produces most goods needed to support life, and what it cannot produce for itself, it acquires in co-operation with others or by purchase and barter. It regulates relations among its own members, for which function it relies upon its chief's authority, but it is in turn bound by the rule of the village in the ultimate control of relations between households. It produces goods for ceremonial and religious occasions, according to its own requirements and to those laid down by the village. And it must contribute to the production and maintenance of village property and to the security of the village from external hazards. In other words, the household, under its chief, enjoys considerable independence in matters which primarily concern its own members; but in many ways it is dependent upon the village and therefore has community responsibilities which limit its freedom. Unless these responsibilities are fulfilled, the household, or some of its members, may be ostracized by the community or even expelled from it.

*Village organization*

With few exceptions, the village and its constituent parts perform those localized activities which are considered indispensable to life in Samoa,[14] so that it is important that the village, in contrast to larger territorial units, should be controlled by a central political authority. For its stability and continuity, and for the immediate implementation of its decisions, Samoan village government depends largely upon the principle of chiefly hierarchy and upon the membership of every villager, excluding pre-adolescents, in some formal status group which cross-cuts all domestic households. The first of these features of village government also pertains to larger territorial units but is not a strong force towards their administrative centralization. The second and perhaps more significant feature, the existence of status groups, represents, in contrast to chiefly hierarchy, a unique Samoan departure in the development of political institutions in Polynesia.

A Samoan chief has a 'title' or name which belongs to his descent group and cannot properly be held by him without that group's approval. As a matter of course, the title conveys to its holder the office of headman and representative of his household and descent group, and in so far as these duties are localized, they pertain to the village in which the descent group owns its principal ancestral lands. More than this, however, each title is related to others, and all are graded in rank.

Among the chiefs of a village there may be acknowledged ties of kinship, but this does not mean that all their titles are necessarily linked

14 Until very recently the largest single local enterprise was the building of a church, a project well within the capacity of the average village. Now, however, the Samoans have begun to want certain facilities and amenities which single villages cannot always provide and maintain, e.g. hospitals, motor roads and upper-primary schools, and in many cases, for lack of government funds, adjacent villages have organized among themselves to supply these wants.

directly to common origins. It may be found that the chiefs of a village
are divided into two or more groups, and that only within each group
are there cognatic ties which determine or validate the graded rank or
seniority of the related titleholders. But in turn, many village chiefs are
related by common descent, through branched but non-localized lineages, to chiefs outside the village. Therefore, whatever the ties among
the chiefs of the village, there are always ways in which rank can be
graded on a village-wide basis: the relative seniority of all chiefs may
be seen in terms of their common descent, with one chief senior to all
others; or one village chief may be ranked in relation to another in
respect of the comparative seniority of their positions among different
groups of related groups. The latter type of ranked relationship, which
is common in Samoa, means that two or more village chiefs may be of
virtually equal rank. In consequence, it is all the more cogent that the
Samoan village should have a government based not simply upon the
principle of kinship seniority but also upon local status groups.

Households whose chiefs are related by acknowledged ties of common
descent often form a sub-division of a village over which the senior
chief (*matai sili*) of the group exerts authority in matters of joint
interest. The related chiefs may discuss issues concerning ceremonial,
land rights and the clearing of new land, house-building, inter-
household disputes, participation in village affairs, and church affiliation;
and if there is a difference of opinion among them, the views of the
senior chief will generally prevail. In addition, the *matai sili* is his sub-
division's leading representative in village government, though he may
be junior in rank to other *matai sili* of the village.

In village government, the degree of a chief's authority and influence
is related directly to the seniority of his position in the village hierarchy.
The village is a sufficiently small unit to ensure that, in spite of the
complexities of Samoan kinship, there will often be only one chief at the
apex of its hierarchy; and yet it is sufficiently large to have several
chiefs of relatively high rank. The result is that, while one chief may
exert more influence and authority than any other, effective decisions
may still require the agreement of several chiefs of high rank in the
village. Village government, then, is seldom an autocracy of one and
never a loose, indecisive confederation of household chiefs.

The rank of village titles, however determined and justified, is
rigorously institutionalized in several ways, the most important of which
centre in the *fono*, or council meeting, and the *fa'alupega*, the village's
honorific phrases of address. The governing body of the village is the
council of chiefs who, when they convene, must observe certain fixed
formalities which denote their rank. When they enter the meeting-house,
they sit by the posts at the perimeter, forming an inward-facing circle.

Each post is associated with a specific title in the village, and its position in respect to the other posts symbolizes relative rank.[15] A chief may take no position other than that associated with his title.[16] The meeting opens with the set recitation of the *fa'alupega*, put in the form of greetings to the chiefs.[17] These phrases refer to descent groups, titles, place names, famous events, and traditional privileges and relationships; and they again symbolize rank. A kava ceremony is then held, with each chief receiving his cup in an order and manner which accord with his title and rank. When the meeting is opened for business, discussion proceeds in an order which again reflects seniority of rank. There is no vote, but when the views of the highest chiefs appear to agree, the decision is regarded as taken. When the business session is over, a meal is served to the chiefs, again in a manner which symbolizes their various ranks. This multiple recapitulation of village political structure occurs every few days,[18] and in addition, special feasts and ceremonies proceed in similar fashion as far as the formalities go. No one in the village, therefore, can have any doubt about the relative status, rank and privileges of the titled heads of the various households.

All village affairs—at one time war was among them—are governed by decisions of the council. If projects require contributions of materials, food or cash from the households of the village, quotas and deadlines are set by the council. If church affairs, including affiliations, are considered village business, the council deals with them; otherwise they are left to member chiefs to arrange privately. The council settles village disputes, legislates in matters of a criminal nature, and determines punishments and tries offenders. Punishments include fines (payable to the council), the confiscation or destruction of property, corporal punishment, and exclusion from village affairs. The death sentence and banishment were once permissible, and the latter is still surreptitiously enforced in some places; but imprisonment has never been adaptable to village conditions.

The council must concur in the appointment of a successor to chiefly office; and ensuring that it is consulted in such matters, it has the power to prohibit the ceremony of title-bestowal and refuse to seat anyone whose selection has not met with its approval. In this way the council is protected against known troublemakers and other undesirables. Moreover, if a member of the council proves unco-operative or irresponsible,

---

15 If it is an outdoor meeting, there are corresponding 'stations' on the *malae*.
16 Some minor chiefs may have to sit between posts.
17 Versions of these phrases may be found in Krämer, *Samoan Islands,* I; in London Missionary Society, *O le Tusi Faalupega*; and MS., Churchill.
18 At present most councils meet once a week for their regular business sessions, and on special occasions for trials and other emergency business.

he may be expelled, thus forcing his descent group to depose him and give their title to someone else. No villager is wholly immune from the police and judicial powers of the council, but there is a practical limit to their effectiveness. In particular, action against a high chief can be taken only in the most exceptional circumstances. A village would have to be thoroughly aroused and strongly united before it could successfully discipline a high chief, and in doing so it would probably have to face considerable pressure brought by the chief's outside connections.

In general, however, the council acts along regular and fairly predictable lines and is capable of reaching clear decisions in matters of everyday concern to Samoans. Moreover, it can act quickly when necessary; for in a small community, items of business can be discussed prior to council meetings, and members can be prepared to state their views without having to refer again to those whom they represent.

While the *fono* of chiefs unites the village households at the highest level, other status groups perform their own village functions, principally the labour involved in economic and ceremonial activities. Taken generally, and disregarding changes which have been occurring recently in the organization of some villages, these latter groups are: the *'aumāga*, the untitled men (*taulele'a*); the *aualuma*, the women who belong to the village by birth or adoption and are living there, wives of local men excluded; and women who have married into the village from outside or who, by virtue of marrying within the village, have acquired the local status of affines.[19] The third group is divided into wives of chiefs and wives of untitled men, but both sections may meet together. The members of the first two groups are ranked and exercise authority and influence generally in accord with the rank of their respective household chiefs, while women of the third group take their rank from that of their husbands. In varying degrees, the meetings of the non-chiefly status groups proceed along lines similar to those applying in the *fono* of chiefs. The *'aumāga*, *aualuma* and affinal women work as instructed by the village council of chiefs, but they are usually left to organize the details of their work and, as far as they can, to solve their own disciplinary problems. Individual members of the three groups are responsible to their household *matai*, but the latter are accountable to the chiefly council for the conduct of members of their households.

---

[19] In general, it is strongly preferred that local women should marry out of the village and reside virilocally, hence some definitions of the *aualuma* that envisage it, ideally, as a group of unmarried female members of the village. Women in the village may be regarded, in practice, as categorized according to their principal roles, either as members of the village by virtue of descent, residence and rights of inheritance, or as resident affines.

Through the media of these various groups, service to the village is obligatory and must be rendered outside the bounds of the separate households. This means that the individual is thrown in with all other villagers of his own status, and he must work in full view of the 'public' in a context in which seniority of rank, on a village-wide basis, determines the standing of the participants. In the case of the 'aumāga, the pressure to obey and conform is especially great, for among the untitled men are many of the village's future chiefs. To prove themselves fit for chiefly office, these men must serve the village faithfully in addition to rendering service and obedience to their respective chiefs. Thus, the system of village government makes for stability, entrenching relationships of rank and authority and confining every individual to a public office associated with his status. The individual who is expelled from his status group for refusing to conform is entirely cut off from the public life of that village, for there is no alternative position open to him there. He may go to another village, but in doing so he scarcely increases the distance between himself and the community affairs of the village he leaves behind.

There are many other formal relationships among the people of a village but only two of these are of immediate relevance to the present discussion of local government at the village level. The first concerns the fixed division of chiefs into two specialized and interdependent categories, ali'i and tulāfale. Generally, a chiefly title identifies its holder as having a certain rank and, in most cases, conveys to him rights and duties as matai of a household and descent group. But the personal status and inter-group functions of a matai differ according to whether his title is of the class of ali'i or of tulāfale.

An ali'i is a chief with personal sanctity to whom, in that respect, belong certain exclusive privileges and the right to be shown special deference by others.[20] The public conduct of an ali'i is, moreover, circumscribed in various ways that ostensibly protect his sanctity from defilement by acts or associations of a 'profane' character. Supernatural sanctions apply to the maintenance of these privileges and prohibitions, but their intensity, as well as the degree of respect to be shown the ali'i, varies with rank, only the more senior ali'i—those ritually nearest the seat

---

[20] e.g. the right to be addressed in polite figures of speech; the right to elevate his house on a high platform, to receive 'sacred' fish and special cuts of pork reserved for him, to be served his kava cup with a special greeting or title. The highest-ranking ali'i of a village may appoint a daughter as tāupou, the village 'virgin' or hostess and head of the aualuma; and a son may be mānaia, the village's leading young man and head of the 'aumāga. The tāupou and mānaia may have ceremonial names and head-dresses, and their respective marriages are occasions of great pomp. The village offices of tāupou and mānaia are not, however, often filled now in a formal manner.

of supernatural power—having a very marked aura of 'sacredness' about them. Today, the ideological basis of chiefly sanctity is rather different from what it was early in the nineteenth century when the Samoans simply held that ancestor deities had ordained *ali'i* status and created and handed on the senior titles of that category, from which titles lesser ones had subsequently come into being through supernaturally-sanctioned processes of segmentation. With regard to the *ali'i*, however, the pattern of formalized dignity and respect is still entrenched in the social system, one feature of which is the dependence of the honour of a village upon the dignity of its highest-ranking *ali'i*, while the ideology has been transformed with little if any loss of effective substance, the Samoans declaring, as if it had always pertained, that their chiefly institutions were given and are upheld by their Christian God.

It is conceivable that such an outlook upon chieftainship might, in some circumstances, lead to a considerable concentration of power. That this has not happened in Samoa may be due, at least partly, to the absence of a prescriptive rule of title succession, a subject which is discussed below. But the *ali'i* of all ranks have been, and are, further contained by the existence and role of the *tulāfale*, the men popularly termed 'orators' or 'talking chiefs', whose responsibility it is to do for or on behalf of the *ali'i* things which the *ali'i* may not do but which, none the less, need to be done. For example, it is beneath the dignity of an *ali'i* to address a public ceremonial gathering. A *tulāfale* does this, concocting and delivering an ornate speech calculated to honour the people who are present, particularly those whom he serves. Again, only a *tulāfale* may preside over the distribution of food and ceremonial exchange goods. For these and other similar functions the *tulāfale* expect payment from the *ali'i*. If the service is an important one and the parties concerned are of fairly high rank, the *tulāfale* will receive fine mats, Samoa's most highly valued traditional article of exchange.

The *tulāfale* must work hard to acquire a knowledge of Samoan lore, for the satisfaction of his audience depends upon the richness, precision, aptness and fluency of his allusions to legends, proverbs and genealogies. He must stand before the people and be judged by his performance, while the *ali'i*, sitting back and looking dignified, receives the tokens and gestures of respect. Superficially, the relationship between *tulāfale* and *ali'i* might seem, then, to be one of service and payment, with the latter chief in the superior position. This impression might appear to be strengthened by the Samoan view that *tulāfale* titles were created by a supernatural agency and by high-ranking *ali'i* to meet the need of the *ali'i* for executive assistants and spokesmen.

In practice the *ali'i* do not, as a group, have the 'supreme power' in Samoan affairs, nor do the *tulāfale*; for on those occasions when they exercise their separate functions, chiefs in each category are dependent upon the other. No *ali'i* may carve and divide a pig; therefore, there can be no feast without the *tulāfale*'s participation; and without the feast, the honour of the *ali'i* is not served. Similarly, no chiefly title can be finally bestowed without a *tulāfale* acting as master of ceremonies. Thus, while the *tulāfale* is paid to serve the *ali'i*, whose sanctity is regarded as stemming from a supernatural source, he has, as a keeper and manipulator of Samoan lore, the capacity not only to honour the other chief's dignity but, alternatively, to degrade it. It may be noted that in the past some *tulāfale* also performed valued priestly functions, including that of augury on the eve of war.

In some spheres of activity the interdependence of the two categories of chiefs may occasion delay and even stalemate, but it seldom impairs the efficiency of village government. The distinct public functions of *ali'i* and *tulāfale* are almost entirely confined to ceremonial activities, which as far as the village is concerned are governed by set procedures and relationships with which all residents are familiar. Errors and disagreements often occur in formal relations between people of different villages, but this is partly because many inter-village relationships are less rigorously institutionalized than are the structure and organization of the village. Within the village, the position of each person and part is established and known, including the pairing or grouping of *ali'i* and *tulāfale*.[21] Adherence to the conventions is more than a question of dignity and the complementary interests of *ali'i* and *tulāfale*; it is also a question of village unity and survival, in which all chiefs have common interests.

It is reasonable to expect, however, that as a village grows in size, the number of its chiefs and households may increase to the extent that serious factions develop and government becomes unwieldy. This does not mean that the factions must divide *ali'i* and *tulāfale* as such; occasionally they do, but the division may also cut across both groups. Whatever the circumstances, should village unity become impossible to maintain—or impracticable, in the sense that it entails reduced efficiency in government—the village may divide into separate parts, but with each being of sufficient size, as a rule, to ensure that essential tasks can still be performed.

21 *Tulāfale* and *ali'i* are usually paired in groups rather than title by title. Within the limits of the paired groups there will be differences of rank, but any *tulāfale* might act for any *ali'i*, though a high-ranking *tulāfale* would prefer to act for a senior *ali'i* and then only in an important capacity. When a *tulāfale* receives payment from an *ali'i*, he must announce the fact publicly and give an account of the goods received. If a *tulāfale* considers an *ali'i* niggardly, he may refuse to act for him; conversely, an *ali'i* may exclude a certain *tulāfale* from his service. A *tulāfale*, because of his right to receive goods, will often try to create situations which might lead to demands for his services.

Another important feature of specialized chieftainship is that its functions within the village do not apply directly to the business side of government. When the council of chiefs convenes, the *ali'i* and *tulāfale* are seated in separate groups, and there is a kava ceremony during which recognition is given the separate status of each; but after the meeting opens for business, all chiefs participate in discussion and contribute to decisions in accordance with rank.[22] It is in the work of government, when both kinds of chiefs assume the same role, that their relative rank becomes most apparent. If Samoa is taken as a whole, and titles are compared in terms of putative seniority, *ali'i* and *tulāfale* vary almost equally in their respective scales of rank, except at the apex of the hierarchy, where the senior titles are those of 'sacred' high chiefs, or *ali'i sili*. Among the villages, gradations of rank are not consistent for both types of titles: an *ali'i* may be the highest-ranking chief in one place, a *tulāfale* in another; or chiefs in each category may be of similar high rank. Disparities of rank between the *ali'i* and *tulāfale* groups will not alter or jeopardize the observance of ceremonial relationships between village chiefs, but they will figure in determining which chiefs have the greatest authority in village government.[23] Therefore, despite their intense preoccupation with ceremonial, the Samoans retain the capacity to deal with essential issues of government in a practical and straightforward way.

The second of the formal relationships referred to is that which has developed between villages and Christian pastors (*faife'au*). In pre-Christian times, as far as is known, many functions of a priestly order were performed by chiefs. They were responsible, first, for the maintenance of satisfactory ritual relations between their descent groups and their lineage gods. Some of the higher-ranking lineage deities, however, were thought to have influence in matters of concern to Samoans generally, regardless of considerations of kinship, in which cases the relevant lineage leaders, or those acting on their behalf, might perform ritual functions of interest to a great number of Samoans, perhaps even all. One may instance as an example of the latter situation the role of the *alataua* of south-western Savai'i, *tulāfale* who interpreted and influenced the goddess Nafanua, one of the deities of war, who was associated with

---

[22] There are, of course, exceptions to this rule. Differences of age, ability and experience—and, now, education and success in commerce—may also influence the taking and implementation of decisions. But in the villages, rank is still the most important factor of all.

[23] Villages in which *tulāfale* are greatly superior in rank to *ali'i* are sometimes referred to in the literature as 'orator' villages. Some of these had special functions in inter-village activities, e.g. in war and in the appointment of 'kings'. In a few of these villages the senior chiefs were *tulāfale* who also possessed *ali'i* status and privileges, and whose titles were distinguished as *tulāfale-ali'i*.

the extensive lineage Sa Tonumaipe'a.[24] There were also various healers, mediums and prophets—they did not have to be chiefs, nor were these offices closed to women—who by virtue of their training or personal idiosyncracies were considered capable of controlling or interceding with supernatural beings, particularly the spirits of the more recent dead, in matters related to life crises and unforeseen events. There is no evidence to suggest, however, that every village had a priest whose position was wholly and consistently analogous to that subsequently taken by the Christian pastor. Nor would it appear that any of the specialized priestly functions—not even that of the *alataua*, of whom there were several groups—was readily subject to monopolization by single individuals or villages.

The Christian pastors are Samoans who have been trained in local mission schools or seminaries and who have agreed, as a condition of their entry into their ministry, to renounce secular offices and chiefly titles. Procedures vary somewhat among the missions; but generally, a pastor's appointment must be approved or sanctioned by the village to which he is assigned,[25] and he must go there as a 'stranger', his own village being closed to him as regards his official pastoral duties. In return for his services as minister and elementary-school teacher, the village must agree to support him and his family: to provide food and housing, and to make him periodic payments of cash in the form of 'voluntary' contributions. The village has, moreover, to guarantee the secure tenure of land for the church site and to provide and maintain the church and its fabric.

On the surface, the pastor may seem to function solely as 'God's representative' in the village. He may not attend the *fono* of chiefs, unless they request his presence, and he is subject to dismissal by the village or, if not that, to loss of support and effective leadership should he neglect his church or interfere in secular affairs contrary to the wishes of the village chiefs. This specialization of function, however, has been absorbed into a complementary relationship between church and village to which recognition is given when, on the occasion of village ceremonies, the pastor receives the first share of food and exchange goods. It is also expressed in the Samoan term *feagaiga*,[26] which signifies, in this case, that priest and village stand opposite and apart

---

24 There were other war deities besides Nafanua and other *alataua* besides these of south-western Savai'i.

25 If a village is divided among two or more denominations, appointments may be referred to the individual congregations; but the village *fono* may intervene if a pastor is not acceptable to the village as a whole.

26 This term also describes other social relationships, notably between brother and sister; and it is used of a contract, treaty, understanding or agreement, and Biblical testament.

from each other but serve one another in reciprocal or complementary ways. As will be shown in discussion of mission activities, the pastors have perfected means of playing upon the social and political susceptibilities of their congregations which have entailed the acceptance of so much of the traditional order and mores, especially in matters of church government, that Christianity has in no sense been a revolutionary or disintegrative social force in Samoa. If, thereby, the pastor's position has become secure, so have the chiefs entrenched themselves in church affairs, largely by virtue of their local authority and rank. As lay officers they carry to the church their social conservatism and their love of ceremonial; and as members of the village *fono* they enforce in public life the Christian prohibitions they endorse and treat church activities as essential business of government. Public manifestations of religion, as measures of piety and of the efficacy of church affiliation, have become as characteristic of Samoan Christianity as they were of the system which the missions superseded. And village government has come to depend as much upon the village church for its stability and validation as upon the kava ceremony and *fa'alupega*.

# 2

## ELEMENTS OF SAMOAN SOCIAL STRUCTURE

### Corporate descent groups

THE BASIC Samoan descent group, variously termed *faletama* or *itu
'āiga*, is a non-localized cognatic corporation headed by a *matai* and
consisting of people born or adopted into his household and, beyond
them, of their descendants outside the village of the household, which
extension is usually limited to one or two generations. Most of the land
occupied and cultivated by the *matai*'s household is subject to rights of
use and control inherited by the members of his descent group, who
retain these interests regardless of where they reside and who, if of
adult age, may expect or demand to be consulted by the *matai* on any
question of land alienation that may arise under his authority within the
group.[1] The *matai*'s chiefly title is property in which the same people
have rights. If possible, they gather just prior to the death of an
incumbent *matai* in order to hear his final pronouncements, including
his proposal of a successor, and after his funeral rites have been conducted, they nominate for the *matai*-ship some one of their number, in
which proceedings they consider but do not necessarily carry out the
dying testament they may have witnessed. Other corporate activities of
the descent group include participation in ceremonial exchanges between
affines.

The descent group usually bears the name of the title it possesses, with
its initial point of genealogical reference being the ancestor who is
reputed to have been the first to hold or acquire that title. Theoretically,
anyone descended from the ancestor-founder by birth or adoption may
be a member of the group, but some cognates must, of course, be
excluded, unless the *matai* title has been very recently created. The
Samoans have no specific rules, however, to establish in advance which
kinsmen shall be excluded from the joint inheritance, nor must those
excluded always remain so as a matter of strict principle. Incorporation

---

[1] The spouse of a member of the descent group may occupy and use land belonging
to the group, but his continued occupation might be questioned after dissolution
of the marriage tie by separation or death. A distant cognate may occupy some
of the group's land, by permission granted on the basis of an acknowledged tie
of kinship; he would not have a right of use comparable to that of one of the
group's original members unless he had been adopted.

of the descent group reflects, rather, a number of circumstantial conditions and preferences.

First, it is generally true that the inheritance does not pass through an individual who has not maintained active participation in the affairs of the group; his rights wither away, as it were, and he can then transmit them to his offspring only as remote claims, to be pressed in case of need, perhaps, but subject for their realization to the will of the group's active members, its *matai* in particular.

Secondly, Samoans should not marry if they acknowledge a close common ancestor, first-cousin unions being regarded as incestuous and marriage within a collateral span of about four or five generations being considered improper, while in all events, intra-village marriage is discouraged. Partly for these reasons, cognates are widely affiliated and scattered. It is hard enough to participate actively in many groups concentrated within a small area; it is impossible to do so over a large area, which assures, with respect to a given descent group, that some cognates must 'fall away'.

Thirdly, women, though not absolutely excluded from chiefly succession, very rarely become *matai*, a distinction which is supported, more generally, by sharp sexual divisions of personal and social roles. At the same time, a man's qualifications for *matai*-ship include his record of service in the household and village of the titleholder whom he may be in line to succeed. If, however, he is related to that chief through a woman, he may, as shall be explained, have certain rights over him and his descendants that, in their eyes, would render his succession to the chiefly office a difficult and even undesirable change of role. Other things being equal, then, long-term marital residence is preferably virilocal and patrilocal and, with the same qualifications, succession is largely agnatic. Consequently, the inheritance, unless something unusual happens, is not transmitted through females past one or two descending generations, while it tends to continue indefinitely through males. Finally, descent groups are inclined formally to divide when they become internally disunited, which grows more likely as their size, or the number of their adult members, increases. As well as dividing land and titles, segmentation has the obvious effect of keeping corporate descent groups relatively small and, therefore, numerous. On the other hand, it seldom results in the immediate freeing of junior *matai* and their respective descent groups from the control or influence of their *matai sili*. In practice, one often finds *joint* descent groups, like joint households, in each of which there may be several *matai*, with *matai sili* exercising some superior degree of control over land use and the succession to junior titles. Still, the junior *matai* and their branch descent groups have a measure of responsibility for their affairs, while the overall effect of segmentation is to differentiate cognates and create new, if not entirely distinct, lines of descent, succession and inheritance which may or may not continue to diverge.

It is an implication of the foregoing conditions that agnates will tend to remain together locally, making up the core of the household associated with a given descent group, dominating the title succession, occupying the land, representing the descent group in village affairs and continuing the inheritance primarily through agnates. This weighing of preferences enables one to regard Samoan lineages as predominantly agnatic, particularly in respect of the genealogical history of title succession and rank; but it must be emphasized that this generalization represents the cumulative effect of many individual choices and decisions relating to succession and inheritance, for strict principles of unilineality, as such, are not characteristic of Samoan social structure.

In one sense, the individual's interest in a descent group is conditioned by the advantages which he receives, or can receive, as a member. By accident of birth he has immediate rights in at least two groups— one through his father and one through his mother—and less immediate rights or claims in others. His first interests in land convey to him no direct negotiable value, in the Western manner, unless the controlling parties decide to sell or lease, which processes are alien to Samoan custom. Otherwise, the principal economic value of land lies in its occupation and use for purposes of residence, subsistence and ceremonial —and, now, for cash crop production. Secondary economic values attach to the rights of absent members of the descent group to receive produce from the land-users on request and, also, to assume an active part in the use of the land at any time. Less immediate interests are the transmission of land rights to one's descendants, and the opportunity to clear bush land in the village of residence. In this regard, then, the individual's choice, if he is in a position to make one and does so, is largely a question of where to reside—perhaps where the land is richer or easier to cultivate, or where it is more plentiful or more favourably situated. At the present time some Samoans maintain plantations in two villages, producing cash crops in both; but generally, land use is still confined to the locality of one's residence, and where there is no shortage, the availability of land is not a very important reason for moving from one place to another.

Title succession is, for men, a more significant aspect of descent group membership. Succession is not bound to the observance of primogeniture nor is it necessarily confined to the agnatic line; rather, any adult male member of a descent group may be chosen as *matai*. The dying wish (*māvaega*) of a deceased titleholder will be a first consideration and will be ignored only if his choice of successor is clearly
D

unsuitable or if there is a serious dispute over the title. Otherwise, the character and ability of the contenders will be taken into account, along with their ages, the rank or influence of their mothers, their past service and the nature of their genealogical connections with the previous *matai*. Other things being favourable, Samoans like to see a title go to the eldest adult male in the agnatic line; hence it may pass from one brother to the next, and then return to the son of one of the brothers, moving in rough relation to age and experience, and setting off the rights of remaining brothers against those of sons.[2] If one man should hold the title for many years, though, it is obvious that other contenders may die or leave the group without ever holding its *matai* title. When contenders are likely to be passed over, or are unwilling to await their turns, segmentation may occur.

Title succession through women usually comes about as the result of special circumstances: there may be no agnatic descendant to contest the *matai*-ship; a *matai* may for purely personal reasons nominate the son of a female relative; a uterine descendant may have proved himself so capable a leader that other contenders are passed over in his favour; or a title may split between agnatic and uterine successors.[3] There are no general statistics to refer to, but material from Samoan genealogies and local surveys suggests that the ratio of uterine to agnatic succession is about one to three.

A man who seeks a title may thus have alternative prospects, which in either case may be influenced by his residential associations and his record of participation in household and village affairs. Accordingly, Samoans may change their residence in order to contend for titles. But while permanent marital residence is usually patrilocal and virilocal, it does not necessarily follow, in respect of uterine succession, that the man selected to be *matai* had voluntarily chosen to live, say, in his mother's home village, or that he had ever lived there. Adoption aside, he may have been taken to the village as a child, growing up there and regarding that place as his original home; for a divorced or widowed woman often returns to her father's village and may take some or all of her children with her. The individual's choice is reversed in this case: whether to stay where he is or to go to his father's village. Secondly, prior residence in a village is not a wholly essential condition of succession there, though once a man becomes a *matai* he is usually ex-

---

[2] The succession rights of a remaining brother are expressed by the Samoan phrase *toe o le uso*.

[3] There is a great deal of variation among Samoans regarding selection of *matai*. Among some groups there is alternation of succession between agnatic and uterine descendants, according to prior agreement (BMG, Misc., Sec. of Native Affairs to R. Tate, 12 February 1919).

pected to live a good deal of the time in the village where his title belongs. Therefore, localities of residence and succession do not always coincide, but in so far as they do, the coincidence is governed by no fixed rule of unilineality as a limitation upon succession and residence.

In the long run, the individual's performance in matters of residence, succession and group participation must influence the course of effective descent, or descent group membership. By birth he has immediate rights in the descent groups of two grandparents, with residual rights in the groups of the other two, and still more distant associations with other groups. If he lives in his father's village, participates in the affairs of his father's household and the descent group of that household, and succeeds to a title through his father, his associations with the affairs of other descent groups will be relatively less active, especially on the death of kinsmen who link him directly to them. Only if his mother and father—and/or two or more grandparents—come from the same area can he maintain close and regular contact with more than one group, and even then his everyday connections will be closer with one than with the others. This means that his inherited rights and claims will be utilized most intensely in one direction. His child, unless taken away, will fit in turn into the pattern the father has established: he will live and work in the village of his father's father, while in the household and village of his father's mother and in the villages of other kindred he may be only an occasional visitor, with rights and claims gradually dying out through infrequent use. Meanwhile, this child will have acquired associations elsewhere through his mother, and so he will repeat the experience of his parents, pressing some of his rights and letting others lapse. After several generations of this process, some descent group ties will be forgotten. Some will be remembered but activated only on special occasions, as when exchange goods are being collected and distributed, when political alliances are being formed or when refuge must be sought. At least two groups, though, will regard the Samoan as a member, with land rights and interests in title succession pertaining in each. These ties will normally be through his father's father, first, and his mother's father, second; but the connections and their precedence will vary in individual cases.

The position of the individual with regard to descent and rights of inheritance has been illustrated by a variety of conditions and preferences, but perhaps its potentialities and limits may be seen most clearly against the background of the brother-sister relationship in Samoa.

From the time of puberty the interests and activities of the brother and sister begin to diverge. This is natural enough, of course, but in Samoa differences between siblings of opposite sex are very strongly institutionalized. In their personal relations, brother and sister must

observe strictest propriety, avoiding familiarity and all references to
sexual matters, and taking care not to be together except in the company
of others. In the village they join separate inter-household status groups,
the 'aumāga and the aualuma. And in the affairs of a descent group they
will assume, as adults, different positions which reflect the divergence
of their interests—and those of their respective descendants—in the title
and property of the group. This third aspect of their relationship should
be examined more closely.

A brother and sister share rights in a descent group—that of their
father's father, say—but in the implementation of their rights their
prospects differ substantially. The sister cannot expect to succeed to
chiefly office; and unless the locality of her husband's household is
situated very near that of her father's, or unless her husband consents
to neglect his own interests in order to live in her father's household
for extended periods, she cannot keep a regular watch on the affairs and
property of her descent group. In contrast, her brother may contest and
hold the matai title and, barring bad conduct, may always live on the
group's land and use its other property. Further, the sister has less
chance of passing to her own son a share in the immediate advantages
which her brother's son will probably enjoy in the group's title and
property.

But while the Samoan woman, through 'foreign' residence and exclusion from title succession, is generally deprived of some of the effective
rights which her brother exercises in their father's descent group and
household, she has others which, in effect, compensate her for the 'loss'.
These include the right to consider and disagree with her brother's proposals concerning title succession and the alienation of land, a first choice
of the fine mats, siapo and other goods acquired by the descent group in
its exchange relations, and the right to demand food and other produce
from her brother. The sister is thus able to retain a measure of control over
the administration of the local affairs of her father's descent group and
to share goods which she has not helped to produce. And through the
medium of her brother, she can obtain for her husband and children
articles which they may want for their personal use or to help meet
their commitments in the descent groups and village in which they are
active. At one time the rights of the sister were upheld by the belief that
she had the power to curse her brother and his children, bringing
sterility, illness or death upon them if her interests and demands were
disregarded. This belief is not widely or intensely held today, but the
sister is still influential and highly respected. The latter circumstance is
due partly to the importance of her marriage and the consequent exchange relations between affines. But no doubt it also arises from the
development of modern transport, which enables a woman to visit her

home village more frequently and to interfere more regularly in the affairs of her brother's household.

The relationship between brother and sister is extended to their respective children, so that a woman's son,[4] for example, may demand goods from her brother and her brother's children and exercise a voice regarding questions of land and *matai*-ship in which she herself is concerned. The effects of this relationship continue after the brother and sister, between whom it originated, have died, the parties involved still belonging to a common descent group but usually differing in the manner in which they exercise rights therein.

In view of what has been said, it must now be clear that a descent group divides along two quite different, but often complementary, lines: (1) according to residence, between members who live in the village where the group's title and ancestral land are located and those who live elsewhere; and (2) according to the sex of the member and/or the sex of the person through whom he is connected with the group. The division between brothers and sisters, and between their children, is a formal one, the 'male' and 'female' sides being distinguished by the terms *tama tāne* and *tama fafine*, respectively.[5] At any given time, then, the two sides of a descent group may be geographically separated. Furthermore, as already implied, an individual will be *tama tāne* in one group and *tama fafine* in another, though his being one or the other will still not, of necessity, deny him a choice of residence.

If its development over a period of time is considered, the brother-sister relationship emerges as a fairly complex one. For example, in the accompanying schematic diagram, which could be extended indefinitely to either side of A and H, it may be noted first that A, B and C are *tama fafine* to D, E and F and that, similarly, G, E and F are *tama*

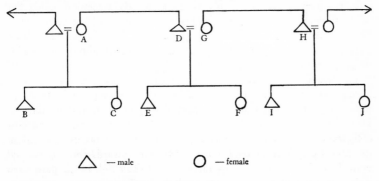

△ — male          ○ — female

[4] Who is her brother's *tama sā* or 'sacred son'.

[5] Meaning 'male children' and 'female children', with reference to the original division between siblings.

*fafine* to H, I and J. Between B and C, E and F, and I and J there are, at the same time, brother-sister relationships which will become important in the affairs of their respective descent groups only when the brothers are mature enough to assume some kind of responsibility for matters in which the sisters have an interest. Until that happens, the more crucial brother-sister links are those between D and A, and H and G. When the members of the second generation are of mature age, and their parents are dead, B and C will still be *tama fafine* to E and F, and all four will remain co-members of a descent group. A similar tie will persist between E and F, and I and J. If E is a *matai*, he will be administering land in which B and C have an interest, and he may even have the title which A had hoped B would have. If B has a title through his father, his relations with E will be influenced by his wanting to get for his use, as a *matai*, all of the fine mats and other goods that E can be induced to supply.

In normal circumstances, B and C will suspect that once they are dead, their surviving descendants will stand to gain very little from the brother-sister link established by D and A. In most cases, children of B and C would not share active descent group membership with the children of E and F, and they would be outside the usual line of title succession passing from the father of D and A. It may be anticipated, then, that the D-A link will lose much of its force in the third generation, to be 'replaced' by the B-C and E-F links, which in any case will have been operating during the adulthood of B and C, and of E and F. Therefore, one may say that the effects of a single brother-sister relationship will tend to persist during two generations, at least, but that there will be a network of overlapping relationships of that order.

Within the descent group the brother-sister relationship that matters most is generally the one involving the senior sister (senior among her own sisters and senior in terms of her generation) and her descendants. It was this sister whose cursing power was believed to have been strongest, and it is she who still figures as the leading *tama fafine* influence in the affairs of the group.

The senior *tama fafine* element will ordinarily pass out of the descent group and outside the line of *matai* succession. When this happens, its influence declines but need not vanish altogether. In fact, it is common for the members of an *entire* descent group to observe formal *tama tāne* obligations towards people outside—not towards all others who might theoretically qualify as their *tama fafine*, but towards those connected with them through some memorable brother-sister link in the past. Such a tie may sometimes persist as a result of segmentation or some formal covenant binding brothers and sisters and their descendants. To the outsider, it appears to link two *matai* and their descent groups—those of their fathers, if succession has been agnatic[6]—in the giving and receiving of fine mats, for example, or the rendering of mutual assistance in political affairs.

It must be apparent that the brother-sister relationship in Samoa helps to maintain contact between kinsmen who would be separated structurally, as well as geographically, in a purely agnatic system. In many cases it may be a highly integrative force in social relations, but it is hardly conceivable that a bond characterized by a division, even an opposition, of interests within the descent group—again, a *feagaiga*—will always be a secure and harmonious one. The two sides can maintain a delicate balance if they adhere to what are, ideally, their separate roles in their descent group meetings and exchange obligations; even in these spheres there may arise tension and exploitation. Only too frequently, though, one side tries to usurp or ignore the rights of the other. The ensuing breach of relations, involving people of a non-localized group, may have far-reaching effects, threatening the stability and security of several villages and perhaps even endangering the general political order.

From the standpoint of this study, the most important objects of contention between *tama fafine* and *tama tāne* are the control of land use and production, *matai* succession, and positions to be taken regarding large-scale political issues and controversies. A dispute over land may be an integral part of a dispute over *matai* succession; but this is not always the case, for it may transpire that one section of a descent group attempts to withdraw or withhold from the *matai*'s authority a portion of the land which his title would ordinarily empower him to administer. Any members of a group may be responsible for such a dispute, but discord between *tama tāne* and *tama fafine* is particularly common. For example, a woman may want for herself, her children and even for her husband or his relatives the chance of using land belonging to the descent group to which she is affiliated through her father. If she and those with her are prepared to submit to the authority of the *matai*—her brother, say— then they might use the land without difficulty. The trouble arises if she goes beyond this, claiming independent rights in land by virtue of descent from her deceased father, and possibly of his testamentary gift (*tofi*). Such a claim would deny the authority of the woman's brother to control the allocation of land and the recruitment and organization of those who use it. If she were to get her way in the matter, establishing permanent rights for herself and her descendants, a portion of the land of her father's descent group might be completely alienated from the control of the future members of the group. The land itself

[6] Except for its origin, the *tama fafine* would not necessarily have any greater matrilineal bias than would the *tama tāne* group.

might not be so important, unless there were a shortage or unless the graves of ancestors were located there. But it would be a serious blow to the dignity of a *matai* if some of his *tama fafine* and affines were to use land in his village without his permission; and furthermore, their doing so would introduce a foreign and potentially troublesome element into his village.[7]

The title pretensions of the *tama fafine* may also have serious consequences. It has been mentioned already that uterine succession may be acceptable in certain circumstances, especially when the man to be chosen has proved his merit by living and working in the village to which the title belongs. But one may take the example of an 'outsider' who wishes to succeed, against claimants among his *tama tāne*, to the title which has been held by his mother's father or her brother. He knows that if he does not get the title, no son of his will be likely to get it. On the other hand, his *tama tāne* know that a shift of the succession to his side may cut them out of the *matai*-ship altogether, unless the title is split. However, they do not regard segmentation as desirable in itself, for it might introduce a divisive element into village affairs and also compromise the status of the title, leaving unsettled the question of the seniority of the branches. The *tama fafine*, on the strength of their own personal influence, might never achieve their aim; but if the sister's husband's people are powerful, and if the title or the political orientation of the *tama tāne* is worth quarrelling over, the *tama fafine* demand may pose an immediate threat to the safety of the household and village of the *tama tāne*. Because of kinship connections and/or the political implications of outside interference in the *matai*-ship, the entire village or surrounding district in which the *matai* title is located may enter the controversy and may even divide on the issue. When *tama fafine* claims reach such proportions as this—or threaten to do so—they cannot be ignored. The choice is between a peaceful settlement and violence—or at the present time, an appeal to a central government authority. Since the Samoan process of mediation has never worked very successfully in the absence of strong neutral forces, the above crisis might well have been carried to the battlefield in former times.[8]

[7] Disputes of this kind are numerous in Samoa. They may be taken to a land court now, but during the nineteenth century there was no tribunal capable of dealing with them effectively save for the Land Commission of the early 1890s, which decided issues arising from alienation to Europeans.

[8] It was precisely this kind of situation which led to fighting over the Mauga title in Tutuila late in the nineteenth century. The dispute between the *tama tāne* and *tama fafine* was aggravated by the fact that the two sides supported different parties in a wider controversy over the Samoan 'kingship'. This case was given much publicity partly because a British warship stopped the fighting, but otherwise it was not exceptional.

Leaving aside for the moment the political implications of the dispute and the aftermath of a decisive battle, one may consider what might happen if the point of war were not reached. In that event, action concerning the *matai*-ship could take one of the following courses. First, a *tama fafine* contender might succeed to the title, with or without an understanding that upon his death it must revert to someone on the *tama tāne* side. Towards his *tama tāne* the successful contender, in this case, would probably have to abandon his active role of *tama fafine*, which would clash with his performance of the duties of *matai*. Otherwise he would invite further dissension, leading to violence, to his loss of the title or to segmentation of the descent group. Secondly, the descent group might divide forthwith, splitting the *matai* title and forming two groups, one headed by a *tama fafine* chief and the other by a *tama tāne* chief. Or thirdly, the sister's son might, with the permission of his father's people and of his mother's home village, bring to the latter place a new branch (*ma'apū*) of his patrilateral descent group, complete with title, which would create a new descent group related as *tama fafine* to his mother's brother's group. The last form of settlement might, of course, just as easily arise from title contention in the village of the sister's husband.[9] Still, the host village would always have to concede something, for land would have to be made available and, more important, the new title would have to be incorporated into the organization of the village, including its chiefly council and *fa'alupega*.

A decision based upon the reversionary rights of the *tama tāne* could lead to a reopening of the controversy at a later date, title succession and, perhaps, change of residence having bolstered the position of *tama fafine* elements of the descent group. Such a dispute might, to be sure, lapse with the *tama fafine* chief's succeeding to another title through his father. But while, until recent years, he would probably have given up the first title upon assuming the second, now he would be inclined to hold both concurrently, travelling by motor launch or bus between his two households in order to retain active and transmissible rights in both places. Alternatively, the problem of future succession might be resolved by the dying out of one of the opposing sides, in which event the original division of the descent group would disappear. But if the *matai*-ship dispute persisted, segmentation would no doubt occur eventually.

## Lineages

The Samoans are among the few Polynesian peoples who considered themselves to have originated in the islands where Europeans found

---

[9] Such contention may be the initial reason for the *tama fafine* pretensions, for an unsuccessful competitor for one title may seek opportunities elsewhere within the limits of the groups to which he is directly related by descent.

them.[10] In their view, Tagaloa, the principal deity, created the islands, and from him were descended the founders of the most ancient human lineages, villages and political institutions.[11] First there was the primeval void, giving way to natural phenomena which in several generations produced Tagaloa and the forces and materials with which he created Samoa and begat mankind. With the coming of Christianity the Samoan creation myth has undergone outward change, but its social orientation remains virtually unaltered, the expression 'Samoa is Founded in God'[12] having the same implications for the social structure as the Tagaloa myth once had.[13]

At their remotest points, some thirty or thirty-five generations back, the best-known Samoan genealogies merge into the pantheon of deities and account for the reputed origins of the highest-ranking titles. The ensuing 'lines' record subsequent title succession, the origins of subsidiary titles and putative links of marriage and adoption. For reasons already given, the genealogies are principally agnatic in so far as they purport to record title succession; but when such lore is employed to support remote title claims or to demonstrate that several titles are connected through marriages, female links may be given greater emphasis than would otherwise pertain.

Although chiefly titles pass through descent lines and integrate descent groups, Samoan genealogies cannot be regarded as complete or accurate representations of relations among people who lived in the remote past. Even if the more obvious mythical elements are discounted, particularly in the earlier generations, little of what remains should be taken as historically correct in the strictest sense. Since the Samoan language had no written form before the arrival of European missionaries, genealogies and other lore had to be remembered and passed along by word of mouth, leaving considerable room for error. Beyond this, however, there are many alternatives or variables in Samoan descent, succession and descent group affiliation, making for changes of social and political alignments, not all of which will be remembered. Moreover, descent, rank, succession and inheritance are readily subject to controversy, so

---

[10] Some immigration was acknowledged, e.g. from Fiji, Tonga and Wallis Island, but the main part of the population was held to have been of autochthonous Samoan ancestry.

[11] There are many recorded versions of this descent: e.g. Krämer, *Samoan Islands*, i, 318 ff; Pratt, *Genealogy of Kings*, 657-60; MS., Churchill.

[12] 'Fa'avae i le Atua Samoa', the motto of Western Samoa.

[13] Sir Peter Buck related an amusing example of the rendering of the Bible to conform to Samoan dogma. Some of his Samoan informants, pressed to defend their belief in Samoan autochthony, held that their islands had been the site of the Garden of Eden (*Vikings of the Sunrise*, 286-7).

that at any given time there may be conflicting versions or interpretations of the same people's genealogies. These latter differences persist
until the contenders settle their disputes and forget or suppress information which has been shown up as 'incorrect'. Therefore, the chief
importance of the genealogies lies not in their value for purposes of
historical reconstruction but, rather, in the way they expound former
relationships and ties which, actual or not, conform to and validate
relations among chiefly titles and descent groups in the present and
recent past.[14]

In theory, going by the Samoans' first preferences, lineages oriented
round the progress of title succession should be agnatic, but in fact,
they usually incorporate some *tama fafine* links and so may be regarded,
in the long run, as 'ambilineages'. But while strict unilineality is not the
rule, either in practice or ideology, it is none the less true that a given
*tama tāne* element, or lineage, usually has the greater continuity in time
and place, members at a particular period tending to form a local group
and to dominate succession to the title of their descent group, which
title generally belongs permanently in a certain village. Besides, when a
*tama fafine* link does occur in a chain of succession, with a corresponding
shift in the reckoning of descent *vis-à-vis* a corporate group of kin, it is
usually followed by reassertion of the dominance of the agnatic principle.
In other words, then, Samoa may be said to have a system of lineages
whose various corporate extensions into the present are predominantly
agnatic and locally oriented, while a given *tama fafine* to *tama tāne*
relationship may be viewed more as a transitory phenomenon arising
from differences of sex between siblings than as a persistent characteristic of individual descent lines. The Samoan lineage system is
further defined by the relationship of chiefly titles which are formally
ranked in terms of their segmentation from, or affiliation to, parent
titles or lines, and in turn, by the fact that the members of the groups
which own these titles acknowledge descent from a common named
ancestor, taking for their genealogical lines of reference those through
which the titles are reputed to have passed. This means, of course, that a
formal relationship of titles and descent groups in the structure of rank
and in lineage affiliation exists within a range of possible relationships,
implying scope for realignment; but taken together, the choices represented by actual conditions strongly favour common descent through
agnatic lines of a segmentary character.

The standing of chiefly titles and their holders, and so of lineages too,
is not absolutely fixed, exigencies of political contention and personal

14 Irrelevant or unimportant events, such as the dying out of lineages and the
deactivation of titles, are seldom recounted in the genealogies, except with regard
to recent generations.

prowess having obviously led to shifts in the hierarchy of rank in Samoa. Within a lineage complex, however, the titles and lines of highest rank are usually those alleged to be the oldest and/or, with reference to lineage ramification, those purportedly named as senior on past occasions when segmentation occurred. Implicit in the name of a lineage and of its title and associated descent group, this conception of rank is grounded in the belief that the lineage, or at least the line of title succession, is the channel through which have passed the ascribed status, rank and *mana* (or supernaturally-based efficacy) of the chiefly title and of those who, by virtue of their descent, control it. If rank is disputed, *de facto* power may 'prove' the seniority of a particular lineage, perhaps with the result that 'history' is recast or reinterpreted; but the Samoans consider the logic of this process perfectly sound.

A ramified lineage of the largest scale, which may be reputed to have originated directly with the deities, can be termed a maximal lineage. Its span includes titled lineages which are thought to have segmented from the parent line or to have joined it by means of incorporation or merging. The people belonging to a maximal lineage may number several thousand, and even the *tama tāne* may be dispersed among many different villages; but they share the belief that their titles are graded relative to the parent or senior line and that the holder of their highest-ranking title represents the dignity of the maximal lineage. They gather for feasts and ceremonial exchanges when an important marriage or the bestowal of their senior title is being celebrated. And ideally, though often not in fact, they formerly joined in war to defend the honour of their senior titleholder, whom they regarded as their closest human link with the deities.

Between the maximal lineage as a whole and its most junior sub-branch there are named lineage complexes of greatly varying span and seniority. Specific genealogical references are required if the constituents of each are to be described exactly. Broad terminological classifications are of little assistance, for in Samoa the formal recognition of common origin and of a single titular head does not alone determine the extent to which the members of a segmented lineage actively cohere. When lineage ramifications are concentrated locally, the degree of lineage unity may be very great indeed, especially at the village level, where unity is essential to many group activities and where there are effective means of determining and maintaining the relative seniority of branch lineages. But lineage complexes whose elements are territorially dispersed may have little inclusive unity. Their affiliates may come together for cere-monial exchanges and yet diverge in such matters as church member-ship, ascription of rank, appointment of a senior titleholder—and, in the past, warfare. For example, it is very common, when Samoans gather from different villages, for chiefs of the same as well as of different lineages to contest rank and precedence. A *tulāfale* must be adroit to satisfy everyone and keep the gathering intact. At one time, title disputes were a more serious source of difficulty,[15] particularly with regard to the senior titles of maximal lineages. The identity and ritual importance of the titles were clearly acknowledged, but members of important sub-lineages frequently fought for the control of them. For the present, then, the village, where most segmentation initially occurs, may be taken as the principal focus of lineages of intermediate span, provided it is quite clear, first, that only a few villages are seats of senior titles of maximal lineages and, secondly, that the remaining villages differ considerably with regard to the span and seniority of the largest and/or the oldest sub-lineages represented within them. Thus, villages, as localities, may also be graded according to the rank of their senior titles, but the village (or, in some cases, a group of neighbouring villages) is still the largest locality within which the seniority of lineage segments and their titles generally supports an effective and persistent hierarchy of authority, even though some village chiefs may owe their positions in that hierarchy to their ties outside the area.[16]

Lineage segments of relatively narrow span—up to five or six generations, say—are more frequently confined to single villages with regard to the titles which they link to common origins. A complex of similar extent is that comprising a long-established lineage and its more recent branches, while excluding the more remote branches. Sub-lineages of the latter order, whatever the respective rank of their titles, are the bases of many of the intra-village groups of closely related households.

Finally, there are the unbranched sub-lineages, often termed minimal lineages. These are comparable to other single lines, exclusive of branches, in that each is represented by one title, one domestic household and one descent group. Unbranched sub-lineages also vary in span and hence in the seniority of their titles, depending on when segmentation last took place; but over all, their genealogical range is smaller than that of the lineage segments already described and seldom exceeds five or six generations. Thus, while the household and descent group of a minimal lineage may be relatively independent of others in questions concerning land and title succession, this is not common.

As represented thus far, a titled lineage usually differentiates by segmentation, with the members of a descent group splitting up to form

---

[15] Title disputes are still numerous, but now, when they get out of hand, they usually come before government officials for mediation or adjudication.

[16] In the control of most group activities the village usually represents the upper limit of inclusive, hierarchically-ordered lineage unity, inter-village affairs more often proceeding on a basis of voluntary participation and joint direction.

two or more groups, each under a separate male chief. Whether the existing title is divided, its name being retained for each of the resultant parts, or whether one or more new titles are created in addition to the original one,[17] one branch will generally be regarded as a direct continuation of the ancestral line and the others as offshoots founded by members of the group which divides at the point of segmentation. Conversely, when lines disappear, by dying out or merging, their titles go out of use or combine with others; but among lineage branches with a common origin, only the relatively junior lines are allowed to lose their separate identity.[18] As a rule, segmentation reflects strong competition for the *matai*-ship and the control of descent group affairs, but that does not mean that the members cease to work together after their formal division. If segmentation has taken place because a dying chief wills it —for example, in order to distribute his authority and title among his children—relations may be quite harmonious and the graded rank of the branch lineages settled and agreed. In any case, if the households of the branches remained in the same locality, as would happen much more often than not, disputes over the position of *matai sili* could be settled by their village.

It would appear that during the course of many generations entire villages, or large sections of villages, as well as groups of neighbouring villages, have developed from one or more parent lineages, mainly through the process of agnatic segmentation. The complexities of Samoan descent and marriage, however, have also facilitated other types of formal lineage differentiation. The first of these has arisen from uterine succession, which Samoans consider permissible, though preferably avoided. As noted, many lineages have some acknowledged female links in their records of title succession, but some branches are actually reputed to have been founded by, or through, women at points of segmentation, in the manner already described. The same principles of seniority apply to this form of segmentation as to the other; but the resulting titles are distinguished as *tama fafine* and *tama tāne* to each other, with the passing of special rights and obligations to their holders.

Lineage differentiation may also arise from marriage, which in each case represents the intersection of two lineages, leading in the first instance to a set of formal relationships between affines. When a marriage is publicly celebrated, affines gather to exchange goods, the bride's people putting up fine mats and other articles produced by women (*tōga*), and the man's side presenting food, boats and other

[17] Or unused titles may be revived.

[18] This tendency may be checked against *matai* lists, which show that recorded titles which are now defunct are nearly all of low rank.

items, now including cash, which are produced by men (*'oloa*).[19] Since the extent of intra-lineage participation in marriage ceremonies is a function of rank, a balance is achieved in the number of participants and in the amount of goods exchanged only if the bride and groom are of similar rank. For this reason, among others, wide discrepancy of rank between the parties is most undesirable; to avoid it, the most important marriages are arranged by *tulāfale* among whose first concerns is the equivalence of the affinal relationship.[20]

The formal exchange relationship persists for the duration of the marriage, being activated on a smaller scale when a child is born and when the affines attend or contribute to one another's ceremonial functions. In the past, the two sides also approached one another with exchange goods when canvassing for help in war. Marriage itself conveyed no absolute right to political support; but once a child was born of a union, bridging the two lineages by virtue of his dual descent, conditions for the formation of an inter-lineage alliance were especially favourable.

Marriage ties between people of high rank have often led to the territorial dispersal of lineages through the formation of *ma'apū* branches. When a chief has had sons of several legitimate unions, he or his heirs may arrange for one son to be the principal title successor, while one or more sons of other marriages establish titled junior branches in the villages of their respective mothers. When a high-ranking chief was able to contract polygynous or numerous successive marriages, this kind of segmentation was a means of exploiting conjugal and *tama fafine* relationships in order to establish permanent rather than transitory ties between scattered villages and, at the same time, of reducing the pressure towards segmentation within the chief's own village. The missions, however, have discouraged divorce and polygyny and have influenced Samoan ideas of legitimacy, with the result that the number of recognized connections through women has tended to diminish in proportion to adult population, while elementary families have been increasing in size. Therefore, the relative significance of *ma'apū* branching has probably declined.

Marriage, *ma'apū* segmentation and relations between *tama tāne* and *tama fafine* are links which in special circumstances may lead to the

19 In general, *'oloa* articles have utilitarian as well as symbolic value, as suggested by application of the term *'oloa* to European trade goods. Articles of *tōga*, in contrast, have little direct utilitarian value. They do, however, represent large expenditures of time and labour and are the only traditional goods which can be readily stored away and used, in the manner of currency and coin, to pay off obligations, such as those incurred in the building of houses. The oldest fine mats, distinguished by special names, are very highly valued.

20 Some marriage ceremonies are very costly, involving the accumulation and use of thousands of pounds, hundreds of mats and enormous quantities of food.

reorganization of formal lineage affiliations. This was particularly true
when contestants for senior titles were allowed to proceed to war; for
in warfare, Samoan chiefs and would-be chiefs found some of the most
valued opportunities to prove their stature, and in the building of their
alliances, they always endeavoured to exploit their inter-lineage connections. For example, if the senior title of a maximal lineage was being
contested, not only would the members of that lineage be divided in
their political loyalties, but each contender would gather supporters
through his personal kindred ties in other lineages.[21] This meant that a
village whose dominant lineage was not directly involved in the struggle
might join one of the contenders because it possessed a title that was
ma'apū, tama tāne or tama fafine to his agnatic line. Alliances constructed in such fashion tended to be loose and impermanent, held
together only with respect to individual controversies and the ceremonial
exchanges which were involved in title succession. Nevertheless, they
placed considerable strain upon established lineage orientations, particularly since every successful war party had the power to create new
honours and privileges in the name of its titular head. In one instance,
the chiefs of a branch of one maximal lineage, in recognition of their
support, might be given the right to be consulted in the bestowal of a
title in another maximal lineage. Or one or more tulāfale of one village
might acquire the right to use the name of a tulāfale of another. Distinctions of this kind were mainly ceremonial and honorific in substance,
but the Samoans prized them highly and always remembered them,
and were influenced by them in the shaping of future alliances.

When a successful alliance enabled Samoans to acquire privileges, titles
or rank superior to those which they enjoyed among their own lineage
affiliates, the way was opened for the formal realignment of lineages.
A notable case of this kind arose late in the nineteenth century when
the first Tamasese founded 'Aiga o Mavaega, with branches in Upolu
and Savai'i. Tamasese was a leader of high birth who, after achieving
considerable renown as a warrior, proceeded to contest the paramount
chieftainship or 'kingship' of Samoa, basing his claims upon agnatic
descent from a great-grandfather. Among his most faithful supporters,
however, were several villages to which he was related through women,
both by tama fafine ties and by ma'apū offshoots of his own agnatic
lineage.[22] In acknowledgement of this assistance, Tamasese willed that a
new sub-lineage[23] should be founded in the villages concerned. His wish

[21] A contender for a high-ranking title was tama'āiga (the son of the families or
kindred) to his supporters.

[22] The village of Tamasese's own mother opposed him.

[23] As an affiliate of Sa Tupua, a maximal lineage of which Tamasese was for a
time the titular head.

was carried out, and owing to his high rank as founder, 'Aiga o Mavaega[24] came to occupy a senior position among formal Samoan lineages.

This is but one example, but it indicates that descent through women, though of secondary importance among Samoans, may also extend in some circumstances to the rearrangement of ranked relationships through the shifting of lineage affiliations. The same may be said of adoption, which may formally unite the lineages of a parent and adopting parent (not necessarily two of the same sex), with one of the parties becoming the founder of a new branched lineage.[25] It should be clear, however, that formal lineage realignments merely reflect the instability of Samoan lineages in their widest span. At any time, established affiliations may give way, in action, to connections which cut across or conflict with them; and as long as the people who make the change are still able to recognize some senior titleholder as their head, they may move from one maximal lineage or sub-lineage to another. It would appear, then, that in addition to locality and the established system of ranked and titled lineages, immediate kindred ties play an integrative role in Samoan group relations, but that only at the village level and below have all these considerations normally been accommodated in such a way that stable group organization has been maintained. This should become more apparent when district organization and Samoan political movements are examined.

## The extent of village autonomy

Every adult resident of a village is clearly involved in a network of relations with people elsewhere, who may include affines, *tama fafine* and even *tama tāne*. If a villager has been adopted, his biological parents may also be outsiders with whom he maintains contact. If he is a chief of high rank, he may have a direct interest in the bestowal of the senior title of some important lineage centred in another village; or conversely, other lineage chiefs outside his village may have interests in the title which he holds. Far from being an isolated community, then, the Samoan village is the scene of frequent coming and going on the part of people engaged in such activities as the exchange or distribution of mats, the selection of titleholders, the celebration of births and the performance of funeral rites. It is in the course of this visiting between villages that Samoans expend much of their energy and resources and

[24] Literally 'the family of the dying testament'. This is one example of a lineage bearing the name of a special event in place of that of its founder.

[25] e.g. Sa Fenunuivao of Atua (Upolu) is related to Sa Tupua as the 'mother of Tupua'. The original relationship was reputedly one of adoption, the child Tupua being given by Sa Fenunuivao.

E

find much of their pleasure and pastime. The relationships herein concerned, however, may confront a village with political problems, some affecting its internal order and others relating to formal inter-village organization. In the handling of these problems a paramount consideration is the village's desire to maintain its independence from external interference and control, enforcing its local regulations among residents and visitors alike and exercising freedom of choice when determining which, if any, outside political causes to support.

Many external links are potential sources of local disorder. Disunited descent groups may cause disputes over land and titles which disturb the peace of the village. People may come in as visitors, new residents or *matai*-elect who for personal or political reasons are unwilling to accept the way village affairs are run. Or residents may be subjected to outside pressures which divide their loyalties and cause them to exert discordant influence in the village. Whatever the source of disagreement, events may lead to open challenges to existing authority within the village, and when this happens, attempts must be made to punish the dissidents and, if necessary, to expel them. There is no custom which exempts anyone, visitor or resident, foreigner or Samoan, from conforming to the decisions and regulations of the village when he is there.

In the nineteenth century, when there was usually no effective central government of any kind, the village itself was chiefly responsible for keeping order. Some of the steps taken to achieve this end were often severe. For example, when a village was irreconcilably divided on any important issue, local or otherwise, the weaker party might be driven out in order to restore village unity. Individuals who committed serious offences were treated no less harshly. When travellers or visitors stirred up trouble or acted disrespectfully towards the village, even unintentionally, they were liable to immediate attack and expulsion by the 'aumāga. The Samoans were so sensitive about village honour and the enforcement of local customs and regulations that their reaction against transgressors was inclined to be hasty and violent.

From the local point of view, these measures were about the only ones which could have been taken, and in so far as they freed the village of divisive elements, they were effective. But they had their limitations, for the forcible expulsion of offenders, and to a lesser degree most other punishments, concerned people in other places: an attack upon visitors was an insult to their own village and invited retaliation. A person badly treated by his affines, for example, would look to his other kin for vengeance; and Samoans expelled from their village of residence would ask their connections elsewhere to restore them to their land by force. For an aggrieved party there were great advantages in the far-flung relationships which Samoans maintained, since refuge and sympathy were nearly always available somewhere. For the village there were obvious disadvantages because local conflicts, however and wherever they originated, were likely to involve outsiders sooner or later. The village could choose whether to act in the first instance, but once having acted, it had no immunity from the consequences save what the strength of its own numbers and that of its outside supporters might lend it. Nevertheless, the village was generally prepared to act immediately, even without alliances, to preserve local order, whether or not this entailed the risk of war. At other levels of political action, especially where long-term questions of high-ranking titles and other honours were concerned, the Samoans were more given to circumspection. In the village, however, they could less easily afford delay, for against the uncertainty of war there was always the assurance that failure to re-establish the unity of the village and validate its hierarchy of authority would undermine its efficiency in the performance of its necessary functions. In this regard it was just as important to deal with those who spoke disrespectfully of village chiefs as with those who stole from other people's houses, for either act, if left unpunished, weakened Samoan confidence in village government.

If, as a result of action taken to restore internal order, a village was confronted with a threat of attack, it usually prepared to do battle, gathering whatever outside support it could at short notice. When matters reached this stage, there were only two traditional means of avoiding war. The first was to offer compensation, together with a formal gesture of self-degradation (*ifoga*).[26] To perform the *ifoga*, the highest chiefs of the village had to go to the village which threatened aggression and there, on the *malae*, bow down and offer fine mats and the humbling of their dignity in satisfaction of the offence. Since this gesture was the greatest loss of face which a Samoan could suffer voluntarily—one out of proportion to the seriousness of most transgressions—it was never viewed lightly by either party to a dispute. A village would often choose flight in the face of attack, leaving its houses and plantations to be destroyed, rather than apologize so abjectly. But when an *ifoga* was undertaken, it was customary that the other party should accept the gesture and agree to a peaceful settlement. A refusal, of course, meant that war was inevitable.

The other means of preventing war required the presence of a neutral party which would take the initiative in standing between the disputants and proposing terms of peace. Originally this party was a village or some chiefs related to both sides, but after the development of substantial

---

26 The *ifoga* could be performed in respect of any dispute, but it was particularly effective in small-scale disputes between villages, which in the nineteenth century were very numerous.

European influence, the mediators were more often headed by missionaries and pastors, or by consuls and naval officers. These foreign-led
parties were usually more persistent than Samoans alone would have
been; for if unsuccessful in preventing war, they kept at the belligerents
to try to stop the fighting. Though many disputes were merely prolonged by this kind of intervention, the missions, in particular, must be
credited with a number of settlements which Samoans could not have
achieved by peaceful means. In larger issues, however, mediation was
very seldom successful unless backed by European threats of force.

When inter-village disputes led to hostilities between parties more or
less equally matched, skirmishes might continue on land and sea until
the two sides had suffered losses sufficiently comparable to enable both
to withdraw without dishonour. By mutual agreement, a formal meeting
of reconciliation might then be held, officially ending the conflict. With
or without the formal peace settlement, however, the parties remained
cool towards one another and found it difficult to co-operate in matters
of joint concern, while for years afterwards, the slightest incident might
renew the old controversy.

Between parties of unequal strength or strategic advantage a decisive
battle was more likely. In this case, the losers were driven away and their
village looted and burned, forcing them to take refuge elsewhere. They
would then try to get outside help sufficient to enable them to reoccupy
their abandoned village, a move constituting a challenge to the victors
and causing the war to spread. If the refugees could get no such support,
they had to make the challenge alone or else wait until the other side
would agree to a peace settlement. From start to finish, wars of this
nature could last several years.

Therefore, while village autonomy was jealously guarded, it was never
absolute. The government of the village might be capable, initially, of
maintaining or restoring order in the face of external pressures; but
between villages which refused to respect each other's decisions and
actions, the final arbiter was force rather than the authority of a regular
government. When villages did co-operate, then, it was because their
leaders believed in a common cause or were, on one side or both,
subject to coercion.

These features of village government—its strength and its weakness—
were of utmost significance in relations between Samoans and Europeans
during the nineteenth century. The Samoans quite naturally assumed
the right to control the conduct of Europeans living in their villages, but
they were often challenged by consuls and naval officers when they
exercised such control. On the other hand, Europeans made demands
upon the villages which, if met, would have invited war: the villages
were supposed to punish their Samoan visitors against whom foreigners

had lodged complaints, whether or not they agreed with the charges; and they were expected to go outside their individual jurisdictions to search for sailors who had deserted and for Samoans who were wanted by the European authorities. The Samoans were denied some of those functions of government which were theirs by tradition and told that they must assume others which conflicted with their traditions. When Europeans gained little satisfaction from dealing with the separate villages, they turned to the organization of central government and failed again—and for comparable reasons.

*Inter-village political organization in the nineteenth century*

Though in some respects very elaborate, traditional inter-village political organization had few functions which Europeans regarded as properly belonging to government. After the villages had taken care of public works, the production of all subsistence and other goods, the control and use of land, the keeping of order and the bestowal of most *matai* titles, little remained for the larger units to do. In their *fa'a-Samoa* guise, their formal purposes were chiefly restricted to the maintenance of ritual and ceremonial relations between villages or members of dispersed lineages and to the control and support of some titles of high rank.

The principles of association by common locality and by common lineage affiliation often coincided, in effect, within small numbers of adjacent or nearly-adjacent villages, though two or more lineages would be present there. Within such an area—it may be called a sub-district— there would usually be a joint hierarchy and *fa'alupega* and also a joint council of chiefs but no other status groups (for example, *'aumāga*) of the sort found at the village level. Drawing the sub-district together were such considerations as the people's involvement in the bestowal of a senior title of an important inter-village lineage or performance of the complementary ceremonial functions of *'ali'i* villages' and *'tulāfale* villages'. In addition, a sub-district might participate as a unit in larger territorial groupings and in the presentation of gifts (*ta'alolo*) to a high chief representing its predominant maximal lineage affiliation; and in so acting it sometimes had, as will be shown, exclusive rights and privileges that distinguished it from other sub-districts.

Matters of common concern to the villages of a sub-district were administered by the joint *fono*, whose members were the highest chiefs of the respective villages. What have already been described as village affairs were not normally submitted to the sub-district council for over-riding control by it; but it frequently happened that member villages agreed to common policies in such matters or that one or two villages dominated the affairs of the others by sheer force. Sub-district organization was generally less stable than that of the single village, putative differences of seniority being more open to challenge, especially when one member village tried to interfere in the local activities of another, and factionalism was more likely to develop serious proportions.

Organized sub-districts appeared throughout Samoa, but they did not combine to a uniform degree in distinct and permanent districts. In this regard their cohesion varied with the extent to which maximal lineages were geographically concentrated; for as one of the principal functions of large-scale inter-village political organization was to orient Samoans towards their highest-ranking chiefs, an area was clearly delimited as a district only if most or all of its villages or sub-districts were associated with the same maximal lineage and took part in supporting the same senior title. Nearly every title of the highest rank was, of course, a focal point of non-local grouping, affiliated lineage chiefs (and, at all times, descent groups) being more or less dispersed territorially. Only one district, that consisting of the three islands of Manu'a, was a complete 'lineage area'. Several others, however, were so dominated by single maximal lineages that their sub-district components and boundaries were relatively fixed, while their senior titleholders superficially resembled 'district chiefs'. Districts of this order were Atua (the Tui Atua title), Tuamasaga (Malietoa, Gatoaitele, Tamasoāli'i), and A'ana (Tui A'ana) in Upolu; the combination of Manono, Apolima and Mulifanua, known as 'Aiga-i-le-Tai[27] (Malietoa); and Fa'asaleleaga in eastern Savai'i (Malietoa).

Tutuila contained mixed lineage elements, including many related to Atua, but had no titled maximal lineage of its own.[28] It had ten small, fairly cohesive sub-districts which in turn were formally grouped, five on each side, to make up two larger but less cohesive divisions, the east Falelima and the west Falelima.[29] Tutuila itself, however, did not constitute a formally-structured, all-inclusive district. Rather, the island emerged as an apparent entity only when a single party, among two or more, had forcibly established or defended its claim to represent itself as 'Tutuila'. Such a party, impermanent in its composition, would be centred in one or the other of the Falelima but would usually contain elements from both.

[27] Mulifanua is situated at the western tip of Upolu, facing Manono. 'Aiga-i-le-Tai means 'family in the sea'.

[28] For ceremonial purposes, and in the fa'alupega of all Samoa, Tutuila was regarded as a 'dependency' of Atua. But during the period covered by this study, the distinction had very little meaning, for Tutuila was not regarded by its inhabitants as related to Atua alone, nor did the island ever unite as a district to support all or any part of Atua in anything. It is true, however, that lineages of Atua were represented in Tutuila only by junior branches.

[29] Literally 'five houses', meaning the five sub-divisions of each area.

The island of Savai'i was no less mixed in its lineage components. Some of these, like 'Aiga o Mavaega, were important branches of maximal lineages that were also prominent in Upolu, while others represented maximal lineages that were restricted mainly to Savai'i but widely dispersed there. Only in the Fa'asaleleaga area did one maximal lineage—in this case, Sa Malietoa—have connections strong and pervasive enough to provide a basis of fairly permanent district structure centred in one place. During the nineteenth century the rest of Savai'i was nominally divided into two districts, Itu-o-Tane in the north and Itu-o-Fafine in the south. These districts, however, bore a closer resemblance to Tutuila than to Fa'asaleleaga in that each had, as well as numerous villages and several small sub-districts, two major inter-village structures rather of the order of the Falelima, through one or the other of which district ascendancy was exercised.[30] It is perhaps more satisfactory to think of Savai'i, east of Fa'asaleleaga, as composed of villages and 'sub-districts' linked non-locally by formal lineage affiliations, and locally by the exigencies of intermittent warfare, though at any given time there was never a great deal of practical difference between district organization in Savai'i and that in Upolu.

Some examples from Tuamasaga may be taken to illustrate the functions and limits of district and sub-district organization, together with the complex lineage and other traditional affiliations which cut across territorial boundaries in Samoa. Tuamasaga is the central district of Upolu, lying between Atua on the east and A'ana on the west and bounded by the sea on the north and south. The town and harbour of Apia are situated on the north coast of this district and are flanked on either side by some of the largest commercial plantations in Samoa.

The sub-districts of Tuamasaga are: Vaimauga to the north-east, extending from Apia to the border of Atua; Faleata on the central north coast, from Vaimoso to Puipa'a; Sagaga to the north-west, from Fale'ula to Sale'imoa, and including Malie, the Tuamasaga home of the high chief Malietoa; Safata to the south-west; and Si'umu to the south-east. But for a few settlements in the vicinity of Apia, all the villages of Tuamasaga were located on or near the shore during the nineteenth century. Direct communication between the two coasts lay through the uninhabited interior.

Each of the five sub-districts contained several villages, and with the exception of Si'umu, each had formal inter-village sub-divisions—three in Vaimauga and two in each of the others. Further, each sub-district except Sagaga had a joint council of chiefs and *fa'alupega*.

In every sub-district lineage affiliations with Sa Malietoa predominated; these were attributed mainly to segmentation and were reinforced by

---

30 But Tutuila did not, of course, have a titled maximal lineage of its own.

such traditional links as the granting of special honours and privileges by former Malietoa chiefs. Formal connections with other maximal lineages were not, however, excluded. In Vaimauga there were important ties with Sa Tupua of A'ana and Atua, through the Sa Tui A'ana and Salevalasi branches, respectively. In Faleata one of the leading chiefs, Faumuinā, was descended through Salevalasi of Atua and was related to Mata'afa,[31] while one of the Matai'a lines was connected with Sa Fenunuivao of Atua and with the ancestors of the first Tamasese. In Safata the outstanding lineage Sa Tunumafono was a direct offshoot of the Malietoa line, but its chiefs, as a privilege granted in war, had the right to be consulted in the bestowal of the senior title of 'Aiga Taua'ana and Sa Tuimaleali'ifano, branches of Sa Tupua in A'ana. Further, the powerful chief Su'atele of Safata was descended from Sa Tupua. These were but a few of the outside affiliations recognized in the fa'alupega. In addition there were other ties, including many of marriage and of descent through women, which were less formally acknowledged but which still had considerable bearing on inter-village associations and activities.

The sub-districts of Tuamasaga were related to one another in a number of different ways. Several major titles of Vaimauga and Si'umu were closely linked to a common origin, binding parts of the two sub-districts in a lineage and military relationship more intimate than, for example, any existing between Vaimauga and Safata. Parts of Safata and Faleata were similarly related, and Safata and part of Si'umu shared oracular functions as alataua.

The relationship between ali'i and tulāfale has already exemplified the importance of role specialization in certain joint activities. The formalities of district activity may better show how really elaborate Samoan specialization could be. In Tuamasaga, a traditional district fono was usually concerned in some way with the Malietoa title or its holder: for example, with the bestowal of the title or the marriage of the chief; or with the raising of war to defend the honour of the chief or to support his claim to other titles. Meetings for peaceful purposes were held at Malie; those relating to war convened at Afega, a village adjacent to Malie. No district meeting could properly be held anywhere else.

When any party wanted a district meeting, an approach had first to be made to the tulāfale of Malie and Afega. If the proposal proved acceptable there,[32] the holders of certain tulāfale titles of those villages were sent throughout Tuamasaga as messengers, putting it to particular

[31] The Mata'afa title of Salevalasi is said to have originated in Faleata.
[32] Among other things, the tulāfale had to consider the problem of accommodating a large number of visitors for several days.

sub-district chiefs, whose right it was to receive such messages, that a *fono* be held. In turn, each sub-district usually conducted a formal meeting to decide whether to support a district *fono* and, if concluding that it should, what views to advance on the subjects on which deliberation was being called for. If representation was forthcoming from each sub-district, the district meeting could be held.

On the day of the *fono*, parties from every sub-district gathered on the appropriate *malae*, taking set positions there. The recitation of the district *fa'alupega* and the performance of the kava ceremony came first, taking the elaborate and rigorous course essential to such formal occasions. Then there ensued discussion on matters of business during which the assembled parties expressed their views in an established order through appointed spokesmen.[33] In some cases the speakers had to be the holders of certain specific titles. In others there was room for some choice, allowing for substitution or rotation in the role of sub-district orator.[34] Needless to say, Malietoa did not speak.

In the district *fono* an issue was clearly decided only when all sub-district parties subscribed to a similar point of view. No vote was taken. Nor, for that matter, was there any hierarchy of authority within the district that gave certain sub-districts an overriding voice in the deliberations. Indeed, the various delegations and their spokesmen were disinclined to concede a right of superior place to any other except, perhaps, Malietoa or one of his rivals for high honours. If, however, such a title-holder succeeded directly by his own efforts in substantially swaying the chiefs of villages other than his own, it was due more to the stake they had in his acquiring or retaining a position of ceremonial and ritual pre-eminence than to any authority or power actually inherent in his office, which was largely that of a respected but 'captive' figurehead. A further aspect of the district's relatively low degree of centralization was the fact that the sub-districts, or elements within them, independ-

---

33 Some European observers have written incorrectly that the 'real power' in the sub-districts was exercised by the formal spokesmen, or that the power over a district rested with the *tulāfale* of the village in which the district met. Views of this kind may have been based upon the prominence of these chiefs in the formal proceedings. Had the performance of Samoan governments of the nineteenth century been considered more critically, such misconceptions might not have been formed, for the active participation of these sub-district and district spokesmen did not, in itself, make for more effective legislation and administration. When the Samoans refer to the rights and privileges of an office, they may use the term *pule*, which means power or authority; but they do not always mean power *over* others, as such, for *pule* may refer simply to a person's right to perform a public function *on behalf of* others.

34 When several chiefs were qualified to speak, they often engaged in a conventionalized 'argument' (*fa'atau*) on the *malae*, each asserting his right, though the choice would have been determined in advance.

ently performed specialized yet essential and complementary functions
in the implementation of decisions jointly taken at a general meeting
in Malie or Afega. As to military ventures, for example, leading *tulāfale* of Safata, together with Li'o of Si'umu, were once thought to have
oracular power to consult the war gods. If the views or susceptibilities
of these chiefs were disregarded, they could withhold their support from
the rest of the district, forcing a pro-war party to abandon its schemes
or look outside Tuamasaga for the services of *alataua* specialists. Similarly, Faleata was Tuamasaga's *itu'au*, the vanguard in battle, and in no
issue, much less one that concerned war, could its representations be
lightly ignored. Of the many other comparable functions, some of the
most important belonged to the *tulāfale* of the meeting centres of
Tuamasaga, who, like their counterparts in Savai'i, were called the
district Pule, as distinguished from the term Tumua, which designated
the *tulāfale* of the meeting centres of A'ana and Atua. The Pule were
not only responsible for the proper conduct of district assemblages,
including those devoted to ceremonial exchanges, but also led the proceedings entailed in the bestowal of the *pāpā*. In addition, the Pule
were Tuamasaga's principal spokesmen in formal meetings and negotiations between districts.

That is not to say, however, that the whole of Tuamasaga had to be
united, voluntarily or otherwise, before a district *fono* could be held or
action taken on the basis of decisions reached at such a meeting. In
practice, control of the district apparatus, including key roles and
titles of the order mentioned, was usually an object of contention
between parties whose components represented sections of all or most of
the sub-districts, the ascendant party acquiring the power to fill the
positions essential to the working of that apparatus and to operate it
in the name of 'Tuamasaga'. In this sense, district politics in Samoa
rather resembled party politics in the West; but the analogy might
break down if carried farther, for the honour simply of being in the
ascendant had a greater traditional appeal for the Samoans than did
the power of material exploitation which that position conveyed.

The prospects for district unity were compromised not only by the
absence of a district-wide hierarchy of authority and of status groups of
the village type, but also by the dispersal of maximal lineages, which
circumstance would have made it extremely difficult, in any case, to
create and maintain a stable district hierarchy without the use of force.
The problem is perhaps best seen in the context of certain senior lineage
titles which were, collectively, the focus of Samoan 'national' politics
in the nineteenth century. The Malietoa title may be taken as the first
example. As shown already, most of Tuamasaga comprised branches of
Sa Malietoa, with the parent lineage being centred at Malie. In every

sub-district, however, there were important titles related to various branches of Sa Tupua. On the other hand, Sa Malietoa had widely scattered lineage connections outside Tuamasaga, notably in certain villages of Fa'asaleleaga (where the parent line had its second centre), in 'Aiga-i-le-Tai, and in Faleapuna, Saluafata and part of Falealili (all the latter three being in Atua). As far as numbers went, Sa Malietoa was, then, amply compensated for the inroads of Sa Tupua in Tuamasaga.

If it may be assumed, now, that the Malietoa title concerned Sa Malietoa exclusively—a purely hypothetical proposition—representatives of the parent and branch lineages would have consulted one another about a successor, perhaps approving the candidate named by the deceased Malietoa in his *māvaega*, or struggling among themselves until agreement had been reached. Ideally, the *tulāfale* of Malie and Afega were supposed to initiate the consultation by canvassing in Upolu, and then the question was to be referred by them to certain chiefs in Fa'asaleleaga and Manono. When all parties had accepted a candidate, they were to meet in Tuamasaga to bestow the title upon him. On that occasion, and whenever homage was paid to the Malietoa by his maximal lineage, it was intended that *all* sections of the three 'Malietoa districts' should participate, regardless of the greater complexity of their actual lineage connections. In turn, it was considered appropriate that two honorific titles (*pāpā*) which had originated with women of the Malietoa line should also be given to the new Malietoa; these were Gatoaitele and Tamasoāli'i, which were bestowed by the *tulāfale* of Afega and Safata, respectively, after consulting others of Sa Malietoa.

Sa Tupua, embracing the lineage complexes of Sa Tui Atua and Sa Tui A'ana, theoretically bestowed its senior titles[35] in similar fashion. Neither side of Sa Tupua was restricted to a single district, but the senior components of each were rather more concentrated territorially than Sa Malietoa, in spite of their connections in other districts. Finally, if the titles of the other maximal lineages, for example, Sa Tagaloa and Sa Tonumaipe'a of Savai'i, Sa Lilomai'ava of A'ana and Savai'i, and Sa Tui Manu'a, were bestowed, the roster of sacred chiefs would have been complete.

If the Samoan political system had really operated in this way, the districts—those of Upolu, at least—might conceivably have represented the separate interests of their predominant maximal lineages. Allowing for intra-lineage title disputes, there might still have developed some measure of political equilibrium between the districts (as localities in which the principal lineage titles were based) and the non-local descent groups and dispersed lineage elements which had interests in the titles;

[35] Tui Atua and Tui A'ana.

and in time the districts might have emerged as true lineage areas, with their dispersed affiliates being absorbed in other localities. Development of this kind was possible in Polynesia, even without European interference, as the political isolation of Manu'a may suggest. But in the western islands of Samoa there were institutional complications which (1) made general war an almost indispensable formality in traditional politics, establishing Samoan parties circumscribed neither by district boundaries nor by segmentary lineage ties; (2) created and perpetuated the dispersal of formal lineage affiliations on the flimsiest genealogical grounds; and (3) made it virtually impossible for the Samoans, excepting those of Manu'a, to stabilize the inclusive unity of districts and maximal lineages, either separately or coincidentally.

Apart from the absence of a prescriptive rule of title succession, such as one of male primogeniture, the condition which probably contributed most to the foregoing effects was contention for the position of Tafa'ifā, that designating the chief who at once held the titles of Tui Atua, Tui A'ana, Gatoaitele and Tamasoāli'i. The Tafa'ifā—'supported by the four'[36]—became the highest-ranking and most sanctified chief in Samoa; for by virtue of his formally holding the four titles, there were united in him several of the most direct links with the deities. Among the other senior lineage titles there was no such connection, nor was any of them associated directly with the Tafa'ifā. On the other hand, only the Tui Manu'a title was totally isolated from the others, both politically and geographically.

The ostensible origin of the office of Tafa'ifā is related in the most famous of Samoan legends, that of the woman Salamasina,[37] who in consequence of warfare and of ties of marriage and adoption is reputed to have acquired the four pāpā of Sa Tui Atua, Sa Tui A'ana[38] and Sa Malietoa. It is held that Sa Tonumaipe'a, through assistance[39] it rendered in warfare, gained control of the titles and was responsible for the female succession. The Tonumaipe'a title was not united with the others; but the occasion would still seem to have been a most exceptional one, in that the principal lineages of Upolu had allegedly never before been formally brought under a single titleholder, male or female. From then

---

[36] The Tafa'ifā was also called Tupu o Samoa, paramount or highest-ranking chief of Samoa.

[37] e.g. Krämer, *Samoan Islands*, I, 22-3; MS., Henry, 37-64; Freeman in *J. Polynesian Soc.* Krämer also used the legend as the basis of a fictionalized account of 'old' Samoan culture (*Salamasina*).

[38] Salamasina is said to have lived about fifteen generations ago, long before Sa Tui A'ana and Sa Tui Atua were united by Tupua.

[39] Allowing for interpretation of the legends, this assistance may have included the ritual support of *alataua* villages. Safata was allegedly given its *alataua* powers soon afterwards.

on, the holding of a single *pāpā* title was not the highest honour but, rather, a means of contending for the Tafa'ifā, which distinction would therefore appear to have enlarged the scale of the Samoans' political activity. And if, in the broadened arena of controversy, Sa Tui Atua, Sa Tui A'ana and Sa Malietoa were mainly involved, the legends nevertheless maintain that representatives of the other maximal lineages, excepting Sa Tui Manu'a, also joined in, leading to the formation of widespread multi-lineage parties as the contenders in war.

According to oral tradition, it was not until comparatively recently that any holder of the Malietoa title became Tafa'ifā; perhaps, before then, none was even considered eligible to contest the honour. As for the *pāpā* of Sa Malietoa, which were *tama fafine*[40] to the Tui Atua and Tui A'ana *pāpā*, they were reputedly given to whoever contended successfully for the others. In the eighteenth century and early in the nineteenth century, however, a complex series of events gained the Malietoa chiefs greater prominence, with fortuitous ties of marriage, the *māvaega* of a former Tafa'ifā[41] and various shifts of lineage affiliation allegedly culminating in the first acquisition of the four *pāpā* by a titular head of Sa Malietoa. This was Malietoa Vai'inupō, who was actually engaged in his 'war of succession' when the pioneer missionaries of the London Missionary Society arrived in Samoa in 1830. All subsequent disputes over the Tafa'ifā involved both Malietoa and Tupua chiefs as the ultimate contenders.

Whatever happened before 1830, it is clear that in that year the Tafa'ifā did not represent a merging of the four *pāpā* and their lines of succession. The titles themselves were quite separate, each bestowed by different groups of Samoans; and every individual who was eligible to contest one of them was eligible to contest them all. Had succession to the Tafa'ifā been limited to within one lineage, there would still have been complications, for the Samoans had no sanctions or rules restricting title succession to a specific heir—to the eldest son, for example. Any male heir was eligible, so that personal qualities, including leadership in war, and the exigencies of marriage and other forms of alliance were of great importance in determining who was best suited for a title. Even so, evolution of a single Tafa'ifā line would have represented a considerable step towards formal political centralization, for it would have brought the largest maximal lineages together under one title and, perhaps, predisposed the Samoans to accept European ideas about kingship and royal succession.

To make the position even more difficult, individual titles of the

40 With respect to the origin of the Tafa'ifā.
41 I'amafana of Sa Tui A'ana, which by then was merged in Sa Tupua, asked that he be succeeded by one of the Malietoas.

highest rank, including the *pāpā*, were subject to conflicting claims not only by members of single lineage segments, for example, brothers, which might split their maximal lineages, but also by heads or other members of distinct branches of maximal lineages. This phenomenon reproduced on a smaller scale the situation which pertained to the Tafa'ifā, though ostensibly for reasons of intra-lineage segmentation and disunity rather than the incomplete merging of lineages. In Sa Tupua, however, both mechanisms of lineage differentiation, branching and merging, influenced the course of major title disputes. According to Samoan beliefs, Sa Tui Atua and Sa Tui A'ana were joined in Sa Tupua, but the two *pāpā* remained separate, with the result that, even lacking the Tafa'ifā, each of the Sa Tupua titles might have been very widely contested. Legend holds that Tupua was Tafa'ifā, and that his son Galumalemana was also. Galumalemana appears to have restricted subsequent succession to the *pāpā* by providing in his *māvaega* that his male descendants should be styled *aloali'i,* 'sons of the high chief', somewhat in the sense of 'princes of the royal blood' of Tupua. In effect, this excluded his collaterals and their descendants from the succession, but as the generations passed, 'descent from Galumalemana' became just another basis of numerous and varied claims to the *pāpā*. Through marriages and *ma'apū* relationships, virtually every important sub-lineage throughout Sa Tupua acquired an *aloali'i* line, each of which was oriented towards the Tui Atua or the Tui A'ana title, and ultimately towards them both—and through them, towards the Tafa'ifā.[42] Some formal lineage affiliates of Sa Malietoa also had *aloali'i* claims to the Tui Atua and Tui A'ana titles.

The Malietoa title, not having been associated directly with the Tafa'ifā, was itself subject to fewer claims, the main division being that between the Malie and Sapapali'i (Savai'i) branches of the parent line. Furthermore, the eventual accession of a Malietoa to the Tafa'ifā enabled Tuamasaga to bestow its two *pāpā* upon a chief within that district and established a precedent for the subsequent holding of the three Sa Malietoa titles by a single contender for the Tafa'ifā. Vai'inupō's victory, which for the time being assured the greater coherence of the Malietoa side, occurred just as Europeans were beginning to settle in Samoa. It appeared to many foreigners, then, that the Malietoa had the soundest claim to the Tafa'ifā and to 'kingship', and for this reason, among others, the first attempts at central government were made through a Malietoa. This approach was, of course, inconsistent with Samoan

---

[42] If a member of Sa Tupua was able to acquire the Tui Atua and Tui A'ana titles, he was also called the Tupua. Today the *pāpā* are no longer bestowed formally, but there is a Tupua, which fact may suggest some 'advance' in the formal integration of the maximal lineage.

practice, for whatever the apparent or theoretical rights of the claimants, the issue of the Tafa'ifā had ultimately to be resolved by force.

On the death of a chief, his title returned to the people whose right it was to bestow it. When a Tafa'ifā died, the four *pāpā* and any other titles he may have held were 'scattered amongst the families', as the Samoans expressed it, and efforts to gather them had to commence anew. In the case of each senior title, the choice of a successor was an involved and protracted process. No single village or local group of chiefs had the sole authority to appoint a new Tui Atua, Tui A'ana or Malietoa, so that unless a maximal lineage could voluntarily unite, its title might be disputed by force. For example, Sa Malietoa of Tuamasaga could seldom pull together in support of one candidate for the Malietoa title, to say nothing of the entire maximal lineage. One sub-district might disagree with another, according to parochial interests or the personal connections of the contenders, and often the sub-districts themselves were internally divided. To break a stalemate, one party had to pro- claim its leader to be in possession of the title. This was a challenge to the opposition which if taken up would lead to war—but between no more than two parties at once. Since every proclamation of this kind was aimed at the ultimate restoration of the Tafa'ifā, the contenders would from the very first try to exploit all their connections in order to acquire the support of people concerned in other titles. In this way, a battle between Malietoa parties, say, could establish strong claims to the *pāpā* of Sa Tupua; and if Sa Tupua were deeply committed in the Malietoa struggle, a single war could decide the Tafa'ifā succession. However, a series of challenges was more likely, with the focus shifting to other titles and with the parties reconstituting after each battle.[43] In the end, it was possible, for example, that the Malietoa faction which had lost in the first encounter could finish on the victorious side.

Political contention of this character could continue sporadically for a long time; in fact, it was almost bound to, for many of the factional commitments were voluntary and the arrangements elaborate and time- consuming. But finally, a Tafa'ifā would emerge at the head of a party which, because of the extenuation of kindred ties and alliances of expediency, cut across most or all of the districts and maximal lineages of Upolu, Savai'i, Manono and Tutuila. This party was the Mālō: the strong.

[43] But any Sa Tupua contender who sided with the losing Malietoa party would find it difficult to overcome the dishonour of defeat. Some candidates for the Tafa'ifā might remain neutral during the opening phases of a war. There was some advantage in doing this if their followers were few in number, for it enabled them to choose a winning side and then wait for a few years till the *pāpā* were vacant again.

Samoan warfare did not ordinarily entail the confiscation of land, but
it did lead to the widespread destruction of villages and plantations,
with the result that both sides could be faced with months of rebuilding
and replanting after a war had ended. It was customary for the Mālō to
re-establish itself on its own lands first, forcing the losers (the Vaivai,
the weak) to remain in exile[44] for several years. This permitted the
Mālō to entrench itself in power and to prepare to make the most of its
victory when all villages were reoccupied.

The main advantage to be gained from war was the power to call
the tune in matters of a ceremonial and ritual nature, which were
largely of prestige-making significance. As well as dominating the formal
organization of sub-districts and districts, the Mālō controlled the pāpā,
assuring elevation of their favoured contender (their tama'āiga, 'son
of the families') to the Tafa'ifā; and they could govern the distributions
of fine mats attendant upon the bestowal of those senior titles. At the
same time, however, lesser titles, prominent in village affairs, might
pass to members of the Mālō, especially by way of resolving outstanding
disputes over succession;[45] or the relative standing of chiefs of the Mālō
might be enhanced within their villages or lineages, as by the shift of
seniority between holders of related titles, constituting changes in the
designation of matai sili. Withal, the Vaivai, plundered of positions of
dignity, honour and authority, were also subject to repeated chiding and
insult which, as long as they were too weak or timorous effectively to
counter with force, further added to their degradation.

Among the victors there was no formal council or other body corresponding to a central government, nor was there any party-wide hierarchy
of authority. Inter-district meetings were held on the district malae of
the prospective Tafa'ifā or of his principal protagonists to effect a peace
settlement and arrange for the bestowal of titles and the creation of new
honours and dignities concerned in the formation or preservation of the
conquering alliance. But the Mālō was not a government in the Western
sense. Its members had no formal right to interfere in one another's
local affairs; indeed, to have attempted such a thing would have been
to risk the dissolution of the alliance. On the other hand, the Mālō did
interfere in the affairs of the Vaivai at practically every level, but this
occurred in relations between neighbours and between individuals and
groups related by lineage affiliations or as tama tāne and tama fafine,
and not as a matter of policy laid down by a central organization. That

[44] Living in the bush or among neutrals, or scattered among the Mālō as prisoners
at large.

[45] As when members of a descent group were divided in war, with those on the
winning side gaining control of the group's title. This was one way in which
tama fafine claims were implemented.

is to say, the emergence of a general Mālō party involved the enforced settlement of many of the small-scale, often localized, differences of the kinds already referred to, the principal exceptions being those between factions that, as neutrals, remained aloof from the war. Every Samoan knew who the Mālō were, and it was understood that if any members of the Vaivai resisted the pretensions and demands of those of the Mālō with whom they were associated, further conflict was liable to ensue. Unrelenting resistance was in effect a new challenge to war. On balance, then, the relationship of the two parties was one of force and domination amongst decentralized groups and localities and was subject to change at any time.

As soon as the villages which had been deserted in time of hostilities were reoccupied and rebuilt, the Samoans began intriguing to contest the distinctions of Mālō and Tafa'ifā once more. Many different situations could arise to strain the alliances formed during the previous war, among them the appearance of new claimants to the pāpā. It was quite possible for war to start again before the death of the new Tafa'ifā, but if avoided till then, it was almost certain to break out after his death. On this occasion, the contenders would have connections differing somewhat from those pertaining before, the pattern of subsidiary and incidental conflicts would have changed, and there would have been consequent shifts in the make-up of the opposing alliances.

This, in general terms, was the cycle of Samoan 'national' politics. Large-scale wars were relatively frequent, while, since there was no stable party organization, the integration of groups by locality and lineage, and by other principles of association, was being repeatedly compromised and upset. Factions were created and sometimes formalized as 'branch lineages' during or after a war; and they were capable of resisting local assimilation, even at the price of being expelled by their neighbours, because the formation of inter-district war parties gave each an opportunity to finish on the side of a Mālō.

It must be obvious that the Samoans, with their diverse lines of succession and the importance which they attached to personal kindred ties in the formation of alliances, had a long way to go before evolving stable political relationships capable of standing up to the responsibilities of centralized government. At the same time, it must be recognized that the development of the Tafa'ifā, although it entailed frequent warfare, was a jump beyond the centralization of individual districts. Disputes over the separate titles might have mobilized inter-district combinations, but not on the scale characteristic of conflict over the Tafa'ifā. From the European viewpoint, the Samoans of the era of Vai'inupō had reached an intermediate stage of political 'progress': in order to stabilize the districts as the largest units of government, the abolition of the Tafa'ifā would probably have been necessary; but to facilitate the creation of an effective central government of Samoa, the Tafa'ifā, to serve as a position of supreme dignity, required further development, including stricter rules of succession and the funnelling of all the *pāpā* and associated titles of high rank into a single royal line.

Early in the nineteenth century, however, the Samoan political system seemed to accomplish all that was demanded of it. At the level of the village, where people had to live and work together harmoniously, the chiefly hierarchy—its structure if not its personnel—was relatively fixed, and senior chiefs and lineage affiliations were few in number. Relationships of rank extended outside the village, but barring exigencies of war and coercion, the control of titles, land and corporate activity within the village was not generally dispersed throughout the wider hierarchy nor concentrated at its apex. Groups of larger scale than the villages were of more diverse make-up, but their activities were more concerned with questions of dignity, prestige and ceremony. Considering the insecurity to which the village and its constituent parts were exposed, they functioned quite well and adhered to fairly regular procedures; and they could often expel troublesome members in order to maintain their local unity. The larger aggregates could function much more slowly and discontinuously, with less rigorous rules of membership, and still satisfy the Samoans' requirements. But regarding the 'proper' scale and operation of government Europeans obviously had different ideas, the impact of which is one of the major themes of this study.

# 3

## DISCOVERY AND MISSION SETTLEMENT

*Early contacts with Samoa*

BEFORE THE arrival of the first Europeans, the Samoans' knowledge of
the outside world extended only to near-by islands inhabited by people
whose social and cultural attainments were similar to their own. They
may once have been intrepid navigators, as suggested by the Polynesian
migrations that emanated from Samoa; but latterly, at least, their relations with other islands owed more to the initiative of their neighbours.
The Tongans were particularly venturesome at sea and, early in the
nineteenth century, were often sending parties to Samoa to secure fine
mats,[1] to contract marriages and to be tattooed. Samoa also received
and assimilated settlers or refugees from other islands, some of the more
recent pre-European immigrants being Wallis Islanders and Fijians
living in Savai'i.[2]

Though accustomed, then, to sighting foreign craft off their shores,
the Samoans faced quite a new challenge on the advent of Europeans.
So much about the strangers was awe-inspiring, from their light skin-
colour, which in Polynesia symbolized high rank,[3] to their material
culture. But more than this, they appeared to have come from beyond
the horizons of the world of men, and so were named the *papālagi*, they
who burst the heavens. Whether the first Europeans were seriously regarded as 'sailing gods', as some writers have claimed,[4] it is impossible
to know; but if they were, the Samoans must soon have gained a more
balanced perspective.

The earliest European visitors to Samoa—Roggewein in 1722 and

---

[1] Europeans saw few ocean-going canoes in the possession of Samoans. Those
which the people had were double-canoes of a Lau Islands design, apparently
supplied to them or built for them by Tongans (Wilkes, *Narrative*, II, 144).

[2] At Falealupo and Fagamalo, respectively.

[3] In many of the islands, including Samoa, people of high rank did relatively
little outdoor work and otherwise avoided direct exposure to the sun. A stranger
with light skin might have appeared, then, to be a person of privilege and high
rank.

[4] e.g. Rowe, *Sailing Gods*. John Williams recorded, however, that some Samoans,
astounded by his voyage from Manono to Keppel's Island and back in an elapsed
time of six days, concluded that Europeans must be 'spirits' (SSJ, Williams,
1832).

Bougainville in 1768—did not proceed ashore, nor would the Samoans leave their canoes to come aboard the ships. Provisions were brought out and exchanged over the side for cloth; but otherwise the contact between Europeans and islanders was so limited that the accounts of the voyages give scarcely any vital information concerning the people or their customs.[5] By the time of Lapérouse's visit in 1787, however, some Samoans, at least, were prepared to confront Europeans at close hand.[6] Indeed, the people at Asu, in Tutuila, showed no inhibitions in swarming aboard Lapérouse's vessels to trade for glass beads, while, in turn, some of the Frenchmen went ashore. With several villages and travelling parties congregated, the behaviour of the Samoans became boisterous and sometimes audacious, inviting the incidents and mis-understandings which culminated in the massacre of the scientist Lamenon and eleven of the French officers and men. Lapérouse was unable to punish the aggressors—a party from A'ana, it was later alleged[7]—and declined to act indiscriminately against the innocent; but he vented his rage in his journal, describing the Samoans as fierce and treacherous savages who, none the less, inhabited 'one of the finest countries of the universe'.[8] He left the islands convinced that their people felt nothing but contempt for the weakness of Europeans; and many who followed him to Samoa took him at his word and prepared for a hostile reception.[9]

The killing of Lapérouse's men was never avenged, yet over the next half-century the Samoans learned that Europeans commanded mysterious sources of power and were capable of extremities of violence and

[5] Behrens, *Expedition de trois vaisseaux*, I; Bougainville, *Voyage round the world*, 278-84.

[6] Possibly through the influence of reports of Cook's protracted sojourn in Tonga (Wilkes, II, 145).

[7] Erskine, *Cruise among the islands*, 57-8; Stair, *Old Samoa*, 27-31; Wilkes, II, 73-4.

[8] Lapérouse, *Voyage round the world*, III, 65-125.

[9] Early in the 1840s the captain of a British merchantman, the *Lloyd*, took an armed guard ashore at Apia as 'protection' against the Samoans. But Lafond de Lurcy, a shipwrecked mariner travelling aboard the vessel, was convinced that the Samoans' bad reputation was a myth kept alive by ships' captains to discourage desertions. He noted that the effort was fruitless because of the obvious charm of the islands and their people (Lafond de Lurcy, *Archipel de Samoa*, 7-8). Giving details of his stop in 1834 at Savai'i, which he described as the finest island for whalers in the whole of the South Pacific, the master of the American whaler, *Howard*, stated that 'no danger need be apprehended from the natives, provided the precaution be taken to keep the head chief on board as a hostage, day and night—a requisition very willingly complied with, when two or three of the natives, and an interpreter, are also allowed to remain'. The editor of the newspaper printing this report regretted that few mariners gave out such infor-mation (*New Bedford Mercury*, 22 May 1835 as cited in CPIP).

destruction. The first lesson of which there is a record came in 1791, when H.M.S. *Pandora* touched at Samoa during its cruise in search of the *Bounty* mutineers. The vessel's tender was attacked—also at Tutuila —but on this occasion the Samoans were driven off by gun-fire and suffered heavy casualties.[10]

In the years immediately following, as the Pacific was opened to the whaling fleets, the sandalwooders, the seekers of bêche-de-mer and shell, and the victuallers to the Australian penal colonies, Samoa was usually by-passed in favour of Tahiti, New Zealand and Hawaii. Some ships called, no doubt in answer to Lapérouse's glowing report of the islands' productivity and wealth,[11] but the resultant publicity was slight and, in general, gave little assurance of Samoan good will towards foreigners. George Bass, the supplier of provisions to Botany Bay, might have given the most favourable account, for in 1802 he visited Tutuila to trade for fruit and vegetables and found the Samoans he encountered friendly and receptive. Moreover, he found an Englishman there, a man who claimed to have drifted to the island from Tonga several years before and who, when offered his passage back to civilization, elected to remain where he was.[12] But as late as 1823, when Tahiti was already the metropolis of the South Pacific islands, another voyager recorded in his journal that Samoans at Manu'a had tried to kidnap him and his companions. The people appeared to have had little contact with Europeans, he said, and while less savage than Lapérouse had pictured the Tutuilans, were still not to be trusted.[13] Kotzebue, who in the following year[14] traded for provisions off several of the islands, concurred in

10 Edwards and Hamilton, *Voyage of the* Pandora, 12 (note by Basil Thomson ed.); Erskine, 58.

11 In 1788, soon after Lapérouse called at Botany Bay, Governor Phillip proposed sending a government supply ship to Samoa for pork and other foodstuffs. The scheme was abandoned, however (HRA (I), I, 61, Phillip to Stephens, 10 October 1788).

12 Bowden, *George Bass*, 112; Oceanus pseud. in *Nautical Magazine*. The castaway said he had deserted from an American trading ship at Tonga some time before 1795. However, he was probably off the *Otter*, a Boston vessel that sailed through the Tongan group in 1796. The *Otter's* captain, Ebenezer Dorr, spirited away a party of convicts from Botany Bay and landed them at 'Eua, near Tongatapu (HRA (I), I, 568, Hunter to Portland, 30 April 1796; and from information supplied by H. E. Maude).

13 MS., Elyard, IV. The author of the journal and the name of his ship have not been identified. The call was made at Manu'a in search of provisions. See Erskine, 411-12, for reference to another case of kidnapping at Manu'a. Cf. also the *William Penn* affair, described in chapter 6, below.

14 Also in 1824, the American whaler, *Maro*, called at Samoa for provisions, according to Stackpole (*Sea-hunters*, 279), probably the first vessel of its kind to do so. The captain reported that the Samoans were fond of large blue beads (USCP, 23 C., 2 S., House Ex. Doc. 105, 20).

Lapérouse's judgement of the Asu people. In contrast, he found the people of Manono courteous and well-disciplined; but when invited to go ashore there, he none the less declined.[15]

Until the arrival of missionaries, the foreign settlers whom Samoa attracted were mainly of the refugee classes—the escaped convicts and deserted seamen who, for one reason or another, were desperate enough to try their luck among a reputedly hostile people. It was thus from the poor and illiterate, and often the dissolute and violent, that the Samoans began to acquire a more intimate, if incomplete, knowledge of Western civilization. Excepting their personal gear and what they may have received from passing ships, these men had no goods to give or barter, but they had the command of new techniques—in carpentry, the working of metals, and the use of firearms. Their skills, even if mediocre by European standards, qualified them as experts among the Samoans. Prestige, protection and a life of comparative ease were available to them in return for their services, for which there arose a considerable demand.

From the scanty record of their deeds, none of the earliest settlers emerges as the 'white chief' of romantic fiction.[16] A few tried to dominate the Samoans by acts of terror, but they were killed. Others fell in with local factions and gained influence by supporting the projects and aspirations of the chiefs with whom they lived; but they probably exerted little power in their own right. There is no evidence that any of them seriously affected the course of Samoan politics, or acquired any land, or for that matter, that the introduction of a few firearms caused any change in the system of warfare prior to the 1840s. The hey-day of the adventurer was yet to come.

From passing ships and from Polynesians of neighbouring islands, Samoans were soon hearing of developments occurring elsewhere in the Pacific. Other islands, according to reports, had been enriched by contact with Europeans to a degree that Samoa had not yet experienced. Into some quarters the news of mission activity penetrated, and Samoans, pragmatic about their religion, began to wonder whether a supernatural being of surpassing power was at work in the islands. In the late 1820s some Samoans visiting Tonga witnessed the successful establishment of the Wesleyan mission in that group and returned home as nominal converts to Christianity, while another Samoan, after visiting Tahiti,

[15] Kotzebue, New voyage, 258-85. Kotzebue discovered the entrance to Pago Pago harbour.
[16] In some islands, notably in Micronesia, European convicts and sailors did acquire much influence, but the extent of it has probably been exaggerated. One of the better accounts of this development is contained in FSD, Blake to Maitland, 5 February 1839, a naval officer's report on the activities of renegades in the Carolines.

established a Christian-inspired millenarian cult in Upolu. In 1830 the missionaries John Williams and Charles Barff came to Samoa unaware that that benighted, heathen land was 'white unto the harvest'.

## The arrival of Williams

John Williams, a Ulysses of Protestantism in the Pacific, led the first successful westward expansion of the London Missionary Society from its stronghold in Eastern Polynesia. After introducing Christianity in the Cook group in the 1820s, he built the *Messenger of Peace*, a craft of some seventy tons, and set sail for Fiji, the New Hebrides and Samoa, where he hoped to land Polynesian teachers from Aitutaki and the Leewards. En route to Tongatapu, however, he received such discouraging news of the perils of Melanesia that he cut short his voyage and headed straight for Samoa.[17] His change of plan seemed all the more auspicious when a Samoan chief, one Faueā, who had been living more than ten years in Tonga and Fiji, asked to accompany the missionaries and introduce them to his relatives in Savai'i, among the Malietoa people.[18]

The *Messenger of Peace* arrived off Savai'i in mid-July 1830 and, on Sunday the eighteenth, anchored near Sapapali'i, one of the home villages of Malietoa. Faueā was greeted as a chief, and he proceeded to explain to the people that the ship was a *va'a lotu*, a ship of religion or prayer, bearing a message which had already been heard in many other islands. If the Samoans would accept Christianity, he said, it would ensure peace among them, and in its wake would come vessels carrying an abundance of goods, which must prove that Jehovah was indeed the most powerful of gods. The logic of this argument, though disagreeable to the missionaries, seems to have appealed to the villagers.

---

17 At the request of a Fijian, some L.M.S. teachers were sent to Fiji aboard a trading schooner (MS., Williams, Journal 1830).

18 It was Williams's preference to use introductions of this kind when approaching an island for the first time, but in this case, rather more has been made of it than the evidence warrants. It has been claimed that Faueā was a *tulāfale* of Sapapali'i who had been exiled from Samoa, and Rowe (42) goes to the length of attributing much of Williams's success to his having had the services of a 'talking man', in the traditional manner of Samoan *ali'i*. Williams referred to his companion as a chief but did not say he was a *tulāfale*; and since 'Faueā' was a personal name, it is not clear what the Samoan's status actually was in 1830. However, Williams did not speak through Faueā when addressing Malietoa. A European resident of Apolima, one John Wright, performed this service and received payment for it. In 1843 Faueā held the *ali'i* title of Mulipola in the village of Salua, Manono (SSL, Mulipola Faueā to L.M.S. Directors, July 1843). He may have come originally from Sapapali'i, but it is equally possible that he merely had relatives there. If he had lived on Manono but had sided against Tamafaigā, it is very likely that he would have been exiled from that island or that he would have fled for his life. But that would not necessarily explain his presence in Tonga nor, of course, his eagerness to return to Samoa.

At the time, it appeared that the hand of divine providence was truly guiding the missionary enterprise; for a certain chief, Lei'ataua Tonumaipe'a Tamafaigā of Manono, whom Faueā had anticipated as the main obstacle to Christianity in Samoa, was found to have been killed only a few weeks before Williams's arrival. Tamafaigā had been assassinated by people of his own Mālō in A'ana, and in preparing for the subsequent war of vengeance, much of Savai'i and Upolu had joined with Manono in a powerful alliance headed by Malietoa Vai'inupō. While the *Messenger of Peace* was standing off Sapapali'i, the Malietoa forces were engaging their enemies in northern A'ana, and Vai'inupō was said to be assured of victory and the Tafa'ifā.[19] Upon hearing that Tamafaigā was dead, Faueā told Williams that the people were now free to embrace the new religion. Therefore, when Malietoa came from A'ana, where many of his opponents were later cast alive into a pit of fire, he found Samoa's eight Christian teachers waiting in his village to deliver their message of heaven.[20]

Malietoa expressed pleasure at having been sought out by the *va'a lotu* and, once he and Williams had exchanged gifts,[21] was quite ready to receive the teachers. It was agreed that he and his half-brother, Taimalelagi of Sapapali'i, would protect them and allow them to conduct services, and that every effort would be made to end the war quickly and to avoid fighting in future. In return, Williams intimated that if these promises were kept, the London Missionary Society would send European missionaries to reside in Samoa. Its purpose accomplished, the *Messenger of Peace* then sailed away, having stayed less than a week. On the day it left, Malietoa took a new wife, giving in the ceremonial exchange a portion of the goods he had received from Williams.[22]

*Conversion*

Writing later of his visit to Samoa in 1830, Williams held that the key to the successful landing of the London Missionary Society teachers had been the timely death of Tamafaigā, whom he described as virtual

---

[19] A'ana received little or no assistance from its Atua allies, who had been defeated in a previous campaign (SSL, Slatyer, 1 March 1844).

[20] It has become a legend in Samoa that Malietoa had received a prophecy from the oracles of Nafanua enjoining him to await the coming of a new religion from the heavens (MS., Henry, 125). Some versions of this legend are elaborate and appear to draw heavily upon biblical material. In the 1830s a similar prophecy was attributed to a Tutuila chief who had seen or heard of Europeans but who had died just before the arrival of missionaries on that island (Murray, *Forty years' mission work*, 50-1; Prout, *Memoirs of Williams*, 525).

[21] Williams reluctantly parted with a musket and later with a blunderbuss, which Malietoa insisted on having for the sake of prestige (MS., Williams, Journal 1830).

[22] *loc. cit.*

'king' of Samoa and as a 'devil chief' reputedly possessed of great super-natural powers. The suggestion was that Tamafaigā, had he lived, would have repulsed the London Missionary Society, regarding it as a challenge to his own religious leadership, and that if he had died much earlier, his position might already have been taken by someone else who would have reacted similarly to the mission.[23] This view, which recalls that of American missionaries towards the abolition of *tapu* in Hawaii,[24] gained wide currency, and eventually the name of Tamafaigā came to stand for all that was repugnant to Christianity. In the process, the history of mission development was almost certainly distorted, the Samoans being credited with reservations to Christianity which were probably more characteristic of a later period, when they were subjected to the demands of Christian doctrine and discipline.

By Samoan standards, Tamafaigā had indeed been powerful. A prominent chief of Manono, he had figured in a series of wars from which that island, with its sea-fortress Apolima and its fleet of canoes, had emerged leader of the Mālō; and it has been alleged that Tamafaigā, by skilfully playing off the Malietoa and Tupua factions, had by the end of the conflict gained control of the Tafa'ifā titles, much as the Sa Tonumaipe'a people were said to have done in the time of Salamasina.[25] Whether Tamafaigā ever held the titles himself is not clear, but by all accounts he was still the leading member of the Mālō. Also, he was said to have acquired superhuman powers through the war goddess Nafanua of Sa Tonumaipe'a, a belief whose truth his success in war might well have demonstrated; and missionaries reported that, for a time, some Samoans venerated, even 'worshipped', his relics, as if he were a deity —or, perhaps more correctly, the chosen instrument of the deities, a wielder of great *mana* in human affairs.

That is not to say, however, that Tamafaigā would necessarily have opposed or even rejected the overtures of the London Missionary Society. To be sure, he had once defeated a Malietoa war party in Savai'i, which fact Faueā may have considered an obstacle to his proposed introduction of the missionaries to Vai'inupō. But Tamafaigā was neither the 'king' nor the supreme religious leader that Williams envisaged. Moreover,

23 Williams, *Enterprises,* 280-1; SSL, Heath, 16 April 1838, with an account of Tamafaigā's death and the war that followed.

24 In 1820, shortly before the arrival of American missionaries. The event was hailed as an act of divine providence, working through the agency of the Hawaiian chiefs.

25 MS., Henry, 120-1; Krämer, *Samoan Islands,* I, 28. In 1824 Kotzebue met a high chief of Manono whom he described as a man of imperious bearing, greatly respected by the Samoans. This chief, who may have been Tamafaigā, claimed to have visited Tonga in his own canoe. Such a visit may have accounted for Faueā's presence in Tonga (Kotzebue, 278-84).

various forms and derivatives of Christianity actually appeared in Samoa while he was still alive, and there is no evidence of his having tried to suppress them.[26] It is more likely that the mission would have prospered regardless of Tamafaigā or Faueā. A polytheistic and practical people, the Samoans were tolerant of the gods of other men[27] and inclined to judge a deity at least partly in terms of the favours he lavished upon the living. When confronted with undeniable evidence of European superiority in material culture and 'magic', they were disposed to look to Jehovah for revelation, for a share in the new marvels, and for a greater measure of power and efficacy in the working out of their own traditional activities and relationships. That being the case, the missionaries' willingness to have others join in the worship of Jehovah may have been, in Samoan eyes, a gesture of good will and generosity.

The Samoans' materialistic approach to Christianity, revealed in Faueā's statement at Sapapali'i, also appeared in a 'hymn' to Sio Vili, an early Samoan cult-leader who was influenced by experience of shipboard life and by contact with religious movements in the Society Islands. The inclusion of the concept of 'cargo' is striking:

> Behold, come is Sio Vili.
> A man-of-war will present itself on the sea
> With knives and musket balls and ramrods.
> Run in haste and be saved.
> She will bring for us blue beads.
> How long is our ship coming on her watery way.[28]

More specific in its comparison of Samoan and Western material cultures was the following speech made by a chief who favoured the formal adoption of Christianity:

> Only look at the English people. They have noble ships while we have only canoes. They have strong, beautiful clothes of various colours while we have only *ti* leaves; they have iron axes while we use stones; they have scissors, while we use the shark's teeth; what beautiful beads they have, looking glasses, and all that is valuable.

[26] There were Methodist converts in northern A'ana and southern Fa'asaleleaga (Dyson, *Samoan Methodism*, 12). The above-mentioned millenarian cult was probably established in Atua prior to Williams's first visit (SSL, Slatyer, 1 March 1844).

[27] In 1829 three L.M.S. converts from Raivavae drifted to Manu'a, where they lived unmolested for three years before being found by Williams. During that time they espoused Christianity but acquired only one convert (MS., Williams, Journal 1832). These castaways had had no obvious European connections or support. Once the L.M.S. arrived on the scene, however, the majority of the Manu'a people soon became nominal Christians.

[28] MS., Williams, Journal 1832.

I therefore think that the god who gave them all things must be good, and that his religion must be superior to ours. If we receive this god and worship him, he will in time give us these things as well as them.[29]

The beads, the cloth, the ships and the knives, ostensibly beyond the capacity of men to produce, seem to have been regarded by Samoans as made by Jehovah and distributed by His agents on earth.

Moreover, Williams and his colleagues, having witnessed similar responses from other Polynesians, fully appreciated the impact of an advanced technology upon primitive peoples. And though they claimed to deplore worldly motives in religion, few of them had any compunction about exploiting the healing power of medicine, the mechanical intricacy of a time-piece, or the 'magic' of writing to inspire awe,[30] or any hesitation in turning the desire for European goods to the advantage of the mission. In the early stages of the mission work in Samoa, gifts of coveted articles were made liberally in the hope that villages would turn out to hear the exhortations of visiting missionaries, and on at least one occasion Williams told a chief that European vessels would not come to trade at his harbour unless he and his people became Christians.[31]

In fostering their cause, the missionaries found it to their advantage that Samoa lacked the idols, temples, and powerful priesthood which had been encountered in eastern Polynesia. There were, of course, mediums and oracles, but many religious rites were led by men who were also *matai*, so that Christianity does not seem to have threatened to demote or ruin very many people whose prestige and position derived principally from specialized ritual knowledge. Besides, the burden of mission work proved so great in Samoa that new converts, chiefs included, were enlisted as exhorters and assistant teachers among their own people. Without idols or sacred *marae*, the Samoans, unlike the Tahitians or Raiateans, could also avoid the traumatic test of destroying *en masse* the paraphernalia of their old religion. It is true that the first Polynesian teachers, left to their own devices, required Samoans to desecrate their *aitu* objects in evidence of the new convictions, but this appears to have presented no great obstacle. When, for example, a family harboured doubts about the relative power of the deities, a single member could be assigned to kill one of the group's *aitu* species, and if no harm befell him, all would be free to profess Christianity. In the

---

[29] *loc. cit.* A more elaborate version of this speech is contained in Williams, 490. A similar statement was attributed to Faueā (ibid., 282).

[30] ibid., 101-2; Nightingale, *Oceanic Sketches*, 88-9; Prout, 554.

[31] MS., Williams, Journal 1832. The harbour concerned was that of Apia.

Malietoa family it was Vai'inupō who insisted on making this test of faith.[32]

It may be noted, furthermore, that the missionaries in Samoa deliberately tried to make nominal conversion as easy as possible, marking many practices for eventual proscription but meeting the people's enthusiasm for Christianity with a superficial tolerance of sin. When asked by Malietoa which acts were forbidden by Jehovah, Williams named only warfare and the rudest of the traditional songs and dances. As he wrote in his journal, a people drawn to Christianity by a desire for worldly gain must not be subjected immediately to sweeping condemnations of their behaviour lest 'they take a total dislike to a religion that prohibited that in which their whole life and comfort consisted'.[33] First they had to be gathered into classes to hear sermons and to learn to read the Scriptures in their own language; then they might judge for themselves what was inimical to Christian belief and practice, so that church discipline, when introduced, would appear reasonable and just. Consequently, the form of 'conversion' devised by Williams in 1832, at the time of his second visit to Samoa, was simply a public declaration of Christian adherence or intention. This part of the religious transformation could not have been made much easier, but there were other obstacles for which Williams did not allow.

## Chieftainship and the London Missionary Society

Although the London Missionary Society, an undenominational Protestant society, was not committed to any particular form of church government or 'church-state' relations, most of its missionaries in the Pacific, at least at the time Samoa was being Christianized, were opposed in principle to establishment, episcopacy and hereditary political power.[34] The large majority were Congregationalists and Free Presbyterians, non-conformists of the lower middle-class to whom a considerable degree of democracy was a preferred condition of ecclesiastical and secular life. But as events in New England had shown, dissent could readily turn to theocracy and authoritarianism when carried abroad; and so, too, in the Pacific did the propagation of the Gospel entail the compromise of non-conformist ideals originating in Britain.

[32] MS., Williams, Journal 1832. It is sometimes suggested that the Samoans were impressed by the impunity with which foreigners desecrated the *aitu* objects. This is not likely, for a Samoan was bound to observe taboos only with respect to his own.

[33] *loc. cit.* To some extent this superficial tolerance of sin could be rationalized by the belief that the Samoans were more civilized, if no nearer salvation, than some other island peoples. It was held, for example, that they did not practise cannibalism, infanticide or human sacrifice.

[34] See Williams, **xix.**

Of all the problems that worried the London Missionary Society missionaries and precipitated controversy among them, and between them and their Directors in London, none was so crucial to their progress nor so difficult of solution in terms of strict principle as that of their attitude towards and relations with the Polynesian chiefs. On the one hand, chieftainship was anathema to them, owing to its suppression of personal liberty, its association of religious sanctions with the privileges and maintenance of rank, and the frequent wars which it seemed to occasion. On the other hand, chieftainship represented the protection, patronage and power which the mission needed to open heathen lands, stimulate mass conversions, punish the wicked and repulse its enemies. Even if it meant bargaining with the Devil, the mission had to start off by courting chiefly favour. But once it had formed this alliance, could it maintain its integrity and its standards and, perhaps, gain the upper hand? Or if not, could it disengage itself? If it did acquire a measure of power or influence over its patrons, was it to try to preserve and possibly 'improve' the institution of chieftainship, thus keeping itself out of the forefront of politics, or was it to try to usurp the functions of government? If it did the latter, was it to establish and maintain a mission theocracy or use its powers to introduce democratic reforms? All of these questions arose in Polynesia and various answers were given, none of which fully squared with non-conformist principles.

In dealing with chiefs, Williams was probably guided more by considerations of expediency than was any other London Missionary Society missionary of his time. Certainly, no one placed a higher value on the patronage of chiefs—or, for that matter, of British royalty and nobility[35]—nor did any display greater confidence in being able to gain it and use it to advantage. To interpret his attitudes and actions, one must realize first of all that Williams was in fast pursuit of great achievement. For reasons of vain ambition as well as pious devotion, it was his self-appointed task to scatter the seed of Christianity throughout the Pacific, leaving the tedious work of cultivation to those who followed. In the vanguard of the mission, he sought to make the most spectacular first impression, that mass conversion might occur in the shortest possible time. Thus, it was his standard practice to put the initial resources of the mission at the disposal of the most powerful chief he could win over. Secondly, Williams was not the fearless, almost reckless, pioneer that his eulogists made him out after his death. In 1830 he not only avoided Melanesia, but while in Samoa restricted his movements because of the war and the Samoans' record of hostility towards Europeans. Of course, he considered Malietoa the 'principal chief of the Leeward Islands' and the chief best able to safeguard the lives of missionaries and teachers. But whereas Tamafaigā had ruled with 'uncontrolled sway', wrote Williams, Malietoa had 'no real authority but at his own Place except in case of war or anything which concerns the People as a body, when they look up to him as their leader'.[36] No doubt Williams hoped that religion was within the scope of the chief's general leadership, but had excessive caution not kept him from testing his assumption, he would surely have found openings in addition to, and independent of, that at Sapapali'i. In that event he might not have left the full contingent of teachers at one place.

Returning in October 1832, to stay a little longer and to make wider contacts, Williams discovered that the war had been over for several months and that the Malietoa side had emerged victorious. The major barrier to the settlement of European missionaries had therefore been removed. He found too that interest in Christianity was running high. However, certain developments were threatening the mission's prospects of a clean sweep of the islands. First, Malietoa had erected a virtual fence around the eight teachers, regarding them as his alone and so resisting requests to distribute them or to let them travel freely throughout the islands. People who had been prepared to pay their respects to him had been permitted to hear the Christian message, but only by way of formal visits. Others had been cut off from the *lotu*. Almost without exception, the Samoans who were ready to declare for Christianity refused to congregate at a mission centre but, rather, wanted their own teachers, stationed in their own villages, or at the very least, frequent and regular visits on circuit. Outside Fa'asaleleaga, Mulifanua[37] and the vicinity of Malie, however, Williams's agents could do little more than temporize. Samoans had been enlisted to organize classes in their home villages and to see that chapels were built,[38] but otherwise it was 'wait until Viliamu comes back'.[39]

Secondly, and more disturbing, there had emerged a number of other *lotu*, all of which were in some way inspired by Christianity. The largest of these was the cult originating with Sio Vili, who had seen the London Missionary Society and the Mamaia at work in Tahiti. The latter, a millenarian movement with spirit-medium 'prophets', had started as a 'visionary heresy' among people who were or had been London Missionary Society adherents; and fed by dissatisfaction with the London Missionary Society, as well as by the charisma of its own

[36] MS., Williams, Journal 1830.

[37] Mulifanua, at the western end of Upolu, is affiliated with Manono. Taimalelagi's title belonged there.

[38] Buildings of traditional design.

[39] Some of the teachers slipped away on an 'unauthorized' visit to Upolu and were sharply reprimanded on their return to Sapapali'i (MS., Williams, Journal 1832).

leaders, it developed into a persistent and widespread rival to orthodox Christianity. In contrast, the Sio Vili cult was not a breakaway movement from the London Missionary Society. In fact, it was probably established in Upolu before Williams's first visit to Samoa. It resembled the Mamaia in other ways, however, becoming bitterly antagonistic to the London Missionary Society and incorporating, in its rites and doctrines, prophecy, spirit possession, miracle-working and the millennium.[40] By 1832 it was well entrenched in Savai'i as well as Upolu, drawing its followers largely, but by no means exclusively, from the Vaivai. Rejecting European leadership, retaining Samoan customs and practices, and yet promising all the blessings of Christianity and more besides, this cult represented, in recent London Missionary Society experience, opposition of a kind most difficult to overcome.

The remaining *lotu* were different. For the most part, they too countenanced 'heathen abominations' but were led by, or drew their inspiration from, Europeans. Short of mission teachers and apparently convinced that any European was capable of drawing something from the fountainhead of true knowledge, many Samoans had turned, not always spontaneously, to resident foreigners. They were also kidnapping sailors or persuading them to desert in order to teach Christianity. These 'sailor sects' were usually identified with individual leaders, not with groups comparable to missions, and so were numerous and, with some exceptions, small and localized.[41] Some represented serious attempts to prepare the people for Christianity, but most were simply convenient sources of influence and means of livelihood for the men who conducted them. Accordingly, religious worship tended towards the use of a copybook as a 'Bible', the singing of sea-shanty 'hymns', and the delivery of 'sermons' in any language the preacher happened to know. That such movements should exist annoyed the London Missionary Society, but that the Samoans should be so eager to *lotu* and so ready to trust Europeans was encouraging. The sailors themselves, so obviously inferior in attainments, were not very redoubtable foes, if indeed they held out against the mission at all.[42]

It is not clear just what support the various sects had in 1832 or how far knowledge of Christianity had spread. There certainly were many

40 The concept of cargo does not seem to have been a part of earlier Mamaia doctrine, but as previously mentioned, it had a place in Sio Vili-ism (SSL, Slatyer, 1 March 1844; Freeman in *Anthropology in the South Seas*, 185-200).

41 Some of these sects may have arisen before Williams's first visit. However, the first reference to them was made in 1832; and thereafter, the L.M.S. assumed that they grew up as a consequence of mission activity in Samoa.

42 Since there was considerable turnover among the foreign population, some of the sects were abandoned and hence easily absorbed by the mission. Of the rest, few were led by men prepared to hold out very long against mission pressure.

Samoans still confirmed in their heathenism and others who were ready
to make a new profession but undecided as to which sects to join. It is
certain, too, that London Missionary Society efforts were directed largely
towards Malietoa's neighbours, kinsmen and political connections.
Otherwise, several general trends appear. First, it was within the village,
where there were centred those religious interests and activities nearest
the everyday life of the people, that the decision to *lotu* was ultimately
taken. That does not mean that the village was necessarily united, even
though it seems to have had a general deity, common to all who lived
or belonged there. The kin groups of the village had also had their own
gods, and in the course of the religious upheaval something comparable,
if not parallel, to this configuration of polytheism again appeared, with
the *matai*, together with their respective families, often splitting several
ways. Thus, a single village might have *fa'atevolo* (the heathens, following the Devil), Sio Vili-ites, supporters of a sailor sect, and people of
the *lotu taiti* (the London Missionary Society, the religion of Tahiti).

At one level, these village groups were self-contained. Given teachers
or other leaders, they functioned as separate congregations, answering
the religious needs of the people in relation to life crises, fishing, agriculture and the like. At the same time, however, the London Missionary
Society, the Sio Vili cult and some of the sailor sects had characteristics
of inter-village denominations, so that people in scattered localities might
share the same *lotu* name and look to the same leaders for supplies and
teachers or, at least, for inspiration and guidance in the conduct of
religious activities.

If the sect-leaders kept out of politics, served the Samoans primarily at
the class or congregational level, and did not allow their causes to be
captured by high chiefs, chance and the relative merits of the various
*lotu* could play large parts in shaping their support. If, in two villages
fifty miles apart, there were adherents of a particular sect, this could
have been due simply to the fact that in each place the same exhortations were made first or to best effect. Or if several sects were represented
in each of the two villages, any one could simply have figured in the
maintenance of local distinctions. In either case, the people in one village
could answer their own needs and interests without being concerned
about events in the other.

But sectarian associations between villages were also consciously
made, avoided or broken, sometimes on the initiative of the Samoans
themselves, at other times in reaction to the sect-leaders' conduct. In so
far as there was any system in Samoan sectarianism, this was probably
its most complicated aspect, owing to the wide range of factors that
influenced the people's decisions. For example, unity in a *lotu* could be
built up on the basis of kinship, to join chiefs who were related affinally

or who were collateral kin, perhaps even *tama tāne* and *tama fafine*. Such a movement might go so far as to associate titleholders in two or more major branches of one of the largest families.

There was also the question of territorial unity—whether all the people of a given area, regardless of kinship, should be joined in one *lotu*. To achieve this sort of unity there might be some element of force involved, with the strong asserting their power to drive out and keep out opposition sects. Thus, for the sake of unity itself or to avoid some undesirable interference from without, a village might become a single-*lotu* area. During the latter half of the nineteenth century many villages did, in fact, achieve this form of unity; and although violence and banishment have since been prohibited and the principle of religious freedom often enforced by European administrators, some still maintain it.[43] Unity could also become an issue within a group of adjacent villages, in which case its protagonists would probably be the chiefs of a joint meeting centre, the leaders of the Mālō party, or the local chiefs of highest rank, with the *lotu* being taken as another context in which their leadership should prevail. At this level, however, there were usually jealousies and conflicts of interest that could be suppressed only by the frequent use of force, which missionaries opposed. The same was true of the general Mālō-Vaivai relationship, which was not based upon locality. Strictly speaking, this was a relationship of political domination, but at the beginning of the Christian era in Samoa, the work of the London Missionary Society was organized in such a way that the question of unifying the war parties in one sect might have arisen, as it did in the Society Islands, Tonga and elsewhere. Prior to unification, however, the following conditions would have been required: the sharing of London Missionary Society facilities by the leaders of the Mālō in order to avoid or eliminate jealousies among them; and agreement by the Mālō chiefs to convert their enemies by force. As it happened, Malietoa's monopoly of teachers precluded the first condition, so that even without the mission's intervention the second was also ruled out.

When Williams visited Samoa the second time, most or all of these forces were at work. Of course, he could not be expected to know precisely what was happening everywhere, but he had had enough experience in Polynesia and had acquired sufficient information from his teachers to get at some of the major problems facing the mission. He realized that progress had been held up by restrictions placed upon the teachers, but eight teachers were still too few to have prevailed over the other sects. Indeed, where the London Missionary Society was best

---

[43] GCA, Census Returns, 1911; BMG, Misc., Statements by Tuimaleali'ifano and Te'o (Komisi), 5 March 1919; MS., Deihl, Minutes of discussion between the Acting Administrator and chiefs of Falelatai, 27 October 1937.

G

represented, right in the vicinity of Sapapali'i, other *lotu* were flourish-
ing, although Malietoa was opposed to them. The invasion of Malietoa's
area by opposition sects concerned Williams more, for it seemed to
mean that the chief had even less power than originally supposed.
Malietoa's acceptance of the *lotu taiti* had undoubtedly given the London
Missionary Society considerable prestige, but getting the Samoans to join
up was another matter. Apparently the 'king' had general power and
influence only in time of war—so Williams now assumed. Otherwise,
his high position was honorific. The large residue of power belonged to
the many 'petty chiefs', who ruled the family groups and villages and
of whom Malietoa was virtually one. It seemed that there were simply
too many small, independent villages for tyranny to thrive. The factions
were too numerous, and voluntary exile was too easy an escape from
oppression.[44]

Nevertheless, Williams was sure that a struggle for power was then
in progress. In this contest, Malietoa was a principal figure, trying on
the one hand to exploit his monopoly of teachers to bring other chiefs
more firmly under his control, and on the other, to use his association
with Williams and the *lotu taiti* to avoid certain traditional responsibilities. If defeated on either count, he might be stripped of what little influence he did have. However innocently, the mission was inextricably
involved in the struggle, and whatever the outcome, there could be a
shift in the balance of power that would affect the mission's prospects.
There was something to be said for abandoning Malietoa as well as
for supporting him. The apparent incongruity between rank and power
suggested that the mission might be comparatively free of chiefly influence and hence more able in these islands than in some others to
develop a democratic system of church government. It might also mean
that the mission would not be embarrassed or helpless if its highest-
ranking supporters turned to drink and immorality, as happened in parts
of eastern Polynesia. Religious liberty and the judgement of individuals
on their personal merits were principles of the greatest importance, not
to be compromised without grave cause. But was freedom of any
present use to the Samoans if, in their ignorance and degradation, they
were ready to accept false creeds or adhere to their paganism? And was
it not better to have Malietoa for a friend, as a supporter who shared
Williams's contempt for Sio Vili-ism and the other sects, than for an
enemy? After all, he was influential in war and might turn to war
again if alienated from the London Missionary Society camp. Moreover,
his opponents were not united politically or ideologically, and so they
could not be counted on for protection and patronage.

[44] MS., Williams, Journal 1832.

If Williams was tempted to modify or withdraw from his arrangement with Malietoa, he may have turned against the idea on discovering that the chief was at odds with Manono. Williams felt that this was a breach that had to be repaired, owing to Manono's prominence in the Mālō; and he set out to effect the reconciliation himself. That he succeeded was probably due in part to his offering each side some advantage from the mission. First, he struck the following bargain with Malietoa. The chief would meet and discuss his differences with Manono. Manono would receive the one teacher that Williams had brought on this voyage and would be asked to pledge itself to support the London Missionary Society. There would be no more war. Subject to these conditions, Malietoa was to retain the eight teachers who had been left with him in 1830, placing them where (and if) he saw fit; and he was to receive teachers and missionaries sent to Samoa in future and be consulted regarding their stations. Samoan neophytes were to be gathered at Sapapali'i for training as temporary assistant teachers to their own villages. With the exception of war and the obscene dances and songs, there was to be no campaign against sin. A special effort would be taken to stamp out the false sects. For its part, Manono got the teacher, patched up its quarrel with Malietoa, and gave its undertaking to support the propagation of the true faith.[45]

In effect, Williams proclaimed to all that Malietoa, with Manono's backing, was in charge of the London Missionary Society mission in Samoa. If the people wanted to be saved, if they wanted teachers and, later, European missionaries, if they wanted to win the favour of Viliamu, they would pay their attention and respect to 'their' high chief. Williams, settling doubts on this score, told applicants for teachers that they must ask for one of Malietoa's or wait for more to be brought. To advance his mission's cause he was directing the Christian appeal to the antithesis of individual conscience.

*The Wesleyan mission in Samoa*

Williams did not refer to the subject in his journal, but he claimed later that in 1830 he and Barff had come to an agreement with the Wesleyan mission at Tongatapu assigning Fiji to the latter and Samoa to the London Missionary Society. The objects of this division, according

[45] MS., Williams, Journal 1832. This teacher was actually brought in fulfilment of a promise given in 1830 to Tuilaepa Matetau, one of Malietoa's closest kinsmen on Manono (the title was *alo*, or 'son', to Malietoa, suggesting agnatic segmentation). But the placement was made as part of the reconciliation, and to get the different chiefs to pledge their allegiance, Williams said that the teacher should not be tied to Matetau's village. Had Williams known beforehand that the war would be over and the islands ready to accommodate a larger mission staff, he might have brought more teachers in 1832.

to Williams, were to prevent duplication of Protestant effort and to minimize sectarian conflict among the islanders. Since the Wesleyan missionaries denied, however, that there had been such an understanding, and since no written evidence of one was ever produced, the truth of the matter cannot be ascertained.[46] But it is fair to say that, whatever the missionaries thought or did, it was hardly within their power to keep Methodism, as a sect or allegiance, out of Samoa; for they could not sever the contact between Samoans and Tongans nor destroy the affinity of the two peoples.[47] Indeed, Methodism had reached Samoa before Williams, though he had not sensed its presence. In 1832 it was still there—a potentially powerful force, destined to become a greater challenge to the London Missionary Society than Sio Vili-ism or the sailor sects.

During his second visit, and after he had made his bargain with Malietoa, Williams was asked to station one of the teachers at Satupa'itea, on the Mālō side of Itu-o-Fafine, southern Savai'i. The petitioner was a holder of the Lilomaiava title, one of the three or four highest honours in which Savai'i people were principally concerned. This chief had recently returned from Tongatapu, where he had shown an interest in Christianity. While there, he had been given religious instruction and, before leaving for home, a supply of books, but his urgent plea for missionaries had so far been unsuccessful.[48] Lilomaiava

---

[46] Williams, 259-60. Williams's book and his journals differ in relevant points of fact and emphasis. In the former, the alleged agreement is described, and the despatch of L.M.S. teachers to Fiji is given as one of the terms, that the L.M.S. should try to create openings there for Wesleyan missionaries. One would think that such an agreement might have seemed important enough to record, but the 1830 journal makes no note of it, though the departure of the teachers is reported in some detail. The 1832 journal mentions a conversation with Wesleyans at Tonga concerning Fiji and Samoa, but no formal agreement is described. On that occasion Williams wrote that he had promised to withdraw three unsuccessful L.M.S. teachers from Fiji—teachers who, according to other evidence, were working in opposition to Wesleyan interests. The withdrawal was not actually effected until much later, a fact which the Wesleyan missionaries complained of and which they used to argue that there had been no pact with Williams. And even if there had been one, they said, the L.M.S. had broken it in Fiji before the Wesleyan mission commenced work in Samoa. Some L.M.S. missionaries felt, too, that the teachers' presence in Fiji seemed to justify Wesleyan 'intervention' in Samoa. The most likely interpretation of the evidence is that remarks passed in personal conversation were taken by Williams as binding, perhaps only at a later time, and by the Wesleyans as nothing more than a discussion of possible arrangements (SSL, Barnden and Murray, 26 November 1837).

[47] Those who allegedly negotiated the agreement also lacked the authority to commit their parent societies.

[48] But at some stage, possibly on a second visit to Tonga, he was promised a missionary (SSJ, Buzacott, 1836-7); SSL, Heath, 1 December 1836).

had already approached Malietoa, asking for one of the teachers, and had been turned down. Williams, though aware of the chief's contact with the Wesleyans, told him he should make some arrangement with Malietoa or wait for more teachers to be brought to Samoa.[49] In doing so, he confirmed Satupa'itea in the *lotu toga*, the Tongan religion.

This affront to Lilomaiava was not the only stimulus to pro-Methodist feeling. Other Samoans, including some in Upolu, had also seen the mission at work in Tonga, and there were many more who, through ties of marriage, descent and trade, had connections with that group of islands. Moreover, there were Tongan immigrants and visitors in Samoa who were ready to exploit any opportunity to spread the religion that bore their name. At about this time, Methodist chapels were built in several villages, and with Tongan assistance, services of a rather crude order were being conducted on Sundays. Most important of all, the Wesleyan missionaries began receiving messages from Samoa begging them to come and look after their people, who were resolved never to join the *lotu taiti*.

In mid-1834, the London Missionary Society missionaries Aaron Buzacott and Barff stopped briefly at Samoa on a tour of inspection, during which they visited those areas in which their mission had its main support. From what they could gather, little had changed since 1832. In particular, the Sio Vili and sailor sects were still in business. Barff, like Williams, attributed this to the independence of the villages —an independence which the agreement with Malietoa had not weakened. This being the case, he and Buzacott concluded that the teachers, whom Malietoa had not yet released, must be dispersed to every part of the group if they were to combat their rivals to good effect. Malietoa promised to comply with this order as soon as he had been able to abolish night-dances *in his own villages*, but it was against his wishes that some of his teachers subsequently left him. As for the pro-Wesleyan sentiment, the missionaries left without even detecting it.[50]

Waiting for additional staff from England, the London Missionary Society neglected a ready harvest of souls and indirectly strengthened the Methodist interest in Samoa. About the time of the Barff-Buzacott visit, the Wesleyans were laying plans for the establishment of a branch mission in the group, and in June 1835 the Vava'u missionary, Peter Turner, together with some Tongan teachers, arrived at Manono aboard an American whaler.[51] Meanwhile, the Manono people had honoured their commitments to Williams, but the prospect of having Samoa's

---

49 MS., Williams, Journal 1832.

50 SSJ, Buzacott and Barff, 1834.

51 They disembarked at Manono because the whaler captain preferred to put in there.

first resident missionary for themselves was too great a temptation to resist. Some of the chiefs immediately laid claim to Turner, and even the London Missionary Society teacher, Teava, indicated his willingness to work with the *lotu toga*. When they heard, however, that Lilomaiava and Satupa'itea had a prior claim, they tried to direct Turner to Malietoa instead, on the ground of that chief's high rank in Savai'i.[52] Turner rejected this advice as well as Manono's claim, but he left two Tongan teachers on the island. A year later Matthew Wilson, the next Wesleyan missionary, settled there, making Manono the second centre of Methodism in Samoa.

Turner set up his first station at Satupa'itea and commenced his labours with several tactical advantages over the London Missionary Society. Accustomed to working through high chiefs in Tonga, he might easily have fallen into the error of 'king-making' had Williams's failure not been obvious to him or had the Tongan Wesleyan teachers not been acquainted with Samoan conditions. True, he may have passed up several early chances to take over the solid core of the *lotu taiti*, but he denied that it was his object to do so. In any case, a much larger field was open to him—a field prepared by the jealousies and political animosities that had already turned some Samoans against the London Missionary Society; by the tendency of the villages to divide among the *lotu* and by the islands' undoubted ability to accommodate another sect; by the longstanding relations between Samoans and Tongans; and by the fact that many Samoans had yet to hear the Word or see a European missionary. In exploiting these openings Turner tried to avoid the exclusive identification of his mission with a few chiefs or villages, and on the whole, he was fairly successful.[53] He had teachers to distribute or to assign to circuits, and he himself travelled extensively throughout the western islands. He had books printed in Tongan, which was more familiar to the Samoans than the London Missionary Society's Tahitian or Rarotongan, and he and his teachers, by speaking Tongan, were able to make themselves understood from the day they arrived. He was also able to capitalize on the impression—the London Missionary Society later alleged that he had been the originator of it—that Williams was dead or, at any rate, would never return to Samoa.

[52] SSJ, Buzacott, 1836-7.

[53] There was a notable exception, occurring when Turner set up a second station at Matautu in northern Savai'i. Since the people there were of the Vaivai, Turner's move was particularly abhorrent to Satupa'itea, which then belonged to the Mālō. When it appeared that the *lotu toga* might lose support or become the excuse for an attack on Matautu, Turner left again for Satupa'itea, but not before acquiring and organizing converts. Subsequently, he made Satupa'itea his 'official' headquarters but moved about freely on tour (MS., Turner, Journal 1836).

Like Williams, Turner was easy on sin—and for the same reason. Actually, his forbearance was greater, for he baptized new converts with little or no delay, whereas the London Missionary Society normally waited until they had been thoroughly tried and tested. He was also flexible in his attitude to Samoan ideas and customs at the congregational level. He did not try, for the sake of his own convenience or sense of propriety, to force the Samoans into inter-village or other combinations to which they were opposed, nor did he require a village to unite in the *lotu toga* before holding regular services there.[54] Moreover, he looked for local chiefs—usually among the higher-ranking *tulāfale* —to serve as the exhorters and organizers of their respective classes or congregations. Thus Turner, not a local chief, was at the head of the mission, but underneath, the organization was still largely Samoan.[55]

Ideological change was undoubtedly slow, but in numbers of converts Turner's gains were impressive. According to his estimates, there were about two thousand adherents of the *lotu toga* soon after his arrival. Twenty months later he reported a total of about thirteen thousand, or roughly one-third of the population of the entire group. At the end of the same period there were eighty Methodist chapels, suggesting followers in at least as many villages; and there were one thousand Samoans serving as exhorters, assistant teachers and the like.[56] If one considers that this progress was made in the three leeward islands, where London Missionary Society effort had also been concentrated, there is some reason to believe Wesleyan claims to an early lead over the other mission. For a short time the Methodists probably constituted the largest sect of all in those islands—perhaps outnumbering the *fa'atevolo*, or heathens, too.

Unfortunately it was on a territorial basis that the missionaries usually

54 As will be seen, most L.M.S. missionaries took the same attitude, but Turner, who preceded them, was the first to approach Samoan conversion in this way. Malietoa was given to using his control of the teachers in an effort to suppress sectarian rivalries. Subsequently, the L.M.S. missionary, Slatyer, used similar tactics in Tutuila, but he was an exception (MS., Slatyer, Journal 1841).

55 Turner admitted that certain aspects of this policy were developed by his Tongan teachers. He was not in full accord with their views but allowed himself to be guided by their superior knowledge of Samoa (MS., Turner, Journal 1839).

56 Dyson, 14, 19; MS., Turner, Journal 1836. Turner claimed that soon after his arrival he found the *lotu toga* in sixty-eight villages. That was more than double the number of L.M.S. openings claimed by Williams in 1832. The first estimates of the L.M.S. following were made a year after Turner's second count and two years after the first L.M.S. missionaries were settled in Samoa. Eighteen thousand adherents were claimed in the leeward islands and seven thousand in Tutuila, (SSL, Heath, 1 December 1837). The L.M.S. figures were exaggerations, that for Tutuila exceeding even the total population of the island. Turner's estimate was probably more realistic, as suggested by the fact that the L.M.S. credited him with ten thousand converts. Of course, the two missions must have been claiming some of the same people.

described their support, so that the pattern which emerges from their accounts is largely a crazy-quilt of divided villages, bearing out the importance of local differences (not necessarily rivalries) in the acceptance of *lotu* but missing or blurring other details. One may, however, discern some areas of concentration and some non-localized associations.

It appears, first, that the principal stronghold of Methodism was Savai'i, where Turner settled—but also where Malietoa and the majority of the London Missionary Society teachers spent most of the period 1830-6. Unlike the London Missionary Society, it soon acquired substantial support in every corner of the island. Its greatest success came in Itu-o-Fafine, starting at Satupa'itea and sweeping through most villages along the south coast. These results were achieved in the Savai'i district least noted for political unity—in contrast to Fa'asaleleaga, where no sect had a commanding lead. Resentment against Malietoa, weak competition from the London Missionary Society, Satupa'itea's status as *alataua* and as *pule* centre of the district's Mālō side—all may have contributed to the success of the *lotu toga*. There was, however, another factor that may have been most important, and that was the unique locations of Turner's headquarters in relation to the lineage and territorial subdivisions of the district. If Methodism grew within either division, or within both, he was always in a position to take advantage of the fact. For although Itu-o-Fafine had two main sub-districts and four great *'aiga*, all were represented in the vicinity of his station. Satupa'itea and Palauli,[57] the centres of the two sides or halves of the district, were contiguous—in contrast to Safotu and Sale'aula in Itu-o-Tane, for example. At or near these two places were branches of Sa Lilomaiava, Sa Tonumaipe'a, Sa Moeleoi, and Sa Muliaga. Of course, a London Missionary Society station at Palauli, say, would have altered the picture; but as long as there was none, Turner enjoyed a strategic advantage that could not have been paralleled in any other district in the western islands. One suspects, too, that the great *'āiga*, which had branches in other districts, may sometimes have been the means of spreading or consolidating the *lotu toga* elsewhere.[58] Thus, some of Turner's converts in southern Fa'asaleleaga may have been gained through connections with Sa Moeleoi.[59] Also, Manono, though formally an *'āiga* of Sa Malietoa, may have been inclined towards division by virtue of a link between the Lei'ataua chiefs and Sa Tonumaipe'a, whose title they used.[60] The case of Manono indicates that formal lineage con-

---

[57] Comprising the Falelua, the 'house of two'.

[58] No other district had the same combination of *'āiga* as Itu-o-Fafine's.

[59] And in the Itu Vaisigano through Sa Tonumaipe'a.

[60] It cut both ways, for later the L.M.S. used this connection to win over Methodists in Itu-o-Fafine (SSL, Heath, 1 December 1837).

nections were not the only factors determining the choice of *lotu*—as the pro-L.M.S. bias of Sa Lilomaiava in Upolu would confirm—but the evidence suggests that if they were strengthened or at least unopposed by other forces, they might prevail.

Turner also did well in Atua, where the London Missionary Society had not been very active. He encountered many other sects there, including that of Sio Vili, whose home village was said to have been Eva, at Saluafata Bay. In some places he also found a stigma attaching to the London Missionary Society, and, as in parts of Itu-o-Fafine, may have been helped by it. At any rate, he made good headway against heathenism and the sailor sects, and he managed to get on reasonably friendly terms with certain Sio Vili people, some of whom he converted.[61] Initially, his best openings in Atua were in the sub-district of Falealili and within the *'āiga* Salevalasi of Aleipata, Falefā and Salevao, whose titular high chief, Mata'afa, was a contender for the Tui Atua title, and hence no friend of Malietoa's.[62] On the subject of Turner's progress only two other observations need be made: that, in general, he was more successful than the London Missionary Society in gathering support at the district meeting centres;[63] and that contrary to allegations later made against him, he worked much harder at pulling in the heathens and 'deluded' cultists than at proselytizing among the followers of Viliamu.

Like the Wesleyan mission, the London Missionary Society had a widely scattered following and a reservoir of tentative openings, promises and inquiries, but the solid core of its support was more limited in scope and size. The underlying reason for this was that Malietoa, upon assuming control of the mission's teaching staff, had embarked on a campaign which, if it could have succeeded at all, would have taken a

61 Turner (MS., Journal 1836) said that Eva was Sio Vili's home village but he described Lefaga (in southern A'ana) as the 'centre' or 'chief place' of the cult. Buzacott (SSJ, 1837) was informed that Lefaga was Sio Vili's place of residence, but L.M.S. missionaries were not welcome there. Turner was told by some Sio Vili people that their religion was also Tongan and therefore the same as Methodism, whereas the L.M.S. was quite alien. This statement may have been pure sophistry or an expression of respect for the Tongan people. It should be noted, however, that Sio Vili had visited Tonga before going to Tahiti and that he had travelled in the company of a Samoan chief who became one of the earliest Methodist leaders in Upolu (SSJ, Barff, 1836; Dyson, 14). Moreover, the followers of Sio Vili were generally more friendly towards the Wesleyan mission than the L.M.S.

62 There were also Methodists among Salevalasi people outside Atua, e.g. in Tuamasaga.

63 In the long run, this distinction between the two missions did not trouble the L.M.S., but the Wesleyans' achievement is still remembered and discussed by Samoans. It did not apply in Tuamasaga, but in Safotulafai (Fa'asaleleaga) Turner had a strong congregation.

long time and required that alternatives to the *lotu taiti* should not have been readily available. In brief, he proposed to consolidate Sa Malietoa under the London Missionary Society banner and to offer teachers in consideration of new family connections and political alliances. He got a fair way towards realizing the first objective in Manono, Mulifanua (where his half-brother's title, Taimalelagi, originated), northern Tua-masaga, and in parts of Fa'asaleleaga, but as to the second, he was frustrated by the dispersal of the teachers by Barff, Buzacott and other missionaries. Considering that Vai'inupō was to become the first Tafa'ifā in the Malietoa line, Williams had arrived at a most auspicious time for him and had played right into his hands. Turner, taking a different course, not surprisingly incurred the wrath of the chief, who was said to have asked why the Wesleyan missionary should come to convert people who had already become Christians.[64]

## The establishment of London Missionary Society stations

Three months after Turner's arrival, the London Missionary Society missionaries George Platt and Samuel Wilson came to Samoa from the Society Islands. It was their responsibility to prepare the way for resi-dent missionaries due from England—to learn the Samoan language, commence translating the Scriptures, canvass for likely station sites and, generally, to provide the assistance which men new to the Pacific would find useful in adapting to conditions there. Platt and Wilson were aston-ished to find Turner in Samoa, but they did not enter into controversy with him. At times their relations with him were even cordial, marked by the exchange of supplies and the sharing of Christian company.

Platt, the senior member of the London Missionary Society advance party, saw through Malietoa's intrigues and went as far as he dared to put the mission on a different basis. More teachers were distributed, but to take up the slack, Platt made Sapapali'i his own headquarters. Wilson, on the other hand, lived in a number of different villages, penetrating the remoter frontiers of heathenism, among them Tutuila, where it was discovered that one or two sailors had actually endeavoured to make converts on the mission's behalf. Platt travelled too, but his contacts with other villages were briefer and his itineraries more limited in scope.

By the time Platt and Wilson had the means of communicating with the Samoans, Turner had forged well ahead of the London Missionary

---

[64] SSL, Platt, 15 February 1836. It will be understood, of course, that 'Malietoa' in this context refers also to those around the chief who were manipulating his claims and connections. As for the Tafa'ifā titles, these were also accumulated slowly. As late as 1835-6, Vai'inupō was being invested with the 'authority of another district'—in this case, Atua (SSJ, Platt, 1835-6; MS., Turner, Journal 1836).

Society, but eventually they slowed his progress and began to close the gap. The two missions worked as comfortably side by side as any missions might, with Platt admitting to himself that Turner had advanced the cause of Christianity against the 'devilish' sects and Turner showing no sign, at least not in his journals, of taking the defensive. The field was large, and if the missionaries and their Polynesian assistants covered some of the same ground, it was more to complement one another's work than to negate it. One may picture many of the Samoans receptive to both missions, even when nominally committed to one. One may see them weighing up the two according to the demeanour of the men who approached them and, while doing this, taking full advantage of both. Whose gifts were the more valuable, whose medicines the more effective, whose oratory the more impressive, whose manner the more dignified, whose injunctions the more reasonable? The effect was enhanced by the missions' near-equality in staff and resources and by the wide distribution and intermingling of their supporters and inquirers. Accounts on both sides tell of 'joint congregations' at the village level—of Wesleyan and London Missionary Society converts who of their own volition met together to hear Platt or Turner preach. People of some of the other sects displayed similar curiosity and interest.[65] In some places tension and hostility did exist between *lotu*, but as yet these were not general attributes of Samoan 'sectarianism'. Perhaps religion and the different ways of practising it were not matters which, left to themselves, the Samoans would necessarily have treated as factional issues.

Early in June 1836, in the company of Barff and Buzacott, the first contingent of London Missionary Society missionaries arrived from England. They were five in number, soon to be joined by a sixth, so that, including visitors, the London Missionary Society now had nine Europeans on hand to set its future course. In addition, the staff of Polynesian teachers was augmented. There were two immediate problems facing this Christian army: how to deploy its forces most effectively; and what to do about the Wesleyans. One aspect of the first problem was the question of the mission's relations with Malietoa, especially in view of Williams's promise that he should have a say in the choice of station-sites. The promise was kept, but as will appear, not in a way that could have given the chief much satisfaction. After he was consulted privately and then in the company of some other chiefs, it was decided that six missionaries should be distributed in the following manner: two for Tutuila (Pago Pago and Leone), owing to recent political unrest which, it was thought, would have prevented one man from ministering to the entire island; one at Apia, where the harbour

65 SSJ, Platt, 1835-6; MS., Turner, Journal 1836.

looked inviting and where Williams had converted the chief Seumanutafa Pogai; one at Tuilaepa Matetau's village of Apai in Manono, in
recognition of that island's Mālō status and of its proximity to Falelatai,
a stronghold of the London Missionary Society in southern A'ana; one
at Sapapali'i, where the mission's Savai'i interests were centred; and one
at Safune, a village in northern Savai'i, on the Mālō side of Itu-o-Tane.[66]
Atua was passed over, but it was hoped that the north coast might be
canvassed from Apia. Except for the stationing of a Raiatean teacher at
Palauli, Itu-o-Fafine was conspicuously disregarded. Northern A'ana was
not forgotten, but as the people were still in exile,[67] no systematic effort
could be made among them until their reinstatement. Manu'a was left
out, pending further exploration of its possibilities.

Within the next few years the more obvious gaps were filled, with
new stations being set up at Matautu Bay in north-central Savai'i, at
Lepā in Salevao (southern Atua),[68] at Ta'ū in Manu'a, in northern
A'ana (first at Fasito'otai and later Leulumoega), at Falealupo in Itu
Vaisigano (western Savai'i), and at Palauli. The station at Manu'a was
unusual in that the person in charge was an English deserter, one
Matthew Hunkin, who joined the church in Tutuila.[69] It should be
noted, too, that before the A'ana station was opened, the London
Missionary Society engineered or at least hastened the return of the
exiles, thus establishing itself in the good graces of the vanquished.

When the London Missionary Society distributed its missionaries in
1836, Malietoa was living in Malie, having left Sapapali'i following a
quarrel with Taimalelagi. His interests were therefore largely neglected.
Although it was reported that he agreed to the assignments, on condition
that the missionary at Apia visit him regularly and often, it is quite clear
that he had no choice.[70] There was no Williams present to plead his
cause, and among most of the missionaries then on hand, he was out
of favour. His early mismanagement of the mission was held to have
been responsible for the 'farrago of teachers [and] runaway sailors'. He
lacked the power to destroy the opposition sects, as he had promised to
do. And even now he was far from being a good Christian himself.[71]
Of course, had he remained at Sapapali'i, there might have been no

[66] But not the *pule* centre, which was Safotu (SSJ, Barff, 1836).
[67] Living in the bush or among their kinsmen in other villages. From the standpoint of comfort and convenience, northern A'ana and Apia were regarded by
the missionaries as the best locations in Upolu.
[68] A station was later opened at Saluafata in northern Atua. Some of these mission
stations were relocated, while others were abandoned or left unoccupied from
time to time.
[69] Hunkin had the status of an assistant missionary.
[70] SSJ, Barff, 1836 and Hardie, 7 April 1837.
[71] SSL, Platt, 15 February 1836.

question of offending him. However, the very fact that he had left seemed to demonstrate the limits of his power and suggest that the mission's territorial commitments should not be subordinated to political considerations. By having a restricted number of missionaries to place, the London Missionary Society must favour some Samoans and perhaps slight some others; but if it appeared that 'every village [had] its king or chief not subject to any other' *except in war*, the policy of courting high chiefs for purposes of political advantage stood condemned. Thus, Williams's arrangement with Malietoa was rejected—as, indeed, similar arrangements had been in other islands.[72] In Samoa, the London Missionary Society was beginning to develop an attitude of political impartiality and to acquire the disregard for high rank that it maintained for many years.

That is not to say that the missionaries repudiated Malietoa outright or that they delighted in exposing him to ridicule. It was rather that his rank and titles did not intimidate them nor, as a rule, excite their respect. On only one occasion do they seem to have backed down. That was when Malietoa, at odds with Taimalelagi, tried to break up the mission's following at Sapapali'i. He did not succeed, but his efforts undoubtedly suggested that he might renounce his nominal conversion to Christianity or switch to another sect.[73] Samuel Wilson, who had stayed on in Samoa as a resident missionary, was then assigned to Malie. Wilson, unlike most of his colleagues, looked up to Malietoa and took an interest in the family's legends and genealogy, but he was soon transferred and subsequently dismissed from the London Missionary Society, owing to the nature of his private life and his neglect of mission duties, and the Malie station was abandoned.[74] Thereafter, Malie was left behind by the march of events, to become a centre of the traditional intrigues which later culminated in warfare—or, as the missionaries thought, a reversion to heathen conditions. Sapapali'i remained neutral, a haven of

72 SSL, Heath, 26 February 1842. A similar situation had arisen in Rarotonga, where Williams had treated one of several high-ranking chiefs as 'king'. Like Malietoa, this chief had been the first Williams had contacted upon his arrival at the island. Moreover, there was at this time a body of opinion within the L.M.S. that was critical of the mission's attachment to the Pomare régime in Tahiti.

73 SSL, Hardie, 9 February 1842. Malietoa Vai'inupō's successor did renounce his L.M.S. affiliation. See Chapter 5, below.

74 Wilson, the son of the missionary Charles Wilson of Tahiti, had grown up in the islands and had been trained in Sydney, not in England. His long association with islanders may have disposed him towards 'going native', as he was alleged to have done in Samoa. Until the L.M.S. adopted the practice of removing missionaries' children to England at an early age, which change was made prior to the establishment of the mission in Samoa, there were many embarrassing 'relapses' similar to Wilson's.

Christian peace. Apia, to the east of Malie, became the centre of trade and commerce, the symbol of Samoa's material progress. Malua, to the west, became the site of the London Missionary Society seminary, a symbol of spiritual and educational advancement. Most ironic of all were the circumstances of Williams's return, for in 1838-9, on his last visits to Samoa and during several months' residence there, he who had brought the *lotu* to Malietoa stayed in northern A'ana and became a protector and hero of the Vaivai.

The allocation of missionaries in 1836 was the last occasion on which an important matter of London Missionary Society policy was referred to Malietoa. With the stations set up, each resident missionary assumed responsibility for his own area, subject to general instructions from London and to the decisions of the Samoan District Committee, a body composed of all the missionaries meeting to settle questions that affected them all. If he wanted Samoan advice in mission affairs, he went to the people among whom he lived and worked. No headquarters station was designated. Moreover, the Committee offices rotated among the missionaries, and the Committee met at the different stations in turn.

At the same time, the group of converts within a village was accepted as the basic unit for purposes of religious instruction, not because the missionaries wanted it that way but because the Samoans did. This arrangement overcame some tendencies towards sectarianism but was not in itself an answer to that problem; for as long as more than one mission was present in Samoa, social and political divisions could always be expressed in differences of religious affiliation. Also, with two or more missions in the field, all would be exposed to exploitation by swinging support, and the Samoans might be encouraged by rivalry among missionaries to make sectarian politics rather than Christianity the principal focus of their religious interests and activity.

The Wesleyans were prepared to accept the *status quo*, but the London Missionary Society was not, demanding that the former leave in order that the Samoans, once they had cast aside Sio Vili and the sailors, should have to accept a single *lotu*. However, events had moved beyond the stage at which unification could be the logical consequence of a Wesleyan withdrawal, even if the missionaries had had the temper and wit to discuss their differences privately and dispassionately, which they certainly did not.

Like Platt and Wilson, the London Missionary Society missionaries who arrived in 1836 had no power to force Turner out. Nor, for that matter, did Turner have the right to abandon his post without permission, save in case of emergency. At most, the missionaries could have reported to their respective societies, requesting instructions and offering recommendations. The fairest and most practical course would have been to propose the sending of a joint deputation to Samoa, unless it could have been agreed that both missions should remain. But among the newly-arrived London Missionary Society missionaries were some hot-heads obsessed with the so-called 'agreement of 1830', with 'Wesleyan perfidy' and other issues that time had made irrelevant. Between them and Turner a hostile correspondence developed, culminating in Turner's being challenged to appear in Manono to answer for his conduct. Held in a spirit of good will, the hearing might have done no harm, but excitement and animus prevailed. Turner, who said he had no objection to the London Missionary Society's presence in Samoa, was put on the defensive and was overruled when he asked that Samoan chiefs be excluded from the meeting. Chiefs and teachers came to testify and to witness the proceedings—and to gather the very clear impression that the *lotu taiti* had put the *lotu toga* on trial for its survival. The hostility between the missions was thus communicated to the Samoans long before the issue between them could be resolved.[75]

Meanwhile, news of Turner's appointment to Samoa reached London, where the two mission societies had their headquarters. Williams in England writing his book and raising funds, was the only person available with first-hand knowledge, and of course, he could tell only of jurisdictional rights, not of events in Samoa itself. None the less, the Wesleyan authorities ruled in February 1836 that Turner's appointment should be cancelled, and they instructed their representatives in Tonga to that effect. An appeal was lodged against this decision and, in the interim, reports of Turner's Samoan activities reached both societies in London. Once again, however, the 1830 agreement, as described by Williams, was confirmed, and soon afterward Williams sailed for the Pacific, reaching Samoa late in 1838 with the first news of the London Missionary Society victory. Turner, rather than leave at the command of the Society, insisted on awaiting official orders from London or Tonga, and while he waited, the controversy grew more heated and Samoan loyalties hardened. For the Samoans, it had now become more a political than a religious issue.[76]

What happened next was probably inevitable, though the Wesleyan missionaries may have been in a frame of mind to take advantage of it or, at least, to stand aside and let it develop. Early in 1839 Turner finally received orders to disband his mission, but the message was brought not by a whaling ship or trader but by a party of Tongans travelling in two ocean-going double-canoes. Led by Joel Tupou, brother of King George Tupou Taufa'ahau, this party also bore a second message, one directed

[75] MS., Turner, Journal 1836; SSJ, Buzacott, 1836-7; SSL, *passim*.
[76] SSL, Resolutions of Wesleyan Committee, 6 December 1837, MacDonald, 4 December 1838; MS., Turner, Journal 1837-9.

to the Samoan Methodists by the king, who promised that, whatever the mission societies did, Samoa should still have Wesleyan missionaries if they were wanted there. They would, of course, be Tongans!

An imperialistic people, the Tongans were always prone to meddle in the affairs of their neighbours, but on this occasion their interference was welcomed, at least by Samoan Methodists. It added a dimension to the cause of Methodism that had no counterpart in the London Missionary Society, and to some extent it compensated for the disparity of resources that had grown up between the two missions. The greatest 'Christian' mass rally of the 1830s was held at Manono to protest the orders sent from Tonga and to hear Joel Tupou speak of Samoan-Tongan friendship and proclaim his brother's intentions. Turner, resigned to defeat, appealed for unity, but his voice was lost amidst threats of violence and the hatching of plots to detain him by force. He and the other Wesleyan teachers and missionaries eventually got away, but the *lotu* did not go with them. King George received Samoan deputations and, true to his word, sent more teachers and also begged the Wesleyan society to post European missionaries to Samoa again. The latter appeal failed, but the supply of Tongan teachers did not. In 1842 and again in 1847 the king himself visited Samoa, encouraging the disheartened and assuring all Methodists that he would continue to fight on their behalf. And so, with or without the approval of the Wesleyan mission in Tonga, Methodism lived on in Samoa.[77] It was more than a thorn in the London Missionary Society's side, for rooted in Samoan factionalism, nourished upon pride and a sense of injustice, and cultivated by King George's fiercely loyal subjects, its hostility became an end in itself; and engaging the support of thousands of Samoans throughout the 1840s, it derided all hopes of Protestant unity.

[77] MS., Turner, Journal 1837-9; SSL, Heath, 3 May 1839, Mills, 3 November 1842, Harbutt, 25 November 1842, P. Turner to Bullen, 1 December 1842, Pratt, 31 March 1838, Heath, 1 April 1848. Meanwhile, Methodism had been taken to Tutuila.

# 4

## THE CHURCH

### London Missionary Society objectives

BY THE late 1830s, the Wesleyan and London Missionary Society missions had made similar progress in their respective activities. For the most part, conversion had been nominal, and the elucidation of Christian doctrine and the application of new moral precepts had only begun. If obscene dancing—for some reason a most exceptionable sin[1]—had been suppressed in a few places, the achievement only emphasized the enormity of the task that remained. By that time both missions had devised a written form of the Samoan language and had made and printed a few tentative translations of religious writings. Congregations and classes had been formed, but the development of the churches lay ahead. It was at this stage, when neither mission had made much change in the Samoans' traditional way of life, that the Wesleyan leadership was assumed by Tongans, who by virtue of their own limitations and their lack of European support were incapable of carrying the work forward.[2]

Thus, it was the London Missionary Society, with a large and growing staff of missionaries and teachers, plus an educationist and printer, that made the first serious attempt to Christianize the Samoans in belief and action. Immediate attention was given to the problem of illiteracy, for the London Missionary Society missionary was 'merely a Bible Protestant'.[3] Indeed, the ability to read was made a prerequisite of church membership, a rule to be waived only when blindness or old age made it inapplicable. Years of toil went into mastering the language and translating the Bible, catechisms, sermons and other indispensable literature; and no effort was spared to provide reading lessons for all who would attend.

Side by side with the literacy campaign the mission intensified its preaching on religious themes and began to isolate the more responsible from the general congregations of adherents. This isolation was progressive, the initial stage being that of 'inquiry', which entailed special classes and meetings. When the inquirer's personal life and statements

---

1 Not less for being dancing than for being obscene?

2 Dyson, 36-7, 51.

3 The *Colonist*, 4 August 1838, a statement criticizing the mission's stress upon the Bible to the exclusion of 'the authorized traditions'.

H

of belief could pass close scrutiny, he was baptized. He then became a
candidate for church membership, and after some months of consistent
Christian conduct, he might be admitted to communion. Finally, an
exemplary record of church membership might qualify him for a deacon-
ship or for enrolment in a teacher-training class.

Another object of London Missionary Society teaching and preaching
was to Christianize the law of the land—to ban the activities and relationships, social and personal, that by mission standards were immoral
or tainted by 'heathenish' associations, and to prescribe the ethics and
conventions of puritanism. As envisaged, the first reforms would follow
in response to the mission's magic, *mana* and material goods—occurring
from wrong motives and beliefs, perhaps, but serving a useful end,
especially if warfare and similar obstacles to mission progress could be
eliminated. More profound and lasting reform would emanate from the
Christian 'change of heart' and the church's discipline of its members,
the rapidity of change depending partly on the church's strength in
numbers and also on whether it had to overcome chiefly opposition. The
ultimate reform would be realized when a future generation inherited
as its birthright a code of unalloyed Christian values.

For the sake of godliness and decency the Samoans would have to
mend many of their ways. Needless to say, the mission gave top billing
to sex and family relations, as featured in the following examples: the
abolition of polygamy and, in most cases, divorce;[4] the celebration of
monogamous marriages in church; the prohibition of certain customary
marriage rights, including the exchange of goods and the public test of
virginity; the prevention of political marriages and of marriages between
Christians and non-Christians; the prohibition of adultery, fornication
and prostitution;[5] the prohibition of obscenity in word and action; the
imposition of new standards of dress, including 'full coverage' for
women and, when at worship, shirts or coats for men, but not shoes for
either; the adoption of hair styles 'appropriate' to the individual's sex,
meaning long for women and short for men, the reverse of traditional
styles; the internal partitioning of houses and more liberal use of the
external blinds.[6]

---

[4] A Samoan who already had two or more wives was supposed to 'put away' all
but one. Existing customary marriages were recognized but, subsequently, the
marriages of church members and candidates had to be celebrated in church
(MS., Dyson, Journal 1858).

[5] The English meanings of these terms are intended.

[6] Coral-lime houses, of the type adopted in the eastern Pacific, were not an
essential part of the scheme, though some were built in the early years. With
suitable modifications, the traditional Samoan house was acceptable to the
mission, and it is likely that the carpenters, then as now, would have been
reluctant to build anything else (SSL, Stallworthy, 15 August 1857).

Action was also to be taken under many other headings: for example, to forbid war and violence, except in defence of life and property; to prohibit the introduction of liquor, the drinking of kava (which was considered intoxicating), gambling, and the use of tobacco (which sailors had popularized); to abolish tattooing, mediumship, and the treatment of illness by divination and magic; to prohibit funeral feasts and to require that the dead always be buried in the ground and without delay.[7] It was intended, too, that the Sabbath should be strictly kept and that habits of industry should be encouraged. In the latter aim was enshrined the dignity of work, and with it the assurance that the people would be able to clothe and house themselves properly and contribute to the support of their mission and church. The above list is by no means exhaustive, but its range is sufficient to suggest why the missionaries would object to the presence of irreligious whites and how they could become so preoccupied conveying their own sense of propriety and shame that they would neglect the teaching of civilization's more useful arts and crafts.[8]

## The congregation and the church

It will be recalled that, apart from its political blunders, the London Missionary Society initially erected few barriers to the accumulation of a mass following.[9] Moreover, it learned to handle its congregations in a manner that conformed to Samoan ideas of how public functions should be run, enabling rank and status, for example, to be deferred to in the making of speeches and exhortations, the gathering and distribution of gifts, the conduct of feasts, and the provision of housing for guests. At first, then, the Samoans could easily adjust to the practice of Christianity, or what appeared to be its practice.

The situation then began to change, following the lines already described. The inquirers' classes were usually easy enough to enter, and so, of course, were the reading classes. Both were popular, the latter especially so. In fact, books and the knowledge of their contents were among the mission's most powerful attractions, giving those who acquired them the sense of being better than those who did not. The London Missionary

---

7 With Christian obsequies, when applicable. Mummification, the despatch of corpses to sea in canoes, and similar practices were banned.

8 Bull, *Trip to the South Seas,* 33; USCD, Apia/1, Swanston to Cass, 31 March 1857.

9 War and the night dances were, of course, proscribed, but the mission had no means of discipline short of withdrawing its services. After Vai'inupō's war, however, a period of relative calm could have been expected. And in areas where mission activities were well developed, the demand for night dances, as diversions, may have slumped.

Society classes and literature excited the envy of followers of other sects and won the mission many converts.

But education helped set in motion the machinery of selection, with the more intelligent and attentive being singled out for praise and moving to the top of their classes. Heading towards baptism and communion, the criteria of personal conduct and conviction were added to that of knowledge, making the processes of selection more rigorous and advancement a rarer privilege. Being a privilege, 'belonging' was desirable for social and political as well as religious reasons, but the qualifications were not tailored to satisfy social and political ends as such. That this was a source of friction hardly needs stating. However, it might have been made a more critical issue for more Samoans if the mission had been able to form and administer its churches within the limits of single, undivided congregations.

One way of achieving single-congregation church districts would have been to resettle Christian converts around the mission houses or station headquarters. This system, reminiscent of that instituted by Catholics in Paraguay, was adopted by London Missionary Society missionaries in several Pacific islands, some of the Society Islands and southern Cooks, for example. Its main purpose was, of course, to facilitate the instruction, moral improvement and protection of people who would otherwise have been out of frequent contact with the mission and, if not actually exposed to physical danger, at least subject to anti-Christian influences. As a rule, these settlements were made up of people drawn from several political jurisdictions—from villages or districts that had been independent in their own right or associated in combinations different from those effected by the missionaries. If, among these people, there were traditional political ties, they did not run to centralized government. It was, therefore, a feature of these settlements, at any rate where they became permanent, that the missionaries established governments of their own conception or strengthened and elaborated existing political relationships. The almost inevitable outcome of either course was mission-dominated theocracy.

The Samoans would pay brief visits to mission centres, but for the most part they refused to abandon their villages. Moreover, they insisted upon having their principal units and places of public worship in their villages. Since their attitude did not change, the London Missionary Society would have had to go to the other extreme—that of creating village churches—if it had been determined to administer church business at the congregational level. Considering that the number of missionaries never exceeded sixteen, and was usually less, that course would not have been feasible, even in the larger congregations, unless Samoans had been taken on as ministers. The missionaries, however, were afraid that the ordination of Samoans would unduly lower standards and so put it off for many years.

The first London Missionary Society church was formed in 1837, and others followed shortly thereafter. Since the initial formula was one station, one church district, traditional boundaries were not always adhered to, but as mission staff increased and the Samoans made their wishes felt, the original church districts were divided or altered until most of them coincided with Samoan territorial units. Until the 1870s, these were traditional districts or sub-districts.

The church district was both a unit of ecclesiastical government and an area within which followers of the London Missionary Society gathered for special mission festivities. For both purposes its centre was the station headquarters or, if it had no missionary in residence, a village selected by the Samoans and the missionary in charge. In the first case, the centre was relatively fixed or permanent and, having been chosen by the London Missionary Society to suit its own convenience, was not necessarily a traditional inter-village meeting place. Thus in Fa'asaleleaga, Safotulafai was for many years by-passed in favour of Sapapali'i. It was also possible for the mission to select a key village for its headquarters and still break with tradition, owing to the fact that some areas, such as the eastern district of Tutuila, had several centres of equal importance. In either event, some Samoans would have been offended and perhaps inclined to follow other sects if existing political divisions had not already led them to do so. Even so, the mission was seldom prevented on such grounds from holding joint meetings of its church members. In the 'detached' church district, or 'outstation', which a missionary visited on circuit, Samoan ideas were more likely to prevail, with meetings restricted to an important *malae* or conducted in rotation at different places.

Although the people who lived in a church district, and with them communicant Christians, may have united for certain traditional purposes, the London Missionary Society would not have considered their unity, either in degree or kind, a suitable qualification for the task of governing an independent church. This, quite apart from spiritual and moral issues, would have induced the missionary to organize his church along episcopal lines. It is true that the early church had deacons and that its members met occasionally to consider admissions, questions of discipline, and other business, as well as to take communion together. Before 1875, however, the deacons and other members could not act in the name of the church unless the missionary first approved, while on the other hand, the missionary reserved to himself such powers of administration and discipline that his views usually prevailed, even when they were unpopular. That is not to say that the missionary was aware of all that was happening, but as far as the official acts of the church were concerned, he was the 'mainspring' without which nothing could be done.[10] In fact, it was not really necessary, in order to transact business, that the full church should meet at all, though for the sake of morale and propriety the membership was usually convened at least once a year. The missionary's purpose in assuming such power was, of course, as much that of educating the people as of protecting the purity of the church.[11] His reason for retaining the power became, as time passed, the fear that the Samoans were not responding fully enough to his efforts to Christianize them.

When it came, however, to the general 'mission meeting' of the church district, held in or about May of each year,[12] the missionary gave way to the Samoans in matters concerning attendance, participation and, to a large extent, leadership. He was wise to do so, for the objects of the meeting—to generate enthusiasm for the *lotu* and to collect gifts from the congregations—were best served by letting the Samoan genius for ceremonial take its own course. Besides, this was a function that was complete in itself, entailing no continuity of organization and activity such as might benefit from or require European supervision.

Regarding the London Missionary Society church-district meetings as inter-village assemblies, it will be obvious that the Samoans would have had few misgivings about representation at a May festival. Anyone, even an adherent of another sect, might attend and take part. The meeting of the church itself was a different matter. True, the Samoans were not so rigid as to require participation *en masse* in order for their views and interests to be upheld, or to leave no room for choice as to who their inter-village representatives might be. None the less, the mission's standards were such that some persons who, in the opinion of Samoans, should have been in attendance at church meetings were bound to be excluded.

If the status of communicant had been, generally, of outstanding importance in relation to the affairs of a village congregation, as the identity of the congregation was in relation to the May mission meeting, church membership would have been a greater issue among Samoans. In this regard it is significant that, until 1855, the London Missionary Society dominated the church even to the extent of forbidding teachers, deacons and members to administer the sacraments. Communicants living near a mission house would be regularly deferred to and consulted by the missionary and, in the course of worship, segregated from adherents,

---

[10] SSL, Pratt, 11 April 1874.

[11] Another purpose was that of limiting interference in church affairs by 'civil government' (SSL, Heath, 26 February 1842).

[12] The meeting acquired the Samoan name 'Me', the month in which it was normally held.

their special status so emphasized that it would become an important local distinction. But farther from the mission house communicants would emerge as a separate body only during the missionary's occasional visit—unless, of course, they assumed unauthorized powers and thereby risked disciplinary action. This is no doubt one reason why for many years church members were more numerous near the station headquarters, where London Missionary Society discipline was nevertheless the most demanding. There was no comparable distribution of adherents.

In the village beyond the missionary's immediate reach, then, the general congregation remained the principal medium of public worship. The teacher, with his limited functions and powers, could not prevent its being organized and run on Samoan lines, even if he had wanted to. Of course, he might solicit mission support in an effort to put across some unpopular measure; but he had to live among the villagers, and to do so on congenial terms he had to serve their interests first. This meant, in effect, that he was subject to the will of the chiefs of his congregation, or of the village council, regardless of who belonged to the church. Thus, if a 'godless' tulāfale wanted to preach, the teacher was constrained to let him. Or, to take another example, the teacher, in his sermons, had to observe the custom which forbade the mention of death or other unpleasant topics in the presence of chiefs.[13] The ten or twelve Eastern Polynesians were not quite as limited as Samoan teachers in their freedom and influence; a few of them were supervisory teachers, senior to the Samoan staff in their respective areas, and all of them had regular (though small) stipends from the mission which enabled them to use European goods to bolster their position. Yet even they, not being ordained, were vastly inferior to the missionaries, who had the lion's share of pastoral powers and who alone could deal with sin without regard for the rank of the sinner.

That the teachers, especially the Samoans, had to depend on their congregations for their maintenance was another important factor in their subjection to local control. This condition emerged as a problem only after the European missionaries settled in and began preparing the more able village exhorters and assistants, together with new recruits, for permanent teaching positions. The terms of assignment, being left to the individual missionaries, varied somewhat, but in many cases the teachers were forbidden to hold chiefly titles and were made to serve outside their home villages, the object being, of course, to try to remove them as far as possible from commitments that might conflict with their mission duties. After 1845, when the Malua seminary was responsible for training teacher-candidates, these two rules were generally applied.

13 SSL, Heath, 30 March 1840.

By 1850 the mission had more than one hundred and fifty Samoan teachers, variously trained, but most of them living where, except for their vocation, they had little claim to permanent residence or support. Nevertheless, these men were expected to devote their lives to this work without receiving any regular salary or allowance from the mission. Several reasons were given to justify their employment on these terms, but the crux of the matter was simply the mission's inability to pay as many teachers as Samoa required. If overseas patrons donated clothing or other goods, the teachers would be given their share, but even if each had been promised 'so large a sum as £10' per annum, the consequence for the London Missionary Society would have been bankruptcy or the drastic curtailment of its programme. The teachers, therefore, were thrown 'for the most part for the supply of their wants upon their own personal management and industry, and the kindness of those whom they [sought] to instruct'.[14] Perhaps this was fair enough, but it was also expected that the teachers should solicit and enjoy the 'kindness' of their hosts without compromising the work of the mission. This was impossible.

## Preaching and practice

According to the general London Missionary Society view of salvation, theological instruction was of crucial importance, first in preparing the individual to receive God's gift of grace, and secondly in helping him, once he had been awakened to the truth of Christianity, to store his mind with the knowledge considered essential to the development and maintenance of true piety and moral self-discipline. Indeed, religion weak in or devoid of this mental activity was scarcely any religion at all, but rather a set of formal observances or barren sentiments. This, at least, was the attitude towards education which the missionaries brought to Samoa and on the basis of which they fashioned their early educational policies.[15] They arrived, however, with little knowledge and no experience of the type of religious system they had come to supplant. What is more, they were so bemused by what they thought to be the universal validity of their own values, and perhaps also by the Samoans' ready profession of Christianity, that they were slow to take stock of traditional beliefs and conditions of life and to adjust their methods of instruction accordingly. Rather, they persisted in preaching 'white

---

[14] SSL, Hardie, April 1851.

[15] Many of the first L.M.S. missionaries to the Pacific were artisans whose principal qualification for the pulpit was religious zeal. Before the Samoan mission was established, however, formal theological training was made a prerequisite for the field, so that the men who came to Samoa were, to all intents and purposes, equipped to build the mission on a solid foundation of Christian knowledge.

sermons' that were 'brim full of good theology' and equally laden with misconceptions for Samoan congregations and teacher-trainees.[16]

There were, of course, analogies between Christian and traditional beliefs, as with respect to the divine creation of the world and man, the existence of a soul and a life after death, and the punishment of forbidden acts and relationships by supernatural means. These, and other parallels, might have facilitated the Samoans' adaptation to Christianity, but they could also entrench and conceal misunderstanding of it. There were, for example, the concepts of sin and taboo, which were easily linked together. The Samoans apparently recognized degrees of wrong, in the sense that one act was more atrocious than another. For them, however, punishment generally occurred in the here and now, through the intervention of the gods and spirits in the affairs of men, to cause illness, death, or failure at important tasks. They could certainly understand the Christian belief in similar acts of intervention by God—as the punishment of the wicked though perhaps not as the testing of the righteous—but if rank, ancestry, and manner of death decided their destination or fortune in the hereafter, as most writers seem to agree was the case,[17] what of the forgiveness of sin and the Last Judgement? If repentance and absolution had a Samoan counterpart, it would have been the propitiation of the gods by some ritual sacrifice or the setting of one god against another to forestall a punishment. The success of the rites would depend on the omens, on the knowledge possessed by the priests, on the amount of sacrifice or payment.

There must also have been apparent contradictions and inconsistencies in the missionaries' presentation of Christian doctrine. For example, the Samoans, who believed in oracles and mediums, were told that prayer was a form of personal communication with God and that much of God's Word had been revealed through prophets; but they were supposed to understand that the Word was complete and, hence, the time of the prophets at an end. Then too, they, who had known no such deity, were told to believe in an omnipotent, omnipresent, all-knowing, independent, consistent, and single God, but at the same time they were confronted with the Trinity and Satan, a potential foursome for a start. Thomas Jefferson, an ardent Christian, saw in the 'Athanasian paradox' a return to the 'polytheism of the ancients', and therefore he rejected it. One suspects that the ancients of Samoa might have shared his interpretation while finding it more agreeable. Paradoxes must also have arisen in the Samoans' reading of the Scriptures, in the propagation of Christianity by rival sects, and in varying presentations of doctrine by Polynesian teachers and European missionaries. In many respects, then, the

16 SSL, Pratt, 31 December 1859.
17 Summary in Williamson, *Religious and cosmic beliefs*, i, xiii.

Samoans' adjustment to Christianity must have been determined by their selection and elimination as well as their adaptation of ideas.

When, in the course of expounding their 'good theology', the missionaries encountered problems of communication, they tended to blame the Samoans before themselves. After only a year in the islands Charles Hardie did not even concede that his knowledge of the Samoan language might have been deficient. Failing to get his message across, he wrote that it was hard for the Samoans 'to form correct or worthy views of divine truth' because they were 'little accustomed to think'. As a result, their notions of Christianity were 'often confused and childish'.[18] After another five years Hardie had concluded that the Samoans did engage in thought, but now he complained of 'the grossness of [their] ideas', which, among other things, 'render[ed] them peculiarly liable to self-deception and . . . easy prey in the hour of peculiar temptation'.[19] The missionary, Pratt, took a similar line, holding that the Samoans had little capacity for 'religious feeling and understanding'. To preach to them as to Europeans was, he observed, 'like trying to fill a small mouthed bottle . . . from a bucket'.[20]

It followed, by London Missionary Society logic, that people who had undeveloped minds must also be undisciplined in their emotions. On two counts, then, it was feared that many Samoans might be incapable of cultivating the means of grace, being deficient in the powers of reason and self-control essential to a state of piety and morality. That is not to say that the missionaries all responded by simplifying their theological discourses, but they did shift the emphasis of their role from that of teacher towards that of father or policeman, concerning themselves less with what the masses understood of Christianity and more with overt conduct. Of course, the Samoans' renunciation of 'heathen depravities' in favour of civilized Christian ways was a transition which the missionaries desired for its own sake, but if they became more preoccupied with controlling the 'volatile and unreliable' Samoans, it was also because such people, like children, seemed unable to appreciate the gravity of their spiritual plight.[21]

For their part, the Samoans also made an issue of 'right conduct', with consequences that were not always pleasing to the London Missionary Society. There was, for example, their 'formalism', which was compounded of their love of regularity and their belief that the efficacy of ritual performances depended partly upon strict adherence to established rules of order.[22] Among such Pharisees it was not difficult to standardize the routine of church service or to enforce the keeping of

18 SSL, Hardie, 1 September 1837.            21 loc. cit.
19 ibid., Hardie, 9 February 1842.           22 SSL, Harbutt, 20 July 1841.
20 ibid., Pratt, 31 December 1859.

the Sabbath, to give but two instances. But on the other hand, it was hard to get them to give up any form that had outserved its usefulness or to prevent the superficial differences between the sects from hardening into symbols of sectarianism, to be condemned or defended for their own sakes.[23] Since ships from England approached Samoa from both the east and the west, even the calendar became a subject of controversy, with opinions differing as to which day was really Sunday. If the London Missionary Society had chosen the wrong day, how could a change be made without alienating the mission's followers?[24]

As for morality, the missionaries soon observed that many Samoans considered 'behaviour . . . the way to salvation'.[25] Depending on what 'salvation' was taken to mean, this belief may have owed something to the traditional religion, but in the event, it was a likely outgrowth of London Missionary Society puritanism. In this regard it may be noted that the missionary, by acting as lawgiver and priest, detracted from his own assertions concerning individual responsibility and prayer, and fostered or confirmed the impression that he occupied the key ritual position between his followers and the Lord, serving each side and interpreting each to the other. On the one hand, he became God's spokesman and His eyes and ears. Being one of several such spokesmen, he would be compared with others, but for his own flock, such as it was at any given time, he remained the man to please. This made him the focus of what he considered hypocrisy, particularly in respect of those rules of conduct that were at once unpopular and subject to violation in private. In his presence the people might behave with utmost propriety, but he could not be sure how firmly he was in mind when he was out of sight. Two of the consequences will be apparent: the encouragement of spying and informing, by which means ambitious or jealous parties used the missionary as their tool; and the development of public 'decency' as an affectation of Christian morality.

On the other hand, the missionary had to serve the Samoans, to help them avoid or overcome trouble, to enable them to enjoy prosperity and good fortune, to see that they were well treated by God. On his performance, and in relation to the performances of other missionaries, he would be judged, and what he delivered would be considered in terms of what he required.

Some of the most serious obstacles to puritan reform arose from the fact that the infant churches were pockets of radical individualism in a reactionary collectivist society. The general idea of church membership appealed to many London Missionary Society adherents, although its

[23] Dyson, 58-9; SSL, Slatyer, 1 March 1844.

[24] ibid., King, 8 May 1864.

[25] ibid., Pratt, 10 February 1841.

ritual as well as social value must have varied with the degree and frequency of contact between missionaries and congregations. However, the Samoan who fully intended to join a church, or who became and wanted to remain a member, had to observe certain standards of personal conduct which many people would neither accept for themselves nor for him. This condition applied whatever his reasons for joining the church and whatever his religious notions. Of course, some of the mission's rules entailed little or no strain. Any man might cut his hair, for example, or wear a shirt and swear off work on Sunday.[26] Rules of this kind could be adopted by whole villages or groups of villages in concert —as 'Christian' laws and earnests of progress. Then, too, there were certain Western conventions, such as those defining limits of consanguinity in marriage and sex relations, which conformed to or were embodied in existing Samoan standards and so were accepted as a matter of course. Other rules might be irksome, in requiring that certain personal pleasures and diversions be foregone, and yet be of a sort unlikely to encounter any other resistance. These would relate to sex, obscenity, smoking, and the like. They, too, might be adopted as general regulations, but whether they were or not, the candidate or church member would still be free to observe them. In a different class, however, were rules concerned with acts and relationships that served important social ends—for example, marriage, ceremonial exchange and war, in regard to which the individual's rights and obligations were not normally his alone to determine. Moreover, such affairs were not locally oriented to the same degree as church membership, so that a Samoan would be free of pressure to participate only if the mission's ideas and influence prevailed throughout the group of islands.

The sanctity of the *lotu* offered some protection against 'public opinion' and secular authority to those who cast off traditional responsibilities that conflicted with the requirements of church membership. As a result, the church attracted not only the pious but also various social misfits and political underdogs and opportunists. Nevertheless, group pressures probably worked more often to the mission's disadvantage, for related to the proscribed activities were also rights and benefits that were difficult for the individual to forego, even if his religious convictions approached London Missionary Society standards. In this connection it should be observed that the mission rules, though ostensibly impartial, demanded greater sacrifices of some people than of others. The obvious victim was the chief, particularly the chief of high rank.

[26] Sabbatarianism was in vogue at a very early date. In 1836 the vessel which brought the L.M.S. missionaries to Samoa was damaged off Sapapali'i on a Sunday, but even in this emergency, the Samoans refused to render assistance, on the ground that it was the Lord's day (SSJ, Barff, 1836).

The untitled Samoan or low-ranking chief could, if he wished, carve out a reasonably secure niche in the church. Membership was in itself an honour, and it helped him to resist the authority of his superiors, should he want to or be required to take that bold step. At the same time, his low rank was not likely to draw him into such 'immorality' as the contracting of successive political marriages or the raising of a war to avenge his wounded pride. On the other hand, the high chief wanted, for the sake of his rank and office, to be a member of the church without being bound to adhere to all of its rules. His position worsened if, in his own village, his authority was challenged or denied from within the church by people who should have obeyed him. But even if he belonged to the church and had no opposition within his village, he was still obligated to his outside connections.

Another episode in the Malietoa saga illustrates the dilemma of the chief. Near the end of his career Vai'inupō, who had not become a church member,[27] arranged a political marriage between one of his daughters and an already married chief of Falelatai. When the commitment was made he turned to his family to canvass for the *tōga*, only to learn that his own son Talavou and his half-brother Taimalelagi would not co-operate. The missionary at Sapapali'i had seen them and told them that the marriage was opposed to the will of God; if they sanctioned it and contributed their fine mats, they would be expelled from the church. The wedding was held just the same, but Vai'inupō appeared as the high chief openly abandoned by his closest relatives and by the mission he had helped to establish.[28]

The same episode also illustrates the missionaries' dilemma, for if they won a victory in Sapapali'i, where the church was relatively strong, they suffered a defeat in Malie. Moreover, the victory, like the defeat, was grounded partly in the shifting sands of Samoan politics—in this case, a division within the Malietoa family. The division remained and so did the crisis for the church, with Taimalelagi and Talavou, in their turn, experiencing the same order of conflict that had confronted Vai'-inupō. Similar crises occurred many times over, in other families and other villages, indicating that chieftainship and the church were to a large extent incompatible. How was the mission to deal with this problem? Obviously, the solution was not to be found in playing Samoan politics if every gain was to be offset by a corresponding loss. Nor did it seem right that the church should lower its standards or apply them in a manner inconsistent with the principle of equality before God.

To combat Samoan conservatism the mission tried to enlarge its

[27] But he had taken a Christian name, Tavita (David), and had presumably been baptized.

[28] SSL, Hardie, 9 February 1842.

influence outside the church while, of course, maintaining discipline within. This influence was pursued in a variety of ways, sometimes for its own sake alone and sometimes as an objective incidental to others. Thus, when missionaries interfered in quarrels between Samoans and Europeans, as some of them often did, their support nearly always went to the former, not only to defend justice or to oppose objectionable foreign elements, but also to establish themselves as the trusted friends and advisers of the Samoan people. Some of the missionaries preferred to remain neutral when that course threatened no harm to their interests nor injustice to the Samoans, but others, by supporting dubious causes or by intervening when their help could not affect the outcome, gave the London Missionary Society the reputation of being pro-Samoan on principle, which accounted for a good deal of European prejudice against the mission. Most of the missionaries were also given to exaggerating the prospects and dangers of French intervention and the protective beneficence of the British Government. Sectarian feeling and patriotism were largely responsible for this, but sometimes the Samoans' fears and aspirations seem to have been deliberately, even callously, exploited. For example, could the missionaries really have believed that a backward, stateless Samoa was especially vulnerable to seizure by a foreign Power? If so, Tahiti should, by that reasoning, have remained independent longer than it did.

One of the most powerful sources of influence was the concept of taboo, which, though associated with heathenism, the missionaries used as a sort of bogy to enforce injunctions against a 'childish' people. The main targets were stubborn sins and political reaction, but also included were 'hyprocrisy' and the belief that the missionaries exerted some control over God's thoughts and actions. The practice was, however, a dangerous one, for as taboo implied some punishment in this world—which was the essence of its value to the mission—it was subject to test. If prohibitions were generally approved, their validity could easily be upheld, since few people would violate them, and those who did would, sooner or later, suffer misfortune of some kind. That had been one basis of social control in pre-Christian times—or, as one missionary wrote, the Samoans had been 'guided by some old established usage which is instead of law' [sic].[29] But clearly, some of the mission's rules were far from being established usage, even amongst its own followers. Moreover, as *new* rules they were likely to be regarded as made by men and only enforced by God, in which case their potency would probably have varied with the apparent *mana* of their makers. In either event, they might be questioned and even discredited from within the *lotu*. And if that was not enough, the *lotu taiti* was but one of several sects and, of them all,

29 ibid., Platt, 19 May 1836.

the most demanding, not only working against communalism and chief-tainship in a society in which those principles were entrenched, but preaching puritanism in a place where freer modes of conduct were also said to represent the will of God.

## The Tutuila 'revival'

One of the prominent features of Christianity in Polynesia was the tendency of converts to show, periodically, intense religious excitement or enthusiasm. In Samoa, such outbursts of emotionalism, frequently reported by the missionaries, varied considerably in duration and in the number of people affected, but there were at least two aspects common to most of them. First, there was usually some recognizable event or condition giving rise to grief or anxiety, for example, a death, a natural catastrophe, an evil omen, or a potent, often disruptive European in-fluence. Among the last were apocalyptic and messianic notions acquired from Christianity. Secondly, spirit possession, in trance, dream or delirium, usually figured among the manifestations. Sometimes the conduct of a medium seemed to be all there was to the 'hysteria', while at other times there might also be contagious outbreaks of weeping, shouting and fainting among spectators or worshippers. The special significance of mediumship was its function, in the traditional religion, as a direct means of canvassing the desires and intentions of the gods, particularly in times of stress. Carried over to Christianity, spirit possession was associated with prayer, divine revelation and, possibly, faith healing.

Mission teaching contained many powerful stimuli to the imagination and emotions, both in expositions of doctrine and explications of God's will in relation to worldly affairs. But whether these seeds of hysteria took root and grew depended greatly on how the missionaries conducted themselves. Of course, no missionary was likely to encourage ritual behaviour which he knew to be founded upon religious views inimical to his own. For example, the visionary who openly expounded an un-orthodox interpretation of his dream experiences would, at the very least, be charged with delusion and, if a candidate or church member, subjected to discipline. If he went so far as to claim miraculous powers or knowledge through divine revelation, he would probably be branded a heretic, and any religious movement or reaction based upon or inspired by his pronouncements would be condemned.

High emotion was not, however, necessarily incompatible with doctrinal orthodoxy, so that one must ask whether the missionaries were ready to take it as a seemly, sincere and reliable expression of Christian conviction and piety and, if so, whether they tried to cultivate it. In other words, were they given to revivalism? The early Wesleyans

undoubtedly were, while the Catholics, for the most part, were not.
In the London Missionary Society, whose missionaries were free to
conduct their services and run their stations much as they liked, very
few, at least in Samoa, treated religious hysteria with anything but the
utmost suspicion. It is of interest, then, that the Tutuila 'revival' of
1839-41, by far the greatest phenomenon of its kind in the history of
Samoan missions, occurred within and around the London Missionary
Society.

In the strictest sense, there could have been little to revive in Tutuila,
for the mission had barely established itself on the island. In other
respects, however, the movement more than lived up to its name. Starting
amongst a small group of inquirers, it quickly gathered force until it
had engulfed most of Tutuila. Outwardly its principal features were
morbid emotionalism, the public confession of sin and the humbling
of all penitents, regardless of rank, station or sex. Ostensibly in con-
templation of hell, sin, the crucifixion and salvation, the people were
reduced to uncontrolled weeping and wailing, followed by prostration,
and many suffered convulsions and catalepsis, with effects lasting for
days. At the mission's frequent meetings, both small and large, the
majority in attendance would usually succumb, among them 'proud,
hard-hearted, haughty, cruel savages, . . . humbled and subdued [into]
mourning over their sins'. Away from the meetings they were said to
have spent much time in prayer, while some, alleged to have gone into
the bush to consult privately with God, would subsequently be found
there unconscious, presumably in a state of trance, as if 'possessed' by
Jesus or Jehovah. The missionary, Murray, who first reported the
movement as a revival, was gratified to think that many experiencing
'violent mental agitation' were 'under deep and real conviction', but he
regretted that his power to console them was unequal to their apparent
need, so heavy was their burden of sin and so great their sorrow in
consequence. Indeed, his mere presence, his opening word, became the
signal for a re-expression of their feeling, until he found it difficult and
sometimes impossible to conclude his sermons. His teachers encountered
similar manifestations and so did his colleague Slatyer, who came to
Tutuila six months after the revival had begun.[30]

That such things should have been observed in one area, when the
London Missionary Society was working throughout the group, must
have interested the missionaries as much as the specific reasons for the
hysteria, but if they had any original ideas on either subject, they

[30] Murray, *Forty years' mission work*, 119 ff.; Lundie, *Missionary life*, 80 ff.; MS.,
Slatyer, 1840-1; SSL 4, letters from Murray and Slatyer. Europeans also caught
the 'revival spirit', among them deserted seamen as well as members of mission
families.

omitted them from their reports. It is possible, however, to discern several peculiarities in the circumstances of the Tutuilans and in the local leadership of the mission itself. First, it is clear that Murray, unlike most of his colleagues, had a background of revivalism in Britain.[31] Unfortunately, there is no detailed account of him in action in Tutuila, but there are some clues. For example, he was known as the mission's toughest disciplinarian, relentlessly hard on sin, always on the watch for it, and adamant in requiring repentance.[32] Archibald Lundie, who came to visit Murray in 1840, described him as 'enthusiastic'[33] in his preaching and 'of a highly spiritual character', possessing those qualities that made 'things prosper' in his church. Inclined towards revivalism himself, Lundie went on to say that other churches and stations in Samoa were not as prosperous as Murray's because other missionaries 'receded' from high spirituality.[34] Before coming to Samoa Murray had not witnessed religious hysteria on a large scale, yet in 1840 he wrote that prior to the outbreak in Tutuila he had been expecting a climax or crisis of religious zeal.[35] When he was finally confronted with the crisis he awaited, the event occurred in his own house, and he was the only missionary in Tutuila.[36] Thereafter the feeling usually ran highest in his presence, as he proceeded in his round of almost-daily meetings.

Events in Aleipata may also throw light upon the movement in Tutuila. Living at the eastern end of Upolu, nearest Tutuila, the people of this Atua sub-district heard of the revival,[37] were said to have been astonished by the reports and, towards the end of 1840, began to act in similar fashion. In this case the hysteria was clearly whipped up by Samoans. In fact, Harbutt, the missionary for south-eastern Upolu, did not live in Aleipata and was quite unaware of the 'awakening' until after it had commenced. When, in the course of his circuit, he witnessed manifestations like those reported by Murray and heard, too, that the people were troubled by their sins, he was forced to review his ideas about religious hysteria. Until then, he wrote, he had not believed in such outbreaks—implying, no doubt, that he had also questioned the authenticity of Murray's revival. Since it was apparent to him, however, that *something* was happening, he resolved to study the situation

31 MS., Gunson.
32 Lundie, 84; Trood, *Island reminiscences*, 32; Wilkes, II, 75.
33 At the time, 'enthusiasm' in a preacher often referred to emotionalism.
34 Lundie, 198-9.
35 SSL, Murray, 20 March 1840. Late in 1839 Murray told Wilkes that his efforts were about to be 'crowned with success' (Wilkes, II, 79).
36 Lundie, 85. Barnden, the missionary originally appointed to Leone, had been drowned. Slatyer arrived in March 1840.
37 The L.M.S. missionaries said that they had heard of it, but it is also likely that some of them had attended mission meetings in Tutuila.

closely before deciding what its religious significance might be. When
he sent his next report, several months later, he had concluded that the
movement was a sham, put on simply to impress him. He denounced
it and it soon died away, after having spread to only a few villages.[38]
Had he been a Murray, however, his station and others might have
been overrun.

To some degree, Aleipata's abortive revival seems to have been an
import, but Tutuila's was not. It may be significant, then, that the
latter developed during an epidemic—the first major epidemic recorded
for Samoa, and certainly the first to occur after the advent of the
mission. This was a coincidence of which the missionaries made very
little, perhaps because the disease in question swept through the entire
group of islands, whereas the revival did not. In the initial phase,
during April and May 1839, something described as 'influenza' affected
most of the people. At this time 'only' one per cent of the population
died—not a particularly high mortality, but according to Murray, enough
to produce a quickening of religious interest in his area. Tutuila's known
dead numbered between thirty and forty, among whom was the high
chief Mauga of Pago Pago. Then, 'after the disease itself was removed,
vast numbers' of those who had had it died of 'pulmonary complications'.
This phase, unlike the first, was spread out over several months and was
reported only by missionaries who had a special interest in medicine.[39]
Murray was not among these, but from data supplied for the western
islands, it would appear that the after-effects must have been felt in
Tutuila during the time in which Murray's anticipated 'crisis' was building up. As for the total effects of the epidemic, there can be little doubt
that, if a mortality of one per cent or three to four hundred was 'not
great', 'vast numbers' must have meant a heavy toll indeed.[40]

Tutuila's revival may well have been stimulated by more powerful
anxieties than Aleipata's, but it would appear that its extent and
duration owed a great deal to the fact that Murray, unlike Harbutt in
similar circumstances, saw the 'power of the Holy Spirit' at work and

[38] SSL, Harbutt, 20 November 1840, 21 April 1841. The missionary, Powell, took a
similar view of a later outbreak of hysteria in Tutuila. This movement—Tutuila's
third revival—may also have been started by Murray (*Samoan Reporter*, January
1857; Lundie, 280).

[39] None of the early L.M.S. missionaries was a fully trained physician, but all
kept medicines and prescribed them. The more successful were renowned for
their cures and, being much sought after, had a fair knowledge of health
conditions.

[40] Murray, *Forty years' mission work*, 108-9; SSL, Murray, 10 June 1839, Heath,
21 October 1839; Mills, 4 November 1839, Pratt, n.d. According to Lundie (83),
the death of Williams, the founder of the *lotu* in Samoa, was announced after
the revival had begun and had the effect of increasing the people's agitation.

set out to intensify and exploit the hysteria he sanctioned. Slatyer, at Leone, came under the same conviction and pursued the same objectives. From the accounts it would seem that, although traditional religious beliefs and expressions were ingredients of the movement, many Samoans accepted as real their accumulation of sin and the peril of their souls. Apparently the new taboos were made to apply retrospectively and the mission's way of salvation made to look like the only way and, therefore, reasonable even at the price the mission exacted.

During the period of the revival the missionaries extended their influence from Pago Pago and from Leone to embrace at least two-thirds of the population of Tutuila, including most of the leading chiefs. There was also a dramatic increase in the number of church members and baptized candidates, who by the end of 1840 comprised about one-quarter of the people in regular attendance at services, or a proportion more than double that in the western islands.[41] From this position of strength the London Missionary Society exerted considerable power outside the strict confines of the church. For example, the highest-ranking chiefs, some of whom had been at loggerheads for years, were brought together to accept mission-inspired 'blue laws'. They also joined in building a wide track between Aua and Leone, via Pago Pago,[42] which according to the Samoans was a new experience in co-operative enterprise. Referring to this 'road', Lundie said that the Samoans' conception of human achievement was being enlarged and that one could expect other new undertakings to follow.[43] He might well have numbered among these the resettlement of London Missionary Society converts, which now commenced in the eastern half of the island. Pago Pago, being 'near the Word', was the focus of this movement—a movement characteristic of Eastern Polynesia, but the only one of its kind ever attempted with any success by the London Missionary Society in Samoa.[44] Along the shore of the bay coral-lime houses sprang up, new taro patches were set out near by, and Pago Pago began to acquire the

---

41 There were eight church members in March 1839, and one hundred a year later. At the end of 1840 there were about two hundred and fifty church members and some three hundred candidates, with congregations totalling more than two thousand people of all ages. Church membership reached five hundred by 1844 and levelled off at that figure. The lag was due partly to the testing of candidates and partly to Leone's having started well behind Pago Pago (Lundie, 84, 195, 280; Murray, *Forty years' mission work*, 104).

42 Aua is several miles east of Pago Pago village.

43 By reducing the people's dependence on canoes, the track enabled adherents to gather more easily and helped the missionaries and teachers to maintain close and more frequent contact with their congregations.

44 The only other mission resettlement scheme was one instituted by the Marists in Apia in the 1870s. There were, of course, numerous school and other training centres.

appearance of a 'metropolis by absorbing the population of the district'.[45] Other innovations included the staging of all-island mission meetings which, though previously out of the question, were now attended without demur. Yet another development was the close regulation of contact between Samoans and visiting seamen. But perhaps the most telling evidence of London Missionary Society power was the Samoans' repudiation of chiefs who stood out against the mission or, having once submitted, relapsed into sin.[46]

Not all such performances were letter perfect, nor was every pocket of sectarianism eliminated. Nor, for that matter, were the mission's power and its effects sustained indefinitely. Indeed, by 1844 Murray was longing for another revival. But while the Samoans' enthusiasm—or their terror—lasted, the London Missionary Society interfered with the privileges of rank, suppressed political rivalries, kept in close touch with its followers,[47] and maintained comparatively strict moral discipline. In short, some of the mission's thorniest problems were solved, at least temporarily, thereby suggesting that revivalism was in some respects well suited to London Missionary Society needs in Samoa. However, if an epidemic contributed to Murray's success, it may be significant that in Samoa such punitive 'acts of God' were relatively few and far between.[48] More frequent, and more prolonged, were the disasters that befell the mission itself. They were the acts of the Samoans.

[45] Lundie, 141.

[46] e.g. Murray, *Forty years' mission work*, 138-9, 205-6, concerning the deposition and banishment of high chief Mauga Manumā after his expulsion from the church. When he repented, Manumā was restored to the title and readmitted to the church.

[47] But for many years the Leone and Pago Pago 'district' churches were among the most highly centralized in all Samoa (SSL, Pratt, 11 April 1874).

[48] cf. the repeated scourges that quickened religious interest in Rarotonga.

# 5

## SAMOAN INFLUENCE UPON THE CHURCH

*The outbreak of war*

By 1840 or 1841 the London Missionary Society had penetrated most villages and, primarily by gaining new converts from heathenism and the sailor sects, had clearly displaced Methodism as Samoa's largest *lotu*. Its principal strongholds, apart from Tutuila, were A'ana and Manu'a, while Savai'i was its area of greatest weakness. In Fa'asaleleaga, Sapapali'i was solidly London Missionary Society, with the strongest church nucleus outside Tutuila, and in several other villages the mission had good support; but Methodism remained a potent force in the district, especially in the south. In Itu-o-Tane the London Missionary Society had several large congregations, including those at Safune and Matautu, and a start had been made in Itu-o-Fafine; but in neither district was it leading. The sectarian picture in Atua and Tuamasaga resembled that in Fa'asaleleaga, except that in some areas, such as Vaimauga, a few Methodists were coming over to the London Missionary Society. In both districts the Society had gained the edge over its rival, but progress was slow and there were no signs of the utter rout of Methodism that the London Missionary Society representatives had confidently anticipated. Manono was almost evenly divided between the two sects, and it remained so, owing partly to the establishment of the Tongan Wesleyan headquarters there.

London Missionary Society and Methodist congregations, which were found side by side in many places,[1] kept strictly apart except for some interchange at mission feasts and medical line-ups. This division was, of course, desired by Samoans, but it was also a product of 'sectarian discipline'—of the missions' refusal to accredit one another's religious observances and standards. Since there were no ordained Tongan Wesleyans in Samoa, except during the period 1848-51, and no Methodist church run on European lines, the exclusiveness worked mainly against the London Missionary Society. Indeed, the ability of the London Missionary Society to attract Methodists on its own merits diminished as its hierarchy, ranging from mere adherents to deacons, developed; for newcomers entered, perforce, at the bottom of the ladder.

However, the political configuration of sectarianism was changing, for the missions, by organizing their congregations at the village level and

1 Within many villages and sometimes between adjacent single-*lotu* villages.

avoiding political commitments, were permitting local events and conditions to assume greater importance in determining the stability and change
of religious affiliations. That is to say, shifts in the wider political associations or alliances were now less likely to upset the balance or makeup of
mission support. Such shifts were in fact occurring, and partly as a result
of them, mission influence was being more widely distributed among
the political factions. Therefore the London Missionary Society, which
was anxious to prevent war, was becoming more likely to have and to
retain influence within each party to a potentially dangerous dispute.

Before Europeans made central government and monarchy issues of
contention in Samoa—that is, before there were 'civilized' grounds for
hostilities—the London Missionary Society took the position that war,
except in the strictest self-defence, was contrary to the will of God.
Anyone who participated in aggression or provoked, instigated, organized, or supported it was, if a church member, liable to be expelled or,
if a candidate, to be dropped.[2] Samoans who 'fell' in this way, as in any
other, might be reinstated, but the process could be more trying than
their previous testing for the church.

Loyal followers of the London Missionary Society had not only to
refrain from fighting but also to work for peace among people whom
they could influence or control. Of course, if they were numerous, their
refusal to subscribe to a warlike measure could in itself prevent war,
either because lack of unity, in what should have had unanimous
support, required that peace be maintained to save face, or because too
few people were left to conduct hostilities. But if war plans proceeded
without them, they set out to mediate, thereby assuming a function of
neutrality which had not been very highly developed in Samoan
society. Led by their teachers and often by their missionaries, they
conveyed the mission's word on war and proposed to the would-be
belligerents alternative means of settling the questions at issue. In this
capacity their *fa'a-Samoa* influence was less likely to be limited to their
own villages, while their passport, the Bible, enabled them to move
about in comparative safety.

During the early years of the mission many disputes and incidents
threatened to culminate in warfare, but in every case the peace was
preserved,[3] with differences sometimes being settled once and for all
by the offering of formal apologies (*ifoga*) or the payment of com-

---

[2] Certain acts incidental to war were also prohibited, e.g. the taking of enemy
heads and the holding of night dances in the war camps. Such acts were
forbidden to aggressor and defender alike.

[3] On one occasion the mission had outside assistance. That was in 1839, when a
vessel of the American exploring expedition intervened in a dispute at Ta'ū in
Manu'a (Wilkes, II, 65-6).

pensation. At first these results were due largely to the missionaries' own efforts. With the development of the churches, however, Samoans joined the ranks of the active peacemakers, and as those ranks grew, so the danger of war seemed to recede. It is true that most of the threats to peace were trivial, small-scale affairs, but when, in 1839, Manono declined to avenge an insult to Malietoa, on the alleged ground that war was sinful,[4] there seemed reason to hope that the Samoans were beginning to value Christian peace even more than the dignity of the Mālō and *pāpā*. This hope was strengthened in 1841 on the occasion of Vai'inupō's death. Having repented his sins and made his reconciliation with Sapapali'i, the chief declared in his *māvaega* that never again should there be war in Samoa. Other interpretations are conceivable, but it was ostensibly to prevent war that the Tafa'ifā was to die with him. The *pāpā* were to survive, but separately and, it was claimed, innocuously. To'oā of Falelatai[5] and another chief of Upolu were to have the Tui A'ana and Tui Atua titles, respectively, and Taimalelagi was to have the rest. The rest included, among others, the Malietoa title and that of Tupu o Salafai, 'Paramount Chief of Savai'i', a dignity created and first assumed by Tamafaigā.[6] This distribution of titles, if effected, was somehow to fulfil Vai'inupō's desire for peace.

In meeting the crisis caused by the death of a Tafa'ifā the London Missionary Society was at two peculiar disadvantages. First, of course, the issues involved were not of a kind that easily lent themselves to mediation. Secondly, the mission, apart from its unhappy association with Vai'inupō, had had little experience of higher politics in Samoa and, therefore, could not be expected to understand the intrigues of the title-gatherers nor to realize that, at such a time, the smallest incident could precipitate a general war. In the foreground, all looked well. Indeed, Manono, leader of the existing Mālō, seemed to accept Vai'inupō's views on war, letting itself be dissuaded from attacking its number one enemy, A'ana, although provoked by a murder.[7] Also

---

[4] SSL, Heath, 3 May 1839.

[5] This To'oā headed a small Mālō faction in A'ana, thus disposing of a rival, another 'To'oā', who remained in exile in Tutuila until 1841. The victorious To'oā, one of Vai'inupō's favourites, was later known as Tuimaleali'ifano Sualauvī, titular high chief of Sa Taua'ana of Falelatai, and held the Tui A'ana title in the 1860s. His mother was *ilamutu* (sister) to Vai'inupō's father, Malietoa Fitisemanu. The To'oā title, bestowed by Manono, actually signified a *tama fafine* relationship to the Malietoa line (Krämer, *Samoan Islands*, I, 302). The most famous To'oā of the nineteenth century was Mata'afa Iosefo, who became Malietoa To'oā in 1888 after the Germans banished Malietoa Laupepa.

[6] After winning a battle in Savai'i.

[7] SSL, Heath, 15 May 1841. About the same time it was noticed that Samoans were refusing arms in trade and disposing of their muskets (ibid., Mills, 17 May 1841).

reassuring was Taimalelagi's reaction to Vai'inupō's *māvaega*. A member of the church at Sapapali'i, he had expressed a fervent hatred of war and such a disdain for worldly honours that, had the choice been his, he would have consigned to the grave not only the Tafa'ifā but all of Vai'inupō's distinctions. That, at any rate, was what he had been overheard to say and what the missionaries thought he believed; and since he was the principal figure in the proposed succession, his word seemed to mean peace. Little notice was taken, however, of the Mālō and *pule*-centre chiefs who openly objected to the terms of the *māvaega* and to the fact that Vai'inupō had not made his dying statement in the presence of everyone entitled to hear it.[8] Even if these people respected the *māvaega* there could still be trouble, for there were contrary claims to the Tupua titles.

For two years the islands were 'unsettled', but not critically so. During this time the Malietoa title was conferred on Taimalelagi. Then, suddenly, a quarrel between people of Palauli and Salelologa villages in Savai'i mushroomed into a threat of war between the Falelua and Fa'asaleleaga. The immediate issue was a case of adultery, which the London Missionary Society took to be the sole cause of strife. Obscured from the mission's view, however, the parties had been disputing the position of first place in Savai'i, and it was now time for the contest to be settled conclusively and in the only way the Samoans knew. The London Missionary Society was caught short, then, in an area in which it was particularly weak.

Being, for the moment, at a military disadvantage, the Falelua party was unexpectedly receptive to the mission's peace overtures; but the leaders of the Fa'asaleleaga party, sensing the prospect of a quick victory, reacted oppositely. Therefore, the only hope of peace seemed to lie in the influence of Sapapali'i and, especially, of Taimalelagi, the new Malietoa. For Taimalelagi, however, this was a time of profound crisis, for he was also under pressure from Safotulafai, the district *pule* centre, to sanction the war and so to act the traditional role of the Malietoa. A further question was whether he was really so little interested in the *pāpā* that he could pass up this opportunity of staking a claim to them.

For the London Missionary Society, too, this was an unusually critical period, owing to the taboo which had been placed on war—and which, in fact, had first been proclaimed by Williams in this very district of Savai'i. If fighting broke out, would those guilty of fostering it be punished in a way that the Samoans could appreciate? Apparently the London Missionary Society church members and candidates were afraid to risk God's judgement, for most of them declared for peace. There were, however, enough people left to support Fa'asaleleaga's cause;

[8] SSL, Hardie, 9 February 1842.

and of these the majority were Methodists, whose Tongan leaders, though not accused by the London Missionary Society of warmongering, could not have regarded war as very sinful. After all, that most devout of Methodists, King George of Tonga, was not only the patron of the Wesleyan mission in Samoa but also the most successful Polynesian general of his time. Hence the reign of peace was probably due to end, but if any doubts remained, they were resolved by Taimalelagi's last-minute defection from the church. His son, Tupapau, had lived in 'secret sin', for which God had taken his life. That, at least, was how most of Sapapali'i's church members interpreted Tupapau's sudden illness and death. But Taimalelagi, in his grief and anger, put the taboo to the test, committing the same sin with the same woman and daring God to kill him for it. He lived and, together with Talavou, renounced the *lotu taiti* and left the village for the war, cursing the mission and the people who refused to follow him. As he had once opposed Vai'inupō, so now he also left behind him an heir-apparent who preferred the church. This was Molī, Vai'inupō's eldest son, the first of his line to both acquire and keep a reputation as a Christian.[9]

When the attack came, the people of Satupa'itea and Palauli heeded London Missionary Society advice and abandoned their villages out of 'Christian conscience'. Given the means of retiring gracefully, they lost their houses to the torch but gained the prospect of fighting later under more favourable conditions. If anything, the mission's intervention had prolonged the struggle. Each side sought allies, acquiring some in Savai'i but very few from the other islands. Manono, which held the military initiative in Upolu, was closely related to both belligerent parties and would support neither. Still claiming to act from Christian motives, Manono kept most of Upolu neutral and took upon itself the role of mediator, with no more success than the mission had had.[10] For three years the conflict proceeded at the rate of one short encounter per year, until finally Satupa'itea and part of Palauli were soundly defeated. The rest of Palauli, having switched sides midway, emerged with Fa'asaleleaga as Mālō. Throughout this time the London Missionary Society kept most of its original following and made some gains in Palauli. The main issue had been lost, however, for the great sinners, far from being punished, had prospered. Safotulafai's claim to be the chief *pule* of Savai'i was upheld, and Taimalelagi was unchallenged Tupu o Salafai.[11]

In Manono and Upolu, meanwhile, the relationship between Mālō

9 SSL, Hardie, 29 September 1843, Mills, 7 September 1846.

10 Some of the Faleata (Tuamasaga) people entered the war.

11 SSL, MacDonald, 13 September 1843, 1844, *passim*, 20 November 1846; *Samoan Reporter*, March and September 1845, September 1846.

and Vaivai had been changing, for under the protective wing of the
London Missionary Society, the people of A'ana had rehabilitated themselves materially and in spirit, becoming relatively prosperous through
trade and assuming an attitude of self-respect which seemed to say that
they considered themselves at least as good as any other Samoans. To
the proud chiefs of Manono, A'ana's recovery was anathema; and that
mission interference had kept them from thwarting it in the traditional
manner in no way appeased their dignity. Related to this same issue was
the question of the Tui A'ana title, which according to custom was the
first of the four *pāpā* to be bestowed again following the death of a
Tafa'ifā.[12] Who was to determine the succession? If A'ana, Vaivai in
name if not in fact, would not submit to dictation in this important
affair of state, Manono would lose its Mālō status by default. Moreover,
Taimalelagi, who had consolidated his position in Savai'i, Manono and
Tuamasaga, had now to contest the Tui A'ana title if he had any pretensions to the Tafa'ifā.

When the war ended in Savai'i, Manono turned away from piety and
began to exchange insults with A'ana. With the initiative belonging to
Manono, A'ana, though stronger in numbers, reacted to London
Missionary Society mediation rather as the Falelua had, condemning the
would-be aggressor on the ostensible grounds that war was proscribed by
God and that all districts should be free and equal. When threatened
with attack, the A'ana people also fled, leaving the Manono party to
take out its wrath on empty villages. This incident, which occurred in
1847, was followed by the forming of alliances on both sides. With
Atua's support, the people of A'ana then returned home, still voicing
a desire for peace. Wrongly assuming from this event that the crisis had
passed, the London Missionary Society allowed its Manono station to be
vacated while the resident missionary visited Melanesia. A series of
complex manoeuvres now ensued, and in 1848 war broke out in earnest,
with most of the people of the western islands being drawn into it.[13]
Roughly, the sides were (1) Manono, most of Savai'i and Tuamasaga,
and minority elements of A'ana and Atua, against (2) the majority of
A'ana and Atua, parts of Tuamasaga, and a small number of Savai'i
people. Most of Sapapali'i and Vaimauga, loyal to the London Missionary Society and Molī Malietoa, remained neutral. So did Tutuila, owing
largely to mission influence. In a few other localities a neutral position
was adopted for political reasons, while Manu'a, as usual, was not concerned in any way.

---

[12] Krämer, *Samoan Islands*, I, 25.

[13] Actually, the first blow was struck by an A'ana party, which attacked a group
of Savai'i warriors at Sale'imoa, Tuamasaga. However, war had already been
declared (MS., Ella, Diary 1848).

The war now in progress marked a transition in the history of Samoan politics, in that it was the last general war in which European intrigues played no substantial part and the first to be influenced by European arms. Through a combination of Samoan organization and Western technology, the traditional balance of power shifted and, in turn, the period of hostility and unrest was unusually prolonged. Manono, whose fleet was said always to have been victorious, found its naval might excelled by the armed vessels which Europeans designed and built for A'ana and Atua. To counter this challenge Manono commissioned double-canoes, similarly armed, and the result was a stalemate at sea. On land other changes were being wrought by the musket, which introduced a concept of warfare to which marksmanship was more important than skill in close combat, and fire-power more decisive than man-power. The Samoans were afraid of firearms and ignorant of how to use them most effectively; yet they wanted them, and they bought enough of them to render obsolete their clubs and spears. Mainly for these reasons their engagements were infrequent, dispirited and indecisive.[14]

In its first phase the war proceeded sporadically for about three years, without issue. This period, 1848-51, was followed by an interval during which some of the participants withdrew and the remaining alliances were slightly recast. At the end of 1853 there was more fighting, again without issue. This ended the actual combat, but a 'state of war' prevailed until 1857, when a peace settlement was finally negotiated. In effect, A'ana's—or rather, the mission's—ideal of district equality and Vai'inupō's scattering of the *pāpā* had been achieved, at the cost of several hundred lives and a decade of strife. But since neither achievement suited the Samoans, agitation and intrigue continued on both sides.[15]

## Mission decline

The London Missionary Society had suspected that Manono's earlier peace policy was based upon political as well as religious considerations, but it had hoped that the chiefs of that island would have been ready to exchange their military pre-eminence for moral leadership. On being disappointed, the mission judged Manono guilty of both treachery and aggression,[16] while A'ana and Atua appeared as the righteous defenders,

14 But the Samoans acquired most of their firearms after the war broke out (*loc. cit.*; Shipley, *Sketches in the Pacific* 23).
15 BCS 4/1, W. T. Pritchard to To'oā, 28 November 1857; SSL, Ella, 22 December 1857.
16 All that the mission could say in Manono's favour was that the principal warmongers were Methodists. This may have been true, yet the island united in support of the war. It was also thought that King George of Tonga might

the protagonists of peace, freedom and equality.[17] The relatively high degree of district unity which then prevailed in A'ana and Atua, as well as Manono, tended to reinforce this view, for as Europeans saw it, such unity gave the quarrel a territorial bias consistent with the objectives that A'ana-Atua espoused. But, in fact, both sides were fighting for the Mālō, not the subjection or liberation of districts as such, and between them there was only one very substantial difference. Manono, having entered the war as Mālō, supported a single aspirant to the *pāpā* and so had only to win the one campaign in order to have the Mālō and Tafa'ifā in hand again. On the other side, however, there were several major contenders for the titles, so that victory for A'ana and Atua would probably have led to the collapse of their 'defensive' alliance and their so-called district unity, with a reshuffling of forces in preparation for another round of fighting.

By the time the war entered its second phase, the London Missionary Society had learned from the intrigues of the A'ana-Atua side that the badge of virtue had been awarded prematurely. A 'corrected' opinion of the political situation now appeared in the mission's news-sheet, the *Samoan Reporter*. Both sides were denounced with equal severity:

> . . . the customs and usages of this people are incompatible with their advancement in civilization. The different parties, on any emergency, are bound together only by fear, and the desire of personal safety and distinction; hence, they are distrustful of each other, knowing that, at any time, any of them may change sides, according to circumstances. There is not among them anything worthy the name of law or government, or any correct principles of justice, honour, or friendship.[18]

This pessimism did not, of course, derive solely from the political upheaval, for the war also had a direct and disastrous effect upon the cause of Christianity. First of all there was the prolonged separation of many Samoans from their congregations. With the warriors and camp-followers spending a good deal of time away from home, the mission could only keep in close touch with its loyal church members and candidates, and with neutrals and some of the non-combatants from the belligerent parties.[19] Attendance at services and classes generally fell off,

have stirred up trouble during his visit in 1847, but for his part, the King claimed to have worked for peace, only to be out-talked by the 'unreliable' Samoans (Adm. 1/5590, Maxwell to Sec. of Adm., 18 March 1848).

[17] But while the missionaries sympathized with A'ana-Atua and handled church discipline accordingly, they generally tried to avoid open expressions of partisan bias that would commit them politically.

[18] *Samoan Reporter*, January 1854.

[19] Some missionaries visited the war camps occasionally, but they were unable or unwilling to remain there.

and in some areas, such as plundered and deserted A'ana, whole congregations were broken up. Considering the duration of the war, comparatively few people left the church, except in Manono and one or two other centres of intense political activity. But considering the length of time the mission had been working in Samoa, church members and candidates still comprised a small segment of the total population—at the outbreak of war, less than ten per cent for the entire group, and only about five per cent in the western islands alone. The mission was hard-pressed even to keep this nucleus of its following intact, for although war leaders would grant that baptism and church membership were honourable grounds for neutrality, they tried every means they knew to set up defections from the church.

In the war camps, at the 'front', and in their travels to and fro, many London Missionary Society adherents joined other Samoans in sin. It was not claimed that heathen religious rites were revived, though they may have been, but it is clear enough that heads were taken, forbidden pleasures and distractions indulged, the Sabbath profaned, traditional modes of undress readopted—in short, that many of the mission's restrictions and requirements were thrown off. When it was noticed that this reaction became general throughout both war parties, one missionary went so far as to suggest that the Samoans were deliberately postponing a settlement of their differences in order that they might escape the 'proprieties of a well-regulated Christian village'.[20] Other missionaries observed, however, that it was not always a question of escape, for many people, on returning home during lulls in the fighting, openly 'pursued activities leading to sin'.[21] In some places, then, the proprieties virtually ceased to exist.

Dealing with a people whom they now considered devoid of decent impulses, the missionaries must have wondered whether the decline of their influence, and therefore of their cause, was a process which the termination of the war would halt and the course of peace reverse. Occasionally a hopeful forecast was made, to the effect that the miseries and ruin of war must conclusively demonstrate to the Samoans the inferiority of their customs and usages and the blessings of Christian peace and order.[22] But for this argument to have carried much weight it should have been supported by evidence of progress in neutral areas, where 'Christian peace' ostensibly prevailed. This it was not. Indeed, by 1851 there were unmistakable signs of 'relapse' in Manu'a and Tutuila, the London Missionary Society strongholds farthest removed

[20] SSL, Turner, 28 September 1855.
[21] SSL, Nisbet, 8 September 1851, Drummond, 13 December 1851, Stallworthy, 31 December 1851.
[22] ibid., Turner, 26 April 1851.

from the scene of the war. In Manu'a the trouble consisted only of a 'weakening of the church' by the members' indulgence in smoking, kava-drinking and ceremonial exchange.[23] In Tutuila, however, events were taking a more serious turn, especially when seen against the background of Murray's revival. First, the chiefs were growing casual about enforcing London Missionary Society standards of behaviour.[24] Powell, who had succeeded Murray at Pago Pago, was shocked to hear 'dirty songs' sung right at the mission house and, because of this and other improprieties, cancelled the district's May festival, lest the gathering of large numbers of people increase the incidence of sin.[25] About the same time Sunderland reported from Leone that tattooing, which the mission claimed to have abolished in Tutuila, was becoming popular again.[26] Secondly, political unrest began to develop once more, with threats of war arising at the rate of one or two a year. With the exception of a minor outbreak in 1854, the mission met and overcame each of these crises until 1858, when most of the island became embroiled in a local war.[27] Finally, church members began to fall away, their numbers dropping from about five hundred to two hundred and fifty during the 1850s.[28] This toll was not taken by sectarianism but rather by sin— particularly by the sin that resulted from the Samoans' 'attachment to family and friends'.[29]

Thus, the war was but one aspect of a more general decline of London Missionary Society influence. What, then, of the other sects? Perhaps the Society could take some solace from the fact that they too were encountering troubles. First, there was the 'containment' of Roman Catholicism, which French Marists brought to Samoa in 1845. Long before any attempt was made to establish the Catholic mission, the London Missionary Society had assumed that the arrival of priests was imminent and so had set out to condition the Samoans to repulse them. The Wesleyan mission had acted similarly. The earliest anti-Catholic propaganda had dwelt upon 'Mary worship', idolatry, the private lives of priests and nuns, and like themes and was virulent enough to make some European observers wonder whether the Samoans were being incited to a dangerous degree.[30] It is not likely, however, that the people found much meaning in abuse of this kind. A new and more effective point of attack had been created by the French seizure of Tahiti.

[23] ibid., Powell, 1 September 1851.

[24] Before 1850 the mission's disciplinary standards were incorporated largely in unwritten regulations, but in that year Murray proposed, and the chiefs accepted, a code of written laws. According to Powell, few of the code's provisions were properly enforced (SSL, Murray, 25 December 1850, Powell, 12 July 1854).

[25] ibid., Powell, 1 September 1851.          [28] loc. cit.; Samoan Reporter, March 1861.

[26] ibid., Sunderland, 25 December 1851.     [29] SSL, Stallworthy, 31 December 1851.

[27] ibid., Powell, 12 July 1854, 1 July 1859.    [30] Wilkes, II, 129.

Accounts of French atrocities had now sounded from the pulpit and echoed from *fono* to *fono*, crossing sectarian boundaries and reaching to the farthest recesses of heathenism. To protestant missionaries, of course, the French Catholics were now more than ever the agents of the anti-Christ, but to the Samoans the prospect of invasion was the most convincing demonstration of the falsity of Catholicism.[31]

Although not united politically, the Samoans came near to sharing a single view of the subject of French intervention. In 1845 the Marists found only two openings, the first at Itu-o-Tane (Savai'i) among some Sio Vili people and other dissident elements, and the second at a place near Apia. At the time, even this slight success alarmed the London Missionary Society missionaries; yet they need not have worried unduly, for in addition to the popular sentiment that had been stirred up against France, the Marists were handicapped by having arrived after the period of mass conversion was over. Heathenism was only a scattered remnant, while the major Christian sects were more resistant to attack. The priests would have proselytized anyway, but being forced to concentrate on this means of building their support, they could not achieve spectacular gains. Starting with a small staff was another disadvantage. Finally, they made the mistake of doing in Upolu what Williams had done in Savai'i, taking a patron of high rank. This was Mata'afa Fagamanu of the Salevalasi, a claimant to the Tui Atua title. Within Mata'afa's party the Marists gradually accumulated a following, won largely from the Wesleyans and the declining Sio Vili cult, but they undoubtedly missed opportunities among other Samoans, especially as the French menace receded. By 1853, after eight years of work, they were said to have had only five hundred adherents.[32]

Another development of some importance to the London Missionary Society was the belated decline of Methodism, which was initiated by Benjamin Latuselu, a Tongan chief and ordained Wesleyan pastor. Latuselu, who came to Samoa in about 1848, made the mistake of engaging in war-time politics.[33] Whether he helped instigate the war,

---

[31] In Tutuila the Samoans were prepared to abandon their villages and negotiate with the French invaders from a mountain refuge. Considering Pago Pago harbour the island's most valuable attraction for Europeans, they were going to offer it to France in exchange for a guarantee of independence for the rest of the island (SSL, Murray, 8 August 1844).

[32] *Samoan Reporter*, January 1854.

[33] Latuselu had been in Samoa as one of Turner's teachers. He was later ordained in Tonga, and in 1847 he was assigned by the Wesleyan mission to the island of Niuafo'ou. However, he left this post for Manono and, without authority, remained there, assuming the leadership of the *lotu toga* throughout Samoa. He was the only ordained pastor in Samoa during the period in which King George sponsored the mission (from information supplied by W. N. Gunson).

or whether the second visit of King George was in any way connected with his political activities, is not clear. It is known, however, that he favoured the Taimalelagi side, or at least that part of it centred in Manono, where he lived and had relatives. The object of his intrigue is also obscure, but it is probable that he hoped to advance Methodism by force, perhaps through the creation of a Samoan kingship patterned after Tonga's. If, indeed, that was his aim, his commitment would have been occasioned by Manono's reputed invincibility and Taimalelagi's claim to the Tafa'ifā and dislike for the London Missionary Society. But whatever Latuselu was after, his meddling discredited the *lotu toga* on the 'enemy' side, where it had had considerable support, and gained it few if any followers on his own. Then, in 1851-2, King George, under pressure from the Wesleyan Society, finally disbanded the Tongan mission in Samoa, thus aggravating the reaction against Methodism. By 1855, the *lotu toga* survived as an organized sect only in southern Savai'i and in one or two villages on Upolu, where Samoan teachers carried it on.[34] Its adherents were down to about three thousand, the rest having associated themselves with other sects, at least nominally. The principal beneficiary of the collapse was the London Missionary Society, but since the event had occurred so much later than expected, the Marists were also on hand to take a small share of the spoils, particularly in Atua and western Savai'i.[35] That was not the end of the story, for in 1857 the Australasian Methodist Conference established a new mission in Samoa, staffing it with both Europeans and Tongans.[36] However, Methodism did not regain much of its lost ground, for during the latter half of the nineteenth century its peak strength, reached by 1863, was only about five thousand.[37]

Had numbers been the sole measure of its prospects, the London Missionary Society could have looked towards the future with confidence, as it had the nominal support of something like three-quarters of the Samoans. But as the Marist Bishop observed, the people, regardless of sect, had sunk into a religious indifference that was 'worse than paganism'.[38] This phenomenon, which in London Missionary Society parlance was a 'hardening in sin', represented the resurgence of social forces that were more durable and more universal than the ignorance, self-interest and fear exploited in the campaign against them. Religious

[34] The most hostile reaction occurred in Tutuila, where the Wesleyans had had four village congregations. A chapel was burned, and the *lotu* was banned from the island.
[35] The Marists acquired about a thousand converts from the Methodist collapse.
[36] The Australasian Conference took over the Pacific missions from the Wesleyan Society in London but refused to countenance the agreements with the L.M.S.
[37] Dyson, 26-54.
[38] APF XXVII, 386, Bataillon, 3 April 1854.

sanctions, supported neither by an effective system of political oppression
nor a monopoly of foreign influence, had failed to sustain the Christian
revolution and had themselves been subverted. But while they could not
get all they asked for it, the missionaries still had much that the
Samoans wanted.[39]

## The Samoan church

Now, more than ever, the London Missionary Society dreaded the
competition of 'easy' brands of Christianity. On this count, at least,
they should have welcomed the establishment of the new Wesleyan
mission, for with Europeans in charge, the moral and religious requirements of Methodism were brought into approximate line with those of
the London Missionary Society. However, that still left the Marists, who
tolerated such customs as tattooing and ceremonial exchange and asked
little of their converts in the way of material support. This comparative
leniency invited public controversy, being condemned by the London
Missionary Society, who feared its attractions, and advanced by the
Marists as one reason why the Samoans should and would abandon the
stricter sects. 'I thank them', wrote one priest of his Protestant rivals,
'for by their exaggerated or ridiculous prohibitions they have made our
work much easier.'[40] Yet the hedonistic flight to Rome never occurred,
not even when the Marists lost much of their original political stigma.
Indeed, Catholics were consistently fewer than the Methodists, their
number increasing only to about four thousand by the 1870s, by which
time the Sio Vili cult was defunct. That this was the case may have
been due, in part, to the Marists' tolerance of certain customs being
outweighed by their strictness in such matters as marriage, and to their
long delay in meeting the Samoan demand for village teachers and
schools.[41] But it was probably more significant that the puritans of the
London Missionary Society, under pressure of sectarianism, Samoan
conservatism, and certain developments within their own mission,
gradually acquiesced in a Samoan reformation.

[39] Writing of this conflict, Robert Swanston, a consular officer, described the Samoan
as 'a utilitarian, . . . attentive to forms and outward observances in his daily
intercourse with foreigners, where he can perceive the actual benefits arising
therefrom, but in heart unconverted' (USCD, Apia/1, Swanston to Cass, 31
March 1857).

[40] ASM, (I), II, Poupinel to Dupont, 8 December 1861. Poupinel wrote that the
Samoans' unusual resistance to mission control made Samoa a refuge for other
Polynesians who wished to escape the laws of their own islands. He referred
especially to Tonga, where King George and the Wesleyan mission enforced
restrictions similar to those which the L.M.S. would have liked to impose in
Samoa.

[41] loc. cit.

K

The first notable instance of Samoan effort to reform the London Missionary Society was a revolt of teachers in 1850, which, though confined to eastern Tutuila, was recognized as being symptomatic of grievances more widely held. To appreciate what was involved it must be recalled that the Samoan village teachers now possessed some formal theological training, yet received no salary from the mission, even though they might be 'strangers' in the villages to which they were assigned. A related issue arose from the mission's regular collection of cash and saleable goods.[42] This equivalent of plate-passing consisted of monthly collections taken up in the villages, and of annual appeals launched at each station during the joint meetings or mission festivals. The Samoans were supposed to understand that the proceeds were credited to the general funds of the Society in London and that total contributions were insufficient to cover the mission's actual costs in Samoa.[43] It is not likely, however, that they fully grasped either point. They were aware, for example, that some of the goods they gave were being sold to local merchants, but they may not have known that the returns were remitted overseas or deducted from the Samoan Committee's London accounts. Also, the volume of their contributions, which was increasing with the growth of export production, must have seemed large by their standards. Finally, criticism emanating from the commercial community, and from the missionaries who levied no 'tax', was calculated to raise doubts in the minds of London Missionary Society supporters.[44]

The Tutuila revolt was sparked by a petty incident—by the mission's decision that teachers' wives and assistants should pay for their Testaments, as the rank and file of Samoans had to do. Thus provoked, the nineteen teachers at Powell's station united and drew up a list of demands which revealed deep-seated resentment of their inferior status in the mission. With one of their ringleaders[45] declaring that 'the missionaries were not everything', they threatened to resign in a body

---

[42] Tutuila's first collection was taken up in 1840. Murray, *Forty years' mission work*, 153-4. The system was introduced in other areas about the same time.

[43] There were also collections for special purposes, e.g. to help support Samoan teachers in Melanesia and to buy and operate mission vessels. In addition, payment was required for books, and a nominal charge was usually made for medicines. Chapels were, of course, built and maintained by the Samoans.

[44] The Marists did not take up collections, but they looked to their converts for other kinds of assistance. The Wesleyan mission introduced a system of contributions after 1857 (Dyson, 68).

[45] This was a man who had survived a period of voluntary L.M.S. service in the New Hebrides, where many Samoan teachers died, and had returned home with allegations of neglect against the mission. In some villages these charges became an issue during the boycott.

unless (1) given free books and clothing and (2) promised that missionaries' salaries would be financed by British donors and that all local contributions would be paid out to the trained Samoan teachers. Feeling that any concession granted in these circumstances would be attributed to weakness, and knowing that other stations would be affected by the outcome of this dispute, Powell refused to bargain and summarily dismissed the four organizers of the revolt. If he assumed, however, that he would thus intimidate the others or leave them without effective leadership, he was mistaken. Five backed down, but the other ten resigned forthwith.

This was by no means the extent of the disaffection, for when Powell set out to replace the fourteen teachers he had lost, he discovered that they had done the rounds before him and had induced the congregations to take up their demands and insist upon their reinstatement. In some places the refusal to receive new teachers was accompanied by village regulations forbidding the taking of collections for the London Missionary Society. What is more, the church members, who Powell thought could have prevented the boycott in all the villages, had joined or acquiesced in the measures taken. Occurring in a single-*lotu* area, this was a movement of village councils to deny the mission its control of the teachers and congregations. Once again Powell was uncompromising, but meanwhile he had learned the value of patience. He now worked chiefly through the district church, convening it frequently and exposing the dissident members to the pressure of loyalist opinion and the threat of disciplinary action. Many members were excluded from the sacraments, pending the assertion of their influence against the boycott, and a few ringleaders were expelled; but Powell resisted any urge he might have had to expel large numbers, lest he destroy his main link with the rebel villages and wreck the church into the bargain. One by one the villages dropped their demands, and after two months the boycott was over.[46]

Powell's actions were endorsed by his colleagues, and the existing conditions of employment for teachers were confirmed.[47] However, the grievances expressed in the Tutuila revolt kept re-emerging, and not just at Powell's station either. In one place the mission contributions would be meagre; in another, the people would refuse to support their teacher adequately; and in yet another, the teacher would resign or turn sour on his job. Meanwhile, the religious zeal of the Samoans was waning, and the peace, thought to have been re-established in 1851, was broken

---

[46] SSL, Powell, 1 September 1851.

[47] Had the Samoans been willing to form larger congregations, thereby reducing the number of teachers required, the question of an annual allowance for teachers would have been considered favourably (SSL, Hardie, April 1851).

again. It was during this period that the London Missionary Society Directors, largely for reasons of finance and growing commitments, started cutting down on European staff in Samoa.[48] Thus, the London Missionary Society, with fewer missionaries and enormous problems of reconstruction, had to look to its teachers for better service than ever and, accordingly, had to consider how to build up their morale and strengthen their hand in the villages.

A first move was made in 1854, when it was decided that the villages or congregations, in addition to supplying their teachers with housing, food, and facilities for conducting classes and worship, must also pay them the allowance which the mission itself could not afford. To achieve this end, the London Missionary Society altered its system of annual Samoan contributions, retaining the mission collections but providing that separate collections should be taken up at the same time for the benefit of the teachers alone. The idea was that the teachers would receive only the cash and goods[49] given by their respective congregations, perhaps as an incentive for them to work harder in advancing the Christian cause. In substance, if not in appearance, this innovation represented a partial acceptance of the demands made of Powell during the teachers' revolt, for it could be expected that the mission would receive less than it would have otherwise. In practice, however, more was conceded than had been intended, for when, after some initial resistance,[50] the new scheme went into general effect, the teachers often received as much as, and in some places even more than, the mission, though the collections for the mission were taken up first and were supposed to constitute a first lien on the people's generosity.

One reason for this result was that the teachers, more than the missionaries, were exploiting the Samoans' competitive spirit—increasing contributions by pitting chief against chief and perhaps even village against village. Still, they had to earn their keep, in which respect their position improved as the retrenchment of European mission staff proceeded. This was almost bound to happen in any case, for with the

---

[48] Some missionaries were transferred, and vacancies caused by deaths or resignations were left unfilled. Retrenchment began in the early 1850s, and by 1862 the number of missionaries was down from sixteen to six (Murray, *Missions in Western Polynesia*, 456).

[49] Or an equivalent from the mission.

[50] In Manu'a, for example, 'the spirit of anger' developed when Powell proposed that the people make a second contribution. After some negotiation, he got them to agree formally to give a minimum of one hundred 'assorted articles' each year (SSL, Powell, 1 August 1857). This may have been the best time to initiate the scheme, for with the Wesleyans out of the way only momentarily, and the Marists destined to commence training Samoan teachers and catechists, the L.M.S. had a temporary monopoly of teachers and hence was in a relatively strong position, from the sectarian standpoint, to force reluctant villages into line.

missionaries forced to run outsize stations and carry heavier loads of preaching and translation, many of the teachers and congregations were freer of European interference and control. The effect was enhanced, however, by a decision of the London Missionary Society to authorize selected teachers, particularly in the remoter churches, to administer the sacraments and to act as the missionaries' chief agents and advisers in other matters of church business. Though carefully chosen, were these senior teachers efficient and reliable enough to do even this much to the mission's satisfaction? Nisbet, who had to cover Fa'asaleleaga and most of Itu-o-Fafine, had no doubt about their efficiency, for he cited it as one of two reasons for an increase in the number of candidacies at his station. The other reason he gave was the large demand for the first complete Samoan version of the Bible, which was then in short supply and hence initially available to church members and candidates only.[51] Pratt, who had the rest of Savai'i, said it was reliability the teachers lacked, especially when it came to recommending people for admission to the church. With the missionaries now unable to interview and investigate all candidates, it was becoming easier to enter the inner circle of the *lotu*.[52]

However, the London Missionary Society representatives, alarmed by the renewed Wesleyan activity, soon began to agitate for another build-up of European mission staff.[53] To help their case they set out to raise additional funds, doing so by making their local collections more competitive. Some, it is true, found the appeal to 'base motives' distasteful, but such objections were overridden by the favourable results. The first innovation, tried in 1860 at the time of the May meetings, was the recording of total contributions by villages and of individual contributions exceeding ten pence. The final lists were posted or read out so that their contents became general knowledge. Approximately doubling the previous year's revenue at the stations where it was first introduced, this system soon became universal.[54] Pratt, who took a cynical delight in its success, had this to say of its impact on the Samoans:

[51] SSL, Nisbet, 8 September 1859; Powell, 1 August 1847.
[52] ibid., Pratt, 31 December 1859; MS., Ella, Correspondence and Papers, Pratt to Ella, 5 March 1861.
[53] For two or three years the L.M.S. and Wesleyan missions worked together fairly well, but when Dyson, the first of the new Wesleyan missionaries, rejected a proposal that he join the L.M.S. and merge the two sects, relations between them broke down. In 1860 Dyson was accused of proselytizing, and from then on, L.M.S. missionaries assumed that the Wesleyans meant to recover their lost support by every possible means. Of course, this threat never materialized (MS., Ella, Correspondence and Papers, Murray to Ella, 6 August 1860; MS., Dyson, Journals 1858-65 and 1867-72; SSL, Whitmee, 7 August 1867, Pratt, 26 November 1867).
[54] ibid., Murray, 3 October 1860.

The result of the new plan . . . exceeded my utmost expectations, and disappointed a whole host of false prophets. The whole herd of 6d and dime contributors vanished. A neighbour of mine had procured three dollars, meaning to give one himself and break up the other two amongst his wife, children, and retainers—ample according to the old plan. But now comes a rebellion in the family—says a little pet niece, an orphan, 'Such a girl is going to give half a dollar, of course, I can't give less'. Two old men living in the family must have a dollar each. Nay, the chief himself can't give silver. What to do? Says a young man, his son, 'What is the use of two horses? Some of your family are already talking of coming to ask for one, and you will not be able to refuse them. Why not sell?' Accordingly, like gentlemen's plate at home, the horse is melted into cash and all are satisfied, and your funds increased . . . to some 2 years' salary of the Missionary.[55]

Over the next few years other refinements were developed, again by the more eager fund-raisers. The most lucrative was the inter-village or inter-district challenge, which was won, of course, by the side that made the larger contribution. Again among the pioneers, Pratt wrote in his usual forthright manner of the first challenge to be directly inspired and sanctioned by European missionaries:

I have been 'hauled over the coals' for exciting such a spirit among the natives; if the Directors think with these, that this is filthy lucre, obtained by improper appeals, they have only to deduct the average of former years and credit my acc't with the remainder. I don't suppose that next year there will be cause for complaint as to the amount.[56]

With competition an accepted feature of the system, another effective innovation was that of reopening collections, allowing supplementary contributions to be made up by those who fell behind or who, for the sake of tactics or drama, wished to be the last to display their generosity. One may envisage proceedings akin to those of the auction room— or, as the missionary, Drummond, suggested, a spirit of giving rather like that which carried the Samoans to war. Drummond gave this description of a collection taken in 1871, during a period of political unrest:

. . . we have had . . . glorious meetings and splendid collections. Indeed, from the appearance and conduct of the people a stranger would never have supposed that the majority of them had but lately returned from the battle-field, unless it might be in the warlike spirit which seemed to urge them to strive with each other in trying who

[55] ibid., Pratt, 19 September 1860.

[56] ibid., Pratt, 19 September 1868; Murray, 22 May 1868. Pratt's Itu-o-Tane people raised over $3,500 in a contest with southern Tuamasaga and Atua.

could give most. . . . Of one thing I am certain: if their motives were too much mingled with striving for the mastery, they did not give grudgingly, but with the highest delight and enjoyment. . . . One of the most amusing scenes which I witnessed in my progress was at our meeting at Lepā. . . . I was requested by one of the teachers, at a certain stage of the meeting, to give the people an opportunity to add to their contributions if they chose. Among those that came forward to pitch their additional dollars into the plate was a young chief . . . dressed in a suit of warm clothing, . . . with boots and a blue cap adorned with gold lace. He first shook hands with me across the table, then stood bolt upright and rifled every pocket, beginning at his trouser ones and ending at the left breast of his pea-jacket. He had hard work getting his hands into his pockets, but he brought some dollars out of each and threw them one by one into the plate as if he liked to hear the ring of the silver departing from him. I think I hear you saying, 'That looks like vanity'. Yes, rather much so: but people do not get wise in a day.[57]

Indeed, the appeal for funds, once regarded by its critics as a 'dying system',[58] was so perfected by the London Missionary Society that it became one of the main public activities of the *lotu* and one of its principal attractions. Whereas the Samoans had once expected to receive lavish material gifts through the London Missionary Society, they were now reversing the relationship, and doing so with 'delight and enjoyment', not so much to support the mission as to seek the favour of God and the respect of men in the volume of their sacrifices. This principle of liberality, not unknown in the Western world, also applied in due course to the construction of their chapels.

As London Missionary Society finances improved, the number of missionaries increased, rising during the 1860s from six to thirteen, or to only three short of the peak strength of the 1840s.[59] On the other hand, church membership fluctuated inversely, though not in strict proportion. During the period 1854-62, when missionaries were leaving, membership rose from 1,835 to 4,200, or from roughly seven to seventeen per cent of all adherents, including children.[60] Heaviest gains were made in Savai'i and southern Upolu, but only in Tutuila was the mission actually losing ground. During the same period Tutuila was also the

---

[57] ibid., Drummond, 14 June 1871.

[58] ASM (I), II, Poupinel to Dupont, 8 December 1861.

[59] Murray, *Missions in Western Polynesia*, 456; *Samoan Reporter*, February 1870.

[60] *Samoan Reporter*, January, December 1854, January 1857, March 1861, May 1862. According to mission census returns, the percentages would have been about one and a half times as great if figured only in terms of people old enough to be church members. This is allowing for about 16,000 adults among 25,000 adherents, in a population that hovered around 34-35,000 during the period 1853-80 (*Samoan Reporter*, January 1854; McArthur, IV).

area in which the teachers were given the least initiative—and where, of course, a delayed reaction to the mission was occurring.[61] After 1862 the mission rules were more rigorously enforced, partly because more missionaries were on hand and also because a growing number of chiefs were discovering that prestige and revenue were to be gained from the enactment of petty 'blue laws' and the establishment of courts and police forces. But the Samoans' actual observance of the rules was not so rigorous, for the number of communicants declined—to 4,000 by 1870 —and there developed a 'great lack of stability in church membership'.[62] The latter phenomenon, characterized by wholesale expulsions and suspensions and equally wholesale applications for readmission, indicated that the Samoans still valued the church but that a good many of them were settling for part-time membership, perhaps in an effort to reconcile conflicting obligations and interests. Consequently, the total number of members was not a true index of mission progress.

It was during the late 1860s that the London Missionary Society Directors, impressed by glowing statistics as well as guided by congregational principles, began to counsel the early formation of independent Samoan churches. For both political[63] and religious reasons this proposition, to which the other sects were not committed, was then unacceptable to the missionaries in the field. That is not to say, however, that all of them defended the *status quo*. There was the veteran, Pratt, for example, who liked strict standards of discipline but not what he called his role of bishop. There were also some recent arrivals who leaned towards moderate reform, possibly because they had been raised and trained in a more liberal environment than the elder missionaries and were less confident of their own insight into the divine plan for Polynesia.[64]

Having concluded that the dangers of proselytism had been overestimated, the self-styled 'radicals' proposed, as a tentative step towards increasing Samoan responsibility for the churches, that the European mission staff be cut back to about the 1862 level. The 'conservative' majority opposed this measure, but in 1871, in the absence of the local 'Disraeli' and his followers, the Samoan District Committee enacted it.[65]

[61] MS., Ella, Correspondence and Papers, Powell to Ella, 14 April 1862.

[62] *Samoan Reporter*, February 1870; SSL, King, 19 October 1869.

[63] Early experiments in central government were proving unsuccessful, and there were rumours of impending annexation.

[64] Pembroke and Kingsley, *South Sea Bubbles*, X.

[65] SSL, Pratt, 11 May 1871, Whitmee, 11 May 1871. The measure was passed at a meeting attended by only four missionaries, all 'radicals', whereas the District Committee then had nine active members. The 'Disraeli', so termed by Pratt, was almost certainly Powell.

The Directors applauded the 'reform bill' and upheld it against subsequent protests from Samoa. It was not, however, enough to satisfy them, the real radicals. Thus, when Pratt, ostensibly on grounds of his old age and infirmity, allowed several churches in western Savai'i to conduct business meetings in his absence, they said that the other churches should have the same right.[66] A good deal of cross-fire and wrangling ensued, but finally the Samoan mission agreed to ordain some of the teachers as pastors and to give the deacons more responsibility.

The missionaries still envisaged only the gradual diminution of their powers, but not so the teachers, who on seeing the old hierarchy giving way, rushed in to demand more far-reaching and, to them, more equitable concessions. This clash of interests came to a head late in 1875, when the District Committee first called teacher-delegates to a discussion of future mission policy and organization. The most important Samoan demand was that *all* teachers, rather than a select few,[67] should be ordained and permitted to exercise full pastoral powers. As a corollary, the existing churches would have to be broken up into smaller units. Apparently fearing a boycott or breakaway movement, the missionaries gave in, leaving themselves little with which to bargain in future.[68]

In an effort to keep up standards, the missionaries retained control of the Malua Institute, where Samoans were prepared for ordination, and they developed a new system of church government that was supposed to give the enlarged clergy the ultimate authority in most other spheres. Not that they fully trusted the Samoan pastors, but they considered them better equipped than the laity to transcend their island background and environment. The deacons and other members of the laity were to have *some* voice in church affairs. Indeed, provision was made for congregational rule by the membership of the churches—but as in inferior order of government, subject to directives and overriding decisions from above. Immediately above the churches were sub-district and district pastors' committees, bodies formed within the respective mission stations and meeting frequently under the chairmanship of the missionaries to discuss problems of church administration and to co-ordinate church activities. Next came a general assembly of pastors,[69] meeting annually, which received remits from the district committees and forwarded them, with recommendations, to a Samoa-wide Mission Committee, which also met annually. The Mission Committee, composed of the missionaries and some eighteen or twenty pastor-delegates, was meant to be the supreme

[66] ibid., Powell, 26 September 1873.

[67] There had been much resentment over the earlier selection of only a few teachers to administer the sacraments.

[68] SSL, Pratt, 29 September 1876.

[69] All pastors could attend, but many were represented by delegates.

governing body of the London Missionary Society church—that is, of all the affiliated local churches in Samoa.[70]

But try as they might, the missionaries could not avoid retreating farther. When the Committee prepared its disciplinary code, for example, the pastors' influence sometimes tended towards 'laxity'.[71] Thus it became permissible for a communicant or candidate to participate in war if ordered to do so by his 'government'[72]—in practice, by any authority he recognized. He might also tattoo and be tattooed, smoke, and play cards, but he was forbidden to gamble or sell liquor or, presumably, to consume liquor himself. He could be married in any church or at a traditional ceremony, provided his partner was deemed by his pastor and church to be a 'godly' person. He might also join in a marriage exchange, now termed a raising of dowry, if the wedded persons were 'godly'. In certain circumstances he might elope and still escape church discipline, and he might divorce a 'delinquent' spouse, doing so on his own authority. So while adultery and polygamy were still condemned, it was possible for a *manaia* or chief, say, to reconcile church and custom in a series of marriages.[73]

Even so, the missionaries might have been reasonably satisfied with the Committee's proceedings had decisions been taken with an assurance of being enforced. They discovered, however, that the *lotu*'s presbyterian superstructure, rather like Samoa's central governments, possessed flaws that greatly limited its sovereignty. One of these was the absence of a settled hierarchy, which aggravated factional tendencies among the pastors and sapped their strength as an executive body. Had the pastors been ready to carry out every Committee decision, they would also have needed a position of power in the churches comparable to that which the missionaries, now simply *ex officio* members, had formerly occupied. This they did not have. To be sure, their ordination gave them ritual power—a near monopoly of it within their sphere of pastoral duties—but they were still fed, housed and paid by their congregations and were, in effect, subject to local 'call' and dismissal. Moreover, the churches were reconstituted at the village level,[74] where the Samoans were particularly

[70] SSL, Powell, Minutes of mission meetings, 7 November 1875; Lovett, *History of the L.M.S.*, I, 400-1. Now there is also a central committee representing lay officers.
[71] But towards strictness in such matters as public decency and the keeping of the Sabbath.
[72] This rule was made before Samoa had a central government which the missionaries considered worth defending.
[73] SSL, Minutes of Mission Committee meetings, 12 December 1875, 2 December 1876, 17 January 1878, 7 November 1878, 31 December 1879. Needless to say, the Catholic Mission attacked this policy on marriage and divorce, all the more because Samoan central governments and the L.M.S. took the same line.
[74] Some of the smaller congregations combined to form united churches, so that strictly speaking, not every village had a self-contained church. Nevertheless, the members in each village had their own pastor and conducted their own

well organized, both to manage their local affairs and to resist outside interference. With all essential functions of the *lotu* now performed within the villages by Samoans, the *feagaiga* between pastors and congregations became a closer, stronger and more stable relationship than that between the pastors and the European stewards of the mission. That is to say, congregational rule, though meant to be subordinate, tended towards independence—or as much independence as the churches wished to have.

Here, then, was an opportunity for the Samoans to resolve on more favourable terms some of the main conflicts between their own ideas and those of the missionaries—in effect, to merge the best of both worlds, as they saw them. Pastors and deacon-chiefs, rather than the members at large, assumed control of the local churches. Disciplinary procedures took greater account of differences in rank and status. Pastors supported the political adventures of their congregations, even to the extent of canvassing allies in war, and once again their stipends exceeded the amounts contributed to the mission itself.[75] In all, the church was oriented more towards the community than the individual. Church membership grew rapidly, soon reaching a level near six thousand, at which it remained during the rest of the century.[76] The missionaries were, of course, grieved to witness such deviations from their original objectives, but they could rejoice in the fact that, while some Samoan rivalries would continue to be expressed in sectarianism, independence farther entrenched the *lotu taiti* among the large majority of the people. They could also be thankful that the *lotu* was still motivated, in some degree, by the 'force of Christian principles'. But at the same time, they could appreciate the magnitude of the task they had undertaken and, no doubt, agree with the conclusion drawn by a London Missionary Society deputation in 1888. As the deputation's report stated:

> Subjection to the mind of Christ has advanced as rapidly as the circumstances surrounding these people would permit. We place no limit on the power of the Spirit of God, but we do not forget that the effect of human environment is still seen in those who are manifestly the subjects of the Spirit's power.[77]

business meetings, and if belonging to a united or inter-village church, they submitted their decisions to that body as a formality. In a united church the celebration of communion was a joint function, with services being held at the constituent villages in rotation (SSL, Powell, Minutes of mission meetings, 7 November 1875; Lovett, I, 398).

[75] Mission Committee rules sanctioned the raising of pastors' stipends by competitive collections and compulsory subscriptions.

[76] SSL, Pratt, station statistics, 4 December 1876.

[77] Lovett, I, 402-3.

# 6

## SIN, SETTLEMENT AND SOVEREIGNTY

*Christianity and commerce*

IN 1838, near the end of an extensive fund-raising campaign, John Williams went to the London Guildhall to ask the City Corporation to invest in his proposed expedition to Melanesia. His 'prospectus' had only recently appeared as the final chapter of his book, *Missionary Enterprises*, in which he had confidently asserted that the evangelist, by taming and sophisticating the savage, was creating the conditions most essential to commercial progress in the Pacific. Indeed, the commercial interests of mankind had *never* been served more effectively, he had written, than by the introduction of Christianity among the heathen. Surely, then, the merchant and the shipowner would want to embrace the mission cause. Hearing this argument elaborated, the hard-headed aldermen and councillors responded even more favourably than Williams had hoped for, voting him £500 and expressing their assurance of an ample return.[1]

As a sermon on geography and the expansion of foreign trade, Williams's appeal at Guildhall was well conceived. It did not, however, depict the working relationship between commerce and Christianity in the Pacific. There were, for a start, ventures that flourished without the benefit of clergy—and sometimes all the better for lack of it. The exploitation of sandalwood, for example, was undertaken in several

---

[1] Williams, 582-4; Prout, 494-9. Mission undertakings in Africa were the subject of similar claims. In 1857, for example, Livingstone, speaking at Cambridge University and before various civic and municipal bodies in Great Britain, referred to himself as the vanguard of both commerce and Christianity. Neither he nor Williams, however, spoke for the L.M.S., which as a society disavowed all interest in commercial or imperial expansion. L.M.S. missionaries were permitted, sometimes grudgingly, to air their personal views on such secular issues, as Williams did at the Guildhall, but they were not free either to trade for profit or to divert their time and energies to the specific advantage of those who did. Also discouraged was exploration beyond the limits of the territory which the mission had the means to evangelize. It was in accord with the latter policy that the Directors criticized Livingstone's first expedition, deeming it 'connected only remotely with the spread of the Gospel'. Williams was similarly inclined towards independent exploration and was, according to conversation reported by the Wesleyan missionary, Turner, resolved to continue his voyages irrespective of L.M.S. opinion, being prepared, if necessary, to found his own mission society, as Livingstone did in 1858 (Monk ed., *Dr Livingstone's Cambridge Lectures*; Simmons, *Livingstone and Africa*, 69-70, 74, 79; MS., Turner, Journal 1838).

island groups prior to the advent of Christianity, though not strictly on condition of its absence. Often dangerous, progressively so in view of repeated clashes between Europeans and islanders, the work still proceeded, for the returns were great. Had there been sandalwood in Samoa, the early history of that group would almost certainly have been different. The labour recruitment or 'blackbirding' of later years was a venture that thrived particularly in heathen areas, owing to the furtiveness that often attended it. Again there was a high incidence of brutality. But, of course, Williams's conception of commerce was not typified by such undertakings as these. Rather, he envisaged the opening of secure harbours and the establishment of permanent trading posts, regular shipping services and commercial plantations. To *this* order of development the missionaries were undoubtedly capable of making valuable contributions. Through their influence, many islands *were* made safe or safer for Europeans, and through the notice they gave little-known islands, the reputations of some peoples, including the Samoans, were redeemed and the existence of natural resources and trading opportunities made known. Also, the missionaries stimulated the production of exportable goods, first by introducing new crop plants and processing methods, and secondly by encouraging their converts to take up mission collections and to imitate Europeans in the use of manufactures. But granting such effects of mission activity, the Pacific was still a frontier, a vast region of widely dispersed resources, remote from the world's chief centres of trade, and imperfectly charted and virtually unpoliced. It was a region that imposed many hazards and few restraints upon enterprise and competition, and it was also a place of refuge for the hunted and relief for the downtrodden. The settler and the mariner of the mission's ideal—pious and teetotalling, or at least scrupulous and orderly out of long-term self-interest—were not absent from the Pacific; but it was too much to expect that they should predominate in numbers or, if consistently well behaved, necessarily prosper, when conditions were so admirably suited to men of less saintly bearing. Thus in the practice of commerce, and in the channels of communication associated with its practice, most missionaries saw not only the means of improving their converts' material standard of life, but also that of exposing them to the influence of the ruthless, debauched and godless elements of Western society. Assuming such prospects, these crusaders against sin determined that the islanders' contact with passing ships should be controlled and the settlement of Europeans restricted. In spite of Williams's dictum, then, the missionaries stood to reduce the value to commerce of the peace, order and industry they fostered.

There were some missionaries who advocated a policy of economic self-sufficiency in direct opposition to commercial development; that is,

they would have controlled their people's demand for goods and enlarged
the mission's programme of industrial training to the point of blocking
foreign trade at its inception, at least for the time needed to complete the
process of Christianization. However, the introduction of new arts and
crafts, aimed originally at satisfying the simpler requirements of 'propriety', had never proved an unqualified success, even when trading
opportunities were few. For a policy of autarchy to prevail *against* trade
was even less probable, for island peoples soon learned that it was often
easier and, in terms of quality and variety, more efficient to barter for
manufactures than to produce their own.[2]

By 1836, when the London Missionary Society settled its first contingent of missionaries in Samoa, the futility of the autarchic approach
to economic development had been exposed. This was just as well for
the mission, for the provisions trade was already well advanced in Samoa,
with European vessels, mostly whalers, calling in appreciable numbers.
The missionaries' clear course, now, was to educate the Samoans' taste
in trade goods, which had been running to blue beads, ancient firearms
and cast-off garments, and to find political means of regulating the
growth and effects of foreign commerce. Contrary to common assertion,
they did not press for imperial rule, British or any other. Indeed, to be
governed by a friendly Power was very nearly their last wish, preferable
only to being governed by a Power or local clique they distrusted, and
regarded chiefly as a final hedge against such catastrophes. For they
knew only too well that some of the measures they wanted imposed
would have contravened accepted practice among Western nations and
on that ground, if no other, would not have been entertained by a
colonial or protective government. To curb the activities of merchants
and mariners—and where applicable, of beachcombers and rival missionaries—they tried instead to exploit the ostensible sovereignty of the
islanders. In Samoa it was this problem of governing Europeans, more
than that of disciplining the Samoans, which first led the missionaries
to seek the reform of traditional political institutions.

## The London Missionary Society and governmental reform

When they entered the arena of politics or government, the missionaries aimed to wield their influence as covertly as possible, eschewing
above all the emblems and forms of public office. (The major exceptions
to this rule occurred in time of emergency or when they proceeded on
grounds generally accepted as humanitarian.) If taxed with interfering
in civil affairs, the missionaries could then say, using the standard
euphemism, that they did not exceed their right, as respectable and

[2] This was a major cause of the failure of the cotton textile industry in the Cook
and Society Islands.

responsible citizens, to render free 'advice' to the local authorities whom they recognized. Their caution sprang, in part, from the need to please their overseas supporters and superiors, many of whom thought that the Church and the State were separable in any society.[3] But as the Samoan District Committee made clear enough, they also meant to foster the impression that the political forces of which their own influence was a component really constituted a non-European sovereignty:

> ... it ought to be understood [said the Committee to the London Missionary Society Directors] that the native government has the right to prevent any foreigner settling whom it may please, and to prevent the introduction by foreigners of any religion which it does not approve. The question here is not whether this is consistent with our views. ... We speak simply of the acknowledged laws of nations.[4]

The effect of the missionaries' 'advice' was obviously dependent on the religious sanctions at their command and on the extent and kind of opposition they faced. They needed to be early on the spot and to make rapid headway in building up their churches, while, as both a means and end of mission policy, excluding or discrediting the Europeans of whom they disapproved. But there was also a constitutional problem to be solved, namely that of finding the most efficient means of distributing the responsibilities of government among the islanders.

As already shown, the majority of missionaries in Samoa considered no chief or party capable of forming any central government in a manner or for a purpose acceptable to them. What, then, were the alternatives? A similar question had arisen in Rarotonga, sometimes regarded within the London Missionary Society as the island of the 'model mission'. There, too, the people had had no central administration other than that based upon a shifting military supremacy. There, too, Williams had tried to raise a 'king' and inspire, through him, the establishment of a general government; and there he had also been overruled by the resident missionaries, for some of the same reasons which later applied in Samoa. But in contrast to Samoa, Rarotonga was a single island, and a relatively small, compact one at that. Also, no Europeans were in residence there when the London Missionary Society representatives first arrived, and few had visited the island or even seen it. Furthermore, the major territorial sub-divisions of Rarotonga were about as highly integrated politically as Samoan villages and yet numbered only three for a total population roughly the equivalent of Tutuila's. With these advantages, among others, the missionaries did not have to promote sweeping

---

3 Williams, 127, for a laboured defence of an advisory course in relation to the civil affairs of Rarotonga.

4 SSL, Stair, Minutes of the Samoan District Committee, 25 February 1841.

constitutional reforms. They had only to treat the three districts as equal and separate jurisdictions and to assume, for themselves, co-ordinating functions of central government, exercised largely through the churches. It was this régime which, despite Rarotonga's considerable productivity and its position on a main Pacific trade route, kept the island virtually free of commercial settlers and beachcombers until the 1850s, and which continued, until superseded by a British protectorate government in the early 1890s, to forbid the sale of land and restrict its leasing, to prohibit intermarriage between Europeans and Rarotongans, and to exclude all mission societies but the London Missionary Society.[5] Rarotonga was, indeed, the island of the 'model mission', though London councillors might not have thought so.

Would the London Missionary Society in Samoa also be satisfied to work through the existing political system—that is, mainly through the villages? At the very outset, that course was not only necessary but also reasonably well suited to mission requirements. Of course, it was then a time of peace, a relatively unblemished peace, which the missionaries dared to think might last; and there was hope, too, that all the opposition sects would soon be put down. In those circumstances, the villages seemed adequate to the task of governing the Samoans. Secondly, the mission's immediate problem of controlling foreigners had not assumed very serious proportions, apart from its sectarian aspect.[6] True, many fugitives and castaways had landed at Samoa before the missionaries, and the influx was continuing, indeed growing, as ships called in increasing numbers. Not all of these men intended to stay very long, or did so, but at almost any time during the 1830s there were probably several dozen of them in the group. They did not, however, establish themselves in very secure positions. Seldom able to stand one another's close company for long, and preferring in any case the maximum of Samoan hospitality, they scattered widely, so that, considering their lack of overseas connections or support and their participation in Samoan village life, which limited both the degree and extent of their influence, they did not pose, either individually or collectively, any serious challenge to Samoan political supremacy in any quarter. Their freedom could thus be attacked through the existing powers and institutions of government. In this regard it was important that the convicts and sailors were often so deficient in manners and attainments that their ability to make their way among the Samoans tended to vary inversely with the people's ex-

---

[5] British protection did not lead to any substantial change in the laws concerning land, but the other two restrictions were dropped.

[6] Which in this context was limited mainly to the missionaries themselves, for the character of the beachcombers was not a subject of contention between the Wesleyan and London societies.

perience of Europeans. They failed, in particular, to stand comparison with the missionaries, who, though by no means of the gentry, surpassed them in wealth, ostensible power, personal dignity and even practical skills, and whose relative stature was further enhanced by the testimony of Polynesian teachers. The missionaries also exerted wider influence among the Samoans, owing partly to the detachment they gained from having independent means and non-Samoan wives, and also to their own group organization. With the growth of mission activity, then, the standing of many beachcombers declined, and with it their various *lotu*, while the personal licence allowed them was curtailed, though not always as much as the missionaries would have liked.[7]

Some of these men, either harrassed or neglected by the Samoans or fearing that European law would follow in the wake of Christianity, left their adopted villages, and often the group itself, to search for new havens. Of those who remained, many worked as pilots or boat-builders, by which means they eked out the period between sailor *lotu* and village store. A few, however, actually joined the missionaries and prospered. Matthew Hunkin, a British deserter at Tutuila, was the most prominent of these. A London Missionary Society church candidate before the commencement of Murray's revival, and a preacher in the midst of it, Hunkin was rising in the esteem of the Samoans while other Europeans of similar origin were on the down-grade. Unlike most of the others, he also acquired a wife of high rank, his marriage being blessed by the mission and, no doubt, sanctioned in Samoan custom by a sufficient payment of goods.[8] After passing London Missionary Society probation in Tutuila and leading an abortive attempt to open Niue island to the mission, Hunkin was put in charge of the Manu'a station. In 1849 he resigned from the mission staff and became a trader, consular agent and landowner at his wife's village of Leone. Today, Hunkin is remembered as the founder of what may be the oldest recognized lineage of mixed European and Samoan origin. There are two or three others of similar

[7] MS., Whittle; USN, WE, Stuart's Journal 1841; Wilkes, III, 382, 434-8.

[8] He married into the Fai'ivae family of Leone. The L.M.S. generally opposed the marriage of Samoans to Europeans, unless the latter were judged to be of 'good character' and intended either to remain in the group or, if leaving, to take their families with them. Such conditions determined whether or not a European might be married in church. Sometimes the mission had sufficient influence to prevent the *fa'a-Samoa* marriage of foreigners, but if not, there were still the considerations of rank and exchange to be satisfied. A man who had neither valuable service nor *'oloa* to offer could not marry into a high-ranking family, if he could marry at all. And unless he continued in good standing in the community, his wife might desert him (USN, WE, Anonymous Journal kept aboard the u.s.s. *Vincennes* 1839, and Briscoe's Journal 1839, for mention of the Samoans' refusal to let deserters 'intermarry' at Manu'a). That does not necessarily mean, however, that foreigners were wholly deprived of female company.

L

antiquity, but there might have been more had the early settlers been able and willing to adjust more readily to the Samoans' changing conception of European respectability and rank.

Shipping contacts were difficult to control, especially with the Samoans eager to trade and rather inclined to look up to the skippers of foreign craft. But apart from the whaler resort of Pago Pago, these contacts were also scattered and, desertions excepted, brief, owing to the absence of commercial centres and to the slow accumulation of knowledge concerning Samoa's reefs and harbours.[9] Until well into the 1840s, in fact, many ships simply skirted the coasts for supplies, stopping off at villages that sent out canoes to trade.[10] Thus, while the missionaries might disapprove of some of the traffic into which the Samoans were being drawn, they did not have much of a 'waterfront' problem—not yet.

However, commercial activity could be expected to increase in volume and differentiate in type, with pressure mounting on the Samoans to alienate land and relinquish some of their 'sovereign' power to foreigners of 'some wealth and little religious principle'. Much of this pressure would be concentrated at a few ports, a consideration which had figured in the missionaries' siting of station headquarters. In the process, a heavy strain would be placed on a small number of villages. Could they cope, given the proper 'advice'? Even if they could, the problem would still be more general than that. Immigration, for example, could not be controlled effectively if barriers were raised only at the ports. Besides, some foreigners would probably want to settle in the outer districts, to become planters or traders, which would raise the question of general restrictions upon land alienation. A related problem would be the control of intermarriage, especially that of a *fa'a-Samoa* character; for men of means would be able to offer considerable *'oloa*, or goods for ceremonial exchange. If allowed to marry, they might acquire land from their affines, and also exercise political influence. Wherever they resided, comparatively wealthy foreigners, once settled in, would be far more difficult to govern against their will than were the destitute beachcombers.

Looking ahead, the London Missionary Society representatives had to ask themselves whether the villages, as they had found them, could be relied upon to meet the foregoing pressures and problems. In this con-

[9] Pago Pago and Apia harbours were first used by whaling ships in 1836. For several years thereafter, Pago Pago was the more frequented of the two, especially by ships stopping over for some length of time, as the harbour was well protected yet difficult of egress for sailing vessels. Towards the end of 1839 Wilkes noted that fifty ships had called at Pago Pago within the previous four years (USN, WE (letters), Wilkes to Paulding, 24 October 1839, no. 52). By the mid-1840s Apia had become the more popular, by reason of its development as a commercial port and centre of European settlement.

[10] At Upolu, particularly.

text, the prospect of government by villages seemed no more appealing than that of the king-making which had been overruled to minimize the Samoan urge to war and factional controversy. For the villages, however well-organized within, were far too numerous and scattered, and relations between them were distinguished by too much jealousy, for the uniform adoption and policing of the necessary laws to be entrusted to their agency alone. Consideration had also to be given to the interests of the Powers, which were unlikely to appreciate dealing with a multitude of 'tiny republics' and might not take very seriously the claims to independence voiced by a people so disunited politically. Hence, there had to be reform, entailing political centralization above the level of the village and, perhaps, leading eventually to national unity. As previous mention of A'ana will have suggested, the London Missionary Society took an early interest in the traditional districts, trying to promote their independence and internal unification, that stable, centralized administrations might be created within them. On some occasions they seem to have gone higher, trying to join two or more districts at an island level; and on others, lower, to the level of the sub-district. As shall be seen, however, they were defeated at every turn, if not by internal stresses then by the political relationships that cut through the chiefly hierarchies and across the geographical boundaries of the units upon which they endeavoured to build.

## Samoa's first port regulations

Out of regard for evangelical and humanitarian objectives, and for Britain's reputation and influence in foreign parts, however remote, British officialdom echoed many of the nobler sentiments uttered by Williams and other missionaries. One of the most outstanding instances of this occurred in 1837, when the Parliamentary Committee on Aborigines deplored the villainy imputed to foreign renegades in Samoa and, with reference to it, departed so far from earlier estimates of the Samoan character and condition as to declare that their hearts bled for 'the poor Samoa people, . . . a very mild, inoffensive race, very easy of access'.[11] Consistent with such compassionate views, if not solely because of them, British governments came to espouse as policy aims the establishment of order and, generally, the promotion of Christian civilization among the Samoans. But in choosing the means of pursuing those ends, they applied the less exalted considerations of empire.[12] Already heavily burdened with imperial commitments, Britain, unlike France, was not anxious to acquire more territory for reasons either of investment or

[11] GBPP, No. 425, VII, 1837, 27.

[12] For detailed discussion of these imperial questions see, for example, Brookes, *International rivalry* and Ward, *British policy*.

prestige; but even if it had been so inclined, neither Samoa nor any of the island groups near by would then have represented a very substantial asset. Nor, again, had Samoa any particular strategic value to recommend it. That is to say, the immediate self-interest which might well have conflicted with a policy of Samoan welfare, had Britain assumed control of the islands, was too slight to warrant that most direct means of implementing such a policy. Of course, it could be argued, as indeed it was in the Australasian colonies, that the foreign rule of Samoa would eventually serve both the private and public interests of the nation exercising it, with all the cost and trouble of early intervention being repaid many times over. As later events were to suggest, that claim would probably have been borne out in respect of Samoa itself. However, territorial accretion, notably on the part of the maritime Powers, proceeded not so much by isolated acts of intervention as by a progression of moves and counter-moves that could entail losses as well as gains for the governments undertaking them. Britain could certainly have acquired Samoa, but without assurance that the issue would have rested there. Another Power might well have reacted, for example, by taking Hawaii, thus inflicting relative disabilities upon British entrepreneurs in a commercial centre which, during a period of open competition, they had successfully penetrated. On balance, such an exchange would have added nothing to the sum of British interests, at least not in the short run.

For several reasons, then, it was expedient, notwithstanding the attributions of blind indifference and lofty principle to which their restraint variously gave rise, for British governments to recognize the islands as politically independent (though not necessarily sovereign) communities, and to endeavour to maintain them as such, subject to the local rulers' observance of the 'laws of humanity' and their grant to Britain of the privileges of the 'most favoured nation'. The rendering of Britain's most conspicuous official service to the cause of Samoan welfare, as to the advancement of commerce, was thus left initially to naval commanders and to resident consuls and consular agents. As shown, this position accorded with certain London Missionary Society interests, in that the assumption of so little responsibility allowed British governments to support or overlook mission-inspired measures which they themselves could not have adopted. On the other hand, they limited the scope of their proceedings in Samoa to an extent better suited to that orderly state of affairs they hoped to foster there, and they chose to act through agents who, their consuls in particular, often had private commitments that conflicted with official policy.

Britain did not have a distinct policy towards Samoa, as such, until the mid-1840s, when the Foreign Office first posted a consul there. However, the above approach to Pacific islands affairs was demonstrated in the group as early as 1837-8, on the occasion of the visit of H.M.S. *Conway*, the next British naval vessel to appear in Samoa after the *Pandora*.[13] Out to recapture escapees from the Australian penal colonies, the commanding officer of the *Conway*, Captain Charles Drinkwater Bethune, had his ship instated to resemble a whaler, the better to surprise his quarry;[14] but he is remembered less for this police action, which was frustrated by an efficient 'coconut wireless', than for his informal and unratified acts of state, in which proceedings the influence of the London Missionary Society—his interpreters and leading informants—is readily apparent.

Bethune's first negotiations with Samoans were conducted in December 1837 at Pago Pago, where, at his request, the 'principal chiefs of Tutuila' gathered to join in 'relations of amity' with 'Great Britain'. In addressing this meeting Bethune spoke as if the two 'Powers' allegedly represented therein were of similar status as nations, if somewhat unequal in size and resources. He went on to imply contempt for the majority of British subjects then in the islands, asserting that his government would protect only those who obeyed the Samoan laws and would remove any against whom the chiefs had 'just cause of complaint'. On the other hand, he made a point of praising the missionaries and said that they enjoyed the confidence and support of the British Government. The question of enacting port regulations was then brought up—according to Bethune, by the chiefs; according to the interpreter Murray, by Bethune; and according to sailors and beachcombers, by Murray, or at least at his instigation. Bethune professed to believe that the chiefs 'were not yet quite in a state to put . . . [laws] in execution', but he lost no time in presenting draft regulations for them to adopt.

The port code that emerged from this meeting was clearly aimed at protecting 'the poor Samoa people' and at furthering the interests of the London Missionary Society, for apart from the levy of pilot and port fees,[15] the provisions were of the 'blue law' variety, similar to those enacted years before in the Society Islands.[16] On a Sabbath, for example, no work connected with shipping was to be done on shore by anyone or, aboard ship, by any Samoan, except in case of emergency. The liquor

---

13 Which, as previously mentioned, called there in 1791.

14 In 1829 Captain Laws of H.M.S. *Satellite*, also engaged in hunting for convicts, had heard in Tonga that a boatload of escapees had reached Samoa. Rather than go after them, he had left them to what he had imagined to be their certain fate at the hands of the Samoans, who at that time were still considered a 'desperate' people (Adm. 1/194, Laws to Owen, 3 May 1829).

15 At rates of seven and five dollars, respectively. In practice, naval and mission vessels were exempted from payment of these fees.

16 FO 58/38, port regulations of the 1820s, Huahine, Borabora and Raiatea During the course of this same voyage Bethune assisted in the codification or port controls at Rarotonga.

trade was prohibited, and all seamen were required to be aboard their
vessels by 8 p.m. and to remain there all night. To restrict foreign immigration it was provided that ships' passengers and members of crew
should not be discharged without prior sanction of the 'government'.[17]
Desertion was also forbidden, and rules were laid down for the shipping
of captured deserters by order of the 'government'. Since these regulations were enacted by the chiefs—Bethune's part being merely that of
assuming to countenance them on Britain's behalf—they were meant to
apply to all foreigners, regardless of nationality. Thus, it was stipulated
that *any* captain who refused to obey any part of the code would be
denied refreshments for his ship and reported to his government, while
most violations were also punishable by fines in cash or goods, con-
vertible into terms of hard labour. For their part, the Samoans undertook
only to provide pilot service and water and other supplies, with the
regulations being so phrased that even these few concessions were in
no way mandatory.

With the Samoans not in 'a state to put . . . [laws] in execution', the
question of governmental reform was also due for consideration. The
available record of the Pago Pago meeting refers only to 'government'
in a general sense—and in English, not Samoan—so it is not clear what
Bethune and Murray had in mind for Tutuila, beyond their acceptance
of the island as a self-contained political unit and the assembly of its
'principal chiefs' as an incipient form of representative parliament and,
possibly, executive council. However, at Apia, where Bethune invited
the 'chiefs of Upolu' to meet him in January 1838, another code was
produced which incorporated not only the regulations previously adopted
in Tutuila,[18] but also some clauses on the subject of their enforcement.[19]
The first of the new provisions stated simply that: 'All chiefs of districts
or towns off which vessels shall call or where boats shall be sent on shore
shall enforce the rules relative to the landing of foreigners.' This was
appropriate to the villages, but how were the districts, which lacked the
regular machinery of enforcement, to play their part? And what higher
authority, if any, was to ensure that all Samoans adhered to the code?

[17] It is ironic that some of the foreigners who caused the L.M.S. the most trouble
in Tutuila had been discharged there in 1837 by the pious Captain Morgan of
the British whaler, *Duke of York*. Morgan later became a skipper for the mission
society (Unsigned MS. in MS., Buzacott).

[18] With one slight alteration, specifying a curfew hour of 9 p.m. in place of 8 p.m.

[19] Although Bethune's invitation was directed to Upolu, all districts of which were
allegedly represented, it is likely that Manono and Savai'i chiefs also attended.
Five days were required to organize the Apia meeting, and over a thousand
people gathered for it. Manu'a was not concerned in any of these negotiations,
but being small, remote and subject to the influence of a single mission, its
exclusion did not matter a great deal.

An approach to the latter question was made by authorizing the Mālō to levy fines upon chiefs who refused or neglected to enforce regulations, but as no means were proposed of giving it effect, this provision probably asserted no more than the pretensions of the Mālō, the party in attendance at the meeting. Where the code *did* specify innovations in government, it was rather to say that the districts should make them—that within each separate district *all* chiefs, meaning regardless of party, should meet and elect a magistrate, who was to hear cases arising under the code. Apparently dodging the issue of a general government for all Samoa, this proposal was almost certainly inspired by the London Missionary Society.[20]

As it happened, Bethune conducted his negotiations in such a way that in the western islands, and possibly in Tutuila as well, the recognition of his code by the Samoans became more a factional issue than he seems to have anticipated. Most important, the code was discredited among the Vaivai, whose high chiefs, though included in Bethune's invitation, would not or could not join in its adoption at the Mālō village of Apia. Perhaps, in all events, the scheme of district courts would have failed, for no matter how or by whom judges had been elected—it appears that none were—their jurisdiction would have been limited by party conflict and village particularism. But if Bethune had negotiated harbour by harbour, rather than island by island, he might at least have had the 'blue laws' amicably received by more of the people whom they were meant to protect.

A write-off in some respects, the *Conway* code still made an impact at Apia and Pago Pago harbours, where the circumstances of its adoption, unprecedented in Samoan experience, impressed the chiefs quite as much as its revenue provisions. Of some force, too, at least for a time, were the mystique of the written word—the code was printed for distribution to incoming vessels—and the preaching of missionaries, who represented the code's enforcement as a Samoan duty to God. From the scanty record it appears that some of the regulations, notably those concerning liquor and 'prostitution', were well enough enforced to inconvenience the beachcombers and mariners against whom they were directed and, moreover, that such foreigners were unable to induce the principal Samoan adherents of the code to abrogate it.[21] Yet it is also true that there were

20 Adm. 1/218, Bethune to Maitland, 9 February 1838 (with enclosures); BCT, Misc./1, Samoan port regulations, 1837; Murray, *Forty years' mission work*, 72-3; SSL, Hardie, 6 January 1838, Murray, 29 August 1838, Murray, 10 June 1839. The Pago Pago code was dated 27 December 1837; the Apia code, 5 January 1838.

21 Dumont d'Urville, *Voyage dans l'Océanie*, IV, 99-103; Murray, *Forty years' mission work*, 79. D'Urville was asked to pay port fees at Apia, though naval

many evasions, some, no doubt, because Samoans profited from allowing
or committing them, but others simply because the police power of the
villages was unequal to the demands made of it. If, for example, a sailor
deserted his ship and went to a place where the code was discountenanced or where, for some other reason, he was allowed to remain, chiefs
from elsewhere were unlikely to get him back short of taking measures
too opposed to their own interests to be freely entertained by them.
Also, a small community that had no monopoly of trade, no regular
contact with foreign governments and, as a rule, no means of its own to
overpower a European vessel, could scarcely intimidate an intractable
skipper into obeying the law nor, unless it happened to capture offenders
or take hostages on shore, into paying or working off a fine. The latter
problem was aggravated by the fact that, while vessels of several
different flags shared in Samoa's foreign trade, only Great Britain
appeared to endorse the code. On this ground American whaler captains,
in particular, were sometimes ill disposed to the observance of port
controls. That the *Conway* code made no absolute concessions or guarantees in favour of visiting mariners was yet another source of their
antagonism towards it.

### Samoa acquires resident consuls and a second code

The next foreign official to mix in the affairs of Samoa was George
Pritchard, a former London Missionary Society representative turned
British consul at Tahiti, whose jurisdiction extended, legally if not very
effectively, through western Polynesia. Visiting the group in May 1839
in the company of John Williams, Pritchard proceeded, as expected, to
act in full consideration of London Missionary Society interests and
ambitions. He would have liked, above all, to persuade the Samoans to
adopt and enforce a general code of domestic law, complementary to
Bethune's code; but the advice he rendered to that effect—he raised the
subject at a London Missionary Society mass meeting in Manono—was
not pursued.[22] He did, however, appoint a resident vice-consul, Samoa's
first officer of the kind, whose attention he felt should be devoted at least
as much to projects of political reform and to the control of Samoa's
'worthless whites' as to the development of the group's commercial
potentialities for Britain. The man chosen to thus exploit and enlarge
British influence was one W. C. Cunningham, who had been a London

vessels were supposed to enter free. He was indignant in his refusal and, in
writing of the incident, charged the L.M.S. with proposing the code in order to
increase mission funds and Bethune with approving it in order to enlarge British
influence. He also wrote that Apia women were available to his officers but not
to his crewmen, who had to go to Faleata to find female company.

[22] SSL, Heath, 3 May 1839.

Missionary Society artisan-teacher in Rarotonga.[23] Cunningham's former mission associates had accused him of 'living in sin', for which reason he had been forced to leave Rarotonga, but somehow he managed to redeem himself in the eyes of Pritchard and Williams and, through them, gained the support of the Samoan District Committee.[24] It was at the next hurdle, where the Foreign Office failed to confirm his appointment, that Cunningham was, strictly speaking, disqualified. But as the Foreign Office did not specifically disallow his appointment either—and, in fact, took no cognizance of it whatever—the way was open to Cunningham to act informally as the agent of Pritchard, who was quite unable to attend personally to consular business in Samoa.[25] Cunningham kept up this pretence for more than two years, creating in some island circles an impression of official British activity which a knowledge of normal consular procedure would have dispelled.

Towards the end of the same year, 1839, Samoa's relations with the Powers were carried forward another step. The prime mover on this occasion was Lieutenant Charles Wilkes, naval officer commanding a scientific expedition sent into the Pacific by the United States Government, whose early interests and proceedings in Samoa were to develop along lines rather similar to those taken by Britain's. Aware of the growing importance of the islands to the New England whaling industry, and having general instructions to promote the advancement of commerce and civilization wherever he called, Wilkes accepted Bethune's port regulations and matched Pritchard by appointing an American consular representative. He was not content, however, to rest at that, for having also to investigate the killing of several of his countrymen by Samoans, Wilkes concluded that the chiefs must, for their part, explicitly guarantee foreign residents and visitors certain fundamental rights and agree to protect their lives and property.[26]

23 FO 58/15, Pritchard to Palmerston, 14 May 1839.

24 SSL, Heath, Day and others to Palmerston, 14 May 1839, Williams to Directors, 16 May 1839.

25 Pritchard was justified in appointing an unpaid agent to start acting immediately, as Cunningham did, but he should have notified the Foreign Office of his course and of the reasons for it, that instructions might have been returned approving or disallowing the appointment. Instead, he wrote recommending the creation of a salaried consular post in Samoa and the selection of Cunningham to fill it. This quite different proposal, for which Pritchard then offered no support sufficient to persuade his superiors, was held over until 1844, when Pritchard himself was appointed British consul to Samoa.

26 Some British subjects had also been killed in Samoa, but unlike the Americans, they had reputedly been escaped convicts, for which reason little official interest had been taken in their demise. But the mistreatment of convicts aside, European authorities usually took a serious view of Samoan violence against foreigners, regardless of the provocation offered. No doubt foreigners were occasionally the

Of the two cases that concerned Wilkes, one, involving the death of
an American deserter in Upolu, was easily disposed of. The alleged
murderer, a young man apparently unaware of being sought for any
misdeed, was taken prisoner without fuss or delay and subsequently
tried at Apia in the presence of various chiefs, who were required by
Wilkes to approve the sentence of exile handed down.[27] But the more
important of the cases had quite a different outcome. Dating back to
1834, it concerned an assault made at the Savai'i village of Palauli on a
landing party from the Nantucket whaler, *William Penn*. Responsibility
for the incident, in the course of which three sailors had been killed and
two of the whaler's boats stolen,[28] was generally attributed to Tualau
Tonumaipe'a Popotunu, a prominent Mālō chief with a reputation for
antipathy towards Europeans.[29] In this instance, the culprit undoubtedly
knew he was wanted, an attempt at his capture having already been
made by an American commander,[30] so that Wilkes resorted to strata-
gem, hoping to cut Popotunu off from the protective cover of the bush
and force him to surrender. Acting on the advice of beachcombers,
Wilkes's next in command, Captain William Hudson, undertook to
deceive the Palauli people by arriving at their village with an armed
party disguised as surveyors. So carefully did Hudson lay his plans that

innocent victims of treachery or misunderstanding, but the provocation which
some of them gave admits of no such extenuation. A particularly harrowing case
of the latter kind is described in Wilkes, III, 434-8.

[27] Initially, the chiefs wanted to settle the case by payment of compensation, but
their offer was declined. A death sentence was then passed, and they agreed to
it. It was Wilkes's intention, however, that they should carry it out, and that
they refused to do. Rather than order a naval execution, Wilkes commuted the
sentence to one of exile from Samoa. The defendant was duly left at Wallis
Island, from whence he probably returned home (Wilkes, II, 88-91, 157-8;
USN, WE, Stuart's Journal for October 1839).

[28] The surviving crewmen were detained at Palauli and, with the exception of a
Hawaiian, were later ransomed by the captain of another American whaler.
Their release, allegedly prompted by a threat of intervention by Manono, was
completed upon the payment of three muskets and a book (USN, Cmdr L.,
unsigned statement forwarded with Aulick to Dickinson, 6 June 1836; *Daily
Atlas*, 19 May 1835 (as cited in CPIP)).

[29] Popotunu was of the Savai'i-Manono line of Lei'ataua Tonumaipe'a. His Tualau
title was that of an *aloali'i*. He was said to have killed many Europeans,
including some of the convicts who disappeared in Samoa before the establishment of the missions (Krämer, *Samoan Islands*, I, 351; Wilkes, II, 92-3; SSL,
Heath, 1 December 1837). However, reports of the *William Penn* affair suggest
kidnapping and plunder more than murderous intent on the part of the Samoans
responsible.

[30] The u.s.s. *Vincennes*, then the leading vessel in Wilkes's squadron, had come
for Popotunu in October 1835. Palauli, deserted by the inhabitants on the arrival
of the warship, had been burned by order of the commander, then J. H. Aulick
(USN Cmdr L., Aulick to Dickinson, 6 June 1836; SSJ, Platt, 1835).

not even the members of his own party were taken fully into his confidence, yet he was wasting his time and, as one of his junior officers wrote afterwards, only making a farce of his campaign by his efforts to keep it secret:

> ... about noon the war party left for the shore. I accompanied it, and heavens, what a fight we had with fried bread, pork and eggs; we either sat in the boats, arms concealed, chilled thro' with the rain, or in some cases, straggled about town in small partys [*sic*], whilst Capt Hudson paid a visit to the Missionary. Thus ended my first grand effort in the defence of my country. At sunset we got aboard the schooner, having killed two pigs and broken fifteen eggs. I am exact as regards numbers, because it is a matter of some importance, that every circumstance in connection with this brilliant affair should be recorded. The whole town was crowded with fierce natives who were better acquainted with the object of our visit than we were, and they were armed accordingly and seemed at one time inclined to begin the play themselves.[31]

Hudson, more serious in his own account, reported to Wilkes that Popotunu could not possibly be found in his 'fastness in the mountains' and that in any case, owing to his extensive influence, he would always be defended by a force much stronger than any the American squadron could muster.[32] It would therefore be advisable to negotiate for the chief's surrender.[33]

What he had thus taken up in the cause of justice Wilkes resolved to pursue farther for the sake of deterrence as well, lest he leave behind him an impression of weakness or indifference that might invite other attacks upon foreigners. His next course was in fact one of negotiation, chosen in conformity with Hudson's report and also with general instructions from the Navy Department, which, *inter alia*, observed that 'the obligations of justice and humanity are always and everywhere imperative in our intercourse with men, and most especially savages ... [who] long ... remember benefits, and never ... forget injuries'.[34] According to the spirit of the *Conway* code,[35] Wilkes might have met with the chiefs

31 USN, WE, Sinclair's Journal, 1839.
32 In contrast, Aulick, on hearing that his men had found Palauli deserted, had concluded that the Samoans were afraid to mount resistance to a naval force, and he had expressed confidence that they would remain so (USN, Cmdr L., Aulick to Dickinson, 6 June 1836).
33 USN, WE (letters), Wilkes to Paulding, 6 November 1839, no. 53. Far from being in a mountain 'fastness', Popotunu was hiding just outside the village (Wilkes, V, 24).
34 Wilkes, I, xxviii f.
35 With its stress on the responsibility of village and district. But Savai'i was not within the area for which the code had been specifically negotiated.

of Palauli or Itu-o-Fafine, but in the circumstances, he had good reason
to think that discussions in either quarter would have been futile.
Instead, he looked beyond both 'town and district' for some vestige of
a 'general government', and guided by the missionary, Williams, for
whose character and advice he professed the highest regard, he found
the Mālō.[36] It was that party[37] which he now approached, inviting its
leaders to meet with him at Apia to discuss new port regulations. When
the chiefs gathered, however, only part of the Mālō was represented,
the most conspicuous absentees being Popotunu and his principal
connections.[38]

Wilkes opened his negotiations by submitting the draft of a new code
which, with additions and amendments, incorporated and was designed
to supersede Bethune's regulations. Oddly, this document contained
nothing original on the means of law enforcement to be employed by
the Samoans, though the old provisions had obviously failed and did not,
in any event, strictly apply to the present situation. Perhaps Wilkes was
simply too preoccupied with the Popotunu case to think of constitutional
questions, or perhaps, like many of the Europeans who presumed to
instruct the Samoans in government, he was in need of instruction
himself. Anyway, he concentrated on the rights of foreigners, proposing
that they should be entitled to use any harbour or anchorage in return
for the payment of dues, that they might remain in the islands if granted
the 'consent of the Government', that they should, if 'conforming to the
laws, receive the protection of the Government', and so on. For the most
part, Wilkes simply invited the Samoans to assume and carry out certain
obligations wholly within the scope of their 'sovereignty', which, incidentally, he had already violated or denied by his direct intervention at
Palauli. Embedded in the draft, however, was a single provision of
quite a different order, stipulating that anyone who killed a foreigner
should be surrendered, on demand and without delay, to a naval commander of the victim's nationality. As for the conduct of trials and the
execution of sentences, no regular procedure was laid down nor, it
appears, was any envisaged. Considering that the Samoans were not
given to punishing those who killed Europeans, though they might take

36 Wilkes regarded Williams, who was then sojourning in A'ana, as the head of
the L.M.S. mission in Samoa, and soon after arriving at Apia, went to see him.
According to Wilkes, Williams approved of the Palauli expedition, while Wilkes
himself returned from their meeting resolved to 'have some understanding with
the Malo party or ruling chiefs'. It was after Hudson's failure at Palauli, however, that Wilkes devised his plan for getting at Popotunu through the Mālō
(Wilkes, II, 92-3; USN, WE, Wilkes's Journal, 1839).

37 To which, in his *Narrative* (II, 152), he attributed the 'whole power' of government, despite much evidence cited to the contrary.

38 e.g. Lei'ataua Tonumaipe'a of Manono.

vengeance without particular regard for individual guilt, this proposed concession of extra-territorial jurisdiction had some justification. But it was also pretentious and, as diplomacy, visionary, for neither would the Samoans readily relinquish their own people for punishment by strangers, European or Samoan.[39] Nevertheless, the entire code was duly enacted by the chiefs and witnessed by various persons claiming to represent Great Britain and the United States.[40] Then Wilkes insisted, as he had planned from the start to do, that the Mālō observe the new law by producing Popotunu.

Malietoa's initial reply to this unexpected demand was cleverly evasive. Popotunu was certainly a wicked man, he said, but the 'regulations now enacted could not apply to his past misdeeds'. Pressed farther, however, Malietoa tried to beg off on the ground that to do Wilkes's bidding would break up the Mālō party and plunge Samoa into war. That there would indeed have been fighting can scarcely be doubted, for in addition to the fact that assault upon chiefly personages customarily led to war, it also happened, owing to the unrepresentative nature of the meeting, that Wilkes was powerless to impose a settlement for which the Samoans might hold the United States solely responsible. At any rate, the assembled chiefs supported Malietoa's prediction, right or wrong, and from what Hudson had reported, Wilkes must have believed it too. He repeated his demand, however, and discovered that some of the chiefs seemed less concerned than Malietoa to keep the peace. Some even urged war for the declared purpose of cementing relations with the United States, though if they really contemplated hostilities, it is more likely that they hoped to draw the American squadron into the service of their traditional political ambitions.

The London Missionary Society representatives on hand for this meeting[41] had, at the outset, given Wilkes their assistance in the hope of strengthening the administration of the port code; but then, confronted with the prospect of war, most of them marshalled their influence against him.[42] Only Williams seems to have vacillated, being loath to permit or advocate war yet anxious that the Mālō, in which he reposed more faith than his colleagues, should assume responsibility for Samoa's good government and continued independence.[43] Subjected, then, to

---

39 The provision was so worded that it could also apply to non-Samoans who killed foreigners. This broader interpretation of the Samoans' responsibility figured prominently in a later case, discussed in another chapter.

40 Cunningham presumed to witness on behalf of Great Britain.

41 Heath, Day, Mills, Williams and Wilson. Heath served as interpreter until the question of war arose, after which Williams took over.

42 The meeting was adjourned overnight, allowing time for much argument and intrigue.

43 SSL, Heath, 7 November 1839.

conflicting European pressures, and probably riven by faction anyway, the chiefs could not agree to do Wilkes's bidding. The initiative was thus returned to Wilkes in circumstances which forced him to weigh the possible consequences of his failure to catch Popotunu against the effect upon American interests should he alienate the people he had befriended—as, for example, by trying to intimidate the Mālō chiefs into taking action.[44] Having manoeuvred himself into this invidious position, he withdrew his demand and, rather than attempt reprisals against Palauli, simply offered a reward for Popotunu's capture.[45] Wilkes claimed that this measure would either secure the murderer, dead or alive, or drive him into hiding, where he would no longer be a menace to foreigners; but in fact, the offer achieved neither object, and so was eventually withdrawn. Yet Wilkes later wrote of the Apia meeting that 'everyone present evinced the greatest satisfaction that the whole of the business before it had been concluded in so satisfactory a manner'.[46]

In terms equally redundant Wilkes overestimated the effect of his 'commercial regulations', stating, among other things, that they 'secure[d] our whaleships a certainty of protection and security'. Actually, 'incidents' continued to occur. Only a few months after Wilkes left Samoa, another American was killed there, while a regulation forbidding the looting of wrecked ships was, according to Samoan custom, repeatedly violated, even though allowances for salvage had been guaranteed. A new provision in respect of desertion, offering a reward of eight dollars in cash or goods for each crewman returned, was yet another failure, first because the amount payable was too small to generate the inter-village co-operation which enforcement would often have required, and also because the very idea of a reward was subject to misinterpretation.

[44] According to Heath (op. cit.), Wilkes did use threatening language and urge, repeatedly, that the chiefs go to war—all to no avail. There is no evidence, however, that he threatened the extreme measures of which he was capable—e.g. the taking of hostages from the meeting he addressed. On the question of war, it is also possible that Wilkes was restrained by the nature of his visit, in that unsettled conditions could have obstructed the completion of scientific enquiries. But as members of the expedition had nearly ended their first stay in the group, this is not likely.

[45] Bethune had considered posting a reward for the convicts he sought but had concluded that it would have been beneath the dignity of the Crown for him to have offered such an inducement (Adm. 1/218, Bethune to Maitland, 9 February 1838).

[46] Wilkes, II, 92-3, 101-6; USN, WE, Wilkes's Journal, 1839, and WE (letters), Wilkes to Paulding, 6 November 1839, no. 53, for his account of these proceedings. Popotunu was never brought to justice—not, at any rate, by the agency of man. But when, years later, he died of an accidental fall from a precipice, the event was attributed by missionaries and Samoans to the avenging hand of the Lord (SSL, Schmidt, 31 December 1852).

If the promise of eight dollars disposed the Samoans to return a deserter to his ship, his offer of ten might well purchase his freedom. A more serious abuse was the ransoming of sailors at premium rates, which, according to one report, ran as high as forty dollars for a valued member of crew.[47] Finally, Wilkes's code, like Bethune's, was enacted by chiefs who were unable, even if they had been willing to try, to impose its terms upon all the people they claimed to represent.[48]

That is not to say that the new code had no bearing upon events, for as it will appear, it was eventually demonstrated to the Samoans that European governments meant such undertakings to be honoured, if not out of regard for 'law and justice', then out of respect for power. This condition applied even though the port regulations were never formally recognized in law as anything but local enactments.[49] In the short run, however, Wilkes's main contributions to the keeping of order seemed to be, first, his placing of American merchant ships on the same footing as the British in the matter of observing the laws of Samoa[50] and, secondly, his provisional appointment of an American consul, pending further action by the State Department.[51] In choosing a consul he favoured the London Missionary Society even more than Pritchard had, for the man he appointed was John C. Williams,[52] the missionary's son,

[47] USCD, Apia/1, Jenkins to Marcy, 15 August 1856, concerning the enforcement of the regulations.

[48] Wilkes, II, 428-30, or St Julian, *Official Report*, 18-19, for the text of the code, which was proposed and adopted only at the Apia meeting.

[49] By appearing to give naval officers jurisdiction in murder cases, and also by allowing for the payment of certain rewards to the Samoans, the Wilkes code bore some resemblance to a treaty, but it was not recognized as such by the Powers. The Europeans who endorsed it were not authorized to negotiate a treaty, nor was it then the desire of either Britain or America to accord Samoa the formal status of a sovereign nation. See St Julian, *Official Report*, 18, for a theoretical interpretation of the code as a treaty.

[50] Several American ships had used Apia harbour and taken provisions without paying. As a good will gesture Wilkes offered to compensate the chiefs, but as a return gesture, they declined. He did, however, pay dues for his squadron, and members of the expedition dispensed gifts rather lavishly. Wilkes did not mention the evasion of any charges by American vessels except at Apia (Wilkes, II, 91).

[51] USN, WE (letters), Wilkes to Williams, 4 November 1839. That Wilkes was able to supply Williams with copies of American statutes and regulations respecting the office of consul suggests that he had authority to make the provisional appointment. On the other hand, it was not until 1844, apparently, that the State Department first heard of the appointment, and then from Williams, not the Navy Department (USCD, Apia/1, minute from Williams to Upshur, 18 January 1844).

[52] Williams was appointed just before the new code was negotiated and so participated in the Apia meeting as an American representative. He and Wilkes witnessed the code for the United States.

who had recently come from England to enter upon the career of 'Christian trader'. The selection of Williams, a British subject, was to some extent dictated by a shortage of suitable candidates, but it was Wilkes's desire, none the less, to associate the influence of the mission with the protection of Americans and their interests.

## How else to defend 'the poor Samoa people'?

On balance, then, the London Missionary Society had been fortunate in its initial dealings with naval officers and consuls, yet some of the major problems associated with European-Samoan relations still remained to be solved, in which undertaking the coolness of the chiefs to political advice was an enormous handicap. As for controlling immigration, time seemed to be running very short when, as early as 1840, the missionaries learned of 'representations . . . made in Sydney relative to the ease with which fortunes may be made in Samoa'.[53] Although excessively optimistic, or at any rate premature, these reports contained sufficient truth to be taken seriously. For Samoa *was*, by Pacific standards, potentially rich, and it was also close enough to the Australasian colonies to become a focus of commercial activity and migration originating in that quarter. Thus it seemed that a tide of 'worthless' adventurers might soon rush upon Samoa. Desperately searching for counter-measures, the missionaries concluded that, if Samoa was destined to go the way of Hawaii, it ought to be carried forward by means of planned colonization, such as to avoid the freebooting pioneer stage of development. In a resolution of the District Committee they stated that 'free settlers . . . of piety or good moral character' should come as merchants and tradesmen, establishing first claim to the ground which less desirable immigrants would otherwise occupy. They added that they were

> . . . in favour of native labour and against the bringing out of a host of foreign labourers, and that whoever came ought to comply with the laws of the Islands in matters between themselves and the natives.[54]

But this modified Land or Wakefield proposal was only a fond dream, for the London Missionary Society was not a colonizing mission, and the British societies engaged in promoting the type of colonization invited by the District Committee were interested in the temperate zones, not the tropics. The first of these problems was actually anticipated in the foregoing resolution, while the second was confronted some two years later by the missionary, Heath. Pious settlers were always to be preferred, said Heath, but Samoa could not expect to get them in sufficient numbers nor in a systematic way. Better, then, a chartered commercial

[53] SSL, Mills, minutes of Samoan District Committee, 30 March 1840.
[54] *loc. cit.*

company—a monopoly which might keep out some of the undesirable 'stragglers'.[55] However, this proposal was no more tenable, for the economic conditions that would have supported it were not to arise in Samoa for many years.

During the early 1840s there also developed the French 'menace', an alleged crisis which must have caused the London Missionary Society to regret keenly the recent passing of Malietoa Vai'inupō, and not only because of the Samoans' distraction by that event. For as the Samoans, united or not, were deemed incapable of thwarting French designs upon their freedom, an appeal had to be made for British assistance; and in matters of this kind, the representations of a 'national' figure, of a high chief whose name was already known abroad, might be expected to carry the most weight. Vai'inupō had, moreover, expressed some interest in an 'alliance' with Britain and, in the present emergency, would prob- ably have been disposed to affix his mark to the requisite petition. But as matters stood, with Vai'inupō dead and no successor in sight, other and lesser chiefs would have to attest to the fears and wishes of 'all Samoans'. According to Heath, the French question was discussed at a large meeting, apparently of the old Mālō, wherein it was resolved to seek closer ties with Britain, lest the fate of Tahiti befall Samoa. All that ensued, however, was an informal letter from several Manono chiefs who, though vaguely proposing an alliance, mentioned no meeting and made no specific allusion to France. Whatever their intention, the chiefs gave the appearance of representing only themselves and of being troubled only by beachcombers, whom they wanted taken away. In an accompanying memorial to Lord Aberdeen, the Foreign Secretary, Heath tried to expand and embellish the 'petition', but to no avail. The chiefs were not even sent a formal acknowledgement of their effort.[56]

In the following year, 1844, a second appeal was made to Queen Victoria, this time by some of the leading chiefs of Tutuila.[57] More to the point, and more suggestive of London Missionary Society super- vision, this document declared the pro-British and anti-French sentiments of the signatories and begged, accordingly, that Tutuila be granted British protection and the status of a *fully* self-governing community within the Empire. It expressed the hope that Great Britain would be moved by love and compassion to gratify this prayer, it being under-

[55] SSL, Heath, 26 February 1842.

[56] FO 58/23, Lei'ataua Tonumaipe'a, Taupa'ū and others to Queen Victoria, n.d., Heath to Aberdeen, 14 August 1843. Heath forwarded the Manono petition from London.

[57] The Tutuila petition was presented to Captain Bell of H.M.S. *Hazard*, who called at Pago Pago on cruise (FO 58/33, Bell to Thomas, 20 May 1844).

M

stood that there was nothing in Tutuila to give that country any material incentive for doing so.[58] This petition, unlike the preceding one, was given serious consideration in London, where, occasioned partly by the reckless conduct of French naval authorities at Tahiti,[59] suspicion of France's intentions and sympathy for the islanders' fears were mounting. Not that Britain's reply satisfied either the chiefs or the missionaries, for no outright guarantee of protection was forthcoming—for example, no promise of a warship to be stationed in or near the group. Yet on closer examination the petition may be found to have had some practical consequence.

It will be clear, first, that the chiefs meant to offer Britain no more than the ceremonial sovereignty of Tutuila, and perhaps not even that much. Their terms were construed, however, as an invitation to Britain to rule under a protectorate agreement, and it was to that proposition that Lord Aberdeen addressed his reply. For his government to accept such a responsibility, he observed, would not be to the advantage of either side. Rather, the Samoans should remain free of imperial control, which would best suit them, while being subject to no foreign influence greater that Britain's, which was all the guarantee that British interests really seemed to require. On the question of maintaining their freedom he was, however, most circumspect.

> It is unnecessary to add [wrote Aberdeen for the advice of the Samoans] that Her Majesty's Government would not view with indifference the assumption by another Power of a Protectorate which they, with regard for the true interests of those islands, have already refused.[60]

Not only was it to have been a protectorate, but a protectorate of the 'islands'—of the whole Samoan group! From the Samoan viewpoint it could scarcely have mattered now what had been read into the petition in London. On the diplomatic front, though, it mattered a great deal. The misinterpretation may, indeed, have been calculated. For Aberdeen advised the French Government—which, incidentally, had intervened in Tahiti on the pretext of a petition even less plausible—that Britain had been asked to establish a protectorate of Samoa and was prepared to decline. Then, having offered this 'concession', he arranged what amounted to an Anglo-French undertaking of mutual respect for Samoa's independence—without, it may be added, implying any formal recognition of a Samoan government.[61] As it happened, Aberdeen's French

[58] FO 58/33, Mauga, Tuitele and others to Queen Victoria, 23 April 1844.
[59] Notably in regard to the imprisonment and subsequent expulsion of George Pritchard, the British Consul at Tahiti.
[60] FO 58/38, Aberdeen to Pritchard, 15 January 1845, no. 2.
[61] ibid., Aberdeen to Pritchard, 15 January 1845, no. 3 (conf.).

counterpart, Guizot, could easily reciprocate, for his government then had little or no interest in ruling Samoa.[62] But it would appear that Aberdeen, influenced by tensions existing between the two countries, had negotiated on the assumption that the opposite might be or might soon become true, exploiting the Tutuila petition to secure assurances favourable to Samoan as well as British interests.

[62] Newbury in *Pacific Historical Review*,

# 7

## FOREIGN SETTLEMENT AT APIA BAY

In the early 1830s many of the Samoans in the Apia area lived inland,[1] leaving the foreshore of the bay almost deserted. Along the 2·5-mile sea front there was, indeed, only one village, that of Apia itself, which lay between the Vaisigano river on the east and the outlet of a small stream (Mulivai) on the west (map, p. 425). Elsewhere at the bay conditions were then less favourable for Samoan habitation: at Matautu, east of the Vaisigano, because that place was the haven of spirits;[2] between Mulivai and Sogi because an extensive waste of mangrove swamp (*taufusi*) lay between the beach and inland cultivations; and on the narrow peninsula of Mulinu'u because, in addition to being cut off from the interior, the position was highly vulnerable to attack. By the end of the decade, only Mulinu'u, apart from Apia, had been settled by Samoans—and then as the 'health resort' of a Faleata chief who suffered from elephantiasis.[3] Thus, Apia Bay stood to attract foreign settlers not only because of its harbour and central location, but also by reason of a substantial surplus of beach land.

### Early settlers at Apia

To one another, and to the beachcombers who lived among them, the Samoans voluntarily conveyed various rights in land but not, as a rule, in a manner corresponding to European practice, for example, to the gift, sale or fixed-term lease of freehold. They were, however, quite capable of understanding such transactions and, on certain conditions, willingly and effectively entered into them with Europeans, whose residential and business requirements often necessitated more than a temporary tenancy or one subject to arbitrary termination by the Samoans. Partly because they classified land among their least expendable possessions, the Samoans preferred to lease or sell it only to Europeans whose presence and enterprise seemed to them likely to prove congenial and rewarding. If, in practice, they were sometimes less restrictive, it was usually on account of an emergency constraining them

---

[1] At Vaimoso, Lepea and Vailoa villages in Faleata, and Moto'otua, Tanugamanono and Magiagi in Vaimauga.

[2] The area was known as Matautu Sā, the sacred or forbidden point of land.

[3] This chief was Matai'a Lalu (SLC 2739, Memo by J. M. Coe, 24 June 1891). Faleata people occupied Mulinu'u on and off until it became the capital of Samoa.

to use land as an article of trade.[4] As for the realization of foreigners' claims or titles, it was important, at least until the Powers commenced intervening in land matters,[5] that proposed sales or leases should be openly discussed; for the Samoans could not effectively dispose of land or grant its secure tenure without the consent and support of their respective villages. If the land in question had been previously developed or occupied, they would probably have to consult their *tama fafine* connections as well. When the interested parties were scrupulously canvassed and the terms of agreement fully explained, foreigners were seldom disturbed in their occupation or claim, though of course their holdings were exposed, as in time of war, to the same hazards as anyone else's.

It was to help secure for themselves the services of the missions that Samoans first made land available to Europeans on secure tenure. When it was proposed, for example, that a London Missionary Society centre be established at Apia, the chiefs of that village gave the mission the free use of sufficient land for as long as it might be required.[6] At Pago Pago and elsewhere the Samoans reacted similarly to the missionaries' requests for land. At the same time, the whaling captains who speculated in real estate, and European residents who had like interests or perhaps an inclination towards commercial agriculture, were refused the land they sought to buy. This cautious approach to land alienation may have owed something to mission advice,[7] but of course, such advice would have been easy to take while the Samoans' demand for foreign goods was being met by the trade in ships' provisions.

Shortly after his appointment by Pritchard, Cunningham also acquired land at Apia, probably on lease; and by 1840 he had erected a 'consulate' and storehouse, the latter for use in connection with some commercial venture which he proposed to undertake.[8] Next came J. C. Williams,

---

[4] cf. chapter 12, below.

[5] A common practice from the 1870s on.

[6] A few of the mission's early holdings were secured under title deeds, e.g. the land occupied by the seminary at Malua, but until the 1870s, most of them were informally conveyed, at least as far as European law was concerned. It was commonly understood that the mission had, during the period of its actual occupation, every beneficial right in its land except that of disposal to third parties. Such terms were later formalized in deeds of trust.

[7] Europeans blamed the L.M.S. for it and also accused the missionaries, quite unjustly, of speculating in land themselves (SSL, Harbutt, 17 June 1844).

[8] Cunningham seems to have searched for openings in a variety of commercial fields, including plantation agriculture, sandalwooding and saw-milling; but there is no mention in the literature of any business actually established by him in Samoa. It is probable that his commercial exploits there were limited to the provisions trade.

who moved to Vaimauga from Fasito'otai (A'ana) in about 1841. Associated with Wilkes and the London Missionary Society, and being the son of a missionary whose memory many Samoans revered, Williams had sufficient influence to buy land outright, becoming, if not the first European landowner in the area, then certainly the first of any consequence. At Fagali'i, four miles east of Apia, he acquired a house-site and some acreage for gardens and pasture, while at Apia village he purchased a site for his consular and commercial headquarters.[9]

Williams's relations with the government he represented in Samoa were never very close. For example, he received no American naval support between Hudson's final visit in 1841 and his own departure from Samoa in 1850—and, indeed, was so isolated during that period that despatches took as long as three years reaching him from Washington.[10] Further, his commission did not arrive until 1848, much of the delay being due to the failure of the naval authorities to inform the State Department of his provisional appointment by Wilkes; and then, when the commission did come, in response to Williams's own inquiries, it was for the post of commercial agent, not consul. Unsuccessfully holding out for the consulship which Wilkes had led him to expect, Williams never actually accepted the appointment offered him by the State Department.[11] He continued, however, to act for the United States, styling himself consul—in Samoan, the Fa'amasino Amelika, or 'American judge'—and serving mainly as interpreter and arbiter in matters relating to port control and trade. Regardless of the technical informality of his position, his functions qualified him locally as an important official, particularly in view of the growing volume of

9 Lucett, *Rovings in the Pacific*, II, 155.

10 USCD, Apia/1, Williams to Upshur, 26 December 1843, Williams to Buchanan, 8 October 1846.

11 Williams objected to the post's official title as well as to its being unsalaried (ibid., Williams to Buchanan, 16 June 1848, Pritchard to Webster, 26 February 1851). Depending on the terms of their respective commissions, an American commercial agent and consul might exercise the same powers. The essential difference between them was that the commercial agent, unlike the consul, was not accredited to a foreign government. That is to say, the appointment of a consul entailed a definite acknowledgement of sovereignty, whereas the appointment of a commercial agent did not. Britain's consular representatives in the islands were, however, designated consuls and could be formally accredited or not, as determined in each case (USCD, Apia/1, draft of State Dept to Dirickson, 25 September 1857, as regards American practice). The American commercial agent in Samoa was subject to discrimination in respect of protocol. For example, he, unlike a consul, was not entitled to a salute from a British naval vessel, which, among the formalistic Samoans, sometimes worked to his disadvantage (Adm. 1/5672, Fremantle to Osborne, 15 November 1855). Except where meaning requires that distinctions of title be made, officials with consular powers are usually referred to as consuls in the following text.

American whaler traffic.[12] Meanwhile, the prestige and influence of the British consular service declined in Samoa. This occurred partly because Cunningham reverted to the easy way of life he had adopted in Rarotonga, thereby gaining the antagonism of the London Missionary Society. Also, he was absent from his post for prolonged periods. Finally, in 1842, he left the group for good,[13] and three years passed before Britain had another (and, this time, a regularly-appointed) representative in residence there. But even so, the number of British ships then calling at Samoa was too small to have given a British consul much standing as a commercial functionary.

With his schooner *Samuel and Mary*, which he himself had built,[14] Williams engaged in itinerant trading in the central Pacific, gaining a good deal of his business through mission contacts. At Apia he joined in the provisions trade, in which he supplied produce acquired from the Samoans as well as what he raised on his own land; and soon he was also buying coconut oil for export. Since the Samoans' method of extracting oil was suited only to their own limited needs, technical innovations had to be made before production could be undertaken on any substantial scale. For this reason, and also because special shipping and marketing facilities were required, the inauguration of the oil industry in Samoa was more dependent upon European initiative than was that of the more familiar and straightforward provisions trade. This initiative was first taken by Williams,[15] closely followed by the London Missionary Society representatives, who envisaged monthly collections of oil as the mainstay of the contributions system they were about to establish.[16] Commencing with a monopoly of the oil trade, Williams made his first shipment in about 1842—the modest quantity of fifteen 'tuns'[17]—

12 During the period 1842-6, annual shipping calls at Apia increased from a total of twelve to seventy-two, of which American vessels accounted for five and forty-four respectively and British vessels (including naval and mission craft) four and sixteen (USCD, Apia/1, Williams to Buchanan, 12 May 1845; *Samoan Reporter* for 1845-9, *passim*).

13 SSL, Mills, 14 April 1842. Having received no commission, Cunningham did not appoint an acting successor. Williams, however, assisted British subjects when the occasion demanded.

14 Williams also built another vessel, the *Samoa*, which he sold to the L.M.S. (SSL, Williams Sr, 12 November 1839). He commenced his trade with other groups before he came to Apia.

15 Supplying leak-proof containers and devising crude methods of extracting oil in larger quantities (e.g. Erskine, 59).

16 SSL, Stair, 14 April 1843. The oil industry got its best start in A'ana, Tutuila and Vaimauga, but stimulated by mission as well as secular interests, it soon spread into most parts of the group.

17 In 1842 or late in 1841. The sources, all giving information supplied by Williams, differ slightly as to the date and the amount of the first shipment (*Samoan*

and by 1844 he had done sufficiently well in his various enterprises to have a general store at Apia.[18] Through these developments the Samoans learned the peculiar advantages of shore-based trading and of supplying non-perishables for which there was constant and virtually unlimited demand. Williams's success was also, of course, a standing invitation to other speculators, his competitors-to-be, whose services the Samoans would prove eager to have and whose wealth they would be anxious to share.

On the Samoan side, the principal figure concerned in the early commercial development of the bay area was Seumanutafa Pogai, whose village of Apia controlled much of the sea frontage within easiest access of the anchorage. Until the 1850s Pogai was commonly treated by Europeans as the highest-ranking chief in the vicinity of the harbour. During that time he received all the port fees and, very often, he was the first chief consulted by foreigners who wanted land, food supplies, firewood, fresh water, labour, women or police assistance. From 1842 he was also an outstanding member of the London Missionary Society church, being regarded by the missionaries as 'a very religious man' and, hence, expected to heed their advice.[19]

But, in fact, Apia was not the only village with interests at the bay, for some, perhaps all, of the inland villages near by had land, fishing and 'navigation' rights there. Nor did Pogai outrank all other chiefs in the neighbourhood. Of comparable standing was To'omalatai Toetagata, his 'brother chief' in the Vaimauga hierarchy, who lived at Moto'otua, about half a mile behind Apia.[20] By about 1850 Toetagata and his people had, no doubt owing to London Missionary Society influence, sufficiently overcome their dread of the pagan spirits to move to Matautu, where they could share more fully in the benefits of commercial activity. Also of high rank were Faumuinā and the holders of the Matai'a title, all of Faleata. As mentioned before, the occupation of Mulinu'u by Faleata people began in the late 1830s for reasons which may have had little or nothing to do with foreign shipping. Subsequently, however, Faleata's settlement at the bay grew in response to the commercial stimulus, spreading to Savalalo as well. The latter area, which was nearer Apia and situated more favourably than Mulinu'u in respect of shipping and trade, was occupied from 1840 on.[21] Subsequently, the adjacent

　　　*Reporter*, March 1861; Murray, *Missions in Western Polynesia*, 467; BCS 3/2, Williams, trade report, 31 December 1859). The cask normally used for shipping oil held about a ton by weight. In their reports the consuls used the measures 'ton' and 'tun' interchangeably.

[18] Lucett, II, 155; Adm. 1/5548, Home to Cochrane, 15 October 1844.

[19] Walpole, *Four Years in the Pacific*, II, 387-8; SSL, Mills, 14 April 1842.

[20] SLC 2739, Memo by J. M. Coe, 24 June 1891.

[21] USN, WE, Stuart's Journal, 1841; FO 58/59, notes on case of Pritchard *v.* Tui Papali'i, with Blake to Seymour, 30 March 1847. In the 1850s Pogai and

sector of Matafele was also inhabited by Samoans, some of whom came from the Vaimauga village of Tanugamanono.[22]

Needless to say, such changes in the pattern of Samoan settlement[23] increased the scope for friction and rivalry at Apia Bay, in turn weakening the administration of port controls. Indications of this process emerge from several known cases of European immigration, the first of which relate to the transfer of consul Pritchard to Samoa and to the advent of French mission and mercantile interests.

Early in 1844 George Pritchard was arrested and deported from Tahiti by the French, whose wrath he had provoked by opposing their intervention there. By this precipitate and high-handed action he was deprived of a position of great prominence, for he had been not only British consul, but also merchant, clergyman,[24] magistrate, self-appointed diplomat, and principal European adviser to the Pomare government. His expulsion outraged his sense of dignity as well and, for the time being, embarrassed him financially. To find, after returning to England, that the Foreign Office was prepared to abandon Tahiti to the French and to remove him, without vindication, to the relative obscurity of Samoa was yet another blow; while to make matters still worse for him, his first assignment, on being transferred, was to decline Tutuila's request for British protection.[25] It was therefore a disillusioned and humiliated Pritchard who, in July 1845, arrived at Apia to establish new consular headquarters.

Pressed for time, the commander of H.M.S. *Daphne*, which brought Pritchard, put him ashore at Apia without introducing him or proclaiming him Britain's official representative.[26] According to Pritchard, this

Toetagata claimed paramountcy over the bayside area between and including Matautu and Sogi, so that Samoans settling at Savalalo and Matafele may have had to secure the permission of one or both beforehand (USCD, Apia/1, Rules of the Apia mixed court, 27 April 1857).

22 By the mid-1850s, Matafele had become the focus of commercial activity on the west side of the Vaisigano, and Pogai himself was reported as living there (USN, Pac. Sqd., Van Camp to Bailey, 18 September 1855, statement by Bailey, 1 October 1855).

23 At first within northern Tuamasaga. But later, Samoans were attracted to Apia from all parts of the group. Except in the case of Moto'otua, this resettlement did not entail the movement of entire villages.

24 Though no longer a member of the L.M.S. staff, he had continued to preach and had conducted himself in such a manner that European visitors occasionally took him for the 'leader' of the mission in Tahiti (e.g. MS., Whittle, Journal 1839).

25 *Samoan Reporter*, September 1845; SSL, Murray, 23 July 1845.

26 The meeting with the Tutuila chiefs at Pago Pago, where the *Daphne* called en route to Apia, had been conducted with considerable pomp, but no meeting was held at Apia (FO 58/57, Pritchard to Palmerston, 17 April 1847).

neglect of the forms observed earlier by Wilkes made such an adverse impression on the Samoans that he entered into his new career on a footing scarcely superior to that of a common deserter—and this in a place lacking in the civilized amenities to which he was accustomed. No doubt it suited Pritchard, especially in his role of martyr,[27] to so fix the blame, though judging from what happened later, there may have been something in his complaint. But this was by no means the whole story, for being a friend of the London Missionary Society and having been well received on his previous visit, Pritchard anticipated some personal following among the Samoans, regardless of protocol. Now, however, they were generally cool towards him, even though Williams and the London Missionary Society representatives vouched for his character and his credentials. There were probably several grounds for the Samoans' negative reactions, including Pritchard's appointment of the unpopular Cunningham and, in some circles, his sectarian bias. Most important, perhaps, he was 'Vaivai', the vanquished leader of the anti-French movement in Tahiti, whose transfer to Apia was taken by the Samoans as a bad omen and possibly as an insult. Then, by reacting with arrogant hostility to what he chose to regard as the Samoans' disrespect for the Crown, Pritchard worsened his position. Unable to acquire land on *any* terms, even from the London Missionary Society chiefs of Vaimauga, he was thrown upon the hospitality of Williams. After the passage of a year, during which he repeatedly threatened to leave his post, he was allowed the unsecured usehold of some land at Savalalo, where he built a shack that reflected no credit upon either himself or the government he served.[28]

In September 1845, only a few weeks after Pritchard's arrival, Fathers Roudaire and Violette, Samoa's first Marist missionaries, came from Wallis Island aboard *l'Etoile de la Mer*. They made their initial contact at Falealupo in Savai'i, and from there canvassed the north coast around to Fa'asaleleaga, finding only one definite opening. That was in Lealatele (Itu-o-Tane), where a holder of the prominent Tuala title turned to the new *lotu*. Apia Bay was the next call—and, the priests hoped, the future site of their second mission centre. It was, of

[27] See Lucett, II, 156-7, 174, for a colourful account of Pritchard's 'mental suffering', likening him to a 'tree in autumn, suddenly blasted by a frost', and so on. Lucett, of Papeete, was one of Pritchard's agents, appointed to represent him in pressing the French authorities for payment of damages.

[28] FO 58/38, Pritchard to Aberdeen, 11 October 1845; FO 58/45, Pritchard to Aberdeen, 28 May 1846; FO 58/59 (or Adm. 1/5577), Blake to Seymour (with enclosures), 30 March 1847. Also, Lucett, II, 156-7; Erskine, 69-70; Jore, *George Pritchard*, 90; and Walpole, II, 360-1. The British Government did not undertake to supply land or a building, and Cunningham's house, if still standing, was not available.

course, much too soon for Pritchard, the arch-enemy of the Catholic French, to have established himself with the chiefs or to have recovered his fighting form. Denied, at the outset, the role of Samoa's saviour, he greeted the Marists with uncharacteristic civility, somewhat tempered with embarrassment, and then withdrew to write alarmist despatches.[29]

As mentioned before, anti-Catholic propaganda was purveyed by *both* of the Protestant missions and owed much of its effectiveness to that fact. The London Missionary Society defence, however, was the stronger because of that mission's larger staff of trained clergy and perhaps, too, because of a greater emphasis upon the political aspect of French expansion. It was among those Methodists who felt most keenly their lack of European missionaries that the Marists were most likely to make headway, and such were the Methodists of Mulinu'u and of Vailele, a village several miles east of Apia. These people had little interest in Catholicism as such and certainly no desire whatever for French rule. On the other hand, they, who had only Tongan teachers, envied their London Missionary Society neighbours, who had a European missionary, and so were sorely tempted by the Marist offer to eliminate the inequity. At one point, when Faumuinā and several other Mulinu'u chiefs agreed to turn *lotu pope*, it looked as if the priests had succeeded in establishing themselves right on the London Missionary Society door-step, but then something happened and the decision was reversed.[30]

Mata'afa Fagamanu, a contender for the Tui Atua title, came on the scene and, because of a rather remarkable coincidence, decided the issue in the priests' favour. It had happened, about ten years before, that he and a number of other Samoans had been overtaken by a storm while travelling between Upolu and Tutuila. Blown off course, they had drifted to Wallis Island, where the chief Lavelua, then a heathen, had received them, given them hospitality, and assisted towards their return to Samoa. Several years later, Marist missionaries had settled at Wallis, and in 1842 Lavelua had been converted to Catholicism. Now, in a message conveyed by *l'Etoile de la Mer*, this chief was asking Mata'afa to repay the long-standing obligation by finding a secure place for Catholic missionaries in Samoa. The coincidence lay in the fact that, of all the Samoans in the Apia area, those closest to Mata'afa were among the very people with whom the priests had made contact.[31] Mata'afa was therefore brought from Atua to Mulinu'u to hear Lavelua's request. He too was a Methodist and in no hurry to change his affiliation, but

[29] Monfat, *Les Samoa*, 223-59, for a Catholic account of the priests' arrival; *Samoan Reporter*, September 1845; SSL, Pratt, 13 September 1845, for L.M.S. versions.

[30] MS., Darnand.

[31] The *ao* title or dignity of Mata'afa had once belonged to Faleata.

he was honour-bound to protect the priests and to urge Faumuinā and others to do the same.[32]

Roudaire took up residence at Mulinu'u, where he was given the use of a Samoan house and a guarantee of personal safety and religious freedom. Yet, for a missionary, he was in the rather unusual position of having no adherents and of being held suspect on the ground of his nationality. It was at this stage that Williams, aided by Pritchard, tried to erect new barriers to French intervention, which according to rumour was due any day.[33] In the state of emergency that was assumed to exist, the consuls focused their attention upon Upolu, the island which France might be expected to seize first, owing to its being the richest and, in other respects too, the most important. To a gathering of Upolu's 'principal chiefs'—how many or how representative is not known— they proposed that the British Government be petitioned for an un-equivocal guarantee of protection and, further, that some sort of central government or general law code be proclaimed and a 'national flag' adopted, such as to give the island at least the outward semblance of unity and order.[34] The idea behind these measures was, presumably, that if France did move in, so soon after the Tahiti crisis, there should be the maximum of international furore. To the Samoans, however, the issue was not so simple and straightforward. They were particularly concerned about the flag, first because to have and retain one in common would require a measure of unity which did not then exist even on a Mālō basis, and secondly because the custody of such a symbol would confer, or constitute a claim to, a position of ceremonial leadership. There had been, for some years, a flag used by the European masters of un-registered vessels and referred to as the 'Upolian colours',[35] and it was proposed that it might suit the present purpose. But as that flag was either the exclusive property of foreigners or a mere party banner, perhaps of the deceased Vai'inupō, the suggestion solved nothing. It led, rather, to a new difficulty, in that elements of both the American and British flags were to be found in the so-called 'Upolian colours'.[36] The resemblance, which was probably not fortuitous, gave Roudaire a valuable talking-point, especially among people who already had strong *fa'a-Samoa* aversions to the above proceedings. The flag in question was,

[32] MS. Darnand; Monfat; 262-4.

[33] It was rumoured, from the time the priests landed in Samoa, that they were to be followed by a French warship carrying a large contingent of marines. It was claimed that such a ship had been sighted off the coast, but the threat never materialized (FO 58/38, Pritchard to Aberdeen, 11 October 1845; SSL, Mills, 11 October 1845, Nisbet, 27 November 1845).

[34] FO 58/45, Pritchard to Aberdeen, 28 May 1846.

[35] Adm. 1/5548, Home to Cochrane, 15 October 1844.

[36] *loc. cit.*; FO 58/45, Pritchard to Aberdeen, 28 May 1846.

he said, of obvious foreign design, and to adopt it formally and raise it over Upolu would automatically bring the island under American and British rule. He added that France, out of concern for Samoa's independence, was as antipathetic to that course of events as were the Samoans themselves.[37]

Roudaire's interpretation of the protectorate scheme was, of course, far-fetched, but hardly more so than many of the things being said against France. In this case, then, it was what the Samoans believed or feared that mattered most, and they were sufficiently apprehensive of foreign domination and ignorant of the ways of the Powers to give serious thought to what Roudaire said. If Pritchard, a man of notorious indiscretion, said openly or even hinted at what he had been writing to the Foreign Office, he too may have helped defeat the proposals put to the meeting of Upolu chiefs. Only if a foreign Power took possession of Samoa, he had claimed, would conditions there change for the better. As for effecting such a takeover, he had observed that the Samoans were too divided among themselves to make any resistance.[38] The clear implication, made explicit in later despatches, was that Britain should immediately annex the islands outright, with or without petitions to that effect. Judged in the light of such sentiments as these, Roudaire's statement might have seemed well-founded indeed. At any rate, the meeting of chiefs broke up without adopting a flag or code or producing any petition.[39] If agreement was reached on any point, it was that the Samoans wanted to secure the benefits of contact with Europeans while remaining free of *all* foreign governments, British and American included.

Having argued his case within the framework of Upolu's 'higher politics', Roudaire became, perhaps unwittingly in this instance, an 'ally' of people inclined towards Mata'afa, whose pretensions would most likely have been passed over by any movement towards 'national' unity that the consuls might have instigated. Roudaire may, indeed, have served these people's interests better than they could have done themselves, in that their views on matters relevant to traditional politics were less widely shared than the fears to which he had appealed. Certainly, he emerged from the controversy with greater influence than before.[40] And within a few months his position was further strengthened by another French challenge to established interests, this time in the field of commerce.

For some time prior to the appearance of *l'Etoile de la Mer*, vessels

[37] Monfat, 270-1.
[38] FO 58/38, Pritchard to Aberdeen, 31 December 1845.
[39] Monfat; FO 58/45, Pritchard to Aberdeen, 28 May 1846.
[40] Monfat, 271-2.

from various ports had been visiting Samoa in search of coconut oil
and other non-perishables. Among these had been vessels from Le
Havre, which—as London Missionary Society officials correctly assumed
—were also surveying the ground for Catholicism.[41] What had not
been known in Samoa, however, was that French mercantile interests
and Catholic missionaries were preparing to join forces. Negotiations
came to a head in 1845 with the establishment at Le Havre of the
Société Française de l'Océanie (S.F.O.), an organization dedicated to the
planting of mission stations and trade stores throughout the Pacific
islands. The scheme did not envisage joint management of the two
enterprises but, rather, the sharing of certain facilities, such as transport,
and the symbiotic exploitation of the islanders' religious and economic
susceptibilities. In the latter regard, the S.F.O. was determined to offer
better terms of trade than its competitors, one object being to attract
bargain-hunters to the Church, which in turn would try to assure the
stores a monopoly of Catholic business.[42] Thus, the opening of a cut-
rate store was due to follow the settlement of Roudaire at the port of
Apia.

Vessels run by the S.F.O. first called at Samoa towards the end of
1846, bringing merchandise for barter and more staff for the mission.
The initial foray into commerce, conducted from the ships *Anonyme*
and the more appropriately named *Arche d'Alliance*, resulted in the
random purchase of some coconut oil in exchange for powder and shot.
This was followed by the landing of a merchant and his stock at Apia
Bay, where it was proposed that a trading station should be established.[43] If any attempt was made to secure land from Pogai, nearest
the anchorage, it failed, but at Mulinu'u there was no difficulty.[44] In
fact, Roudaire was now given a block of land, which the S.F.O. partners
proceeded to occupy.[45]

This new French incursion produced consternation farther along the
bay, at least among Europeans. Pritchard, for one, was thrown into a
virtual state of panic, not least because he was trying to start his own
trading business in circumstances already unfavourable enough. Despatches reaching the Foreign Office told of a flood of 'cheap' goods,
supplied at 'little more than cost', that threatened to wreck British
enterprise, mission as well as commercial—this in addition to and

[41] SSL, Harbutt, 17 June 1844. Monfat, 183-212, for reports by Captains Marceau
and Morvan.

[42] Brookes, 175-6; Koskinen, *Missionary Influence*, 139-40; Walpole, II, 369.

[43] *Samoan Reporter*, September 1846; FO 58/45, Pritchard to Palmerston, 16
November 1846.

[44] FO 58/59, Blake to Seymour, 30 March 1847 (notes on case of Pritchard *v.*
Pua Matai'a).

[45] SLC 2739, Broyer to DHPG, 16 March 1891.

irrespective of the alleged danger of political intervention by France.[46] Pritchard implied, first, that the French stores would be and, indeed, would have to be subsidized as long as they had competitors to under-cut. Considering, however, that the scale of retail mark-ups had been ranging from a minimum of about one hundred per cent, the S.F.O.'s competitors, mainly Williams and Pritchard, were probably concerned not so much about the question of subsidies as that of how many mer-chants the Samoan trade could sustain and, in all events, about the S.F.O.'s larger resources and the possibility of its achieving greater operating efficiency. Secondly, Pritchard seemed to contend that the Samoans would take the bait—that the S.F.O. price formula would work for both the missionary and the merchant. This, from his mission experi-ence and from the poor reception given him as consul, Pritchard may well have believed or suspected, though as a trader he adopted no such course to gather influence for himself or for his government or religious sect.

From the events which followed it would appear that Pritchard and some other Europeans misjudged the Samoans. True, there was a rash of conversions to Catholicism, but as already shown, the number involved was smaller than that expected by the priests and, for that matter, by their foreign antagonists.[47] It is likely that this movement, along with Roudaire's acquisition of land, owed something to the development of French trading activity. The most influential of the con-versions, including Mata'afa's, had, however, been pending for some time, and one suspects that when they finally materialized, the S.F.O.'s merchandising policy, as such, played a smaller part than the overall strengthening and clarification of the French position in Samoa. The question of turning *lotu pope* had involved not only sectarian con-siderations but also critical issues of confidence, and the latter were in the process of being resolved. First, had the Marists come to stay? Methodists, in particular, could well ask this, seeing that they had already been let down once. By the end of 1846, it must have been fairly clear to all that the priests had no intention of leaving. Moreover, the alleged threat of French invasion was wearing thin, at least in some places. This was partly a function of time, of the inability of the London Missionary Society representatives and others to maintain indefinitely the state of high suspense. Another contributing factor was the conduct of foreigners who actually possessed the sort of power about which the Samoans were concerned. These were the French naval officers who supported Roudaire's interpretation of their government's attitude to-

---

[46] FO 58/45, Pritchard to Palmerston, 16 November 1846, 31 December 1846; Lucett, II, 157.

[47] Walpole, II, 370-1.

wards Samoa and, after them, the British commanders who, by treating the Marists with respect and by refusing to mix in local controversies, also impaired the credibility of anti-French propaganda.[48]

But if the Samoans, when offered a choice in each sphere, had actually mixed trade and religion in the manner anticipated by some Europeans, Catholicism would have forged ahead of its rivals, for the S.F.O., at least in its trade with Samoans, was soon the leading mercantile house in the group. As it happened, though, the Samoans had the sense to take advantage of a bargain without necessarily feeling bound to the Church on account of it. By early 1847, most of their coconut oil, excepting what they produced for London Missionary Society collections and their own use, was going to the French store at Mulinu'u.[49] Of the remaining business open locally to other merchants—that is, to Williams and Pritchard—only the trade in provisions and the custom of Protestant missionaries were of much consequence. In respect of British commerce, then, if not of the London Missionary Society position, there was some ground for Pritchard's concern.

However, the S.F.O. merchant, one M. Chauvel, had not cleared every obstacle, for some of his antagonists were quite ready to pursue elsewhere what they were unable to accomplish in the market-place. There was, of course, much petty controversy, especially between Pritchard, the British consul, and Chauvel, who claimed to represent France but showed no credentials.[50] The slanging match in which these two and their partisans engaged was typical of much of the so-called 'international rivalry' in Samoa prior to the 1870s. That is, it was essentially a private quarrel in which the names of the Powers were taken in vain by the participants. This invocation of higher authority, like a certain form of blasphemy, only stimulated the spirit of malice. The outcome, in this instance, was arson, by which means the S.F.O. store was destroyed within a year of its erection.[51] Curiously, the fire, which was attributed to a European of unknown identity, was never reported officially by either Williams or Pritchard.

The store was rebuilt on the original site and trading operations were resumed,[52] but the S.F.O. was thenceforth dogged by misfortune. Next it was the war, which within a few days of its outbreak saw Mulinu'u occupied by a large party of belligerents. With his competitors based in neutral Vaimauga, Chauvel was put to an enormous disadvantage.

[48] APF, XXII, 107, Vachon to his mother, August 1848.
[49] FO 58/59, Blake to Seymour, 30 March 1847 (notes on case of Pritchard v. Pua Matai'a).
[50] BCS 2/1, Worth to Chauvel, 1 June 1848.
[51] *Samoan Reporter*, September 1847.
[52] Bérard, *Campagne en Océanie*, 21.

Then, in 1850, it was a gale or hurricane, which destroyed the second store-building and practically finished the firm in Samoa.[53] The *coup de grâce* was delivered in 1852, when the parent organization was dissolved.[54] Thus ended in ignominy an experiment in Catholic commerce.

Meanwhile, at Apia, Pogai and his people were exercising considerable control over European enterprise and settlement. In this respect, of course, the interests of the London Missionary Society gave some direction to Pogai's leadership. Not that he satisfied the mission's every wish or demand, but on several counts he acquitted himself very well indeed, notably in preventing the commercial importation of spirits at Apia Bay and in barring all missionaries but those of the London Missionary Society from settling on land controlled by his village. When he did accommodate Europeans, Pogai was inclined, on his own account, to drive a hard bargain—hard even by their standards. To be sure, he was still anxious to gain wealth and prestige through his contacts with foreigners, but from his experience of shipping and trade he was learning what his concessions and services were worth to them.[55] At the same time, he had some idea of the dangers to his position attendant upon the development of a mixed community, while in all events, he was a proud man of forceful personality, one not easily awed into forgetting or abandoning what he conceived to be his own interests. Finally, the scarcity of good harbours in Samoa added to his bargaining power.[56]

Seen in this context, Pritchard's early difficulties assume another dimension. If Pritchard, like the S.F.O. people, had had friends, partisans or debtors among the Samoans at Apia Bay, his initial efforts to lease or purchase land there might have succeeded by dint of personal influence or local rivalries. Lacking them, he might still have acquired land at Apia on reasonable terms had he had a choice of ports at which to make his headquarters; for in spite of what has been said about him, the removal of the British consulate to another part of Samoa would have occasioned Pogai and his fellow chiefs an unwelcome loss of face. Pritchard *did* threaten to leave, no doubt hoping thereby to bring pressure on the Samoans as well as the Foreign Office; but according to his despatches, he meant, if he had gone, to quit the group altogether.[57] As it was, he remained without a show of doing otherwise; and once allowed to occupy land at Savalalo, he proceeded to develop

[53] Cazalis, *Rapport*, 17.

[54] Brookes, 175-6.

[55] Walpole, II, 387.

[56] But not in every circumstance. See chapter 10, below, concerning Saluafata's efforts to attract Europeans away from Apia Bay.

[57] e.g. FO, 58/38, Pritchard to Aberdeen, 31 December 1845.

N

it as a store-site, though the terms of rental were hardly more secure than might have been offered a beachcomber.[58] True, his initial outlay of capital was modest; but whatever it was, he laid himself open to exploitation by entering into commerce on such a basis, and so further compromised his position as consul. Pritchard anticipated as much, but in desperate haste to supplement his consular salary, he accepted the risks, only to appeal for outside help that he might escape the consequences of his decision.

Effective aid came to Pritchard through the agency of the Royal Navy, which fact he took as vindication of his complaint against the commander of the *Daphne*. In 1847, at Pritchard's urgent request, Captain Blake of H.M.S. *Juno* issued a written proclamation ordering the Samoans to show the British consul 'proper consideration and respect'.[59] In the following year, Captain Maxwell of H.M.S. *Dido* repeated the performance, with extra flourishes.[60] With this backing—essentially a show of force—Pritchard was released from some of the restrictions that had bound him. In particular, he was now able to buy land: a building-site at Mulivai and a tract outside the bay area. In turn, he invested more heavily in his business and, in anticipation of continued naval support, began to assert himself more confidently in his quest for power.[61] As will appear, he did achieve some influence, but scarcely of an order consistent with his past record.

It was after the outbreak of war in 1848 that the peace-loving, Protestant teetotallers of Apia village were put to their greatest defensive test. In one respect the war worked to their advantage, for with Mulinu'u virtually out of bounds to prospective settlers, Pogai's power to regulate European activity was enhanced. However, that activity was on the increase too. This was due partly to the trans-Pacific gold rush,[62] which stimulated certain forms of trade and facilitated migration to Samoa. It was also a consequence of Vaimauga's neutrality, which drew to Apia not only new arrivals but also Europeans forced out of areas affected by the war. Samoan laws and rulings in restraint of commerce were therefore bound to come under heavier attack—and all the more so considering that speculative pressures were growing more rapidly than the economy upon which existing forms of business were based. For obvious reasons, the liquor law was especially unpopular; but with the British and American consuls doubly committed to uphold it (as officials *and* church-members), there should have been a fair chance

---

[58] FO 58/59, Blake to Seymour, 30 March 1847.

[59] BCS 2/1, Blake to Samoan chiefs, 13 March 1847.

[60] Adm. 1/5590, Maxwell to Sec. Adm., 18 March 1848; Erskine, 71.

[61] After Pritchard moved to Mulivai, two of his sons came out from England to join him in business—in the firm of Pritchard and Sons (FO 58/60, W. T. Pritchard to Palmerston, 22 November 1847).

[62] Which gave Samoa a direct link with North America.

of preventing at least the open traffic in spirits at Apia. But the consuls were also merchants, and in the case of one, it was the pursuit of profit that prevailed. That one was Pritchard, the ex-missionary, who in 1850 imported the first cargo of spirits for the Apia port trade. In so defying the law he entirely destroyed its force, for in effect, he put the liquor business under his consular protection. When, in 1852, he brought in a second shipment, he was forthwith expelled from the London Missionary Society church, but such disciplinary action, however drastic as far as he was concerned, could not make Apia a 'dry' port again.[63]

Until about 1850 it was difficult to buy land at Apia suitable for commercial purposes. The position eased, however, when Toetagata and his people moved down from Moto'otua; for the effective control of the port was further divided, and Apia and Matautu villages, both well situated in respect of the anchorage, could be played off one against the other. Between them there was, in fact, a good deal of competition to attract prospective storekeepers and other 'wealthy' settlers. This, of course, entailed some conveyance of land and often the supplying of wives, two transactions which were frequently related, ties of marriage being a means of 'capturing' Europeans and also a channel through which negotiations for land might be conducted.

That is not to say that Pogai and Toetagata threw caution to the winds, but neither were they so strict as to avoid compromising their long-term interests. Foreigners of ostensible means now seldom experienced the insecurity of tenure of which Pritchard had complained some years before, while a few were able to purchase even more land than required for their own use. Although extremely limited in scale, this speculative accumulation of freehold, plus the occasional disposal of land by departing foreigners, gradually undermined the chiefs' power to control European settlement within their villages. Indicative of this trend was Pritchard's sale of his Mulivai land to the Marists, giving them a strategic site for the cathedral they planned to build. Executed in 1852, shortly after Pritchard's removal to a newly-purchased section at Matautu, this sale constituted yet another of his 'betrayals', for at the time there were no influential Samoan Catholics on that side of the bay and no other European landowner who might have supplied a foreshore block of sufficient size. Indeed, Pritchard claimed that it was really on account of the Mulivai land case, and not of his traffic in liquor, that he was excommunicated.[64]

It was in the 1850s, then, that Apia clearly emerged as Samoa's

[63] SSL, Mills, 12 October 1852.
[64] ibid., Mills, 12 October 1852, Hardie, 11 June 1853; MS., Darnand; Adm. 1/5672, Fremantle to Osborne, 12 December 1855. The sale of land to the Marists was made in the name of W. T. Pritchard, a son, but consul Pritchard acknowledged responsibility for it.

emporium. As the business community expanded, the predominant elements were, at first, British and American. At Matautu the leaders in trade were Pritchard, W. C. Turnbull and a branch of the Papeete firm of Hort Brothers, all British—and V. P. Chapin, an American. Their counterparts on the other side of the Vaisigano were the Americans John Sargent and Aaron Van Camp, both at Matafele—and on his return from Australia in 1855, John C. Williams. The Samoan branch of Godeffroy and Son, the Hamburg house that was to surpass them all, was established at Matafele in 1857.

Each side of the Vaisigano also acquired its grog shops, boarding houses, billiard parlours and bowling alleys—'amenities' supported largely by transient trade. In addition, blacksmiths, coopers, mechanics and auctioneers set up at Apia Bay, some independently and others as employees or associates of the mercantile houses. The medical profession was also represented, with two 'surgeons' in practice during the 1850s. And contrary to the hope expressed earlier by the London Missionary Society, there was a large proportion of unskilled labourers among the immigrants. In 1856, about seventy-five foreigners were in more or less permanent residence at Apia Bay, and in 1860, more than one hundred; and these were often outnumbered by visitors and castaways.[65]

Meanwhile, other Europeans acquired small tracts of land in the environs of Apia and began to raise produce for the provisions trade. Still others took up trading with the Samoans in the outer districts, wherever the course of the war permitted. The first village stores included several branches of Apia firms and a few serious independent enterprises, like Matthew Hunkin's at Leone;[66] but most of them represented the casual and often unremunerative efforts of beachcombers, trading with small, irregular consignments of goods supplied to them on credit. When the war ended, however, the number of permanent stores increased fairly rapidly, and by the late 1860s village trading was a firmly established feature of the economy in every part of the group.[67]

By the mid-1850s much of the vacant foreshore between Sogi and Matautu had been occupied, giving Apia—the 'town', not the Samoan

[65] Bull, 23; D'Ewes, *Pacific Islands*, 129, 164-5; Trood, 29-33, 48-53; USCD Apia/1, Van Camp to Marcy, 1 October 1855; USN, Pac. Sqd., Van Camp to Bailey, 26 September 1855, Foreign Residents of Apia to Bailey, 28 September 1855; Adm. 1/5672, Fremantle to Osborne, 12 December 1855; *Samoan Reporter*, March 1860.

[66] In 1855 one of Pritchard's sons was running a trading station and store on the south coast of Upolu. About the same time Van Camp had an agent, Elisha Hamilton, at Matautu in Savai'i (D'Ewes, 181; SSL, 15 December 1854).

[67] BCS, 4/1, W. T. Pritchard to To'oā, 28 November 1857; SSL, Murray, 6 January 1866; BCS 3/3, Williams, Trade Reports, 24 December 1870, 22 December 1871.

village—some continuity of length but as yet little depth. In appearance the settlement was of 'a most mixed character'. Indeed, the only regularity was to be found within the Samoan villages, where the traditional orientation of *malae* and buildings had been retained, along with the traditional architecture. In contrast, the Europeans had no overall plan as regards arrangement, while their dwellings and business premises varied from the crudest huts of cane and thatch to substantial buildings constructed of stone and imported lumber. Apia may have had 'quite a business look about it', but judged by most aesthetic standards, its rating was low.[68]

Lower still were many estimates of the state of society at Apia—particularly of the Beach, which comprised the European element (clergy excepted) and its various Polynesian dependants, mainly women, sailors and labourers. The missionaries, their dream of a pious, orderly, exclusive community shattered, were righteously severe in their judgement, but no less so were visiting naval officers, whom the ill-disciplined conduct of the 'people' offended. Owing largely to criticism from these two sources, Apia became known far and wide as a 'little Cairo', a 'hell of the Pacific', a 'St. Giles'. Few indeed of the foreign settlers and transients passed the test of puritanism or lived up to 'what England expects'. This was true even of those who 'knew better'—for example, the consuls, Williams included, who degraded themselves as 'representative[s] of Majesty' by trading in arms.[69] As for Pritchard, he turned the British consulate into a 'pot-house' and maintained premises 'unfit for a respectable Englishman to live in or for the English flag to fly in front of'.[70] One British naval commander, investigating some disputes among the merchants of Apia, was 'ashamed and disgusted to be involved in the exposure of so much falsehood and dishonesty', while the foreigners in general he considered the most 'unruly, disreputable community' imaginable.[71] Many of the European dwellings and shops were described as 'vile sinks of corruption', whose occupants and patrons were 'scoffers living in open licentiousness, and setting examples of immorality by gambling, drinking, and double-dealing in all shapes'.[72] The most violent critic of all was Commodore William Mervine of u.s.s. *Independence*, who disposed of the Beach in these terms:

> [In] Apia . . . I found a state of society existing that beggars all description; composed of a heterogeneous mass of the most immoral

[68] Bull, 23.
[69] Shipley, 23.
[70] SSL, Mills, 12 October 1852; Adm. 1/5617, Home to Stafford, 20 December 1852.
[71] Adm. 1/5672, Fremantle to Osborne, 15 November 1855.
[72] *loc. cit.*

and dissolute Foreigners that ever disgraced humanity, principally composed of Americans and Englishmen, several of whom had been Sidney [*sic*] convicts. Responsible to no law for their conduct—certainly none that the natives have the power or disposition to enforce against them—there exist anarchy, riot, debauchery which render life and property insecure. . . . Among the evils . . . are grog-shops kept by Englishmen and Americans, where are sold the most poisonous liquors; connected with these are obscene dance houses, very demoralizing in their character.[73]

For the part they played in this the Samoans were not so harshly judged, nor was the criticism so single-minded. True, they were supplying the dancing girls and were said to be giving women in exchange for muskets. But they were children of nature, easily misled. On the other hand, they were sometimes commended for shrewdness, as when they gained an advantage over the new storekeeper, a licentious fellow who got his 'wife' but then found to his chagrin that he had 'married the family'.[74] It was also true that some of the young men were going to work aboard foreign ships, 'floating dens of vice'. But was it not amusing to see them come back and 'strut about, very much to their discomfort, in trowsers, jacket and coat, shoes and socks'?[75] Yes, but out of greed the Samoans were becoming beggars and money-grubbers, cadging 'presents' from visitors and demanding unreasonable prices for their goods and labour.[76] Still, the eagerness with which they sought to entertain their foreign guests was flattering and (therefore) charming, even if they did expect rewards for their unsolicited hospitality. And while they were acquisitive, their use of foreign-made goods was often more ridiculous or pathetic than wicked. Imagine Pogai, a proud giant of a man and once a fearsome warrior, wearing

> . . . an old hat, that seems to stand off his round grizzled head; a light shooting-coat forced over his fat arms, the two buttons showing his shaggy breast and flappy belly; an old coverlet—one of those wraps which people say hide the dirt, and are certainly never supposed to cover the clean.[77]

When it came, however, to the *'ava papālagi,* the white man's kava, the Samoans preserved their dignity. Certainly, a few would drink spirits, especially if Europeans were paying, but the large majority acquired no taste for it. Indeed, they were offended by heavy drinking, or at any

[73] USN, Pac. Sqd., Mervine to Sec. of Navy, 30 June 1856. See also Bull, 28-9, and D'Ewes, 164-5, for similar comments.
[74] Bull, 29; Trood, 135.
[75] Walpole, II, 387.
[76] Bull, 24-5.
[77] Walpole, II, 387-8.

rate by its effects, which was more than one could say for most of Samoa's foreigners.[78]

In at least one conclusion, though, there was a good deal of agreement among observers. It was that the Samoans were at fault for the weakness of their political institutions—for the 'selfish and jealous feelings which they cherish[ed] towards each other' and which made them the victims of 'internal discord and external apprehensions'.[79] If they unwillingly succumbed to the pernicious designs of wicked whites, the blame rested partly upon them.

## Economic prospects

In his *Island Reminiscences*, published in 1912, Thomas Trood wondered why foreigners had wanted to settle in Samoa as early as the 1850s, when he had first seen the group.[80] He was not thinking of the fugitives or the aimless; nor, at the other extreme, was he inquiring into the motives of the Godeffroy management, for whom Samoa was then chiefly a convenient *entrepôt* in a growing network of Pacific enterprise. He was thinking, rather, of the 'independents' of commerce and the trades, men who deliberately chose Samoa as the place in which to invest their limited resources. The time was, of course, one of large-scale migration and fortune-hunting in many parts of the world, but what were Samoa's special attractions? Trood supposed that Europeans were captured by the 'easy life', which was no doubt true of many, including him. But, as he had asked himself, why did they go to Samoa in the first place?

It is not likely that the existing state of business in Samoa appealed to very many, for conditions were far from prosperous. This was due in part to the fact that the Samoans would not supply agricultural land in sufficient quantity for commercial plantations. Even if the land had been available, however, its improvement would have been discouraged by the hazards and uncertainties of the political situation.[81] There would also have been a labour problem, for scarcely any Samoan labour[82] was to be

---

[78] Bull, 24; Adm. 1/5672, Fremantle to Osborne, 12 October 1855; *Samoan Reporter*, February 1870; SSL, Pratt, 6 October 1869, Whitmee, 5 January 1872. The missionaries' first mention of a serious problem of drunkenness among Samoans was made early in the 1870s, and then mainly in respect of Apia. War, which was then in progress, was given as the main reason, the idea being that the people lapsed into all manner of bad habits when they left their villages to fight. Whatever the circumstances, however, the problem was short-lived, except among half-castes, of whom there were by then a substantial number of adult age.

[79] *Samoan Reporter*, January 1854; Adm. 1/5672, Fremantle to Osborne, 12 December 1855.

[80] Trood, 39.

[81] BCS 3/2, W. T. Pritchard to Malmesbury, 8 May 1858.

[82] Excluding domestic labour, of which there was a sufficient supply.

had except on a casual basis, and then at uneconomic rates of pay.[83]
For the time being, then, the settlers' economic prospects depended
largely upon Samoan export production, the sale of fresh provisions and
general merchandise to ships and their companies, and trade and other
speculative ventures in near-by islands.

The supply of Samoan produce, mainly coconut oil, was not very
dependable. In 1848, when the war commenced, the annual output of
oil for the local trade had reached one hundred tons—at a gross profit of
about £20 per ton, hardly a sound basis for much speculation. During
the war, production stayed 'up'. In fact, the combined domestic exports
of the various firms rose to about two hundred tons per annum in the
early 1850s, though local selling by the London Missionary Society
accounted for some, if not most, of the increase.[84] The continuation of
production was facilitated by the neutrality of some of the Samoans and
by the sporadic nature of the fighting. Also, contrary to later practice,
arms were not generally available on credit or in exchange for land,
owing to the reluctance of the Europeans in the first instance and of the
Samoans in the second. Merchants who participated in the arms trade,
as most did, were therefore able to sustain their volume of business,
subject only to the effects of competition. But would the Samoans have
made more oil if there had been no war—or, more to the point, would
their output increase rapidly once the war was over? The merchants
were inclined to think that it would, and for that reason, among others,
were anxious for an early peace settlement.[85]

But when peace was declared, quite belatedly, and regular village life
generally resumed, trade with the Samoans showed no marked improvement overall, even though the destructive effects of the war had
been concentrated in the early years and largely effaced by the mid-
1850s.[86] A major problem confronting the merchant was the limited

[83] Bull, 24. Samoans usually demanded the equivalent of the wage paid to Europeans
—except for domestic tasks, for which Europeans did not hire out. An unskilled
labourer was paid one dollar per day, a real wage greater than that paid many
islanders now. By 1865, however, Samoan wages had been driven to a lower
level, to about half the rates for Europeans.

[84] When possible, the L.M.S. sent its oil direct to an overseas market, thereby
cutting out the middleman in Apia. In 1847, for example, a shipment of ninety
tons went direct to England by the *John Williams* (Adm. 1/5590, Maxwell to
Sec. Adm., 18 March 1848). During the 1850s, however, the mission encountered shipping difficulties, losing two vessels in quick succession, and so was
forced to sell at least some of its oil locally. It was at this time that the switch
to cash contributions was begun.

[85] FO 58/65, Pritchard to Palmerston, 31 December 1849; USCD, Apia/1,
Swanston to Cass, 31 March 1857.

[86] A'ana, where most of the damage was done, was rehabilitated during the period
1851-3 (SSL, Turner, 26 April 1851).

range of the Samoans' trade requirements. They were not yet interested in expensive durables, such as imported lumber and gear for the building of schooners or houses, or large-volume consumables, such as imported foodstuffs; nor were they yet engaged in the high-pressure raising of funds for the London Missionary Society. Cottons and hardware accounted for the bulk of their demand, with trade for these goods increasing hardly more than enough to compensate for the decline of the arms traffic. Then, as well as being slight, the Samoan demand was also unstable. During the war, many of the people traded compulsively for arms, of which the belligerents were estimated to have three thousand 'stand' by 1853.[87] Moreover, there were always some Samoans under obligation to the missions to purchase clothing or piece-goods—and some, too, who were driven by considerations of rank and dignity to indulge in 'conspicuous consumption', though not of a very costly kind. Such demands were not, however, constant or frequently-recurring, so that at any given time, there were relatively few Samoans who simply *had* to accept whatever terms of trade were being offered. The merchant's scope for sharp practice was, of course, limited by fierce competition on the Beach and by the knowledge of arithmetic and the conceptions of value and 'fair dealing' which the Samoans were acquiring from the missionaries. He was similarly affected by the nature of the Samoan demand but, more than that, might also be the innocent victim of it; for any market fluctuation that worked to the Samoans' disadvantage could, whether it originated in London or Apia, radically curtail his rate of turnover. Indeed, the Samoans were quite capable of conducting a systematic boycott—of one store or all, according to the provocation.[88]

The port trade was not in a healthy state either. True, cargo and passenger vessels, some of them in trans-Pacific service, called fairly regularly throughout the 1850s, providing adequate links with foreign ports and bringing in retail business. Meanwhile, however, the whaler traffic was declining, with the final collapse setting in during the year 1856.[89] Since the whaling ships often remained in harbour for protracted periods—for repairs as well as for purposes of recreation and victualling —their departure from Samoa's sector of the Pacific deprived the

[87] HFO, Chapin to Wyllie, 9 June 1853.

[88] Adm. 1/5672, Fremantle to Osborne, 15 November 1855; USCD, Apia/1, Swanston to Cass, 31 March 1857.

[89] The traffic was at its peak in the mid-1840s. By the early 1850s it was halved, with some fifteen to twenty ships calling at Apia each year. Whaling vessels also used Pago Pago and Saluafata harbours, but there is no record of the numbers visiting there in the 1850s. After 1856, calls were few, mainly casual and brief; and after 1866 no whalers came to Samoa at all. The decline was due to a northward shift of whaling activity (BCS 3/2 and USCD, Apia/1-2, Trade Reports, *passim*).

merchants and tradesmen of a valuable source of income, and the Samoans of their chief market for provisions. This development probably contributed to, and certainly cancelled out much of the effect of, the increase in coconut oil production over the same period. It may be noted, in particular, that domestic exports of oil levelled off at three hundred tons per annum after 1856, just as the whaler trade gave out.[90]

The extension of operations to other island groups thus acquired, for the business community at Apia, a relative significance out of proportion to Samoa's potentialities. High on the list of itinerant enterprises was the search for pearl-shell, which offered the prospect of a quick fortune in the event of success and which, largely for that reason, was launched in an atmosphere of secrecy and intrigue. Another was the search for sandalwood, to which similar conditions pertained. Neither of these products was to be found in Samoa—nor, to any great extent, was bêche-de-mer, a less profitable item, but one much in demand for the China trade. Some bêche-de-mer was brought in, but with one notable exception, to be mentioned later, the other speculations seem to have failed.

Of quite a different order was the far-flung trade for coconut oil conducted from Apia, some of it on a purely itinerant basis, the rest through agencies in various islands. This trade accounted for at least half the oil exported from Apia during the 1850s but was still of insufficient volume to ensure the solvency of the general merchant. Again, a major problem was competition, particularly after the establishment of the Godeffroy branch at Apia. This Hamburg house, whose resources no other firm in Samoa could begin to match, was most aggressive in the inter-island trade and import-export business, to which it devoted a large and growing fleet of ships. Secondly, the conduct of itinerant and remote out-station trade was usually more hazardous than operations confined to the Samoan group, while capital and overhead costs, if not always higher, certainly added more to the outlay of the Apia-based merchant than he would have been occasioned by a comparable expansion of his domestic market. Considering, then, that little trade was available in any one field, the diversification of competing firms only increased the tendency towards their over-capitalization. While these conditions lasted, a substantial reserve was the only reliable guarantee of survival.

[90] USCD Apia/1, Swanston, Trade Report, 31 March 1857; BCS 3/2, Williams, Trade Reports, 1 January 1859, 31 December 1859, 1 January 1861. Since there were no customs duties and no official check on cargo except through the various consulates, Samoan trade reports are not very detailed and cannot be relied upon for accuracy. Taken together, however, they do give a general impression of the state of business which is sufficient for present purposes. Of the reports cited above, Swanston's offers the most valuable insights into the economic and allied problems of the 1850s.

Since most firms lacked this endowment, it is no wonder that several failed or were induced by imminent threat of failure to close down. Among these casualties were Pritchard and Sons and the Samoan branch of Hort Brothers.[91] It is more surprising that others no better equipped were prepared to fill the breach, to help maintain the pressure of competition and, in turn, to suffer the effects of it. This recalls Trood's question.

Obviously, those who invested in Samoa in the face of such grim reality must often have been gambling on the immediate future. What basis was there for thinking that prosperity might be 'just around the corner'? One suspects, for a start, that many of the leading settlers, like J. C. Williams and George Pritchard, were ambitious far beyond their means or hope of advancement at home—that theirs was the restless, filibustering spirit of middle-class builders of empire, theirs the urge to seek wealth, power, privilege and honour in a new world and perhaps, in the event of success there, to win greater recognition in the old. Given its latent resources, chiefly its surplus of arable land, Samoa was, in any case, a likely target for such ambitions; but given the exaggeration endemic to accounts of its potentialities, it acquired for the unwary the appearance of a target almost too large to miss.

At mid-century the news of a Samoan Eldorado was, at its source, the product of design as well as misjudgement and wishful thinking. One may consider, in this regard, the case of Charles St Julian, a Sydney court reporter, who during the 1850s held the unlikely office of 'His Hawaiian Majesty's Commissioner to the Independent States and Tribes of Polynesia'. St Julian had never seen *any* of the tropical islands of the Pacific, yet he was an acknowledged 'authority' on the internal affairs and prospects of them all, and of Samoa in particular. This reputation was built up partly by St Julian himself—by his assiduous collection of information from men who *had* been in the islands, and by the self-assurance and persistence with which he expressed his views, both verbally and in print.[92] But it derived mainly from the testimony of

91 Pritchard and Sons failed in 1855. Hort Brothers over-extended their Samoan operations and withdrew in 1862 to cut losses. Their interests were taken over by the firm of A. and C. MacFarland, which also experienced financial troubles. Sargent and Co. was yet another firm that had a precarious existence. Chapin and Van Camp disappeared from the scene in 1856—but, as shown in a later chapter, not because of insolvency. Williams returned to Samoa from Australia in 1855 and engaged in commerce until 1858, when he accepted the post of British consul on terms that forbade him to trade.

92 St Julian, *Latent resources of Polynesia* and *Official report*; HFO letters from St Julian to Wyllie (Hawaiian Foreign Minister), *passim*; MS., Horn. St Julian was an employee of the *Sydney Morning Herald*. He did not visit any of the islands until about 1870, when he went to Fiji. Afterwards he became a judge in the Levuka government.

influential parties in Sydney who, by gratifying his love of pomp and
his desire to mingle with the great, made him a front for their interests.
From their viewpoint, St Julian's chief function was to attack the political obstacles to commercial progress in the islands, to which end,
among others, the Hawaiian Government allowed St Julian the use of
its name. As will be shown, his proposals for Samoa, which he represented as a promising field for investment, were naive and highly mis-
leading. They were also still-born, though St Julian had the satisfaction
of having some of them received and commended by British naval and
colonial officials.[93]

One may also consider the fantastic claim repeatedly made by George
Pritchard to the effect that 'hundreds of thousands of acres of the most
fertile soil [were] lying waste' in Samoa, and that it was the opinion of
'persons well acquainted with these islands . . . that Upolu alone would
support Five Millions and leave plenty of land for the natives'.[94] An
account of his own financial difficulties would, of course, have been
more informative to persons not so 'well acquainted' with Samoa, yet it
was largely because of his insecurity that Pritchard was so irresponsible
in his estimate of the group's resources. This was a grand inducement, a
calculated effort to stir a lethargic Britain into annexing another 'West
Indies' and, in the process, to improve the fortunes of its consul there.
There is even some suggestion that Pritchard envisaged himself as
colonial governor,[95] whereas if he achieved anything at all, it was to
enlarge his troubles by encouraging European immigration.

Also tending to misguide prospective settlers were the many accounts
of mission activity which exaggerated the advance of Christianity in
Samoa. For as John Williams's view of the civilizing process was widely
accepted, even among Europeans who opposed certain mission practices,
such reports suggested the existence or early promise of commercial
opportunities which were, in fact, remote. Some of this misinformation
was spread by visitors who had misjudged what they saw or accepted
uncritically what they were told. One such observer was Wilkes, whose
influential *Narrative*, though inconsistent in some details, generally overrated the London Missionary Society achievement. But more of the fault
belonged to the missionaries themselves. Their object was not, of course,
to encourage indiscriminate immigration but, rather, to express their
faith in their work and to give a good account of it, both for their own

[93] On a few minor points his advice was heeded by the British Foreign Office, e.g.
on the appointment of consuls to Samoa, Fiji, etc. (FO 58/86, Memo by T. B.
Alston, 7 May 1857).

[94] BCS 3/1, Pritchard to Granville, 1 January 1852. Pritchard made similar statements on other occasions.

[95] *loc. cit.*

satisfaction and for that of their overseas connections. Their estimates of the number of their adherents, their reports of educational progress, their selection of events to record, their interpretation of those events and their intimations of the future—all, more often than not, tended towards the brighter side, especially in the early years of mission activity in Samoa.[96] This emphasis was most pronounced in the books they wrote and in the public addresses they delivered when on leave, while their published letters, though more frank in the original, were carefully edited to conform to similar standards of optimism.

Finally, one may consider the tendency of many Europeans, not only missionaries, to over-estimate their own ability to influence the Samoans. There was more to this than faith in God, the concept of white supremacy, or the flattering illusions prompted by Samoan hospitality and etiquette. Equally important was the inspiration of events in Pacific islands longer-settled by Europeans—of the knowledge of this advice or that example to which Hawaiians, Tahitians, Tongans or Mangaians had seemed highly susceptible. That Williams had entrusted the *lotu taiti* to the care of Malietoa, that Wilkes had presupposed the enforcement of his commercial regulations, that Pritchard had anticipated a position of influence among the chiefs was, in each instance, due partly to projection upon the Samoans of the apparent reactions of other Polynesians. Such, too, was the case when Europeans sought a political formula for conditions essential to commercial progress.

[96] As noted in Bull, 33-4; Pembroke and Kingsley, 308; Walpole, II, 388; USCD, Apia/1, Swanston to Cass, 31 March 1857.

# 8

## PROSPERITY AND THE POLITICAL ORDER

ON THE political side, where it bogged down, the quest for Eldorado had as minimum objectives the destruction of organized Samoan resistance to foreign economic penetration, and the preservation of peace and order, that life and property might be secure and the Samoans freer to develop the 'civilized' tastes and habits conducive to the growth of industry and trade. The business community would have been even better pleased if government had offered more positive inducements to enterprise—if, for example, the development of plentiful supplies of cheap land and labour and the improvement of internal communications and other facilities had also become aims of public policy.

Commercial settlers saw Samoa, as they found it, verging upon a state of 'anarchy'—that is, a state in which neither the form nor the conduct of government was consonant with the above objectives. One of their proposed solutions to this problem was that Samoa should follow the course taken by Hawaii. This would have entailed the creation of a centralized kingdom—centralized because the unification of the group was considered essential to the conduct of external relations as well as to the maintenance of internal order, and a kingdom because monarchy, apart from being 'naturally' suited to Polynesians and traditional with many settlers, represented a form of entrenched and concentrated authority through which Europeans might hope to exert influence generally upon the Samoan people. If the ascendant party could have established a firm grip on the reins of power, a form of serfdom might have been developed among the Samoans. On the Beach (to pursue the Hawaiian example) a greater degree of personal freedom would have pertained, but there, too, power would have been concentrated in the hands of a few, including wealthier entrepreneurs and consuls. The policies of the central government, affecting the interests of both communities, would have been determined jointly by the leaders of both. There would, no doubt, have been some power conflict between races, but if the Samoan rulers had responded like the Hawaiians to the blandishments of Western civilization, the focus of their interests and aspirations would have shifted away from the indigenous society, while inter-marriage might have contributed further to the merging of *élites* into a ruling class. If, at the same time, the policies of the government had been directed towards the large-scale expansion of private economic enterprise, the foundations of village life would probably have been destroyed in some areas and many Samoans drawn into a multi-racial community organized largely along Western lines.

If they were to set Samoa on the above course, Europeans had obviously to sell their proposals to Samoans able to do something about them, and to lend practical assistance towards implementing them—assistance which Samoans would value and might even regard as indispensable to the objects in view. Thus, one might think that Europeans bent on achieving centralized and stable government, and on establishing their own right to participate in government, would have taken account of the principles of chieftainship and Mālō, and have made it part of their plan to help extend and preserve the power of ambitious Samoan leaders. This course, building up one chief or party at the expense of others, was taken often enough in Polynesia in the early nineteenth century for Europeans in Samoa to be quite familiar with it. When it came to the question of taking it themselves, however, they were put at a disadvantage by the fact that Samoa's traditional political cycle was out of phase with the development of foreign interests and influence in the group. In the early 1830s the Mālō had had a margin of power which commercial settlers of a later period might have tried to enlarge and consolidate, with a view to entrenching that party in office as the Samoan element of a 'general government', at least in the western islands. The chance of success, of lasting success in particular, would perhaps have been small, but the experiment would not have been very dangerous, owing to the weakness of the Vaivai. Instead, the missionaries, the first influential Europeans to acquire a permanent interest in Samoa, had worked in the opposite direction, not only discouraging all violence, but insisting upon the early rehabilitation of the Vaivai. The latter measure put an untimely end to the Mālō's power advantage, while the death of Vai'inupō removed its established figurehead. By the mid-1840s, when the requirements of commerce were no longer satisfied by the port regulations, the Samoan political situation had so far deteriorated that any attempt at general reform was inconceivable unless preceded by war. Hoping to avert war and still achieve some political progress, consuls and traders, like the missionaries, tried to encourage the Samoans to establish independent governments on a district or island basis; but as already shown, the effort did not turn the Samoans' attention from the issues of Mālō and Tafa'ifā. Soon, Europeans would have to accept that war was, in any case, virtually inevitable. How were the would-be ministers and privy councillors of the Beach to react to that revelation? Would they determine to take sides in the struggle, trying to promote the unification of Samoa under a new

Mālō? In the event of their favouring that course, would they be able to agree, between the contending parties, to support but one of them?

What they did was to shrink from war in reality as in prospect, foregoing the opportunity to turn the conflict, once upon them, to a political advantage. Some shared the missionaries' moral viewpoint on the question, but it was more generally a fear that paralysed political action—fear of being burned out or killed by hostile warriors.[1] Thinking, quite rightly at the time, that the danger to their lives and property would be increased by their partisan activity, the foreign settlers—at least those around Apia—resolved as a body to show themselves neutral in deed if not in sentiment. It is possible that they might still have acted surreptitiously to control the supply of arms or ammunition to the advantage of one side, but they were too apprehensive of reprisals to do even that.[2] Besides, there were the day's profits to worry about. If they had just let matters stand at that, leaving the Samoans free to get on with the fighting, they might still have helped themselves. But no, a war whose objects were traditionally Samoan and whose course was directed by Samoans was 'futile' as well as hazardous and so, in the general interests of progress, had to be stopped. Europeans thus presumed to act as mediators and peacemakers, in which roles missionaries and settlers were joined by naval officers. By their interference, however, they only helped to prolong the conflict and prevent the conclusive settlement of the issues that had occasioned it. For all concerned, then, the war was indeed futile.

Aloof from the give and take of party politics, Europeans still demanded concessions and reforms, as if by right. A common feature of this indiscriminate approach was an undue emphasis upon alien and abstruse principles, constituting an attack upon Samoan institutions then closed to exploitation. In other respects, as in that one, there were resemblances to mission preaching. Thus, the names of foreign monarchs, statesmen and other high authorities were intimately invoked. Respectable visitors, especially naval officers, were pressed into giving testimony and guest lectures. And a form of salvation was offered, which in this instance was a place among the lesser nations recognized by the Powers. A few Samoans may have sympathized with this line of argument, but in general there was no reaction except, perhaps, to anger over some of the points that got across. One may imagine, for example, how 'The Chiefs of Samoa' took the following remarks addressed to them by Pritchard:

> Laws . . . must apply to all persons of all classes, not to the common people only. . . . It is not for a few chiefs to make laws for the

---

[1] cf. chapter 10, below.
[2] USCD, Apia/1, Pritchard and Chapin to 'the authorities of Lufilufi and Leulumoega', January 1854.

common people. The laws must be enacted by the consent of the people at large.[3]

The rest of this statement, proposing trial by jury, with foreigners to comprise *half* the jurymen,[4] probably contributed no more to Pritchard's popularity among the Samoans.

In 1849, after much fruitless exposition of such themes, Pritchard begged the foreign minister of Hawaii, an Englishman, to bring his government's wise counsel to bear upon the Samoans. The result was a 'friendly letter' ghost-written in the name of Kamehameha III and purporting to advise his 'brothers' of the superiority of a society in which peace reigned and all persons were equal before the law. 'I myself obey them', said the king of his laws, '[and so do] all who live in my Islands'.[5] By having good laws and by keeping the peace, Hawaiians had won the respect of the Powers and were facilitating the work of foreigners dedicated to their spiritual and material well-being. Samoans, too, could taste the fruits of progress, and at little or no cost to themselves, if they would only examine the latest constitution and statutes of Hawaii—copies enclosed—and proceed in peace to establish a like order in their own islands. If the choice of a king proved a subject of controversy, let district representatives meet and elect one, and let other outstanding issues be settled in similar fashion. In other words, let Samoa be unified from the bottom up, by voluntary negotiation, not from the top down, by force of arms, as Hawaii had been.

This advice was even more hypocritical than that which Pritchard, the ex-chamberlain of Pomare, offered in a less fraternal guise. How false the claim of equality before the law when judged, for example, by the terms and results of the land reform only recently carried out in Hawaii. Granting chiefs, nobles and crown alienable titles to most of the better land, dispossessing many 'commoners' of their customary rights and holdings, and thus clearing the way for the emergence of large plantation estates, it was more characteristic of the system being recommended to the Samoans. Not that it mattered, but the 'Kamehameha' letter was never sent, owing to the reluctance of the king and most of his councillors to meddle in Samoa's affairs.[6] However, its substance was later communicated through another medium, as will appear shortly.

3 FO 58/38, Pritchard to 'The Chiefs of Samoa', 12 August 1845.
4 Without distinction as to the nature of the case or the identity of the parties involved. Concerning issues between Samoans and Europeans, the suggestion would have been reasonable.
5 HFO, Minutes of Hawaiian Privy Council, 2 May 1853, with draft of letter from Kamehameha III to the 'ruling chiefs' of Samoa, dated 13 March 1849; HFO, Wyllie to St Julian, 17 September 1857.
6 *loc. cit.*

O

Meanwhile, leading figures on the Beach, assisted by various overseas connections, were exploring the prospects of imperial rule for an alternative road to peace and prosperity. This activity differed from that aimed at domestic reform in having no intentional support from the London Missionary Society and resembled it in having none from the Samoans either. Since it was largely British-oriented, however, it was in practice strengthened by London Missionary Society and Samoan opinion, thanks to the existence of a common 'enemy', France. For if Britain could have been persuaded to give Samoa the sort of protection which the mission and various chiefs requested, it would almost certainly have gone beyond that to assume some measure of control over the group's internal affairs. Actually, the antagonism towards France died down on the Beach after the collapse of the Le Havre mercantile society, the S.F.O.; and in view of the progress of non-French enterprise in Tahiti, and of the stagnation besetting business in Samoa, intervention by France would have been regarded by some as a positive blessing. True, a strong British preference persisted, and occasionally the French spectre provoked a chorus of cries for protection.[7] One suspects, however, that denizens of the Beach were responsible for some of the haunting— that the lingering fears of the Protestant missionaries and of many of the Samoans were deliberately exploited to build up the demand for British intervention. If so, the effort was wasted, for neither Britain nor any other Power answered the 'call to duty' from Samoa.

So unresponsive were the Powers that none would even give its official backing to efforts being made towards the reconstitution of government in Samoa. The desire to avoid formal commitments was, on this occasion, reinforced by a suspicion of the motives and scruples of some of the foreigners who might have benefited from measures being urged upon the Samoans. But, of course, there was no monopoly of the facilities to advise and sponsor, and so it was, when all else failed, that the Hawaiian Government, a more sympathetic body of officials, came into the picture again. Subjected to importunate requests from St Julian and others, who represented Hawaii as a nation for which Polynesians generally had enormous respect, that government agreed to appoint special agents to promote the political advancement of islands neglected by the greater Powers. Naturally, this decision had some reference to Hawaiian interests, too. Dreams of territorial expansion were probably involved, but if so, only remotely. Hawaii's immediate national interest in the Pacific was more in the line of defence, that its own independence might be better secured by helping other territories establish claims to similar status, either separately or in league with itself. St

[7] e.g. HFO, St Julian to Wyllie, 7 August 1854; Adm. 1/5672, Fremantle to Osborne, 12 December 1855.

Julian's proposals laid particular stress upon the latter consideration, and also upon humanitarianism, upon Hawaii's moral obligation to share with others the secrets of its progress, as the draft of the 1849 letter had set out to do.[8] More mundane, and quite outside St Julian's field of interest, was the desire of Hawaii's commercial proprietors to alleviate, by way of immigration, an acute shortage of labour, a condition aggravated by the decline of the indigenous population. Rather more exalted again was the corollary of this proposition, which captured the enthusiasm of the king (then Kamehameha IV). It was that the Hawaiians should be given a new lease on life, a 'stiffening of the blood', by means of intermarriage with other peoples of their own race.[9] To become civilized and to remain free, do as Hawaii does; and to be sure of doing it well, spend some time in Hawaii, as long as you like—that, ideally, was to have been the approach to the Samoans.

Obviously, the immigration scheme did not square with the objectives of the filibusterers and visionaries who had been trying to bring order to Samoa, but they had no cause to worry about it, for the Hawaiian Government, being too impecunious to pay its overseas representatives, had to rely upon such as they for free and hence largely undisciplined 'service'. Besides, even if the Samoans had been exposed to such early Hawaiian tourist propaganda, which it appears they were not, it is unlikely that many would have responded. Thus, apart from routine consular business, of which there was very little, the only function of Hawaii's agents for Samoa was to pursue their private interests under the cover of an official establishment.

Hawaiian diplomacy in Samoa issued mainly from the Sydney office of St Julian, Commissioner to Polynesia, who reported frequently to Honolulu but seldom received specific instructions from there—or, for that matter, *any* instructions. As farcical as its tenuous legality was the failure of this diplomacy to move the Samoans, the people towards whom it was directed. The only reason for mentioning it, then, is that reputedly knowledgeable and hardheaded men considered it better to have the Hawaiian label on their intrigues than no government label at all. It is true that St Julian, at the hub of this activity, gave it a fanciful gloss, the product of his idealism, inexperience, and love of formality; but he had around him, feeding him facts and impressions, correcting or confirming his basic assumptions, and acting as his agents, men whose interests were highly practical. One of these was J. C. Williams, then commonly regarded as the leading authority on Samoa and the Samoans.

St Julian produced his first constitutional plan for Samoa in 1854,

8 MS., Horn; HFO, St Julian to Wyllie, 7 November 1854 and 11 May 1855.
9 HFO, Wyllie to Chapin, 28 July 1855, Chapin to Wyllie, 24 November 1855.

the year he was appointed Commissioner.[10] Then, as in the 1840s, there was no likely 'monarch' nor any prospect of one's early appearance. Moreover, political conditions were still too unsettled to warrant expectations of immediate reform throughout the group. Facing these obstacles, St Julian proposed, for the interim, the establishment of an independent and representative 'republic of Upolu', the island in which foreigners were most interested. The idea was to appeal to the good sense of the neutrals and 'non-aggressors' (that is, the Atua-A'ana war party), who had been said to predominate among the Samoans of Upolu, and get them to set an example which other islands might follow in due course. It is not clear what was to have been done about the war, though as it was then in the doldrums, St Julian may have thought that a peace settlement was in the offing or that his exciting scheme would divert the Samoans from their hostilities. Looking farther ahead, he readily envisaged the day when the new island governments would confederate and appoint a king to found a Samoan dynasty. This 'union of petty states' would be 'a sort of Lilliputian resuscitation of the Old German Empire, upon which a more perfect system [would] be slowly grafted'. Meanwhile, Samoa would have assumed a place among nations.[11] In effect, then, St Julian's plan was simply an elaboration of the 'Kamehameha' letter of 1849.

To put his ideas direct to the Samoans St Julian commissioned, as his attaché, one Harry De Boos, a British subject and former ship's surgeon, who was heading for Samoa to settle.[12] The arrival of this dignitary in Samoa precipitated a jurisdictional crisis on the Beach, owing to the presence there of a Hawaiian commercial agent with credentials straight from Honolulu.[13] This dilemma, also 'Lilliputian' in character, was amicably and quite properly resolved by a division of diplomatic and consular functions, but all to no purpose, for De Boos could make no impression whatever upon the Samoans. On hearing of this, St Julian protested that he had always thought the Samoans too jealous of one another to consider the 'general good', too immature to accept sound proposals conventionally argued, even when they bore the Hawaiian cachet.[14] A new approach was required—not a different objective, for the existing one was best suited to Polynesians, but some special means of get-

---

[10] St Julian, *Official Report*, 73-5.

[11] HFO, St Julian to Wyllie, 11 May 1855.

[12] HFO, St Julian to Wyllie, 6 November 1854. De Boos was often referred to as 'Doctor', a distinction to which he apparently had no right.

[13] This was Virginius Chapin, who was also United States commercial agent in Samoa. cf. chapter 10, below. Chapin was residing in Honolulu when he received his American commission and, before leaving for Samoa, solicited the Hawaiian appointment (HFO, Chapin to Wyllie, 20 November 1854).

[14] HFO, St Julian to Wyllie, 11 May 1855.

ting the singularly backward Samoans headed in the right direction. Addressing himself to this problem, St Julian, with the help of others, turned up several new ideas, two of which may be examined here for the credulity or desperate perseverance, or both, of those responsible for them.

The first related to St Julian's interest in Tonga, whose king, George Tupou, he had met in Sydney in 1853. Engaged then in unofficial diplomacy, St Julian had advised Tupou on various matters of state and, on being appointed Commissioner, had hastened to pursue the contact on a formal basis, sending De Boos to Tonga as visiting attaché and exchanging correspondence with Tupou. His immediate aim was to drive a wedge between the ruling chiefs and the Wesleyan mission, to make room for 'Hawaiian' influence in Polynesia's 'second-ranking' kingdom. Given this, St Julian proposed to bring Hawaii and Tonga together as the first partners in an extensive Polynesian union, another and larger 'resuscitation of the Old German Empire'. Within this confederation the various kingdoms were to have been largely self-governing, the chief purpose of their association being to forestall the imposition of European imperial rule where internal order could be maintained without it. St Julian idealized this prospective arrangement, seeing in it a logical consistency and beauty of form; but, of course, it was also designed to satisfy the more practical interests of the politicians on the Beaches of the Pacific.

Deceived by Tupou's civility and by optimistic reports from the islands, St Julian actually thought that Tonga was moving into his orbit of influence.[15] So, on considering that the Tongan rulers were highly respected in Samoa and that their ancestors were said to have held sway there in ages past, it occurred to him that Tonga, acting on Hawaii's advice, might help to organize the Samoans and keep them on the right track. In this way Samoa might become a Polynesian kingdom of the 'third rank' and the third member of the projected confederation.[16] This proposal was not wholly unsound, for the Tongans were quite capable of intervening in Samoa's affairs. That was known at the time, and it was probably on that ground that St Julian's efforts were encouraged by Europeans acquainted with the islands. It was absurd, however, to think of the Tongans' submitting to *any* sort of Hawaiian influence or, regardless of that, of their achieving anything in Samoa of satisfaction to St Julian without the substantial use of force, which he hoped to avoid. As for St Julian's personal standing in Tonga, it may be noted that King George and the missionaries, whose confidence he claimed, later opposed his application for the post of British consul there.[17]

15 HFO, St Julian to Wyllie, 1 March 1855.
16 HFO, St Julian to Wyllie, 7 November 1854, 11 May 1855.
17 FO, 58/89, Rabone to Malmesbury, 4 May 1858.

St Julian's hope for Samoa's future did not fade when the Tongan
rulers proved 'slow' to respond, for meanwhile there was suggested to
him a fresh approach, one even more reminiscent of the court intrigues
of Europe. The year was 1856; the inspiring occasion, the failure of the
Samoans to make headway in their negotiation of peace terms. From
somewhere St Julian learned that, with the war's having been a stand-
off, the Samoans were unable to agree on how to dispose of their highest
honours, the 'royal' titles and the distinction of being Mālō.[18] He understood that dignity and ceremonial considerations were at stake, not the
power to govern—that it was a question of neither party's being prepared voluntarily to lose face to the other. What was to be done in a
case of this kind, when it seemed that mere pride stood in the way of
co-operation towards peace and progress? Obviously, one could not do
away with royalty, and besides, one needed a symbol of sovereignty and
nationhood. Neither could one force a settlement upon the Samoans, for
as yet, no foreign government was prepared to intervene to that extent.
But in a deadlock, reasoned St Julian, friendly mediation might be
successful. So, propose to the two parties that they declare themselves
equal and appoint a neutral outsider to be king of Samoa. Surely, if
they were as anxious for peace as they maintained, they would acquiesce
in this plan to preserve honour on both sides and to remove from their
forward path the objects of their jealousies. Who should be the Samoans'
chosen monarch? Kamehameha IV, of course; and his successors in
Hawaii should also occupy the Samoan throne, thereby solving Samoa's
dynastic problem. For their part, the Samoans should retain full rights
to control their internal affairs and have partnership rights in the confederation which St Julian once again saw emerging in the Pacific.[19]

St Julian's surviving despatches do not reveal the identity of the other
parties to the above conspiracy, and considering his usual discretion in
matters of a 'delicate' nature, he may never have forwarded such information. It is very likely, however, that J. C. Williams was in charge at the
Samoan end. He was, in any case, Hawaii's official representative there
from late 1856,[20] and not long before then St Julian had described him
as the most able and co-operative associate he had in respect of Samoan
affairs.[21] The two of them were certainly engaged in other joint activities, one of which was a move, supported by Pogai and Toetagata, to
oust Pritchard from the British consulship in Samoa and to have

[18] Before this he had proposed that Taimalelagi be chosen king (HFO, St Julian
to Chapin, 25 April 1856).
[19] HFO, St Julian to Wyllie, 25 April 1857.
[20] After Chapin's departure.
[21] HFO, St Julian to Wyllie, 11 May 1855.

Williams appointed in his place.[22] Of Samoans who might have been involved in the kingship scheme there is no direct mention either. The despatches say only that St Julian had been advised from Samoa that a formal offer might be arranged.

The intrigue hinged, first, upon having an advance undertaking from Kamehameha to accept the kingship of Samoa if invited to do so. Had this agreement been forthcoming, St Julian would probably have acted on a longstanding desire to remove his headquarters to Samoa, into the centre of his district of 'jurisdiction'. The Hawaiian Government, however, then itself insecure, refused to entertain any measure suggestive of out-and-out imperialism, which, reasonably ignoring the qualifications, it took St Julian's proposal to be.[23] Thus, another grandiose scheme came to nothing. Of course, it is difficult to imagine its ever advancing very far anyway. Surely, no representative Samoan offer would have been made to Kamehameha when, for example, petitions to Queen Victoria, conceding less and asking much more, were hard enough to get from part of a district or island or from one of several political factions; while anything less than a representative decision would probably have been the cause of fresh trouble. Besides—and this is the main point—if it *had* been possible to secure a genuine, widely-supported offer of Samoa's 'royal' titles, political conditions in Samoa would not have been such as to have prompted the idea of seeking one.

After this reversal, confirmed in 1857 by Hawaii's final 'no', St Julian faded out of the Samoan picture, his confidence in his Hawaiian commission undermined and his diplomacy outmoded, in any case, by developments in Samoa. Most important, in the latter regard, was the Samoans' abandonment of the war, which opened the way to freer and sometimes friendlier communication between them and the spokesmen for foreign interests. Timely changes of personnel, notably the retirement of consul Pritchard in favour of the more influential Williams, plus the cumulative impact of naval intervention, also inclined many Samoans to take more serious heed of European demands for political concessions. In the absence of a Tafa'ifā or established Mālō there was still no scope for experiment in central government; but now, at least, it was easier than before to negotiate local, piecemeal reforms. This change represented, for the leading settlers, an improvement sufficient to take the edge off their dissatisfaction and to encourage a more reasoned and practical approach to political subjects. Before pursuing this turn of events, however, it will be necessary to go back and see what actually happened during the intervening years.

22 FO 58/86, Memo by T. B. Alston, 7 May 1857.
23 HFO, Wyllie to St Julian, 17 September 1857.

# 9

## NAVAL JUSTICE

*On the protection of Europeans and the call for naval intervention*

FROM THE 1840s until the late 1860s, relations between Europeans and Samoans were less violent than they had been earlier, during the free-booting convict period, or than they were to become later, when grave differences arose over land and politics. But while 'outrages' were then comparatively few, conditions were still such that even the pettiest issues and grievances, of which there were many, were taken most seriously. This was due, among other things, to shortened perspective, conflicting views of equity and justice and, on the part of Europeans, a keen sense of vulnerability.

As commercial settlement proceeded, the Samoans, for their part, substantially altered their conception of the benefits of contact with foreigners but not their standards of propriety as regards the behaviour of foreigners nor their methods of upholding those standards. Thus, a merchant or tradesman, like a beachcomber, was liable to be beaten, to be subjected to ridicule or insult, or to have his property confiscated or destroyed if, for example, he offended the dignity of a chief, trespassed on Samoan land, quarrelled over women, broke the Sabbath, cheated on his obligations to supply services or goods, introduced divisive influences into the village at which he lived, or otherwise upset the tenor of domestic or village life or overtly threatened the integrity of Samoan institutions. Depending on the nature and circumstances of the case, he might be dealt with summarily by aggrieved parties resorting to self-help, or condemned by a village council and punished by its order. Either way, the personal consequences for him were likely to be the same, except that a village council might, as an alternative penalty, subject him to ostracism, ruling that he be shunned or boycotted if not actually driven away. In practice, then, Samoan justice, partaking largely of vengeance, might affect him in the same manner as if he had been the innocent victim of assault or theft. This was especially true at Apia Bay, whence Samoan visitors were attracted in such numbers by shipping and trade that the local chiefs, regardless of their desire to preserve order, could give the settlers there but little protection against unprovoked attack by strangers or satisfaction in the event of it.

These circumstances did not basically alter the missionaries' attitude towards Samoan sovereignty, except to enhance their concern for the independence of the group; for their sanctity was usually inviolate. However, the view prevailing on the Beach, even among those who experienced little trouble themselves, was that the Samoans had no right of unilateral jurisdiction over foreigners and that, in one way or another, their exercise of initiative must be limited accordingly. If they would not restrain themselves, as proposed in connection with reform projects already mentioned, they would have to be coerced—to be shown, as one of the consuls put it, that the white man was 'taboo'.[1] Needless to say, this view tended to ignore or obscure the Europeans' provocation of the Samoans. Indeed, it was demanded that all Samoans in any way connected with injuring a white man should be treated as criminals regardless of what he had done to them. The Samoans, as customers, in-laws, protectors and neighbours, were to allow Europeans all manner of benefits and privileges while being denied their usual means of safeguarding their own interests.

Failing the institution of more grandiose measures, the leading commercial settlers envisaged, first, the establishment of a government for and by Europeans. As will be shown, some progress could be made in this direction, at any rate at Apia Bay, not least because many of the affairs of the business community, which needed regulating anyway, were beyond the competence and interest of the Samoans. Next, differences between Europeans and Samoans, if resistant to amicable adjustment by the parties concerned, were to be resolved by negotiation between consuls and chiefs, with agreed terms of settlement being enforced on a segregated basis, by foreigners against foreigners, by Samoans against Samoans. Thirdly, all who for any reason refused to submit to negotiation or, having submitted, to facilitate the final settlement of grievances were to be dealt with by the Powers through the medium of naval intervention, by which deterrents might be raised to all classes of 'crime' and local processes of negotiation gradually perfected.

It was the wish of the consuls that this makeshift system of justice should have a legal basis, consisting of magisterial authority for themselves in respect of the nationalities they represented, and of formal extra-territorial rights and immunities for Europeans in Samoa. Foreign governments, however, though intervening in relations between their subjects and Samoans, generally chose to exercise power without responsibility—that is, without acknowledging any local authority but that of the chiefs. Thus, for example, British consuls were refused extra-terri-

---

[1] USCD, Apia/1, Swanston to Marcy, 31 January 1857. Also, ibid., Chapin and G. Pritchard to 'the authorities of Lufilufi and Leulumoega', January 1854; Adm. 1/5672, Fremantle to Osborne, 15 November 1855; BCS 4/1, W. T. Pritchard to To'oā, 28 November 1857.

torial powers on the ostensible ground that none could be granted them except by right of treaty concession.[2] There existed no treaty with Samoa and, until the 1870s, no effort was made to negotiate any. American consuls were left in a similar position, even after 1860, when Congress passed legislation enabling consular officers in primitive or unsettled regions to be given, without sanction of treaty, the authority of justices of the peace with jurisdiction over American citizens. Until the 1870s, the State Department, like the Foreign Office, evaded commitment—on the one hand, that of formally recognizing Samoa as a sovereign nation and, on the other, that of defining the group as a place wherein it was obliged to perform regular duties of government.[3]

In a rather different situation from that of his colleagues was the consul for Hamburg and, later, the North German Confederation, who was allowed to function as a magistrate but had no naval support.[4] An exception of another kind was Britain's unilateral extension of the jurisdiction of certain colonial courts to permit the apprehension and trial of British subjects for kidnapping and other grave misdeeds committed in the Pacific islands. This jurisdiction, which in Samoa had no American counterpart, was not very effective, owing to procedural and other faults; but in any case, it was intended mainly to protect peoples more subject to abusive treatment than were the Samoans.[5] Far more important in Samoan affairs generally were the informal police and judicial functions performed by naval officers of the several Powers, who acted without claiming sovereign rights or assuming a state of war. In some respects this intervention was more effective for being informal, but the same condition, among others, also made it more easily manipulated by foreign residents than the Powers may have intended or even suspected. At any rate, naval power was utilized in a manner that enabled Europeans to gain an increasing measure of influence over the Samoans, first in the settlement of disputes and claims and, subsequently, in the introduction of political reforms.

### Naval intervention and the consuls

From the early 1840s on, Samoa was visited fairly often by warships. These vessels were, until the formation of the German Empire, almost exclusively representative of Britain and the United States, which also maintained regular consular establishments in Samoa, and of France,

[2] BCS, 1/1. Russell to Williams, 28 September 1864.

[3] USCI/10, F. W. Seward to Coe, 11 February and 23 March 1867.

[4] BCS 3/3, Williams to Clarendon, 5 January 1869.

[5] But it may have had some admonitory value in Samoa, as British naval officers commonly referred to it when lecturing British subjects on their conduct (e.g. Erskine, 96-7).

which did not.[6] Of the three navies, Britain's was for many years the most active in Samoa, with calls averaging about one per annum.[7] Emulating the Powers, Tonga also sent an armed schooner occasionally, assuming jurisdiction over Tongans residing in Samoa, whether or not they were assimilated.[8]

Some of these ships came in response to urgent requests or to make special surveys, and a few more made emergency stops for supplies or repairs; but the majority came on routine patrol, that their commanders might 'show the flag' and, if conditions were found to require it, to intervene in the interests of peace and order. Stop-overs were usually brief—a few days to a fortnight, seldom longer. However, warships came without warning and at any time, even during the so-called hurricane season; and it was not unknown for one to double back and put in a second appearance soon after its first. In police work as in war, surprise was part of the naval officer's stock-in-trade.

Few commanders arrived in Samoa without being met by a chorus of complaints and special pleading, mostly from Europeans. And while many of the reported grievances must have seemed trivial in themselves, and even more so in proportion to the effort required to fathom the interests and relationships of the parties concerned, most commanders tried to dispose of issues referred to them, lest their failure to act should open the way to further and more serious troubles. Over the years they dealt with hundreds of cases, most of which they had to tackle without set rules of procedure or specific instructions from their superiors.[9] Their methods of arriving at terms of settlement or punishment included arbitration, mediation, trials, public lectures, threats, and the display and outright use of force. The terms, at least in so far as they set them, were also varied, though running mainly to the heavy-handed. One of the

6 A Prussian warship, the *Eugen*, called in 1869, the only one prior to the unification of Germany (BCS 3/3, Williams, Trade Report, 1 January 1870).

7 But a regular annual routine was not established until about 1865.

8 BCS 4/1, Swanston and W. T. Pritchard to King George Tupou, 3 February 1857.

9 The informality and haphazardness of British naval intervention in the islands were subject to a good deal of criticism, notably by Sir George Grey, the Governor of New Zealand. Grey proposed the appointment and instruction of a single naval commander to act as roving commissioner—'to pursue one uniform and consistent line of policy, and to neglect no opportunity of attaching the natives to British interests, or of promoting their welfare by his advice and assistance in the adjustment of their internal affairs, by recommending the formation of courts suited to their present state of civilization, and for the adjustment of disputes between themselves and Europeans, by acting as mediator for the prevention of their now frequent wars, and by other similar measures'. Grey's scheme was favoured by Palmerston, but the Admiralty was not willing to assume the responsibility (FO 58/65, Sir George Grey to Earl Grey, 7 October 1848, Ward to Addington, 12 March 1849).

more subtly contrived exceptions to the latter rule was the punishment of the offender who was 'decorated with a thief's cap, with [the Samoan word for thief] painted upon it and marched . . . through the town, with a file of Marines, and music playing the rogue's march'.[10]

If they wished, naval commanders could always cite grounds or pretexts for interfering in Samoa. For example, they could act, as it were, at the instance of chiefs, missionaries or consuls to uphold 'local laws' or the 'principles of humanity and justice'. Or they could claim that the Wilkes code gave them the right to intervene, not only in the specific case of murder, but in regard to the protection which that instrument ostensibly guaranteed both foreigners and Samoans. Or, again, they could refer to metropolitan laws, such as the British legislation previously mentioned. Just the same, naval intervention in a police or judicial capacity was usually extra-legal at best, so that it behoved a commander to avoid, if he could, the raising of protests. Perhaps the most effective safeguards against embarrassment on that count were the islands' remoteness and the circumstances of their inhabitants. The Samoans, ignorant of Western law and usage, would never have thought of resisting or protesting on legal grounds, while Europeans, if their own antecedents were dubious, would hardly have thought it discreet to resist at all. Furthermore, the political state of the islands disposed foreigners to accept and even welcome naval intervention, whether legal or not. But if they ignored all else, naval officers still had to consider the views and reactions of missionaries and consuls, at least of their own nationality, for these parties had ready means of gaining the attention of foreign governments. Of the two, the consuls were, in this context, the more influential.

As the local representatives of their governments, the consuls served as intermediaries between naval commanders and the residents of Samoa.[11] Few complaints came to the bar of naval justice except through the consulates; few cases were investigated without one or another of the consuls being present; and few decisions were taken without their having given information and advice. Having no official police or magisterial powers, the consuls could not dictate the course of justice; but as interpreters and witnesses and, in effect, as bailiffs, recorders and general stage-managers, they could substantially influence it, while assuring themselves that the navy could be blamed for any adverse consequences. In this regard it was also to their advantage that most naval commanders were loath to openly disagree with them, lest the foreign governments and their representatives become objects of ridicule.

[10] USN, Pac. Sqd., Bailey (u.s.s. *St Marys*) to Mervine, 1 October 1855.
[11] Consuls who were acquainted with the Samoan language also served as interpreters.

It was of the utmost importance, then, that the consuls not only generally favoured European causes against the Samoans, but also were very often personally involved in the issues brought up for settlement. Naval officers who objected to this bias put it down mainly to financial motives, most consuls being engaged in private business undertakings which identified them with the Beach in matters causing much of the friction between Europeans and Samoans. Convinced that this was the case, the British Foreign Office decided that Williams, who succeeded Pritchard in Samoa, should not be allowed to trade.[12] Yet if a consul was a permanent or long-term resident in the islands, his business, which supplemented his income and through which he was vulnerable, actually implied some check to the grossest abuse of his official position. Certainly, it was no accident that among the most notoriously irresponsible officials to serve in Samoa, there was a predominance of carpet-baggers, which the American system of political patronage occasionally turned out,[13] and (in the late nineteenth century) of career men whose judgement, unrestrained by fear of economic insecurity, was carried away by patriotism and the urge to political power. Still, the early prevalence of merchant-consuls did work to the overall disadvantage of the Samoans, in that naval commanders, however disposed to carry out their duties, were guided or restricted in action by men who shared the frustrations and commitments of the business community.

That the consuls played a key part in the practice of naval justice, which was in turn an indispensable means of keeping order, tended to enhance their influence among Europeans, largely because of the services they could perform, and among the Samoans because of the coercive power they could conjure up. That is, they were in a position to exercise 'gun-boat diplomacy', especially in their relations with the Samoans. In resorting to this tactic, however, they were well advised to be circum-

12 But through family ties he was still involved in the fortunes of two mercantile firms at Apia, one managed by a son and another by a son-in-law. Williams was also a planter, and in the early 1870s he acted as a land-purchasing agent for a real estate syndicate.

13 Owing to this system of appointment, the tenure of office was insecure. Moreover, the salary was, until the late 1870s, too small to attract and hold able men from overseas or to make the post of American consul a satisfactory full-time job. The State Department did not intend that its early representatives in Samoa should have to trade, but they were not prohibited from doing so. Until 1879 the German consuls were also the Godeffroy managers. After that, they were usually career officers sent from overseas, as were most British consuls. The American post was normally filled by political appointees. Towards the end of the century, however, the standard improved considerably, for the office was upgraded to the rank of consul-general and thereafter attracted more experienced men. At about the same time that Germany changed over to career officers, the United States also introduced the ban on private trading.

spect, for the informality of naval justice, plus the fact that the same commanding officer seldom visited Samoa more than once or twice, made it virtually impossible to know in advance just how individual issues would be settled. To promise retribution in very severe or specific terms was to risk 'crying wolf' or being contradicted by ensuing events.

No consul, prior to the 1870s, misused the threat of force more than George Pritchard, who had not only the commitments and outlook of the merchant, but a keen political ambition which the Samoans would not gratify. Accustomed to being taken seriously—'at Tahiti I had power and extensive influence, but here', he complained, 'it is utterly impossible to possess either'—Pritchard seems for a time to have lost his head in an orgy of vindictiveness. On the subject of naval intervention, among others, he became an extremist, determined that 'the last measure of severity' should be exacted for every complaint brought against Samoans.[14]

Some of the cases reported by Pritchard were so trivial that naval officers were occasionally reluctant to act upon them at all. One commander, asked to proceed to Leulumoega to find and punish a Samoan who had stolen a pig, flatly refused on the ground that the Royal Navy had more pressing engagements.[15] Another officer was inclined to the same view when asked to punish an act of 'indecent exposure' at which Pritchard's wife had taken offence, but to avoid a scene he went through the motions of hearing the case.[16] More unjust were Pritchard's claims against Samoans who, in line with their custom, killed the horses and cattle which he and other Europeans permitted to run free, despoiling gardens and taro patches. Several cases of this sort were actually decided against the Samoan defendants,[17] but in 1852, Sir Everard Home (H.M.S. *Calliope*) dismissed a number of them with the recommendation that pastures be fenced. In a private aside to Pritchard, Home added that 'by kind treatment and conciliatory manners shown to the natives . . . there will be no longer any repetition of the acts complained of'.[18] To be lectured on how to 'handle the natives' was perhaps even more of a rebuff for Pritchard than to have the villains, against whom he had promised harsh measures, go scot free.

Pritchard came to worse grief over a so-called act of piracy perpetrated in 1854 at Manono against the *Crescent*, a British-owned and Apia-based schooner that was engaged in the local arms trade. Underlying that event was the fact that Pritchard's firm had previously violated

[14] FO 58/59, Blake to Seymour, 30 March 1847. He sometimes levied 'fines' against the Samoans which he expected naval officers to collect.
[15] BCS 2/1, Maxwell to Pritchard, 4 February 1848.
[16] FO 58/57, Pritchard to Palmerston, 17 April 1847.
[17] Walpole, II, 363-4.
[18] Adm. 1/5617, Home to Stafford, 20 December 1852.

an undertaking to supply two cannons to the Manono war party. The relevant order had been placed against advance payment in full, with the firm promising, for its part, to deliver the goods to the island of Manono. The cannons had, indeed, been imported, but on the way from Apia—perhaps by whaleboat through the A'ana lagoon—they had been confiscated by members of the other war party. According to the terms of contract, the firm was now obliged to replace the cannons or refund payment. Pritchard refused to do either, however, citing in justification the immunity of neutrals from making restitution for the seizure of contraband, which principle he promptly 'established' *post hoc* by public declaration. In doing this, he also abandoned whatever claim he might have had against the A'ana side. When the opportunity arose, then, the aggrieved people of Manono detained the *Crescent*, which was or had been carrying arms to their enemies. No doubt such retaliation seemed to them perfectly just, but of course, they were charged with piracy and, though they soon released the vessel, were told that a warship would still come to deal with them. To be sure, a warship (H.M.S. *Juno*) did come, and its commanding officer, Captain S. Fremantle, did undertake to settle the case. In spite of Pritchard's efforts at concealment, however, Fremantle uncovered the whole story and let the Samoans off with a warning, a remitted fine and a small levy to cover actual material damages. Fremantle was unforgiving only in his attitude towards Pritchard, whose conduct in this and other matters he thought had had a disastrous effect upon British influence in Samoa. He recommended, therefore, that a new consul be appointed, and that that person should be independent of commerce and of the Pritchard family. Fremantle's report figured largely in the Foreign Office's early resolution to release or retire Pritchard, which decision the consul may well have anticipated, perhaps by courtesy of his superiors, for he resigned shortly thereafter.[19]

When Fremantle said that Pritchard had compromised British influence, he was thinking not only of the consul's personal unpopularity but also of the open incongruity between his threats, made prior to the arrival of warships, and the relative moderation which several commanders had felt bound in justice to observe. On the other hand, not many of the complaints brought against Samoans were dismissed altogether or decided in their net favour. In that respect the outcome of the *Crescent* case, however unfortunate for Pritchard, was still more typical of naval justice than was the disposition of the horse- and cattle-killing charges referred to Sir Everard Home. That is to say, even if the terms were not always as onerous as had been promised, the Samoans usually had to pay something for their alleged offences, once arraigned

[19] Adm. 1/5672, Fremantle to Osborne, 15 November 1855; FO 58/84B, Morshead to Bruce, 23 November 1855; FO 58/86, Memo by T. B. Alston, 7 May 1857.

for them. 'What, are you going to fine us again?' asked an orator at Savalalo of a commander whose 'leniency', according to Pritchard, positively invited disorder. 'If that is so', the Samoan added, 'we shall have to leave here and go elsewhere to live.'[20] When it came to discrepancies between words and deeds, the greater or, at any rate, the more consistent contrast related rather to the control of Europeans. Now it was the naval officers contradicting themselves, using hostile or threatening language but, owing to certain jurisdictional blockages, seldom taking decisive action. This is another fact which may help to explain why the Samoans seldom submitted *their* complaints to the court of naval justice, though repeatedly enjoined to do so.

With regard to Europeans, one weakness of naval jurisdiction was implied in differences of nationality. The power of a British commander, for example, was generally limited to cases between Samoans and British subjects or between British subjects alone, and to issues defended by British subjects against European plaintiffs of other nationalities. In practice, these limits were most often exceeded in the prosecution of complaints against Samoans, who, being in no position to precipitate diplomatic crises or even to claim formal national status, did not have to acknowledge naval jurisdiction in order to be subject to it. Provided he had consular support and some urgent cause to intervene, a commander might act against Samoans on behalf of *any* foreign national. But in dealing with Europeans he had to be more careful, exceeding the normal limits of his jurisdiction only with the consent of the parties directly concerned. This meant that aside from cases involving British defendants, the British officer was not likely to come between nationalities except in the following situations: (1) when, as a respected and disinterested outsider, he was asked to mediate in civil disputes; and (2) when foreigners without consuls in Samoa accepted his jurisdiction as a condition of having and retaining British protection. The main problem was, then, that a European would hardly submit voluntarily to an investigation which he thought might go against him. To solve this problem by means of naval intervention, the several Powers would have had to send warships to Samoa coincidentally, as some commanders actually suggested they should. However, this course was not adopted until the emergence of 'international rivalry' in Samoa, when the occasion for it was quite different.[21]

If their reports are any indication, many naval commanders were prepared, within the limits of their jurisdiction, to act against Europeans,

---

[20] FO 58/59, Blake to Seymour, 30 March 1847.

[21] But as shown in the next chapter, an 'international' system of justice was developed locally which supplemented and gradually took over some of the police and judicial functions performed by naval officers.

particularly to clear up grievances harboured by the Samoans. Certainly, many expressed the desirability of curbing the 'anarchy' of the foreign community and of demonstrating to the chiefs the 'correct' processes of justice to be adopted in the governing of Europeans. This, of course, was the position taken by Bethune and Wilkes. In 1849 Captain J. E. Erskine (H.M.S. *Havannah*) followed suit when he advocated the formation of a Samoan central government of Upolu and warned British residents that they could be deported or removed from Samoa for offences committed there.[22] During the 1850s the liquor traffic caused a good deal of anxiety among naval officers, and on several occasions attempts were made to 'clean up' the Beach. In 1856 Fremantle was ready to support a campaign against grog, but when he failed to secure the revival or re-enactment of the defunct prohibition law, he let the issue drop.[23] In the same year, Commodore William Mervine, commandant of the United States squadron in the Pacific, was content to act upon the old law, imprisoning several American saloon-keepers aboard his vessel (U.S.S. *Independence*) and apparently taking one or two away with him.[24]

When claiming or exercising jurisdiction over their fellow nationals, naval commanders often referred to the Samoan chiefs as *de facto* sovereigns in whose behalf they presumed to act. However, it was still through the consulates that they learned 'officially' of complaints against Europeans, and as a rule, they required the active support of the consuls in order to hear such cases. Even with that support, their hands were tied unless the consuls, who were outside their jurisdiction, were themselves innocent of the kinds of misbehaviour with which other foreigners were charged. Assuming, for example, that the arms trade had been the subject of complaint, how could anything have been done to limit it when the consuls, 'who talked very well, were retailing musquets, powder, and shot to both parties'?[25] To take a less hypothetical case, how, considering Pritchard's involvement in the *Crescent* affair, could a British commander have then disciplined other traders accused of sharp practices? With regard to the liquor trade there was a similar problem, which partly accounts for Sir Everard Home's anger at seeing the British consulate turned into a 'pot-house'.[26] Since trading activities in general, and the liquor business in particular, were the principal origins of trouble among Europeans and between them and Samoans—at

[22] Erskine, 80, 94-7.

[23] USCD, Apia/1, Jenkins to Marcy, 18 August 1856.

[24] USN Pac. Sqd., Seumanutafa and Toetagata to Mervine, 19 April 1856, Mervine to Seumanutafa, 21 April 1856.

[25] Shipley, 23.

[26] Commodore Mervine's enforcement of the liquor law occurred soon after the American consular representative at Apia had given up dealing in spirits.

P

least at Apia—the dedication of most consuls to those pursuits assured
the Beach a considerable degree of immunity from naval jurisdiction,
which in turn aggravated relations between foreigners and Samoans.
Caught up in this dilemma, naval officers could do little more than issue
warnings to Europeans and write critical reports of their behaviour and
mode of life.

## Naval intervention among the Samoans

Before the 1870s, the conduct of police and judicial inquiries was
generally free of the conscious political bias which made nonsense of
later pretensions to instruct the Samoans in Western law and justice.
The right of naval officers to intervene was then more widely acknowledged by the Samoans; the problems and disputes which they had to
investigate were less complicated; and the justice which they meted out
was more impersonal and, for the most part, fairer to all concerned.
That is not to say that they acted consistently, one with another, or that
they always understood or were correctly informed regarding the issues
at stake, but at least their actions were not compromised by the involvement of foreign residents and foreign governments in Samoan politics.[27]

As mentioned, the commonest complaint, by far, was one raised by a
European against a Samoan. The identity of the alleged culprit was
generally known or could easily be ascertained. Before the arrival of a
warship, one or more of the consuls would probably have tried to
negotiate a settlement, only to be repulsed altogether or to have some
disagreement arise over the cause of the complaint or the extent of the
losses entailed. When a naval commander took up the case, action would,
as a rule, be initiated at the village level—in the village where the
reported offence had occurred or where the alleged offender was living.
Normally, a conference would first be held between naval and consular
officers on the one hand and the higher-ranking chiefs (if aboard ship)
or full village council on the other, with the complainant and sometimes
the accused being present. If the case was an important one, all the
consuls might be in attendance, thus demonstrating the solidarity of the
foreign residents. When conducted ashore, this meeting would open
with the kava ritual, during which the guests would be seated and
served in order of rank or esteem, naval commander taking precedence
over consuls. In the ensuing discussion, differences might be reconciled
simply through the airing of views and through explanation of mis-
understandings; but if the case required that guilt be established and
an indemnity paid or stolen property returned, discussion and debate
might not suffice. In that event, a naval court might be formed, with a

27 Aube, *Entre deux campagnes*, 179.

panel of officers to take evidence and pass solemn judgment. If the charge was proved against the defending party, then, regardless of provocation, some form of punishment would be ordered. In the usual case —one of theft, restraint or petty assault—this would constitute some payment of goods or cash, which high-ranking chiefs among the offender's connections would be held responsible for raising. If the amount was small, immediate payment in full would be demanded. Otherwise, the Samoans would probably be told, under threat of a heavier penalty, to make payment to the appropriate consul within some stated period, either a definite time or 'before the arrival of the next warship'. In the interim, some of their fine mats or a prized canoe might be held as security.

There were, of course, many variations of procedure. Some of these were dictated by circumstances on the Samoan side, as for example, when a case concerned more than one village—of which more will be said shortly. One of the major variations arising from the European side related to the assessment and distribution of indemnities or fines. Most often it was the injured party alone who benefited, in conformity with the notion of torts or private delicts; and when a settlement *was* exacted on behalf of the 'public' interest, the proceeds usually went towards meeting consular expenses, as if a foreign government or head of state had been the prosecutor in a criminal suit. But as Apia progressed as a commercial centre, a few naval commanders came to recognize the need for 'public' revenue to finance various works and took account of it in the levying and distribution of fines.[28]

A common feature of the above proceedings was the visiting commander's address on the duty of foreigners to keep the peace and of Samoans to act like civilized, Christian people. Of those statements which were recorded verbatim, one of Sir Everard Home's illustrates as well as any the admonitory approach taken to the latter subject.

> Ships of War visit these Islands to see that he [the consul] is respected and that English subjects as well as the natives are not ill-used. . . . The chiefs should keep the people of their tribes in such control as to prevent them from robbing or ill-treating the Foreigners who live upon their Islands; this they will do as Chiefs and as Christians, but if they have not the power or the disposition they cannot be treated as such but as heathens and savages and be made to pay for the damage they have allowed to be done. It is the Chiefs who will be answerable for the faults of the persons under them. . . . The desire of the Queen of England is to be friendly to and to be of use to the people of Samoa and it is on this account that the chiefs have been advised to act pro-

[28] USN, Pac. Sqd., Bailey to Mervine, 1 October 1855; Adm. 1/5672, Fremantle to Osborne, 15 November 1855.

210     SAMOA 1830 TO 1900

perly towards strangers, for there is no desire to injure them, which
will never be done unless repeated acts of violence render it necessary,
when as you have been assured before, the destruction of a whole
village may be the consequence.[29]

As for admonition, it may be noted, too, that some commanders dispensed with the ceremonious and circuitous routine of the Samoan *fono*
in favour of the more direct and frightening procedure of meeting aboard
ship—and perhaps also foregoing the naval court in favour of a summary
judgment and demand or ultimatum. But whatever was said, and however investigations were conducted, the threat of force was still present,
as the Samoans, with their growing knowledge and experience of naval
power, came to realize. Part of their experience was gained from witness-
ing 'shore exercises' or 'field days', a thinly-disguised yet, to the Samoans,
an entertaining form of intimidation. At Apia and Pago Pago, particularly, it became standard practice for the marines to be paraded and
mock battles to be held. These demonstrations were regarded as war
dances and, after being staged a few times, became so popular that the
Samoans felt slighted if a ship left without putting on its show.
Hundreds, sometimes thousands, of people turned out to watch, to be
awe-struck by the sight, sound and effect of cannonades. In this regard
it was important that the Samoans, though divided among many factions
and many small villages, spoke a common language, visited one another
frequently, and congregated in large numbers on special occasions. In
Samoa, unlike the Solomons or the New Hebrides, no one could long
remain ignorant of the potentialities of naval might.

The Samoans had also to learn through being the victims of naval
power. Extreme punitive action was not often taken, yet it was not long
before the Samoans had good reason to believe that any commander
might use force to arrest and punish those whom he accused or, if
thwarted in those objectives, to destroy houses and canoes by way of
reprisal. The Samoans might escape the first by fleeing to the bush, but
as a coastal people they were always vulnerable to the second. This fact,
which may even have discouraged 'crime', disposed them to adjust
their differences with Europeans in a peaceable manner, if not at the
instance of the consuls, then certainly in the presence of naval officers.
However, not every case raised simple alternatives, such as the choice
between delivering a few pigs and having a village destroyed by fire.
Had the issues always been as straightforward, the first few punitive
raids might have been the last. But occasionally the Samoans were told
they must do something which they could scarcely do, either because it
was physically difficult or because it entailed a risk of internal strife or

[29] Adm. 1/5672, Home to 'Chiefs of Samoa', September 1852.

an intolerable loss of face. Some crises of this order could have been avoided without sacrificing any principle of justice. For example, a commander or a naval court, acting on bad advice or following some ignorant whim, might choose, from among all the forms of settlement which would have suited Europeans, one least acceptable to the Samoans. Or the Samoans might be given too little time to meet an otherwise just and reasonable demand. However, as some exceptional examples will show, other crises were brought on simply because the minimum requirements of Western justice conflicted with Samoan beliefs, customs and commitments.

## Some examples of naval justice

It will be recalled that in 1839, at Apia, Wilkes and some fellow officers tried and passed sentence of exile upon a young Samoan who had killed an American sailor but that shortly afterward Popotunu eluded capture. The latter event, according to J. C. Williams, allowed many Samoans to gather the impression that naval officers lacked either the will or the means to enforce judgment against an unco-operative people.[30] Perhaps that impression was strengthened in some quarters in 1841, when Captain Hudson, Wilkes's next in command, made another unsuccessful attempt to get Popotunu, this time by trying to take as hostages a number of prominent chiefs, among them Malietoa himself.[31] On this occasion, too, Hudson's 'secret' plans were anticipated, with results similar to those at Palauli two years before. Meanwhile, however, he had bombarded and burned three villages at Saluafata Bay, where the local chiefs had refused to surrender yet another murderer.[32] Notwithstanding Popotunu's escape, then, some Samoans must have realized already that the killing of a foreigner might have drastic consequences. That, indeed, was the issue raised in 1847 when a party of Vaimauga people, recruited by Williams and sent into the bush to capture some American deserters, was resisted by its prey at the cost of one sailor's life. The death was reported as accidental, but before the killer—an untitled young man—was finally absolved from blame, he begged Williams to take his life, lest his village be destroyed by a warship.[33] Some Europeans, though they may have regretted that a Samoan

30 USCD, Apia/1, Williams to Upshur, 26 December 1843.
31 So much for Wilkes's later assurances regarding the efficacy of his commercial regulations.
32 USN, WE, Stuart's Journal for February 1841; Wilkes, V, 25-6, 31-3, 507-12.
33 USCD, Apia/1, Williams to Buchanan, 4 June 1847 (with enclosures). In the following year Captain Maxwell of H.M.S. *Dido* reported that Hudson's attack at Saluafata had created among Samoans a general fear and mistrust of naval officers (Adm. 1/5590, Maxwell to Sec. Adm., 18 March 1848).

should ever be pardoned for killing a foreigner, felt that the people were learning a valuable lesson—that whatever their own ideas about justice and guilt, they were at least finding it better to surrender the accused than to suffer mass reprisals.

Quite a different situation arose in 1851 when an American sailor was killed in a drunken brawl at Apia. This time the offenders were foreign seamen, a Portuguese and a Tongan, the first of whom was taken prisoner on the spot, while the second got away and took refuge in Savai'i. Who was to be charged with the Tongan's escape and apprehension? Captain G. A. Magruder of u.s.s. *St Marys*, which by chance called within a month of the event, held Pogai responsible on both counts, on grounds of his being the principal chief at Apia and a signatory to the Wilkes code. Pogai protested, arguing that he was neither a chief of Savai'i nor the ruler of the foreign community; but Magruder insisted, none the less, that a party be mustered to search for the accused and, to enforce his demand, took Pogai, Molī Malietoa,[34] and the leading Wesleyan teacher, a Tongan, as hostages aboard his vessel. Some Samoans of Vaimauga did, in fact, go to Savai'i but returned empty-handed, after which the hostages were released. Magruder, however, required the chiefs at Apia to sign a new agreement by which they undertook once more to adhere to the Wilkes code in matters relating to the killing of foreigners.[35] He then issued a statement to 'the chiefs and people of the Samoan Islands' telling them how such cases would be dealt with in future. A village which failed for *any* reason to deliver *any* person charged with killing an American within its boundaries would, said Magruder, be destroyed or have its chiefs 'carried away as captives'; any village harbouring such an offender would be destroyed; and no customary form of asylum would be acknowledged.[36]

The terms of Magruder's pronouncement, though far more severe than the course he took in his abortive search for the Tongan killer, were still moderate in intent, for it was his desire that, if possible, the Samoan people should not be fired upon. In the following year, 1852, Sir Everard Home made, for Britain, a rather similar statement on the subject of reprisals and intimidation.[37] But how was this policy, with its hopeful concession to humanity, to work out in practice? This question was answered by a British officer, Commander Vernon of h.m.s. *Cordelia*,

---

[34] Who lived at Apia after the outbreak of war.

[35] *Samoan Reporter*, July 1851. The Tongan was captured in 1857 and handed over to Matekitoga Tupou, the commander of a Tongan war vessel and a member of the royal family (BCS 4/1, Swanston and W. T. Pritchard to King George Tupou, 3 February 1857; USCD, Apia/1, Swanston to Marcy, 17 February 1857).

[36] BCS 2/1, Magruder, notice to Samoans, 5 July 1851.

[37] Adm. 1/5672, Home to 'Chiefs of Samoa', September 1852.

who came in 1858 to arrest and try a Samoan for the murder of a British trader, the only European reported to have been intentionally and maliciously killed by a Samoan during the period 1841-76. In this case, the prosecuting officer had instructions to adopt the most humane measures consistent with the success of his mission. With regard for these orders, and for advice received from the British consul in Samoa, he acted in close accord with the declarations made by Magruder and Home; and when the case was concluded, he was said to have 'won the respect and love of the people by his gentleness and firmness'.[38] After reviewing the known facts of the case, however, one may wonder what the Samoans really thought.[39]

William Fox had his store at Sala'ilua, a village in the Fa'atoafe section of Itu-o-Fafine, Savai'i. This was in a part of that island which, after Popotunu's death in 1852, attracted a relatively large number of foreigners, no doubt because it was little affected by the war and possibly because it had the advantage for some of being remote from Apia. Fox seems to have been one of the first European residents in the area, if not *the* first, to take up trading on a regular basis; and for that stage of Samoa's development, he had a fairly prosperous business, serving not only Sala'ilua, but also villages on either side.[40] Since Sala'ilua was near the western boundary of Fa'atoafe, his customers from the east were of that side. But on the west his trade extended into the Salega (Alataua) section of Itu-o-Fafine, crossing a boundary between people who, on the one hand (Fa'atoafe), looked to Palauli as a political and ceremonial centre and, on the other (Salega), to Satupa'itea. Palauli and Satupa'itea were, of course, the two sides of the Falelua, the rival *pule* centres of Itu-o-Fafine. This division was an important feature of the present case.

Late in 1856 Fox was shot dead at his store by one Sailusi, a young man of Sagone, a village in Salega. According to report, Fox had provoked Sailusi by accusing him of theft. In turn, the murder provoked the Sala'ilua people, for through it they suffered the indignity of having a man whom they protected cut down within their village, while losing their trader into the bargain. Sagone therefore offered its *ifoga* but was turned away and, had it not been for the timely intervention of the nearest London Missionary Society teacher, might have been attacked forthwith. Subsequently, however, the *'aumaga* of Sala'ilua evened the score by ambushing and killing a Sagone chief who had had nothing to do with Fox's murder.

38 BCS 3/2, Williams to Loring, 22 November 1858.
39 cf. chapter 11, below, concerning threats made against Williams during the *faitasiga* war, which broke out in 1869.
40 The Sala'ilua reef passage was the safest in south-west Savai'i.

When the consuls—W. T. Pritchard and R. S. Swanston, acting for
Britain and the United States respectively—arrived on the scene to
investigate, the Samoans were in a state of excitement, the issue being
whether Sagone would take the offensive or agree with Sala'ilua and
the mission that one round of vengeance was quite enough. Into this
situation the consuls intruded the obvious demand: they had to have
Sailusi, not the life of an innocent pawn taken in the customary Samoan
fashion. Either Sagone had to give up the killer, or Sala'ilua had to go
after him. But Sailusi was not a common man, as the killer in Williams's
Vaimauga police party had been and as it now occurred to the Samoans
to think that Fox had been. He was a 'young chief'—probably a *manaia*
—of Sa Lilomaiava, one of the two outstanding *ali'i* families[41] represented in his village, and Sagone would never surrender him. Indeed,
echoed Sala'ilua, the ambushed chief had also been of higher rank
among Samoans than Fox had been among Europeans, and so Britain
should be more than satisfied. Besides, if fighting broke out between
the two villages, it would spread throughout Itu-o-Fafine and thence to
all Savai'i, and on to encompass the whole of western Samoa, which was
only just emerging from a prolonged period of warfare. Very well, said
Pritchard, but when the island trembled with earthquake and the
mountains were rent and the people tottered and fell to the ground,
Samoa would know that Britain herself had come for Sailusi.

Owing to a delay in the assignment of vessels to the Australian Station,
nearly two years passed before a British warship came in answer to
Pritchard's urgent call.[42] Meanwhile, the Samoans concerned in the Fox
case may have concluded that Britain was weak or irresolute; for when
the *Cordelia* arrived, Vernon, together with J. C. Williams, then British
consul, found Sala'ilua less inclined than ever to act and Sagone unwilling even to discuss the case, much less surrender Sailusi. Not wishing to
send his marines into armed conflict with Samoans—that would have
been to endanger the former and mistreat the latter—Vernon bombarded
Sagone and retired, the people of that village having taken to the bush.
The *Cordelia* then proceeded to Fa'asaleleaga, where at Williams's suggestion it was planned to contact Taimalelagi, the Tupu o Salafai, and
require him to get Sailusi from the Falelua or Salega. However, Taimalelagi was gravely ill, and before negotiations with him could be carried
through, he died. Vernon turned next to Molī, who was in line to succeed
Taimalelagi, and demanded, rather prematurely in terms of the title-
bestowals, that he secure the murderer. For some reason, not revealed

---

[41] The other was Sa Moeleoi. The leading chief of the Sagone branch of Sa
    Lilomaiava was Leilua. In early accounts, *manaia* and *taupou* were often described
    as young chiefs and young chieftainesses.

[42] BCS 1/1, Loring to W. T. Pritchard, 31 July 1857.

in the reports but perhaps related to Molī's experience with Magruder,[43] the chiefs of Safotulafai and Sapapali'i took Vernon's representations to mean that their *pule* was at stake—that they were in danger of falling under Britain's domination if they did not achieve what was demanded of them. They did, at any rate, approach the Falelua, only to be met with contempt and accused of trying to curry the favour of England at the expense of others. To add injury to insult, Vernon then judged Molī guilty of 'trifling and delaying', for which he penalized him ten fine mats and $500 in goods or cash.

The centre of action now shifted back to Itu-o-Fafine, where Palauli, head of the Mālō of that district, was to be turned against Satupa'itea and Salega. Offended when Fa'asaleleaga had interfered in the business of Itu-o-Fafine, Palauli, once appealed to direct, boldly promised to deliver the culprit. However, its efforts to make good the promise encountered Satupa'itea's resistance, meaning that the question of hostilities was raised yet a third time. Apparently too afraid or too proud to back down altogether, Palauli then proposed to draw Sailusi into an ambush, at which point Williams advised Vernon that the chiefs were temporizing, just as Molī had done. Since that could not be tolerated, Vernon destroyed Palauli's forty houses, its large war canoe and, by accident, one of its chapels. Subsequently, the whole of Fa'atoafe, including Sala'ilua, was promised the same treatment unless Satupa'itea and Salega were made to submit; and for protecting a criminal Satupa'itea was itself bombarded.

Vernon went back to Fa'asaleleaga to collect part of the fine imposed upon Molī and to compel him and his supporters in that district to intervene once more. Possibly in a desperate attempt to have the whole issue dropped, they offered Britain one of their most precious fine mats, one of the 'crown jewels' of Samoa, but it was declined. They had to act, and somehow they succeeded without resorting to violence. Satupa'itea and Sagone may or may not have been paid compensation; but whatever was done, it is not difficult to imagine the influence of events upon the proceedings. One village had been destroyed by fire; two others had been bombarded by the *Cordelia*; Molī and his people had suffered a heavy fine; and the Samoans had reason to fear further destruction plus foreign domination, the taking of hostages and the loss of life.

The danger of internal hostilities, forced upon the Samoans in the name of mercy, had not been dissipated entirely, for Sailusi had yet to be punished. He was brought aboard the *Cordelia* and actually tried before a naval court; but when the sentence of death was passed, Molī

[43] Meanwhile, in 1855, the *aloali'i* Moegagogo of Faleata had had a brush with the u.s.s. *St Marys* in which the question of hostages had been raised again (USN, Pac. Sqd., Bailey to Mervine, 1 October 1855).

—who for the occasion was taken to be the 'King of Savai'i'—was asked
to concur in the judgment and arrange for Sailusi's execution *by
Samoans*. The acknowledgement of guilt presented no great problem,
for the identity of Fox's killer had never been disputed. From the
Samoans' point of view, however, the murder had already been avenged.
Those concerned had surrendered Sailusi only because they thought they
had to, and they had given him into the custody of Vernon, not of Moli
or any other chief. Therefore, any Samoan who openly shared in the
responsibility for Sailusi's execution would risk setting in train a new
cycle of vengeance. Moli would not accept that risk, but he agreed to
sanction the trial and approve the sentence. He and his younger half-
brother, Tonumaipe'a Talavou, then signed a warrant appointing Vernon
and Williams the executioners, asking in return that the convicted
murderer be taken from Savai'i alive. Vernon granted this request and
performed the final act at Apia, where by the ostensible authority of
'His Majesty, the King of Savai'i', Sailusi was hung from the yard-arm
of the *Cordelia*. According to Thomas Trood, this event had the most
salutary effect upon the 'insolent Samoans'.[44]

More common than murder as grounds for grave complaint by
Europeans were instances of war damage and of threats to life and
property during time of war. Apart from the political adventures of the
late nineteenth century, these were the cases in which naval commanders
were least inclined to affect an attitude of 'gentleness' or to have recourse
to legal myths to justify their intervention. Considering, however, that
naval justice, whatever form it took, was ultimately based upon force or
the inducement of fear, the difference did not always matter in practice.
In that regard, Vernon's proceedings may be compared with those of
Captain H. J. Worth of H.M.S. *Calypso* at the outbreak of war in 1848.

Worth, on tour out of Valparaiso, called twice at Samoa within a
period of several months. He came first in April 1848, when Malietoa
Taimalelagi's party was on the verge of attacking A'ana. Fearful of war,
many of the European residents begged Worth to prolong his stay in
order to prevent it or, if that proved impossible, to protect the foreign

---

[44] Trood, 37-8; BCS 3/2, W. T. Pritchard to Clarendon, 30 January 1857, Pritchard
to Fremantle, 30 January 1857, J. C. Williams to Loring, 22 November 1858,
Williams to Malmesbury, 22 November 1858, Moli to Williams, 18 October
1858, Sapapali'i and Safotulafai to Williams, 28 October 1858, Vernon and
Williams to Palauli and Satupa'itea, 4 November 1858, Vernon and Williams
to Fa'atoafe, 10 November 1858, Warrant of Sailusi's Committal by Malietoa
Moli and Pe'a, 18 November 1858; BCS 1/1, Clarendon to Pritchard, 18 May
1857, Malmesbury to Williams, 31 March 1859; BCS 2/1, Minutes of Meetings
with Sagone and Sala'ilua, 8-9 January 1857, Affidavits by Harris, Purcell, and
Gluvver, 9 January 1857, Judgment by Lt B. Leach *et al.*, 18 November 1858;
USCD Apia/1, Swanston to Marcy, 17 February 1857. Minutes of the meetings
with Sagone and Sala'ilua are also reproduced in Pritchard, 92-103.

community. This petition was favourably received, and as long as the *Calypso* remained—five weeks on this occasion—the Malietoa side stayed its attack. Its leaders would not, however, renounce their ultimate intention to fight, so that Worth, being unable to lie over indefinitely, tried to impress upon Taimalelagi that the foreign residents, as neutrals, should be immune from 'injury and insult', both in property and in person. To assist the warriors in avoiding trespass, it was agreed that houses and land owned or occupied by foreigners should be marked by flags. Worth then announced that he would return in a few weeks' time and that if, meanwhile, any damage had occurred in violation of the above arrangements, he would exact compensation and punish the offenders.[45]

War broke out a few days after the *Calypso* left. The A'ana people abandoned their villages straight away, and the Malietoa forces from Manono, Savai'i and Tuamasaga swept through the district, looting and burning. Several sharp but inconclusive battles followed, after which the Malietoa side withdrew to Tuamasaga and its enemy to Atua and to the bush in central Tuamasaga. Mulinu'u was now occupied by the Manono and Savai'i parties, which comprised many hundreds of warriors, with some women and children as camp-followers. Since food supplies at Mulinu'u were hopelessly inadequate, the people there had to go outside for most of their requirements, foraging near by and sending regularly to Manono and other outlying places. Obviously, they would try to get as much food as they could close at hand, but owing to the proximity of Atua-A'ana forces, their freedom to move by land was limited to the Apia area, where foreign interests were concentrated. Moreover, the fact that some of the Faleata people had joined the opposite side in the war opened the way to the destruction of property in the neighbourhood, exposing foreigners with Samoan-style houses to this additional hazard. The Samoans at Mulinu'u were from outside the district, and many of them probably knew or understood nothing of the flag-posting scheme to which Taimalelagi had agreed. When they went out to scavenge and plunder, they broke up into small parties, any of which could easily fail to recognize European property. Finally, there was a good deal of excitement and confusion among the Samoans and some degree of partisan feeling, but not activity, among the foreign residents, some of whom were, in any case, living with women from Atua and A'ana. Considering the circumstances, then, it is not surprising that some European property was stolen or destroyed.

Worth returned in August to find that thirteen foreigners claimed losses to the total value of $1,625. Of that amount, $1,000 represented

---

45 BCS 2/1, Worth to Pritchard, 12 May 1848, Worth to Malietoa T., 31 May 1848; SSL, Harbutt, 7 August 1858.

the destruction of a London Missionary Society chapel at Leulumoega—a building that had been erected by Samoans but whose nominal value was sought by the missionary stationed in A'ana. The other claims were submitted by Europeans and non-Samoan Polynesians with respect to the loss, at or near Apia, of Samoan-style houses, food crops, pigs and several small items of personal property. A few Europeans also complained of insulting language used by warriors from Mulinu'u. Except for the London Missionary Society claim, the stated damage was insignificant—and even then was probably exaggerated. Indeed, it was so slight in the circumstances that the Samoans could not have intended much harm to foreigners or their property. Nevertheless, Worth and the consuls—Williams and George Pritchard—felt that the Taimalelagi people had grievously and deceitfully infringed neutral rights and had to be taught a resounding lesson. No doubt this attitude was made to seem all the more appropriate by the absence of claims against the Atua-A'ana forces, though it was never proved that all of the reported damage had actually been done by Samoans from Mulinu'u.

Worth set out to act on behalf of all foreign claimants,[46] regardless of nationality or place of origin. In doing so, he accepted as correct in every essential detail the schedule of damages compiled by the consuls,[47] and he assumed that Taimalelagi and all the people at Mulinu'u shared a collective guilt by virtue of sharing a common cause. He found it unnecessary, then, to conduct trials but, rather, proceeded to press Taimalelagi for payment of compensation. Needless to say, Taimalelagi was not much nearer being the 'general' of his army than was Molī, after him, the 'King of Savai'i'. In fact, each side in the war was composed of several parties which were free to participate or withdraw,[48] but owing perhaps to the terms of the ultimatum issued by Worth, his approach to the questions of guilt and leadership—incorrect from the Samoan point of view—was none the less effective.

Within three days Taimalelagi was to have his supporters start raising the $1,625 in goods or cash. Meanwhile, Worth blockaded Mulinu'u to prevent the Samoans there from reinforcing their military position or from escaping—and also to interfere with their food supply.[49] If anyone tried to get away or if the armed bluejackets were attacked, Mulinu'u was to be fired upon by the *Calypso*. If Taimalelagi did not accept the

[46] Including some Polynesians—e.g. Mary Paumotu, Johnny Tahiti, and Ta'a of Rarotonga.

[47] BCS 2/1, Pritchard and Williams to Worth (with attached schedule of claims), 4 August 1848.

[48] There were, in fact, substantial withdrawals from Taimalelagi's side during the following year.

[49] Shipley, 24-5. The terms were later modified to permit some gathering of food.

ultimatum within the allotted time, the entire fleet of canoes then beached at Mulinu'u was to be destroyed, after which the war camp itself, together with north-western Tuamasaga and Manono, were to be bombarded. Lastly, if payment was agreed to, some of the canoes were to be kept as security until the full amount had been collected.[50] Faced with the prospect of hunger, wholesale destruction, and possible loss of life, the Samoans had no choice. They commenced without delay to raise the indemnity required of them, sharing out the cost among them and drawing heavily upon their store of fine mats.[51]

Perhaps Worth would not have achieved his immediate objective had his course of action been different, but it is not likely that he knew that, for he chose the harshest conditions without testing any alternatives. Obviously, few of the local Europeans were going to condemn his proceedings on that ground. Even some of the London Missionary Society representatives, their attitude coloured by the outbreak of war and the loss of a chapel, commended him for his firm *but kind* treatment of the Samoans.[52] What would have been said, though, if the Samoans had misunderstood the ultimatum or for some other reason had not given the satisfaction demanded of them?[53] Was the penalty not out of proportion to the amount of damage that had been done? The missionary, Pratt, some of whose Itu-o-Tane people helped to raise the levy, was one who took this view. The claims were dubious from the start, he said, and the London Missionary Society claim was the most suspect, for the chapel was only 'nominally Mission property'. For so little cause Worth had come 'breathing out slaughter against Samoa', threatening 'starvation or cannon balls', while the mission had stood idly by and let its name be associated with the *Calypso*.[54] Not given to mincing words,

50 BCS 2/1, Pritchard and Williams to Worth, 4 August 1848, Worth to Malietoa, 4 August 1848, Worth to 'chiefs of the Manono war party', 4 August 1848.

51 Goods to the value of one thousand dollars were supplied before Worth left, and the balance was made up to Pritchard later, twelve canoes being impounded at the consulate as security. Fines were not levied for the alleged insults, but apologies were made (FO 58/62, Pritchard to Palmerston, 12 August 1848; Erskine, 68; Shipley, 25).

52 SSL, Harbutt, 7 August 1848, Hardie, 15 August.

53 Europeans sometimes disregarded the linguistic and ideological problems of communication with the Samoans. In 1887 a village in Savai'i was burned simply because one word had been omitted from the Samoan version of a naval commander's ultimatum.

54 Pratt linked Worth's approach to the Samoans with the punitive measures previously taken by the *Calypso* in Fiji, where, between the vessel's Samoan visits, several Fijians had been killed in retaliation for the deaths of two British subjects. Pratt wrote that the ship 'arrived from the Fijis reeking with the blood of the natives murdered' (SSL, Pratt, 3 November 1848; FO 58/62, Pritchard to Palmerston, 12 August 1848; Derrick, *History of Fiji*, 133). Pritchard accompanied Worth to Fiji and was implicated in the action taken there.

Pratt told the Directors that the episode had made the London Missionary Society 'stink as a Mission in the esteem of the natives'.[55]

But Pratt's estimate of the case was incomplete, for he referred only
to the question of redress for damages. In fact, Worth also wanted to
deter violence against Europeans in future and, if possible, to lessen the
occasion for it by clearing the Apia area of belligerents, creating in
effect an unbroken neutral zone around the bay. The latter aim he
could hardly have pursued directly, first because he had no right whatever to evict Samoans from Samoan-owned land, and secondly because
he wished to avoid the appearance of favouring either warring faction,
lest the foreign community be implicated in the hostilities and suffer
*real* damage. This aspect of the case is not fully documented. The circumstances, however, strongly suggest that the war-damage claims
served as a pretext for intervention of a military character—that one of
the chief purposes of Worth's ultimatum, and hence a reason for its
severity, was to emphasize the untenability of Mulinu'u as a fort or
encampment. In any event, when the ultimatum was answered, Worth
proposed, and Taimalelagi allegedly agreed, that the peninsula should
be evacuated in order to minimize the Samoans' risk of further 'difficulties' with Europeans and warships. Worth then contacted the Atua-
A'ana forces and told them that they must not occupy Mulinu'u after the
evacuation or take advantage of the move in any other way. If they
ignored this warning and in that event damaged or appropriated
foreign-owned property, they would be made to pay double indemnity
or, in default, to suffer the fate their enemies had so narrowly escaped.[56]
Worth appears to have assumed that the Samoans at Mulinu'u would
not be willing to leave there unless the other side received an ultimatum,
too; but as it developed, their departure on that condition would still
have occasioned them loss of face. For another two or three years,
perhaps for a longer period than would otherwise have been the case,
they remained at the peninsula, while their enemies built and occupied
several forts near by. However, during this time, despite occasional
fighting in the Apia area, the Samoan warriors there displayed the
utmost respect for the property of Europeans.[57]

From the foregoing cases it would appear, then, that naval intervention sometimes placed heavy burdens upon Samoan political institutions, especially in requiring chiefs to assume duties and responsibilities
beyond their normal functions of office and areas of jurisdiction. Prior

[55] SSL, Pratt, 3 November 1848; Erskine, 87, 92.
[56] BCS 2/1, Worth to 'chiefs and people of Atua and A'ana', 13 August 1848.
[57] Erskine, 79, 97. In 1851 Mulinu'u was blockaded by the Atua-A'ana side, and
the Manono party subsequently withdrew. For an account of various engagements
around Apia, see Pritchard, 62-73.

to the 1870s, however, this strain never culminated in hostilities among the Samoans, possibly because warships ultimately threatened interests common to many of them, while offering no support for the aspirations of one faction in its rivalry with another. In the Fox case, for example, Molī was treated as if he had been the paramount chief of Savai'i, but only as a last resort and for the sole purpose of attaining an immediate objective sought by British officials and of providing a legal cover for their proceedings. Vernon and Williams may well have dreamed of a Savai'i united under a central government, yet there was no suggestion of their raising or backing a movement dedicated to that end nor of Molī's undertaking to exploit their intervention for the sake of his own ambitions.

It should also be clear why, when the Samoans became familiar with the methods and resources of naval commanders, the mere mention of a warship was often enough to enable consuls to obtain redress for damages and to elicit apologies for insults.[58] By the late 1850s, direct naval intervention was largely restricted to cases in which the Samoans could not act voluntarily without risk of trouble among themselves (for example, cases involving two or more villages) or in which Europeans claimed large sums in compensation or made demands that conflicted with the integrity of Samoan institutions. By the same time, thanks partly to naval influence, there had been formed at Apia a mixed court of chiefs and consuls, a rudimentary yet more regular system of joint jurisdiction aimed at resolving issues between Europeans and Samoans. Preceding this innovation, however, was the establishment of the Foreign Residents' Society, a government of the Beach, which by emphasizing the hiatus between the two communities helped to expose the need for permanent constitutional links between them.

[58] Aube, 163; Trood, 38.

# 10

## THE FOREIGN RESIDENTS' SOCIETY
## AND MIXED TRIBUNALS

MANY ACCOUNTS of the Beach, notably those influenced by moral, religious or class bias or by a legalistic view of political order, convey the impression that lawless confusion generally prevailed among Europeans in Samoa during the middle years of the nineteenth century. On closer examination, however, a rather different picture emerges. Moral laxity there certainly was, and an abundance of noise and coarse language; but the insecurity of life and property, the unavailability of credit, and other conditions more properly identified with political chaos, and obviously inimical to commerce, seldom pertained. For while the settlers were technically 'outside the law', they were neither beyond restraint nor beyond recognizing some need for it, however much they may have differed from their critics in their conception of order and justice. The fact is that, although given little encouragement and less recognition, they did organize politically and try to maintain, among themselves, at least that measure of order essential to the functioning and survival of a trading settlement.

### Concerning political influence and leadership after 1850

In any systematic effort to regulate the affairs of the Beach, the consuls were assured leading roles, not only because of their naval and other external support, but also by virtue of the functions which, not then being undertaken or supervised by any 'domestic' authority, belonged solely to them in their respective consular capacities. For example, they alone registered deeds and other legal instruments, issued birth and death certificates, provided for the administration of deceased estates, and enforced maritime law in respect of European vessels and their cargoes and companies.[1] Already, on the strength of their official powers, the consuls occupied positions of great influence and responsibility, from which it was but another step to the assumption of informal powers of a more general political nature. They were not all eager to

---

[1] Their maritime functions included, among other things, the ordering of marine surveys, the disposal of vessels deemed unseaworthy, the maintenance of destitute or stranded seamen, and control of the discharging and signing on of ships' crew. Certain aspects of these powers are discussed below, in connection with the case of Aaron Van Camp.

thus extend their jurisdiction, but all of them did. Neither did they all have enthusiastic and sizeable followings among the foreign residents, yet the Beach could scarcely be governed without their assistance and certainly not against their opposition.

The consuls had, of course, to work together if differences of nationality were to be transcended. From what has been written on the subject of 'international rivalry', however, one might well imagine that the national limits of consular jurisdiction, and the support of the Powers for the interests of their respective nationals, were almost invariably grave weaknesses in the political structure of the Beach. Indeed, one might envisage British, American and other national groups, forced by circumstances of geography to live cheek by jowl in place of having their own separate enclaves,[2] engaged in a Punic struggle for supremacy and, in the course of it, unable even to resolve the cases of indebtedness, assault, theft and the like which arose between people of different nationalities. In the long run, the politics of the Beach did tend to develop in that direction. At no time, though, did the principal political factions form strictly along national lines, while not until the 1870s was there among Europeans *any* sort of cleavage conducive to organized party politics. The latter phenomenon, when it appeared, related directly to problems encountered in time of economic expansion, chiefly the prosecution of conflicting land claims; and the parties which formed were linked with rival Samoan factions in a fight for the control of central government. Until then (and from about 1850) the main line of cleavage lay, rather, between the settlers and the Samoans, first in the context of Samoan warfare and general political 'backwardness', which tended to unite the Beach to resist interference, and secondly in the context of various pressures, chiefly the demand for economic opportunities, which united the leaders of the Beach in the cause of Samoan political reform. Meanwhile, of course, the settlers had their differences—their personal animosities, their patriotic, commercial and sectarian rivalries and, by the late 1850s, even a measure of 'class' conflict, that is, the 'respectables' against the riff-raff. However, these differences were not all persistent or mutually reinforcing. With only one short-lived exception, yet to be discussed, no single issue or combination of issues proved so divisive as to render ineffective the available means of maintaining public order and security.

---

[2] Like the foreign concessions in India, say, or China. At Apia there was some tendency towards the formation of national districts. D'Ewes (169-72), who visited Samoa in 1856, noted, for example, that the Matautu and Matafele were predominantly British and American, respectively; and later on, an area at Sogi, Savalalo and Matafele was commonly known as the 'German part of town'. However, these localities were not exclusive to single nationalities, nor were they territorial units of government.

Starting, as a rule, with some common interest in the welfare of the
Beach, of which they were part, the consuls were further disposed to
co-operate by the reciprocal nature of their functions. Thus, the
American consul, for example, had to acknowledge and investigate
British complaints against Americans in order to receive similar assistance from the British consul when the tables were turned.[3] As will be
shown, the most constructive form of this give-and-take relationship
was the pooling of national jurisdictions in a joint executive and
judiciary. Another aspect of the latter development was the occasional
doubling up of consular representation, with one man having, as well
as his regular commission, an appointment to act *pro tem* as the agent
of a second government. In a sense, the informality of the police and
magisterial powers assumed by the consuls also contributed to their
effectiveness, for there was seldom any reason, then, to postpone action
pending advice or instructions from abroad. Perhaps equally important
was the fact that the consuls received no fees for their unofficial services
and so had relatively little cause to stir up or prolong litigation for its
own sake. On the other hand, the consuls' liability to censure for
'illegal' acts, in the event of complaint to their superiors, limited their
scope for imposing unpopular standards of conduct and justice upon
Europeans. It is conceivable that they might still have gone quite some
way towards authoritarianism had they been able to strengthen their
position by such 'legitimate' means as the attraction of Samoan support
or acquisition of dominant economic power. Over the years their
influence did tend to ramify in such faction, but as already indicated,
there also developed among them issues which overtaxed their ability
or inclination to co-operate.

As for economic influences in politics, it may be noted, first, that
before the late 1860s, no vital sector of the economy came under
monopoly or near-monopoly control, except during brief periods such
as might ensue from shipping irregularities or other chance or incidental
circumstances. Meanwhile, the control of employment was perhaps the
major internal economic force capable of being translated into political
power. This power was, of course, dispersed and the economy highly
competitive for employers. Apart from certain skills, however, the job
market was also competitive, and until the mid-1860s, when the way
was opened to plantation development, there was a surplus of labour
as well as of capital. Not that all Europeans lived wholly on a money
economy or that all wished to, but neither did many care to or find it
possible to depart from it altogether. Drink, clothing, certain imported
foodstuffs, materials for the construction and upkeep of dwellings, goods

[3] BCS 5/1, Williams to Coe, 6 July 1866, 21 December 1868, on the history of
joint consular courts and the need for reciprocity between consuls.

for presentation to Samoans—all were in fairly general demand and so, accordingly, was a cash income, at least on a part-time or periodic basis. There was considerable scope, then, for the intimidation of employees, the political implications of which will be obvious. Suffice to say here that one of the most popular forms of gossip among Europeans was that of attributing political action or allegiance to that order of economic pressure: for example, X, as an employee of Y, had to sign the petition against Z, but he does not really think that way.

In the political affairs of the Beach the missionaries sometimes exerted influence too, mostly indirect and divisive. Their principal contacts were not with the 'masses', whom they could rarely if ever sway, but with the 'oligarchy', notably the consuls and prominent merchants, who had secular means of attacking moral and social problems. Since these leaders were not numerous, the missionaries might well pin their hopes on two or three. Moreover, their prospects might radically alter with a few strategic changes of personnel or shifts of loyalty or interest. As will be shown, such changes did in fact occur, sometimes entailing the intake or defection of church members or adherents, and at other times involving commitments of a more strictly social character, which had fewer implications of sectarian bias. Needless to say, the missionaries were not the only ones whose interests were at stake, for their goodwill or enmity was of some consequence, too, not least to those who sought the mission 'accounts' or the confidence of Samoans. Indeed, it will be suggested, without undue cynicism, that the course of relations between missionaries and leading settlers was, in so far as the initiative of the latter was concerned, greatly affected by economic and other material considerations.

## The deviations of George Pritchard

Cunningham, Pritchard's unofficial agent, fell out with the London Missionary Society over his associations with beachcombers and sailors, but he did not stay long enough to compromise seriously the mission's campaign against 'vice' at the port of Apia. When Pritchard himself threw over the same traces a decade later, the results were quite different. So too, of course, were the circumstances in which he acted, but the dissolution of his London Missionary Society loyalties and his assumption of popular leadership on the Beach were no less remarkable or significant for that.

It was towards the close of 1847 that the first recorded move was made to organize the foreign settlers and drifters around Apia. The leaders were the consuls, chiefly Pritchard, and the reason for their initiative was the threat of general warfare among the Samoans. Recollections and accounts of the benighted past, which readily came to mind then, suggested that Europeans might not be immune from attack if the people 'reverted to savagery'. That missionaries and others had been cultivating the Samoans' fear of various foreign interests and influences was another source of concern. Yet another was the prevailing doubt as to how far Europeans were considered collectively responsible, in the Samoan manner, for the actions of individuals. To discuss such questions as these, and to determine some common course of action, the consuls invited the foreigners in Upolu to meet with them at Apia. It is not clear how widely representative the ensuing meeting was, but for the environs of Apia, at least, the attendance was good.

Pritchard took the fore on this occasion and proceeded to give vent to his chronically poor opinion of the 'native character'. Samoans might give the appearance of being friendly towards strangers, but he maintained that they were still barbarians at heart, which judgement the rising tide of traditional conflict strengthened, while also suggesting to him, then, a greater risk of treacherous assault upon the weak and the helpless. In the event of war, said Pritchard, Europeans should remain neutral so as to offer the least provocation. That course was also consistent, in his view, with their being unable to rely upon Samoans for protection; but it did not dispose of his fear of wanton attack. To meet the latter possibility, Europeans would have to arm, he said, and be ready to close ranks and fight in one another's defence. At this juncture Williams demurred, holding that military measures would be more apt to invite attack than to deter it and would almost certainly be futile, in any case, against the numerical superiority of the Samoans. Unarmed neutrality was the sole and probably a sufficient warrant of safety, he thought, provided that all foreigners observed it. However, most of those present agreed with Pritchard, and finally, though reluctantly, Williams fell into line too, allegedly to ensure the fullest support for the principle of neutrality, which was asserted in the resolution carried by the meeting.[4]

Whatever Williams or Pritchard may have intended, one suspects that if it had come to the point of resisting attack, the Europeans would have abandoned their position of neutrality, suing for Samoan help rather than chancing the hazards of standing alone. But as it happened, the Beach militant never saw action.[5] On only one occasion were foreigners directly victimized, and that was at the beginning of the war, when 'neutral rights' were infringed in the manner already described. The desire to resist was no doubt present then, but the unexpected concentra-

[4] Halligon, *Six mois à travers l'Océanie*, 32; Adm. 1/5590, Maxwell to Sec. Adm., 18 March 1848.

[5] Pritchard (62-3) tells how, instead, European residents of Apia took refuge at the British consulate whenever fighting was expected to break out. The building was barricaded with tiers of empty casks.

tion of Samoan forces around Apia, where most cases of theft or damage occurred, amply bore out Williams's objection to Pritchard's proposal to arm. Equally important, it was observed that the belligerents respected Vaimauga's neutrality, while the forthcoming return of Captain Worth with the *Calypso* offered hope of early action to recover property losses and to bring home to the Samoan warriors the gravity of their misdeeds. Probably irrelevant, but still of interest, is the fact that Pritchard was not present when the war started. On the eve of hostilities he had left aboard the *Calypso* to visit Tonga and Fiji.[6]

Worth's harsh terms of settlement in the war-damage cases were, at the time, widely applauded among Europeans; but afterwards, when the belligerents refused to shift from the environs of Apia and when some of the Malietoa party threatened reprisals, there was concern as to whether his intervention would backfire. Among foreigners with London Missionary Society connections there was still another ground for anxiety, namely the presence of a Catholic priest within the Mulinu'u encampment. Here it may be noted, parenthetically, that from the start the Marists had been conspicuous among Europeans for their optimistic reaction to the war, which, though deploring the violence, they regarded as indicative of a London Missionary Society collapse. For all the Society knew, they could have been right, and if they were, the priest at Mulinu'u was well-placed to capitalize on the crisis. He was, needless to say, credited with that intention for staying there, and it was conceded that he must surely gain *some* influence among people whose interests he had tried to defend against Worth and whose hardship he had been ready to share.[7] How would he use his influence? Would he counsel peace? London Missionary Society representatives thought not, expecting instead that he would try to turn the war to sectarian advantage. In that case he would hardly oppose the continued occupation of Mulinu'u; and there was some doubt as to whether he would even discourage assaults upon his foreign enemies and rivals.

Given these conditions and assumptions, the consuls and London Missionary Society officials were inclined to adopt, in addition to their policy of neutrality as regards the war itself, a conciliatory approach to some of their more powerful or influential antagonists. Thus, for example, the immoderate expression of anti-French sentiment went out of vogue temporarily and so, for Pritchard's part, did 'gunboat diplomacy'. Following urgent representations by the consuls, it was also

---

[6] Tonga was within Pritchard's consular district, and Worth had been instructed to offer him a passage to that group. Fiji, where Pritchard was implicated in reprisals taken by Worth, was outside his jurisdiction.

[7] As a result of his protest, Worth allowed a few canoes to go out for food and water (Shipley, 24-5).

agreed that London Missionary Society sectarian propaganda must be toned down, in which regard an extravagantly anti-Catholic pamphlet, just ready for distribution to the Samoans, was suppressed.[8] And with a view to placating Taimalelagi and his warrior chiefs, some of whom (including Taimalelagi himself) were renegades from London Missionary Society churches, the missionaries went so far as to propose returning the indemnity exacted for the destruction of the Leulumoega chapel. Not surprisingly, however, their offer was haughtily declined.[9]

Meanwhile, every effort was made to restrain the urge to war that was present in some circles in Vaimauga. This undertaking had perhaps its strongest support from Moli Malietoa, then a London Missionary Society teacher, who came or was brought to live at Apia.[10] How necessary it was is another question, but at any rate, the sub-district did keep out of the fighting and so continued, in the customary role of neutrals, to give refuge to those who sought it, Europeans as well as Samoans. Vaimauga's status as a sanctuary was not, however, an unmixed blessing from the London Missionary Society viewpoint, for through the influx to which it gave rise, it stimulated the 'cosmopolitan' development of the Apia area. Among other things, it let in 'undesirables' who in different circumstances might not have come, or might have been kept out; and it contributed to the greater concentration of commercial activity at Apia. As already shown, this critical phase of Apia's development was to continue over the next few years, with war-caused dislocations being followed by the trans-Pacific gold rush traffic and the opening of Matautu to Samoan and European settlement. It was during this period that Pritchard's sympathies changed.

Soon after the war broke out, Pritchard, accepting the frustration of his lingering hopes for an illustrious career in Samoa, conveyed to the London Missionary Society Directors the desire to leave and take up mission work again.[11] He wanted first, however, to make certain family arrangements, and before he was able to complete them, he had offended the London Missionary Society by keeping the wrong company. Pritchard entered upon his course of 'inconsistency' largely by way of efforts to promote, as a war-time expedient, greater harmony among Europeans. To a point, he had London Missionary Society representatives in agreement with him, but he went too far, his undue fear or mistrust of the Samoans disposing him to overlook too many of the 'errors and shortcomings' of people whom in the past no one had condemned more severely than he. Once out of line, Pritchard was carried farther astray by other forces. On the one hand, the men whose good will he now canvassed also cultivated him, desiring his assistance

[8] SSL, Nisbet, 20 June 1849.
[9] Erskine, 87, 92.
[10] SSL, Mills, 29 January 1849.
[11] ibid., Pritchard, 22 November 1849.

or, in any event, preferring his friendship to his enmity. To a hard-pressed merchant they could offer business, and to an unappreciated consul, a degree of recognition, to which temptations Pritchard yielded. In doing so, he was influenced partly by one or two of his sons whose discipline seems to have been a problem for him. On the other hand, Pritchard, who strongly resented criticism, was repelled by that to which his fellow missionaries subjected him. Those who made little or no allowance for differences from their own opinions weighed in early on relatively minor issues, as Pritchard himself was accustomed to doing, and from there the antagonism grew and spread, until the whole mission was denouncing him for major derelictions. In the process, his desire to resume his London Missionary Society career was frustrated and his church-membership revoked, while he in turn took out vengeance on the mission.[12]

With his spectacular record of anti-French and anti-Catholic crusading, Pritchard's latter-day relations with the Marists in Samoa constituted a striking about-face. Commencing with self-conscious expressions of regard for the priests as individuals, he was next displaying tolerance of their religion and willingness to provide facilities for its propagation, and eventually, he came to show respect for other French interests and for France itself.[13] So far did he shift his ground that he took up the defence of the Catholic mission against 'persecution' and, no doubt partly for that reason, was requested to act as French consular agent in Samoa.[14] He assumed the latter responsibility in the mid-1850s, and about the same time, several members of his family were said to be interested in Catholicism.[15]

But if one considers that Pritchard also had a record of rampaging puritanism, embellished by such details as the public use of stocks to punish offenders at Papeete, his becoming a champion of the Beach at Apia seems an almost equally radical reversal of form. In this case, too, he graduated from tolerance to indulgence, as his assault upon the prohibition law will have indicated. And again, he received appropriate recognition. His first notable advancement, made early in 1851, was his

12 SSL, Mills, 12 October 1852, Hardie, 11 June 1853.

13 Bérard, 26; Cazalis, 19.

14 USCD, Apia/1, Van Camp to Chapin, 13 November 1854; Adm. 1/5672, Fremantle to Osborne, 15 November 1855. The agency, apparently offered by a French naval commander to suit the convenience of the Tahitian authorities, was assumed by Pritchard without consultation with the British Government. Like his American agency, which he had acquired in 1851, it would have been unsalaried and, viewed from outside, would have represented no more than an exercise of 'good offices'. Sometimes, however, an appointment of this kind substantially augmented a consul's influence in Samoa.

15 MS., Darnand.

succession to the post of acting American commercial agent, which had
been vacant since Williams's departure a few months before. Having
had only the most tenuous hold on that office, Williams had been free
to abandon it without leave and, strictly speaking, had had no authority
to name anyone else to act in his place. Had Pritchard not lost his confidence, however, he might at least have handed over to him, as another
consul, which would have been in line with common practice in the
islands. Pritchard came to office, rather, as the 'people's choice', a
petition in favour of his provisional appointment being raised by American settlers and mariners and successfully presented to the commander
of the visiting u.s.s. *Falmouth*.[16] Whereas Wilkes, in selecting Williams,
had been guided by the London Missionary Society, Petigru of the
*Falmouth* deferred to the Beach, and for over two years Pritchard represented the two nationalities then predominant in Samoa.

With both consulates removed from the London Missionary Society
sphere of influence and with Matautu opening up across the Vaisigano
from Apia village, the foreign settlement was freer not only to expand
and to develop the more venal amenities, which Pritchard came to accept
as natural features of seaport life,[17] but also to organize politically and
claim the right of self-government. Efforts in the latter direction came
to a head in 1852, about the time Pritchard let the Marists in at Mulivai
and was excommunicated. Another distinction was now added to his
growing list, that of holding office in the Foreign Residents' Society.
Finally, in circumstances rounding off the travesty of the position he had
enjoyed in Tahiti, Pritchard returned to the pulpit. It was after his
excommunication, at a time when the London Missionary Society was
temporarily without a missionary at Apia, that he received a petition
inviting him to become the Protestant chaplain to the foreign settlement.
For his church he was to take over the seamen's chapel, which had
been built with subscribed funds some years before. Since most of the
services there had been conducted by the local London Missionary
Society representative, Pritchard was, in effect, 'called' to succeed the
man from whose communicant church he had been expelled. Responding to this 'congregational' gesture, he pre-empted the chapel and, with
support from the Beach, refused to stand aside for Murray, the next
London Missionary Society incumbent to reside at Apia.[18]

## The Foreign Residents' Society

According to St Julian, the Foreign Residents' Society, in its original
form, was an association for the protection of foreigners from the 'natural

---

[16] USCD, Apia/1, Pritchard to Webster, 26 February 1851.
[17] BCS 3/1, Pritchard to Bruce, May 1856.
[18] SSL, Murray, 6 December 1854.

consequences' of Samoan warfare, and in his view, no influence aside from Christianity played a greater part in the achievement of that object.[19] The fact is, however, that when the Society was founded, the war was no longer regarded in Samoa as much of a threat to European lives and property, there having been no repetition of the initial 'outrages', no reprisals on account of the *Calypso* affair, and not much more fighting either. Rather, the Society, in so far as it was the product of a hostile environment, represented mainly the settlers' desire to be free of restraint and interference in their everyday activities and affairs; and it was not only their Samoan neighbours they had in mind, but also missionaries, to whom St Julian gave so much credit on their behalf. The Society made no discernible contribution to the settlement or smoothing over of differences between Europeans and Samoans. If anything, the leaders, given an organization to back their claim of extraterritoriality, took a more intransigent line with the Samoans. Certainly, naval intervention, an influence overlooked by St Julian, remained in great demand, and the threat of it was in common use. Of course, the Society, merely by endeavouring to keep order on the Beach, may have prevented a certain amount of trouble between the two peoples. Not that it paid much attention to acts which provoked the Samoans, but it did give Europeans a better chance of settling disputes among themselves without resorting to Samoan assistance. Perhaps St Julian would have been nearer the truth, then, if he had described the Society as an association to protect foreigners from one another.

Basically a government of the town-meeting type, the Foreign Residents' Society was open to the participation of all settlers and claimed jurisdiction over them all. Its activities were confined largely to the Apia area, but no territorial limits of jurisdiction were set, presumably because the only other governmental authority acknowledged to apply locally to Europeans was that of consuls and naval commanders. The port code was considered null and void, except for the levy of fees upon shipping and for the obligations imposed upon the Samoans. The consuls, not the Society, assisted in the collection of port fees and the provision of a pilot service, and it was mainly they who took up matters at issue between Samoans and foreigners. Also, the consuls, rather than the Society, assumed jurisdiction over merchant seamen and passengers off visiting ships, hiring Samoans or European residents as police when need arose. Visiting naval personnel were, of course, under the authority of their commanding officers.

The entire membership of the Society—that is, the adult male 'public' in voluntary assemblage—constituted a legislature. This body periodically elected a chairman or president, laid down principles or rules for

[19] St Julian, *Official Report*, 73, or *Sydney Morning Herald*, 30 March 1855.

the maintenance of order and the conduct of trade, and elected executive councillors and judges. The president of the general meeting was also the executive head and, together with his councillors, was responsible for the investigation of civil complaints, the conduct of police activities, and the administration of the Society's funds. Revenue, consisting of collected fines, was appropriated by the Society to finance minor works such as the building of foot-bridges in the vicinity of Apia. The officers, including judges, served without pay.

The court was composed of a presiding judge and up to six associate judges, with the latter performing some of the functions of a jury or panel of assessors. It was the practice for consuls to be elected to this judicial body, but there was, of course, an 'unofficial' majority. Court procedure was neither elaborate nor rigid, nor were decisions and settlements reached according to hard-and-fast rules. Rather, procedure, substance and even jurisdiction were determined in each case with regard to whatever seemed just, necessary and enforceable. 'It was more a Court of Equity than of law.'[20]

Despite recognition allegedly given it by 'the chiefs', the Society had no legal status, so that settlers were obliged only by personal necessity or inclination to participate in it or acknowledge the jurisdiction claimed for it. Therefore, it was, wrote St Julian, 'only . . . a respectable system of lynch law'.[21] Still, its leaders—in the first instance, Pritchard and an English boat-builder named William Yandall—had the firm support of at least half the settlers in the Apia area; and excepting a crisis yet to be mentioned, the Society performed reasonably well its chief functions of keeping order and settling grievances among Europeans. A pious teetotaller would not have thought so, as the missionary, Murray, railing against the 'mimic State' and its 'notoriously godless' officials, clearly did not; but by then, the general run of foreigners in Samoa were not such a desperate lot as to countenance just any sort of behaviour. One person who discovered this was Harry Miller, a saloon-keeper tried and condemned for having, in the course of a drunken brawl, bitten off an opponent's ear. Another was the defendant who, also in his cups, had been dared to 'fire, you Irish bog-trotting bugger', and had. On one occasion, rather later, the Beach proved that it could even rise to gallantry and punish the peeping Tom seen in the grounds of the convent. More usual, needless to say, were cases of theft, petty assault and property damage and, on the more strictly civil side, indebtedness and breach of contract. In no category

[20] USCD, Apia/1, *passim*; Murray, *Forty years' mission work*, 336; BCS 3/3, Williams to Russell, 1 April 1864.

[21] Of which there were other examples in the Pacific, e.g. in New Zealand and Fiji.

was the 'crime' rate very high, while acts of a really serious nature, or cases of habitual offence, were exceedingly few. Fewer still, in a place like Apia, were the crimes that went unsolved. As there was no gaol, most offenders were fined or, in the event of default, had some of their property confiscated; and in appropriate cases, damages were awarded at the same time. The more severe penalties included deportation and flogging. A variation of the former was the sentence of banishment handed down in the 1860s, the prisoner being taken to Apolima and the Samoans there paid to maintain him in custody. There seems to have been no case of intentional homicide (that is, 'first-degree' murder) during the mid-nineteenth century, and no sentence of death.[22]

## The Van Camp affair

In 1853 'judge' Pritchard and 'president' Yandall were joined by Virginius Chapin, sometime of Virginia and subsequently of the California goldfields and Honolulu, who came to Samoa as the first regularly appointed and salaried commercial agent for the United States. Chapin also came to trade and, by the way, to act as commercial agent for Hawaii. Working closely with Pritchard, as the Hawaiian foreign minister had advised him to do, and serving as one of the judges, Chapin added considerably to the strength of the Foreign Residents' Society.[23] It was a different story with 'Doctor' Aaron Van Camp, who in 1854 succeeded to the American post. Calling himself a doctor of dentistry, and claiming to have a son at Georgetown University and to have had a 'Professor' Nooney as a business associate, Van Camp looked down upon and despised many of his neighbours at Apia for their inferior attainments and antecedents. His allegations regarding his own may have been true. However, his letters and despatches do not reveal a man of great refinement—for example, 'I am very well aware of what I done'—while his reputation in the South Seas was not that of a passed doctor but a past master, and that of cunning and deception. Indeed, from most accounts Van Camp emerges as Samoa's first American adventurer of note, a worthy forerunner of others equally betitled.[24]

22 BCS, 2/1, 3/1-3, 5/1, *passim*; USCD, Apia/1, *passim*.

23 HFO, Wyllie to Chapin, 3 May 1853, St Julian to Chapin, 25 April 1856; USCD, Apia/1, Van Camp to Chapin, 13 November 1854.

24 Concerning Van Camp and the foreign residents at Apia: BCS 3/1, Pritchard to Clarendon, 11 July 1854; FO 58/84B, Fremantle to Osborne, 15 November 1855 (with enclosures), Morshead to Bruce, 23 November 1855 (with enclosures); HFO, Chapin to Wyllie, 24 November 1855 (with enclosure); USCD Apia/1, Van Camp to Marcy, despatches and enclosures for period 16 February 1854 to 13 November 1854; USN, Pac. Sqd., Bailey to Mervine, 1 October 1855, Mervine to Dobbin, 30 June 1856 (with enclosures); SSL, Pratt, 15 December 1854; and D'Ewes, 169-72.

Before he was appointed commercial agent, Van Camp had been engaged in buying provisions for the California market, a venture which had brought him to Samoa at least twice, once to be left stranded at Apia for several months.[25] From what he had then seen of the islands, he had apparently concluded that he might make his 'pile' more easily there than in California, especially if he had an official position.[26] At any rate, he had successfully applied through 'channels' for Chapin's job and then set out to establish a general trading business at Apia. His arrival produced a flurry on the Beach, as Chapin, not unreasonably, took offence at being dismissed without notice and after such a short time in office.[27] This crisis was brief, however, for Van Camp proceeded otherwise to make himself amenable, not least by recognizing and supporting the Foreign Residents' Society.

The trouble really started when, after a few months, Van Camp had occasion to exercise his power, as a consular officer, to have American merchant ships surveyed for fitness and to seize and auction, with their cargoes, those condemned or wrecked inside his district of jurisdiction. The one occasion was followed by another, and by several more after that, with grave charges developing against Van Camp on account of his proceedings. It was alleged, first, that he defrauded the lawful beneficiaries by fixing his auctions, misappropriating receipts and falsifying his records. Secondly, it was charged that, in some instances, he conspired with captains and others to have sound vessels condemned for his disposal, sharing the proceeds with them. In other words, he was said to be using his official powers to facilitate the commission of barratry and embezzlement. That was the opinion voiced by absentee owners, underwriters and shippers, and it was widely supported at Apia, where Van Camp was also accused of rigging his auctions so as to corner supplies of goods that should have gone on the open market.[28] To be fair to him it must be noted that he was not proved guilty in a competent court of law. Some of the circumstances suggest, however, that if he were entirely innocent he must then have been, also contrary to the impression he often gave, extraordinarily inept and naive. How

25 USCD Apia/1, protest of Van Camp before Pritchard, 9 August 1852, Van Camp to Marcy, 16 February 1854.

26 ibid., cutting from *Plattsburg Republican*, 6 June 1857.

27 ibid., Van Camp to Marcy, 15 April 1854.

28 He was accused of brutal mistreatment of Samoans, and missionaries brought various charges of immorality against him (Murray, *Forty years' mission work*, 316-18; *Sydney Morning Herald*, 3 October 1856 (article by Murray); SSL, Pratt, 15 December 1854). Pogai petitioned an American naval commander for Van Camp's removal (USN, Pac. Sqd., Bailey to Mervine, 1 October 1855). It may be noted that Van Camp's land at Apia was purchased from a European, not from Samoans.

was it, for example, that he employed for his own private purposes one of the vessels condemned and sold as unseaworthy? There was much adverse comment over this at the time, but in Apia a subject of greater concern was the venture in which he used the vessel. For soon after he entered the 'shipping business', Van Camp branched out into what was then the most promising field of speculation, namely pearling at Penrhyn Island, and by virtue of superior wit and more effective skulduggery outdid his influential rivals, the Papeete and Apia firm of Hort Brothers. That he outdid them was no doubt the main consideration, overshadowing the cut-throat methods adopted, but once again he was accused of the foulest misdeeds and, ostensibly because of them, opinion ran heavily against him.

Van Camp did not suffer attack in silence but rather, for his part, issued a barrage of counter-charges as well as denials which, though perhaps not as convincing as the case against him, added to the heat and confusion and helped to frustrate the efforts of naval officers to find out what was going on.[29] Nor was he standing alone, for being a political power unto himself and also one of the few prosperous businessmen in Samoa, he was assured of some following, whatever he did. Several of his party were men who came out from the United States especially to work for him, but there were others, chiefly idle tradesmen and hard-up merchants, who went over to him at Apia, sometimes questioning his scruples but still attracted by offers of employment or joint speculation. Among the latter was Chapin, who was associated in the pearling enterprise. Van Camp's men were of various national origins, more American than anything else but, for reasons partly related to the shipping scandals, by no means fully representative of that nationality at Apia. Meanwhile, Pritchard, the British and French representative and a failure in his own business, was taking the part of Van Camp's enemies and competitors, which side attracted the majority of Europeans.[30]

Within a year or so of Van Camp's arrival in Samoa, the consuls had virtually ceased to reciprocate in the settlement of disputes, and the only sphere in which they could usually be counted on to co-operate was in taking up complaints against Samoans and in resisting Samoan interference in the affairs of Europeans. With its chief prop removed, the Foreign Residents' Society all but collapsed. The remnants belonged

29 Two British and three American commanders investigated Van Camp's proceedings in Samoa during the period 1854-6. At the request of the French governor in Tahiti, one of the British commanders was also investigating on behalf of French interests. Of the five commanders, only one, Mervine, was sympathetic towards Van Camp, but none was able to gather conclusive evidence against him.

30 USN, Pac. Sqd., petitions from foreign residents to Bailey and Mervine, 1854-6.

to Pritchard and Yandall, but in effect, the Society was replaced by a system of consul-led gangs, the make-up of which was determined more by local issues than by straight-out considerations of nationality. With regard to nationality, it may be noted in passing that a settler's true origins were often unknown or unproved, passports, naturalization papers and birth certificates seldom being carried. In determining consular jurisdiction, declarations of national allegiance commonly served in place of such documents; and these were subject to repudiation and change, particularly when the consuls were at loggerheads and so had occasion to steal one another's 'subjects'. The position of the United States as a nation of immigrants facilitated this process of conversion, which operated now as Pritchard received into his protection Americans antagonistic to Van Camp.[31]

In spite of the rivalry of these groups, which generated the most hostile feelings within a confined space, it was only in the field of commercial activity that relations between them became really chaotic, serious incidents of physical violence being avoided. This restraint may have been due partly to fear of international repercussions in the event of attack upon the person or property of a consul. As one naval commander hinted, common fear of Samoan intervention may also have been a factor.[32] Perhaps most important, though, was each side's hope of being upheld by an external authority. So many complaints against Van Camp were filtering back to Washington—from American commercial interests, from official British sources and also, on the Horts' account, from the French administration at Tahiti—that he must surely come to grief soon, or so his enemies thought. On the other hand, Van Camp survived investigation at close range, several naval inquiries being conducted without proving any serious charge against him. Whether that was because he was innocent, as he claimed, or because he took advantage of his consular position to suppress evidence, as others claimed, is probably irrelevant. Either way, he must have anticipated an inquiry by the State Department, if not some form of court action in the United States, and yet he proceeded as if perfectly confident of his defence. His chance of retaining his commission was another matter, since he had no more security of tenure than Chapin had had. Van Camp had had time to make his 'pile', however, so that being summarily dismissed, as he in fact was, should in itself have been no disaster. But a disaster it was, for the State Department, perhaps unwittingly, appointed as his successor a man who was determined to ruin him.

The new office-holder was one Jonathan Jenkins, a retired judge, who

[31] BCS, 2/1, Van Camp to Pritchard, 12 April 1856.
[32] Adm. 1/5672, Fremantle to Osborne, 15 November 1855.

at some stage fell in with shipowners aggrieved by Van Camp's proceedings in admiralty. It is not clear whether his appointment was
arranged by them or whether he was approached by them afterwards,
but there is no doubt that prior to his arrival in Samoa he was firmly
committed to act in their behalf. Indeed, he left San Francisco in their
company and on the voyage out was engaged in drafting writs and
orders to effect the seizure of Van Camp's property and the criminal trial
of the man himself. Jenkins produced an impressive array of documents
and, to justify their use, an argument likening himself to an American
consular magistrate in China or the Ottoman Empire. Neither by writ
nor interpretation, however, could he alter the fact that his assumption
of magisterial powers was wholly informal and never intended by his
superiors.[33]

Early in May 1856, as Jenkins approached Samoa, the unsuspecting
Van Camp received an offer of passage aboard u.s.s. *Independence* and
took leave from his post to visit the United States. It was another
coincidence that Commodore Mervine, the commanding officer of that
vessel and of the Pacific squadron, had been blindly influenced by Van
Camp to interfere in a number of petty controversies and had conducted
himself in such an irresponsible and provocative fashion that existing
animosities had been intensified and new ones created.[34] Had he come
a week earlier, Jenkins would have encountered both Mervine and Van
Camp, and the working of 'justice' would almost certainly have been
thwarted. As it was, Van Camp departed at the height of his unpopularity, leaving the way quite open to his successor. Chapin, who
had been appointed to act as commercial agent, was pushed aside and,
with Pritchard's help, Jenkins sequestered all property ostensibly belonging to Van Camp. The 'United States Consular Court' then proceeded to
try and convict Van Camp *in absentia* and to order the disposal of his
property for the benefit of the shipowners who had come to Samoa
with Jenkins. At the auction which followed, some satisfying bargains

---

33 Legislation implementing treaty provisions granted American consuls in China
and the Ottoman Empire certain magisterial powers with reference to American
citizens in those countries. Just before leaving San Francisco, Jenkins wrote to
the State Department saying he assumed the legislation to apply equally to
consuls in Oceania. The Department's negative reply was received in Samoa
after Jenkins had left again for the United States (USCP, 35 C., 2 S., House Rpt.
212; Ryden, *Foreign policy*, 31).

34 USN, Pac. Sqd., Mervine to Dobbin, 30 June 1856; BCS 3/1, Pritchard to
Bruce, May 1856; BCS 2/1, Van Camp to Pritchard, 12 April 1856; 'Foreign
Residents of Upolu' to Mervine, 19 April 1856, Mervine to Seumanutafa, 21
April 1856; *Sydney Morning Herald*, 3 October 1856. Prior to the 1870s,
Mervine was the only naval commander whose intervention in Samoa was the
subject of strong protest to his superiors.

were knocked down to residents of Apia, whose pleasure would have
been greater only if the 'Doctor' had been present to witness his downfall.

This was by no means the end of the affair, for whatever Van Camp
had done, assets worth about $20,000 had been openly and unlawfully
confiscated by Jenkins, a thriving business had been ruined, and
aggrieved parties not present at the trial had been put to a disadvantage
as to the prosecution of their outstanding claims. Moreover, Van Camp
had not been the sole owner of all the goods seized and sold. Among
others to suffer was Chapin, who soon left for the United States to
submit a report and join Van Camp in laying charges of felony against
Jenkins. Of all the cases in which informal magisterial powers might
have been exercised in Samoa, this was one most likely to have repercussions abroad and to cause trouble for the consul concerned. Eventually, time and distance and the limitations of metropolitan jurisdiction,
which had in the first place contributed to the emergence of 'kangaroo
courts' in Samoa, combined to frustrate the efforts of private parties to
take legal action in the United States, while the American Government,
which might have helped them, decided not to bring charges of its own
and not to assume responsibility for the wrongs attributed to its agents.
In effect, the cases involving Jenkins and Van Camp were allowed to
cancel one another out. In the interim, however, Jenkins also lost his
commission and, besides that, suffered a period of imprisonment in the
United States pending the dismissal of Van Camp's charges against
him.[35] As seen in Samoa, then, this affair lent urgency to the plea of
other consuls for an enlargement of their formal powers. Otherwise,
they seemed to be faced with the choice of relying upon chiefs and naval
officers for the conduct of judicial proceedings among European residents, or of continuing to exceed their terms of appointment at the risk
of their jobs and their freedom.[36] Yet in the long run, the more serious
problem was that posed by the consul who permitted or fostered disorder by declining to co-operate with his colleagues or by misusing
his powers, formal or not. Given the political state of Samoa, there was

[35] The internal affairs of Samoa were then outside the cognizance of American
courts, there being no unilateral assumption of formal extra-territorial rights and
no treaty granting such rights. Charges relating to piracy and the like collapsed
for want of evidence, while the State Department, after a half-hearted investigation, declined to prosecute either Jenkins or Van Camp for malfeasance in
office. Jenkins, assisted by a government attorney, was released from prison
following his application for a writ of *habeas corpus*. Concerning the Van Camp-
Jenkins affair: USCP, 35 C., 2 S., House Rpt. 212; USCD, Apia/1, Swanston to
Marcy, 19 January 1857; Apia/2, Dirickson to Cass, 1 July 1859.

[36] USCD, Apia/1, Swanston to Cass, 20 April 1857. Swanston's report contains one
of the clearest accounts of a consul's position in Samoa.

simply no immediate way of countering such an influence short of violating the 'immunity' which consuls claimed and were generally thought to have.

## A Samoan boycott

Trouble of a different kind developed in 1855 when the chiefs at Apia Bay, including those of Faleata at Mulinu'u, banned Samoan patronage of the trade stores in that locality. Not since the war-damage claims of 1848 had any single issue arisen in which the interests of Samoans and of most Europeans were so directly and actively opposed or in which the very foundations of the foreign settlement were imperilled. In some respects the present affair had more serious implications, as the Samoans responsible for it were not from outside the area but, rather, were those among whom the foreigners lived. Moreover, a boycott, unlike looting, entailed a continuity of purpose and organization that was reminiscent of government—of sovereign rule in practice as well as theory.

Some time before the boycott was ordered, the chiefs met and jointly enacted a law purporting to lower retail prices at Apia by a substantial margin—according to one report, by twenty-five per cent, and to another, by fifty. The specific reasons for this measure are not clear. Certainly, relations between the Beach and the Samoans had been poor for some time, as indicated by the high-handedness of the consuls in dealing with disputes and complaints, and perhaps even more by the open arrogance which both peoples were said often to have displayed in their everyday contacts with one another. Moreover, there was growing discontent on the part of Pogai and other chiefs over certain foreign encroachments, notably in the use of the waterfront and harbour.[37] But as an economic weapon, the price-control law was probably more immediately related to the rise of import prices during the early 1850s, and also to the decline of the whaler traffic, which left the Samoans more dependent on the resident merchants for their trading outlets. In any event, the chiefs presented their demand, only to have it rejected on both economic and political grounds. Their next move was to order the cessation of Samoan trade at existing prices and rates of barter exchange. To enforce this boycott, the various Samoan settlements and villages, acting separately, were to post 'constables' at the stores.

[37] For example, Van Camp and various Samoan chiefs had only shortly before the boycott come into conflict over his closure of a customary right-of-way across his land at Matafele. Van Camp, who had also acted against the opposition of many of his European neighbours, was required by an American naval commander to reopen the track to public use (USN, Pac. Sqd., Bailey to Mervine, 1 October 1855).

R

A month after the enactment of the price-control law, Captain
Fremantle of H.M.S. *Juno*, calling on routine patrol, found the chiefs
resolved to make good their demand and the merchants, with their
hangers-on, convinced that the Samoans were out to destroy them. The
posting of several guards had already led to minor clashes and to
instances of 'trespass', and in Fremantle's opinion, such a state of
excitement had been reached that, but for his auspicious arrival, there
might have been a serious outbreak of violence. A naval party was sent
ashore to disperse angry demonstrators and pacify the leaders on either
side, and then Fremantle called a meeting of chiefs and traders. He
warned them of the dangers of continued ill feeling and unrest, and to
the Samoans he explained that commercial buying and selling were
private transactions in which the governments of civilized countries did
not normally interfere. The chiefs would not forego their traditional right
to control the production and consumption of goods by their own
people—and for that matter, were not told that they must—but to please
Fremantle, the 'real representative of the Queen', they promised to withdraw their guards and leave Samoans from elsewhere free to trade at
Apia. The merchants gratefully accepted the compromise and soon
witnessed the total collapse of the boycott.[38]

## Satan's stronghold breached

Following Fremantle's settlement of the price-fixing dispute, several
events occurred which had important bearing on the political situation
at Apia. Reference has already been made to some, including the opening of peace negotiations among the Samoan belligerents, the return of
J. C. Williams, and the departure of Van Camp and the succession of
more congenial men to the office he had held. Another was the recovery
of the London Missionary Society as an influence among the foreign
settlers. This was due partly to the arrival of people who were well
disposed towards the mission in any case—notably Williams and, somewhat later, August Unshelm, a Godeffroy manager, who, perhaps as a
matter of policy, made himself agreeable to both Catholics and Protest-
ants. But it was also associated with the repentance of some of the older
hands who, according to Murray, a veteran of the Tutuila revival, were
induced partly by financial and other personal misfortunes to seek
spiritual salvation. Among the first to come forward was George
Pritchard, a fact which no doubt made a strong impression on others.
In 1856 he gave up his opposition preaching, asked for a reconciliation
with the mission, and exhorted his friends to come with him to Murray's
English services. About the same time, his son, William, became a

[38] FO 58/84B, Fremantle to Osborne, 15 November 1855 (with enclosures).

church member and was reported as being 'thoroughly reformed' and
'quite steady'. After the Pritchards, others entered the church, including
Yandall and two former employees of Van Camp. The number of
adherents also 'greatly increased'.[39]

Another bond between Murray and the foreign settlement grew out
of the question of establishing a school for Europeans and half-castes,
that parents who were unable to send their children abroad should not
be forced to let them grow up virtually as Samoans. It was not the
policy of the London Missionary Society Directors to appropriate funds
specially to sustain work among Europeans, but the mission was none
the less concerned to help form and civilize some of the future leaders
of the community. Most of the interested parents were, for their part,
prepared to accept help from the London Missionary Society, if not on
grounds of religion, then of language, the great majority of foreigners
being English-speaking.

In order to provide a school it had been proposed as early as 1846, by
Mills, Pritchard and Williams, that parents subscribe funds to cover
expenses and that the London Missionary Society locate a qualified
teacher and undertake to keep up standards and maintain a regular
schedule of instruction. Money had in fact been collected and a school
site acquired, but too little had been raised then to guarantee the salary
of a teacher. The next attempt was made in 1856 and, under stimulus
of greater demand and of improved relations between the mission and
the settlers, culminated in the establishment of the Foreign Children's
School at Apia. Although ostensibly independent of the London Missionary Society—and certainly so in the financial sense—the successful
operation of the school depended heavily on Murray's initiative, particularly as to staffing. The first of a series of mission-approved teachers
was a new convert, an American whom Van Camp had brought to
Samoa.[40]

## Mixed courts and other innovations

In August 1856, on the occasion of another visit, Fremantle observed
a great improvement over the state of affairs he had found at Apia a
year before and concluded that the time was ripe for him to mediate
between chiefs and consuls, that they might work together more closely
in matters of interest to both Samoans and Europeans. Accordingly, he
invited Pogai, Toetagata, Jenkins and the repentant Pritchard to meet
with him to review the provisions and enforcement of the Wilkes code.
One of his main objects was the revival of the prohibition law, a

[39] Adm. 1/5684, Fremantle to Osborne, 4 October 1856; SSL, Murray, 25 June
1856, 1 December 1856.
[40] Murray, *Forty years' mission work*, 321-2, 332-4.

measure which Pritchard was now prepared to support. However,
Jenkins, rather ironically in view of his illegal court proceedings,
demurred on the ground that he allegedly had no authority to countenance departures from American law and practice unless they were undertaken by a fully sovereign government, which Samoa clearly lacked.[41]
If not genuine, his argument was at least a friendly one, though the
proposal was too impractical anyway for that to make much difference.
What Fremantle did achieve at this meeting was a written amendment
to the code providing that Pogai and Toetagata would help the foreign
residents build and maintain a bridge over the Vaisigano River, between
the villages of Apia and Matautu.[42] In this case it was the Samoans who
had reservations, for while the bridge would be of use to them as well as
to Europeans, they viewed such concessions in terms of their harbour
rights, of which they were exceedingly jealous. For some years, as the
business community had grown and the Samoan provisions trade had
become less important as an attraction to shipping, the consuls and
others had been at them to improve the harbour and its attendant
facilities in consideration of the fees they collected. They had consistently
refused, however, to grant any favours or supply any services unless
paid extra for them, contending that the harbour was theirs and that
Bethune and Wilkes, by virtue of that fact alone, had acknowledged
their right to collect fees. Now, but for Fremantle's influence, Pogai and
Toetagata would probably have refused again, for the new agreement
allowed them no increase in revenue.[43]

After some further negotiation, mainly to settle a dispute between
the chiefs as to the division of port fees, the Vaisigano bridge was
built.[44] Meanwhile, in April 1857, chiefs and consuls embarked upon a
much more important undertaking, namely the establishment of a mixed
court to decide cases between Samoans and Europeans. Significantly,

[41] USCD, Apia/1, Jenkins to Marcy, 15 August 1856.

[42] FO 58/86, Vaisigano bridge agreement, 11 August 1856 (encl. in W. T. Pritchard
to Clarendon, 30 August 1857).

[43] Adm. 1/5684, Fremantle to Osborne, 4 October 1856. In 1854 Pogai had made
several standing concessions, but only in return for an increase of one dollar in
the fee paid for each vessel (USN, Pac. Sqd., Van Camp to Bailey, 17 September
1855).

[44] USCD, Apia/1, Swanston to Cass, 18 July 1857; BCS 3/2, W. T. Pritchard
to Clarendon, 30 August 1857, 30 September 1857; BCS 4/1, Swanston and
Pritchard to Seumanutafa and To'omalatai, 2 February 1857, 7 June 1857,
Swanston and Pritchard to Seumanutafa, 15 July 1857, Pritchard to Seumanutafa,
7 November 1857. The dispute concerned a demand by Toetagata (To'omalatai)
to receive, by right, a full half share of the fees, all of which had been going
first to Pogai and disposed of or distributed by him. A new agreement was
reached whereby the consuls collected the fees and divided the proceeds equally
between the two chiefs.

this step, calculated to lessen dependence on naval justice, was taken in the absence of a warship. That this was possible was due partly to additional changes which had occurred in the make-up of the consular 'corps'. Pritchard, whose dismissal in favour of Williams was still advocated by Pogai and Toetagata, had gone off to England with prospects of remaining there.[45] His 'thoroughly reformed' son was acting in his place, but Williams, now permanently resettled in Samoa, had applied to succeed him and, pending the outcome, was accorded the rank of consul on behalf of Hawaii.[46] The American post had also changed hands, Jenkins having left to follow up the Van Camp affair. R. S. Swanston, the young Australian whom he had appointed to act, was outstandingly able and, as a visitor to Apia, had the additional advantage of being uncommitted on many of the issues that had come between Samoans and European residents. Another development which disposed the chiefs to negotiate was the campaign launched by Samoans at Saluafata Bay to entice the consuls and traders away from Apia. Having, through the collapse of the whaler trade, lost their market for provisions, the Saluafata people were offering free land, free use of their harbour, and a guarantee of self-government for Europeans, against which the cost and other disadvantages of moving were to be reckoned. This offer, though later rejected, was being given serious consideration, and the chiefs at Apia Bay knew it.[47]

The mixed court was the subject of a written agreement of a quasi-constitutional nature by which the consuls endeavoured to impose definite responsibilities upon the contracting parties and to establish, by authority of the 'ruling' chiefs, the legality of their own jurisdiction, lest they ever be called to answer for their proceedings. The competence of the court was limited to issues between Samoans and foreigners, and its jurisdiction was defined geographically, covering the area between and including Matautu Point and Sogi, where Pogai and Toetagata, the signatory chiefs, claimed to be paramount. The court was to be called into session by either of the two chiefs, acting for a Samoan complainant, or by any one of the consuls on behalf of a foreigner under

45 George Pritchard returned to the ministry and later became L.M.S. agent for Scotland and Ireland. Fremantle, who had recommended his dismissal from the Samoan consulate, noted that his son William would have been a suitable successor but for having a Samoan wife and having been involved in the mercantile affairs of Pritchard and Sons. It was partly on the strength of Fremantle's favourable report that William Pritchard was appointed first British consul in Fiji (Adm. 1/5684, Fremantle to Osborne, 4 October 1856).

46 Acting for Chapin, who had returned to the United States. De Boos succeeded Williams when the latter became British consul.

47 USCD, Apia/1, Swanston to Marcy, January 1857, Swanston to Cass, 15 August 1857.

his protection. The two chiefs and the consul for the foreign party had to be present as judges to constitute the court, while the other consuls were, if they wished, to sit in judgement as *ex officio* members of the panel. Other rules authorized the levy of fees and collection of costs, and one provided the option of trial by a jury of three Samoans and three Europeans. Without a comprehensive body of law to define the issues that might be adjudicated and the decisions that might be taken, this court, like that of the Foreign Residents' Society, was to perform as the judges thought expedient and fair. An issue would exist when a party complained, and a judgement would be handed down if and when the members of the court could agree to one. As for enforcing the terms of judgement, the chiefs would be responsible for Samoans and the consuls for Europeans.[48]

One of the problems encountered by the consuls in putting the mixed-court scheme into effect was that of securing the simultaneous support of Pogai and Toetagata. Both chiefs had insisted on being judges, but in place of a court for each, there was a 'central' tribunal, matters being arranged so that a case involving Matautu, say, was heard at Toetagata's house, with Pogai present as guest judge. This pooling of responsibility probably simplified the question of jurisdiction. Moreover, both chiefs stood to share in all the glory, which encouraged the one to participate if the other did, and to share in the division of all court fees, which encouraged them both. On the other hand, they tended to project their extraneous differences into the joint proceedings and to be hypersensitive about their dignity when in one another's presence. For the consuls, then, the exercise of diplomacy was still an essential part of the quest for ready justice—and all the more so considering that most of the patrons of the court were Europeans.

In dealing with charges against local Samoans, the original mixed court achieved considerable success, but it usually bogged down when the consuls, referring to its territorial jurisdiction, brought charges against strangers to the Apia area.[49] Whatever the chiefs had understood by the terms of the agreement they signed—and one may question whether, in any circumstances, they would have qualified their authority in writing—they would seldom apprehend and try visiting Samoans, however long or short the visits, and never on behalf of Europeans would they pursue offenders elsewhere, except occasionally to help negotiate for the restoration of stolen property or the payment of compensation. Many of the cases in this category had to be held over pending naval assistance, but sometimes the consuls were able to per-

48 USCD, Apia/1, Swanston to Marcy (*sic*—Cass), 1 May 1857, with court rules dated 27 April 1857.
49 e.g. BCS 4/1, W. T. Pritchard to Seumanutafa and To'omalatai, 8 April 1858.

suade other chiefs to follow the example of Pogai and Toetagata and join in special mixed courts, either at their own villages or, for preference, at Apia.[50] Needless to say, this procedure was slow and cumbersome, and what advantages it had disappeared as Apia attracted more and more Samoans from other places. Thus, there was still room for judicial reform at Apia as well as in the outer districts.

Turning back to 1857, one finds that Williams and the other consuls proposed, in addition to the establishment of the mixed court, the enactment of certain general laws for the Apia area. Their principal aim was to clamp down on the sale and consumption of liquor—not to attempt prohibition, as Fremantle had suggested, but to eliminate the excessive and disorderly drinking that most offended their sense of propriety and gave rise to much of the trouble between Samoans and Europeans. To be 'legal', the laws were to be passed by the chiefs, and to be effective, they were also to be policed by Samoans, who were to act at the instigation or with the approval of the consuls. Thus were the democratic principles of the Foreign Residents' Society and the solidarity of the Beach to be overthrown.[51] However, the consuls did not, on that occasion, make good their 'gross assumption of power', for the opposition so confused and divided the chiefs with threats, bribes and conflicting advice that it proved impossible even to get the laws passed. And so, once again, the Foreign Residents' Society survived. True, there developed in place of the original organization a simpler combination of consular board and public meeting, but the system remained basically unchanged and, judged by their own standards, the settlers remained 'firm supporters of law and order'.[52]

[50] When such hearings were conducted at Apia, Pogai and Toetagata were, as a matter of courtesy, invited to attend (BCS 4/1, Pritchard to Seumanutafa and To'omalatai, 23 April 1858).

[51] USCD, Apia/1, Swanston to Cass, 30 June 1857, 15 August 1857.

[52] USCD, Apia/2, Dirickson to Cass, 25 November 1859.

# II

## THE 1860s: A PERIOD OF TRANSITION

*'Honest people' and a runaway reform*

IN 1860 Samoan chiefs were again asked by Europeans to pass laws for general observance and to help enforce them. The laws proposed on this occasion, however, were to be more comprehensive in subject matter; they were to apply as widely as possible throughout the group of islands, not simply in the Apia area; and their enactment and the Samoans' share of their administration were to be undertaken by united sub-districts or districts, not by separate villages. In due course, several regional codes were in fact adopted. Unfortunately, no copy of any has come to light, but there is, at least, a record of the subjects taken up in the first and most important of them. This was Vaimauga's code of 1860, which contained seventeen 'simple laws' relating, among other things, to property and trading rights, land sales, shipping, marriage, adultery, keeping of the Sabbath, assault and murder, the carrying of lethal weapons, disorderly conduct, and regulation of liquor sales. No provision was made at this stage for the levying of duties or taxes, but fines were, of course, to be collected for offences, part of the revenue from which was to be spent on public works.[1]

As in connection with the abortive liquor-control scheme of 1857, so now were the consuls to be the principal custodians of European interests. Thus, while it was intended, once again, that the Samoans should provide the requisite police facilities, they were to employ them against foreigners only as sanctioned by the consuls. Foreigners charged with violating the general laws of a given area—of Vaimauga, for example—were to appear before a mixed tribunal, and so, too, were Samoans whose offences had given rise to complaints by Europeans. Issues to which the laws did not pertain were, if between Samoans and Europeans, to be decided by a mixed tribunal, as before, and if between Europeans, by the consuls and other foreign residents.[2] Public works, harbour control and

[1] BCS 3/2, Williams, Trade Report, 1 January 1861; USCD, Apia/2, Williams to Seward, 12 May 1862; Hood, *Cruise in H.M.S. 'Fawn'*, 93-4.

[2] BCS 5/1, Williams to Cowley, 3 April 1861, concerning court procedure in cases brought against Samoans on behalf of British subjects:

> All you have to do is to lodge your complaint with me. I appeal to the chiefs as the charge is against their people. They appoint the day and place, name the time when the Court will sit, you the complainant being present, I as H.B.M. Consul on your behalf to see that justice is given you.

allied matters of concern to both Europeans and Samoans were to be—
at Apia, to remain—the joint responsibilities of consuls and chiefs.
Finally, no law or subsequent amendment thereof was to apply to
Europeans unless endorsed by their consuls—a condition which, in
practice, required that *all* of those officials should agree to the enactment.[3]

It was J. C. Williams, the British consul, whose ideas largely inspired
the present reform and who worked hardest to promote it. In this
undertaking he no doubt benefited from having, late in 1859, again
become acting commercial agent for the United States, a position he was
to occupy until 1864.[4] Recalling, however, the failure of the consuls'
combined law-making efforts in 1857, what success Williams had then
probably owed less to his dual consular role than to the wider appeal
of his new proposals, especially for members of the foreign community.
For while he placed sufficient emphasis on questions of morality and
propriety to gain the support of missionaries, including Marists, his chief
purpose this time was to create a political climate more conducive to
economic growth. To gain the latter object he looked not only to the
passage of laws protecting property and enterprise, but also to the
gradual unification of the Samoans under a system of government that
would stimulate industry among them.

With a draft code in hand, Williams set out first to negotiate with
the chiefs of the Vaimauga sub-district, whose boundaries embraced most
of the foreign settlement at Apia Bay and among whose people there
appeared sufficient good will and common interest to encourage hope of
exemplary reform. In Vaimauga, too, Williams had many of his most
influential Samoan contacts. The details of the proceedings are not well
documented. It is clear, however, that Williams's appeal, which probably
emphasized the prestige- and revenue-making potentialities of the code,
was taken up not only at Matautu and Apia but also to the east, where
Vaimauga's principal meeting centre was situated and where its highest-
ranking title (Tofaeono) belonged. Vaiala, Matafagatele and the Catholic
stronghold of Vailele certainly joined in, and if Williams's reference to
the united 'district' of Vaimauga may be taken at face value, so did
the other villages, right up to the Atua border.[5]

Preparations for Williams's reform in Vaimauga were made in two
stages. The first was completed in November 1860 when an assembly
of chiefs adopted his draft laws, with minor alterations, and agreed to
the appointment of executive and judicial officers to administer them.

---

[3] e.g. BCS 4/1, Williams to Tui Atua at Lufilufi, 14 June 1860.

[4] USCD, Apia/2, Williams to Black, 30 January 1861, and Coe to Seward, 15
September 1864.

[5] USCD Apia/2, Williams to Seward, 12 May 1862.

It was decided then that the laws would go into effect on 1 January 1861, so that as far as Europeans were concerned, the experiment was ready to proceed.[6] For the people of Vaimauga, however, it was also desirable that the new code should be celebrated and proclaimed, as it were, before the whole of Samoa, for which purpose they set out to organize a great formal gathering. At this point, certain other Samoans took offence and tried to suppress the code.

Here it should be recalled that the enactment of written laws of European origin or conception had previously been undertaken in the name of territories or parties of greater magnitude than Vaimauga. In the western islands that activity had, in fact, been monopolized by the Mālō of Malietoa Vai'inupō, in which Seumanutafa Pogai, Vaimauga's signatory to the Wilkes code, had had only a subordinate position, however highly he may have been esteemed by Europeans. The questions which arose now had little or nothing to do with the enforcement of laws but related, rather, to subjective values associated with the possession of them. Had the chiefs of Vaimauga, in acting alone to acquire a new code, taken over a privilege to which they had had no exclusive or separate right? Were they trying to make themselves out as better or more advanced than other Samoans? Did they mean to take independent action in other matters which did not solely concern them?

The feeling elsewhere in Tuamasaga was that the chiefs of Vaimauga were guilty on all counts and that, if allowed to have their new laws, they would claim pre-eminence in the district. Consequently, pressure was put on them to abandon their scheme, that a code might be adopted on behalf of Tuamasaga as a whole. Having considered Tuamasaga, which was divided over the choice of a Malietoa, incapable of taking conclusive *district* action on his proposals, Williams now saw his more modest and 'realistic' approach in danger of being subverted by intrigues and possibly by hostilities. Aware, however, that the Vaimauga chiefs were determined to go ahead with their plans, he urged them, accordingly, to avoid offering their neighbours any gratuitous provocation. In turn, he warned the other Samoans of Tuamasaga not to obstruct, lest the Powers be required to intervene, and suggested that they would be better occupied improving their own laws and methods of government.[7] On that note the proclamation of Vaimauga's code came off without further incident.

During the next year or two, chiefs in other areas, notably A'ana and north-western Tuamasaga, also adopted codes and appointed judges. It is probable that they did so mainly to emulate Vaimauga and, in the

---

[6] *loc. cit.*

[7] BCS 4/1, Williams to Malietoa, 6 May 1861; BCS 3/2, Williams, Trade Report, 1 January 1862, Williams to Russell, 14 May 1862.

process, to lend superficial variety to traditional activities; for thus far, the Samoans generally had shown little interest in overhauling their machinery for governing themselves, while those in the 'outer districts' had yet to contend with the chronic political problems occasioned by foreign settlement and commercial development. At any rate, these later codes and judicial appointments do not seem to have had much bearing, constructive or otherwise, upon the course of European-Samoan relations.[8]

In Vaimauga, events took a different turn. Not that the Samoans there proved themselves in full accord with Williams's objectives, but they did take a keen interest in at least one aspect of his reform, that of enforcing stricter standards of public order and morality against the 'worthless element' on the Beach. Mainly to deal with this problem, the one most in evidence at the time, the chiefs at Apia Bay built a detention prison and established a regular Samoan police force. Now, at long last, observed a Marist at Mulivai, one could go out during the day and sleep at night without being disturbed by the revelries of sailors and beachcombers. The police were perhaps over-zealous, he thought, but 'honest people' could only be grateful to them for curbing excesses which had become so annoying and irksome.[9] A similar view was expressed by Williams, who said that the first effects of the laws had been 'salutary' and that only the riff-raff opposed the new order.[10]

It is not clear from the records how much, if any, of the task of controlling foreigners was undertaken by or in behalf of Vaimauga as a whole.[11] It *is* clear, however, that no change occurred in the manner of governing the Samoans of the sub-district and the *malaga* parties visiting there. Though capable of joint action of a quasi-legislative character, the Vaimauga chiefs remained too jealous of one another, said Williams, and too partial to the interests of the people they represented to form and maintain a central Samoan administration. This meant that most complaints brought against Samoans by Europeans, whether under the new laws or not, still had to be taken up at the village level. It meant, too, that the enforcement of the laws against Samoans lacked consistency and was often neglected altogether.[12]

In so far as they took their duties seriously, Samoan judges and police

8 With the possible exception of Faleata, of whose code and law-enforcement methods there is little record.

9 ASM(I), II, Poupinel to Dupont, 8 December 1861.

10 BCS 3/2, Williams, Trade Report, 1 January 1862; USCD, Apia/2, Williams to Seward, 12 May 1862.

11 e.g. whether the Samoan judges and police at Apia Bay were appointed by the sub-district and ever acted strictly on its authority or direction, or how far their jurisdiction, or that of any other officials, may have run.

12 BCS 4/1, 1861-3, *passim*.

probably acted in part from economic motives, the collection of fines being a convenient source of income. This may have been true not only in Vaimauga but also in places where most victims of the laws would have been Samoans. But in addition, there were political ends to be served, notably the discharge of grievances against foreigners, which 'respectable' settlers encouraged by tolerating and, in some cases, inviting police initiative against the 'worthless element'. At one time, missionaries would have been about the only foreign residents to concede the Samoans such jurisdiction; but now, given a code and other trappings of the 'rule of law', which ostensibly protected the 'law-abiding', the Samoans were more generally regarded as having some practical measure of authority over Europeans. But while it may not have been anticipated, the danger was, of course, that the Samoans' 'zeal' might give way to 'arrogance'—that they might try to control the 'honest people', too.

Such was the trend of events at Apia Bay by 1863. In that year, the consuls not only experienced greater difficulty in convening the mixed court to hear complaints against Samoans, but also found the local chiefs acting without their approval, and sometimes without their prior knowledge, in matters which, they maintained, should have been administered jointly. On one occasion, for example, a Samoan party was directed or allowed to tear up part of the 'government road' which had been laid out according to agreement between the chiefs and consuls. On another, Matautu and Apia unilaterally enacted and proclaimed new laws for general observance. Exception was also taken to the chiefs' recruitment of 'ruffians' to augment the local police force and, again, to the despatch of so-called police parties from beyond Matautu to intimidate traders and other Europeans at Apia Bay.[13] The quarrels attendant upon these acts were patched up, but good will was ebbing away and Williams's experiment in 'good laws and government' was approaching its ultimate crisis.

The end came after some policemen of Apia forcibly entered and caused considerable damage to the Godeffroy premises at Matafele, where they had allegedly pursued a Samoan woman wanted on a morals charge. The firm's local manager, August Unshelm, also consul for Hamburg since 1861, had once been a supporter of Williams's reform;[14] but concerned by liberties the police had been taking, and now their

---

[13] BCS 4/1, Williams to Tofaeono and the *faipule* of Vaimauga, 13 January 1863, C. MacFarland to Seumanutafa and Toetagata, 8 July 1863, Affidavit of Timote (of Aleipata), 7 November 1863; BCS 5/1, C. MacFarland to Unshelm, 19 August 1863.

[14] Being a consul without naval support from his home government, Unshelm had been particularly dependent on local means of securing and advancing his interests. Among other things, he endeavoured to remain aloof from factional and sectarian controversies.

innocent victim, he lost patience and himself ignored the 'due process of law' he had advocated. His complaint should first have been submitted for hearing by the mixed court, but instead, he summarily demanded that the Apia chiefs pay him an indemnity and fine, the total amount of which he set at one thousand dollars. The circumstances of the case, to say nothing of his influence as consul and merchant, gained Unshelm the support of most European residents. He was unfortunate, however, in having to do without the advice and help of Williams, who was then on a visit abroad, and was unwise to approach the chiefs in a manner which their mission, the London Missionary Society, could scarcely approve. To make good his claim Unshelm naively counted on assistance from Murray, with whom he was friendly, but the missionary would not take his side. The police had exceeded their legal powers and had acted with undue violence, Murray thought, yet they had been engaged in making a justifiable arrest and were, in any event, entitled to be heard. The chiefs readily took the same attitude, insisting on a 'fair trial' to determine who should pay compensation and how much.[15]

Unshelm did not test the chiefs' sincerity. Rather, he settled on a course which they and many others were bound to regard as even more reckless and retrograde than his first: in the absence of support from his own government, he asked the French authorities at Tahiti to send a warship to his aid. The chiefs, who until then may have thought themselves in no danger, were appalled, and so was Murray. In their view, Unshelm had become madly obsessed by a desire to 'crush the Samoans' and, to realize it, was playing into the hands of French 'annexationists', including, of course, the Marists. It is likely that Unshelm *did*, in fact, want to crush the Samoans, in the sense of freeing 'respectable' Europeans from their police jurisdiction. As for his immediate complaint, however, what choice of action did he have, once his bluff had been called? Surely, the chiefs' offer to submit to or participate in a trial was unpromising, quite apart from the demands it made upon Unshelm's pride; for with the whole community up in arms over the case, it would have been virtually impossible to constitute a local court acceptable to both sides. Unshelm could have waited for Williams, who might have negotiated to some effect, but otherwise, his only substantial hope of a favourable settlement lay in obtaining naval assistance. If he preferred to look to the French for that (rather than to the British, again with help from Williams), it would probably have been because he was well known to the officials in Tahiti and could easily contact them through his own shipping organization, while, in the meantime, putting the French bogy to work in his behalf in Samoa.

15 SSL, Murray, 27 June 1864.

Soon after he announced that he was appealing to France, Unshelm left on a westward trading voyage and was lost at sea in a hurricane, a fate which Samoans did not fail to attribute to divine justice. That the available records do not refer again to Unshelm's claim suggests that it, too, may have died when he did, but not so the hostility provoked by the Matafele and other 'outrages'. Two notable features of that hostility clearly emerge: first, a decline of Murray's popularity and influence among Europeans, occasioned by his refusal to support them in a time of crisis; and secondly, a closing of settler ranks in reaction to Samoan interference. Certain events of this period recall those associated with Pritchard's career on the Beach. For example, attendance at the foreigners' Protestant chapel fell off considerably, and a petition for Murray's transfer, originally inspired by Unshelm, his erstwhile friend, was directed to the London Missionary Society headquarters in London. More important, the Foreign Residents' Society was actively revived, though in a simpler form and under a different name, that is, the Association for the Mutual Protection of Life and Property.[16]

Williams, who returned to Samoa just before Unshelm's fateful departure, conceded the failure of his attempt to associate Europeans and Samoans in a joint government and took a prominent part in the establishment of the new settlers' society.[17] In doing so, he too strained his relations with Murray, who, owing mainly to the emphasis the Samoans had given the suppression of vice, opposed the dissolution of the existing régime. Not that Williams had grown indifferent to loose living, but he was not prepared to sacrifice the security of property and trading rights just to facilitate the punishment of it. It was up to him, then, to counter Murray's influence and convince the local chiefs that Europeans should again be independent of their jurisdiction, with matters affecting both peoples to be regulated according to agreements made prior to 1860. In this task Williams was successful; and thereafter, when the prevalence of vice was reported by London Missionary Society representatives, he took the side of the Beach, admitting that strict moral standards were not generally observed but insisting that Apia was, contrary to the implications of the 'libel', a perfectly safe place in which to do business.[18]

The foreign residents formed their Association in March 1864 and elected Williams their judge, with instructions to conduct each trial

[16] BCS 5/1, Williams to Weber, 11 January 1865.

[17] According to Williams, there was 'no dependence to be placed on the native authorities' (BCS 3/3, Williams to Russell, 1 April 1864).

[18] SSL, J. C. Williams to Tidman, 9 January 1867, in reply to attack appearing in the *Chronicle,* June 1866.

before a panel of jurors. Soon afterwards, Williams notified the Foreign
Office of the new development and asked that his assumption of magisterial powers be approved.[19] He knew, of course, that the British Government denied having the right to confer such powers itself; but he thought
that 'the chiefs' should be acknowledged as having that right, and that
the Association should be recognized as their legal instrumentality,
having been founded with their consent. Williams's case did not, however, satisfy the requirement for a treaty, nor could his statement of the
Samoans' unreliability, made to emphasize the need for the Association,
have stimulated confidence in the practical force of any agreement that
might be reached with them. For that matter, he did not even offer
supporting evidence of an agreement in the present instance or name the
chiefs with whom he had negotiated. Finally, his court jurisdiction was
to extend to *all* foreigners, an expedient certain to horrify those who had
to consider the international implications. The Foreign Office might
have been prepared to shut its eyes to the conduct of informal judicial
proceedings, if relating only to the interests of British subjects and
Samoans; but it was not British practice—as it was then that of the
United States[20]—to invite consuls to assume even that degree of private
responsibility, much less to countenance any disregard of instructions
when official notice of it was given. Thus, Williams was ordered to
decline or relinquish the office of judge and was offered no advice
beyond the hint that it be taken by someone unconnected with the
British Government.[21]

When Williams was elected judge, the only other consular officer at
Apia had been Theodore Weber, who acted for Unshelm, and was
destined to succeed him as Hamburg consul and Godeffroy manager.
Within a few months, however, there was a third, an American settler
named Jonas Coe, who was commissioned United States commercial
agent. Coe's appointment deprived Williams of a source of local influence and made it more difficult to maintain a foreign residents' court
under the presidency of a single consul. That is not to say that American
interests, adversely affected by the Civil War and the northward shift
of whaling activity, were now of very much account, but the American
element on the Beach was still quite large, and Coe's support of the
Association correspondingly vital to its success. Williams's position as
judge was insecure, then, before he ever received his instructions to
give it up. When the instructions arrived, he did as he was told; but
without advising the Foreign Office, he continued, as consul, to perform

[19] BCS 3/3, Williams to Russell, 1 April 1864.

[20] USCI 10, Seward to Coe, 29 November 1869; BCS 1/1, Rice to Williams, 23
August 1869.

[21] BCS 1/1, Russell to Williams, 28 September 1864.

magisterial functions, which he had always undertaken anyway.[22] The difference was that the consuls, unless dealing only with their own nationals, acted in concert as equal and *ex officio* members of the foreign residents' court, in effect sharing the position to which Williams had been elected. The influence of the settlers was maintained by the provision for trial by jury. This arrangement, facilitated by the long tenure of all three consuls, worked quite well until the 1870s, at least within the terms of reference laid down by the Association.

## The cotton boom: false dawn of prosperity

As suggested, Europeans considered the Samoans' factionalism and sense of pride inimical to the growth of commerce, thinking not only of the obstacles they presented to the remodelling of Samoan society and enterprise along Western lines, but also of such practices as 'civil' war and the 'purchase' of brides and titles which the people were said to pursue virtually to the point of impoverishing themselves and their resources. Yet the fact is that rivalry among the Samoans was one of the most powerful forces capable of being turned to the advantage of the merchant. It is perhaps understandable why this was not appreciated during the 1848-57 war, when the arms traffic actually helped sustain the volume of trade; for among other things, it was easy to imagine that the Samoans would have produced much more had they been at peace. But in 1861, when, chiefly in response to the new London Missionary Society fund-raising techniques,[23] their tempo of production *did* quicken, suddenly and very substantially, the relative economic significance of *fa'a-Samoa* rivalry seems still to have made little impression in commercial circles. Williams, in his reports, did not even refer to the mission's drive for contributions, much less cite its influence on trade. The supply of Samoan-produced coconut oil had nearly doubled in volume within the span of a year, with cash payment being required for much of it, yet all he said by way of explanation was that European goods were gradually becoming more popular.[24] Williams had, of course, pinned faith on 'good laws and government' as the best prospect for commercial development[25] and was then hopefully engaged in promoting them; but as shown by the results, he was in that regard, too, misjudging the Samoans' motivations and intentions.

[22] BCS 3/3, Williams to Clarendon, 5 January 1869, Williams to Granville, 18 October 1870; BCS 4/1 and 5/1, *passim*; USCD, Apia/2, Williams to Coe, 6 July 1866 (and other enclosures with Coe to Seward, 15 November 1866).

[23] See chapter 5, above.

[24] BCS 3/2, Williams, Trade Report, 1 January 1862. Samoan production rose to about six hundred tons in 1861.

[25] BCS 3/2, Williams, Trade Report, 1 January 1859.

The next economic development of importance, the cotton boom of the mid-1860s, owed no more to legal or political reform nor, again, were the local conditions which made it possible given full due in commercial reports of the time. The principal overseas stimulus was, needless to say, the world shortage of cotton brought on by the American Civil War.[26] Some years before the outbreak of that conflict, inquiries had been made on behalf of Manchester textile interests as to whether cotton might be cultivated in Samoa,[27] but apart from the ideal climate and soil, which promised a quick and heavy yield, the indications had been unfavourable.[28] Commercial planting by Europeans had been out of the question, for they had neither significant quantities of land nor access to labour cheap enough to enable them to compete in a distant market against the slave-owning producers of the southern United States. If the land had been available, not even the higher-priced long-staple cottons could have been grown economically by Europeans in Samoa. As for the Samoans, they could not be persuaded to take on something unfamiliar in addition to or in place of their production of coconut oil and food-stuffs, which already satisfied their trade demands. The subsequent rise in cotton prices was great enough to compensate for high cost of transport from Samoa and to enable Europeans there to pay moderate wages. It did not in itself, however, dispose the Samoans to sell more land or to provide a dependable supply of labour, nor did it induce them to plant much cotton for themselves.

At first, then, the change in the overseas cotton market had little practical effect in Samoa. Commencing in 1863, European small-holders developed pocket-handkerchief 'plantations', which, after about a year, totalled no more than one hundred acres in extent and produced a crop that one small gin and press could easily prepare for shipment.[29] Since too little Samoan labour was forthcoming to support the industry, even on that scale, some of the 'larger' planters, which included Williams, brought in Niueans and Rarotongans on one-year contracts, paying them five to ten dollars per month, plus rations.[30] This experiment did not

26 By the Union blockade of the Confederacy as well as by the neglect or destruction of many southern plantations.

27 One inquiry had been prompted by the submission of samples of Samoan-grown cotton to the Foreign Office, another by the request of the Cotton Supply Association of Manchester for information on the cotton-growing potentialities of tropical areas generally (BCS 1/1, FO to Pritchard, 20 July 1857, 12 September 1857).

28 BCS 3/2, Pritchard to FO, 8 May 1858.

29 BCS 3/2, Williams, Trade Report, 28 January 1864; Trood, 54.

30 Williams started by paying ten dollars per month, plus rations, but found this rate too costly. Subsequently, the contract wage dropped to five dollars, with rations. BCS 3/3, Williams to Russell, 19 November 1864. Williams had seventy acres planted in cotton in 1865. Brenchley, *Cruise of H.M.S. 'Curacoa'*, 63-4.

solve the labour problem, however, for after the developmental stage, which was soon passed when land was hard to get, most of the work of producing cotton was concentrated in the twice-yearly harvesting and processing of crops. In other words, the indenture system, unless reduced to conditions of virtual slavery, could have been permanently adapted to cotton cultivation only if the Samoans had supplied periodic drafts of supplemental casual labour or if the planter had sufficiently diversified his interests to have full-time productive work for a force of contract labourers. The latter course, if confined to agricultural pursuits, would have entailed investment in crops maturing more slowly than cotton, for which long-term commitments most settlers lacked capital reserves as well as land.

During the second half of 1864, however, the outlook changed radically, as Samoans began offering Europeans an abundance of labour and arable land at reasonable prices and, throughout the group of islands, started taking up cotton as a cash crop. European accounts purporting to explain these phenomena stress influences which, if relevant at all, must surely have been marginal or superficial—namely, the example of enterprise set by foreign planters; mission advice on agriculture and trade; the Samoans' anxiety to purchase copies of a revised edition of the complete Bible as translated by the London Missionary Society; the building of weatherboard houses by a few chiefs around Apia, taken as evidence of a growing desire for a Western living standard.[31] Without doubt more significant was a series of natural disasters which so depleted the Samoans' traditional food resources that they could not maintain former levels of trade in coconut oil and provisions. By the time they went to the rescue of the cotton industry, the Samoans had been in reduced circumstances for about a year, and their position was rapidly worsening. They were then in the grip of a drought, Samoa's longest on record, which ruined such crops as taro and yams and made possible large bushfires that destroyed natural food reserves in several areas.[32] After the dry spell came an unusually severe storm, reputedly a hurricane, which took another heavy toll, especially of coconuts and the oncoming breadfruit crop; and in the wake of that disaster, a blight or pest ravaged coconut palms and other vegetation.[33] The whole cycle of destruction, lasting the greater part of two years, had cumulative effects from which the economy did not recover until 1868. Meanwhile,

[31] e.g. BCS 3/3, Williams, Trade Report, 1 January 1868.

[32] BCS 3/3, Williams, Trade Report, 1 January 1865.

[33] USCD, Apia/2, Coe, Trade Report, 1 January 1866; SSL, Murray, 9 January 1866. A plague of caterpillars sometimes followed a severe storm (SSL, Hardie and Turner, Annual Report, September 1850). The nature of the blight in 1865 was not described.

Samoans made up some of their requirements of cash and manufactures and perhaps, in some measure, supplemented their stocks of food by cultivating cotton, which throve in the prevailing conditions, and by selling land and performing wage-labour.[34] None of the reports suggests that, apart from a few individual cases, the Samoans' income or wealth was augmented by the cotton boom.

The total income of Europeans, too, probably increased little, if at all, especially in view of the decline of the local trade in coconut oil; but the rise of the cotton industry had, none the less, profound and lasting economic significance for them. For in Upolu, notably in northern Tuamasaga and A'ana, hitherto a fertile 'waste', several thousand acres of arable land were sold by the Samoans, not only to the larger firms and entrepreneurs, such as the house of Godeffroy, but also to men of small capital, tradesmen and shopkeepers, whose part in the cash economy had been slight and of whom there was now an exodus from Apia.[35] With labour in over-supply, and with many Samoans engaging in cotton planting themselves, cultivation of the new crop jumped from 400 acres in 1865 to 1,700 in 1866, and to 2,400 in 1867, while at Apia, the processing and shipment centre of the industry, the number of horse- and steam-driven gins increased, during the same period, from four to about twenty.[36] Although the cotton boom did not last, then, a major breakthrough was made into the fields of land speculation and commercial agriculture, entailing a sharp rise in capital investment and the expansion of economic enterprise into some of the 'outer' districts.

Cotton was Samoa's leading domestic export in 1866-7, during which time it brought, locally, a top price of five cents per pound in seed, with labour on European plantations being remunerated at full-time rates up to ten dollars per month and a casual rate of one cent per pound for picking.[37] The prospects appeared so bright then that Williams declared

---

[34] USCD Apia/2, Coe, Trade Report, 1 January 1865. Coe wrote that 'the present difficulty is, when a person requires laborers, . . . to be able to keep only the laborers he requires, so great is the anxiety to obtain work'.

[35] USCD, Apia/2, Coe, Trade Report, 1 January 1865; SSL/30, Murray, 9 January 1866.

[36] The following is a percentage breakdown of production during the period June 1865 to May 1866: Upolu, 78.7%; Savai'i, 13.6%; Tutuila, 6.1%; and Manu'a, 1.6%. The European plantations were concentrated in Upolu. No separate figures were given for Samoan production (BCS 3/3, Williams, Trade Report, 2 January 1867).

[37] The daily wage for casuals was fifty cents. Both daily and monthly rates excluded rations. Prior to the drought the Samoans had demanded about twice what they accepted in time of hardship. The Gilbertese who, from about 1867, were recruited to work on German plantations received only one dollar per month, plus rations (BCS 3/3, Williams to Clarendon, 9 December 1868).

## COTTON PRODUCTION 1863-8[38]

| | Acreage planted (cumulative, at end of year) | Local buying prices (in seed), per lb | Quantity exported | Rated value of exports, f.o.b. Apia |
|---|---|---|---|---|
| | | | | $ |
| 1863 | 12 | — | 6 bales | — |
| 1864 | 180 | 6 to 10 cents | 4 tons clean | ca.   3,000 |
| 1865 | 400 | 3 to 4 ,, | 40 ,, ,, | 21,000 |
| 1866 | 1,700 | 3 to 5 ,, | ca. 150 ,, ,, | 77,500 |
| 1867 | 2,400 | 4 to 5 ,, | 230 ,, ,, | 115,000 |
| 1868 | 2,500 | 2 ,, | ca.  60 ,, ,, | — |

that Samoa seemed destined to become a 'cotton-growing country'.[39] In 1868, however, the overseas market eased, particularly for the short staple but heavy-bearing kidney cotton, which Samoa's planters, influenced by Britain's requirements, had taken up almost exclusively. Sea island, a long staple variety used chiefly by French mills, was still selling for a relatively high price, but only in Fiji and Tahiti, among the principal South Pacific islands, had it been cultivated extensively. Kidney, now at two cents per pound in seed at Apia, could still be harvested without loss, even by European planters paying pickers the accepted piece-wage of one cent per pound. But meanwhile, the Samoans' food supplies had nearly returned to normal, and a large surplus of coconuts was available for commercial purposes. Only recently, moreover, the Godeffroy manager, Theodore Weber, had begun to encourage copra-making in preference to oil-extraction, which was more tedious and wasteful. Copra was also easier to produce than cotton and, at prevailing prices, offered a greater return for effort expended.

Circumstances having thus changed, Samoans fairly generally refused to pick cotton for European planters and would not harvest their own. In some areas, chiefs demanded that the merchants raise the buying price of cotton to five cents per pound, the previous year's maximum, but this was of course impossible. At least three-quarters of the 1868 crop, the most abundant yet, was therefore lost.[40] A few Europeans switched to sea island, but when the Franco-Prussian war broke out, resulting in the shut-down of textile mills in Alsace, Samoa's favourable

[38] These are rough figures extracted from consular reports. USCD, Apia/2-3, and BCS 3/2-3, *passim*. The yield of clean or ginned cotton from cotton 'in seed' was about thirty per cent. The local price ratio between the two was, however, about five to one, which induced some Samoans to hand-clean a small quantity.

[39] BCS 3/3, Williams, Trade Report, 1 January 1866.

[40] BCS 3/3, Williams, Report on the Cultivation of Cotton, 6 November 1868, Trade Report, 1 January 1869.

market for that strain was also gone. Even so, cotton production continued, and actually increased during the 1870s and 1880s, the copra
industry alone outranking it in terms of domestic output values. Cultivation was largely undertaken, however, by the Godeffroy firm, which
used cotton as a secondary or cover crop on its new and extending
plantations of coconuts. Having a large force of indentured labour,
otherwise occupied in clearing land and planting nuts, the firm could,
at little extra expense, grow cotton, which by itself would have been
uneconomic. Without capital to develop substantial coconut plantations,
most landowning settlers were also unable to produce cotton in significant
quantities.

## The origin and outbreak of the war of 'unification'

Thus, it was not by force of local political circumstances but, rather,
through vagaries of climate and overseas markets—'accidents' of history
—that European settlers acquired their first big economic stake in Samoa.
The protection of their land titles and investments, however, and the
development of their holdings were still matters in respect of which they
looked to the government for assistance, and accordingly, the question
of political reform gained new urgency for them during the mid-1860s.
Late in 1865, Williams, having decided that 'the present state of Samoa
without either a responsible Government or laws' was a problem which
had to be attacked once again, proposed calling a meeting at Apia of
'the principal chiefs and tulafales' of all the districts,[41] that the adoption
of a republican constitution and code of laws might be considered. 'If I
find the majority of the chiefs are willing to entertain my proposition,'
wrote Williams in his letters canvassing mission support, 'I shall render
them every assistance in my power, and the minority must submit.'[42]

Out again for 'national' reform, which had proved so elusive in the
mid-1850s, Williams was making little headway until Captain Charles
Hope of H.M.S. *Brisk* undertook to help him.[43] Hope, visiting the group
in July 1866, tried to frighten and shame the Samoans into taking
Williams's advice. The incidence of disputes between them and Europeans, the risk of internecine war, and the likelihood of prolonged
economic stagnation were so great, in the absence of sound government
and laws, that the freedom and independence of Samoa were thereby
jeopardized. At any time, Hope told various high-ranking chiefs, an
imperial Power might find a ready cause or excuse to take over the
islands. Then, look at the Hawaiians, he said, with their own ships

---

41 BCS 5/1, Williams to the missions (to each separately), 11 December 1865.
42 *loc. cit.*
43 Adm. 1/5969, Hope to Wiseman, 5 September 1866; MS., Hope, Journal I,
   account dated 14 July 1866.

under their own flag, and their own accredited representatives abroad. See how well the Tongans governed themselves, and also the Raro- tongans. Even the Niueans, among the last Polynesians to be converted to Christianity, were ahead of the Samoans, having adopted good laws and built a network of roads. The Samoans, with their 'many districts', all 'perfectly independent', were falling behind. To catch up, they must first create a strong central government or, if that proved impossible, individual island governments. Or, at the very least, the principal chiefs[44] should agree to a single code of laws for the whole group and meet once a year to settle outstanding disputes, though a more highly centralized authority would improve Samoa's chance of recognition by foreign Powers. In addition, the Samoans would have to be more industrious, working harder at 'useful' tasks and putting less time into such pursuits as the making of fine mats.[45]

A few months after the call of the *Brisk*, Williams reported that 'the chiefs of A'ana' had 'established' laws for that district and levied a poll tax of one dollar on every male. Tuamasaga, he wrote, was preparing to follow suit, and should it succeed in doing so, similar measures would probably be taken in Savai'i and Manono.[46] Within the next year or so, other district codes were in fact proclaimed in the western islands, and Samoans there began considering proposals for confederating the districts. Europeans regarded these developments as the most encouraging to date: the Samoans, moved by such arguments as Hope's, were making their most serious effort to 'advance' politically. The evidence suggests that they probably were. None the less, legal and constitutional innova- tions undertaken by them, if not always intended mainly as a new guise for the expression and working out of *fa'a-Samoa* ambitions and rivalries, still ran up hard against those forces at some vital stage, as happened in the present instance.

One of the major obstacles to the reforms now attempted had been touched on by Williams when writing, prospectively, of the submission of a minority of chiefs to a majority government. Not that he would have opted for war, if necessary to achieve that end, or that he even appreciated the strong probability of its occurrence, but how else were dissidents, unless few, to be ruled against their will? Later on, Williams and others wrote of the new district codes as if their enactment had, in each case, been widely considered and had met with little or no opposi- tion.[47] That may have been so, outwardly at any rate, but their enforce-

[44] Of whom he named Tui Manu'a; Mauga and Tuitele of Tutuila; and Tui A'ana, Tui Atua and Malietoa. These were chiefs he had met.

[45] BCS 2/1, Hope to Chiefs of Samoa, 25 July 1866.

[46] BCS 3/3, Williams, Trade Report, 2 January 1867.

[47] *loc. cit.*; SSL, Whitmee, 7 August 1867.

ment proved quite a different matter. If left to the separate villages, as had been done in Vaimauga with regard to the laws of 1860, enforcement might not have raised dangerous factional issues. Undertaken at the district level, however, it clearly did. What happened then was that one of two or more inter-village parties took the *pule* centre or some other place as its headquarters, appointed officials and demanded, without always observing the laws itself, that others obey the decisions of a 'government' in which they lacked, and may not have wanted or have been offered, representation.

Events in Tuamasaga help to illustrate the point, but first it should be noted that the political situation generally was complicated by a division of the Malietoa title, in which that district had a large interest. When Molī had died in 1860, Talavou, Vai'inupō's son by a different wife, had been the strongest contender for the succession and, in terms of Samoan custom, an ideal choice, as both Taimalelagi and Molī before him had been. The only other contender of consequence had been Molī's son Laupepa, a youth who might ordinarily have been expected to succeed after Talavou's death. Talavou, however, had still been *persona non grata* to the London Missionary Society, for which he was said to have retained a 'heathenish hatred',[48] whereas Laupepa, perhaps influenced by his father, once a teacher for the London Missionary Society, had been a student at the Malua seminary. Particularly fearful lest Talavou, like Taimalelagi, should sanction war if he became Malietoa, the missionaries had thrown their weight behind Laupepa, reputedly a man of peace like his father. This had been the first instance of the mission's involvement in such an important title dispute.

With European backing, which some accounts say was crucial to his then having a persistent claim at all, Laupepa had secured an edge over Talavou in Upolu (mainly Tuamasaga), but not in Savai'i or Manono. In the ensuing negotiations, each side had stood firm against the other, and a compromise proposal by the missionaries, that the Malietoa title should go to a third member of the family, a woman, had also failed.[49] The parties had agreed, however, to the sharing of the *pule* and dignity of the title by Laupepa and Talavou, the former to live in Tuamasaga and the latter in Savai'i or Manono. This uneasy arrangement, for which there were temporary precedents in the history of the Malietoa line, was still in effect when there arose the questions of district reform and confederation.

In Tuamasaga, as in other districts, at least some of the paraphernalia of central government was acquired without the appearance of factional strife. That is to say, the Samoans seem to have been capable of agreeing

48 HFO, Genealogy of the Malietoas, 1887.
49 Aube, 170-2; Hood, 75-7.

on the form, if not the substance or implementation, of certain measures which Europeans urged upon them. Thus, a code of laws, drafted by the consuls, was enacted at a district meeting early in 1868; a representative council was formed and plans laid for the establishment of a district court; and the working centre of government was placed at Matautu village, allegedly by reason of the commercial advancement of the Apia area.[50] However, district cohesion, such as it was, did not survive long enough for the central government to be fully constituted, much less to assume the actual business of ruling. For at an early council meeting the explosive issue of choosing a head of state was raised, quite probably on European advice, and the action taken on it divided the district reform movement into hostile factions. The supporters of Laupepa, taking advantage of superior strength, pushed through a resolution proclaiming that chief *sole* Malietoa and the 'king' or paramount chief of Tuamasaga. They then brought him from Malie to live at Matautu. Samoans favouring Talavou immediately dissociated themselves from the Matautu government and brought their champion and many of his Savai'i and Manono people to Mulinu'u, to which access was given by Faleata chiefs loyal to him. Talavou's supporters subsequently issued their own proclamation, affecting to bestow on him alone the honours already claimed for Laupepa, and they set up a rival Malietoa 'government' at Mulinu'u. For several months thereafter the two factions glared at one another across Apia Bay, both threatening war but neither taking an irrevocable step towards it, until the *faitasiga* or union of the districts became the subject of partisan negotiations.[51]

Among Europeans the idea of a confederation of districts was linked with the apparent disinclination of the Samoans, following the 1848-57 war, to take up the dispute over Mālō status and restore the Tafa'ifā. On only one occasion, and that shortly after the close of the war, had any serious attempt been made to reopen those issues, and it had received too little support to raise a threat of hostilities. Meanwhile, the constituent titles of the Tafa'ifā had gone to the leading claimants, Mata'afa Fagamanu becoming Tui Atua, and Tuimaleali'ifano Sualauvī acquiring the Tui A'ana title and the two pāpā of Tuamasaga. That the Tuamasaga *pāpā* went to Sualauvī, a close relative of Vai'inupō, was probably due to the division of the Malietoa title, which, of course, had also been contested without resort to force. Not that these titles belonged strictly to districts, but Europeans tended to think that they did, or should, and to regard the continuation of peace as evidence of widespread desire that the districts should be equal and largely self-contained. This impression

[50] BCS 3/3, Williams, Trade Report, 1 January 1868; SSL, 'The War on Upolu' by George Turner Sr, 16 April 1869.
[51] SSL 1869-70, *passim*; Aube, 172-5.

gained more force when early discussion of confederation took place in an atmosphere relatively free of inter-district partisan intrigue. It seemed feasible then to envisage the districts as unitary elements of a state peacefully evolved and their internal rule as the principal focus of power politics in Samoa.[52]

These prospects were apparently dimmed by the 'kingship' crisis in Tuamasaga. Towards the end of 1868, however, some chiefs of A'ana and Atua came to Apia Bay ostensibly to mediate in the Malietoa dispute and to promote, by peaceful means, a union of districts in the western islands. Since these visitors were pro-Talavou, it is not surprising that their first undertaking was fruitless, if indeed they pursued it at all seriously; but the confederation they proposed was agreed to by the chiefs at Mulinu'u, and a joint headquarters or seat of government was established there.[53] At this point it was widely believed among Europeans that Talavou's supporters had chosen to assert his pretensions through participation in the *faitasiga* movement, as an alternative to war. It was thought, too, that all of the districts but Tuamasaga were sufficiently united internally and well enough represented at Mulinu'u to satisfy the requirements of confederation, and that the Laupepa government at Matautu, hopelessly overshadowed by the Unionists (or *faitasiga* people), had no sane course but to join them and make the confederation complete. Accordingly, influential Europeans, including London Missionary Society representatives, tried to effect a reconciliation of the Matautu and Mulinu'u régimes, seeking terms that would leave no disparity of status between Laupepa and Talavou nor cause either any embarrassment.[54] Their efforts were not, however, successful.

The two so-called governments continued in separate session at Apia Bay, and as they did so, it emerged that the Mulinu'u confederation was not retaining, if it had ever had, all the support originally claimed for it. Manono may have been united, but none of the districts of Savai'i was, while in A'ana and Atua, reform movements which Europeans had hailed as progressive were breaking up, partly under the influence of the Tuamasaga rift. With the Malietoa title dispute as an initial focal point, inter-district alliances were forming that eventually would fight for the Mālō and, after the deaths of Mata'afa Fagamanu and Tuimaleali'ifano Sualauvī, for the reconstitution of the Tafa'ifā.

Of the two sides, the Unionists enjoyed greater favour among local Europeans: they seemed much the stronger and hence likely to prevail in the event of a general war; they had taken the initiative in forming

[52] SSL, Whitmee, 7 August 1867; MS., Brown, Letterbooks, entry of 21 June 1870.
[53] ibid., Turner Sr, 7 May 1869.
[54] BCS 3/3, Williams, Trade Report, 1 January 1869; SSL, Turner Sr, 16 April 1869.

Samoa's first 'central government', which helped give their cause an aura of legitimacy consonant with Western principles; and they were allegedly the party of the district *pule* centres. The first argument proved to have some validity. In the opening battle of the war, which Laupepa's Tuamasaga party entered without active allies, the Unionists were far superior in numbers and easily won; and though their lead was later reduced, they remained the *itū taua tele*, the large war party, and but for foreign interference, might have had a decisive victory. The second argument was more dubious. The confederation had a capital, and probably a written constitution, but as yet it had made no substantial change in the manner or system of rule in Samoa. The legitimacy of the confederation was therefore nominal, and if Europeans recognized its having any, surely it was more because the Unionists showed greater promise of being able to carry out the reforms for which both sides professed a desire. That some such desire existed among Samoan leaders need not be doubted. The collection of taxes, the building of roads, the regulation of trade, the punishment of acts previously sanctioned—these and other functions of political authority that interested Europeans *did* appeal to the imagination of Samoans, quite contrary to the view, often expressed since, that their new ideas on government mostly concerned gun salutes, badges of office and other symbolic uplifts to their dignity. But events suggest that much of the Samoans' interest in such substantive measures derived from the obvious fact that they could be onerous for those on whom they might be imposed and advantageous for those who might impose them. In effect, foreign residents and visitors, apparently without fully realizing it, were educating the Samoans in new ways of persecution and self-aggrandizement. In that connection it must be recalled that, by Samoan standards, the Mālō-Vaivai relationship was one of exaction and oppression on the largest scale, no more compatible with the principle of equality before the law than were the prerogatives of chiefly rank, yet it was towards the establishment of such a relationship that the present Samoan power struggle was oriented.

As for the third argument, it is true that the Unionists were stronger in the *pule* centres. Only at Malie, in Tuamasaga, was the other side ever the favourite, and at an early stage, perhaps consequent upon Laupepa's removal to Matautu, the Unionists, through Talavou, seem to have gained the upper hand there too. According to the Wesleyan missionary, George Brown, however, the *pule* centres were the 'ruling towns' in their respective districts, and the *faitasiga* movement, which he described as the only hope for an independent Samoa, was really theirs.[55] For generations, wrote Brown, these centres had been at odds with one another, but now they had agreed 'to sink all their old

[55] MS., Brown, Letterbooks, entry of 21 June 1870.

differences and unite to establish one firm government for Samoa and make a code of laws like those in Tonga', only to meet opposition from 'villages owing allegiance to them'. In other words, voluntary unity was taken as a *normal* political attribute of the districts, their present internal divisions being put down to rebellion against a 'reasonable' extension of the authority of the *pule* centres and past disturbances being regarded as contention between united districts. Most Europeans, said Brown, came to accept this view, which purported to prove, in terms of Samoan custom, the correctness of the district reform and confederation schemes. But it was not sound. As will be clear already, the districts were *not* normally united by force of allegiance or loyalty but, if at all, by force of arms, while opposing parties in larger conflicts were usually of an *inter-district* composition. Moreover, the *pule* centres were *not* 'ruling towns'. In the traditional affairs of the districts they had several of a larger number of specialized functions, all of which were essential to the proper performance of the activities concerned. Only in the sense that they were the sites of district meetings could they be regarded even as 'capitals'. The opposition they may have encountered was not, therefore, in the nature of a rebellion, as defined by Europeans. And since Brown's formula, as applied to the operation of 'settled' district governments, would have given the *pule* centres power in certain matters generally controlled at the village level and in other matters new to Samoan political experience, any pretension to such power could hardly have failed to arouse antagonism. But were the *pule* centres really out to become 'ruling towns'? If they were, they might well have agreed 'to sink all their old differences', but how could they have mustered so much support in other villages, which, in that case, would have been due to become their dependencies? Whatever was said—and one must allow for the Samoans' having played on the uninformed hopes of Europeans—actual political developments leave no doubt that the Unionists, like their opponents, aimed to establish a Mālō which, though perhaps engaging in some new activities, would dispose of power in traditional fashion. Consistent with that fact, at least some of the *pule* centres themselves were internally divided, as Leulumoega and Lufilufi, for example, had been during the 1848-57 war.

There were many provocations to war, but that which finally touched it off was the Laupepa party's expulsion of *faitasiga* delegates from Mulinu'u early in 1869. This rash move, coyly represented as a 'sovereign' act against encroachment on Tuamasaga territory, further demeaned Laupepa's cause in the eyes of Europeans, not simply because it led to hostilities, but all the more because it seemed timed to frustrate the Unionists' efforts to develop uniform laws and judicial machinery, discussion of which had just opened at Mulinu'u. There had, in fact, been a lingering hope that Laupepa and his supporters might still relent and participate in this discussion, some of their earlier statements having been taken as indication of willingness to compromise and so more readily construed now as groundwork for treachery.[56] It was understood that the chiefs in the Matautu government had lost face on account of the Unionists' proceedings, but Europeans would not grant that they had any rational reason for inviting war, especially one they appeared unlikely to win, nor of course acknowledge their having any right to so imperil foreign lives and interests. Feeling on the latter point was intensified by the fact that fighting threatened to centre in the Apia area, as it had during the previous war.[57]

In 1868, at a time when the danger of war had seemed particularly acute, the consuls had reached an agreement with the two sides on the subject of neutral rights and immunities. There was to be no fighting on the beachfront between Matautu and Sogi, or in the area behind it inhabited by foreigners, and though combatants might enter there, they were not to be armed with rifles or similar weapons. Samoans within the neutral zone were also to refrain from the use of liquor. Lastly, foreigners were to have immunity from assault, as to property as well as person, provided they remained neutral; and their land and buildings were to be marked with flags identifying them as out of bounds to marauders. Now, as *faitasiga* warriors prepared to attack their enemies in northern Tuamasaga, these terms were conceded again.[58] In this regard, the present situation resembled that pertaining in 1848, when Captain Worth of H.M.S. *Calypso* had required various chiefs to agree to limits on the war-time use of force. But how neutral were the foreign residents? Certainly, Europeans had no intention of bearing arms, except perhaps in their own defence, but in 1869, unlike 1848, they were deeply involved in some of the issues at conflict and had been so free with their criticism, advice and encouragement that part of the responsibility for events leading to war could reasonably be attributed to them. Moreover, some of the merchants were thought to be selling their stocks of arms on a basis of party preference.[59] For reasons soon to be explained, this practice was not in evidence once the war was well in progress, and the appearance of it before then may have been illusory, arising more from the fact of the Samoans having their favourite

[56] *Samoan Reporter*, February 1870.

[57] Brown, *op. cit.*; BCS 4/1, Williams to Meafaifua, 18 February 1868.

[58] BCS 4/1, Williams to *ali'i* and *faipule* at Mulinu'u, 22 February 1868, Williams to Malietoa and *faipule* at Matagofie (Matautu), 8 December 1868, Williams to Malietoa Pe'a (Talavou), 8 December 1868; BCS 5/1, Williams to Weber and Coe, 5 March 1869.

[59] Brown, *op. cit.*

suppliers than from any effort by Europeans to strengthen one or the other of the parties, each of which managed, in any case, to get an abundance of arms. Still, the accusation of biased selling was cast, giving Europeans further cause to ask whether their claim to neutral status was sound by Samoan standards and, if not, whether they would be victimized for that reason, apart from any other.[60]

These were questions of special consequence for Williams, who, with members of his family and a few other British settlers and some missionaries, was among a minority of Europeans to sympathize with Laupepa's side.[61] Williams's position was determined at least as much by the implications of his past actions as by personal convictions. During his long association with the affairs of northern Tuamasaga he had developed close ties with chiefs who now supported Laupepa and who, though for the most part neutral in the previous war, intended to join in this one. It was with these people that Williams had negotiated many of the concessions, settlements and reform measures sought in behalf of foreign interests, and his apparent influence with them, judged by his outstanding ability to secure such agreements, had helped gain him the almost universal respect of Europeans in Samoa. If Weber of the house of Godeffroy was acknowledged supreme in matters of trade and finance, Williams had acquired the reputation of being the best man to consult on political questions, especially those involving Samoans of Tuamasaga.[62] It would appear now that Williams's influence was greatly overrated, possibly by himself as well as by others, and that this contributed to his ultimate embarrassment, even his disgrace. For if he was trusted to advise and negotiate, he also ran the risk of being blamed when any of his proposals and ideas, once agreed to by the Samoans, failed to have the desired results or had quite the opposite results, and this risk increased as his schemes grew more ambitious and his part in their implementation more prominent. So it was with the proceedings of the Tuamasaga government at Matautu. Williams was never shown to have planned the intemperate moves which led to the 'kingship' crisis, and it is most unlikely that he would have consciously added to the chance of war. Recalling the outcome of the Vaimauga reforms of 1860, it is more probable that whatever influence he may have had at Matautu

[60] BCS 4/1, Williams to Malietoa Pe'a (Talavou), 8 December 1868.

[61] 'Williams and Murray who live in the driven district [Tuamasaga] . . . are red-hot partisans, as Mr. Williams does not scruple to affirm himself. . . . Williams is a first-rate, kind-hearted fellow but in this matter he himself well acknowledges that he cannot take an impartial view as all his sympathies are bound up with the people amongst whom he has lived so long.'
(Brown, *op. cit.*) See also SSL, Murray, 15 March 1870, indicating support for Laupepa's side.

[62] Aube, 161-2.

was gone, or at least ineffective, by the time Laupepa was proclaimed
'king' and sole Malietoa. None the less, Williams had done more than
any other European to promote the reform movement in Tuamasaga;
he had closely advised the Matautu régime, had often been consulted by
its leaders, and had tried to persuade foreign residents and visitors to
recognize and support it as the *de facto* government of the district, in
preference to the local minority party based at Mulinu'u; and he was
known to have backed Laupepa's original claim to the Malietoa title.
Given these undisputed facts alone, Williams would have been lucky
indeed to have avoided suspicion of complicity in controversial decisions
and actions taken by his Samoan acquaintances. Add certain other disabilities, including a son and a son-in-law, both merchants, who had
numerous enemies, and an element of sectarian conflict leading to
Talavou's identification with the Catholics; allow for an atmosphere of
war frenzy with wild rumours circulating in it; envisage Williams in
a panic on finding himself the target of threatening abuse—then it may
be even clearer how much of the blame for this war happened to be
off-loaded upon Williams.[63]

The London Missionary Society came in for criticism too, having also
been associated with Laupepa's claim to succeed his father in the
Malietoa title. With the approach of war, however, a sharp division of
opinion had developed among the missionaries as to the merits of the
contending parties,[64] which in itself ameliorated the position of the
Society in Samoa and behoved it for reasons of internal solidarity, as
well as those of sectarian interest, to maintain an official attitude of
impartiality during the hostilities. Having the personal immunity
accorded them by their sanctity, the missionaries suffered no great loss
apart from the incidental effects of war on church discipline and
membership and on attendance at London Missionary Society functions.
Williams's case was different. Initially, he faced not only criticism
but also threats of violence, the latter from members of the *faitasiga*
alliance.[65] Regarded as having aided and abetted a party bent on war
and having, in the process, abandoned his European status for the role
of a Samoan chief, he was in danger of being treated as a belligerent.
Williams avowed himself neutral, but perhaps owing to the prevailing
excitement and to his being on the defensive, he did not try to come to

[63] Brown, *op. cit.*; Adm. 1/6192, Stirling to Sec. Adm., 1 November 1871; ASM(I),
   III, 125-6, Elloy to Comtesse de N—, 1 March 1872.

[64] SSL, Murray, 10 May 1869.

[65] USCD, Apia/3, Coe to Seward, 2 January 1868; BCS 5/1, Williams to Weber
   and Coe, 5 March 1869. Some of the Samoans who threatened Williams cited
   as grievances his support of Wilkes's attempt to arrest Popotunu and his involvement in the execution of Sailusi, the murderer of Fox.

terms with the Unionists but, rather, acted in a manner tending to confirm their suspicions of him. For he simply met their threats with some of his own, promising intervention by the Royal Navy to avenge the menacing insults he had received and to punish any hostile acts that might be committed against British subjects. In spite of this warning, and of statements issued jointly by the consuls relative to the rights of foreigners generally, the agreement establishing the neutral zone was repeatedly violated,[66] and Williams became a victim of one of the more notable 'outrages' of the decade.

The limits of the neutral zone were probably untenable from the start, for while they excluded Mulinu'u, which the Unionists wanted to reoccupy, they embraced Apia and Matautu villages, Laupepa strongholds in the midst of the foreign settlement. Considering that the destruction of enemy villages, defended or not, was a customary feature of Samoan warfare, and that Matautu was actually the headquarters of the Laupepa government, the danger of belligerent activity within the zone must always have been present. As it happened, Laupepa's warriors invited it by holing up there and refusing to leave. Indeed, they erected a barricade near Mulivai, and since they had firearms with them, it was really they who first violated the agreement made with the consuls.[67] The Unionists might not have been provoked in this fashion had their opponents in A'ana and Atua gone straight into the war in support of Laupepa, as promised. These 'rebels' eventually took part in the fighting, but as the opening battle approached, Laupepa's Tuamasaga party stood alone against a combination of forces from Manono, Savai'i, Atua and A'ana, and also from Tuamasaga itself. In these circumstances, Laupepa's warriors took the neutral zone as a convenient sanctuary, perhaps counting on foreign intervention on their side or hoping for time to bring in their reluctant allies before engaging their enemies. But the Unionists attacked without delay, and in several encounters over the Easter period in 1869 they retook Mulinu'u, stormed the barricade at Matautu, destroyed villages throughout northern Tuamasaga, and drove the vanquished into the bush, from whence many went into exile as guests of their A'ana and Atua allies.[68] During the fighting and also afterwards, when the Unionists were in control of the Apia area, some foreign-owned property was inadvertently damaged and some was plundered, part of it by Samoans of the defending side. Invading warriors, however, were responsible for the crowning incident, the destruction and theft of pro-

[66] BCS 4/1, Williams to *ali'i* and *faipule* of Leulumoega, Lufilufi, Pule of Salafai, and Aiga, 1 April 1869.

[67] BCS 5/1, Williams to Bishop Elloy, 27 February 1869.

[68] Trood, 61-3. Laupepa's warriors later built a new fortress at Mulifanua (BCS 3/3, Williams, Trade Report, 1 January 1870).

perty belonging to members of the Williams family and some of their friends, in the course of which a British flag was torn down and destroyed.[69]

This mishap to the flag occurred in the heat of battle and, if meant specifically as an affront, was directed mainly against Williams. Talavou and other leading *faitasiga* chiefs realized, nevertheless, that the British Government might take the most serious view of what had happened, and to make amends, they went to the extreme length of performing the customary ritual of abject apology, the *ifoga*, in Williams's presence. It was reported that they also offered to surrender into slavery the young man who had cut down the flag.[70] By a magnanimous gesture in return, Williams might have gone a long way towards squaring himself with the Unionists. These were, after all, some of the most honoured and powerful chiefs in Samoa, come to humble themselves before him. But no, he declined the apology, foolishly acting the outraged patriot, the consul whose Queen had been symbolically assaulted and whose 'vice-regal' dignity had been offended. Thus humiliated, the Unionist leaders were virtually compelled to carry on their feud with Williams, who, by resorting to gunboat diplomacy, was himself shown up, British naval commanders refusing even on account of the flag incident to take the forcible action the Samoans had been led to expect of them.[71] This downturn in Williams's consular career reached its low ebb in 1870 when Talavou petitioned the Foreign Office to remove him on grounds which included his being of the Vaivai, a conquered enemy.[72] Latterly, then, Williams's proceedings and experiences in Samoa recapitulated those of George Pritchard, upon whose official conduct he had vowed to improve.

[69] BCS 3/3, Williams to Clarendon, 1 April 1869; 5/1, Williams to Lambert, 24 July 1869.

[70] Adm. 1/6096, Lambert to Sec. Adm., 8 September 1869.

[71] *loc. cit.*; Adm. 1/6192, Williams to Stirling, 27 May 1871, Montgomerie to Stirling, 1 July 1871, Stirling to Sec. Adm., 1 November 1871; BCS 4/1, Williams to Tumua, Pule and Aiga chiefs at Mulinu'u, 1 February 1871, and Tumua, Pule and Aiga to Williams, 22 February 1871.

[72] BCS 4/1, Williams to Malietoa Pe'a, 21 April 1870; MS., Brown, Letterbooks, entry of 21 June 1870; Aube, 173-80.

# 12

## LAND AND POLITICAL CONFLICT

*Before the land rush of 1870-2*

PRIOR TO the onset of the *faitasiga* war, Samoan land amounting to a few thousand acres, most of it on the north side of Upolu, was sold to Europeans for residential and agricultural use. The most active period of alienation, it will be recalled, was the mid-1860s, when the Samoans' economy was disrupted by a drought and other adversities. At that time, the per-acre purchase price in Upolu ranged up to ten dollars in trade or cash, the rate varying with the distance from Apia harbour and with the extent to which the land was already bearing useful products, notably breadfruit and coconuts. Both then and before, land was usually sold in small blocks. It was difficult, wrote Jonas Coe in 1865, to purchase more than three or four acres at a single transaction, owing to the extensive sub-division of land among the Samoans. To acquire a relatively large, unbroken section, suitable for development into a plantation, it was therefore necessary to negotiate for a number of adjoining but variously-owned parcels.[1] Remoter bush land, most of which was owned in common by village or sub-district units, might have been available in larger blocks, but there was then little demand for it.

Land transactions were thus fairly numerous in proportion to the total area involved. At the same time, no system of registration or general law of conveyance and title was in effect to regularize and protect European land interests. The written deed of sale that went with each property might be deposited at the appropriate consulate, or a record of it be made and kept there, but this procedure merely gave informal notice of the existence of a claim, on which basis the purchaser might argue his rights if disputed or endeavour to prove them when offering to resell his land. To *defend* his claim he had to resort either to force or to the usual media of negotiation and settlement—to a mixed court or an *ad hoc* meeting of chiefs and consuls, if challenged by Samoans; to the foreign residents' court or a consular hearing, if confronting a European challenger; or perhaps, in either case, to a naval inquiry. Without any

[1] USCD, Apia/2, Coe, Trade Report, 1 January 1865. Williams noted several years later that 'land in small portions from five to ten acres' could be bought 'at a moderate rate from twelve to twenty dollars per acre uncleared' (BCS 3/3, Williams, Report on Conditions in Samoa, 14 November 1870).

T

legal guarantee of title, the settler who 'owned' real property felt insecure, and was especially concerned lest Samoans confiscate his land or otherwise deny him rights in it. But while it is true that Samoans occasionally disputed a boundary location or objected to such action as the closing of what had been a public right of way, before the 1870s they very seldom repudiated a land sale on the ground that it had been improperly executed or that the transfer of an effective title had not been intended. It would appear, particularly in the light of what happened after 1868, that the earlier land sales were usually negotiated by Samoans who had authority to sell, and that these people had a fair understanding of the conditions which Europeans attached to such transactions.[2] Whether they anticipated all the finer points of European ownership—that, for example, they should have no say in the realienation of the land nor any reversionary right should it be abandoned—lack of evidence makes it impossible to determine, though it is probable they did not. None the less, the settlers could have gained little *practical* advantage, at that time, from having formal and protected titles of freehold, so extensive were the land rights they enjoyed without them.

Of the various considerations affecting the security of European landholding, one of the most vital was the measure of control exerted by the Samoans over the actual process of alienation. As noted already, Samoan land rights and interests were diverse and, with regard to any given block, were normally shared by a number of people, not all of whom would be living on or near the land in question. For a land sale to stand the test of time, it was perhaps unnecessary—and certainly impracticable—to consult all of the interested parties. Some would have rights largely dependent on the will or authority of others—for example, remoter kinsmen whose residual claims might never have been pressed anyway, or people who had the temporary tenancy of borrowed land— and they might be ignored without undue risk. But the power of disposal was still shared, as a rule, by several Samoans, and a sale made without their joint consent, or in the absence of agreement among them as to the division of the proceeds, was very likely to be challenged sooner or later. To buy a small agricultural section a European might need to negotiate with a *matai sili*, say, and a junior *matai* in the village where the land was situated, and also with a spokesman for their more immediate *tama fafine* connections. In addition, he would be well advised to make sure that his purchase of the land was generally agreeable to the villagers among whom he proposed to live or, at any rate, to invest his capital.

---

[2] It was then Williams's practice to investigate land purchases before registering the deeds. If he found that the 'true owners' had not been consulted, he required that a sale be re-negotiated before he would accept the buyer's deed for registration (BCS 5/1, *passim*).

According to consular records, the wisdom of these scruples was appreciated by Europeans, but if the earlier land sales were usually transacted with such care, this was due to the initiative of the Samoans as well as to that of the consuls and other settlers. It was of the utmost importance, in this regard, that most of the land was sold during a period of relative political calm, when the Samoans were spending much of their time in their home villages, where their principal land interests were centred. For in these conditions, they were best, though not fully, able to prevent abusive or negligent land-sale practices. Developments during the *faita-siga* war indicate how much more open to exploitation the Samoans were otherwise, and how Europeans stored up trouble for themselves by taking excessive advantage of this fact.

Had there been advance signs of a land rush, foreign settlers might have been more amenable to the prospect of war in 1869, and some might actually have tried to precipitate it on that account. The Samoans had nearly always preferred to barter with produce, however, and their experience during the period 1848-57 had shown that they were capable of continuing on that basis in time of war. In 1868, even though arming at a considerable rate, the contending parties had still relied on coconut products to cover most of their trade needs, not only keeping their land-holdings intact but allowing their cotton crop to go unharvested and the foreign planters' call for labour to go unanswered.[3] The same pattern of trade, the same attitude towards land alienation, generally persisted for some time after the war started, with conservatism being strengthened by the changeover to copra production, which enabled the reduced labour force more easily to maintain the Samoans' income of cash and trade goods. Regarding the disposal of land as unnecessary as well as undesirable, but probably recognizing some danger of irregular transactions occasioned by the upheaval of war, chiefs on both sides soon adopted laws wholly forbidding the sale of Samoan land to Europeans. Because these laws undertook to restrain commerce, they were refused endorsement by the consuls, as were Unionist laws banning the sale of arms to Laupepa's supporters.[4] In giving the Unionists his reasons for objecting to their land laws, however, Williams claimed they were invalidated simply by not being enforced; but when asked for evidence of evasion, in which Europeans were clearly prepared to connive, he could cite only three trivial cases for the whole of the period concerned—April through

---

[3] BCS 3/3, Williams, Trade Report, 1 January 1869.

[4] BCS 4/1, Williams to Moepa'ū, 22 April 1869, Williams, Coe and Weber to judges of Tumua, Pule and Aiga, 3 May 1869. Williams was in favour of the consuls' refusing to recognize land purchases at this time, but no proclamation to that effect was issued, apparently because Weber would not co-operate (BCS 5/1, Williams to Weber and Coe, 6 April 1869, Williams to Coe, 7 April 1869).

July 1869.[5] It would seem to have mattered little, at first, that the laws were not readily enforceable.

There was gradually developing, however, a new threat to Samoan land interests, a highly speculative and undiscriminating market, characterized by the readiness of Europeans to buy more varied types and larger quantities of land, with less regard for its location or for the authority of the people affecting to sell it. The fever of this market was to increase, in turn, the tempo of the arms race and the inclination of both vendors and buyers to gamble on dishonest contracts, and the result was to be a land rush of quite unprecedented proportions. Encouraging this speculative activity, in that it made land ridiculously cheap, was the high Samoan resale value of firearms scavenged from foreign battlefields. But its chief basis, a psychological factor which made an attractive proposition of a dubious land claim, was the opinion, widely shared by Europeans, that Samoa was about to come under foreign rule or control. By the early 1870s enough had happened to give this assumption an appearance of near-certainty. In Samoa itself, political conditions had deteriorated so far as to kill confidence in the capacity of any Samoan-led movement to constitute a satisfactory central government.[6] Having won a resounding victory in the opening battles of the war, the Unionists had neglected to press their advantage. First, Laupepa and his warriors had been made an impossible offer: if they would lay down their arms and recognize the *faitasiga* party as the Mālō, and if Laupepa would renounce his claim to the Malietoa title and to the paramountcy of Tuamasaga, the war might end forthwith and the exiles might return home.[7] After these terms had been refused, the Unionists had proceeded to dawdle until their enemies had brought in substantial reinforcements, and from that time on, military honours had been more evenly divided.[8]

Like the progress of the war, so had the results of various Samoan laws and agreements run counter to early hopes or expectations. A particular case in point had been the belligerent parties' procrastination over paying for the damage inflicted on foreign-owned property early in 1869. Naval officers of various nationalities had investigated the claims and, though employing methods less drastic than those adopted by Captain Worth in 1848, had exacted promises of prompt indemnification. Several years and a succession of naval visits ensued, however, before satisfaction was finally given.[9] Meanwhile, there had been other incidents, giving

[5] BCS 4/1, Williams to Moepa'ū, 28 July 1869.
[6] USCD, Apia/1, Coe, Trade Report, 2 January 1871. cf. chapter 13, below.
[7] MS., Brown, Letterbooks, entry of 21 June 1870.
[8] *loc cit.*; *Samoan Reporter*, February 1870.
[9] BCS 5/1, Williams to Coe, 24 May 1871, Williams to Stirling, 27 May 1871, Williams to Puthrie, 24 August 1871; Adm. 1/6261, on a visit of H.M.S. *Clio*, 1873; Adm. 1/6303, on visit of H.M.S. *Blanche*, 1874.

rise to new claims and harsher naval action. And while the centre of fighting had shifted away from the Apia area, there had been further violations of the neutral zone.[10] Of greater concern to Europeans had been the *faitasiga* government's neglect of law-enforcement in areas where it had seemed to have the power to rule—notably in northern Tuamasaga, where for many months it had been quite unchallenged. Although judges had been in residence at Mulinu'u and had had men on whom they could call for police assistance, the grievances of Europeans, including those nominally covered by the laws, had seldom been taken up until the consuls had demanded action, and not always then.[11] Some cases had had to be held over for prosecution by naval officers, while the approach to the rest had been substantially the old process of negotiation and haggling by chiefs and consuls, so far had been the Mulinu'u régime from having developed an independent judiciary and the impartial rule of law. Only the facade of government had changed. As Europeans ought to have foreseen, the proper functions of the *power* were still regarded by Samoans as the protection and advancement of what they conceived to be their own interests, which conception had not greatly altered. Thus had the question of whether the Samoans would be able to unite under a central government given way to another: would such unity, in the unlikely event of its being achieved, really serve any purpose of much value to Europeans, apart from the maintenance of peace?

If conditions in Samoa in the mid-1860s could have been seen as inviting imperial intervention by one Power or another, how much more reason for that outlook, then, given the local political events of the next few years. And if it could be seriously believed that Samoa must soon lose its independence, Europeans were bound to view their own prospects in a different light, too, and they did. They anticipated, above all, greater security of property and enterprise and more consideration for their interests in matters of land policy. This forecast in itself encouraged speculation, which further strengthened the original impression, that Samoa was ripening for dependent status. But if so, which Power was to reap the harvest? Clearly, international interest in Samoa was mounting, but its pattern was becoming more complex, as may be noted, especially, in the increase of naval activity. From the late 1860s, British warships visited Samoa more regularly and frequently than before; American warships, long absent from Samoan waters, resumed patrols about the same time; French naval influence, though never so

---

[10] BCS 4/1, correspondence of 1871-2, *passim*.

[11] USCD Apia/3, Coe to Fish, 1 August 1869; BCS 4/1, Williams to Moepa'ū, 9 August 1869, Williams to Moepa'ū and judges of Tumua, Pule and Aiga, 23 November 1869.

pervasive, was maintained; and following the unification of Germany, that Power also became active in Samoa through the medium of naval intervention. Meanwhile, foreign investment in Samoa, which it was one of the main objects of this naval activity to protect, was growing under conditions fostering the development of irreconcilable conflicts of interest, some between speculators of different nationalities.

## German and American land speculators

The first major participant in the rush on Samoan land, which occurred during 1870-2, was Theodore Weber, the local Godeffroy manager. Weber's purchases, counting a few made in 1869, totalled more than twenty-five thousand acres and included large and valuable holdings in northern Tuamasaga, within easy access of Apia.[12] There was talk, at the time, of his intending to settle German colonists on some of this land, but no such scheme ever went into effect.[13] Rather, Weber turned his firm's resources to the development of coconut and cotton plantations. From the mid-1860s he had been engaged in planting, having acquired some hundreds of acres during the drought and its aftermath, but agriculture did not become his main line of business in Samoa until the 1870s, following the land rush of the *faitasiga* war period.

In contrast to the solid presence of the Godeffroy establishment, the Central Polynesian Land and Commercial Company (C.P.L.C.C.) had only a brief and most tenuous existence in Samoa, yet in certain respects it had quite as much impact on events there. Some impression of why that was so may be gained from the fact that, during 1871-2, agents of the company acquired interests in Samoan land then estimated at more than three hundred thousand acres in extent—an area almost half that of the entire group of islands. Before examining this phenomenal speculation, however, one should look into the origins of the company itself. These may be traced back to negotiations for a trans-Pacific steamer link which, in conjunction with the newly-completed railway across America, was to facilitate more rapid communication between Britain and its Australasian colonies. In a prospectus issued in September 1869, the San Francisco trading firm of Collie, Stewart and Company proposed the formation of a shipping line to provide such a trans-Pacific service, conditional upon the payment of subsidies by the governments of the United States, Hawaii, New Zealand, the Australian colonies, and possibly France and Great Britain; and a few months later, a New York shipowner, William H. Webb, authorized that firm to negotiate mail contracts and subsidies on his behalf, offering to inaugurate a regular

[12] NZPP, A-4, Sess. 1, 1884, Memo by H. B. Sterndale (28 March 1874), 20.
[13] Brown, *op. cit.*

monthly service with four 'magnificent side-wheel steamships'.[14] Complicated by the number of governments to be approached, ensuing arrangements got the Webb line going on a provisional basis only, pending the grant of further subsidies.[15] As it happened, the United States Congress failed to authorize the subsidy which the line critically needed, and meanwhile, Webb's vessels proved incapable of maintaining a satisfactory schedule of sailings, so that the service was soon terminated.[16] It was going long enough, however, for its promoters to proceed with an allied plan, the formation of the C.P.L.C.C.

The chief purposes of this company were to acquire, for eventual resale or development, whatever cheap land was available in Samoa, a likely way-point on the trans-Pacific route, and indirectly to increase the business of the Webb steamship line and to stimulate support for maintaining it. The idea rationalizing the venture was that Samoa must attract new settlers and capital and, with land values rising, develop into an *entrepôt* and agricultural centre comparable to Hawaii, given the prerequisites of regular communication, which Webb envisaged providing, and of political stability.[17] As to the latter, the promoters were angling for intervention by the United States, either to annex Samoa or to exert influence and 'protection' there sufficient to maintain a central government under American control.[18] This effort was not as misguided as it might appear simply in the light of the Congress's known lack of enthusiasm for American expansion into non-contiguous territory. For the executive branch of the federal government had more far-reaching imperialist ambitions and had recently shown, in the acquisition of Alaska, that a reluctant Congress could sometimes be manoeuvred into advancing them. Moreover, Ulysses S. Grant, the president during the early 1870s, was notoriously amenable to the suggestions of his friends and cronies, to some of whom Webb had access. Failing an American takeover, British intervention might have been acceptable to the C.P.L.C.C., notably in view of the fact that Julius Vogel, the New Zealand premier and then one of the keenest protagonists of a British Samoa, had plans for colonizing and developing the islands through which the company, as a major landowner, could hope to profit.[19] Intervention by Germany, on the other hand, would not have suited the company, but though it was rumoured, in connection with Weber's

14 NZPP, E-4a, 1870, 9-10, Collie, Stewart & Co. prospectus of 27 September 1869, and notice of 26 January 1870.
15 NZPP, E-2, 1872, and F-3, 1873, *passim*.
16 NZPP, F-3b, 1873, 1-3, Russell to Vogel, 11 July 1873.
17 Cooper, *Coral Lands*, II, 30-1.
18 USCD Apia/3, Coe, Trade Report, 2 January 1873.
19 NZPP, A-4, 1884, Sess. 1, 81-4, Vogel to Fergusson, 5 February 1874; ibid., 156-7, Report by Wm Seed, 13 February 1872.

proposed scheme of colonization, that that Power did have imperialist designs on Samoa, the allegation was officially denied.[20]

The C.P.L.C.C., with nominal capital of $100,000, was incorporated in California late in 1871 on terms allowing Webb the option of buying, at cost, up to fifty-four per cent of the land that might be acquired. The firm of Collie, Stewart and Company, which had already been acting for Webb, was assigned the Samoan land-purchasing agency, and J. B. M. Stewart, of that company, became treasurer (later, president) of the C.P.L.C.C.[21] Stewart, a British subject masquerading as an American, had previously risen from obscurity in Sydney, where he had been a wine salesman, to a managerial position at the Terre Eugénie cotton plantation in Tahiti.[22] His part in the latter venture, a disastrous failure, had gained him locally the reputation of being a plausible rogue, a confidence man of wide vision, which notoriety the proceedings and subsequent fate of the C.P.L.C.C. were destined to spread. The Samoan agency of the land company was entrusted to Stewart's partner, George Collie, who earlier in 1871 had gone to Apia with a supply of general merchandise, proposing to trade on behalf of himself and Stewart and, as opportunity arose, to purchase land for conveyance to the C.P.L.C.C. Collie, in turn, had selected several local buying agents, Europeans with influential contacts among the Samoans and allegedly unsurpassed knowledge of Samoan land tenure and ownership. One of these men was Coe, American commercial agent, and another, Williams, whom the Foreign Office had forbidden to participate in private trading activity.[23] Also prior to the incorporation of the C.P.L.C.C., a Captain E. Wakeman had arrived in Samoa with a commission from Webb to survey the islands' resources and to investigate the potentialities of Pago Pago as a port of call and coaling depot for naval and commercial steamships. Wakeman's report, which rated Samoa among the richest tropical territories in the world, was printed in the United States for the edification of speculators, politicians and government officials.[24]

Webb and Stewart were endeavouring, meanwhile, to secure the political and financial backing of the American Government. This campaign had its first visible results in Samoa in connection with the proceedings of Commander R. W. Meade of the u.s.s. *Narragansett*, which called early in 1872. Meade's orders directed him merely to 'survey the harbor of Pago Pago and locate a coal depot for American steamers'; but, obviously with the approval and foreknowledge of his

[20] NZPP, E-2, 1872, 7-8, Webb to Vogel, n.d.
[21] Cooper, II, 30-1; SLC 2402, indenture by Stewart, 17 January 1872.
[22] Cooper, II, 28-30; and from information supplied by J. W. Griffin and H. E. Maude.
[23] SLC 2547 and 2815, *passim*.
[24] Wakeman, *Report to W. H. Webb*.

naval superiors and other officials, he went to much greater lengths, both to assist Webb's ventures and, more generally, to further the cause of American expansion in the Pacific. Arguing the need to 'frustrate foreign influence . . . seeking to secure the harbor', by which he referred to Weber's alleged agitation for German intervention, he undertook unofficially to invite an offer to the United States of exclusive foreign naval rights in the port of Pago Pago. Mauga, the chief whom Meade approached, was then resisting involvement in the politics of the western islands and, seeing a friendly bond with America as a potential advantage in that regard as well as a boost to his position in Tutuila, he willingly extended the concession Meade was after. An agreement was then drawn up in the form of a treaty, providing for (but not guaranteeing) American protection in return for the grant of harbour rights; and new commercial and port regulations were enacted and, with Meade's endorsement, promulgated.[25]

Having thus honoured Mauga and stimulated the jealousy of others, Meade offered American recognition and protection to leading chiefs elsewhere in Tutuila if they would join Mauga in signing what was described in the English version as an agreement to confederate. Several chiefs did in fact rise to the bait. According to the terms it contained, however, the document they signed was simply a local treaty of mutual non-aggression and defence and an undertaking to enforce, within the respective jurisdictions of the signatories, the regulations previously adopted for the Pago Pago area alone. No allowance was made for the formation of a representative central government of any kind, nor did the agreement stipulate or acknowledge any disparity of status or privilege among the parties to it. As for the parties themselves, they represented only one political faction or alliance, which was that concentrated in the eastern half of the island.[26] None the less, Meade proceeded to act as if the whole of Tutuila had now become a confederacy, the independence of which the United States would help to maintain, and to treat Mauga as the paramount chief of it. When the *Narragansett* left, Mauga was the proud custodian of the new flag of 'Tutuila', a hastily-designed parody of the Stars and Stripes; and taking continued American support for granted, he fancied his village, Pago Pago, to be the island's capital and the general enforcement of the new laws to be his due, if not his own responsibility.[27]

25 USN, Cmdr L., January-April 1872, papers relating to proceedings of u.s.s. *Narragansett* in Samoa; Rieman, *Papalangee*, 24-5.
26 USCP 44 C., 1 S., House Ex. Doc. 161, 65-6, for copy of confederation agreement of Tutuila chiefs, March 1872.
27 USCP, *op. cit.*, 45-6; sketch of flag as enclosure in the copy in the Mitchell Library, Sydney, of Rieman, *op. cit.* Summary of Meade's proceedings in Ellison, *Foreign Influence in Samoa*, 40-3.

A few weeks after the *Narragansett*'s call, Stewart came on a visit to Samoa and, capitalizing on the impression created by Meade, gathered the signatures of various western Samoan chiefs to a petition specifically requesting, in English, the annexation of the islands by the United States. This document was subsequently forwarded to the State Department through Webb.[28] As such matters went, the petitioners in this instance represented a fair proportion of the Samoan people, but they had not fully understood what they were signing.[29] European settlers clearly had, however, and Williams for one approved, having discountenanced the likelihood of early intervention by Britain and preferring, in that case, American rule.[30] Stewart, of course, maintained that the Samoans had been quite aware of what they were doing. Not that anything came of the petition, or of Meade's treaty, which was never ratified, or of any other move then made to prod Congress into action over Samoa and the Webb-Stewart interests, yet owing to further machinations of the Grant administration and to the intrigues of certain United States representatives in Samoa, there persisted an appearance of American imperialist intent towards the islands. But first, some attention should be given the development of the Samoan land rush of 1870-2 and the nature of the interests which Europeans then acquired.

## Speculative land practices

Apart from the total area which Europeans claimed to have bought— approximately 350,000 acres—the most striking feature of the land rush was the large scale of many single transactions. One schedule of C.P.L.C.C. claims, covering an alleged area of about 250,000 acres, listed purchases averaging more than two thousand acres each.[31] Where bush or 'back' land was involved, some of the tracts put up *en bloc* were, by the estimates given, of extraordinary size—for example, at Falealili in southern Atua, 38,400 acres; at Sale'imoa in northern Tuamasaga, twelve square miles; at Malie, eight square miles.[32] Land near the villages was more often sold in small pieces, but there were notable exceptions. At Vaitele, to take a well-known example, Weber purchased as a single property five hundred acres of the choicest land, including the very site of the village itself.[33]

[28] USCP, *op. cit.*, 3-4, Stewart to Webb, 28 June 1872, with petition of 9 April 1872.

[29] As explained below, the petition was circulated among leaders of both war parties (USCD, Apia/3, Coe, Trade Report, 2 January 1873).

[30] Williams helped to circulate the petition.

[31] This was generally referred to as the '414 square miles contract'.

[32] SLC 2402, agreement between Samoan chiefs and Stewart, 10 April 1872.

[33] SLC 3061.

In many cases, especially with regard to C.P.L.C.C. claims, acreages were only estimated, never surveyed; and a large number of these estimates were later shown to have been quite excessive. Thus, half the country had not been sold by the end of 1872, as the figure of 350,000 acres might seem to imply. Still, going by the descriptive material available, enough land had ostensibly been alienated to confront the majority of Samoans in Upolu and many in Savai'i with a potential shortage, in that bush reserves had been sold holus-bolus, while in some villages, particularly around Apia, virtually all the land was now claimed by Europeans. Missionaries, even a consul or two, bemoaned the fate which the Samoans were apparently inviting with open eyes: on the way to becoming landless, they must inevitably live as squatters or toil for wages and, like the Hawaiians, lose their dignity and coherence as a people.[34] But would the owners of the land really have acted so foolishly? Or, to put it differently, was the land sold on the authority of those entitled to dispose of it? Did the vendors, whoever they were, understand what they were doing? And why did they deal so liberally in land anyway?

Taking these questions in reverse order, it will be recalled, first, that the land rush was closely associated with the arms trade. But as shown, it did not assume ruinous proportions until the war had been in progress a long while. The war was actually fought in two stages, the first lasting from April 1869 to August 1870 and the second from February 1872 to May 1873;[35] and during the first period, the sale of land, though on a considerable scale, seems to have been of an unsystematic character, largely undertaken to meet occasional emergency requirements for arms which could not be satisfied soon enough through the sale of produce alone. Only from late 1871 was the Samoans' demand for arms so general, so urgent and competitive, that land was alienated at a wholesale, apparently suicidal rate.

The immediate development with which this arms race was identified was, of course, the onset of the second stage of the *faitasiga* war. In mid-1870 a truce had been arranged on terms which allowed all warriors and exiles to return home but left open the main issues which the parties had been contesting. Because they had grown tired of fighting, said Williams, they had stopped; but because they had settled nothing, they were likely to fight again.[36] And so they did. This time, however, they took up the war with quickened interest and keener determination,

34 ASM(I), III, 132, Elloy to Poupinel, 6 June 1872; MS., Brown, Letterbooks, Brown to Nettleton, 4 June 1872; BCS 3/3, Williams, Trade Report, 1 January 1873.
35 SSL, Turner Jr, 27 February 1872, Turner Jr, 10 May 1873.
36 BCS 3/3, Williams, Trade Report, 1 January 1871; SSL, Nisbet, 18 April 1872.

for which change foreign influences were partly if not wholly responsible.[37] Indeed, there emerges here the first clear instance of the inten-
sification of the Samoans' high-level political rivalries by Europeans
endeavouring concertedly to exploit rather than suppress them. These
agitators were the agents of the C.P.L.C.C., who, among them, had
'friends' in both war parties and whose chief activities involved the
playing off of one side against the other.[38] So it was, obviously, when
it came to buying land. Whereas other Europeans usually awaited
offers or went out after specific properties, the agents of the C.P.L.C.C.
canvassed wherever and whomever their contacts permitted, urging
Samoans to take arms on account and, by way of covering the cost of
present and future supplies, to sign over as much land as they would
consent to alienate.

A similar approach may be discerned in the campaign for American
intervention. Whatever their previous ideas on that subject, Samoans
gathered from Meade's visit, and may have been deliberately led to
believe, that the United States would protect Samoa without ruling
there and, to the extent that it intervened at all, would recognize and
support the Samoans capable of dominating negotiations with its representatives. By analogy with Mauga's 'treaty' position in Tutuila, the
inference was that the party in the ascendant in the western islands
when an American protectorate was established there would be perpetuated as Mālō, upheld against its local enemies and safeguarded against
the demands and encroachments of foreign navies and other agencies of
imperialism. But needless to say, this was far from being what the promoters of the C.P.L.C.C. had in mind. As an indication of how they
pursued their ambition, it may be observed that Stewart's petition for
annexation was signed by leaders and members of both war parties to
whom he was, on that very occasion, dispensing arms in exchange for
land, that they might prosecute more vigorously a war in which the
power to exploit American intervention had become an issue. Facilitating
this combined operation were Williams and Coe, the former in negotiations with the Laupepa side, the latter with the Unionists. To be sure,
Stewart's petition was later repudiated by the signatories when the
meaning of 'annexation' was explained to them; but expectation of an
American protectorate, Tutuila style, remained, and so, with much
anxiety as to the outcome of the Samoan power struggle, did the desire
for one.[39]

[37] ASM(I), III, 124, Elloy to Comtesse de N—, 1 March 1872; MS., Brown, Letterbooks, Brown to Austin, 1 April 1872.

[38] ASM(I), III, 306, Vidal to Fraysse, 15 June 1873; USCP, *op. cit.*, 47, Steinberger to Fish, 9 February 1874; Barnes, *Story of Lauli'i*, 37-8.

[39] ASM(I), III, 132, Elloy to Poupinel, 6 June 1872; Cooper, II, 32-3; Rieman, 38.

A further measure of the Samoans' will to acquire arms is evidenced by the amount of consideration they now accepted for land. In terms of the local retail value of the goods they received, which was how land prices were usually expressed in deeds and contracts of sale, they were taking as little as fifty cents per acre, and sometimes less. Admittedly, much of this property was covered in bush, yet for crop-bearing land the price ranged from only one dollar per acre to about two and a half, as against the five to ten, or even twenty, dollars paid prior to the war.[40] However, the cost to the purchaser, if he was an importer or trader, was actually much less, owing largely to profiteering in muskets, the main line of goods exchanged for land. For these weapons, as relics of foreign wars, could be bought for about fifty cents each, while the charge to the Samoans was of the order of ten to twenty-five dollars, depending on supply and demand and, presumably, the condition of the muskets, many of which were faulty.[41] The cost of land was therefore down to only a few cents per acre, exclusive of surveying expenses, consular registration fees and the like. Considering, then, the speculator's small outlay and, conversely, the high cost of war, the dimensions of the land rush would appear somewhat less remarkable than the figures of total acreage alone might suggest.[42] From the same viewpoint, another aspect of the C.P.L.C.C. speculation is also exposed. For, apart from reimbursement of incidental expenses, the basis on which Collie and Stewart were buying land for the company was not that of true cost plus commission but, rather, of the retail value they placed on the goods supplied to the Samoan vendors. Thus valued, their land acquisitions and claims were converted to capital investment in the C.P.L.C.C., netting them, by indenture of exchange, seventy per cent of the share issue of their so-called principals.[43] By this rags-to-riches yet superficially respectable approach, through what may be regarded as initially their dummy corporation, Collie and Stewart emerged with shares they could sell at a large profit and, if they wished to keep it, the controlling interest in the C.P.L.C.C.'s assets, including the capital invested in cash by other shareholders.

Among the Samoans there was, as will be explained, too much vocal opposition to land alienation, too much abortive effort to stop it, for one

---

[40] e.g. deeds of conveyance in SLC 2402, 2547, 2815, 3061.

[41] SLC 3061, testimony of Carruthers; Barnes, 37.

[42] GCS, Zembsch to A.A., 29 April and 23 May, 1880. Zembsch estimated that three-quarters of the one hundred thousand acres claimed by the Godeffroys in 1880 had been paid for 'in guns and kind at enormously inflated values', whereas the average price, according to the bills of sale, had been less than one dollar per acre.

[43] SLC 2402, indenture by Stewart, 17 January 1872. Collie and Stewart allegedly paid cash for another ten per cent of the C.P.L.C.C. share issue.

to imagine that many land-sale contracts were entered into quite blindly by the vendors. Some of the crucial details of such transactions, however, were often misconstrued by the Samoan parties concerned, or never mentioned to them in advance, with the probable effect that agreements were occasionally signed which would otherwise have been reconsidered.[44] Perhaps not in every case of this kind were the purchasers guilty of intentional misrepresentation. For one thing, contracts were drafted by amateurs, there being no qualified lawyer in Samoa at the time; and for another, the local facilities for the conduct of surveys were quite unequal to the pace of the land rush, leaving many sales to be arranged with less definitive regard for the location of boundaries. These conditions, plus language difficulties, no doubt led to some inadvertent defects and innocent misunderstandings. One may ask, though, whether the omissions characteristic of most of the C.P.L.C.C. contracts were wholly unintentional. Pertaining to the bulk of the land claimed by the company, and to nearly all in which it acquired some interest in 1872, the documents in question described the land in the crudest fashion, stated no total or unit price to be paid for it, required by way of immediate payment only nominal deposits pending the outcome of surveys, and stipulated no time limit on the company's right or obligation to complete the surveys or its purchases.[45] It was later alleged by European claimants that a price of fifty cents per acre had been offered and agreed to, but no proof of this was produced. Nor could it be shown, as argued, that the deposits alone entitled the C.P.L.C.C. to a *pro rata* share of the land originally contracted for.[46] After buying about twenty-five thousand acres outright, Collie and Stewart were, one suspects, spinning out their remaining resources with the object of tying up the maximum area of land, hoping for the establishment of a sympathetic government in Samoa and a greater inflow of capital, which conditions might have made it both possible and worthwhile for them to complete their purchases and perfect their titles.[47] Though expecting '12,800 acres' in Falealili, for example, to net more than the one or two muskets given as first deposit, the Samoans who signed such slapdash contracts did not realize how much potential lee-way they were giving the C.P.L.C.C. For lest it be assumed that the looseness of the terms was bound to invalidate the sales, it must be observed that vast

[44] GCS, Zembsch to A.A., 29 April 1880.

[45] SLC 2402, agreement between Samoan chiefs and Stewart, 10 April 1872.

[46] Which allegations were made in SLC 2815, Hetherington to Sherwood, 8 October 1884. Steinberger claimed that the company was supposed to pay the balances within two years, but no limit whatever was stated in the agreement (USCP, *op. cit.*, 47).

[47] MS., Brown, Letterbooks, Brown to W.M.S., 28 September 1872.

areas of land were acquired from other peoples, including the American Indians and the New Zealand Maoris, through transactions showing no more deference to legal form and propriety.

By comparison with the C.P.L.C.C.'s land-sale contracts, Weber's gave the appearance of being models of scrupulous care, for which quality he had, in any event, a considerable reputation among Europeans. None the less, he too engaged in some highly dubious practices in the course of his land dealings. In the present context the most objectionable of these, from the legal standpoint, was the taking of vendors' and witnesses' signatures on contracts from which the description of the land had been left out, to be added only after surveys had been made.[48] In this way, of course, Weber was able to buy land which might otherwise have been reoffered to someone else, but it will be just as apparent that the short-cut increased the risk of misunderstanding and the room for abuse. Because of it, a German consul—the only one to remain independent of commercial interests in Samoa—later condemned a number of Weber's land transactions, and when this official, Captain Zembsch, was subsequently recalled, it was rumoured in Apia that his strict regard for legal procedure had been the reason.[49]

But all the malpractices mentioned thus far—the exploitation of Samoan rivalries, the profiteering, the rigging or phrasing of contracts to favour the purchasers—might have availed little but for trafficking in land by persons who had no exclusive right or authority to dispose of it or, in some cases, no right of disposition at all. Considering that the sale of land to Europeans was by no means a new form of undertaking, that Samoan objections to it now were relatively far more numerous and strenuous than ever before, and that the assignment of land to European trustees was commonly sought in the hope of frustrating its sale,[50] the fact that much land was wrongfully alienated cannot be attributed entirely to ignorance or oversight. Some vendors as well as purchasers were plainly guilty of deliberate fraud, and possibly of conspiring together to perpetrate it. One may assume that some Samoans were tricked or misled into signing away land in excess of the amount they had meant to alienate, yet in many transactions the *whole* of the land in question was, by Samoan standards, sold without sufficient authority. One *matai sili*, for example, might sell part or all of his

---

48 GCS, Zembsch to A.A., 29 April 1880.

49 BCS 3/4, Malietoa Laupepa and Selu to Knorr, 7 May 1886, in which Zembsch was extolled at length for fairness in handling land disputes.

50 The idea was that foreigners could register trust deeds at the consulates and claim consular protection for their interests, though their 'titles' had no more legal force than those of the Samoans for whom they acted. There were several cases in which alleged trustees were charged with having usurped the rights of the Samoan owners.

village's bush land without the approval of the other leading chiefs of the village, which he would know to be in violation of their rights. Such was the nature of some of the 'on deposit' sales to the C.P.L.C.C., while others were made by lesser chiefs whose rights in matters of this kind would have been consultative, not deliberative. Or, to take another example, all the chiefs of a village might agree there should be no sale of land within its boundaries, only to discover later that someone living beyond the jurisdiction of the village, but having or at least claiming a connection there, had presumed to dispose of some of their land to Europeans. Such was the experience of the people of Lefaga, who anticipated the danger but could not prevent outsiders from contracting to sell their land—to the extent of nine thousand acres!—to the C.P.L.C.C.[51] Or, again, people absent from their homes during the war might return to find that in the interim some of the land in which they had had a controlling interest had been sold by a chief of their village who had joined their enemies, or by an interloper from the enemy side, someone who may have been related to them but had not been a resident of their village. Cases of this sort were fairly common, especially in northern Tuamasaga, where members of the Unionist side took advantage of their position as conquerors to alienate land belonging wholly or in part to exiled supporters of Laupepa.[52] This practice, it must be said, was in no way consistent with or a logical extension of the rights of conquest customary among the Samoans, nor did Europeans, as a rule, insist that it was.[53] Rather, it was held that the vendors, by virtue of their chiefly titles and kinship connections, would have had the authority to sell at any time—a principle perhaps safer for Europeans when the occurrence and progress of war were so unpredictable. It was not, however, a principle having many advocates in central Vaimauga where, during the exile of Laupepa's supporters, one of the few local Unionists sold Weber nearly eight hundred acres behind his own and neighbouring villages. Called upon later to explain his action, the vendor, a prominent chief with the title of Asi, said: 'I sold these lands because I was angry, because I was in a different war party. . . . I had no right to sell. . . . I used all the [guns and] ammunition during the war'.[54]

[51] ASM(I), III 132, Elloy to Poupinel, 6 June 1872. Numerous Samoan regulations were made at this time prohibiting the sale of land (e.g. BCS 4/1, Williams to *ali'i* and *faipule* of Tuisamau, 29 November 1871, Williams to *ali'i* and *faipule* of Safotulafai and Salea'ula, 20 May 1872).

[52] Barnes, 28-9, 37-8; SSL, Murray, 6 September 1870.

[53] e.g. testimony in SLC 3061.

[54] SLC 3060, Asi's testimony. During the war this chief also sold other land which became the subject of dispute (BCS 4/1, Williams to Asi (at Mulinu'u), 10 December 1872).

The previously-mentioned sale of five hundred acres at Vaitele, a solidly pro-Laupepa village of Faleata, was an even more flagrant example of misappropriation. In this case, most of the land had been under cultivation, and some of the rest consisted of burial and dwelling sites, with which Samoans were scarcely ever willing to part. Almost needless to say, then, the two vendors were outsiders. The principal one (upon whose alleged ownership or control the purchaser, Weber, based his informal title) was Tamasese, an *aloali'i* from A'ana and a war leader on the Unionist side. The second was Faumuinā, the highest-ranking Unionist in Faleata, but of a different village. Also supporting Tamasese's action, and sharing in the distribution of the fifty-one guns received in exchange, were other chiefs of the same party, two of whom signed the deed as witnesses. Attempts to justify Tamasese's sale of the Vaitele land were based on acknowledged lineage connections between him and the most important *ali'i* of the village, Galumalemana. One of these ties related them both to the Matai'a family of Faleata, members of which had once supported Tamasese's father, Moegagogo, as their *tama'āiga*, and from which Tamasese, in turn, might have claimed similar consideration.[55] Whatever he *might* have done, however, Tamasese had never resided in Vaitele nor been given support from there for any political pretensions he may have had; and even if the opposite had been true in either or both respects, he would still have lacked sole authority to sell land in the village, excepting perhaps some small area set aside for his personal use. If, on the other hand, Tamasese's transaction with Weber had been permissible by Samoan custom, a few well-connected high chiefs would then have possessed, among them, sufficient authority to dispose of all the land in Samoa. This implication of the Vaitele case, the first outstanding one of its kind, was not lost upon Europeans, as accounts of later speculations in land will reveal.[56] Few Samoans, though, would ever accept it as valid. Even Tamasese shrank from it when confronted by the wrathful people of Vaitele, but while he tried, he could not induce Weber to return their land to them.[57] For many years they were dispersed, living among friends and on the former margins of their village, kept at bay by the force of indentured labourers employed on what had become the Vaitele plantation.

[55] SLC 3061, *passim*. Galumalemana and Tamasese were both descended from the original Galumalemana, a son of Tupua, but in the case of the former, not through an all-male line. They also had a common link, through a woman, with the Matai'a family, branches of whose title passed in their respective lines.

[56] cf. chapter 16, below, concerning the claims of Frank Cornwall, some of whose vendors were involved in Tamasese's sale of the Vaitele land.

[57] SLC 3061, proceedings of mixed court inquiry in 1883. Tamasese was assaulted at Vaitele 'because he stole our land'.

It was a further implication of the Vaitele case that such sales of land would tend to conflict—indeed, that the same high chiefs who might have alienated all Samoan lands could have done so several times over, owing to the intersection or overlapping of their complex connections. Thus, a Malietoa, Tuimaleali'ifano or Mata'afa might as easily have sold the Vaitele land, if so inclined; for all had kinship ties with members of the village. But the same tendency was inherent in the presumption by any people, regardless of rank, to ignore or split up the customary *pule* over land. In terms of the rank of the vendor, the Vaitele case may not have been typical of many sales made during the land rush of the early 1870s, but as an example of the usurpation of controlling rights in land, it was quite unexceptional. Wanting to keep intact what they themselves used or required by way of reserves, Samoans were commonly offering, instead, land that was not theirs to sell and, in turn, were sometimes victimized in similar fashion by others. In the process some land, almost inevitably, was sold more than once— perhaps in a few instances intentionally, but not necessarily so. Adding to the effect, of course, was the lax manner in which many transactions were negotiated, especially regarding the measurement and description of the property.

## Political implications of land sales

It is not possible to determine precisely the extent to which the land claims acquired by Europeans during the *faitasiga* war derived from transactions inconsistent with Samoan principles of ownership and control; for, among other reasons, the 'on deposit' sales to the C.P.L.C.C., originally estimated to account for about two-thirds of the land in question, were never tested by those criteria before a competent tribunal. From the available information, however, one may conclude that only a very small proportion of the land—perhaps a few thousand of what might, on survey, have totalled some two hundred thousand acres— would have been free of fundamental objections as to the Samoan vendors' rights to sell. This, it must be emphasized, was also the impression which Europeans had at the time, as indeed it should have been, considering their knowledge and experience of previous land-sale practices. Their inclination to resist Samoan interference in their affairs, particularly the jurisdiction of any truly independent Samoan government, was correspondingly strengthened.

In the absence of full and accurate surveys, it cannot be ascertained, either, how much land Samoans had sold more than once. But again, Europeans were aware that a problem existed; and, given the many extensive tracts sold as single properties and the secrecy that had often pervaded land negotiations and, for lack of compulsory registration of deeds,[58] continued in some cases to surround the consequences, they had cause to think a large area might be subject to conflicting claims by purchasers. This problem, brought on inadvertently by haste and greed and enlarged more systematically over the ensuing twenty years, greatly complicated the task of finding an alternative to a Samoan-controlled government, the early accomplishment of which Europeans had taken for granted. The multi-national character of foreign settlement and enterprise, including speculation in land, was of course a standing invitation to international rivalry over Samoa. But the conflict of European land interests, far advanced by the time any of the Powers was actually ready to assume control of the islands, was to aggravate that tendency and become perhaps the major issue leading to the prolonged international impasse for which Samoa achieved renown.

Failing direct imperial intervention, and starting some years before any Power would have undertaken it, Europeans turned to filibustering tactics for the solution to their political problems. In so far as they aimed at the establishment of a Samoan central government under their influence, and in which they might participate, their approach bore the mark of earlier reform movements launched or advocated by Pritchard, Williams, St Julian and others. But owing chiefly to the economic conflicts which had developed in the interval, these later endeavours not only failed to get the concerted backing of the principal foreign elements in Samoa, but actually stimulated opposition, resulting in the alliance or identification of rival European interest-groups with Samoan parties contesting the Mālō. Although the division among Europeans was not, as a rule, strictly according to nationality, the opposed factions, and through them their respective Samoan allies, more often than not had on each side the support of one or more Powers. This alignment of forces, usually within two contending sides whose composition was subject to shift and change, so limited the margin of ascendancy that no general government could be formed which had sufficient strength and stability to realize and preserve the programme of its partisans, short of there being a head-on clash among the Powers themselves. If the pattern thus imposed on the struggle for power was one of alternate revolution and stalemate, so did the prevailing moods of the foreign populace tend to extremes, to unrestrained optimism and morbid frustration. Every movement to grasp and hold the reins of government was accompanied by

---

58 Various attempts were made by Samoan governments to limit Samoan land sales to those approved by executive authority, but the regulations were not widely enforced. The Tamasese-Brandeis régime of 1887-8 tried to compel all foreign land claimants to register their deeds, but it was overthrown soon after the measure was announced (USCD, Apia/15, Sewall to Rives, 29 February 1888).

wild speculation in land and armaments, representing investment in special privileges and preferences and, often, the hope of recovering what had been risked before. And every movement that collapsed or declined carried with it the wealth, spirit and even the sanity of intense, ambitious men. Perhaps in no other islands of the Pacific were talent, time and effort so meanly rewarded as in Samoa.

# 13

## THE STEINBERGER RÉGIME

*Peace and confederation*

By 1873 the fervour with which the Samoans had resumed the *faitasiga* war was spent, without either side having gained an advantage. Again, the unsuitability of the customary organization and tactics of warfare to the common use of firearms had sapped the belligerents' confidence and morale. Moreover, foreign naval intervention, occasioned by numerous complaints of property damage and trespass, had repeatedly distracted the Samoans from the course of their struggle and had been, also, a dispiriting influence, portentous of the trouble implicit in the burgeoning of European land interests. This dilemma of pursuing a futile war, for which foreigners were partly to blame, was one from which the Samoans seemed incapable of extricating themselves, especially as there were few Samoan neutrals, and none of very great influence, to mediate between the two parties. Assuming, then, that the conflict might otherwise drag out indefinitely, to no constructive purpose, Europeans took upon themselves the responsibility of engineering a final, face-saving settlement.

The initiative behind this undertaking came chiefly from the missions. Among the consuls and leading merchants there was perhaps less enthusiasm for it; yet there were no overriding objections either, for the war was no longer regarded by them as more immediately beneficial than peace. In particular, the land market had contracted, there now being greater concern about the enforcement of existing claims than the acquisition of new ones. If only for lack of funds and supplies, no more land was being purchased for the C.P.L.C.C., and Collie was having to refuse requests for further advances of arms and other goods against the company's unfulfilled contracts.[1] The peace campaign was thus able to proceed without serious obstruction by Europeans. Indeed, as it gathered force, something approaching a common front developed, with negotiations being conducted by representatives of the three missions together with all three of the consuls.[2]

The Samoans gave way to this combined pressure, possibly glad of the opportunity to do so; and on 1 May 1873 the leaders of the two

---

[1] MS., Brown, Letterbooks, Brown to W.M.S., 28 September 1872; USCD, Apia/3, Coe, Trade Report, 2 January 1873.

[2] SSL, Davies, 15 January 1874.

parties, in conference with European mediators at Apia, agreed to
disband their fighting forces and declare the war at an end. It was
decided, too, that another attempt should be made to establish a central
government in the western islands, this time a true *faitasiga* régime,
with its headquarters at Mulinu'u.[3] Europeans, though endorsing the
latter agreement, had little faith in it, expecting in any case that imperial
intervention would soon make it irrelevant.[4] Yet, as far as Samoan
politics went, there had never been a better time for trying to form a
united government by voluntary means. For, with the war having ended
in a draw and the opposing alliances having been *acknowledged* equal
and then broken up, the Samoans could hardly have been less prepared,
in terms of organization, confidence and sense of provocation, immediately to adopt the Mālō principle as a basis of experiment. No present
move of theirs, short of putting their islands under the control of a
foreign Power, would have been likely to rule out future recourse to war.
For the time being, however, their choice was not so much between
violent and peaceful avenues to governmental reform as between a
peaceful attempt to initiate reform and no attempt at all. As it happened,
they *did* try forthwith to carry out their agreement.

That the first members of the new Mulinu'u government included no
contenders for any of the constituent titles of the Tafa'ifā, all of which
were now vacant, was reported by the Catholic bishop as evidence of
extreme caution on the Samoans' part. They were afraid, he said in
recollection of the Malietoa kinship controversy, that the appointment
of such a chief would appear as a challenge to others and lead straight
to conflict.[5] But again the picture was distorted, the risk of trouble
exaggerated; for given the political conditions then pertaining, open
challenges of this kind would have been out of place anyway. There
simply was not, as yet, sufficient organized support for claimants to the
*pāpā* titles, the movements concerned in the *faitasiga* war having dissolved and new ones not having had time to develop. If confederation
did not have to be (and could not then be) pursued by way of conflict
between inter-district alliances, as it had been in the late 1860s, the
Samoans' determination to realize it mainly on a basis of voluntary
district-by-district representation would seem to have been more expedient
than cautious. For this representation they looked first to the Tumua and
Pule chiefs of the six districts of Upolu and Savai'i, plus the leading
chiefs of Manono in the seventh district, 'Aiga-i-le-Tai. On questions
relating to confederation there evidently was, within these groups, a

[3] ibid., Turner Jr, 10 May 1873; ASM(I), III, 318, Vidal to Frs Fraysse, 4
October 1873.
[4] BCS 3/3, S. F. Williams to Granville, 17 October 1873.
[5] USCP, 44 C., 1 S., House Ex. Doc. 161, 64, Elloy to Steinberger, 29 September 1873.

considerable degree of harmony facilitated by the quiescence of such divisive issues as that of the Mālō. Similarly, it was feasible that within the respective districts there should be, if not wholly active unity in support of confederation, little or no effective opposition to it, provided the functions of the Mulinu'u régime did not clash with or usurp those of traditional units of government. It is significant, then, that the central government was meant to have, in its own right, no direct authority over Samoans, except at Mulinu'u and on the Beach at Apia Bay. Rather, it was to try to settle Samoan disputes referred to it and to negotiate uniform laws and rules of administrative procedure for local enforcement and observance.[6]

But functions so modest, though helping to explain why confederation might be achieved without force, scarcely explain the Samoans' effort to achieve it, which stemmed principally from a desire for a central authority to strengthen their hand in dealing with Europeans, including the representatives of foreign Powers. In this respect, the Mulinu'u government formed in 1873 more closely resembled the Vaimauga government of the early 1860s, when European interests were still heavily concentrated around Apia, than Talavou's so-called *faitasiga* régime, the main object of which was partisan domination founded on the Mālō-Vaivai relationship. To be sure, forces could yet evolve to shift the new government's focus from that of cleavage between Samoans and Europeans to one of cleavage between Samoans and Samoans, so altering its make-up, perhaps even destroying it. One of the clearest dangers was that foreign intervention might assume an actively partisan character, tending to stimulate and accelerate the development of militant *fa'a-Samoa* causes. But if directed towards the fulfilment of the main purpose for which the Samoans had confederated, foreign interference might then strengthen the bonds of unity among them. This was a lesson soundly demonstrated by Albert B. Steinberger, American filibusterer extraordinary to Samoa.

## Steinberger, a man of promises

In August 1872 the American Secretary of State was advised by the White House that Steinberger, an acquaintance of both Webb and President Grant, would be 'a competent person to visit the Navigators Islands and report upon their condition'.[7] The occasion for this recommendation was the frustration of efforts to move the Congress in matters relating to Samoa. Meade's treaty, approved by Grant despite the informal manner of its negotiation, had failed to secure the favour of the

[6] FOCP 2849, 66, constitution of 21 August 1873.

[7] USCP, *op. cit.*, 3, endorsement by Horace Porter to letter of Steinberger to Grant, 17 August 1872.

Senate. Proposals to annex Samoa or extend American protection to the group had also been lost. And Webb was still waiting for the House of Representatives to authorize a mail subsidy of his Pacific steamer service and had no assurance of its ever doing so. Were there any inducements, previously overlooked, that might be offered the Congress to whet its appetite for Samoa? Grant, particularly anxious to get Pago Pago harbour for the United States Navy, was prepared to have a special agent of the State Department go out and search for some, and it was ostensibly for that purpose that Steinberger was appointed.[8]

Like Meade's mission, however, Steinberger's had more behind it than his official instructions alone would suggest. After all, Wakeman and others had already reported at length on the character and condition of Samoa, and further information, if really required, could easily have been solicited from the American consul or a naval commander. Why should Steinberger, a private citizen wholly unacquainted with the islands, be sent out merely to produce another descriptive account of them? Why should he himself have argued a pressing need for this inquiry and have volunteered to conduct it, given only a daily expense allowance and an otherwise unpaid commission from the State Department? Surely, it was no mere coincidence, either, that Steinberger, as well as having Webb's recommendation, knew some of the investors in the C.P.L.C.C. and had a brother on the company's board.[9] Circumstantial evidence points, indeed, to his having had an initial interest in Samoa transcending the collection and recording of information. How much more he envisaged doing, or exactly what, is a matter of conjecture; perhaps he started with no specific plans. Whether Grant or members of the cabinet anticipated, much less intended, Steinberger's exceeding his instructions, using his appointment as a front for unofficial activities, is also uncertain. When it came to his doing that, however, he had support from within the government, especially from the War and Navy Departments, the administration of which was grossly corrupt and loose during the early 1870s. If not conspiracy, there was at least connivance on the part of senior executive officials at the bypassing of the Congress by way of a private political adventure in Samoa.

When Steinberger's appointment was first mooted, the affairs of the C.P.L.C.C. were in a desperate state, and drastic action was needed if the speculation were to be salvaged. One cause of difficulty was the grave doubt hanging over the future of the Webb shipping line. Even in the best of remaining circumstances Webb might not have been willing, as he was not, to take up his 'cost-price' land option and so to encourage

---

[8] ibid., 5-6, Fish to Steinberger, 29 March 1873.

[9] ibid., 47; S.P., Steinberger to McCrellish, 30 October 1875; and from information supplied by J. W. Griffin.

the sale of other land on terms more advantageous to the company's shareholders. More fundamental, however, was the fact that knowledge of the insecurity and irregularity of many of the Collie and Stewart land contracts, which Stewart had palmed off as sound, had got back to the United States, seriously damaging the reputation of the C.P.L.C.C. At this, Webb relinquished his option altogether and, perhaps as a further indication of loss of confidence in Collie and Stewart, transferred the San Francisco agency of his shipping line to another firm.[10] Stewart endeavoured to resolve the crisis by offering land to capitalists in Britain, where he hoped the truth about the C.P.L.C.C. would not be known, but he canvassed there in vain. To retrieve the interests of those who had already invested in the company, it seemed clear, then, that some government authority must first help make good its land claims. This problem was one which Steinberger was no doubt expected, if not actually committed, to follow up.

Seven months passed before Steinberger was finally commissioned. Grant's scrupulous Secretary of State, Hamilton Fish, would not appear to have been animated by a sense of urgency. If anything, he had to be pressured into making the appointment at all. Fish's hesitance may have been due simply to his viewing the proposed mission as a fact-finding tour of doubtful value or necessity. On the other hand, it may have arisen from his suspicion of the aims and proceedings of the C.P.L.C.C., which is reflected in his instructions to Steinberger. For aside from gathering information, Steinberger's only significant duty was to advise the Samoans against selling or granting land to 'individual foreigners', while, at the same time, telling them that foreign governments, if called upon to investigate such transactions, would probably be disposed to invalidate them.[11] This advice was so obviously at variance with the expectations of European land claimants and, to a large extent, with the inclinations and practices of the Powers that one may wonder why Fish chose to give it. Certainly he was striking out at the C.P.L.C.C. But was he also trying to win the favour of the Samoans, about whose land problems no other government had officially expressed concern? Whether or not that was his object, his statement was thus used by Steinberger.

Thus it might appear that Steinberger betrayed the land interests of his brother and friends; but as will be shown, he did not. Meanwhile, these speculations had been so overtaken by disaster that their future seemed black anyway. The first casualty had been the Samoan steamer connection, on the strength of which a C.P.L.C.C. trading depot had been established at Pago Pago. In March 1873, when Steinberger had been on the verge of receiving his commission, Webb had given up the

10 NZPP, F-3, 1873, 7, Raymond to Vogel, 26 October 1872; Cooper, II, 35-6.
11 USCP, op. cit., 5-6, Fish to Steinberger, 29 March 1873.

fight for a United States mail subsidy and, with it, his Pacific shipping service, on which he had incurred a substantial loss.[12] By that time, the C.P.L.C.C. had been beyond saving, too, so thoroughly had Collie and Stewart—by their trading activities in Samoa, their use of land deeds as security for private debts, and other operations conducted chiefly outside United States jurisdiction—plundered its assets and undermined its credits.[13] The company had been in the process of liquidation when, late in June, Steinberger had taken passage from San Francisco, and it had been wound up shortly after his arrival in Samoa in August.[14] Therefore, Steinberger was ostensibly free of responsibility for the C.P.L.C.C. land claims, but in fact, he retained a secret interest in them, while exploiting Fish's invitation to condemn them.

'Who is Steinberger?' The obscurity of his past makes that question almost as apt today as in 1876, when it captioned a leader in a West Coast newspaper.[15] Was he a mining expert, a retired manufacturer of rifles, an ex-Army officer of the rank of colonel, which title he used? Had he ever been an eight-dollars-a-week clerk in Stewart's San Francisco office? Had he known 'Sam' Grant in the 1850s, caroused and travelled with him, accumulated such a wealth of knowledge of the future president's delinquencies that he, Steinberger, would be gladly packed off later to distant Samoa? Did contemporary reports of his identity and background sometimes confuse him with his brothers?[16] Much uncertainty remains. Of Steinberger's character and personality, however, the record is more vivid.

That he was an unprincipled, self-seeking opportunist there can be little doubt, though it is still probable that he had some warmth of feeling for the Samoans, some sympathy for their problems, despite his battening off them. In his manner and capabilities he was, *par excellence*, a politician. Highly articulate in speech, persuasive in expression, expansive in his views, keen to sense and then to play upon people's weaknesses and aspirations, master of the innuendo from which commitments might be inferred, a gifted *raconteur*, a consummate actor in his affectation of sincerity, withal a man of charm, flexibility and self-assurance, at his ease and to the fore, whether at tea with the bishop or at kava with the Samoans, whether in waterfront saloon or senior naval officers' mess—such were some of the qualities of this very 'special agent'.

[12] NZPP, F-3b, 1873, 1-3, Russell to Vogel, 11 July 1873.

[13] SSL, Turner Jr to Parrott & Co., 27 November 1873; USCD, Apia/3, Collie to Coe, 27 February 1874.

[14] SLC 2537.

[15] *Daily Post*, 31 July 1875.

[16] *loc. cit.*; BDCS, Misc., draft articles by J. L. Young (with Williams to Gordon, 9 May 1876); Cooper, II, 38; and from information supplied by J. W. Griffin.

In keeping with his instructions, Steinberger did submit a report on Samoa, a comprehensive and quite informative document, though containing some data already available elsewhere.[17] His posture and conduct in the islands, however, were by no means circumscribed within the terms of his appointment, which enjoined him from acting as a diplomat or political agent, even from discussing in a general way the interests and policies of the United States Government.[18] Participating freely in local affairs and neglecting to define or explain his official powers unequivocally, he let it be thought, rather, that he was preparing the way for an American protectorate or was somehow in a position to determine whether one would be established.[19] One of the impressions he fostered was that he and President Grant had to be sure American intervention would be well received in Samoa before it would be undertaken, by which approach, among other means, he sought to raise a clamour for such intervention. He also made the effort to ingratiate himself among people of influence, to persuade them of the soundness and value of his leadership, that they might welcome, even solicit, his return to Samoa in an administrative or political capacity.[20]

Steinberger's greatest difficulties arose, needless to say, from his encountering rival interests, often in competition for his favour. When, on such occasions, he was required to give advice or take a stand, he tried first to satisfy the Samoans and the missionaries, but without provoking unduly adverse reactions from the Beach.[21] An advantage to him in the latter regard was the attenuated state of the Beach's consular leadership, compared with what the strength of it might have been. Weber was on protracted leave, and in his absence Germany was represented by acting consul Alfred Poppe, a man of less force and influence. Coe was also away, and acting on his behalf for the United States was another American settler, Elisha Hamilton, whose inexperience and inferior status made it easier for Steinberger to usurp consular and diplomatic functions. Moreover, Hamilton, though another of the C.P.L.C.C.'s former buying agents, was less touchy than Coe on the subject of land, possibly because his own land interests were neither as extensive nor as controversial. But if Steinberger was fortunate not to be confronted by Coe, later one of his rivals for influence among the Samoans, he was even more favoured on this occasion by the absence from Samoa of S. S.

---

[17] USCP, *op. cit.*, 13-69, Steinberger's report to Fish, 9 February 1874 (unless otherwise indicated, subsequent citations of this volume refer to the main text of Steinberger's report).

[18] ibid., 5-6, Fish to Steinberger, 29 March 1873.

[19] e.g. MS., Brown, Letterbooks, Brown to Chapman, 11 October 1873.

[20] e.g., ASM(I), III, 317-18, Vidal to Frs Fraysse, 4 October 1873.

[21] MS., Brown, Letterbooks, Brown to Watkin, 24 December 1873.

Foster, the manager of the C.P.L.C.C.'s store at Pago Pago, who had
been chosen to succeed Coe as American consul and was to become one
of the bitterest enemies of the Steinberger régime.[22] Foster's appointment
actually dated from April 1872, before the C.P.L.C.C. had lost its good
name, but he did not take office till the beginning of 1875.[23] This left
Williams, who, though present to meet Steinberger in 1873, was mortally
ill and about to retire to Sydney for medical treatment. Already installed
as acting British consul was his unpopular and inept son, Samuel.

It is significant, too, that when conciliation proved or appeared impossible, Steinberger was given to dealing separately with rival parties,
making them promises or letting them assume conditions that were
essentially contradictory or illusory, which may have pacified them, but
only in the short run, while the extent of his successes was correspondingly exaggerated. So it was when, during his visit to Upolu, there issued
from Mulinu'u Samoan-prepared drafts of a constitution and various
laws, discussion of which brought into focus some of the most vital and
potentially disruptive questions of the time.[24] Pending the establishment
of a protectorate, the Samoans proposed no changes of court jurisdiction
over Europeans or their interests; the consuls' separate and joint tribunals
were to continue functioning as before, and so were mixed courts. But on
certain matters of concern to Samoans, the government chiefs wished to
enact and execute general laws, subject to consular approval if their undertakings were to affect Europeans. In other words, they wanted, without
necessarily depriving the Beach of all rights of self-government, to
return to the system of joint jurisdiction which had been tested and
then upset in the early 1860s and, during the ensuing years of political
experiment and discord, never readopted. This proposal did not, in itself,
arouse much antipathy among foreigners, but of the draft code there
was some severe criticism.[25]

Missionaries asked, for example, why there should be no provision for
the control of the liquor trade and the stamping out of 'vice'. What did
Steinberger think? And what line would the American government
take? Perhaps the Samoans, having once bungled the policing of morals
on the Beach, were chary of claiming that responsibility again, lest
their whole scheme be overturned. It might well have been, too, and

[22] USCD, Apia/3, Coe to Hunter, 28 July 1874 (with enclosure).

[23] ibid., Foster to Fish, 25 October 1872, and Coe to Cadwalader, 5 January 1875.

[24] USCP, op. cit., 49-51. The drafts had been prepared by the chiefs of the
Mulinu'u government and their failautusi (secretaries), but they had taken some
of their ideas from non-Samoan sources, including law codes of the Society
Islands.

[25] FOCP 2849, 66 and 68-70, constitution and code agreed to at Samoan fono of
21 August 1873; SP, Samoan copies of constitution and code, the latter effective
from 1 November 1873.

Steinberger seemed to realize that, for while he professed to share the missionaries' concern, he suggested the postponement of remedial legislation excepting the prohibition of Sunday liquor sales, provision for which was added to the Samoans' draft.[26] The code, as presented, was only a beginning, he said, and among the improvements to come was the introduction of thorough-going controls on the liquor trade and related activities, towards which he promised to exert his utmost influence. In the meantime, he told the Samoans, they should not 'recognize' —presumably not patronize or frequent—the 'liquor-shops'.[27] Whether the issue arose then on the Beach, requiring Steinberger to mollify opinion there as well, is not apparent, but later it did arise generally, becoming one of the reasons for opposition to him. Meanwhile, soon after his first visit, the Mulinu'u chiefs were pressured by the consuls and publicans into amending the 'law for the Sabbath' to allow liquor sales during limited hours.[28]

A more crucial problem was uncovered by the government's proposal to investigate all prospective land sales by Samoans and to require that none be concluded without its express permission. The consuls and other foreigners were prepared to agree to such a restriction, but some among them insisted that the government, while imposing it, should exempt past sales from being questioned by Samoans, leaving to some other authority the task of sorting out conflicting European claims. In reply, the Mulinu'u chiefs took the position, in which the missionaries generally concurred, that existing but unproved claims must be quite open to review, not necessarily by the Samoan Government acting independently, but certainly by a tribunal acceptable to it.[29]

Steinberger quickly perceived that his handling of the land issue was going to be of supreme importance in determining both his own prospects in Samoa and local attitudes towards the United States. From the moment he arrived at Apia he was bombarded with questions by Europeans seeking, above all else, his advocacy of their land interests.[30] As for the Samoans, they had come to realize, by the end of the war, how extensive the land rush had been, while naval intervention occasioned by numerous European complaints of violated property 'rights' had acted as clear warning to them of how their objections to past land sales could be ultimately met and possibly overruled, if the Powers so determined.

26 cf. the original version of Tulafono XI in SP and the English version printed in FOCP 2849, 69.

27 USCP, op. cit., 57-8, Steinberger to Samoan chiefs assembled at Apia, 1 October 1873.

28 ibid., 70, Turner Jr to Steinberger, 29 October 1873.

29 ibid., 46-7, 51; FOCP 2849, 69.

30 USCP, op. cit., 47.

Already there had been heated controversy in Vaimauga over the trans-action between Weber and one of the holders of the Asi title, involving land then being developed into a Godeffroy plantation; and acts of 'theft' and 'trespass' committed by Samoans there had elicited from German naval officers demands for compensation.[31] Similar action, predicated on the assumption that the sales made by Samoans were valid, had been taken with regard to land claims of various British and French residents.[32] In search of a reasonable alternative to the steady whittling away of Samoan interests by intimidatory means, the govern-ment chiefs had wanted to establish a special mixed court to settle land questions arising from sales made since the outbreak of the *faitasiga* war, but strenuous objections from Poppe had prevented action from being taken on the proposal.[33] When Steinberger arrived, shortly there-after, the Samoans' outlook on foreign protection was coloured quite as much, then, by desire for help in saving their land as it had ever been by any consideration of political rivalry or jealousy. Could the United States be counted on for such support? That its navy—and its navy alone—had not intervened recently in European-Samoan land disputes was a point in America's favour. But Coe had complained bitterly of this 'neglect';[34] and if his pleas for a more energetic course of inter-vention were heeded, might the Samoans not find that Power their greatest exploiter? For the ominous fact remained that the C.P.L.C.C. and other American land claims far exceeded in extent those of all other nationalities combined.

To allay the Samoans' fears and doubts, Steinberger made liberal use of Fish's comment on land sales, from which they were able, and were surely encouraged, to draw the most optimistic conclusions: that the United States government held no brief for the C.P.L.C.C. land trans-actions and would do nothing to save them, and that under American protection the interests of the Samoans would outrank those of Euro-peans in the processing of land claims. The effect of his conveying this message, reported Steinberger, was to stimulate the Samoans' confidence in the United States—and, of course, in him.[35] But what of the Euro-

---

[31] SP, Minutes of meetings of 1-5 June 1874, concerning various proceedings relating to Vaimauga land; BCS 3/3, Williams to Derby, 24 June 1874.

[32] BCS 4/1 and 5/1, Correspondence for early 1870s, *passim*.

[33] BCS 2/1, resolutions passed at *fono* of 4 July 1873 (also in BCS 2/4, with proposals by Williams to the *fono*, 4 July 1873). In 1869 Williams had been in favour of the consuls' refusing to recognize war-time land sales to Europeans, but later he had become a land-purchasing agent himself. Now, in 1873, he sponsored the Samoans' plan for a land court.

[34] USCD, Apia/3, Coe to Fish, 1 August 1869 (and periodic despatches thereafter).

[35] USCP, *op. cit.*, 46-7; MS., Brown, Letterbooks, Brown to Watkin, 24 December 1873; USCD, Apia/3, Coe to Davis, 28 August 1874.

pean residents, many of whom would have been inclined to react oppositely? In his official report Steinberger professed to have given them no satisfaction, beyond saying they should have the opportunity to place their claims before a competent tribunal.[36] By itself this assurance could have carried little weight, and scarcely any at all if, as he alleged, he openly described the recent land rush as an imposition on the Samoans, exempting no specific purchases or purchasers from criticism. But whatever he told Fish, he still managed somehow not only to put down the objections of Europeans, but to acquire a considerable following on the Beach.

Soon before the end of his two months' stay in Samoa, Steinberger met with the Mulinu'u chiefs, together with mission representatives and consular officers, for final deliberation on the draft code, and only the discussion of land led to a crisis, and this was too easily resolved to have been as serious as the issue might seem to have warranted. It arose, said Steinberger, on the reading of the proposed land law, at which time Poppe and Hamilton called for the acknowledgement of past sales as valid. Steinberger reported having intervened here on behalf of the Samoans, to insist that their text be accepted without modification and to scold Hamilton for having moved to amend it. 'This', he wrote with engaging deception, 'was the single extra-official and arbitrary act upon my part during my intercourse with the Samoans.' Someone—patently Steinberger, though he did not admit to it—then suggested that land claims deriving from past sales be allowed to rest for a period of one year, after which moratorium an 'enlightened board of commissioners might adjudicate them'. These terms, embodying no obvious compromise, were made the substance of an oral agreement, and thereafter, said Steinberger, harmony prevailed, with the code being passed in a form virtually that of the submitted draft.[37] To some observers, preoccupied with the complexity of Samoa's land problems, the result of this meeting and the apparent ease of its attainment represented feats of wizardry by Steinberger.[38] Description of the proceedings suggests, however, a more conventional turn of magic, carefully practised and prepared. But how? Moreover, what lay behind the petition addressed to Steinberger by foreign residents, mostly Americans and British subjects, begging for the protection or annexation of Samoa by the United States?[39] And what had happened between Steinberger and Poppe, who

[36] USCP, *op. cit.*, 46-7.

[37] ibid., 51.

[38] e.g. ibid., 63, Turner Jr to Steinberger, 7 October 1873.

[39] ibid., 55-6, European residents to Steinberger, 19 August 1873, and Steinberger to European residents, 6 October 1873. S. F. Williams said the signatories represented a majority of foreign settlers (BCS 3/3, Williams to Granville, 11 October 1873).

had held private discussions prior to final consideration of the code, to induce the German consul to change his mind and join the American and British representatives in recognizing the new Samoan Government?[40]

From the available clues it would seem, for one thing, that Steinberger made a scapegoat of the C.P.L.C.C., that concentration on the general question of enforcing European land claims might be prevented or broken up. The company was undoubtedly a ready and likely candidate for this sacrificial role, even without the lead given by Fish. For it figured in many of the known cases of duplicated or overlapping land sales.[41] It was in liquidation, vulnerable to criticism and attack. The land-purchasing methods of its officers and agents commended those of other Europeans as fair and honest by comparison, while depreciation of the interests of the company or its successors might, in any event, lessen the Samoans' anxiety over land, perhaps disposing them more favourably towards the remaining claimants. Finally, there was not a single person of influence then present to defend what had been done in Samoa by or on behalf of the C.P.L.C.C. Collie, to be sure, was still living at Apia, but he had broken with Stewart and become one of his bitterest, most vocal detractors.[42] According to Collie, as well as Steinberger, Stewart was an arch-swindler, preying on business associates and Samoans indiscriminately; and Collie's house was a place where Samoan chiefs met Steinberger and talked about the iniquities of the land rush.[43]

Again, it would appear that the proposal for the founding of a land court was actually made by Steinberger well before the final consideration of the draft code and was put in terms so loose and vague that most of the parties concerned might see or be persuaded of some potential advantage in it.[44] To the Samoans it would have come as a repetition of their recent proposal for a mixed tribunal of the type they knew, but one backed now by the 'friendly' government of the United States, which would have been thought likely to help administer the proceedings and to take their part in them.[45] Europeans, on the other hand, were led to expect some kind of international commission, or at any rate a body whose composition, rules of procedure and guiding principles of law were agreeable to all the governments represented in Samoa.[46] At least a year would have been needed to put such a scheme

[40] USCP, op. cit., 49-50.
[41] USCD, Apia/3, Foster to Fish, 19 October 1874.
[42] ibid., Collie to Coe, 27 February 1874.
[43] USCP, op. cit., 46-7.
[44] loc. cit.
[45] USCD, Apia/3, Coe to Davis, 28 August 1874.
[46] ibid., Foster to Fish, 19 October 1874.

into operation, which requirement might have seemed reason enough
for a moratorium. For Steinberger, however, a moratorium meant chiefly
the present relief of tension and the avoidance of detailed discussion that
would have pointed up conflicts he could not have resolved. To dodge
issues if possible—that, he told Fish, was one of his main concerns. That
is not to say that Steinberger had no real interest in land or land
disputes. He most certainly envisaged the establishment of some jurisdiction in such matters; but first he was intent upon acquiring personal
privilege and power in Samoa, and to that end he readily subordinated
all other considerations. There is no more telling documentation of his
methods than his secret pact and correspondence with the Godeffroy
management in Hamburg, relative to his accepting, at a price shortly to
be described, that firm's support for a private filibuster in Samoa. He
entered into this arrangement in 1874 with the knowledge, and partly
for the reason, that the United States would not assume official responsibility for the governing of Samoa, though it might conceivably want port
concessions there. But when Steinberger visited Samoa in 1873 he had
already been advised by Fish of what America's position would be,[47] a
fact suggesting that his private conversations with Poppe, leading to
nominal recognition of the Mulinu'u régime by 'Germany', may have
been the first step in the negotiation of his agreement with the house of
Godeffroy.

It was in his approach to Samoan politics that Steinberger acted
most constructively, successfully endeavouring not only to gain the
people's confidence but also to strengthen the foundations of the new
central government. Only through a united Samoan government, one
resistant to local attack and subversion and accorded at least *de facto*
status by the Powers, could Steinberger hope to retain any political
position of authority and prominence. That an unprecedented measure
of unity was actually achieved was, as already noted, due largely to the
Samoans' apparent need for it, too. No doubt they had some illusions
of grandeur, some shared sense of pride in claiming a place among the
organized nations of the world, but it was fear of what might happen
if they did not unite, a fear felt much more acutely at that time than in
the 1860s, that drove the Samoans hardest to rise above their factional
particularism. They worried most, of course, about foreign incursion
upon their land and their political autonomy, for which Steinberger
offered a specific and seemingly practical remedy. With a strong central
government, created by them and guided by the United States, the
Samoans could surely stop the unwanted encroachment and, besides,
recover much of the land which had been put in jeopardy by unauthorized sales. It was further implied, though it did not come out

47 USCP, *op. cit.*, 5-6, Fish to Steinberger, 29 March 1873.

V

clearly until later, that they might also assume full power to govern foreigners residing in Samoa. To the Samoans, who conceived of a protectorate strictly in terms of aid given at their request, an argument demanding from them so much initiative and responsibility was quite consistent with opinion favouring American intervention.[48] An adventurer such as Steinberger might reasonably plan, then, to simulate that intervention, knowing that his services would probably suit his protégés better than the real thing would have.

Steinberger, in addition to meeting various chiefs assembled at Apia Bay, carried the discussion of politics and government direct to the 'country', calling at a majority of villages throughout the group, all the way from Manu'a to Falealupo. The mere fact that he took this trouble, such as few if any distinguished visitors had ever taken before, made a most favourable impression on the Samoans. Sometimes Steinberger was accompanied, introduced and vouched for by missionaries, with whom he got on well, regardless of sect. Perhaps even more helpful to him in the villages were the London Missionary Society teachers, who regarded him as a special friend, believing that he sympathized with their struggle for ordination.[49] In the course of his talks and travels Steinberger scrupulously shunned the temptation, often thrust upon him, to get entangled in Samoan politics himself, and he was sufficiently sensitive and well-advised usually to avoid breaches of Samoan etiquette and petty yet damaging acts of discrimination, traps into which European visitors frequently fell for lack of care or knowledge. In particular, he made it a rule never, if possible, to present himself to leaders or members of only one or two or more rival localities or groups and never to gratify one side, to uphold its material interests or defer to its dignity, at the expense of another.

Although not satisfied with the Samoans' new constitution, which roughly described the form and functions of the government already established, Steinberger did not tamper with it. Rather, he sought to ensure political stability along existing lines, until there should arise a more auspicious occasion for advanced constitution-making. To a European, perhaps to an American especially, the Samoans' effort was indeed a crude one. Officially, the Mulinu'u government was headed by an oligarchy of seven chiefs, the Ta'imua or paramount rulers, each of whom represented one of the districts of the western islands. The member for Atua was also recognized by many of the leading chiefs of Tutuila— excluding Mauga, among others—as that island's representative, in acknowledgement of its ties with Atua. As mentioned, six of the Ta'imua

[48] APF, XLVIII, 222, Elloy to Central Council, 5 September 1875.

[49] USCP, *op. cit.*, 62, L.M.S. teachers to Steinberger, 1 October 1873. cf. chapter 5, above, concerning the question of ordaining Samoans.

came from the Tumua and Pule groups, but all were chosen, or their appointments approved of, in district meetings and were held to have the backing of the majority of their 'constituents'. To the reasons already given for the latter circumstance, namely, the fluid state of Samoa's 'higher politics' and the government's intended role as regulator of Samoan-European relations, may be added two more: the fixing of the term of office of the Ta'imua at one year, which promised scope for the ambitions of other chiefs; and the contact maintained between Mulinu'u and the districts through numerous local representatives known as the Faipule, who shared legislative responsibility with the Ta'imua and who themselves, in keeping with the constitutional undertaking to preserve the customary rights and privileges of individual *matai* and chiefly councils, assumed the additional task of putting up for local action all relevant matters of government business, including the drafts of proposed laws. Empowered by the constitution to determine how many Faipule there should be, the Ta'imua set a limit of forty per district—in practice, the total approximated two hundred, the bulk of them *tulāfale* —which was sufficient for every village to have a representative at Mulinu'u. Within the remaining limits of the government's functions the authority of the Ta'imua predominated, ranging from the promulgation of laws to mediation in case of 'serious trouble' anywhere in Samoa, and from the negotiation and ratification of treaties to the performance of ceremonial duties as joint heads of state. Discretionary power was also given the Ta'imua to select some member of Sa Tupua or Sa Malietoa as chief executive—in effect, as their claimant to the titles of the Tafa'ifā—but this provision was not exploited during the period the constitution was in force. The Ta'imua did, however, act under a further clause which entitled them to appoint up to four official deputies called Pule (in this context, controllers or governors) whose role, only generally described, was advisory and administrative. Also appointed under the constitution were many lesser officials, including district and sub-district judges and police, who were chosen locally but commissioned by the Ta'imua in the name of the Mulinu'u government.[50]

As will emerge, this government worked rather more effectively than many Europeans anticipated, though too little is known about the conduct of its principal office-holders for one to ascertain in much detail just how power was distributed and responsibility discharged. Clearly and more predictably, though, it lacked the differentiation of form that an American statesman-in-the-making might fancy. But if Steinberger, through the preparatory stages, did envisage constitutional refinements, he proceeded for the moment only to advocate the fullest backing for

[50] MS., Westbrook, E. W. Gurr's translation of the 1873 constitution (a much more complete version than that contained in FOCP 2849).

the new régime, while trying to popularize the idea of American intervention. By all accounts he was highly successful. Sentiment on the
Beach may have been somewhat less than enthusiastic; but the government was at least recognized there, and some of the more influential
British and American settlers signed a petition favouring a United
States protectorate. To a man, the missionaries were won over and were
pleased to record the fact. The London Missionary Society, Steinberger
was assured, held the Samoan desire for an American protectorate to be
both widespread and genuine and would consider its realization to be
the 'saving of the race'. The mission would also welcome Steinberger's
appointment to administer the protectorate.[51] The London Missionary
Society representative, G. A. Turner Jr, declaring his most sanguine
hopes for Steinberger's visit to have been more than justified by events,
prayed for the success of the next undertaking, namely the arrangement
of American intervention. Steinberger's 'honest spirit', said Turner, had
won him the esteem and love of all Samoans.[52] George Brown, for the
Methodists, expressed similar views, claiming that pro-American feeling
was universal among the Samoans and promising always to remember
fondly his association with Steinberger.[53] Bishop Elloy of the Catholic
mission praised Steinberger's handling of a delicate assignment and
came out, too, in favour of an American protectorate.[54] Among the
Samoans—always excluding the people of separatist Manu'a—the only
significant element rejecting Steinberger's call for recognition of the
Mulinu'u régime was that led by Mauga and several others of Tutuila,
who, none the less, still wanted American protection, provided their
independence of Upolu was guaranteed.[55] As for what American intervention meant to other Samoans, the Ta'imua and Faipule no doubt
spoke with the greatest authority. 'The body is whole,' they said of their
laws and government, 'but it is only lying on the ground; it has no
living breath in it.' Would President Grant breathe into Samoa as God
had breathed into man upon creating him? Would President Grant
please send Steinberger back to help them?[56]

## A new constitution and government

Steinberger's report, to which were appended numerous letters and
petitions complimentary to him and solicitous of American interest in
Samoa, impressed Fish and others in Washington as both enlightening

[51] USCP, op. cit., 63-4, Whitmee and Turner Jr to Steinberger, 4 October 1873.
[52] ibid., 63, Turner Jr to Steinberger, 7 October 1873.
[53] ibid., 63-4, Brown to Steinberger, September 1873.
[54] ibid., 64, Elloy to Steinberger, 29 September 1873.
[55] ibid., 53-4, Mauga to Grant, 15 August 1873.
[56] ibid., 56-7, Ta'imua and Faipule to Grant, 3 October 1873.

and sound but failed to spur the Congress into authorizing any measure of imperial intervention by the United States. Undaunted by this not unexpected reception, which denied him the office of American commissioner that he had made room for in Samoa, Steinberger set out privately to 'breathe life' into the allegedly inert form of the Mulinu'u government.[57] One of his first steps was to prevail upon Grant to have him appointed again as a 'special agent', this time for the ostensible purpose of delivering the president's reply to the Samoans' petition and reporting their reaction to that reply. Grant's message, it turned out, was quite as flowery and imprecise as the petition itself, obscuring, no doubt intentionally, the official attitude of the United States Government and leaving the bearer free to produce, by side-effects, an illusion of a quite different response. As part of his equipment for this performance, Steinberger obtained from the federal government a respectable quantity of military supplies, to be presented to the Ta'imua in reciprocation of gifts sent to Grant by them.[58] That some of the articles from Mulinu'u had been symbolic of a willingness to accept American intervention, and that Grant's return of goods might appear to signify readiness to intervene, were facts which must have been well known to Steinberger. Also likely to mislead the credulous were the arrangements for transporting Steinberger to Samoa by warship, in contrast to his previous arrival there on a privately-owned schooner, and his appointment to a rank having precedence over that of the consuls at Apia. When the time came, moreover, the commander of the vessel on which he travelled was given the broadest possible orders—to afford him 'any facility . . . for the execution of his mission', the interpretation of which was left for the emissary himself to provide.[59] On the available evidence, it is indeed difficult to believe that President Grant and some of the American cabinet were not knowingly and willingly supplying props for an act of international legerdemain.

But if set up to carry Samoan opinion, Steinberger still had to look for means of staving off interference by other foreign Powers, whose opposition could nip in the bud his plan for assuming leadership of the Samoan Government. For a solution to this problem he obviously could not depend wholly on *sub rosa* support from the federal executive of the United States. Britain, it seemed, would pose no immediate threat; for

[57] He nonetheless proposed an American protectorate and suggested himself for the post of governor. 'I can with facility control these people; and to me it would be a labor of love', he wrote to the State Department (USCP, *op. cit.*, 70-2, Steinberger to Fish, 14 March and 8 April 1874).

[58] ibid., 72-7, concerning official arrangements for Steinberger's second mission. See also Ellison, 56-60.

[59] Ellison, 59; USN, Cmdr L., Erben to Ahny, 22 May 1875.

the senior officer on the Australian station of the Royal Navy, visiting
Samoa soon after Steinberger had gone, had been persuaded by Protestant
missionaries and the acting British consul that the Mulinu'u régime was
the legitimate government of Samoa and had recognized it as such,
pending America's response to the petition for a protectorate.[60] Not only
were the Ta'imua and Faipule thereby acknowledged as having the
authority to invite American intervention, but it could be inferred that
Britain was agreeable to their doing so. On the other hand, it looked as
if Germany might cause trouble. This was probably a fair enough conclusion to draw from the fact of Hamburg's commercial pre-eminence in
Samoa. If there was any doubt, however, it was removed early in 1874
by the action of the German warship, *Arcona*. Despite the moratorium
to which Poppe had agreed, the commander of that vessel took up the
Godeffroy land claims in Vaimauga and threatened force if they were
not immediately granted and indemnities paid. Required to answer for
the Samoan side, the Mulinu'u chiefs insisted on postponing settlement
of the case, reasonably citing the moratorium in justification of their
position, which also squared with their obligations to their Samoan
supporters. Perhaps having misjudged the intent and capacity of the
government—a common failing of German officials in Samoa—the commander of the *Arcona* had then to make good his ill-conceived ultimatum
or retire beaten. So it was that, for the first time since H.M.S. *Cordelia's*
pursuit of the murderer Sailusi, the destruction of Samoan villages was
resorted to, several in central Vaimauga being burned.[61] Accordingly,
the Samoans' desire for American protection grew more acute.

In one sense, therefore, the *Arcona* incident played into Steinberger's
hands, but there remained the question of whether Germany would go
on employing force as the arbiter of the interests of its nationals in
Samoa. This, Steinberger told the State Department, was the main point
of his seeing the Godeffroys in Hamburg. On his representations, he
said, these 'elevated and conscientious people' were going to ensure that
their firm's claims in Samoa were subject, in future, to 'legal adjudication' rather than naval action; and *once Steinberger had returned to the
islands*, they and their agents would endeavour to secure formal German

[60] BCS 5/1, Williams to Goodenough, 10 November 1873; USCP, *op. cit.*, 73-4,
Steinberger to Ta'imua and Faipule, 15 April 1874; Goodenough, *Journal*, 200.
Goodenough, whose flagship was H.M.S. *Pearl*, wanted 'to show everyone in
Samoa, as well to Samoans as to foreigners, that I recognize the authority of
the Taimua, and that as far as I can I intend to give it support'.

[61] Adm. 1/6304, concerning German naval proceedings in 1874; BCS 3/3, Williams
to Derby, 24 June 1874; SP, Lemana (for Ta'imua) to Poppe, 16 April 1874,
von Reibnitz (of *Arcona*) to Ta'imua, n.d., and minutes of meetings of 1-5
June 1874 between Samoan chiefs and German officials Weber and von Reibnitz;
USCD, Apia/3, Coe to Davis, 28 August 1874.

recognition of the Samoan Government.[62] What the special significance
of his forthcoming mission was for Godeffroys Steinberger seems to
have passed over, but it was revealed later by documents taken from
him.[63] Among these papers was a ten-year, renewable agreement between
Steinberger and J. C. Godeffroy by which the former, declaring his intention of creating a 'fixed and substantial government' in Samoa, bound
himself to a set of the most unscrupulous conditions. He pledged himself generally to uphold Godeffroy interests in Samoa, 'to avoid all other
business connections in America, Europe and Samoa', and to consult the
firm on 'all important matters', especially those directly concerning its
commercial operations. More specifically, Steinberger presumed to commit the Samoan Government to the following measures: the admission
of labourers from other Pacific territories, the validation of all Godeffroy
land purchases, appointment of the firm as banker and fiscal agent to
the government, and the levying of taxes to be paid by the Samoans in
produce, all of which the Godeffroy establishment would have the first
right of buying, at rates advantageous to it. In consideration of these
undertakings, which the Godeffroys solicited or exacted from him for
lack of an aggressive German imperialist policy, Steinberger was given
not only the terms which he mentioned to the State Department, but also
the advance of funds towards meeting the cost of his accession to power
and the promise of a commission on all sales and purchases transacted
between the Samoan Government and the house of Godeffroy.

When it served his personal ambition, then, Steinberger readily for-
sook principles on which he had founded his popularity among the
Samoans. But he was equally cavalier towards his responsibility to the
'elevated and conscientious' Godeffroys, with whose confidence the
obvious need for secrecy again enabled him to play fast and loose. For
prior to his departure for Samoa, Steinberger, contrary to his agreement
with J. C. Godeffroy, signed away various business concessions and
speculative rights in Samoa for which he received more advances of
cash and the adherence of other American freebooters to his political
project.[64] His scheming probably went even farther, but the evidence, of
which more account will be given, is quite full enough to show his
assault on power to have been planned with ruthless care. The assault

[62] USCP, op. cit., 75, Steinberger to Fish, 19 November 1874.
[63] USCD, Apia/4, Foster to Hunter, 18 March 1876, sending copies of agreement
between Steinberger and J. C. Godeffroy, 16 September 1874, and of Steinberger-
Godeffroy correspondence of 1874-5. The agreement also appears in FOCP 2849,
27-30.
[64] e.g. FOCP 2849, 29-30, agreement between Steinberger and J. H. B. Latrobe Jr,
2 January 1875, referring to various undertakings of a nature contrary to
provisions of the Godeffroy contract; and SP, draft plan for Samoan-Hawaiian
treaty, 1875, in which certain non-German commercial concessions were proposed.

itself began on April Fool's Day 1875, when Steinberger arrived at Apia aboard U.S.S. *Tuscarora*. Following him on the American schooner *Peerless*, which the Godeffroys had purchased for his 'official' use in Samoa, were his entourage, among them one Major J. H. Latrobe, destined as his military aide and training officer to perform one of the most important functions in the establishment of the new Samoan Government.[65]

Steinberger had returned none too soon. During the first year of his eighteen months' absence, the Mulinu'u government had performed quite well, retaining its Samoan support in the western islands, where local application of the new laws was widespread, and negotiating or adjudicating the settlement of many issues between Samoans and Europeans, other than those relating to land ownership.[66] Although they had experienced some difficulty in getting court decisions enforced against Samoans in favour of Europeans, the consuls had found the Mulinu'u chiefs fairly responsive to their wishes and apparently content with the system of joint jurisdiction.[67] But while the government was superior to anything the foreign residents had come to expect of the Samoans, it had not borne the promise of stability and fair play that was imputed to it later, in apotheoses nurtured by Europeans' grievances against Steinberger's own régime.[68] For, unaided by such a charismatic influence as Steinberger's leadership, the Samoans were not only unable to face up to the land problem, which had continued to gnaw at the vitals of their confidence, but were also at a loss to conduct elections of Ta'imua without risk of disturbance or, at any rate, suspension of government activities.

At the end of their one-year term, when the agreed period of the land-claim moratorium had also expired, the Ta'imua had tried to waive the constitutional requirement for new elections and continue in office pending some word from President Grant, which they impatiently awaited in hope of Steinberger's return.[69] The consuls, with a regard for formality to which their own actions would not have stood up, had insisted upon strict observance of the constitution, no doubt aware, though not acknowledging the fact, that the Ta'imua were driven by more than self-aggrandizement to postpone the elections.[70] Once opened

[65] BDCS, Misc., draft article by J. L. Young, 24 January 1876.

[66] SSL, Davis, 15 January 1874.

[67] BCS 3/3, Williams to Derby, 27 October 1874. In consideration of the Samoans' attempts at law-enforcement, the consuls allowed poll tax to be collected from Europeans, a measure which had been accepted in principle in October 1873 (BCS 5/2, Williams to Brown, 23 May 1874; FOCP 2849, 70).

[68] e.g. BDCS, *loc. cit.*

[69] BCS 3/3, Williams, Trade Report, 1 January 1875.

[70] BCS 4/2, Coe and Williams to Mulinu'u chiefs, 26 August 1874, and Coe, Williams and Poppe to Mulinu'u chiefs, 28 October 1874.

by the consuls' refusal to deal with other than a 'legally' constituted government, the election issue had indeed led to unrest, becoming the occasion, now, for serious talk about the selection of a 'king', for which Europeans may also have had some direct responsibility. Early in 1875, after several months of discussion and intrigue among the Samoans and between them and the consuls, measures had been taken to replace the 1873 constitution with another. Proposals originating with the consuls would have reduced to six the number of Faipule appointed by each district, while making the reformed 'house' of Faipule, instead of the districts, responsible for choosing the seven Ta'imua. The same scheme would have required the Faipule to elect a king who, it had been intended, should exercise very substantial powers as chief executive and head of state. Withal, the Ta'imua, though formally retaining most of their legislative and executive functions, would have been downgraded, or so the consuls had supposed. But the Mulinu'u chiefs, though anxious to escape the dilemma which demands for new district 'elections' of Ta'imua had raised, had been opposed to the degree of centralization desired by the consuls, with the result that a compromise had been worked out. Making no change in the number of Faipule, this plan had provided, however, that the Ta'imua should be chosen by that body. On the other hand, the number of Ta'imua had been doubled, and the same principle had been adopted with regard to the kingship, power being given the Faipule to select one Malietoa chief and one of Tupua to form a duumvirate, preparations for which had actually been made in advance by the Samoans. The two kings, it had been stipulated, should jointly convene government councils, supervise and participate in the proceedings of those bodies, and determine whether or not measures passed by them should go into force. As a limitation upon these wide-ranging formal powers, it had been provided that the kings might be impeached by the rather unlikely majority of four-fifths of the Faipule. Yet another constitutional innovation, pressed upon the Samoans by the consuls, had been the specific acknowledgement of the right of the consuls to share in all jurisdiction over foreigners, whatever their instructions from their home governments, and to take the initiative in the exercise of this jurisdiction, which was in correspondence with the system evolved in Vaimauga in 1860.[71]

Certain features of the new arrangement had thus had, for Samoans, the purpose of composing or accommodating factional differences, while preserving the government's facade of solidarity in the conduct of rela-

[71] BCS 4/2, Williams, Foster and Weber to Mulinu'u chiefs, 30 December 1874, 7 January 1875; USCD, Apia/3, Foster to Hunter, 8 February 1875; MS., Westbrook, constitution of January 1875 (translation by E. W. Gurr); Samoa Times, 30 March 1878.

tions with foreigners and the Powers. But if the numbers of Ta'imua and Faipule had been great enough to permit representation of diverse interests, leaving little residue of dissatisfaction regarding those particular offices, two kings had proved too few—or possibly too many. On the Malietoa side there had been no trouble, Talavou having been dropped in favour of Laupepa, perhaps partly because the latter, still a resident of Apia, had become increasingly popular and influential among Europeans and had, by now, reached an age better qualifying him for high office among the Samoans. On the Tupua side, however, there had not been such a clear-cut choice, and when Mata'afa Iosefo had been passed up for one Pulepule, an *aloali'i* of northern Atua, angry charges of European interference had been cast. These were directed particularly against the London Missionary Society representatives, whose opposition to Mata'afa, a Catholic, was beyond question.[72] The background details are obscure, but it is evident enough that a considerable faction in Atua, with probable connections elsewhere, had withdrawn from the Mulinu'u government and talked of raising a challenge to Laupepa and Pulepule in the name of Mata'afa, in response to which Manono had threatened war on behalf of the Malietoa cause.[73] Steinberger found, therefore, that the outward-oriented unity he had helped create was breaking up and the country was again drifting towards war.

Steinberger started immediately holding conferences with the Samoans in order to restore harmony and introduce a new constitution. Grant's message, delivered with suitable emphasis and embellishment, seemed to give him that authority and a good deal more, representing the *whole* of Steinberger's earlier proceedings as having the approval of the United States Government and his return as being a concession to the Samoans' wishes. The effect was enhanced by the presence of the *Tuscarora* over a period of some two months, during which Steinberger carved out his new position at Mulinu'u, and by the conduct and attitude of the ship's commander, Captain Henry Erben, who not only backed him at every turn but showed him respect commensurate with his rank, nominally greater than that of the consuls.[74] Erben also undertook judicial inquiries, generally into matters other than land, thus disposing of outstanding disputes in which Americans were involved. This action was limited by Erben's instructions to cases outside the proper jurisdiction of the United States consul, S. S. Foster, whom the State Department had formally

[72] APF, XLVIII, 223-4, Elloy to Central Council, 5 September 1875.

[73] USCD, Apia/3, Foster to Hunter, 8 February 1875.

[74] BDCS, Misc., draft article by J. L. Young, 24 January 1876; SSL/35, Whitmee, 20 March 1876; USCD, Apia/3, Erben to Foster, 20 May 1875, complaining of posters at Apia derogatory to Steinberger, including one entitled 'Hamlet's Ghost'; USN, Cmdr L., Erben to Ahny, 22 May 1875.

invested with magisterial powers, but it was, of course, contrary to the guarantee recently given the consuls by the Mulinu'u chiefs. Being also in marked contrast to the previous inactivity of American naval commanders, the holding of court by Erben therefore added to the local impression that Washington had adopted a more far-reaching policy of intervention than that in force in Samoa prior to Steinberger's return.[75]

That Steinberger came back with the declared intention of remaining to help them was in itself a powerful influence towards the Samoans' reunification, reawakening interest and confidence in the Mulinu'u government. As to his actual proceedings, one of the most effective measures was the establishment of Samoa's first full-time 'national' militia, an enterprise that put Grant's presents to the use actually envisaged when they had been selected.[76] The hundred-odd muskets and small arms, plus a similar number of uniforms and a supply of ammunition, were taken in charge by Major Latrobe as a start towards equipping his recruits, some one hundred men gathered from the various districts; and heavier arms were, with the help of gunnery experts from the *Tuscarora*, mounted on the *Peerless*, that it might serve the government as a 'naval' as well as passenger- and freight-carrying craft.[77] These innovations were meant both to stimulate pride in the Mulinu'u régime and to discourage or put down opposition to it, in which they succeeded remarkably well.

Of no less significance was Steinberger's settlement of the kingship dispute. Aware that the challenges thrown by the supporters of Malietoa Laupepa and Mata'afa Iosefo were commitments from which the Samoans would not easily withdraw, and probably persuaded by what he knew of other Polynesian territories that the Samoans would want a king anyway, he resolved to make room for one when reconstructing the Mulinu'u government. The selection of a monarch to reign for life would, he believed, defeat his purpose of consolidating the régime's support quickly and with little or no violence. Seeing, too, that provision

---

75 FOCP 2849, 73, Robeson to Ahny, 13 November 1874; USCD, Apia/3, Foster to Hunter, 3 July 1875 (with enclosures); USCP, 44 C., 2 S., House Ex. Doc. 44, 26-7, Foster to Hunkin, 11 November 1875, giving terms of his magisterial jurisdiction based upon the previously-mentioned statute of 1860 (cf. chapter 11, above).

76 USCP, 44 C., 1 S., House Ex. Doc. 161, 71-2, Steinberger to Fish, 8 April 1874, proposing an American protectorate, in respect of which Steinberger referred, *inter alia*, to 'equipment for, say, one hundred men as a native guard, clothing, muskets, a battery of four field-pieces (brass) with ammunition'. Also note the following statement made by him to the Samoans: 'In bringing you presents from our Government, I made such selections as I honestly thought would be of the greatest service to you' (*Frank Leslie's Illustrated Newspaper*, 21 August 1875 [cutting in SSL]).

77 USN, Cmdr L. Erben to Ahny, 22 May 1875.

for a duumvirate had failed to achieve a state of compromise and had, moreover, increased ill feeling between Catholic and Protestant missions, whose respective support he wished to retain, Steinberger proposed that the royal tenure be limited to four-year terms, with the office to be held alternately by single representatives of the Malietoa and Tupua families.[78] According to the new constitution, in which this scheme was incorporated, it appeared that from the outset the choice of king was to be made by the members of the Mulinu'u government, but in fact, the re-establishment of the government and its wide acceptance by the Samoans were conditional upon the prior understanding that Laupepa, from the united Malietoa side, should occupy the throne first. The vexed and potentially disruptive problem of selecting a Tupua king was therefore put off, and meanwhile, each of the contenders was given some hope of succeeding. As for the future of the monarchy itself, an entrenched clause of the constitution provided, but did not require, that by the end of two terms the legislature might hold a general plebiscite on the question of whether Samoa should continue to have a king at all.[79]

This arrangement, as far as Samoan aspirations were concerned, was the most agreeable form of compromise ever to be reached over the kingship—a short run compromise, to be sure, but then there was never any that proved satisfactory in the long run. An essential if not so obvious feature of its success, however, was the assurance that the king should be merely a figure-head, having neither great power in his own right nor leadership of a party claiming the traditional status of Mālō. It was a belief that the king *would* have substantial power that had made the prospect of having one a keen issue among Europeans[80]—not only the missionaries, whose sectarian interests brought them into 'national' politics as rivals for royal patronage, but also consuls, merchants, landowners and others who, unless sure of their ability to manipulate it, were suspicious of power highly concentrated in Samoan hands and were bound to dispute access to it. As for the Samoans, they would find it impossible to maintain a central government within which there was contention for the Mālō and the *pāpā* titles. The Samoans' answer to these problems, in so far as it neutralized the kingship, was the appointment of Steinberger to an indefinite term of office as premier, with constitutional power to conduct the executive business of government and to act as 'Chief Judge of the Supreme Court', independent of

---

78 Before his return to Samoa, however, he had thought that a king (and founder of a royal dynasty) might be elected on a basis of universal male suffrage (SP, Article I of Steinberger's first draft of a proposed constitution).

79 APF, XLVIII, 225, Elloy to Central Council, 5 September 1875; FOCP 2849, 63, Constitution of 21 August 1875, Article I.

80 APF, *loc. cit.*; BCS 4/2, Coe, Williams and Poppe to Mulinu'u chiefs, 30 December 1874.

the king, whose duties these were in name only. The premier was also
to take part in the proceedings of the legislature.[81] As Poo Bah of
Samoa Steinberger thus became, both formally and practically, responsible for the government's handling of foreign interests and thereby
assumed the brunt of European pressure aimed at influencing or opposing the government's actions. Until the final stage of Steinberger's career
in Samoa, European interest was thus diverted from the kingship.
Among the Samoans, too, Steinberger acted as a buffer, isolating the
royal office-holder from the affairs of government, while his pursuit of
administrative and legal innovations and his persistent emphasis on the
Samoans' material interests and the dangers thereto preoccupied energy
and enthusiasm that might otherwise have been devoted to traditional
and more divisive issues, such as that of bestowing the titles of the
Tafa'ifā. Needless to say, only a trusted European, without Samoan
partisan affiliations or leanings, could have performed these functions
successfully.

According to Steinberger's constitution, the councils of the Ta'imua
and Faipule (in the English version, the House of Nobles and House of
Representatives) were reduced to the status of a bicameral legislature,
with the two houses having roughly equal powers. The Ta'imua,
members of the upper house, were to be nominated 'by the people' and
commissioned by the king for unspecified terms of office. In practice,
these chiefs, who were to be of high rank, were chosen from among the
most effective and outstanding participants in district meetings—not
aloali'i and tama'āiga, then, but ali'i, tulāfale-ali'i and an occasional
tulāfale, of whom about half came from the pule centres.[82] The existing
basis of representation in the western islands was retained, with pro-

81 FOCP 2849, 63-4, Constitution of 21 August 1875, Article I.
82 Some of these officials are difficult to identify, particularly in view of the repetition
and division of many chiefly titles and, also, of the fluctuation of Ta'imua
membership without the strictest regard for district quotas. Without attempting
an exhaustive list, it may be noted that the fourteen Ta'imua who signed Steinberger's constitution in May 1875 were fairly representative of the more prominent
and active Ta'imua of the 1870s. These chiefs were: Tagaloa Apela of Saluafata,
Atua; Fuataga of Aleipata, Atua; Misa of Falelatai, A'ana; Lemana of Leulumoega,
A'ana; Samoa of Vaimauga, Tuamasaga; Mata'afā of Malie, Tuamasaga; Taupa'ū
Sailusi of Manono; Letufuga of Safotulafai, Fa'asaleleaga; 'Aufa'i of Sale'aula,
Itu-o-Tane; one of the holders of the Lavea title of Safotu, Itu-o-Tane; one of
the holders of the Asiata title of Satupa'itea, Itu-o-Fafine; and individual holders
of the widespread, repetitive titles Ti'a (possibly of Fa'asaleleaga), Tuiā (possibly
of Atua or Tuamasaga) and Mata'utia (possibly of Itu-o-Fafine or Fa'asaleleaga).
Tutuila chiefs who served as Ta'imua under Steinberger's constitution included
Letuli and Le'iato. Most of the foregoing chiefs were of ali'i status, the main
exceptions being the tulāfale-ali'i Lemana and Fuataga. Mata'afā, a tulāfale,
should not be confused with the holder of the ao or ali'i sili title Mata'afa in
Atua.

vision for two Ta'imua from each district, excepting Manono, which
was allowed only one. All the remaining islands to the east were to form
a single district represented by two Ta'imua, but since Manu'a, which
also figured in Steinberger's plans for the lower house, did not participate in or recognize the jurisdiction of the government—an aloofness
from the west that it maintained throughout the nineteenth century—
the number of Ta'imua actually remained as before, the fourteenth
position being allocated to Tutuila.

The Faipule, members of the lower house, were to be 'elected' for
two-year terms 'by the people of each district', which was given a quota
of seats at the rate of one for each two thousand of its population. The
maximum size of the house of Faipule, unlike that of the Ta'imua, was
thus altered drastically, being cut down to about twenty from a working
membership of two hundred or more.[83] This change, partly an economy
measure in that members and officials of the government were now to
receive regular salaries, clearly narrowed the scope for representation in
the legislature, eliminating the opportunity previously given each village
to have one of its chiefs in a position of responsibility at Mulinu'u. If
Steinberger saw this as a disadvantage, he may have felt that his
constitutional provision for popular elections would help compensate for
it. What is more, he proposed that in the process of electing the Faipule
—and, by implication, of nominating the Ta'imua—printed ballots should
be employed. These radical departures were not actually attempted, however, for the government was formed by Samoan methods in the first
instance and did not last out the year allowed for full implementation
of the constitution. Nor is there any record of the enactment of an
electoral law defining 'the people' for purposes of the franchise. Considering Steinberger's otherwise cautious approach to Samoan politics,
it would seem likely, indeed, that the 'democratic' principles enunciated
in his constitution were meant more for display than adoption.

Of potentially greater significance than electoral reform, with regard
to links between Mulinu'u and the people, was the provision for a
district administration. Each district was to have a governor (Kavana),
appointed by the Ta'imua and responsible to the king and premier, to

---

[83] Chiefs of *tulāfale* status were rather more in evidence among the Faipule than
among the Ta'imua, yet in practice there was a good deal of interchange of
membership between the two 'houses', and also between them and other categories
of senior positions, notably judgeships and governorships. The following titles,
whose likely district origins are indicated, were held by Faipule of the Steinberger period: Matai'a (Tuamasaga); Tufuga (Itu-o-Tane); Lealai'auloto (Itu-o-
Tane); Mamea (A'ana); Aiono (A'ana); Tuisalega (Itu-o-Fafine); 'Ape (Fa'-
asaleleaga); Fiamē (Atua); Tupa'i (Atua); Amoa (Atua); Alapalelei (Tutuila);
Leaeno (Tutuila); Mulipola (Manono); Tuatagaloa (Atua); Masua (Atua);
Leapai (A'ana); and others.

direct and account for the conduct of all affairs over which the central government assumed jurisdiction in that area. Among the governor's stated duties were the administration of tax collections and delivery of the receipts, 'execution of the law', appointment of local judges and supervision of court administration, and control of the police or militia of the district. 'All important decisions rest with him,' said the constitution, 'but a subject shall always have the right of appeal as against unlawful or tyrannical acts of a Governor.' The governor was therefore to be, in effect, a vest-pocket edition of the premier. Like Steinberger, he was to have the widest latitude, but perhaps not so much to facilitate authoritarianism, in this case, as to leave ample room for the satisfaction of *fa'a-Samoa* considerations, permitting the work of government to be spread as widely as necessary among the villages, while holding one chief accountable for its being carried out.[84]

The balance of Steinberger's constitution, which was a scrappy, ill-arranged document, covered a large variety of subjects, but seldom in terms clearly conveying their intent or appearing to bind the government to specific courses or limits of action. The section dealing with the supreme court at Mulinu'u, for example, did not state categorically what that body's jurisdiction was to be, but one may infer that it was only to take cases on appeal from the lower courts, that is, those set up by the district governors. The section providing for the latter tribunals expressed no limits of jurisdiction except to prohibit their hearing cases involving land ownership, taxation, and relations between landlords and tenants, which the supreme court, too, was presumably debarred from accepting. Special provision was made for the establishment, within a 'Department of Interior', of a land commission, to which it was probably intended all land cases should be referred for settlement; but the functions, proceedings and make-up of the commission were left wholly to the legislature and executive to determine and govern, no allowance being made for foreign extra-territorial jurisdiction. The explicit exceptions to the jurisdiction of the regular Samoan courts directly recall Steinberger's contractual obligations to the Godeffroys regarding land and taxes. Just as obviously slanted in favour of the Hamburg firm was that section of the constitution permitting 'the introduction of foreign labour upon our islands'. Another guarantee of economic importance was that prohibiting the levy of tariffs,[85] except on the importation of spirits. To take a final example, again at a less practical level, the constitution contained as a

[84] FOCP 2849, 62-6, Constitution of 21 August 1875, *passim.*; SP, Samoan version of same. District governors under Steinberger included: To'omalatai Patiole, Tuamasaga; Afamasaga Moepa'ū, A'ana; Mata'afa Iosefa, Atua; I'iga Papali'i, Fa'asaleleaga; Tuitele, Tutuila; and in Manono, one of the holders of the Le'iataua title.

[85] Financial implications of duty-free trade are discussed in chapter 15, below.

preamble a so-called 'declaration of rights' which, in terms unmistakably reminiscent of the American Declaration of Independence, expressed the signatories' regard for the sanctity of private property and man's inalienable right to life, liberty and the pursuit of happiness, and also their confidence of God's approval of what they had wrought.[86]

Notwithstanding allusions to American revolutionary crises of 1776, this was not for the Samoans a season of solemn dedication, of facing up to problems just emerging, but rather one of emotional yet complacent self-congratulation. It was as if all that mattered had been granted and confirmed that they fell in with Steinberger's plans and proposals. His 'popular mandate' to proceed with the drafting of a new constitution and laws was given him at a festival of welcome held for him and Captain Erben at Apia Bay three weeks after their arrival. Eight to ten thousand Samoans gathered there from far and wide, some of them transported by the *Peerless*, to hear Grant's message and revel in the meaning that Steinberger and Erben were pleased to have them attach to it. Never had the political leadership or guidance of a European been so enthusiastically, so generally or so blindly accepted in Samoa as on this occasion. If, on the Beach, there was some doubt about Steinberger's powers and intentions, there could be, and in fact was, little question that his Samoan support was genuine and formidable.[87]

The constitution of January 1875 continued in force after this gala demonstration, with Steinberger functioning as adviser to the fourteen Ta'imua at Mulinu'u. In consultation with these chiefs, he prepared drafts of organic and statutory legislation, and on 18 May the new constitution was promulgated, Steinberger then being appointed the acting premier. Four days later, Malietoa Laupepa was installed as king and saluted by the *Tuscarora*, which left shortly thereafter. Within the next few months the government at Mulinu'u was gradually refashioned in terms of the constitution, the Ta'imua and nineteen Faipule being chosen or confirmed by the customary methods that were allowed to operate *pro tem* and Steinberger being sworn in as premier for an indefinite period. By October, when the appointment of local officials was completed, the new apparatus of government was fully set up.[88]

In law, if the enactments he inspired may be accorded that status, Steinberger's government represented a clean break from the principles of confederation which had informed previous attempts at political unification. Theoretically, he was, at least in the executive and judicial spheres, the virtual dictator of Samoa, so far had the balance apparently

[86] FOCP 2849, 62-6.

[87] BDCS, Misc., draft article by J. L. Young, 24 January 1876.

[88] BCS 3/3, Williams, Trade Report, 1 January 1876. Steinberger became premier on 14 July 1875.

tipped in favour of centralized authority. But if, as further evidence will be adduced to show, he had the almost universal backing of the Samoans of Tutuila and the western islands, the specific form of the law had little bearing on the fact, despite the occasional claims of Steinberger's critics to the contrary. His hold on office was determined, rather, by his successful pose as an apostle of political 'progress', as the Samoans' defender, not dictator, and by his shrewd accommodation of rival or mutually exclusive Samoan interests. The missionary, Williams, had once made Christian converts by playing down sin, dispensing gifts and conjuring up visions of wealth to come. By analogous means, and with as much facility, Steinberger made the Samoans politically 'enlightened', while, unlike Williams, avoiding the pitfalls concealed in their factionalism. Whether Steinberger, too, would ultimately have sought to impose onerous obligations upon his followers is another matter, a subject upon which one may only speculate, for his government, soon becoming the victim of foreign aggression, did not last long enough for such a phase to develop, even if one had been seriously planned. While Steinberger was in charge, the government, despite an elaborate array of legislation affecting close control of the Samoans' lives, was really the lightest of yokes, asking little of the general run of the people beyond observance of their own standards of peace and order, acknowledgement of loyalty to Steinberger, and payment of taxes to finance the official payroll and a modest programme of public works. The first two of these conditions were satisfied, and the third might conceivably have been too, had the régime survived intact the foreign assaults upon it. A start was certainly made towards collecting a poll tax, which Steinberger had promised the Godeffroys he would see levied, but as in the case of one or two earlier and largely unsuccessful attempts to raise public revenue in this way, no detailed record is available of the receipts or their expenditure.[89]

Discounting Manu'a, the only notable Samoan opposition to the Steinberger régime, once the new constitution had been promulgated, was in Tutuila, where Mauga and several other prominent chiefs continued to insist upon independence from Upolu. This problem involved, as well as Atua's claim to supremacy over Tutuila, the question of Mauga's right to Pago Pago harbour dues, which he was understandably loath to relinquish. During his preliminary visit to Samoa, Steinberger had tried without success to persuade Mauga to recognize the Mulinu'u government, being aware that the division of Tutuila, and the fact that the name of the American naval officer Meade was closely associated with it, might vitiate his own efforts to bring the whole of Samoa under American influence. That had, indeed, been the basis of some of the most serious criticism made of the central government while Steinberger was

[89] loc. cit.; USCD, Apia/4, Foster to Fish, 1 October 1875.

W

away. For if one small faction could hold out, asked Europeans, might
not others break away, too? And why did American officials seem to be
working at cross purposes? Since the visit of the *Narragansett*, however,
European feeling had been running against Mauga, mainly owing to
attempts by him to exact arbitrarily high port fees, which he had claimed,
erroneously, to have been warranted by the terms of his treaty with
Meade. Weber, for example, had gone to Pago Pago on a naval vessel
specifically to warn Mauga against imposing any restrictions or levies
upon German shipping.[90] In turn, Steinberger had informed the State
Department that Meade's negotiations in Tutuila had been ill advised,
tending only to encourage Samoan separatism and bolster up a petty
'despot' whose conduct might harm America's reputation and interests.[91]
By 1875 Mauga had become sufficiently unpopular among Samoans
and Europeans alike, and so isolated politically, that Steinberger had
little trouble bringing him to heel and, with him, several other Tutuila
chiefs who had taken a course similar to his.

To make a show of force, Steinberger went to Tutuila on the armed
schooner, *Peerless*, accompanied by Latrobe's nattily-uniformed and well-
disciplined militia. The presence of the *Peerless*, flying the United States
and the Mulinu'u flags, was also meant to demonstrate America's repudiation of Meade's treaty and support for a united Samoa. A further
sanction employed by Steinberger was the threat to exclude Pago Pago
from among the ports of foreign entry to Samoa, which were to be
designated by legislation already in draft form. But while resorting to
this pressure, Steinberger also offered the 'rebels' attractive inducements,
that they might have positive reasons for recognizing his government and
facilities for doing so without loss of face. Here he was at his shrewdest,
promising Mauga and Satele, another dissident chief of comparable rank,
prominent salaried posts in the 'district' administration of Tutuila and
devising for them a special oath of office and allegiance from which all
mention of the king or a Samoan overlordship was deleted. In effect,
Steinberger himself became the object of these people's loyalty, to which
their acknowledgement of the Mulinu'u régime was incidental. But for
such juggling of terms and conditions, a peaceful solution to this remaining problem of Samoan solidarity might not have been found.[92]

To minimize internal friction in Tutuila, Steinberger went as far as

[90] USCD, Apia/3, Foster to Hunter, 8 February 1875 (with Weber to Foster, 9
February 1875, and other enclosures). Weber had intervened in March 1872,
about the time of the first German naval inquiry into the Vaimauga land
disputes.
[91] USCP, *op. cit.*, 50-1.
[92] SP, 'A Short Journal, to Tutuila and back per Schooner Peerless', n.d.; USCD,
Apia/4, Foster to Hunter, 5 January 1876, criticizing Steinberger's intervention in
Tutuila.

he could, without amending the constitution, towards giving duplicate district offices to leaders of the two principal parties. The division of the island into two separate districts might have been regarded with more satisfaction in some quarters there, but that proposal would almost certainly have had adverse repercussions elsewhere: harsh feeling towards Tutuila and demands for the division of other districts. As it was, the creation of a dual set of offices—apart from the governorship, which it was understood would alternate between the two parties— eased the strain and proved adequate to the small demands that Steinberger made of the district administration. A similar approach was taken to the appointment of local officials in other islands, with results equally conducive to the stability of the Mulinu'u régime.

## The premier's downfall

One of Steinberger's greatest dilemmas was, of course, that of how to keep up the appearance of protecting and advancing the Samoans' interests while, if not actually gratifying every hope or expectation of the Europeans, doing nothing to arouse dangerous opposition among them. This problem, skated over during his visit in 1873, proved quite insoluble when the time came for him to do more than talk and intrigue; and it was on account of it that Steinberger, though retaining the confidence of most Samoans, was eventually overthrown. Some of his commitments to Europeans he endeavoured to meet. For example, the missionaries, already pleased by his constructive intervention in the kingship controversy, had the additional satisfaction of seeing legislation passed to license saloons and restrict their number and their hours and conditions of trade, to tax liquor imports, and to close 'disorderly houses'.[93] But if the missions applauded these enactments, the Beach did not; and when Steinberger made an intrepid stab at *enforcing* them, the outcry from there became very wrathful indeed.

As for his agreement with the Godeffroys, it embodied terms so inimical to the interests of other Europeans, and of the Samoans, too, that one may wonder whether Steinberger ever contemplated trying fully to live up to it. Surely, any arrangement for the Hamburg firm to purchase all produce received in payment of taxes and fines would have been fought to the last ditch by British and American traders,[94] while any move towards confirming all its land purchases would have alienated many Samoans and raised a chaotic welter of claims and counter-claims from other buyers of land. Poppe, once more acting for Weber, was not so immediately concerned about the tax programme,

93 SP, drafts of penal code and licence law.
94 But by late 1875 there would seem to have been some suspicion that such an arrangement might be made (BCS 3/3, Williams, Trade Report, 1 January 1876).

probably realizing that it would take some time to perfect. But as to
the land, he importunately pressed for early results, to which his firm
looked for security of its substantial investment in plantation development, current and projected.[95] Steinberger had to temporize, giving
reasons of political necessity for delaying establishment of the land
commission he had promised and now provided for, only to have his
argument turned back on him when he asked Poppe for further advances
of credit against his Hamburg contract.[96] If Steinberger was so unsure
of his position, said Poppe, the firm of Godeffroy would have to withhold credit till he proved not only willing but able to discharge his
major obligations. Such evidence was never forthcoming. Later, when
the nature of his Hamburg negotiations became public knowledge,
Steinberger claimed to have withdrawn from the Godeffroy contract and
to have done so with Poppe's approval; but the fact that he had not met
all his undertakings was the only known circumstance in support of
his allegation.[97]

If it seemed unlikely to offend the Samoans, then Steinberger did
actually defer to Godeffroy interests but, in the process, he sometimes
encountered trouble on the Beach, where any favouritism was suspect
and seldom escaped notice. A particular point of conflict was his
handling of the question of indentured labour, vital to plantation
development. The presence of labourers from other islands had not as
yet aroused much objection from Samoans, and superficially, the constitutional measure permitting their importation was perfectly fair to all
who might have wished to take advantage of it. British subjects, however, who accounted for the only other plantation-minded element
apart from the Godeffroy interests, had a hidden grievance. They,
unlike the Germans, had to contend with metropolitan regulation of
the Pacific islands labour traffic, and unless the Samoan Government
would impose fairly high uniform standards for the treatment of indentured labourers within its area of jurisdiction, British residents, though
still under a disability themselves, could expect to see the Godeffroys
extend and consolidate their commercial predominance on the basis of
exploited labour as well as superior capital resources. Not that British
restrictions on the Kanaka trade had always been rigorously enforced,
but facilities for policing them had improved from time to time, and
now, in connection with the recent annexation of Fiji, formal arrange-

[95] USCP, *op. cit.*, 84-5, Steinberger to Fish, 28 October 1875.

[96] USCD, Apia/4, J. C. Godeffroy to Steinberger, 1 September 1875 (with Foster
to Hunter, 18 March 1876).

[97] Steinberger's continued correspondence with the Godeffroy management belies his
allegation (*loc. cit.*; USCP, 44 C., 2 S., House Ex. Doc. 44, 79-84, Steinberger
to Fish, 1 June 1876).

ments were being considered for carrying British extra-territorial jurisdiction into most of the independent islands of the South Pacific, to
ensure, among other things, the just and humane treatment of labourers
under contract to British subjects. When the authority to administer
this jurisdiction was later established, as the Western Pacific High
Commission, fears entertained for the prospect of British plantation
development in Samoa were realized. Indeed, it was no coincidence that
the only such venture of substantial proportions, launched in the late
1870s by a former London Missionary Society printer, Frank Cornwall,
should have involved the surreptitious landing and, subsequently, the
slave-driving of indentured labourers and that it should decline after the
High Commissioner intervened and forced the management to observe
the law.[98] Meanwhile, the firm of Godeffroy went on setting its own
terms of employment and benefiting accordingly. It was a glimpse of
this future that British settlers could see in the labour clause of Steinberger's constitution. He gave them another by discountenancing the
reported (and apparently well-founded) grievances of Gilbertese employed on Godeffroy plantations and by jailing those men who left
work or advocated revolt, thereby punishing breach of contract in a way
not provided for in local law.[99]

Steinberger also observed his commitment to consult the Godeffroy
management—meaning, at this time, Poppe—on important measures
proposed in connection with the formation and conduct of the government. In doing this he tried to be discreet, necessarily so in view of
his denying the British and American consuls similar consideration, and
to the extent that he concealed the precise nature of his relationship with
Poppe, his caution succeeded. On the other hand, it was known that he
had frequent private meetings with the German consul, which fact, plus
the latter's singularly tolerant public attitude towards Steinberger, did
give rise to speculative allegations of collusion between the two.[100]
Among the documents which eventually gave the game away was Steinberger's draft of some intended shipping regulations, in the margin of
which he had marked one section for review in the light of objections
raised by Poppe.[101] The other consuls, it could be recalled later, had
not even known such regulations were in the offing, and the same
applied to the larger part of Steinberger's legislative programme.[102]

It was, on balance, Steinberger's differences with the British and

[98] NZPP, A-6, Sess. 2, 1879, 'Native Labourers in Navigator Islands'.
[99] SP, Report of Mixed Investigating Commission to King Malietoa, 14 June 1875,
concerning runaway labourers from the Mulifanua plantation.
[100] BCS 3/3, Williams, Trade Report, 1 January 1876.
[101] SP, Steinberger's draft of customs house and port regulations.
[102] BCS 3/3, Williams, Trade Report, 1 January 1876.

American consuls that contributed most to his ruin. Contemporary reports tended, in this regard, to damn him mainly on grounds of specific incidents, and it must be admitted that these do add up to an impressive sum of grievance. In addition to the cases already mentioned, it is true, for example, that he spread a false rumour among the Samoans attributing to Britain, which had recently annexed Fiji, the intention of taking over Samoa next. This was a charge of somewhat remarkable subtlety, being put across as consistent with the assumption that the islands were already under American protection. It is true, also, that British and American residents were arrested and imprisoned despite the protests of their consuls, and that some were assaulted by government officials without redress being offered or given. Moreover, Steinberger *did* facilitate Captain Erben's disallowance of an American settler's land claim, which decision was later enforced by the Mulinu'u government.[103] Many other cases of comparable nature could be cited, but the particulars would not contribute much more to an appreciation of Steinberger's fate. For, discounting the *post hoc* exposure of his private intrigues, the issues which most exercised his principal enemies could not be given much overt stress, lest it be demonstrated that their motives were no more ethical than his and their activities certainly no more legal.

Irrespective of Steinberger's official connection with Washington— whether that of a responsible administrator, which he affected to be, or of a messenger 'detained' in the course of his errand, which he actually was—the fact remained that his constitution recognized no extra-territorial jurisdiction on the part of the consuls and that in practice, always excepting his relations with Poppe, *he* recognized none either. Contrary to the express provision made early in 1875 for their sharing in all jurisdiction over foreigners, the consuls were now, apparently, to be mere consuls and nothing more, their extra privileges being accorded the premier instead. In the process, Steinberger endeavoured even to swallow up consular functions of a formal kind, challenging the right of S. S. Foster, Coe's successor, to use the magisterial powers given him by the American Government. Allowing for the Samoans' conception of an American protectorate, then, the Mulinu'u régime claimed to possess full local sovereignty; and in the absence of any provision for European representation as such, Steinberger and his entourage were, outwardly, the only foreigners entitled to participate in the exercise of that sovereignty.[104] Undoubtedly Steinberger had personal reasons for

---

[103] e.g. BDCS, Misc., draft article by J. L. Young, 24 January 1876; FOCP 2849, 33-7, Stevens to Hoskins, 5 January 1876.

[104] Steinberger prepared drafts of treaties with Hawaii and the United States in which no allowance was made for extra-territorial jurisdiction in Samoa, though certain guarantees were to be given regarding property rights and freedom to

wanting it that way, but that was also the way he was set upon by the logic of his political circumstances, his affectation of official American support being too insubstantial to free him from dependence on Samoan support. Thus, for example, he had to treat the consuls as his inferiors not only to uphold the illusion of his administering an American protectorate but also to please the Samoans, who welcomed the chance of disregarding them.

It was not, then, simply the occasional law passed without their prior knowledge or the arrest of a foreigner without their approval that agitated Foster and the acting British consul, S. F. Williams. There had been many such incidents before but never, till now, a situation threatening the permanent and almost total eclipse of the consulates by what was, at least in its political orientation, a Samoan authority. As well as the loss of power to act on behalf of their fellow nationals, the consuls were concerned about the fate of their own private interests and commitments. Young Williams, still holding only the provisional appointment left him by his deceased father, had lived for many years under the protective influence of the British consulate, developing a modest trading business with the aid of the patronage that office could dispense, and he was naturally loath to contemplate being stripped of what were, to him, almost customary privileges. He had indeed envisaged himself being commissioned to succeed as consul and undoubtedly had other ambitions inspired by his father's prominence in the affairs of Samoa.

Foster, who was to have the pivotal role in the coming drama of Steinberger's downfall, was more narrowly motivated by private interests. A friend of Stewart's and, like him, a former resident of Tahiti, Foster had originally come to Samoa for the C.P.L.C.C.[105] When the company had gone into bankruptcy, whereby California shareholders purged the enterprise of Stewart and set about to reorganize it, Foster had resisted take-over proceedings in Samoa but later, in his role as consul, he had assumed the right to sell off the former C.P.L.C.C. land interests. Officially, the offer of sale had been made in order to pay the London Missionary Society for bills of exchange that Collie had issued and Stewart had subsequently dishonoured. At the same time, however, the way would have opened for Foster to let his friend, Stewart, resume control of the C.P.L.C.C. speculation for a nominal purchase

trade (SP, Steinberger to Hawaiian Foreign Minister, 30 October 1875 [with draft of proposed treaty]; USCP, *op. cit.*, 3-5, Steinberger to Fish, 30 October 1875 [with draft of proposed treaty]). Erben, despite his own assumption of extra-territorial jurisdiction, had stated in May that the Samoans were a sovereign people whose laws and customs had to be observed by foreigners (USCD, Apia/3, Erben to Foster, 11 May 1875 [enclosed with Foster to Hunter, 3 July 1875]).
105 ibid., Collie to Coe, 28 July 1874.

price; but apparently in anticipation of some such move, Collie had put
the firm's land deeds into the protective custody of the German consulate, where, despite Foster's protestations, they had remained, forcing
the liquidation sale to be cancelled. Steinberger, meanwhile, had continued to denounce the C.P.L.C.C. operation as a wicked plot of
Stewart's to dispossess the Samoans and had appeared to connive with
Collie and Poppe to tie up the land contracts, so inviting Foster's
antagonism and, somewhat ironically, that of the London Missionary
Society.[106]

Other Europeans were also growing fearful on account of their land
interests, partly because of the unilateral note which the constitution
sounded on the theme of a land commission. Moreover, there was mounting suspicion that Steinberger and his entourage were pursuing personal
economic objectives which might threaten existing business enterprise
in Samoa. There were, in particular, rumours of an American conspiracy
to take over the whole of the Samoan copra trade, once the Mulinu'u
government had acquired a firm grip on power. It is not clear just
what substance there was to this allegation. True, it did eventually come
out that Steinberger had gained the assistance of Latrobe and others by
promising lucrative government positions and various trade concessions,
the latter being, of course, in contravention of the Godeffroy contract.
But it also happened that some of these hangers-on themselves complained of being gulled by Steinberger, which suggests again that,
whatever serious business undertakings he may have had in mind, he
mounted his filibuster by means of consistently conning the credulous
and self-interested.[107] In evidence of his ruthlessness his Hamburg
negotiations have always been cited as the most damning of his proceed-

[106] ibid., Foster to Fish, 19 October 1874, and Apia/4, Foster to Campbell, 28
February 1876; SSL/33, Turner Jr, 8 June 1872, Powell, 7 November 1875, and
notice by Foster of 15 October 1875; SLC 2537 and 2815, *passim*. The controversy centred upon the approximately 25,000 acres of land near Apia for
which the agents of the C.P.L.C.C. had paid in full. The L.M.S. claimed to
hold, in security, the deeds to this land, which Foster allegedly intended to offer
parcel by parcel till the mission's cash advance to Collie had been repaid with
interest. Various copies of C.P.L.C.C. land documents were extant, however, and
the originals of the deeds in question were clearly in the possession of the German
consulate, where Collie had lodged them.

[107] Several of Steinberger's American associates, apart from his initial entourage,
came to Samoa where they behaved as if investigating commercial openings and
acquiring business premises and land. Moreover, Steinberger appointed two
'Samoan' commercial agents in the United States, one of whom, R. L. Ogden of
San Francisco, had been instrumental in his gaining control of the *Peerless*
(SSL, Turner Sr, Whitmee and Turner Jr to Fish, 5 October 1875; FOCP 2849,
79-80, notes by C. E. Stevens on Steinberger and associates, n.d.; USCP, *op. cit.*,
3-5, Steinberger to Fish, 30 October 1875, and 73-4, Ogden to Grant, 5 May
1876).

ings, but equally significant was his manipulation of the land issue, about which comparatively less has been written. For, regardless of his influential public criticism of the C.P.L.C.C., the sense of which seemed favourable to the Samoans, he was *not* determined that the firm's claims should simply lapse or be voided. Foster and Stewart were to be cut out of them, certainly, but not the C.P.L.C.C.'s successors and creditors in San Francisco, of whom Steinberger's brother, John, was one. The land for which Collie had paid in full was clearly regarded by Steinberger as having been legally purchased, and from his private correspondence it is plain he believed the property, which was located near Apia, would greatly increase in value, an assumption presupposing the establishment of secure titles.[108] It is less certain what future he envisaged for the claims based on the C.P.L.C.C. options, upon which he concentrated his verbal attack, but considering the later activities of several of his friends, of which some account will be given,[109] it would seem likely that he hoped to have the Samoan Government pay for the cancellation of the contracts. In any case, if Steinberger, almost alone among the principal adventurers in Samoa during the late nineteenth century, went down in history as having firmly pro-Samoan views on land matters, that was only because he did not remain long enough for his objectives to be fully revealed.

As the conviction grew that Steinberger must somehow be removed, Europeans closed ranks around the American consul Foster, intent on giving him, a man of more bravado than spine, sufficient push to tackle the job. But what exactly could be done? If, as Captain Erben had vehemently declared, Steinberger really had some official sanction to interfere in Samoa, direct assault upon him would be too risky, inviting international complications or a repetition of the Van Camp-Jenkins affair, with the possibility of dire consequences for Foster in either event. Even if Erben had been wrong, the Samoans would still have to be reckoned with. They alone would possess a clear legal right to assail Steinberger's position, and if remaining loyal to him, they might in any case prevent others from assailing it. Many Europeans suspected that Erben *had* been wrong, a suspicion which Steinberger would and obviously could not show credentials to disarm, but to be on the safe side, Foster solicited and awaited the State Department's advice on Steinberger's powers and proceedings.[110] Meanwhile, opposition to Stein-

---

[108] SP, Steinberger to McCrellish, 30 October 1875.

[109] cf. chapter 14, below.

[110] USCD, Apia/4, Foster to Hunter, 3 October 1875 (no. 30). Foster said that Catholic and L.M.S. missionaries wanted to know what Steinberger's position was and that, if he had no official backing from the United States, *they* would have him sent away.

berger was concentrated on efforts to subvert the Mulinu'u government, either by dividing its Samoan members or by driving a wedge between them and their premier. Among these agitators, at this time, was Jonas Coe, the unsuccessful party to the land case which had been taken by Captain Erben.[111]

From some contemporary reports one might think that 'progress' was being made, so assuredly did their authors detect signs of unrest among the Samoans.[112] In fact, Steinberger's hold on office was in no way endangered until the consuls obtained the assistance of Captain C. E. Stevens of H.M.S. *Barracouta*, an officer of the reckless breed, one to rank in Samoan history with Captain Worth of the *Calypso* affair. Stevens, in the course of a Pacific cruise, arrived at Apia in mid-December 1875, by which time Steinberger had alienated the majority of foreign residents, including some of the London Missionary Society representatives, who were resentful of his allegedly loose living, his opposition to the C.P.L.C.C. land sale and his overriding secular influence upon the Samoans.[113] Quite as antagonistic to the Mulinu'u régime as the consuls were, Stevens was more certain than they that Steinberger was a complete fraud and was readily persuaded to remain in Samoa to investigate his proceedings and, if possible, expose him.[114] After seizing the *Peerless* in execution of Foster's writ charging violation of American laws of neutrality, Stevens proceeded to conduct a form of inquisition, a series of meetings at which Steinberger, in the presence of Samoan officials, was subjected to systematic and hostile scrutiny. Stevens's main object, apart from laying complaints against the government for certain of its actions,

[111] USCP, *op. cit.*, 28-36, Steinberger to Fish, 8 January 1876.

[112] e.g. BDCS, Misc., draft article by J. L. Young, 24 January 1876, concerning events of late 1875.

[113]    'For the first time the missionaries have lost their influence with the natives. First came the adventurer Col Steinberger, and stole away the hearts of the people, at the same time that he excited their prejudices against us. He condescended to lower himself to their level, took them home to his board and his bosom, and managed to convey the idea that we were proud, because we would not do the same. Perhaps he is right; but then, I fancy, you will require to send out a batch of Dr. Landall's patent missionaries, to submit to such a state of things.'

(SSL, Pratt, 29 September 1876). Pratt went on to describe the L.M.S. teachers' demand for ordination as another indication of the mission's loss of influence. It will be recalled that Steinberger had supported their demand. Pratt lived in an area where the Samoans remained loyal to the Mulinu'u government after Steinberger's deportation.

[114] USCD, Apia/4, Foster to Hunter, 18 January 1876 (with petition to Stevens from fifty-four foreign residents, 28 December 1875, asking for protection). British settlers predominated among the signers of the petition. Very few Germans signed. A copy of a counter-petition, signed by twenty-five Americans including members of Steinberger's entourage, appears in USCP, *op. cit.*, 66-7.

was to prove to the Samoans that Steinberger had no American credentials authorizing him to perform the functions he had assumed. That the demand for such papers could not be met did not, however, concern the Samoans, to whom such technicalities meant very little. For all Stevens's pains, their defence of their premier defied reduction. As Malietoa declared, the country belonged to the Samoans, and they claimed the right to appoint to public office whomever they wished. If Steinberger was giving them satisfactory service, why should they have to get rid of him? What right had consuls and naval officers to interfere in Samoa's affairs and oppose the enforcement of the laws of the Samoan Government?[115] At this, Stevens and the consuls went into conference and agreed that foreigners in Samoa must be declared wholly free of the jurisdiction of the Mulinu'u government.[116] Poppe, who had taken no active part in the public condemnation of the premier, joined the others in proclaiming European extra-territoriality, but only with reluctance, being, if not wholly disillusioned with Steinberger, as unwilling to provoke him as he was unable to defend him.[117]

The premier remained in office, however, and Stevens could not stay indefinitely to check him. This problem was not resolved until February 1876, after Foster had received sufficient evidence from Washington to prove, to his entire satisfaction, that Steinberger was a mere adventurer. Among other things, the actual nature of Steinberger's official mission was revealed, and also the fact that he had, though somewhat belatedly, resigned his State Department commission and requested special dispensation to assume the premiership without jeopardizing his American citizenship.[118] But while the myth of the 'American protectorate' was now exploded, there was, especially in view of Erben's intervention, no reason for assuming that the United States Government actually disapproved of Steinberger's general line of conduct, hence none for thinking that *it* would remove him, much less deny him protection. Efforts were made, therefore, to find a plausible basis in law from which to launch an action against him with the forces then at hand and to do

115 FOCP 2849, minutes of meetings, 24-9 December 1875.

116 ibid., 19-23, minutes of meeting aboard H.M.S. *Barracouta*, 13 January 1876, and consuls' proclamation of the same date.

117 Poppe refused to sign a second proclamation disputing the Samoan government's objection to the first one. He gave as his reason for declining that he did not want to 'injure his business relations', which statement the other consuls and Stevens appended to the printed document (BDCS, Misc., draft article by J. L. Young, 20 March 1876). A German warship was in port during some of the proceedings against Steinberger but did not intervene.

118 USCP, 44 C., 1 S., House Ex. Doc. 161, 124-5, Campbell to Foster, 12 January 1876. This letter, with a Samoan translation, was printed as a broadside and circulated by the consuls.

this before the arrival of another American warship. With the help of the London Missionary Society representative, G. A. Turner Jr, who had so ecstatically praised Steinberger in 1873, Malietoa Laupepa was taken aside and harangued, cajoled and intimidated into denouncing the premier and signing an order for his deportation. This action by the king, taken with obvious distress on his part, was of course 'unconstitutional' and hence a weak link in the chain of legal justification for what followed, but with Steinberger's impeachment being out of the question, there was no better alternative. To the deportation order were attached, by prearrangement, letters of 'request' and delegated 'authority' from Laupepa to Foster, Foster to Williams, and Williams to Stevens, and on the strength of this series of documents a party from the *Barracouta* pounced on Steinberger and took him to the ship to await 'free passage' abroad. Also arrested and held for deportation was the hapless Coe, who had changed sides and was now to suffer for having 'betrayed' Foster. Finally, some of Steinberger's personal effects were confiscated, among them papers relating to his Hamburg contract which, on being disclosed, was cited as a further reason for the measures already set in train against him.[119]

Enraged by what their king had done, and unwilling to excuse him on the ground of his having acted under duress, the Ta'imua and Faipule deposed him and sacked the few officials, including some of their own number, who rallied to his support. Having no doubt promised to guard Laupepa against loss of his throne, an event which would also compromise the already dubious legality of Steinberger's arrest, Stevens resolved immediately to reinstate him, by threat of force if necessary. This was the gravest miscalculation of the Samoans' temper, leading to tragedy; for the armed bluejackets that went to Mulinu'u to effect the restoration were resisted by the government militia, and in the exchange of fire that followed, there were casualties, including several deaths, on each side.[120] So unprecedented a clash between Samoans and Europeans, an affair in which Latrobe had had no hand, drastically altered the perspective of the case. To be sure, Steinberger and Coe were still deported; but Laupepa was still minus a throne, too, and the Ta'imua

[119] FOCP 2849, *passim*; USCP, 44 C., 2 S., House Ex. Doc. 44, *passim*; BDCS, Misc., draft article by J. L. Young, 20 March 1876; Ellison, 66-75. Malietoa Laupepa, whom Young described as 'easily led', responded to pressure from all sides, defending Steinberger and the Mulinu'u government, agreeing with L.M.S. missionary, Turner Jr, that Steinberger's public interrogation had been in the Samoans' interests even though he, Laupepa, had been insulted in the process, and finally being persuaded by Stevens and Turner Jr to denounce Steinberger. Turner's influence upon Laupepa would seem to have been that which ultimately prevailed.

[120] BCS 3/3, Williams to Derby, 13 March 1876.

and Faipule, with a large majority of Samoans to call upon for support, were still ensconced at Mulinu'u. Moreover, an international incident, if avoidable before, was inevitable now, and Stevens, Foster and Williams were ensnared in their own 'legal', profusely documented trap, all three of them destined for official reprimand and dismissal. Lastly, the *Barracouta* episode demonstrated how firmly Steinberger, but for an aggressive act of foreign intervention, had been entrenched in power among the Samoans. He had gone wrong, suggested his brother, John, by underrating the possibility of such intervention. He should have retained the sponsorship of at least one Power other than the United States, which could never have given him sufficient guarantees. But that, of course, had been one of Steinberger's main dilemmas from the start: he could not go on serving European interests and still satisfy the Samoans. As for Washington, said his brother, he might now find no help there even towards securing redress and clearing his name. For the corruption among Grant's cabinet members, which had given momentum to the Samoan filibuster, was being exposed: 'they have all been heavy on the steal, and hell will be to pay'.[121]

121 USCD, Apia/4, John Steinberger to A. B. Steinberger, dated SF, 20 March 1876 (enclosed with Foster to Campbell, 25 September 1876).

# 14

## POLITICAL FREE-FOR-ALL: 1876-9

STEINBERGER, put down at Levuka by the *Barracouta*, could have returned to Samoa forthwith and found a ready welcome at Mulinu'u. But until, and unless, the consuls who had contrived to expel him had been disciplined for doing so, he could not have expected his influence among the Samoans, particularly on the Laupepa side, to be more than a shadow of what it had been; and without great influence he could not have hoped, realistically, to reunite the Samoans and so to gain for himself a position at all comparable to his former premiership. Discretion prevailed and he chose, rather than to go back, to pursue his grievances elsewhere, to seek compensation for his arrest and deportation. During the several months that necessarily passed before the consuls were in fact dismissed, to the indirect vindication of Steinberger, the political situation in Samoa so deteriorated that, whatever his influence, his premiership would probably have been beyond saving. Discretion prevailed again, and he never went back.

From abroad Steinberger tried, none the less, to go on pulling political wires in Samoa. One of his first efforts of that nature was made in a letter to the Ta'imua and Faipule written in Auckland, where he had gone to lay complaints against Stevens. Assuring the chiefs of his innocence of the charges brought against him, Steinberger told them his immediate intention was to sue for redress on *their* behalf in Washington, London and Berlin. Meanwhile it would be up to them, with what little European help they could get, to keep the Mulinu'u régime running. They must for a start, he said, forgive Malietoa Laupepa and that chief's aides, whom he represented as the unwitting victims of a foreign plot to destroy the government and thereby reduce the Samoans to a state of vassalage. He himself, said Steinberger, had forgiven the dupes; now the loyal Ta'imua and Faipule must follow suit if they hoped to preserve Samoa's independence.[1]

But the Mulinu'u chiefs, as it turned out, were inclined towards

---

[1] TFP, Steinberger to Ta'imua and Faipule and chiefs of Samoa, 8 June 1876. In this document, the Samoan translation of the original letter, there is reference to a 'Misi Ataliti' whom Steinberger was sending to gather information on his deportation and related matters. This person was Ebenezer Hadrill, the shipping reporter of the *New Zealand Herald* (USCP, 44 C., 2 S., House Ex. Doc. 44, 93-4 and 107, Hadrill's statement of 31 May 1876, and Ta'imua and Faipule to Steinberger, 22 July 1876).

indulgence only where no harsher course, short of war, was open to them. After all, the government could scarcely afford to foster the appearance of having no hold over its own members, lest it resign all pretence to authority, nor could its remaining leaders easily ignore the insults to their dignity implied in the 'revolt' of Laupepa and still maintain the *fa'a-Samoa* bases of their prestige. Accordingly they had, long before receiving Steinberger's letter, set out to discipline those defectors whom they could reach directly, fining some and committing others to the Samoan-style 'imprisonment' of exile, while all break-away officials of the government, reachable or not, had had their commissions summarily revoked.[2] Laupepa and his closest associates, however, had been beyond the government's ready grasp in that they had taken with them the allegiance of Samoans sufficiently numerous and sufficiently concentrated territorially to assure them comparatively entrenched places of refuge. Still, Laupepa's faction, centred in parts of A'ana and to a lesser extent Tuamasaga and Fa'asaleleaga, was much smaller than the government's, owing mainly to the reluctance of Talavou's people to cross over and join it, so that the crisis, if left to the Samoans alone to resolve, might well have terminated in the early collapse of the 'rebellion', perhaps under fire. But European interference, designed to bolster the Laupepa cause and keep it alive, had from the time of Steinberger's deportation prevented the government from making any progress in dealing with its principal antagonists. On the one hand, naval force had been threatened in the event of war, while the encouragement given Laupepa had, on the other, created a deadlock from which neither side could have moved for a peaceful *rapprochement* without appearing weak rather than magnanimous or statesmanlike.

Caught in an impasse, the two Samoan parties soon adopted towards each other a cautious attitude marked by willingness to avoid further provocative acts, if not to compose existing differences. Consistent with this *modus vivendi*, as with their desire to preserve their remaining support, the Ta'imua and Faipule decided, after discussing the issue of the monarchy, not to appoint a successor to Laupepa, while supporters of the latter, though obviously bent on his 'restoration', made no hasty move to proclaim him 'king'. But if the Samoans thus confounded Europeans who had anticipated war as a sequel to the *Barracouta* incident, their political equilibrium was nevertheless much more

---

[2] TFP, Mata'afa (Governor of Atua) to Steinberger, 19 July 1876, public notice by Ta'imua and Faipule, 31 July 1876 and another undated (in correspondence, the Samoan officials addressed Steinberger as Galumalemana, an honorary title stemming from one of the sons of Tupua); TFP, Meisake's account of government affairs between 7 February and 22 July 1876; TFP, Sworn statement by the Ta'imua and Faipule, 14 June 1876, concerning the treatment of the deposed officials and their supporters.

delicately balanced than when they had had, in Steinberger, a commonly-accepted leader from outside their own ranks.[3] For Laupepa remained a potential focal point of anti-government feeling, to which not only *fa'a-Samoa* aspirations might contribute, but also any egregious failings of the Ta'imua and Faipule, who bore the onerous responsibility of conducting Samoa's official relations with the Beach and with the Powers.[4] With Steinberger's edifice of authority thus undermined, there followed a protracted period of speculative politics during which Europeans sought to exploit the Samoans and, at the same time, to get at one another *through* the Samoans, for some or all of whom, almost needless to say, they piously affected the most profound concern. To balance the account, however, the Samoans' actions and attitudes towards Europeans would have to be described in rather similar terms and the political machinations of them all, Samoans and Europeans alike, as mutually offsetting in the long run.

## Partisan realignments in Samoa

Europeans who had been antagonistic to the Mulinu'u régime while Steinberger was in Samoa found it, once he was gone, hardly more amenable or responsive to their representations. Indeed, the only significant concession given by the Ta'imua and Faipule was their reluctant acknowledgement of the consuls' claim to extra-territorial jurisdiction over foreigners. Demands that the constitution be amended to allow the consuls to participate in the government were turned down flat, along with proposals that certain existing provisions of the constitution be observed or implemented, for example, by the appointment of a king and establishment of a land commission. The general granting of land claims was a proposition that the Ta'imua and Faipule refused to entertain in any form, and they often proved unwilling to take up European reports of Samoan 'offences', most of which related to thefts of property, particularly from plantations. In brief, this was, in most ways that mattered to foreigners, a government of inaction, if not obstruction. Variously described as wilful and weak, it was in a sense both, the stubborn advocate of its supporters' interests and the timorous evader of responsibility for events where its authority did not run.

Some Europeans were of course favourably disposed towards the Ta'imua and Faipule and were in turn trusted by them. Among these were the Catholic missionaries, who, though having had second thoughts

[3] TFP, Record of A'ana meetings between representatives of Mulinu'u and Laupepa parties, October 1876.

[4] e.g. TFP, Ta'imua and Faipule to Weber and Knorr, 20 October 1876, refusing to amend their constitution (*tulāfono sili*) and denying right of foreigners 'to make laws for Samoa'; BCS 3/3, Williams to Derby, 2 October 1876.

about Steinberger himself, stood by the remnant of the government he had established, not least because their champion, Mata'afa, was associated with it as governor of Atua. Otherwise, the foreign friends of the Mulinu'u régime were mostly Americans or persons connected with American enterprises and were generally a feckless, fickle lot. Foster, to be sure, remained *persona non grata* at Mulinu'u, and his conduct as consul may have given the Ta'imua and Faipule some moments of doubt about the United States Government, too. If so, however, their confidence was boosted when, soon after the *Barracouta* left, the *Tuscarora* put in another appearance and the new commanding officer, Captain J. N. Miller, publicly criticized the deportation of Steinberger and intimated that more would be heard from Washington on that subject.[5] To the Ta'imua and Faipule, America must have seemed as faction-ridden as their own country; but with the Steinberger forces evidently in the ascendant in Washington, they had reason to think that Foster's days as consul were numbered and that their premier might return or be replaced by someone else acceptable to them.[6] Actually, a new American candidate for the premiership—Major-General J. J. Bartlett, a friend of Steinberger's—*did* appear on the scene later, but not until 1878. Meanwhile, the Mulinu'u chiefs, nominally headed by Lemana of Leulumoega whom they designated acting premier, took heart from the prompt sacking of Foster and fastened much of their desire for foreign assistance upon his successor, Gilderoy Griffin, who leaned as far the other way on local political issues.[7] Griffin, who came out from California, indeed became fanatically pro-Steinberger in the sentiments he expressed, while participating, behind the scenes, in a movement to realize on the C.P.L.C.C. land claims. Openly engaged in this promotion, which was to lead to one of the most complex and chaotic political episodes in Samoan history, was Griffin's vice-consul J. G. Colmesnil, an appointed agent of successors to the C.P.L.C.C.[8] Colmesnil, one of the more prominent of the carpet-bagging mercenaries that plagued Samoa in the 1870s, also insinuated himself into the confidence of the

[5] In May 1876 Miller of the u.s.s. *Tuscarora* even declined to enforce the few outstanding judgments which Erben had brought against Samoans on account of American complainants, excusing himself on the ground that the Mulinu'u Government already had enough trouble to contend with (USN, Cmdr L., Miller to Robeson, 6 May 1876).

[6] TFP, Ta'imua and Faipule to Steinberger, 24 July 1876. A rather cool letter indicating that they awaited action by the United States Government and would not write again to Grant until they had had a reply to their last petition, which they had given to Miller to forward.

[7] USCD, Apia/4, Griffin to Campbell, 6 October 1876, concerning his withdrawal of the American Consulate from the foreign coalition of consuls and missionaries who were intriguing against the Mulinu'u Government.

[8] ibid.

X

Ta'imua and Faipule. Among the established settlers with entrée to
Mulinu'u was D. S. Parker, a provisional vice-consul to Griffin and the
only American trader then operating on any substantial scale in Samoa.
Coe, soon back from his involuntary exile, also aligned himself with the
government chiefs.

That the Ta'imua and Faipule should accept such advisers whose
interests were, for the most part, so much more obviously European-
oriented than Steinberger's had seemed is in itself indicative of the
altered state of political affairs in Samoa. One change was the increased
incidence and apparent gravity of naval intervention, which the
Mulinu'u chiefs invited by claiming to constitute a central government
but failing to provide the law and order that most Europeans wished
for. True, American and French commanders were friendly and well
disposed towards the government, but they could afford to be, having
relatively few complaints to process. It was different with British and
German commanders, who called more frequently and took up a multitude of claims. Much of the work of these officers was still of a judicial
or quasi-judicial order, leading to many demands for the payment of
fines and indemnities, some for very large amounts. It was not this particular aspect of naval intervention, however, which now had the most
serious implications for the Samoans. Indeed, the Ta'imua and Faipule
were able, in respect of most of the major levies imposed, to resist payment for several years without having extreme measures taken against
them or against people for whom they were held responsible. That they
got away with this dalliance, for which the Samoans had always shown
a tendency, was due mainly to the risks which the use of force might
entail for Europeans. For with settlers, consuls and others splitting up
into factions aligned with rival Samoan parties and with the Powers
acting separately on their behalf, harsh measures taken to dispose of
foreign claims could too easily result in the victimization of the intended
beneficiaries or some crucial loss of local influence on their part; or, it
was sometimes feared, there might be counter-intervention by officials
of other nationalities. Along with these risks had to be weighed the fact
that force, as shown by experience, was not a wholly reliable means of
collecting levies that might have seemed large enough in themselves to
warrant using it. Unless hostages could be taken or some movable property found that was worth confiscating, police action was apt to be
merely punitive. The commander of the *Arcona*, for example, had
burned several villages in 1874, yet the money he had demanded was
still owing. On the other hand, there were issues now arising that were
ultimately to provoke the frequent use of force. These, as will be shown,
were not of a judicial character but involved, rather, the employment of
naval power as an instrument of direct *political* intervention, some of the

general implications of which will already be apparent from the *Barracouta* incident.

Another source of concern to the Ta'imua and Faipule was the growing threat of a local *coup d'état* aided and abetted by Europeans who wanted Laupepa's party to effect a change of government at Mulinu'u. Not all the foreigners who engaged in this campaign were willingly or perhaps even consciously instigating violence, but that, regardless of intent, was precisely what they were doing. Among the 'pacifists' on Laupepa's side were some of the London Missionary Society representatives, notably G. A. Turner Jr, whose name would have been near the top of any black list then kept at Mulinu'u.[9] As closely linked with the 'rebels', but allegedly bent on war, were Williams and Foster, whose intrigues did not end with their dismissal from consular office. Edward Liardet, Williams's successor and a newcomer to Samoa, bull-dozed his way into local affairs and soon aligned himself with the Laupepa faction too, becoming as deeply involved on that side as Griffin was on the other. A man of wildly unsound political judgement, which trait he shared with Griffin, Liardet was to be perplexed and harried into madness by the utter failure of all his designs. Much more remote, guarding himself against similarly fast commitments and unavertable frustrations, was Theodore Weber, who speculated on an uprising by Laupepa's forces but not without playing the other side too. Weber had, as special advantages in this twofold game, a screen of hirelings and double agents such as no one else in Samoa had the resources to maintain, and the most compliant naval support of any of the consuls.

Threatened from both within and without, the Ta'imua and Faipule were inclined to accept uncritically whatever help or promise of it was offered while, of course, Laupepa and his chiefs were being tempted and flattered into doing the same. The political strife that ensued from this division of forces was primarily a local power struggle set on its course by initiative taken locally or, if elsewhere, by private persons interested in Samoa. In so far as contention among the foreign Powers played an active, observable part in what happened, it was occasioned not by aggressive annexationist intent on their part, such as led to the 'Samoan imbroglio' of the late 1880s,[10] but rather by the Powers' endeavouring to keep up with one another in the acquisition of extra-territorial rights and privileges in Samoa or by their being drawn willy-nilly into existing local conflicts, usually through attempts to retrieve their nationals from self-invited difficulties or to afford protection to incompatible or irrecon-

[9] TFP, Ta'imua and Faipule to Directors of the L.M.S., 22 July 1876, complaining of Turner's part in the intrigue against Steinberger and asking for his removal from Samoa.

[10] cf. chapter 15, below.

cilable private interests. But as a concept in the imagination, the effect of faulty reasoning or outright invention for which there were no ready antidotes in the isolated islands, international rivalry was still a potent force.[11] Considering how Steinberger had created the illusion of an American protectorate and how, long before that, the London Missionary Society representatives had transmitted their fear of French intervention, it is hardly surprising that the Samoans could now think their country to be the subject of bitter antagonism among the Powers, given the various partisan alignments of consuls and naval officers. Many foreign residents were likewise beguiled. Moreover, the Samoans' belief could stand up to the chopping and changing of Europeans' loyalties and commitments for, obviously, they evaluated Western imperialism in terms of their own political projects and factions, which were slow-moving and, in many cases, short-lived. If, for example, Steinberger had been taken away by Great Britain and the United States had as yet done little about it, that did not mean that there had never been an American protectorate or that there would never be another.[12]

At this time, and later too, the more serious propositions put to Samoan parties by European speculators in power politics had certain elements in common. Unlike Steinberger's scheme, which rested on the premise of Samoan unity and had therefore to stress the cleavage between Samoans and Europeans, these others appealed mainly to traditional values and pretensions. With foreign assistance, it would be suggested, a given party might be assured of suppressing its rivals, gaining or strengthening its hold on the ascendant position, acquiring for its favourite *tama'āiga* unquestioned right to the office of Tafa'ifā, securing the disposal of the 'fine mats of state', and becoming, in effect, an hereditary Mālō. As for the nature of the assistance to be given, proposals varied. The promise of naval support was a usual condition, and often there was to be some arrangement for the supply of 'superior' types or quantities of arms. There was always, of course, to be ample 'advice', sometimes of a specialized nature, as in the military field, and nearly always with the implication that the recipients would acquire some

[11] '. . . it is almost impossible for any one who has not visited these Islands to understand the way in which the half-developed minds of the natives are worked upon and perplexed by the rumours and reports put about by the adherents of the various parties—political and religious, native and white— which exist in a state of constant rivalry; nothing is too far-fetched or too absurd to be invented and be believed.'

(FOCP 3372, 13 Hoskins to Sec. of Adm., 6 June 1876, relating to the fear of British intervention to which 'Stevens's overbearing dictatorial conduct had given ample scope'.)

[12] Nor did Hoskins himself wholly discount the possibility of Steinberger's being returned by the United States Government (*loc. cit.*).

arcane knowledge of the art of government. The negotiation of a 'bene-ficial' relationship with a Power, or perhaps with more than one, was another inducement regularly offered. Yet others were the special perquisites for prominent chiefs or for the government-to-be: salaries and honorariums, schooners, new and palatial residences, foreign titles of distinction, even marriage into allegedly high-class families overseas.

These were powerful blandishments. They had to be, for Europeans were after large concessions, calling for the Samoans' abandonment of important material interests for the sake of party advantage. One of the conditions commonly demanded was a guarantee of clear title to the land claimed by the foreign 'advisers' and their friends or co-nationals. This undertaking, which if given was often put in writing at the outset, represented one of the more speculative aspects of an intrigue; for the original owners and vendors would not, as a rule, be confined to any one Samoan party, nor would the land be wholly free of European counter-claims. If a new partisan régime was founded or an existing one shored up, then, would it have, as well as some legitimate status as a government, the strength and the will to enforce an agreement unpopular not only on the side of its Samoan enemies and on the Beach, but on its own side too? Or if not that, would the appropriate Power be ready to intervene, on the pretext of documentary evidence, and insist that grants of title be recognized however they had been acquired? Only if the foreigners claiming land did not require possession of it might the question of effective title be avoided, the Samoans then being asked to pay for the relinquishment or cancellation of the relevant deeds. On the other hand, arrangements of this kind would still necessitate the establishment of a strong, friendly government before the receipt of full compensation could be anticipated.

Other concessions sought by Europeans related to commercial and financial privileges (often in the nature of monopolies), to the construction of roads and bridges, provision of facilities for protecting property, the assumption of liability for Samoan offences against property, and renunciation of the right to levy customs duties. Conditions of a political character were always stipulated too—for example, that the Beach, the consuls, or some particular nationality or national representative should have a say in the government; that certain offices should be filled by Europeans, perhaps even reserved for specific individuals; that the government be of a given form; or that one of the Powers be invited to assume some measure of control over the islands or to establish a naval base there.

The Samoans probably never knew, prior to accepting European assistance, all the major undertakings which would be asked of them. With the development of rivalry between Samoan-European factions, however,

it became increasingly difficult to conceal the self-interested motives
behind the offering of that assistance. Sometimes little or no attempt was
even made to conceal them, the implication being rather that European
support refused by one Samoan party might be extended to another,
which was a strong point in favour of accepting it. On the Beach, needless to say, almost any foreign political overture to Samoans was construed by those not involved in it as a bid for some 'unfair' advantage.
One intrigue therefore begot a second, and so on, keeping the islands in
a perpetual state of ferment and turmoil.

Many objects of political speculation were thus defeated. But if each
upheaval was meant, in some quarters, to have been the last, leading to
political stability through imperial intervention or the foundation of a
strong, independent central government of Samoa, it is also true that
disorder itself brought certain advantages to some people or, at any rate,
was thought to. Indeed, a cross-current of fractious, purposeful anarchy
seems to have run through the course of events of the late nineteenth
century. For example, it was often alleged by observers that Europeans
persistently meddled in Samoan politics, or approved of such meddling,
as much to promote the further sale of land as to confirm ownership of
what had already been bought. This was probably true, for regardless
of how much land had been alienated before, there remained a demand
for more, not only by some of the long-established interests, but also
by newcomers who wanted land cheap and, if in large quantities, usually
with the hope of making a fortune on its eventual resale. Some indication of the force of this speculative fervour may be found in the total
of all the acreages represented by European claims brought before the
international land commission in the 1890s—about 1.7 million acres, or
two and a half times the entire area of Samoa.

It was mainly through the influence of party intrigue and conflict,
leading to recurrent arms races, that the land problem was thus aggravated. From the mid-1870s on, Europeans commonly advanced arms on
credit in connection with their political gambles, taking mortgages on
land and produce as security; and periodically, when there was fighting
or imminent threat of it, further wide-open land rushes occurred.[13] These
later sprees saw more investment by the house of Godeffroy and its
successor, the D.H.P.G., which by the early 1890s accumulated claims to
about 135,000 acres in Samoa. British interests entered the race too,
making a triangular affair of what had been principally a German-
American conflict over duplicated purchases, thus adding to the complexity of local politics and the difficulties besetting inter-Power relations.
Compared with the land rush of 1870-2, succeeding ones were characterized rather more by large-scale transactions with chiefs of high rank

13 cf. chapter 16, below.

who asserted, or had asserted in their names, full rights of disposal, either as exclusive owners or as political overlords. The all-time specialist in this form of misappropriation was the trader and planter, Frank Cornwall, who, with a veritable mania for land ownership, built up the first massive block of British claims in Samoa. Dealing principally with his father-in-law, Afamasaga Moepa'ū, the governor of A'ana, and with a few other chiefs, at least one of whom was an *aloali'i* and another a Tonumaipe'a, Cornwall presumed to buy approximately three hundred thousand acres in Savai'i and A'ana.[14]

Another disruptive influence was the activity of European 'Beach' lawyers, *agents provocateurs*, confidence men and straightout goons, of whom there was a considerable increase in numbers from about 1877 on. Many of these professional troublemakers came from Fiji, whence they had been flushed by Sir Arthur Gordon, the first British governor there. To them chaos represented opportunity, which they did not have to look far to find in Samoa; nor did they have to look much farther to discover ways of promoting new opportunity. One observer, taking note of this fact in 1877, archly if somewhat extravagantly remarked that Samoa had acquired several lawyers but, of the law itself, none.[15]

Of a rather similar nature was the influence of a certain element among the Samoan and part-Samoan clerks and interpreters, often mission-educated, who first came into prominence in the 1870s, with the establishment of central government and the advent to consular and other important positions of foreigners unacquainted with the Samoan language. Some of these locally-born people performed their vital functions without unduly abusing the trust placed in them, and there were a few able and consistent ones who spent their working lives in devoted 'public service'.[16] But many others, succumbing to temptations put in their way by bribery and personal ambition or frustration, took advantage of the obvious opportunity to manipulate forces and events. Indeed, the history of Samoa in the latter part of the nineteenth century is studded with 'incidents' set off by the unauthorized acts of various scribes and other go-betweens. The few of these officeholders who bore chiefly titles were not, it should be mentioned, among the more unreliable. Those most complained of—and the complaints grew more numerous as the century wore on—were in fact part-Samoans, from which general class also came other elements reported as troublesome. Among the latter were experts in the handling of firearms who were welcome and privileged

[14] NZPP, A-4, 1884, Sess. I, 215, F. Cornwall's petition, 5 May 1883.

[15] *Samoa Times*, 27 October 1877.

[16] e.g. Te'o Tuvale who on the establishment of the New Zealand administration was the 'last of the old officials'. He commenced as a clerk at Mulinu'u in 1878 (BMG, Misc., Te'o Tuvale to Logan, 8 April 1919).

recruits to any war party. Nevertheless, part-Samoans were seldom prime-movers in any affair of great moment; and if they were rather given to turbulence and treachery, it must be remembered that they often had little credit, status or resource, apart from their personal knowledge and wits, upon which to depend for the achievement of their aspirations, whether these were European- or Samoan-oriented. For with European immigration continuing, if only at a very moderate rate, and with most of the leading Samoan families resisting marriage between their senior women and Europeans or, if not that, declining to pass their higher-ranking titles through such women to mixed-blood offspring, part-Samoans had little chance of forming or entering the social and political *élite* during the nineteenth century and actually did so only in remoter areas, as in parts of Tutuila and Savai'i.

Of the foregoing considerations, the ones bearing most heavily on political developments in 1876-7, at one remove from the Steinberger régime, were the land problem and the question of regaining for the consulates their direct influence in affairs of government. By the time Griffin arrived to succeed Foster, about seven months after Steinberger had been taken away, there had been whipped up by the incumbent consuls and other foreigners the keenest partisan spirit among the Samoans. One of the first major contributions to that movement had been made, quite unintentionally, by the British Commodore A. H. Hoskins, the senior officer on the Australia Station, when visiting Samoa in May 1876 to investigate the Steinberger and *Barracouta* affairs. Hoskins, bound to stand up for the Royal Navy despite his own dis-approval of Stevens's proceedings,[17] had been rather one-sided in his public criticism of the Ta'imua and Faipule and had imposed on them a levy of indemnification which, though moderate in the circumstances, had caused resentment and embarrassment at Mulinu'u. True, his anti-pathy to the conduct of Williams and Foster had come out, prompting Williams, no doubt from fear of dismissal as much as from offended dignity, to protest to the Foreign Office, charging Hoskins with having maligned and insulted him.[18] On the other hand, Hoskins had also taken an unfavourable view of Steinberger's schemes and methods and, accordingly, had told the Samoans they should consider going back to the 1873-5 constitution, expressing the hope that in the process they might resolve their differences.[19] This suggestion had strongly appealed to critics of the existing régime: to Samoans because the previous con-stitution, originally a Samoan creation, now had the endorsement of two

[17] FOCP 3372, 11-14, Hoskins to Sec. Adm., 6 June 1876.

[18] BCS 3/3, Williams to Derby, 7 June 1876.

[19] FOCP 3372, 16 and 54-5, Hoskins to Ta'imua and Faipule, 30 May 1876 and Weber to von Bülow, 17 June 1876.

British naval commandants in a row, suggesting that Great Britain would surely look with favour upon any government formed on the basis of it and to the consuls because that constitution, as amended, had allowed them formal participation in government.[20]

Taking up Hoskins's idea, Laupepa and his supporters, who were then concentrated mainly in Tuamasaga, Fa'asaleaga and A'ana, made known to Mulinu'u their willingness to unite with the side of the Ta'imua and Faipule under the pre-Steinberger constitution and flag—and, of course, under Laupepa as king.[21] Except for a change of personnel, the situation had become rather like that pertaining in 1868, but in this case it was the party at Mulinu'u which was asked to make concessions in the interests of unity. It must have been widely anticipated that the Ta'imua and Faipule would refuse to abandon the 'Steinberger government', as their régime was still called, and this proved to be so. At this, the Laupepa side had determined to observe the old constitution itself and had set up a capital in A'ana under the party name Puletua, a contraction of *pule i tua*, 'authority behind' or, in effect, country opposition government.[22]

The establishment of a second 'central government', which competed with the first for local delegates and support, had made it relatively easier for the consuls to secure consideration for their demands and respect for themselves. The Ta'imua and Faipule were chastened, the Puletua chiefs anxious for approval and it was a simple matter to play one side off against the other. The consuls demanded major changes and concessions from the Ta'imua and Faipule which the latter could not give without loss of position: yet they demanded that the Ta'imua and Faipule should not fight, arranging to prevent this through threat of naval intervention. Having thus strengthened the position of the Puletua, the consuls continued to make all demands of government of the Ta'imua and Faipule.[23] This encouraged the breakdown of the central government or, at least, attempted to force them into making changes and accommodating the Puletua. In the state of continued unrest and political jockeying between parties, there were more frequent 'incidents' giving cause for European complaints and little will or capacity on *either* Samoan side actually to discharge the onerous responsibilities of

20 Commodore Goodenough had, of course, recognized the government constituted in 1873, of which fact Hoskins reminded the Mulinu'u chiefs. cf. chapter 13, above.

21 FOCP 3372, 54-5, Weber to von Bülow, 17 June 1876.

22 BCS 4/2, Williams, Foster and A. Godeffroy to Puletua in A'ana, 12 September 1876.

23 ibid., noting with reference to the Ta'imua complaint about the Puletua that the consuls say that they do not recognize the Puletua *in matters relating to law in Samoa*.

government which Europeans sought to impose. Clearly, there had to be a single Samoan government, which the consuls and many settlers were intriguing for the Puletua to form, counting on that party to absorb or displace the régime of the Ta'imua and Faipule by means of attrition or, if necessary, of force.

Griffin, who arrived in October, reacted violently upon this scene, straightway plunging into politics at Mulinu'u, adding to the confidence of the Ta'imua and Faipule and encouraging fresh hopes of American intervention. Everything Steinberger had done, he told the Ta'imua and Faipule, had been in the best interests of the Samoan people, calculated to guard them against persecution and dispossession by foreigners. Steinberger's enemies, including the 'traitor', Foster, and all the other Europeans who had engineered or desired his deportation, were therefore the Samoans' enemies too. The tragedy now was, according to Griffin, that Laupepa and his chiefs should remain the unwitting tools of such people, letting themselves be diverted by factional jealousies into a course that threatened *all* Samoans with ruin. The cause of the Ta'imua and Faipule emerged, by the same reasoning, as nothing less than that of the people's salvation. Ostensibly in support of that cause, Griffin interposed himself between the Mulinu'u régime and its would-be 'oppressors', notably the British and German consuls. But that, he said, was not enough: the Ta'imua and Faipule needed more help from America than he alone could give. To this proposition they wholeheartedly agreed, and within a few weeks of taking office, Griffin left again for the United States with the hope of promoting 'closer ties' between Mulinu'u and Washington.[24]

Griffin's mission failed but during the more than eight months that he was absent from Samoa, events there were strongly influenced by belief or suspicion that it might succeed.[25] For one thing, British and German encouragement of the Puletua, including the supply of arms, was intensified, the object being to provoke an attack on Mulinu'u that might force a change of government before the United States could intervene. The only let-up in this effort occurred early in 1877 when Liardet, immediately on taking over the British consulate from Williams, suggested to the two Samoan parties that they abandon their respective

[24] USCD, Apia/5, Ta'imua and Faipule to Griffin, 12 November 1876. This commissioned Griffin as ambassador to the United States with absolute powers—Griffin says he turned this down (USCD, Apia/5, Griffin to Fish, 2 February 1877).

[25] There were wild statements and rumours concerning his purpose—even Gordon believed that an American filibuster was in the offing, if not United States official intervention. Fear of Steinberger by Europeans persisted; Weber thought he might be coming back and one object of the Puletua, in European eyes, was to build up a party to resist an American take-over.

constitutions and flags and unite to form a central government.[26] This proposal, which Griffin's vice-consul Parker supported, was favourably received by leaders on both sides, showing that even then they were reluctant to fight if they could reasonably avoid it. Soon, however, Colmesnil arrived to act as American vice-consul and fell out with Liardet, with the result that the unity plan was scrapped and preparation for war resumed.[27] Owing partly to the impression that the Puletua war effort would have invincible European backing, there was, during this period, a drift of Samoan support towards that side, notably in Vaimauga. But the Mulinu'u government still had superior strength, which it effectively mustered; and in July 1877 at Fale'ula, near Apia, its forces met and crushed those of the Puletua chiefs, whose European 'friends' had wheedled them into making a premature challenge and then left them to defend it as best they could. The Puletua opposition did not cease to exist but it lost its previous orientation, Laupepa's cause, and became, rather, a dispersed body of opinion critical of the Mulinu'u régime. As for Laupepa's cause itself, it trailed away into farce, several dozen chiefly supporters of the ex-king, taking asylum in the grounds of the British consulate, where for months they remained as Liardet's unwelcome guests, allegedly afraid to leave.[28]

But while the Mulinu'u régime was victorious among the Samoans, thereby winning the distinction of being Mālō, it failed in the performance of its main function as a government, the conduct of relations with the Powers. Its most serious troubles began some months before the Fale'ula war when Weber, with a German warship in harbour, demanded prompt settlement of damage claims which had been accumulating for several years. These claims, now totalling about $14,000, were actually being used as a bogy, Weber being prepared to relax them if he could get some guarantee of future security for German property and enterprise. The Ta'imua and Faipule concluded or were persuaded to believe, however, that he was trying to create a pretext for the annexation of the islands by Germany, whose importunate unbending representatives had made that Power the one Samoans now most feared. Assuming this state of emergency, also uncertain of their chances against the Puletua, lacking favourable news from Washington, and influenced by Europeans who fancied their trading and land interests would suffer more under German rule than any other, the chiefs appealed for British

26 USCD, Apia/5, Colmesnil to Campbell, 2 April 1877, 12 March 1877 (first with enclosures), re peace moves.

27 FOCP 3535, Memorandum respecting Mr Liardet's recent proceedings at Samoa, by Victor Buckley, 14 February 1878.

28 FOCP 3372, 127-32, Liardet to Gordon, 18 July 1877; Turner to Gordon, 17 July 1877, Brown to Gordon, 17 July 1877.

protection. This they did in spite of the avidly pro-Puletua sympathies of Liardet, which may suggest how desperate they were, though they were not so desperate as to petition through Liardet himself. Rather the Ta'imua and Faipule sent a deputation to Sir Arthur Gordon in Fiji. It returned empty-handed, however, Gordon being prepared only to recommend cession to Britain, which he personally favoured but which the Samoans would not entertain.[29] The Mulinu'u government had therefore to stand alone against the Germans. The result was not, of course, annexation; but, by exploiting his claims and hurling various threats of intervention, Weber did force the government, on the eve of its clash with the Puletua, to acknowledge and agree to protect German property 'rights', which were not described in detail, and to guarantee that no privilege acquired by another nation in Samoa would be withheld from Germany.[30] This local agreement, a hedge to Weber's encouragement of the Puletua and a further offset to Griffin's efforts in Washington, was the precursor of formal treaties between Samoa and the Powers.

For, as the Ta'imua and Faipule were meeting and overcoming the Puletua challenge, German, British and American diplomats were exchanging assurances of respect for Samoa's 'independence'. That is to say, each Power was undertaking to get what it wanted in Samoa by negotiating for it with whatever régime it recognized as the *de facto* government there, which meant, in turn, that the Ta'imua and Faipule, now constituting the only authority in Samoa resembling a central government, would have the inescapable responsibility of dealing formally with all three. The independence of Samoa was, of course, a myth which the Powers, when it came to the negotiation of treaties, soon exposed by the extensive, often sweeping nature of their demands. Still, the Samoans were almost certainly freer under the exploitation of three governments than they would have been if left to the mercy of only one. That all three got comparable rights and concessions—that is, 'most favoured nation' treatment—was in itself an advantage for the Samoans, too, for it left many conflicting European interests and objectives unresolved and undeveloped until the Samoans had more effective means of countering with their own. At the time, however, the Ta'imua and Faipule seemed literally to be giving the country away, and the people judged and censured them accordingly.

[29] FOCP 3372, 90-1, Gordon to Carnarvon, 25 April 1877.

[30] But in May 1877 Colmesnil, after the Fiji deputation failed, was prevailed upon by the Ta'imua and Faipule to hoist the United States flag above theirs. Colmesnil gave them the flag to use but said it must be hauled down if there was any fighting in Samoa and the Ta'imua and Faipule agreed (USCD, Apia/5, Colmesnil to Campbell, 25 May 1877, 15 July 1877, re Puletua war).

In the prologue of events leading to the negotiation of treaties between Samoa and the Powers, intrigue over the C.P.L.C.C. land claims played a prominent part. Through a series of complicated legal transactions and manoeuvres, involving the ostensible sale and resale of assets, the assignment and reassignment of various rights and powers, and the formation of a hierarchy of interests extending from San Francisco and London through Levuka to Apia, J. B. M. Stewart had by 1877 acquired control of a commercial venture in Samoa, G. J. Smith & Co., whose chief object was to realize on the land claims of which he and George Collie had been the originators. There were other people too, in and out of this particular firm, in Samoa and elsewhere, who had or presumed to have negotiating rights in the same land, and before long, within what was an ever-growing number of interested parties, there was to be intramural discord, from which Samoa would suffer ill effects.[31] During the first few months of 1877, however, the intrigue seems to have proceeded harmoniously, at least at the Samoan end, where the main participant then, apart from Stewart, was the American vice-consul, Colmesnil, an agent of San Francisco speculators who had principal rights in the former assets of the C.P.L.C.C. Indeed, it was primarily Stewart and Colmesnil, acting in co-operation, who facilitated the Mulinu'u régime's approach to Sir Arthur Gordon, lest Germany seize the islands and, in consideration of Godeffroy interests, suppress the land claims they were both endeavouring to exploit.

The ambition of these adventurers was, ideally, the establishment of a strong, stable Samoan government which they could be confident would pay for the liquidation of the C.P.L.C.C. claims, either in its own favour or in that of the original owners and vendors. The sum they envisaged settling for was usually put at about $100,000, the nominal value of the C.P.L.C.C.'s capital issue but, it may be recalled, several times the initial outlay for the land itself. Their choice of whom to attempt to gull, the Ta'imua and Faipule, was of course the soundest possible one, justified by the affection those chiefs expressed for America and by the superior strength of their Samoan support. By the time of the Fale'ula war, however, the object of the C.P.L.C.C. intrigue seemed likely to be defeated by Germany anyway, regardless of what the Samoans did, while perhaps partly for that reason, the intrigue itself had degenerated into a fight among the participants. The immediate issue of contention was control of the Smith & Co. assets, which absentee members and creditors of the firm sought, through their agent, G. A. Woods, from Fiji, to wrest from Stewart on grounds of the latter's

---

[31] On complexities of this affair: SLC 2815, 2537, 2547, 2402; BCS 5/2 and 2/2 *passim*; FOCP 3846, 16, Weber to von Bülow, 15 September 1877, on quarrel with C.P.L.C.C.

alleged mismanagement and fraud. From this struggle, which attracted many ruffians and freebooters from Fiji, waves of violence spread that reduced all but the German element of the Beach to a state of chaos reminiscent of the Van Camp fracas of the mid-1850s. The opposed European factions that formed in the process were, like the fragmented interests descended from the C.P.L.C.C., of mixed British and American nationality, with the leaders including, on the one side, the British consul, Liardet, and Stewart, who passed as an American, and on the other Colmesnil of the American consulate and Woods, a British subject. In its initial phase, commencing on the return of the Samoan deputation from Fiji, this rivalry was confined to the Beach, where the Liardet-Stewart faction, the larger of the two, had the advantage, but over an issue of little consequence. With the sudden crash of the Puletua and the abatement of the German annexation scare, however, the prospect of securing compensation for the C.P.L.C.C. land claims, as distinct from merely scoring off campaigns to secure it, grew much brighter, and the emphasis of intrigue shifted accordingly. So did the advantage, which now lay with parties having access to the Ta'imua and Faipule, which Stewart, by teaming with Liardet, had lost.

Seizing the initiative, Colmesnil and Woods together with Frederic Clay, a San Francisco promoter and trustee of Samoan land investments, approached the victorious Mulinu'u government with a grandiose scheme. Woods, who had been a leading member of the Cakobau-Levuka régime, proposed a new constitution which would have let himself and other selected Europeans into the government of Samoa. Clay, too impatient to wait for Woods to make headway, simultaneously put it to the chiefs that negotiable security bonds of a par value of $100,000 should be issued by the government against C.P.L.C.C. land deeds which he had at his disposal. Colmesnil's function, of course, was to assure the Samoans that the United States would be delighted to see the proposals accepted. But this cabal had gone too far—much too far for the chiefs who deferred a refusal until Griffin had come back and given them his advice. They had gone too far even for Griffin, who was by no means unsympathetic to the recovery of investments in C.P.L.C.C. lands.[32] But if the consul, who returned late in July 1877, would not endorse so crude a filibuster, neither would he condemn it. And when it came to the point, it was Griffin, by arranging Samoan-American treaty negotiations, who gave Clay his next chance, doing so in a manner which strongly suggests that Clay was meant to have it. Griffin knew that the United States Government was obliged to forego imperial commitments in Samoa but continued none the less to plug for an American protectorate as an emergency measure. If Germany still had

[32] USCD Apia/5, Griffin to Campbell, 18 September 1877.

some value as a scarecrow, disposing the Ta'imua and Faipule to want such protection, Britain now had more. This was due in the first instance to Liardet, who had become increasingly irresponsible, partly through frustration over the Puletua's poor showing. Some of his more objectionable acts, though taken with aggressive or punitive intent, were actually so absurd and insupportable that, once the Fale'ula war was over, he might as well have been disregarded by the Ta'imua and Faipule. For example, his singlehanded attempt to 'attach' all land in Samoa as security for payment of the *Barracouta* fine ought to have been seen as pure farce or pathetic madness, even where foreign officials regularly put on lofty airs of self-importance.[33] Yet among Samoans, notably the chiefs at Mulinu'u, a quite different impression gathered force; that Liardet was really acting with authority, guided by some diabolical British scheme to seize Samoa.[34] The person cast in the role of 'evil genius' behind the consul was Sir Arthur Gordon. The vehicle of the 'plot' was the forthcoming extension of Gordon's jurisdiction to Samoa as British High Commissioner for the Western Pacific. 'Essential clues' to Gordon's 'real intentions' included his raising the subject of annexation with the Samoan deputation to Fiji and the very fact of that territory's having been taken over by Britain. The *dénouement* was to be expected when Gordon himself came to Samoa, which visit was known to be in the offing. Among the authors of this fantasy, giving testimony to its 'unerring' logic, were Woods and other renegades from Fiji, who had had careers of political opportunism ruined by Gordon's administration and perhaps half believed their own propaganda. On the other hand, Griffin, though politically artless, should not have thought it was true. He professed to, however, and urgently prevailed on the Mulinu'u chiefs to send a representative to Washington to plead and negotiate for preventive intervention by the United States.

As its emissary the government chose an A'ana chief, a holder of the Mamea title at Lefaga, who had been associated with the Mulinu'u régime for several years as chief secretary and interpreter. Also known as M. K. Mamea, a style he had allegedly adopted at the suggestion of Steinberger, this chief had little qualification for his new role beyond a capacity to speak fluent but simple English.[35] His ability to read and write in that language was, if he had any at all, very slight. Of the practice of state-

---

[33] Liardet's 'attachment' was the point at which he went off-balance.

[34] Liardet's support of the Puletua and the *Barracouta* fine case increased the fear of Gordon's visit and propaganda amongst the Europeans added to it. This was certainly a factor in precipitating the Ta'imua and Faipule into a United States treaty move.

[35] The *papālagi* name of LeMamea was John McLeod—M. K. Le Mamea was probably a corruption of the name McLeod (USCP 44 C., 2 S., House Ex. Doc. 44, 38, Waters to Williams, 6 December 1875).

craft, as he was to encounter it abroad, he could have had but the barest notion, and that acquired from the rather dubious examples set by Steinberger and the consuls. Yet Mamea, bearing various elevated titles including that of Secretary of State, was given full and conclusive powers to negotiate with the United States Government, while to accompany and assist him the Mulinu'u chiefs, acting with the advice of Griffin, appointed none other than Colmesnil. From the start, then, Mamea was in the hands of land speculators who, as soon as he reached San Francisco, induced or tricked him into signing a document purportedly authorizing the bond issue that had been unsuccessfully proposed to the Ta'imua and Faipule.[36] Not that Mamea had been empowered to contract such an obligation to private parties, but Clay and Colmesnil apparently hoped that, in the event of his reaching an agreement with the American Government, the irregularity of their proceedings would be discounted or lost sight of.

As it happened, Mamea did strike a responsive chord in Washington. His request for annexation or the establishment of a protectorate, which he seems to have envisaged more in terms of erecting an impassable barrier to British and German intervention than of submitting to American rule, appealed to some members of the Hayes administration, the recent successor to Grant's, but it had to be declined for lack of congressional support and of will to buck the other Powers. Perhaps anxious to avoid the complete 'failure' of his mission, however, Mamea offered to relinquish Pago Pago harbour, which he knew interested some cabinet officials, if he could have at least a formal undertaking of American friendship for Samoa.[37] Also pertinent to this move was the fact that Mauga and his people, to whom the harbour belonged, had broken away from the Mulinu'u government and were at that very time being forcibly brought to heel.[38] What better way to buy American favour than at the expense of one's enemies? For this gesture Mamea was rewarded with a treaty, but one which, to be acceptable to an isolationist senate, was hardly rewarding for Samoa. By the terms finally agreed to, the United States promised, in addition to the maintenance of perpetual friendship for Samoa, only the use of its good offices for adjusting differences that might arise between Samoa and any Power in amity with the United States. For its part, the American Government secured the first (and, if it wished, sole) right to establish a naval station at Pago Pago, a guarantee of duty-free trade through Samoan ports, the privileges of the 'most favoured nation', and certain

[36] SLC 2815, Le Mamea's agreement with S. I. Clay (Mrs Colmesnil), 16 September 1877.

[37] Seward, *Reminiscences*, 440.

[38] FOCP 3846, 88, Liardet to Derby, 20 December 1877.

concessions of extra-territoriality, namely, exclusive jurisdiction in disputes between Americans, joint jurisdiction with the Samoan Government in cases between Americans and Samoans, and the observance of American laws on matters pertaining to the punishment of offenders of that nationality.[39] This agreement, the Treaty of Friendship and Commerce between the United States and the Samoan Islands, was signed at Washington in January 1878 and, consistent with the extraordinary powers which had been conferred upon Mamea, ratifications were exchanged there soon afterwards.

To see this one-sided treaty put into effect, the State Department detailed a commissioner, Gustavus Goward, to go with Mamea to Samoa, and the navy provided transport for the party aboard the u.s.s. *Adams*, whose commanding officer was under instructions to locate a sight for a refuelling depot at Pago Pago. This was Clay's opportunity. Expecting to tag along and reappear in Samoa as if part of the American 'establishment', he met the *Adams* at Panama, but the commander, after referring the question to Washington, refused him passage, to the relief of both Goward and Mamea. His suspicions rightly if belatedly aroused, Goward wondered in a report to his superiors whether the treaty project might really have been conceived and initiated by shady speculators.[40] Had the State Department been manoeuvred and exploited all along by these private interests? It had been indeed, and it would be again.

It was mid-1878 before the *Adams* reached Samoa, where meanwhile a series of crises had occurred. Following Mamea's departure for the United States, and in some degree because of it, relations between Liardet and Griffin had worsened, and disorder had become rampant on the Beach. Griffin, increasingly unpopular among the Europeans, had for reasons of personal safety sought and secured protection from a French naval commander and subsequently he had removed himself and his consular headquarters to Mulinu'u, from which vantage point he had had the Ta'imua and Faipule threaten Samoan action against his enemies in the town.[41] With the death of Liardet in February 1878 —Stewart had died a few weeks earlier—the tension had shown signs of easing; but soon a British warship had arrived, bringing Sir Arthur Gordon, and fresh trouble had arisen. Having particular regard for Mamea's mission, though the outcome of it was not yet known to him, Gordon had tried to negotiate an Anglo-Samoan treaty. The terms he had sought of the Ta'imua and Faipule were more comprehensive and

[39] USCP, 44 C., 2 S., House Ex. Doc. 238, 124-5, Text of treaty, 1875.
[40] USCD Apia/6, Goward to Seward, 6 May 1878.
[41] USCD Apia/5, Griffin to Evarts, 29 September 1877, and Griffin to Campbell, 10 November 1877.

Y

onerous than those just acquired by the United States, omitting provision for a naval station but seeking to establish, for example, the right of British subjects to retain land they had purchased in a 'normal and regular' manner, which was not otherwise defined.[42] Even so, Gordon's proposals had not justified the worst fears held out for his visit by the Ta'imua and Faipule. With Griffin's encouragement, however, they had stood up to the presence of a British warship and stubbornly refused to negotiate. They had determined to seek treaty relations only with the United States, they had said, and had insisted upon their right to make that choice and stick to it. Probably as much from anger over this as for the official reason he had given, which was the taking of security for payment of the *Barracouta* fine, Gordon had then seized and sent away to Fiji a vessel belonging to the Mulinu'u government.[43] This act, an apparent confirmation of what the Samoans had been told to Gordon's discredit, had been answered by Griffin's raising the Stars and Stripes over the Samoan Government's flag at Mulinu'u, a gesture which, because Gordon was leaving anyway, had given the Ta'imua and Faipule the impression of its having thwarted him.[44]

Griffin, far along the well-trod path of megalomania, had proceeded next to cross Liardet's provisional successor, A. P. Maudslay, who on Gordon's authority had tried to take up treaty negotiations again. By that time, news of Mamea's treaty had travelled to the islands, strengthening Maudslay's resolve to score for Britain but also giving Griffin, if not the satisfaction of Samoa's having become American territory, the idea for a further course of obstruction to prevent Britain or Germany from making treaties with Samoa. Observing that a 'difference' existed between the governments of Great Britain and Samoa, Griffin had invoked the 'good offices' provision of Mamea's agreement with the United States and declared that British-Samoan exchanges over the issue at controversy must pass through the American consulate, where an appropriate 'adjustment' might be made. At the diplomatic level, Griffin had thus presumed to exercise a protective function which the chiefs at Mulinu'u had long wanted to entrust to the United States, reinforcing their opinion, already inspired by the flag-hoisting episode, that an American protectorate had indeed been established. Meanwhile, Maudslay, with the help of a warship, had managed to collect the *Barracouta* fine money, and the annoyance of the Ta'imua and Faipule over this also increased their resistance to negotiating a treaty with him.[45]

[42] *Samoa Times,* 2 March 1878—cf. chapter 16, below, for results of this land provision.
[43] FOCP 3846, 103-6, Gordon to Derby, 4 March 1878.
[44] *Samoa Times,* 2 March 1878.
[45] FOCP 3846, 114-26, Maudslay to Gordon, 19 March 1878 (with Maudslay's enclosures including minutes of meetings with the Ta'imua and Faipule).

On the arrival of the *Adams*,[46] disenchantment began to set in at Mulinu'u. In explaining that there was really no protectorate, Goward tried to soften the blow for the Ta'imua and Faipule by saying that America considered it better for Samoa to remain free and independent. But how, ignoring the concessions already made by Mamea's treaty, was that independence to be maintained? Would the United States guarantee it? Perhaps with the intention of leaving some illusion of American support, Griffin's flag of the 'protectorate', still flying atop the government's staff at Mulinu'u, was not required to be lowered immediately. Also, the commander of the *Adams* engaged in some acrimonious interchanges with the British and German representatives in which he defended the Samoans' right to refuse treaty-making overtures. But events were soon to demonstrate how much practical value could be placed on America's friendship. For one thing, the *Adams* brought notice of Griffin's transfer to Fiji which, because he made a public scene about it, was clearly revealed as a disciplinary measure, a repudiation of his mixing in Samoa's internal politics and foreign relations. Much more important, however, was Weber's call of what he had judged to be an American bluff and undoubtedly meant to expose as such. For in the very presence of the *Adams*, Weber and the commander of the recently-arrived German warship, *Ariadne*, put this ultimatum to the Ta'imua and Faipule: the chiefs would forthwith pay the balance owing on German compensation claims and agree to observe all the terms of the convention into which they had entered with Weber in July 1877, or Mulinu'u would be attacked by a naval landing party. This was the acid test, and the American commander, his intervention confidently anticipated by the Ta'imua and Faipule, did nothing but bluster, leaving them to empty out their meagre treasury. Nor was this all, for Weber also had the Atua harbours of Saluafata and Falealili attached by the *Ariadne*. Controlling rights in them were to belong to Germany pending its establishment of formal and 'satisfactory' treaty relations with the Samoan Government.

Whether weak, irresolute or false, the United States now had little *mana* left in Samoa. That of the Mulinu'u régime was slumping too, borne down by the weight of responsibility for serious errors which Samoans, rightly or wrongly, of their own initiative or at the instance of Europeans, were attributing to it: for Mamea's negotiation of a treaty which seemed to benefit the United States alone; for his relinquishment of land and harbour rights at Pago Pago without having consulted the local inhabitants; for his illegal transaction with Clay, which though discountenanced by the Ta'imua and Faipule, was attracting more foreign office-seekers and concession hunters; for exposing the country

[46] *Samoa Times*, 6 July 1878.

to the wrath of Britain and Germany and, perforce, leaving it exposed; and for a multitude of other ostensible shortcomings.

Where was Samoa heading in its relations with the Powers? Were the Ta'imua and Faipule, in view of what had happened already, fit to continue in charge of Samoa's foreign affairs? These issues of 'national' significance were the main points of inquiry at an inter-district meeting of chiefs—Puletua as well as government supporters—that was held at Apia soon after the *Ariadne* affair. Interrogated by Tuiatafu of the Puletua, the outstanding Tuamasaga orator of the time, Mamea suffered humiliation after humiliation until, asked what the Mulinu'u chiefs were doing to ensure respect for Samoa's independence in future, he finally betrayed the hopelessness of their position. What they were doing, he replied, was writing to all the great nations, at which Tuiatafu, in whose eyes Mamea was merely 'the scribe', broke into satire. 'Listen, o ye people', he said, 'do not backbite the Government, for we are now enlightened.'[47]

The Ta'imua and Faipule were in a tight spot. With Griffin's successor, Thomas Dawson, determined to fulfil his instructions not to engage in Samoan politics or to put obstacles in the way of treaty negotiations by the other Powers, they now had no special friend or partisan in the consular corps. As for their Samoan support, it was slipping away, swelling the ranks of the Puletua and the neutrals, especially in Atua, where the German harbour seizures had occurred, and also in Manono.[48] In considering what to do next, the government chiefs, most of whom had been closely identified with the Mulinu'u régime since Steinberger's time or before, had to think of their respective positions in Samoan society. To be challenged, say, by the Puletua, and then defeated would of course bring about the marked decline of their influence; they would become Vaivai. But without that, if they continued coming off second best in their relations with representatives of the Powers—if they continued having to dispose of Samoan interests holus-bolus and being presented with diverse claims that they could neither meet nor beg off to their credit—they might lose favour even among their nearest connections and would certainly suffer much ridicule and scorn. It is hardly surprising then, that there was talk of disbanding the government or, in the absence of an organized challenge to it, of starting a 'king' movement to divert attention from foreign affairs and attract the support of neutral and Puletua elements.[49] Against their resignation or a radical change of focus they had but one new course to

[47] *Samoa Times*, 3 August 1878.

[48] Atua and Manono had been strongholds of the Ta'imua and Faipule (*Samoa Times*, 24 August 1878; USCD, Apia/6, Dawson to Hunter, 1 January 1879).

[49] USCD, Apia/6, Dawson to Hunter, 1 October 1878.

ponder seriously, one means offered them of supposedly keeping the government intact and prevailing against the Powers and the Samoan opposition. If it failed to arouse their spontaneous enthusiasm, that is quite understandable, for it was to another American adventurer that they had been told to look for deliverance. Again there was a link-up with the past, this time with Steinberger, who had seen Mamea in the United States and undertaken to send the Samoans someone to instruct them in the use of the local autonomy which it seemed likely the Powers would be leaving them. Mamea had wanted the ex-premier himself to come back. That had been 'impossible', however, as long as Britain had still to compensate him for his deportation—which, incidentally, it never did. But Steinberger had a friend, General J. J. Bartlett, who would be glad to oblige and this friend had come to Samoa immediately and ready for action, being full of expectations and short of cash.[50]

Slow to take stock of their chances, the Ta'imua and Faipule kept Bartlett waiting impatiently. Obviously, he wanted the premiership—and a substantial salary to go with it—and just as obviously, the consuls wanted him left out of the government. Possibly to free themselves of the prejudice which the premiership question necessarily evoked on account of the past, and possibly to discourage Bartlett too, the Ta'imua and Faipule expediently decreed the abolition of the office of premier.[51] That violence was thereby done to their constitution went virtually unnoticed: there having been no elections since 1875 nor a king since 1876, to mention but two inconsistencies of form, had already robbed that document of all but its emotional value anyway. This done, the chiefs took a recess and, promising to reconvene in a few months and announce their plans for the future, they all went home.[52]

While the Ta'imua and Faipule were away, the initiative was taken by leaders among their opponents, who perfected a large alliance headed by the traditional centres of Malietoa support and, towards the end of 1878, declared that Talavou should be king of Samoa.[53] This, it would seem, was not an immediate or straightout challenge to war, for Talavou stood in well with several of the Mulinu'u chiefs and actually spent some time at the capital while the government's reply was being determined.[54] But after some further alienation of support, the so-called

[50] loc. cit.; Samoa Times, 3 August 1878.

[51] USCD, Apia/6, Dawson to Hunter, 1 January 1879.

[52] Samoa Times, 5 October 1878. When the Ta'imua and Faipule went home, they left some of their number to carry on the government.

[53] USCD, Apia/6, Dawson to Hunter, 24 February 1879; Samoa Times, 4 January 1879.

[54] USCD, Apia/6, Dawson to Hunter, 23 January 1879.

Mālō rejected him and, though unable to agree to a counter-claimant to the throne, drew the line against the 'rebels', the Pulefou (or 'new authority'). At this most unpropitious moment for the Mulinu'u régime, Weber demanded the conclusion of a treaty with Germany and, with two naval vessels lined up to quell argument and a third expected, got precisely the concessions he wanted:[55] the granting of naval rights at Saluafata, guaranteeing Germans the ownership and peaceful possession of land they had purchased in a 'regular' and 'customary' manner, undertaking not to give other foreigners commercial concessions disadvantageous to Germans, and erecting the most elaborate barriers to Samoan jurisdiction over Germans and their employees, for example, contract labourers. This treaty raised a howl of anguish from Samoans, no less from the signatories than from the others.[56]

In this double crisis, the Ta'imua and Faipule finally turned to Bartlett, to whom they gave the rather equivocal title of 'Teacher of Laws'.[57] What followed was sheer travesty. To a government *in extremis* Bartlett recommended legal and constitutional innovations even more high-flown than Steinberger had tried to introduce, proposed with the mercenary's disregard for scruples that bonds be issued on behalf of Clay (whose dirty work he had unjustly accused Dawson of contracting to perform), and boasted of the military magic with which he, an ex-army officer, would save the régime and restore it to a place of glory.[58] Actually, the Ta'imua and Faipule lasted for several months at Mulinu'u; but that was due to consular and naval interference between the Samoan parties, not to Bartlett's leadership. During that 'period of grace' they suffered repeated affronts and ignominies. Called upon by the consuls to help maintain roads at Apia, for example, they had sometimes to engage in that work themselves, having insufficient manpower available to them in the hostile environs of their capital.[59] Finally, in May 1879, they looked on helplessly while people

55 USCD, Apia/6, Dawson to Hunter, 15 February 1879 (says German treaty exacted); FOCP 4127, Houston to Chesson, 15 February 1879, 59-60 (also an exaction of treaty and its immediate use by Weber to give an ultimatum to Vailele to get off the land which he claimed).

56 *loc. cit.*, 60-1; meeting at Malie (Lemana was present to explain the treaty with Germany. Tuiatafu criticized Lemana, who was the principal signer of the treaty and tore him to shreds with sarcasm as he had dealt with LeMamea).

57 USCD, Apia/6, Dawson to Payson, 28 March 1879.

58 FOCP 4127, 92, Bartlett to Gorrie, 29 April 1879, and, 97, Weber and Swanston to Dawson, 17 June 1879. The latter expresses a protest to Dawson about Bartlett who had taken his job in a civil capacity but now became a military adviser, urging extreme action.

59 *Samoa Times*, 17 May 1879. When the Ta'imua and Faipule were doing road work, the Tuamasaga chiefs got commoners to work on a bridge at Mulivai, to show up the Ta'imua and Faipule.

of the Pulefou gathered at Mulinu'u and appointed Talavou king of Samoa. Then ordered out, the Ta'imua and Faipule, months too late, abandoned the place without resistance,[60] leaving their opponents to experience some of the same dilemmas and defeats that had confronted them. For Bartlett, stranded penniless and his family with him, the eventual journey home also began humbly, the price of passage being paid by subscriptions taken on the Beach.[61]

[60] *Samoa Times*, 30 August 1879.
[61] USCD, Apia/7, Dawson to Payson, 13 August 1879. Mrs Bartlett and the children were sent home as charity cases (Dawson to Payson, 12 January 1880).

# 15

# THE FAILURE OF INTERNATIONAL CONCESSIONS

*Extra-territoriality*

THE EXERCISE of extra-territorial jurisdiction by the consuls, acting as resident magistrates for their respective nationalities, was of course established practice in Samoa from an early date. For many years, however, only German representatives had substantial legal grounds for exercising it, being entitled to act within the limits of prevailing custom or usage, an authority of considerable latitude in Samoa.[1] From 1860 there was an American statute enabling a consular officer serving in a stateless or uncivilized country to be invested with judicial powers somewhat similar in scale to those of a justice of the peace, yet Coe, throughout his period of tenure, was denied them. The State Department, it will be recalled, encouraged him simply to conduct informal court proceedings, which he did—at his own risk, needless to say.[2] The British consuls had rather more law behind them, but of a specialized and, in some instances, obscure nature. For them to be commissioned as regular magistrates, the Foreign Office told them, Britain would have first to secure from Samoa a treaty concession of extra-territoriality. In the absence of such a concession, British consuls still performed judicial functions—like Coe, informally, but without the countenance of their superiors.[3]

Supported by naval officers, this furtive, makeshift system of justice worked fairly well till the 1870s, when political disorder among the Samoans, increasing competition and conflict among growing European interests, and the arrival of uncommonly troublesome, litigious foreign elements plainly called for more formal and responsible measures on the part of the United States and Great Britain. Accordingly, the American Act of 1860 was applied to Samoa upon the appointment of Foster, who took office at Apia in 1875. In that same year, in legislation opening the way for establishment of the Western Pacific High Commission, Britain provided for a more extensive extra-territorial jurisdiction than that assumed by the United States. Samoa did not figure very largely in the initial argument favouring such an authority as the High Commission, but conditions there certainly stimulated anxiety to

[1] FOCP 3846, 142-3, von den Brincken to Salisbury, 20 August 1878 (conf.).
[2] USCI 10, Seward to Coe, 23 March 1867.
[3] BCS 3/3, Williams to Clarendon, 12 January 1870.

see it given early effect, once its legal foundation was laid.[4] Of particular
relevance was Britain's embarrassment over the consuls' withdrawal of
Europeans from the jurisdiction of the Steinberger régime. The Foreign
Office regarded the proclamation of withdrawal as warranted and just
in itself, but Britain, alone among the three Powers, then lacked formal
means of sustaining it. Thus Liardet, though permitted by his instructions to express consent or disapproval of Samoan jurisdiction in specific
matters concerning British subjects, could not legally undertake the
judicial functions that he might seek to disallow the Samoans from
performing.[5] Meanwhile, the newly-arrived Beach lawyers, wise to the
limits of the consul's authority, played havoc with his attempts to hold
informal court hearings, for which activity he was severely reprimanded.[6]
But for a few cases referred to Fiji, and involving British subjects only,
the march of British justice, excepting the naval variety, came virtually
to a standstill in 1877. To get it moving again was one of the first jobs
tackled by Sir Arthur Gordon on receiving his appointment as Western
Pacific High Commissioner. The authority of the High Commission was
originally invoked in Samoa early in 1878 and was subsequently exercised
there by a resident deputy commissioner, who as a rule was also the
British consul.

Belatedly or not, extra-territorial jurisdiction in Samoa therefore had
a firm basis in law before the negotiation of treaties formally conceding
its practice as a limitation of the Samoans' sovereignty. To have the
Samoans recognize and concede that such jurisdiction was of some
importance forestalled objection to it on alleged grounds of their
sovereignty, but that was not the main value put on having treaty
relations with Samoa. Each Power was out, rather, to ensure its having
rights in Samoa no less favourable than those enjoyed by other nations
and, at the same time, commensurate with its own interests there, whatever they were. Taken together, then, the three treaties of 'friendship
and commerce'—America's of January 1878, Germany's of January
1879, and that which Britain acquired from the Pulefou régime in
August 1879—perpetuated the multi-national character of foreign influence, cancelling out differences of imperialist outlook among the Powers
and suspending Samoa in a neutral, semi-autonomous state. Even this
stand-off among the Powers, the systems of tri-consular rule and mixed
Samoan-European jurisdiction, though diffuse, unwieldy and inherently
fragile, might have been restored to working order had their breakdown
been due simply to the absence of legal sanctions, the resurgence of
Samoan partisan strife and the uncertainty of Samoa's future status—

4 See Ward, chapter 17.
5 BCS 1/2, Derby to Liardet, 25 October 1876.
6 BCS 1/2, Lister to Liardet, 12 October 1877.

and, equally important, had the government not been expected to perform to a standard much above the highest reached in recent years. For, consistent with what would have been obvious remedies in that case, the consuls were instructed to co-operate, while the Powers not only professed the formation of a stable Samoan government to be their wish but also intervened to facilitate its achievement.

Certain developments occurring in 1879-80 did in fact suggest that some progress might be made towards the establishment of an effective government. Significantly, the leaders of the Pulefou party, once in residence at Mulinu'u, proved more amenable than the Ta'imua and Faipule had been to the advances of foreign officials, an about-face attributable to desire for help in consolidating and preserving factional gains. Claiming to be the Mālō, the Pulefou constituted its own government, its form resembling that of its predecessor but with the kingship restored and bestowed on Talavou for life. A flag was also adopted and various laws were enacted. Having given its pretensions this guise, resorting to *fa'a-papālagi* expressions that were becoming *fa'a-Samoa* too, the Malietoa régime sought the favour and recognition of the foreign representatives; but to satisfy them it, of course, had to do more.[7] Until it had demonstrated its capacity to retain the ascendant position, the consuls wanted to avoid taking sides. Meanwhile, the obligations contracted by the previous Mulinu'u chiefs had to be acknowledged by the present ones and fresh guarantees given regarding the observance of the neutrality of the Apia area in the event of war. Out of the neutral-zone negotiations of this period—May-June 1879—there developed an arrangement whereby the three consuls assumed supreme jurisdiction in the maintenance of public order at Apia Bay and environs, Mulinu'u excluded. Endorsed by both Samoan parties, each now anxious to please, the agreement granting this jurisdiction was to run till the achievement of a stable peace and, on the basis of it, the consuls began issuing and enforcing emergency regulations.[8]

The question of recognizing a Samoan government was brought to a head in August by Sir Arthur Gordon, who came to Samoa determined this time to secure a treaty for Britain. The Mulinu'u chiefs, perhaps trying subtly to play on European rivalries, immediately appealed to Gordon for British protection, arguing that the equal rights and privileges of the three Powers created too great a burden for the Samoans and denied them the benefits of peace which they would expect if under the influence of but one foreign nation. Of course the chiefs wanted not

[7] USCD, Apia/6, Dawson to Payson, 4 June 1879.

[8] FOCP 4127, 96 and 99, Maudslay to Salisbury, 27 June 1879, Agreement *in re* Neutral Territory, 29 May 1879; USCD Apia/7, Dawson to Payson, 19 June 1879.

merely to cut out America and Germany but to gain support for themselves, so that Gordon, though having to discourage their petition, none the less had some power to help them by virtue of his requiring a *de facto* government with which to negotiate; consequently, he had some power to exploit Samoan rivalries as well. Selling the consuls on his pet scheme for a municipality of Apia, for which their emergency powers already supplied a rudimentary basis, he contrived the exchange of this further concession, plus the treaty with Britain for the three Powers' provisional recognition of the Malietoa régime, the obvious choice of party at the time.[9]

The area laid out for the municipality extended, at the beach front, from a point just to the east of Vaiala to the outlet of a river beyond Sogi on the west. As defined, the boundary embraced Mulinu'u but, in practice, the peninsula was normally excluded. By the terms of a four-year convention signed in September 1879,[10] the area was described as a neutral township over which the Samoan Government retained its sovereignty but the terms of the agreement, by debarring the exercise of that sovereignty from the specified functions of the municipality, were clearly meant to create a largely self-governing enclave. In so far as the treaty-bound government had any jurisdiction left to resign, responsibility for public order, civil works, sanitation, harbour control and rating passed to a municipal board to be composed of the three consuls and one resident national of each of the three treaty Powers. Regardless of the presence of Samoan villages within the municipal boundary,[11] only one special allowance was made for Samoans, and that a curious one: every Samoan 'subject' charged with a criminal act within the concession area, 'other than an offence against the municipal regulations', was to be tried by a mixed court consisting of the municipal magistrate—a European—and a Samoan judge. In contrast, the Apia board was to release to the jurisdiction of their national authorities—normally the individual consuls—Germans, Americans and British subjects who offended against the laws of their respective countries, whether or not they simultaneously broke municipal regulations.

The Malietoa régime would be asked to give way even more, but first

9 FOCP 4127, 120-9, Gordon to Salisbury, 15 September 1879 (nos 1 and 2), Malietoa Talavou, Afamasaga Le Auauna, *et al.* to Queen Victoria, 31 August 1879, and Malietoa Talavou and Malietoa Laupepa to Gordon, 2 September 1879; *Samoa Times*, 30 August and 6 September 1879.

10 FOCP 4127, 133-5, Municipal Convention of 2 September 1879. The signatories were: for the Mulinu'u Government, Malietoa Laupepa and Afamasaga Le Auauna; for Great Britain, Gordon and Maudslay; for Germany, [Captain] F. Mensing and [Consul] Weber; for the United States, Captain R. Chandler and Consul Dawson.

11 The villages of Vaiala, Matautu, Tanugamanono, Apia and Vaimoso.

there arose an armed challenge to it. Following their eviction from
Mulinu'u, the loyalist members of the previous *de facto* government had
retired to northern A'ana from whence, egged on by the now desperate
and destitute Bartlett, they had issued a call for war against the Pulefou.
The initial response had been pitiful. In the very district to which they
had fled the chiefs found only two villages[12] prepared to fight for them,
which was less support than they were offered from Tuamasaga, their
enemies' principal stronghold; while their connections in Savai'i—in
Itu-o-Tane and Itu-o-Fafine—had simply countered with 'embarrassing'
questions about their conduct of the government and other matters.
Only from Atua had substantial military backing been promised them.[13]
Obviously, their loss of Mulinu'u and the many indignities they had
suffered had provoked little sympathy or concern. As for the kingship,
they had not been able to make an effective issue of it either, the people
on the Tupua side being divided between two *tama'āiga*—Tamasese,
now or shortly to become the Tui A'ana, and Mata'afa, the Tui Atua.
Despite this poor beginning, however, the chiefs of the 'old Mālō' had
persevered, capitalizing on the exceptionable acts and attitudes of members of the Malietoa party or government and resorting to intrigue at
the lowest level of rumour and insult-mongering; and by September
1879, they had managed to abstract a large number of warriors to their
side.[14] With this support, raised mainly in Atua, A'ana and Itu-o-Tane,
they proposed to overrun their enemies in Tuamasaga and set themselves
up again at Mulinu'u. Meanwhile, the leaders of the Malietoa régime
had been shirking war preparations, apparently persuaded that the
Powers would help them if there were fighting but hoping, in view of
the peacemaking efforts of various naval officers, that there might be
none.[15] When mediation failed, then, the party centred in A'ana took
the field commanding larger forces and imbued with the idea of repeat-
ing the Fale'ula victory of 1876.

Hostilities, which broke out in earnest during October, were regarded
by the foreign officials as a treble threat to their interests and to those of
many settlers. As well as having to contend with the destruction incidental to war over a possibly protracted period, they actually preferred
the present *de facto* government to its predecessor. In addition to being
more tractable, the chiefs now at Mulinu'u had more of their influence

[12] Faleasi'u and Fasito'outa.

[13] *Samoa Times*, 13 September 1879, reporting the proceedings of the 'old Mālō'
in A'ana.

[14] *Samoa Times*, 3 January 1880.

[15] *Samoa Times*, 5 July 1879, on a proclamation by consuls and naval officers
concerning the protection of foreigners and their property and proposals to mediate
in the conflict between Samoan parties.

concentrated in places of particular importance to Europeans—notably in northern Tuamasaga, where Apia and three of the six Godeffroy plantations were situated,[16] and at Mulifanua, the Manono ('Aiga-i-le-Tai) district's mainland village, which was adjacent to two of the remaining Godeffroy plantations.[17] Thus, when the commander of the German warship, *Bismarck*, working in league with the consuls, intervened in December to impose peace terms, he wanted not only to stop the war as such but to save the Malietoa government and, if possible, to extend its jurisdiction.[18] The fact was that the Malietoa party, even if it did start with only scratch forces, had held its own and now, having mustered more of its strength, had a definite prospect of victory.[19] Had this not been the case, the other side, though admittedly confronted with the possibility of naval reprisals, would probably have rejected the terms of the *Bismarck* settlement or refused to negotiate at all. Ostensibly beneficiaries of this foreign intervention, the Malietoa chiefs might therefore have remained at Mulinu'u and enlarged their influence among Samoans strictly on their own party's efforts.

The most important sections of the *Bismarck* settlement dealt with the membership and constitution of the Mulinu'u government.[20] From the terms they contained it is clear that those who framed them—consuls and naval officers—would have liked the Samoans generally to assume responsibility for and towards the government but feared they would not. The settlement provided for broadly representative procedures but laid down alternatives which would tend towards a tight oligarchical rule. On one plainly contentious issue no lee-way was allowed: from the outset Talavou was to be acknowledged as king (Tupu) and Laupepa as regent (Sui Tupu or vice-king but in effect, premier) 'to attend to the work of the king'. Membership of the Ta'imua and Faipule, numbering sixteen and thirty-four respectively and apportioned on a district basis, was, however, to be renewed—this in the hope that adherents of the different parties might participate in the selections. On the other hand, if no one was put forward for a particular seat or no change of representative proposed, the previous member would resume office automatically; while, regardless of how or by whom the Ta'imua and Faipule

16 These plantations were Vailele (1,750 acres then cultivated), Vaivase (375 acres) and Vaitele (100 acres).

17 The Mulifanua plantation (1,000 acres) and Fatuosofia (150 acres). The sixth plantation was Vaipouli (150 acres) in northern Savai'i (GCS, Zembsch to AA, 26 January 1880).

18 *Samoa Times*, 10 April 1880.

19 USCD, Apia/7, Dawson to Payson, 17 and 28 November 1879.

20 Peace was agreed to on 15 December 1879, and on 23 December 1879 a second agreement, in the form of a constitutional enactment, was signed by representatives of the two parties (*Samoa Times*, 10 April 1880).

were chosen, their enactments were to be observed by all Samoans. To
take another example, the people of each district were to try to select a
governor, who would be responsible to Mulinu'u for minor district
appointments and 'the execution of the laws'; but if they could not agree
to a 'single appointee', the question would be taken up by the Ta'imua
and Faipule; and if *they* could not agree, the king or regent would
determine who should be governor. The Ta'imua and Faipule, meeting
separately, were to initiate all legislation but if the two houses could not
reach the same decision on a given measure, the king or regent would
break the deadlock, passing or defeating the proposal on the strength
of a casting vote. It was implied, moreover, that the king, or the regent
in his name, should have absolute power to veto legislation. Finally,
half the members of the Ta'imua—one from each district—were to
form a full-time council to 'assist' the king and regent in 'execution of
the laws', and all 'documents of state' would have to bear the signature
of the chairman (Ta'imua Sili) of that council as well as that of the
king or regent.

Although leaders on both sides solemnly swore to carry out this
agreement, which was the first of its kind to be committed to writing
and signed by the parties to it, the cessation of hostilities was the only
condition of the *Bismarck* settlement immediately realized in full.[21] The
suppression of animosity, to say nothing of the creation of popular,
multi-party government, could hardly be accomplished so easily, especially when the peacemakers presumed to dictate who should be king.
But if most of the people who had been opposed to the Malietoa government continued in opposition, there was one outstanding exception. That
was Mata'afa, who joined the Mulinu'u régime and became Ta'imua
Sili, one of the handful of Samoans managing the affairs of the *de facto*
government. On changing over, Mata'afa left behind much of his former
following in Atua and gave a tremendous fillip to Tamasese's cause on
the Tupua side. But with the Powers apparently favouring the Mulinu'u
government, with Talavou ageing and ill and Laupepa still bearing
some onus for past failures and mistakes, Mata'afa, well-connected on
the Malietoa side and having once been in line for the kingship under
Steinberger's constitution, had a seemingly high chance, on the occasion
of his 'defection', of soon succeeding Talavou. As for the government's
prospects, they would certainly have looked better had Mata'afa been
able to bring all of his original partisans over with him; however, the
fact that three of the four principal *tama'āiga* were now at Mulinu'u
was of great significance in itself, adding weight to the claims of

[21] USCD, Apia/8, Dawson to Payson, 11 March 1880 (with numerous enclosures),
Malietoa Laupepa to consuls, 13 March 1880 (with Dawson to Payson, 13 March
1880).

legitimacy made for the Malietoa government and, given the persistence of party rivalry, strengthening the argument for continued foreign intervention on the government's behalf.[22]

On considering the outcome of the war the consuls, acting with authority from their superiors, gave the Mulinu'u régime in March 1880 formal confirmation of their *de facto* recognition of it and promised to protect it, if necessary calling upon naval assistance. Now that foreign naval vessels were putting in at Samoa with great frequency and often staying for protracted periods, this pledge of support was not to be taken lightly. British and German warships were, in fact, already worrying some of the people who had gone back on the constitutional provisions of the *Bismarck* agreement and over the next few months there would be repeated acts of naval intervention aimed at suppressing resistance or opposition to Mulinu'u.[23] But neither was the consuls' pledge to be *given* lightly, for in return for it, they extracted further concessions. First, the *de facto* government, represented by the two Malietoas and Mata'afa, agreed that the choice of Talavou's successor should be subject to the approval of the Powers. Secondly, an arrangement was made for the king to have an executive council of three Europeans: an American minister of justice, a German minister of finance and a British minister of public works.[24] The convention granting these concessions omitted to define the ministers' powers, but it is evident from what followed that the consuls intended they should take over, in their respective fields, all the executive responsibility ostensibly given the king and regent by the *Bismarck* settlement. In other words, most of the important administrative functions of the central government were to be performed by Europeans—for the whole of Samoa, not simply for the municipality. What is more, the consuls, who were not authorized by the treaties to assume such functions themselves, were to have the ultimate say, for each was to have the right of nominating and dismissing at will the minister of his own nationality. Apart from being permitted to reject nominations and call for others, the Samoan Government was to have only the privilege of paying the ministers' salaries. At that stage, repre-

---

[22] e.g. USCD, Apia/8, Dawson to Payson, 11 March 1880.

[23] Some naval officers, however, disapproved of political intervention, e.g. FOCP 4467, 50-1, Commodore J. C. Wilson (Commandant, Australian Station) to Sec. Adm., 8 April 1880, asserting that the 'capable and strong native Government' envisaged by German diplomats could not be achieved. '. . . in recognizing Malietoa as King, and affording him, in conjunction with the naval commanders of Germany and America, all protection he may require, we may drift into collision with the rebel party, without any possible prospect of gaining credit or of bringing about a settlement.'

[24] *Samoa Times*, 10 April 1880, text of agreement of 4 March 1880 between King and government of Samoa and the three consuls.

senting a high point in the development of extra-territoriality within what was allegedly a sovereign state, the consuls had indeed become the panjandrums of Samoa.

The system of concessions built up by early 1880 was not to remain fully intact very long, for objections by the British and American governments led to the disbanding of the European executive council.[25] The British dissent was based on the belief that involvement of the three Powers in the rule of the Samoans would prove unworkable, while Washington, though recognizing and being prepared to support the Malietoa régime, wanted no part in the administration of Samoa's internal affairs beyond that determined by treaty obligations, which in the present context related mainly to court jurisdiction over United States citizens. The municipality survived the American desire for disentanglement but only on sufferance by the turning of a blind eye towards what the State Department considered a disagreeable necessity.[26] Before the arrival in Samoa of instructions narrowing the consuls' jurisdiction, however, events there were already exposing some of the fatal weaknesses in the existing basis of government, flaws which no elaborate superstructure could ever correct.

Judged by early results, the provision for a municipality of Apia was, on the whole, successful. So it should have been, too, considering that its object was the maintenance of public services and order at the most elementary, indispensable levels. But judged by the amount of time and energy that went into its proceedings and the extent of the scheming and controversy they occasioned, the Apia administration was most inefficient in performing its job. From the Samoan side there was comparatively little trouble, apart from the violations of Apia's neutrality which sometimes occurred during periods of general political disturbance. The internal affairs of the local villages were not the concern of the town board, while the main problem relating to non-Europeans— that of keeping routine order among visitors to the area—was adequately handled by the police force. The board did, of course, assume control of the harbour; but since the Samoan Government had had its eye on that source of revenue, misgivings over its coming under foreign jurisdiction were centred more at Mulinu'u, from whence there would be, partly because of this, abortive resistance to the renewal of the municipal convention. For Samoan villagers in the township, the convention actually produced many advantages; for example, the appointment of local

---

[25] BCS 1/2, Granville to von den Brincken, 7 September 1880; *Samoa Times*, 21 August 1880.

[26] USCD Apia/8, Payson's minute to Dawson, 29 August 1880. The State Department did not approve of the municipal convention, but Dawson was allowed to participate in the municipal government *on his own responsibility*.

chiefs to positions of responsibility in the municipal administration, the provision of employment for Samoans as labourers and policemen, the greater prominence which Apia enjoyed because of its special status and the relative freedom it gained from outside interference. If the affairs of the municipality were unduly complicated, the fault lay, rather, on the European side. It is not apparent from the size and economic development of the foreign settlement why this should have been so. By those standards alone Apia should really have been no more difficult to govern in 1880 than it had been during the days of the Foreign Residents' Society. The European immigrant population of Samoa had certainly grown in the interim—from roughly 150 in 1860 to about 300 or 350—but the number of settlers at Apia Bay, just over 100 according to the first municipal roll, was not much larger than it had been in the early 1860s, prior to the exodus associated with the cotton boom.[27] Nor were there many adult half-castes living independently there in the manner of Europeans: the municipal roll listed only four.

As for shipping and trade, the port of Apia was considerably more active at that time. The predominant element in that growth, however, had been the firm of Godeffroy, which was generally above reproach in its commercial dealings with foreigners and whose German staff were orderly almost to the point of being dull and who, therefore, were not a direct force for disorder.[28] Apart from the build-up of German interests, concentrated in the Matafele-Sogi area, there were few outward signs to distinguish the European settlement of 1880 from that of twenty years before. Some of the hotels, boarding-houses and stores had been established since then or had been rebuilt; a weekly newspaper had recently begun publication; law was being practised, after a fashion; and among the tradesmen and shopkeepers there were many new names and faces. Otherwise there had been little material change.

Spared formidable tasks, then, the municipal government none the less limped along and, for this, its own structure was partly to blame. One source of trouble was the excessive power reserved to the consuls. The Foreign Residents' Society, it will be recalled, had depended on consular leadership but had allowed for popular participation and could not achieve much without a substantial measure of popular support or acquiescence. Now Apia had what was, fundamentally, a consular oligarchy, a circumstance for which the consuls themselves were responsible, the municipal convention having empowered them to set up the government and their own self-seeking and distrust of the mob having led them into taking too prominent a part in it. True, they provided,

27 *Samoa Times*, 7 February 1880 (supplement).
28 GCS, Zembsch to AA, 29 April 1880; Hübner, *Through the British Empire*, II, 361-3.

z

not without pressure from the Beach, that the unofficial members of the town board should be popularly elected but these members held subordinate positions.[29] Without the agreement of the consuls, for example, the board could take no affirmative action, regardless of how voting strength—at first six, later increased to nine—was divided numerically. As an obvious corollary, there could be no quorum unless the consuls were all present. Moreover, the consuls formed a separate board or council of their own, acting in an executive capacity and hearing appeals from decisions of the municipal magistrate, an official in whose appointment they had the most say. Given a régime of such an undemocratic character, plus the aggravating fact that from 1879 on, heads of the consulates were nearly always 'outsiders', men sent to Samoa from overseas—many settlers reacted unfavourably, especially when it came to financial issues such as the levying of rates, the fixing of licence fees and the expenditure of municipal funds.

Another source of difficulty was the excessively complicated legal framework within which the municipality was set. As events of the 1870s had shown, the time had passed when order could be kept through the medium of local instrumentalities and codes lacking the sanction of international recognition. But if there had been, in that sense of formality, too little law before, there was now too much. For there impinged on the municipal regulations not only the laws of the Samoan Government but also, extra-territorially, the laws of Britain, Germany and the United States. For any community such a convergence of jurisdictions would have produced a staggering burden of legal conflict and not the least for a town of only a few hundred people and an annual revenue of a few thousand dollars.[30] It may be conceded that civil causes lay outside the competence of the municipality but that such issues none the less obtruded into the affairs of the town administration, since the representatives of three of the four outside governments were directly involved in it. As for the processing of criminal suits, there was endless complexity, not so much when Samoans were involved—the mixed court arrangement actually worked quite well—but certainly when Europeans were being charged, the municipal magistrate having to contend, on the one side, with the prospect of appeals to the consular board and, on the other, with real or alleged jurisdictional clashes between his own court and the separate extra-territorial tribunals of the consuls.

The most critical point of weakness in the structure of the town administration was, of course, the necessity for joint action by the three

---

29 *Samoa Times*, 27 December 1879, election of three supervisors, assessor, collector and treasurer; USCD, Apia/9, Dawson to Payson, 26 October 1880.

30 FOCP 4467, n.d., 92-3, Memorandum on the state of Samoa, by Vice-Consul Maudslay.

consuls, lacking which no legislative and little executive business could be discharged. This was not an intrinsically unreasonable or visionary requirement, for as experience again had shown, the consuls *could* work together, at least to maintain public order. Not that they had always done so in the days of the Foreign Residents' Society but neither did they always disagree amongst themselves now, when their instructions enjoined them, after all, to co-operate in matters of common concern, to which category municipal affairs clearly belonged. But the position of Apia had changed. No longer were its environs the Europeans' frontier on a comparatively resistant, unexploited hinterland. No longer were Europeans disposed by a sense of vulnerability or danger ultimately to cohere against the Samoans. If the consuls could co-operate in their dealings with the Mulinu'u government or its opposition, if they could take the same line towards the protection and advancement of European interests in Samoa generally, then surely they could join in tackling the problem of governing the municipality of Apia. But if they differed over the former, could they avoid carrying over their contention into the affairs of the town, however routine those might be? If not, could the municipality survive at all?

The consuls were, indeed, headed for disappointment at Mulinu'u. Having halted the war, they then demanded more of the Malietoa régime in the way of facilities for safeguarding and promoting European interests than they might reasonably have expected had it gone on, with or without their backing, to win a clear victory. Ideally, foreigners were to gain most if not all the advantages of imperial rule by having the consuls and others exercise part of the Samoans' sovereignty by right of delegation and guide the Samoans in the use of what autonomy they had ostensibly retained. The days of negotiating with chiefs and haranguing or threatening them afresh in every particular instance in which action of government was desired—days which Steinberger had promised to end—were now supposed to give way to an era of programmed government and administration, of established policies and principles and of continuity of effort to implement them.

One of the major objectives of the European executive council was the development of police and judicial systems functioning by the rule of law. Mixed court jurisdiction in matters involving foreigners and Samoans was to be retained; but it was intended that the government should, on its own initiative, bring Samoan offenders to book and proceed against them without having to be prodded by consuls or naval officers. Moreover, there was to be organized protection for property.[31]

Another objective, towards which there has been less preliminary comment here, was the adoption of new or more thorough methods of

[31] Hübner, II, 372-3, re failure of justice to Samoans in absence of force.

raising and appropriating public funds. It is plain enough that the main
item of expense, aside from the housing and maintenance of government offices, was to be a programme of public works—roads, bridges,
wharves and the like—to facilitate travel and the transport of goods. But
where was the money to come from? Samoa being 'independent', none
of the Powers could be expected to contribute anything but the services
of those officials already posted to Apia plus the cost of any naval action
that might be taken to preserve peace and order. Even had the islands
been under colonial rule, of course, outside financial support would not
have amounted to much more than that in those days; but their government would not, in that case, have been denied the simplest, most direct
local means of acquiring revenue—the levying of tariffs—which the
treaties of 'friendship and commerce' had forbidden. Meanwhile, the
establishment of the municipality had pre-empted what little income
Samoa's chief port was allowed to produce and along with it had gone
the exclusive power to tax property and licence business enterprise at
Apia. That is not to suggest that the funds which might have been
raised from these sources would have been enough to satisfy all the
government's needs. Given, for example, a tariff structure in line with
the free trade principles then widely accepted,[32] the customs duties that
might have been charged against Samoa's imports, which at that time
were estimated to value only about £50,000 per annum,[33] would not have
produced a very substantial revenue. But the prospective tax burden
would have been much more equitably distributed: the treasury would
not have been forced to fall back almost solely on the proceeds of a
head tax, for nearly all the Samoans would have been accountable.
Furthermore, there would have been some assured income from the
start, whereas the collection of a head tax would have depended on the
good will of the Samoans and the extent of the government's authority.
Since the Samoans were acccustomed to subscribe funds only for
specific purposes, a basis of taxation quite alien to the requirements of
annual budgeting, the government could not really have counted on
regular payments even from its own supporters, let alone others.

If they had had a substantial military advantage over their enemies and
had then sustained it through strong police action by their own party
and a guarantee of concerted support by the Powers, the Mulinu'u chiefs
might have made headway with measures of the kind urged upon them.
In that case, too, they might have made an attempt at such reforms, provided they had been offered some clear advantages apart from that of
merely exploiting or enhancing their power as Mālō. But considering the

[32] In the 1890s, when tariffs were allowed, the rate was only 2% on most items.
    cf. chapter 16, below.
[33] BCS 3/4, Hicks Graves, Trade Reports, 20 December 1879 and 31 January 1881.

insecurity of their position[34] and the fact that the European ministers were plainly concerned about foreign interests alone, the chiefs of the government would go no farther than the enactment of laws authorizing the collection of a poll tax and the establishment of a new Samoan judiciary.[35] The question of implementing these measures and adopting others was held over for 'later consideration' and thereafter the chiefs had as little to do with the ministers as they possibly could, short of actually repudiating the executive council agreement.[36] The time-worn system of negotiated 'justice' therefore remained in operation.[37] As for government finance, it continued to be a matter of raising subscriptions from friendly Samoans for purposes of which they approved. The number-one purpose was the purchase of implements of war: nearly every party that occupied Mulinu'u, including this one, had an armed schooner paid for by its supporters. The number-two purpose, not agreed to so happily, was the payment of fines and indemnities demanded by naval officers.[38]

Although discouraged by this setback, the consuls decided, after some argument,[39] to renew their efforts to develop an effective government at Mulinu'u. After all, the people who had been rebuffed had been the ministers, all old settlers, who perhaps lacked the respect of the Mulinu'u chiefs or had approached them in the wrong way. Moreover, they had had the opposition of a British adventurer, W. J. Hunt, who had struck up a friendship with Malietoa Talavou and seemed to fancy himself another Steinberger.[40] Finally the consuls admitted the Samoans' dis-

---

34 This insecurity was partly due to intervention to stop the process of fighting to a clear decision, which was not wanted because of fear that the Samoans would not establish a clear lead by one party, anyway, and fear of damage to property, etc.

35 'Law concerning the organization and operation of the Samoan Government', with USCD Apia/8, Dawson to Payson, 16 June 1880.

36 BCS 3/4, Hicks Graves to Granville, 7 October 1880; GCS, Zembsch to AA, 16 April 1880.

37 FOCP 4467, 92, Memorandum on the state of Samoa by Vice-Consul Maudslay.

38 ibid., 93.

39 The British and American consuls were disgusted with both Samoan parties and would have preferred a larger measure of foreign intervention to further experimentation with the means at hand, but none the less, they adhered to the idea of there being a single central government. Zembsch was for a time in favour of the formation of separate district governments but was talked round by the other consuls. Zembsch, who would have liked Germany to assume control but considered that event improbable, was for a time in favour of the formation of two separate inter-district governments or of district governments (USCD, Apia/9, Dawson to Payson, 8 February 1881; GCS, Zembsch's draft of an unsubmitted report on how to retain and further German interests in the South Seas).

40 USCD Apia/8, Dawson to Payson, 15 May 1880 (enclosing ministers to consuls, 14 May 1880). Hunt's appointment by Talavou was a breach of an agreement made with the German consul promising that no European would be taken into the government without the approval of Germany.

unity to be an extenuating circumstance, confronting the government with issues more urgent than the ministers' reform proposals. The executive council's activities were therefore suspended while German and British naval commanders set out to enforce the *Bismarck* peace settlement. As for Hunt, he was obligingly deported by order of Sir Arthur Gordon.[41]

Efforts to strengthen the government's Samoan support were concentrated on northern Atua,[42] whence Mata'afa had come, and were aimed at getting the Samoans there to agitate against Tamasese's cause. Talavou was to be recognized as king and given the remaining titles he needed to become Tafa'ifā, that is, the *pāpā* of Atua and A'ana; and, though the point is not documented, there was very likely some promise or inference to the effect that the next king would be a Tupua chief. In July 1880, aboard the German warship *Nautilus* at Saluafata, an agreement was reached between representatives of the Malietoa government and the 'rebels' in Atua whereby the latter undertook to come over to Talavou and send Ta'imua and Faipule to Mulinu'u as soon as they had persuaded their allies in A'ana and Savai'i to do the same. This pact, in which A'ana representatives subsequently concurred, bolstered the consuls' morale, but in it there was a hidden pitfall. For, to the chagrin of the Malietoas, the consuls had accepted the proposal of the Atua party that 'peace' negotiations in Savai'i be conducted at the Vaivai centres of Palauli (in Itu-o-Fafine) and Salea'ula (Itu-o-Tane), not fully realizing that the Mālō centres of Satupa'itea and Safune, together with Safotulafai (in Fa'asaleleaga), were almost bound to regard such meetings as challenges to war. Indeed, the Vaivai centres in Savai'i, by formally receiving Tumua chiefs of Lufilufi and Leulumoega, would be accused of having attempted to break into separate parts the joint *pule* of their respective districts, a development which was ultimately to lead to the division of Itu-o-Tane and Itu-o-Fafine into independent districts.[43] The A'ana and Atua parties which proceeded to Savai'i, headed for Palauli, initially, were therefore met by a powerful force of Malietoa supporters over whom the Mulinu'u chiefs professed to have no control. The result was the opening round of a new war, commencing with a Malietoa victory but soon followed by Talavou's death and the subsequent outbreak of general hostilities in Upolu again.

To the consuls, the editor of the *Samoa Times*, on hearing of the war

[41] BCS 3/4, Hicks Graves to Granville, 7 October 1880.
[42] GCS, Zembsch to AA, 6 June 1880. Northern Atua was the centre of the rebel cause with Lufilufi as headquarters. In early June 1880, representatives of the Lufilufi party said they were ready to negotiate with consuls and naval officers and missionaries for a reconciliation—a great surprise, according to Zembsch (*Samoa Times*, 5, 12, 19 June, 17 July 1880).
[43] Information from R. Va'ai.

in Savai'i, directed an 'I told you so': this would teach them, he said, that their influence in Samoan affairs was not as great as they had thought.[44] Had they, in approving the plan for the Savai'i meetings, simply failed to use their imagination? Or had they been misinformed, perhaps made the victims of a belligerent *togafiti*, a provocative piece of trickery? Whatever had gone wrong, the consuls were confirmed in their view that Samoan factionalism was too involved to suit their present approach to the problems of government and their superiors took a similar attitude. It was observed, moreover, that European rivalry had also led to irreconcilable conflicts, of which the most significant was the freezing of foreign land claims. At least ten thousand acres purchased by Germans were also claimed by British subjects. Far more than that was involved in disputes between the successors of the C.P.L.C.C. and various British and German speculators. And most of the land to which Europeans laid claim was, in turn, disputed by Samoans. Yet the concessions granted by the treaties of 1878-9, which acknowledged foreign land purchases without defining the manner and form of alienation to be accepted as legal, made it impossible under prevailing conditions to form a tribunal to dispose of these problems. What, then, could be done? For lack of any new approach which all three Powers would accept, the existing treaties and conventions, minus the provision for the executive council, were retained as the official basis of foreign rights and influence in Samoa, with results that occasioned mounting dissatisfaction and controversy among all concerned.

## German interests and grievances

The death of Talavou removed from Mulinu'u that member of the government whom the consuls had trusted least. Intended to serve as a figurehead, or at any rate to have no more say than either Laupepa or Mata'afa, he had in fact been given to acting without their consent, sometimes in a manner contrary to the government's treaty commitments or allegedly calculated to provoke feelings of hostility among the Samoans, for which delinquencies the consuls had blamed his 'old warrior's' instincts and the malign influence of Hunt.[45] For most Europeans the only seemingly bright political prospect at the end of 1880 was that Talavou might be succeeded by Laupepa. For the latter was almost alone among the highranking chiefs of Samoa in having had some formal education; in his dealing with Europeans he had shown

---

44 *Samoa Times*, 7 August 1880.

45 Talavou had insisted on appointing the Ta'imua and Faipule he wanted, disregarding district choices or adding more than the Bismarck Agreement allowed for (GCS Zembsch to AA, 16 April 1880). He also alienated the Germans by repeatedly refusing to ratify the treaty.

uncommon appreciation of their views and interests, if not always siding with them; and by Samoan standards, he was a man of peace. With a more enlightened king, suggested the British consul, further experimentation in government might conceivably prove worth while.[46] Among the Samoans, Laupepa's qualities were less widely admired, those of Talavou—and as would appear later, of Mata'afa too—being nearer their ideal. But perhaps owing partly to the marked European preference for him and the possibility of naval assistance to be inferred from it, Laupepa gained the backing of most of the Samoans who had supported Talavou; and a disappointed Mata'afa, purportedly disgusted with the way the Mulinu'u government had been run, went back to Atua to try his luck again on the Tupua side.[47]

True to the consuls' estimation of him, Laupepa approached them while his party, which had retained control of Mulinu'u, was still engaged in warfare in Upolu and professed to them his desire for peace negotiations. What he wanted was another settlement like that imposed by the *Bismarck*, one declaring him king at Mulinu'u and leaving to foreign naval officers the task of forcing his enemies to acknowledge him and join or submit to the *de facto* government. On this occasion, however, the Malietoa party, following Talavou's death, had slackened its war effort, leaving its opponents in a much stronger position than they had been at the time of the *Bismarck's* intervention. Indeed, the other side, the so-called 'old party', had declared its intention of forming a separate government under a Tupua king and of fighting relentlessly to uphold and defend it.[48] Fearing that this political conflict might be, for all practical purposes, irreconcilable, the German consul proposed recognizing a government on each side, provided that the Samoans would stop fighting; but his British and American colleagues, arguing that the Malietoa party was the stronger and the more amenable to European interests, brought him round to supporting another attempt at unification.[49] This time, however, a peace settlement took longer to achieve and when terms were finally found which both sides could be induced to accept, Laupepa came off less well than Talavou had. For while the

[46] BCS 3/4, Hicks Graves to Granville, 22 January 1881.

[47] *loc. cit.*

[48] Within a month of Laupepa's selection as king of the Malietoa side, the opposition announced its choice of Tamasese as king and a plan to hoist a flag at Leulumoega (alternating with Lufilufi). They asked consuls to attend, but the consuls refused (BCS 3/4, Hicks Graves to Granville, 12 May 1881). Graves says that the parties were about equal in size, but the Malietoa side refused to fight unless attacked.

[49] GCS, Zembsch to AA, 21 April 1881. Zembsch said that Laupepa seemed eager to please, all German claims having recently been settled, and asked for permission to recognize him.

negotiations which were concluded aboard the u.s.s. *Lackawanna* in July 1881 resulted in Laupepa's being proclaimed king, the 'old party' secured the office of regent or vice-king for a Tupua chief and an understanding that Laupepa's tenure of the throne would be limited to a definite period, after which a Tupua chief would succeed. On these terms, the two sides agreed to form a united government. The Malietoa party therefore emerged with but a very slight advantage, measured by Samoans only in terms of Laupepa's having first chance at the kingship, neither side having won out as Mālō.[50]

The *Lackawanna* agreement stipulated that Tamasese, the Tui A'ana, should be vice-king in preference to Mata'afa; but it was months before he was generally accepted as such by members of the 'old party'—and months more before the houses of the Ta'imua and Faipule were reconstituted to represent most of the Samoans. In July 1882, after further naval action to check unrest, the members of the new government held their inaugural meeting at Mulinu'u, formally declaring the country at peace and promising strong, effective rule. Laupepa's term of office was subsequently set at seven years, numerous laws were enacted and, with considerable reliance upon foreign intervention or the threat of it, the peace was maintained.[51] But of strong rule Mulinu'u gave no display. With no party in the ascendant there, with recent governments having had no record of successful resistance to foreign encroachment, the present *de facto* régime attracted little confidence from Samoans of either the Malietoa or the Tupua persuasion. What there was of centralized rule was, on both sides, exercised rather at the district level, in each case by the strongest local party, usually from a headquarters (*fale pule*) centre. As well as passing their own laws, the district chiefs took those of which they approved from Mulinu'u and enforced them as they saw fit, keeping the proceeds of whatever fines they collected. Most of the proceeds of a poll tax, levied by the Mulinu'u government and collected in part by some of the district governors, were also withheld. The reason generally given for this unwillingness to lend financial support to the central government was the fear that money remitted to it would go straight to the consuls and naval officers in payment of fines and indemnities.[52] That was, no doubt, how many of the Samoans felt; but it was also true that the principal business of the district party régimes was to agitate and prepare for war, to which end funds were wanted for armaments, a commodity that traders gladly supplied.

50 *Samoa Times,* 16 July 1881. While the American vessel intervened to achieve a peace settlement, German forces were actively engaged in restoring peace around the Apia area.
51 BCS 3/4, Churchward to Granville, 31 December 1882.
52 BCS 3/4, Churchward to Granville, 31 December 1882, 6 May 1883.

Excepting formalities, of which legislation was virtually one, the activity of the Mulinu'u government was taken up with mainly *fa'a-Samoa* disputes among various factions, Samoan criticism of the concessions made to the Powers and continual intrigue aimed, in one way or another, at breaking up what was generally agreed to be an undesirable political stalemate. Laupepa, who himself acted as chief executive, was throughout the focus of intense pressure brought by rival and diverse interests, a demeaning position which had been anticipated by the Talavou government in 1879 and from which Laupepa tried repeatedly and of course ineffectually to extricate himself by attempts to secure the protection of a single foreign Power. These appeals he usually addressed to Great Britain, occasionally to America, never to Germany.

That Laupepa did not canvass the assistance of Germany was due quite simply to his distaste for any intervention by that country, an attitude very widely shared among the Samoans. Having already become, by the mid-1870s, the Power least trusted by the Samoans, Germany had continued to decline in popularity with the expansion of the commercial enterprise of its nationals and the growing severity of its representatives' demands for concessions and reparations. The latter two phenomena were, of course, related and in both respects Germany outdistanced both the Americans and British in Samoa. Had the colonization scheme attributed to Weber during the *faitasiga* war been put into practice— there had in fact been such a scheme but it had failed to gain the active support of the German government—the Samoans would have had much more to complain of, for many thousands of acres of newly purchased land would then have been closely settled and cultivated. Godeffroy plantation development, however, had made considerable inroads, if only in a few places, notably Vaimauga, Faleata and Mulifanua.[53] While land approaching in extent the total acreage of Samoa had, by the late 1870s, become subject to American and British claims, no person or firm of either nationality had entered very seriously into commercial agriculture excepting Frank Cornwall, whose two coconut plantations— one at Magia in northern A'ana, the other at Lata in southern Savai'i— had entailed the clearing of a few hundred acres and had been left in neglect following Gordon's invocation of British labour regulations although these regulations did not apply to treatment on plantations.[54] As far as most British and American land interests had been concerned,

---

[53] Weber had also developed a small plantation of his own at Moto'otua, behind Apia. Among other small plantations were several established by the Catholic mission (APF, XLIX, 220-1, Vidal to Germain, 2 July 1876).

[54] British regulations did not then apply to the treatment of labourers on British plantations, but only to recruitment and transport (NZPP, A-4, 1884, Sess. 1, 143, Maudslay to Hicks Beach, 14 May 1878).

then, the only immediate issue had been that of establishing legal titles or of securing compensation for claims, towards which little progress had proved possible. There had been no question of contending with the Samoans for undisturbed occupancy. In contrast, the firm of Godeffroy, though claiming a far smaller acreage than either Cornwall or the C.P.L.C.C. speculators did, had proceeded without unassailable titles to take possession of substantial areas, clear the land and plant coconuts and various secondary crops. By Steinberger's time, this development was occupying about four hundred indentured labourers and had already run to more than one thousand acres. Samoan resistance to it had usually been met by uncompromising naval action or the threat of it, never by readiness to accept the outcome of a fair test in court. By the early 1880s, the developed area had been increased to more than five thousand acres—by the end of the decade it was to be about eight thousand—and the number of imported labourers under contract to German plantation management was averaging between one thousand and fifteen hundred.[55] Meanwhile, the treaty imposed by Weber in 1879, if failing in its object of gaining clear titles to German-claimed land, had none the less deprived Samoans of the privilege of taking their counter-claims to law. Moreover, it had extended to Germany's extra-territorial rights so far as to remove from Samoan jurisdiction the indentured labourers employed on German plantations, which work force was subsequently used, in a sense, as a private army, supplementing naval intervention as a means of protecting the cultivations. No aspect of their relations with Germans more infuriated and frustrated the Samoans than the experience of being chased off land they regarded as Samoan property by Micronesians and Melanesians, people for whom they had little respect anyway yet on whose behalf the extra-territorial status of Europeans had been established by force.

Other German commercial activity, being less localized, affected more Samoans; but, except in so far as it involved further dealing in land, it did not arouse from them such explicit objections. Owing to the per-functory nature of the available reports, the Samoans' contribution to the import-export trade cannot be very clearly ascertained for the period following the establishment of European plantation agriculture. The impression one gains, however, is that the wants stimulating their par-ticipation in trade, though still headed by arms for war and cash for mission collections, gradually grew in both variety and magnitude. Among the influences at work in this process were the maintenance of government establishments at Mulinu'u and in the districts and the more frequent levying of large fines for European property losses. There was

[55] Hübner, II, 363-4; NZPP, A-4D, 1885, Stuebel to Bismarck, 1883; MS., Stout, D.H.P.G. balance sheets, 1886-9.

also increasing interest in the running of schooners and the building of imposing church edifices. Between the early 1860s and late 1880s, the annual value of Samoan-produced exports more than doubled, and by 1888, in which year some fairly detailed commercial figures were compiled, the Samoans were estimated to be producing more than three thousand tons of copra per year, or at least seventy-five per cent of the group's domestic export of that commodity.[56] In value the Samoans' copra, their only important item of trade other than land, was then accounting for about half the domestic export trade. The D.H.P.G. plantations were the main supplier of the balance, producing cotton, coffee and cocoa as well as copra.[57] Apart from trade among foreigners, conducted chiefly at the port of Apia, local mercantile enterprise was therefore almost wholly oriented towards getting the Samoans' copra, a cut-throat business entailing, for those who secured the most produce, the maintenance of chains of permanent out-stations, to which practice the itinerant schooner trade had largely given way by the 1870s.

By 1880, there were four firms controlling most of the trade with the Samoans: the Godeffroy company, the Pacific branch of which was re-organized in 1880 as Die Deutsche Handels- und Plantagen-Gesellschaft der Südsee Inseln zu Hamburg (D.H.P.G.); Ruge, Hedemann & Co., another German house whose Samoan branch opened in 1875; Frank Cornwall's trading concern, which in 1883 passed to his Auckland principals, W. McArthur & Co.; and the American firm under the proprietorship of D. S. Parker. By the late 1880s, a few other merchants had entered the race, notably Grevsmuhl, a German, and H. J. Moors, an American.[58] But the lion's share of the copra trade was always in the hands of the Godeffroy-D.H.P.G. establishment, whose supremacy worked to the Samoans' disadvantage in two distinct ways. First, that company, drawing on its large resources, had by the 1870s flooded Samoa with debased South American dollars which only it and Ruge Hedemann & Co. could supply. Calculating this money locally at par with the United States dollar, though it was worth only sixty-five to eighty per cent as much, the D.H.P.G. thereby gained, among other things, considerable control over the buying price of goods for export. Secondly, the Godeffroy house—and its successor, the D.H.P.G.—could extend the Samoans more credit than any other firm, which practice involved the Samoans in paying high interest charges and inflated prices for consumer goods, while having to give land as security. The only traders that tried seriously to compete in this field were Cornwall and,

[56] USCD, Apia/16, Sewall to Rives, 27 March 1888.
[57] ibid., Sewall to Rives, 15 August 1888.
[58] Grevsmuhl and Moors started as partners in a firm associated with the island trading firm of Crawford & Co. of San Francisco.

after him, W. McArthur & Co., whom it soon crippled, in as much as their business was not sufficiently large and varied to offset the effect of their advances to the Samoans. In some measure, then, the Samoans might have benefited from freer competition among the merchants. If they did not fully realize this, they were still uncomfortably aware of their undue dependence upon the D.H.P.G., a condition which they resented and, with some reason, attributed not only to the firm's management but to the German Government as well.[59]

The D.H.P.G., of course, had grievances too. The firm objected, first, to the Samoans' wastage of their productive resources, a judgement supported by the fact that the much smaller Tongan group was exporting half again as much copra as Samoa and regarded it as one of the Mulinu'u government's primary responsibilities to induce or require the people to increase their output of marketable goods. In this sphere the government gave little satisfaction, being unable to force general tax measures or the paying off of trade debts, unwilling even to try to compel the Samoans to extend their planting of cash crops and powerless to resolve European land claims.[60] Secondly, the government, if not actively hindering German enterprise, did nothing to facilitate it, as might have been done, for example, had the ministerial scheme resulted in the adoption of a public works programme. Most critical of all, German land interests lacked the complete protection which was claimed for them by virtue of the treaty of July 1879. For, in spite of its own precautionary measures, the D.H.P.G. still suffered losses through acts of theft and vandalism. Meanwhile, the Laupepa régime had proved the least effective to date as regards the settlement of claims for damages, having little authority anywhere and lacking, particularly on the Malietoa side, the will to risk alienation of the Samoans by trying to impose adverse judgements upon them. Reflecting the government's embarrassment on this account, there were, in fact, numerous statements by Mulinu'u chiefs advocating repudiation of the treaty with Germany, a course which the terms of that document did not legally permit.

These circumstances—plus the intrigues of foreign adventurers bent on private filibusters or annexation by another Power—encouraged German initiative to upset the present three-Power treaty arrangement and its corollary, tripartite support of the Laupepa régime. A preliminary step in that direction was taken in 1883 when Weber and the German consul, O. Stuebel, prevailed upon the government to agree that Samoans convicted in a mixed court of non-capital offences against Germans or

---

[59] See reports of Commissioners Bates, Thurston and Travers, 1886, in USCP, 50 C., 1 S., House Ex. Doc. 238, 1888, 137-286 (or BCP 5629, 61-75, for Thurston's report and RP 110, 1889 for Travers's report).

[60] BCS 3/4, Churchward, Trade Report, 20 January 1883.

German-protected persons should be put under German jurisdiction to work off their sentences as forced labourers. At the end of the same year, Weber acquired for the D.H.P.G., through a controversial transaction in which Jonas Coe served as intermediary, a claim to the ownership of Mulinu'u; and thereafter, though there were counter-claims to the land,[61] the government chiefs were repeatedly threatened with eviction unless they adhered rigorously to the obligations to which Samoa's various treaties and conventions with Germany formally bound them. The screws were further tightened in 1884 when Weber and Stuebel extracted from Laupepa and Tamasese an agreement providing that the German consul, together with officials of his nationality appointed by him, might assume control of the executive branch of the government at Mulinu'u and that a German magistrate might act for the consul in sharing mixed jurisdiction over Samoans. This executive clause of the agreement was held in abeyance, ready to be implemented at Germany's pleasure.[62]

While its consular and naval representatives were establishing in Samoa a basis for acting without notice, and with ostensible legality, to overthrow or take charge of the Mulinu'u régime, the Berlin government was engaging in diplomatic activity calculated not simply to ensure that Great Britain and the United States would forego sharing in these further encroachments upon Samoan sovereignty, but if possible to effect their resignation of extra-territorial rights, leaving Germany to act as the sole foreign authority in the administration of Samoa's internal affairs. Germany's case was founded on two obvious facts: that tripartite intervention had not succeeded in maintaining order or stimulating progress and that Germans had a preponderant commercial interest in Samoa. The failure of the *Lackawanna* compromise had, indeed, led to increasing difficulty in securing co-operation among the consuls, so that tripartite intervention was actually becoming less workable. In the meantime, the D.H.P.G. had continued to extend its plantations, thus enlarging the German economic stake in Samoa. By the mid-1880s that firm was itself producing about a third of the territory's domestic exports, while German merchants were regularly transacting up to three-quarters of the total import-export business, approximately half of which represented trade with other islands through the port of Apia.

After some controversy, provoked partly by the high-handed treatment of the Samoans by Weber, Stuebel and various German naval commanders, Britain acknowledged the justice of Germany's claim to exercise

[61] But the firm's title to most of the land was later confirmed (SLC 2739).

[62] On the subject of the international rivalry of the mid-1880s see USCP, 50 C., 1 S., House Ex. Doc. 238; BCP 5629; and Masterman, *International rivalry,* Chapter 8; Morrell, *Britain in the Pacific,* 226-32; Zimmerman, *Geschichte,* 288-91; Ryden, *Foreign policy,* Chapter 9.

exclusive foreign jurisdiction in Samoa, envisaging its assumption of the political functions now shared by the three Powers. This understanding was reached in 1885 and was later elaborated in the course of negotiation over division of the Pacific into 'spheres of influence', a form of imperialist horse-trading for which Britain and Germany were well matched. But what of the United States? That Power's interest in Samoa was mainly strategic, centring in Pago Pago harbour, while the more restrictive imperialist policies of its government, which had been only just sufficient to the establishment of American naval rights, did not in any case leave much scope for the mutual exchange of concessions with either Great Britain or Germany. The United States therefore adopted what Germany regarded as a dog-in-the-manger attitude, insisting that the three Powers go on dealing equally and, if possible, co-operatively with the 'independent' government of Samoa. This approach, clearly antipathetic to German interests, was justified by Washington as being better for the Samoans, which it no doubt was, though perhaps not as good as was imagined.

During 1885-6, as the German Government doggedly pursued its case through diplomatic channels, its representatives were pushing ahead in Samoa with their deliberate campaign of aggression against the Laupepa régime. By late January 1885, after a number of niggling measures calculated to impress the Samoans with Laupepa's impotence and the unwillingness or inability of Britain and America to defend him, Weber and Stuebel had provoked Tamasese and his supporters in the government into withdrawing from Mulinu'u, whence they proceeded to Leulumoega, hoisted a flag of their own and repudiated the *Lackawanna* agreement. Encouraged by the American and British consuls' hostile reaction to this development, and now freer of dissident Samoan elements, Laupepa and the other chiefs remaining at Mulinu'u took a more forthright stand against the Germans, only to be required at the close of 1885 to leave their headquarters on the pretext of their not having paid rent to the D.H.P.G.[63] This was the beginning of the end for the Laupepa government, for the Germans, apart from the tremendous damage they had done to its prestige, had deprived it of the only piece of territory generally accepted as a suitable site for a capital of all Samoa. Transferring to Apia village, the evicted chiefs suffered further humiliation by having the flag they raised there, torn down by a German naval party, Stuebel having presumed to deny the existence of any Samoan sovereignty over the municipal zone. For several months thereafter, until British and American protests had counteracted Stuebel's interference in the municipality, Laupepa stayed away from Apia, while the Ta'imua

[63] BCS 3/4 (appendix), Knorr-Malietoa correspondence, May 1886.

and Faipule continued to stay away, assembling rather at the village of Afega, one of the *pule* centres of Tuamasaga.

In the meantime, at the instance of Washington, a three-Power inquiry and conference over the future of Samoa had been called and Germany, having raised havoc with Laupepa, was hoping this would result in a fundamentally new approach to the problem of governing the islands. While these negotiations proceeded, Germany conducted relations with both the Leulumoega and Tuamasaga régimes, thereby emphasizing the parlous political state of Samoa and, in effect, also denying that Laupepa now had any exclusive right to petition for British or American intervention, for which he had shown too great a longing to suit the Germans. More important, Germany had the prospect of an alternative central government to be exploited whatever the outcome of the international conference. Should the conference prove fruitless, the Tamasese party, given its strict adherence to German terms, might receive military and naval assistance and, in the event of its winning out, the use of Mulinu'u as its capital. This, as it happened, was the course Germany ultimately took, endeavouring to create by means of a filibuster the political advantage which, as previously noted, the United States would not concede.

## The Tamasese-Brandeis régime

In January 1887, a whole year after Mulinu'u was cleared, a local employee of the D.H.P.G.—Eugen Brandeis, a former Bavarian cavalry officer—was sent to Leulumoega by Weber and the new German consul, Becker, to act under their instruction as premier to Tamasese whom they recognized as king on the Tupua side, though he had only the title of Tui A'ana. Brandeis's job was formally to constitute a government, to see that various policies and laws favourable to German commerce were adopted and enforced among Samoans acknowledging Tamasese as their *tama'āiga*, to raise and train an army for possible use against the Laupepa régime and to encourage intrigue aimed at augmenting Tamasese's Samoan support. The Germans behind Brandeis undertook, for their part, to supply arms and, by discriminatory acts of diplomatic and naval intervention, to try to foster among Samoans in general the idea that Tamasese's cause represented the 'wave of the future'.

The government which Brandeis formed was similar in several respects to that constituted by Steinberger, who had also been pledged to serve German interests. The Leulumoega régime, too, had a king whose powers were only nominal. To himself Brandeis reserved quite as much responsibility and authority as Steinberger had assumed.[64]

[64] Brandeis's Samoan title of office differed from Steinberger's, being Ali'i Ta'ita'i (later, Ali'i Ta'ita'i i le Mālō, leader of the government), not Ta'imua Sili (e.g. TBP, B/1, Brandeis to Ta'imua and Faipule, 15 February 1887).

There was a legislature of two houses, called the Ta'imua and Faipule, whose members were drawn from the various districts in about the same numbers as in 1875-6 and were amongst the highest-ranking chiefs available, excluding *tama'āiga*. Again, each house had a mixed membership of *ali'i* and *tulāfale*[65] made up of two or three from each district, who formed a 'state' council (Vasega) under the presidency of Brandeis. It was the Vasega, which (unlike the executive council envisaged by the *Bismarck* agreement) was independent of the Ta'imua, that conducted most of the business of government at Leulumoega, not only discharging executive functions but, between meetings of the Ta'imua and Faipule, acting in a quasi-legislative capacity, too. Finally, as in Steinberger's time, provision was made for each district to have a governor and a number of local (that is, sub-district) judges, while at Leulumoega there were Samoan 'high-court' judges to hear cases on appeal from the districts.[66] The holding of mixed tribunals, it may be observed, was required only on behalf of Germans, in as much as the British and American consuls did not recognize the Tamasese-Brandeis régime as having any legal status.

In other ways, Brandeis's project obviously differed greatly from Steinberger's. That Brandeis was both committed and dedicated to a pro-German programme, for example, no one could doubt, so evident were his ties with the D.H.P.G. and the German consulate. That a good many Samoans were prepared none the less, to accept his leadership was not, of course, due to any new-found sympathy for German interests or affection for Germany but rather to political aspirations of an order which Steinberger, by taking the Samoans' side against foreign encroachment, had relegated to second importance. Tamasese and his supporters wanted to contend for and win Mālō status and subsequently to form their own central government at Mulinu'u, and thus motivated, they were willing to risk linking their cause with Germany's plainly aggressive intentions.[67] The apparent advantage of this alliance for the Samoan parties to it did not arise simply from the fact that the D.H.P.G. controlled Mulinu'u or that the Germans could and were ready to supply naval assistance and large quantities of arms. For the Tamasese party, though in no present danger of Germany's reversing its attitude towards Laupepa, had to consider the fact that Mata'afa was still a strong contender for the paramountcy of Sa Tupua and therefore another whose cause the Germans might consider sponsoring should Tamasese prove

[65] Including Tuimaleali'ifano and the *aloali'i* Tualau.

[66] TBP, B/1, *passim.*

[67] After the failure of his bid for power, and shortly before his death, Tamasese asked that Germany pay him an inheritable pension in consideration of the great sacrifices he had made on that country's behalf (MS., Gurr, Tamasese's message to Dr Stuebel).

**AA**

too 'difficult' for their liking. Given this division, it could be argued that, whichever way the Germans went, so might go most of the Tupua people.

The Germans' patronage of him, notably the deference shown him by various officials,[68] and the credit advanced him by the D.H.P.G. for the purchase of arms in violation of municipal and 'central' government regulations did certainly gain Tamasese Samoan support at Mata'afa's expense, but the shift was slow and tentative. On his withdrawal from Mulinu'u in 1885, Tamasese had had strong backing in only two districts, A'ana and Itu-o-Tane. By the time Brandeis took office, however, a Tupua alliance had been formed bringing over to the Leulumoega party strength centred mainly in Atua and western Tutuila;[69] and accordingly Mata'afa accepted from Brandeis an appointment to the governorship of Atua, a position clearly subordinate to Tamasese's. Atua remained divided, though, as to which of the two high chiefs should have the Tui Atua title, vacant since Mata'afa's switch to Talavou in 1880. Had the Germans stepped up the pace of their preparations and been less concerned that Tamasese should secure formal pre-eminence among the Samoans, the Tupua alliance might have remained intact and the issue of the Tui Atua title held over till after the general power struggle, or at any rate the first round of it, had been decided. But early in 1887, in the face of waning Samoan enthusiasm for the Leulumoega régime, Tamasese's claim to the *pāpā* of Atua was ill-advisedly pushed by the Germans,[70] raising a violent reaction in favour of Mata'afa and, at one point, the possibility that war between Tupua factions might be engineered on the Laupepa side. In a desperate effort to prevent the 'Mālō of Tumua' from being 'lost again', Tamasese personally renounced the pretensions argued in his name and Mata'afa was chosen to become Tui Atua.[71] The A'ana chief was left, however, with few militant supporters outside his own district. Though he was still the Germans' favourite, the rest of the Tupua people had taken a neutral position pending further action by or on behalf of his partisans.

Until the onset of the Tui Atua title dispute, Brandeis, with influence built up almost entirely on the basis of the material support he could

[68] e.g. Rear-Admiral Knorr of the *Bismarck*, who visited Tamasese at Leulumoega (BCS 3/4, Powell to Rosebery, 28 May 1886).

[69] A few months before Brandeis went to Leulumoega, war had been narrowly averted by the intervention of the u.s.s. *Mohican*, preventing a strong Tamasese force from launching an attack upon Malietoa Laupepa's supporters and government.

[70] TBP, B/1, Address by Brandeis to the Faipule of Atua, 28 February 1887. Brandeis accompanied Tamasese on a visit to Atua in search of greater support for the Leulumoega régime.

[71] TBP, C/1, Tamasese to Mata'afa, 13 June 1887.

deliver,[72] had been busy trying to restrain the impatience of the Tupua chiefs for a *coup d'état* and to impose upon them and their people an order and discipline consonant with the Germans' idea of 'good principles of administration'.[73] His main advance, apart from the actual formation of the Leulumoega government and militia, had been the institution of a regular tax programme, a district-by-district collection of poll tax in proportion to the number of people counted as Tupua supporters or directly subject to the will of members of the Tupua party. The areas concerned had included, in addition to those already mentioned, a part of Itu-o-Fafine, embracing the village of Palauli and a few others. Most of the money thus accumulated—two to three thousand dollars over a period of about six months—had been paid to the D.H.P.G. on account of guns and ammunition supplied on credit.[74]

The Tamasese-Brandeis *coup d'état*, when it finally occurred in August 1887, was something in the nature of an urgent salvage operation on Germany's part. The long-awaited international conference on Samoa, then in progress in Washington, was turning out most unsatisfactorily for Germany, the United States having continued to oppose control by a single Power, modified its previous position only so far as to propose the formation of a tripartite European executive council to the Laupepa government, a scheme reminiscent of the abortive ministerial agreement of 1880. Furthermore, the proceedings of the Leulumoega régime had stimulated intense counter-intrigue on the opposite side, in which various British and American officials had become involved. This activity, in so far as it aimed at or partook of unilateral intervention or the instigation of civil strife, was discountenanced both in London and Washington, of which fact the German Government was given repeated assurances. But of course it was impossible at such a distance to supervise the conduct of officials in any detail, while the wait-and-see attitude of Britain and America, almost devoid of plan, effectively invited the 'man on the spot' to exercise his own judgement and initiative. The Laupepa government, as a result, was never short of the most strenuous anti-German encouragement and advice. In the circumstances, particularly in the light of what they themselves were doing at Leulumoega, German officials in Samoa, if not in Berlin, could readily imagine their opposition to contain a real threat of British or American intervention. Creating suspicion of British 'duplicity', for example, were various annexationist intrigues

[72] e.g. TBP, F/1, Brandeis to Weber, 21 February 1887, Weber to Brandeis, 17 March 1887; concerning German arms traffic see, e.g. BCS 2/6, W. McArthur & Co. to Symonds, 26 February 1887 (with enclosures).
[73] TBP, B/1, Address by Brandeis to Ta'imua and Faipule, Leulumoega, 1 February 1887.
[74] TBP, F, *passim*.

traceable to Auckland business interests and also to members of the
New Zealand Government, which was passionately hostile to German
claims to Samoa. In fact, these excursions represented wholly unauthorized—and, to the Foreign Office, highly embarrassing—interference in a
field of action that the imperial government reserved to itself.

Equally embarrassing to the United States Government was the
attempt by the American adventurer-premier of Hawaii, Walter Gibson,
to assume control of Samoa by means of a 'confederation' of the two
'kingdoms'. There was associated with this Hawaiian scheme, in its
early stages, a former United States consul, Berthild Greenebaum, who
in 1886 had compromised the State Department and earned his dismissal
for proclaiming an American 'protectorate' of Samoa, ostensibly to forestall what he claimed to have been a German move to seize the territory.
That he had been, as well as the consul, an agent of C.P.L.C.C. interests
had had considerable bearing on Greenebaum's over-liberal interpretation
of the 'good offices' clause of the Samoan-American treaty and it had
been because of the same private connection that, having learned he
would lose his State Department commission, he had solicited a consular
appointment to represent Hawaii in Samoa. At the insistence of Washington, Gibson dismissed Greenebaum but the impression had already
been given in Samoa—and it persisted—that the Hawaiian overture
might be a front for unilateral intervention by the United States. As an
imperialist exploit, probably launched chiefly for purposes of political
diversion in Hawaii, Gibson's approach to Laupepa could be more fairly
described as a piece of Ruritanian drollery, features of which were the
establishment of a legation and the stationing of a gunboat at Apia and
the plying of prominent Samoans with honorary titles and free gin.
There was, however, a serious side to the episode, in that the members
of the Hawaiian legation—the minister, John Bush, and his half-caste
secretary, Henry Poor—became deeply involved in agitation against the
Leulumoega régime. Through this unwanted interference, which was
ended by the fortuitous closing of the legation only a few days before
the Germans struck, the morale of the Laupepa government was raised,
several of Tamasese's more influential partisans abandoned his cause, that
political pendulum Mata'afa was brought to the verge of swinging across
to the Malietoa side again, and Tamasese himself was reported to have
considered breaking off relations with Brandeis and the German consulate. To see their position among the Samoans being undermined in
this incredible fashion infuriated the Germans, in which state they un-
wisely precipitated the Tui Atua title dispute, with results that have bee·.
described.

In no event would Germany have wanted the Tamasese party to have
the initiative in the contest for power, lest there be a protracted war that

might cause extensive damage to foreign-owned property and increase the risk of intervention by Britain or America. The ideal was a German-led surprise assault which, within a few days, would present to the world as a *fait accompli* an effective change of Samoan government. As it happened, though, Tamasese's support had sunk to so low an ebb—he had only about three hundred warriors left to fight for him—that the Germans had virtually to do the whole job themselves. While the Laupepa side was quietly awaiting the outcome of the three-Power conference on Samoa, an imposing naval force was assembled and, on the pretext of insults allegedly cast at the Kaiser, Germany itself was declared to be at war with the Apia government. At this, Laupepa fled to the bush, after which the Leulumoega cabal were installed at Mulinu'u and recognized by Becker and the senior German naval officer, Commodore Heusner, as the sole government of Samoa. Acting throughout against the indignant protests of the British and American consuls, who had no naval support at hand, the Germans then proceeded to round up and bring to Mulinu'u as many of Samoa's higher-ranking chiefs as they could find and require, under threat of force, that they sign a proclamation declaring themselves the loyal subjects of 'king' Tamasese. Impressed by the lengths to which Germany had finally gone, many of the Tupua neutrals willingly joined Tamasese again, but of the nearly five hundred chiefs gathered at Mulinu'u, a majority were none the less opposed to him. All did as they were told, however, and the proclamation was immediately published as 'evidence' that Samoa was united and Laupepa disowned. Not content with mere fiction, the Germans also demanded that each district in the western islands, plus Tutuila, be represented in the Tamasese-Brandeis government by a selection of its most influential chiefs, regardless of whether they had ever been adherents of the Leulumoega régime, and notice was served that these officials must be faithful to the government's decisions and have the obedience of everyone within their respective areas of jurisdiction. A summary example of the penalty for disregarding these orders was soon given when the pro-Laupepa village of Satupa'itea in Itu-o-Fafine was destroyed by a German warship. As for Laupepa himself, the German commodore issued an ultimatum requiring his surrender, and, gaining that, he took that chief into exile abroad. Intended to remove a possible focus of further unrest, this ham-handed act was to have unfortunate consequences for Germany.

Trying to pose as an independent Samoan government with a European premier freely chosen by its members—as a government akin, that is, to the one formed by Steinberger—the Tamasese-Brandeis régime at Mulinu'u remained, during the brief period of its existence, essentially the creature of German interests. For Brandeis went quite some way towards doing what Steinberger had but given a secret promise to do, which course, having been taken on the strength of foreign intervention rather than local conquest, could be maintained by only one means—by the regular employment of German naval power to keep the Samoans in fear and submission. Before the experiment had met and failed its final test, even people who had remained consistently loyal to Tamasese were complaining of the government's policies and regretting their dependence upon Germany for the establishment and preservation of 'their' Mālō.

According to Robert Louis Stevenson, who never met him, Brandeis was genuinely concerned about the Samoans' material welfare and believed he was acting to advance it. From the direct evidence provided by his economic policies, however, Brandeis would seem in fact to have been working chiefly for the benefit of the D.H.P.G. Such evidence is found, particularly in the provisions and consequences of his government's poll-tax measures, the first of which was applicable to the initial six-months' period from the date of the German *coup d'état*. The proclamation of this tax levy, published in mid-October 1887, required that within about four weeks, there must be paid the cash sum of one dollar by or for every Samoan male who was able to climb a coconut tree and every female who was capable of working, for example, of helping to make copra. Only the Samoans regularly residing within the municipality of Apia were exempted. Failure to pay within a specified time was to result in the raising of the tax charge to two dollars, to be paid within an extended period of only five days, beyond which time delinquency would be punishable by one month's forced labour and imprisonment.

Tax lists were methodically compiled and, with only slight delays in some areas, the whole of the envisaged proceeds of this measure—approximately twenty-one thousand dollars—was credited to the government's account. Only the one-eyed could take from this, however, that the Samoans could afford the levy on such short notice or that it was a fair means of encouraging industry and responsibility on their part. For if the people complied with the tax law, it was more often than not because German warships, at one time as many as five of them, were snooping about, their commanders searching for signs of 'rebellion' and issuing warnings against tax evasion;[75] and if the government got all the money demanded from the Samoans, it was because thousands of them went into debt to raise their share of it. One dollar may not seem very much. That was all the Samoans got, however for between fifty and sixty-seven pounds of copra. To put it another way, the tax receipts were, in aggregate, the equivalent of forty to fifty per cent of the value of the Samoans' estimated income from commercial sources, taken on a half-yearly basis. Thus confronted with the early necessity of raising in addi-

[75] Payment was refused only in the Pago Pago area where punitive action was ultimately taken (RP 110, Becker to Bismarck, 31 December 1887).

tion to their other requirements, what was for them a very substantial amount of money for taxes, many of the people looked to traders for credit, which played straight into the hands of the D.H.P.G. No other firm could call upon such large reserves to tide the Samoans over their 'emergency'. As for non-German traders, they had to consider, if they could afford to give credit, whether they should help finance Brandeis's puppet régime and tie up further capital in a place where Germany appeared to have gained political ascendancy. But this was not the whole story, for the D.H.P.G. had a monopoly of the government's banking business which, aside from being profitable in its own right, enabled the firm to cover tax payments without having to circulate any cash whatsoever among the Samoans. When a D.H.P.G. agent allowed credit for tax purposes, the recipients got, instead of negotiable currency, a voucher that could be tendered only in payment of tax and redeemed only at the Apia office of the D.H.P.G., where the government might have it cleared in favour of the account it kept there. Almost needless to say, the D.H.P.G. alone was permitted to operate this tax-voucher system.

To get a tax voucher—here was the nub of the matter—Samoans had to contract for credit as a communal unit, which in practice was usually a village, though in one case, that of A'ana, a whole district was bound. This process involved the leading chiefs of the community in signing a special form of mortgage which the D.H.P.G. had already been employing for some years, particularly in the arms trade.[76] The terms of this mortgage required that all copra produced within the locality concerned in the contract, had to be supplied to the D.H.P.G. until the indebtedness had been discharged, the buying prices of the produce to be determined by the firm. Moreover, the period allowed for full repayment of principal and interest was limited to two years, after which time, the debtors were to forfeit land in liquidation of any balance owing. Thus, the Samoans were not only being made to raise most of the revenue for running the government,[77] which was denied the right of imposing customs duties, but were being spurred on to greater production by means of the principle of 'your copra or your land' and were, at the same time, being roped into granting local trade monopolies. The spur dug deeper in February 1888 when the next tax levy was proclaimed, in this term to cover a full year and to net $47,000, which liability was apportioned among the districts more in relation to their inhabitants' anticipated income than to their actual number. Allowing for previous

[76] The Laupepa government had tried to outlaw these contracts, another move confirming German support of a Tamasese *coup d'état* (MS., Stout, Crighton to Fletcher and Spencer, 22 May 1887).

[77] On which the D.H.P.G. made a further profit for most of the government's purchases were made from that firm.

mortgages still outstanding, most of which were held by the D.H.P.G., the American consul, Sewall, estimated that the Samoans' formally contracted indebtedness exceeded thirty thousand dollars at the end of 1887. According to additional figures supplied by Sewall, the Samoans had by March 1888 been taxed for an amount that, relative to the period of eight months over which the levies were payable, approximated their total average income from copra. As a consequence, he reported, the people's indebtedness had grown to at least eighty thousand dollars. An estimate compiled by Brandeis in mid-1888 gave a rather lower figure— sixty thousand dollars—but, unlike Sewall's, in this case, explicitly referred to debts for which land was held as security. Stating that the Samoans would need up to three years to pay off their mortgages, in addition to meeting their other financial commitments and observing that they were in danger of losing all their land if credit facilities remained freely available to them, Brandeis proceeded in time to introduce a regulation prohibiting the Samoans from assuming any more debts to Europeans and enjoining them to pay off existing ones in the order undertaken.[78] The position was, obviously, that the European demand for copra exceeded that for land and with a net of contractual obligations now woven, the Samoans were to be forced into producing more of that commodity for the benefit of their creditors, mainly the D.H.P.G.

Apart from his manifestly inequitable approach to taxation and related matters, Brandeis actually gave Europeans little direct cause for just complaint, though his critics would never admit it. There is no evidence that, for example, the public works projects he started unduly favoured German planters, a charge which would seem inconsequential in view of the importance of commercial agriculture and the great predominance of Germans in it. As for his influence upon Samoan police and court administration, it was most beneficial to foreign interests, law enforcement and justice being generally both swift and firm. Again, the constant presence of German warships, and their occasional intervention to ensure order, complemented the law, but some credit is also due Brandeis. Certainly no politician, no scintillating personality with Steinberger's gift of swaying the Samoans, he was, rather, a conscientious executive after the military fashion, a man who, within narrow limits, could put to effective use the power he was given. Brandeis kept himself well informed on affairs directly connected with his official duties; he reduced his dependence upon the government councils at Mulinu'u, the form of which had been carried over from the Leulumoega régime, and placed more and more reliance on the district officials, to whom he directly

[78] Sewall reported Brandeis as saying that the law could go into force only if and when all three powers approved of it, but the records of the Tamasese-Brandeis Government indicate that it was invoked, none the less.

dictated policies and even regulations; and he exercised personal control or influence over all government appointments and demanded loyal, competent service, readily replacing those who failed him. That many Samoan members of the government and administration *did* fail him is scarcely surprising; but if the turnover of office-holders was unusually high, Brandeis at least took the opportunity of finding and developing some 'new blood', freeing himself of the exclusive influence of one or another of the small groups of chiefs that in the past had dominated relations between Samoan governments and foreign officials. Moreover, Brandeis was prepared to employ his trusted associates in ways which were, by former standards, unorthodox ones, as instanced by the appointment of an obscure but undoubtedly keen and able A'ana chief, Pa'o, the Richelieu to a decrepit local governor whose political reliability and high-ranking title alone qualified him to remain formally at Apia.

Another responsibility which Brandeis seems to have taken seriously, was that of observing the treaty rights of Britain and the United States and, inasmuch as he was the Samoans' own premier, of Germany too. The one substantial change which his government made in the system of extra-territorial jurisdiction was the revoking of the municipal convention of 1879. Repudiated by Mulinu'u in October 1887, the convention ceased to have any standing in international law as soon as it was renounced by Germany, the only Power to have taken its rights in the municipality as granted by treaty. Britain had never regarded the special status of Apia as more than a matter of local agreement or charter and did not do so now, while the American Government had never recognized the concession at all and so could hardly raise a valid objection to its termination. Owing to the chronic state of disagreement that had developed among the consuls, the municipal régime, as set up under the 1879 convention, had largely outlived its usefulness anyway. But if its formal passing was not, in itself, the occasion of much lament, there was a great deal of agitation at Apia over what followed. For while the Mulinu'u government acknowledged, and allowed to continue in force, the consuls' extra-territorial jurisdiction as established by international treaties and metropolitan law, it presumed, unlike the Talavou régime prior to negotiation of the municipal convention, to put into practice at Apia the residual sovereignty of the Samoans. For this latter purpose, some of the administrative and legal framework of the municipality was salvaged: for example, many of the Apia regulations, pertinent to local problems and to such matters as the raising of revenue and the provision of special services, were carried over as 'laws of Samoa' applicable only within the 'former municipal district', and a European judge—a German —was commissioned from Mulinu'u to exercise the powers that had belonged to the municipal magistrate and police chief. The Mulinu'u government, however, directly assumed the functions of the consular and municipal boards and extended to the Apia area the general laws of Samoa, the poll tax included.

This new arrangement for the rule of Apia was never fully put into effect, owing, in the short run, to the refusal of most of the non-German settlers to accept it and to the government's restraint in not endeavouring to force it upon them. The opposition, which took in more than half the foreign residents, actually had little to complain of as far as the affairs of the town went. The previous municipal régime had not been so democratic that the issue of 'taxation without representation', though a popular rallying cry, had much unique significance now, nor were there the numerous petty annoyances—for example, the irresponsible acts of police repression and trespass—that had marred some other attempts at government reform, including Steinberger's. But among those who felt it, suspicion of Brandeis was all-pervasive, admitting of nothing supportable in his present programme and of no potential advantage to them from his remaining in power. As to the letter of the law, if not always its spirit or consequence, it would appear in fact that Brandeis was impartial towards Europeans, while in certain cases he plainly omitted to employ against non-Germans the legal weapons which he might well have tried to exploit. He did not, for example, intervene at Apia against the settlers who formed a committee of vigilance, a combination of resistance council and mutual protection society, nor did he apprehend Americans and British subjects there who evaded payment of rates. But if he seemed at all impartial or moderate and loudly protested his being so, it was also true that he had not consolidated his political position. As to what would happen when and if he did, Brandeis's local European antagonists, judging by developments thus far, had ample grounds for anticipating German monopolization of trade and adoption of a pro-German land policy, in fear of which they refused to co-operate with him in any way.

Seen in the wider perspective of international affairs, it is most likely that Brandeis's filibuster was aimed at eliminating the United States from the three-Power deadlock over Samoa. This would have been a German *tour de force* which the State Department had long acknowledged as a possibility arising from a weakness in the American treaty position. The point was that, whereas Britain and Germany had acquired perpetual treaties, the United States had taken one binding for a period of only ten years, ending in January 1888, and subject from then on to unilateral termination by either side. Given Samoa's withdrawal from LeMamea's treaty, Germany would then have been free to offer Great Britain an exchange of concessions and would no doubt have emerged with outright control of Samoa. It would have been essential to such a scheme that Britain, at least, should recognize the Tamasese-Brandeis régime as Samoa's *de facto* government, which, unlike the United States, it did, to the chagrin and disgust of the British consul and his fellow nationals in Samoa. But more than that, it would have been necessary for the Mulinu'u leaders to so entrench themselves in power that the United States, having also to consider the British act of recognition, could not reasonably deny the new régime's competence to govern and hence to withdraw from treaty relations. Diplomatic objectives notwithstanding, Brandeis had still, of course, to develop a position of strength among the Samoans and it was precisely there that his plans, whatever else they prescribed, ultimately broke down.

Brandeis, it will be recalled, started off at Mulinu'u working through a Samoan minority party whose claim to govern Samoa had been advanced not by its own warriors but by the German navy. Subsequently, that party's position was also maintained by the German navy, whose frequent intervention—to order that taxes and fines be paid, to subdue symptoms of restiveness, to deport chiefs suspected of 'rebellious' intent —constituted a reign of terror. It is a moot question whether such a government, controlled and supported by Europeans and pursuing policies that were blatantly pro-European, could have lasted very long even if *fa'a-Samoa* political issues had been handled judiciously or, in so far as circumstances permitted, left strictly alone. There was no chance of finding out, for Brandeis proved quite insensible of the Samoans' feelings regarding traditional matters of great moment and treated them with an ineptitude fully as great as the determination he brought to the direct propagation of foreign interests. The result was that a large majority of Samoans, already overburdened by economic exactions and incensed by Tamasese's undeserved position of privilege at Mulinu'u, were whipped into a revolutionary fury that no available force could restrain.

Where Brandeis finally went too far was in trying to make Tamasese the Tafa'ifā, a distinction which the Germans no doubt coveted for him in order to represent him abroad as Samoa's undisputed monarch. Laupepa, of course, was out of the way, the unwilling guest of the German Government. Though the banishment of that chief had been, at the time, in the nature of a punitive and precautionary act, his absence was subsequently taken by Brandeis as favourable to the grabbing of titles in the name of Tamasese. In fact, Laupepa's being in exile was a much greater boon to Mata'afa's cause than to Tamasese's, facilitating the alliance of Mata'afa's Tupua and Malietoa connections, which had been attempted before without success. It remained only for Tamasese's opponents to be so provoked that despite their fear of German intervention, they would unite in revolt against his régime.

Tamasese knew, and so did Weber, that the way to the Tafa'ifā was fraught with far more danger than had been encountered between Leulumoega and Mulinu'u and they were reluctant to take it while the government was largely dependent on warships for its defence; but the parvenu, Brandeis, confident that the Samoans could be kept under control, insisted on pushing ahead and got Tamasese and the other Mulinu'u chiefs to agree to do so. Tamasese's pre-emption of the Tui Atua title was the first move, taken in May 1887 to anticipate completion of the long-drawn-out formalities associated with the bestowal of that title upon Mata'afa. On the pretext of his having been offered it by the minority faction in Atua, Tamasese simply took the title and restyled himself 'Tuiaana Tuiatua Tamasese, le Tupu o Samoa', over which name government proclamations immediately began to appear.[79] This development produced such a hostile reaction in Atua that, with German naval assistance, dozens of chiefs had to be arrested and removed to prison before the people quietened down there. Mata'afa who had renounced his governorship of Atua before the Tamasese-Brandeis *coup-d'état,* was allowed, however, to remain free—perhaps, as Sewall alleged, because the Germans, having already incurred the wrath of the London Missionary Society by deporting Laupepa, were afraid of alienating the Catholic mission, too. Meanwhile, Samoans on the Malietoa side were intriguing with Mata'afa and apparently to get in first there as well, a claim was soon made on Tamasese's behalf to the two *pāpā* of Tuamasaga and, according to some reports, to the Malietoa title itself.[80] At this, the spirit of revolt, only barely contained before, overflowed in Tuamasaga and quickly spread throughout the western islands and Tutuila, with Mata'afa emerging not only as Tui Atua but also as the holder of the Malietoa title, to which he succeeded as *tama fafine* to Laupepa's line.[81]

Reporting the opening battle of the ensuing war, which broke out in September 1888, the editor of the *Samoa Times* took 'great pleasure in stating that during the conflict not a single act of violence was committed'.[82] What he was expressing, of course, was relief at seeing the Samoans, some fifty of whom were killed or wounded in this 'non-violent' contest, confine amongst themselves the hostilities that Europeans had done so much to provoke. The subsequent intervention of German naval forces, however, soon led to an encounter between German marines and Mata'afa warriors in which both sides suffered comparatively heavy

---

[79] MS., Stout, Maben to Stout, 17 June 1887.

[80] The *pāpā* Tamasoali'i was irregularly bestowed on Tamasese by his son-in-law, Su'atele of Safata, on which account Su'atele fled his home village to escape punishment (*Samoa Times*, 10 November 1888).

[81] Fa'alata, Talavou's son, was a counter-claimant to the Malietoa title but he had slight support (RP 110, Becker to Bismarck, 11 September 1888).

[82] *Samoa Times*, 15 September 1888.

casualties; and thereafter, as Germany retaliated in force and private traders 'invested' large quantities of arms in Mata'afa's cause, the war not only developed into the most savage and sanguine yet fought since the opening of the islands to foreign settlement but engaged Europeans in the most open and vehement partisan activity. While a greatly out-numbered Tamasese party made a prolonged and heroic final stand at the inland fortress to which Brandeis had taken it in retreat from Mulinu'u,[83] mounting tension among Europeans threatened to bring into conflict at Apia the warships sent by the Powers to protect the lives of their respective nationals. Whether the celebrated hurricane which intruded in 1889 and broke up this naval concentration thus prevented an international war is one of the more popular conundrums in the history of the Pacific. It certainly did, at any rate, make dramatic news exposing the unavailing effort which the Powers had expended in Samoa and directing attention to the renewed negotiations into which Bismarck, in early acknowledgement of Brandeis's failure, had called them in search of a durable solution of the Samoan problem.

[83] American naval intervention, ostensibly aimed at preventing hostilities in the neutral zone, hastened abandonment of Mulinu'u (RP 110, Becker to Bismarck, 15 October 1888).

# 16

## THE CONDOMINIUM

THE THREE-POWER conference on Samoa was moved to Berlin and resumed in April 1889, by which time the German Government had sworn off active hostilities against the Mata'afa forces and had found, in Brandeis and members of the German consulate at Apia, scapegoats for the failure as much as for the perpetration of what had plainly been an officially-countenanced conspiracy to gain control of the islands. Except for a residue of ill feeling on account of the German *coup* and its aftermath and for the willingness of the United States, increasingly conscious of its 'manifest destiny', to assume a rather more active role in Samoa, the Powers were back where they started in 1885-6. That is to say, Britain, given concessions elsewhere, would probably have got out in favour of a German 'mandate' or have accepted the partitioning of the Samoan group, whereas the United States was prepared neither to abandon any of its existing rights to Germany nor to accept a political position in Samoa inferior to that of another Power. Since there was little point in Germany's making any sacrifice to secure the withdrawal of Britain alone, and since Britain would not have given up its place for nothing, particularly when to withdraw at all would have raised an embarrassing storm in the Australasian colonies, the Powers proceeded to canvass new means of exercising joint jurisdiction, trying, without great expectation of success, to provide Samoa with more effective government and still maintain parity of privilege among the three nationalities. The arrangement they hit upon was a form of condominium supported not only by rights they already had by virtue of treaty concessions, but also by others for which they now provided without first consulting the Samoans. Admittedly, the agreement reached at Berlin and embodied in the conference's General Act of 14 June 1889, was not to go into force until it had been seen, accepted and signed by the king of Samoa. This did not mean, however, that Samoa was to be an equal party to the negotiations, for the Berlin Act itself, though it declared the 'free right of the natives to elect their Chief or King', stated which one of the several contenders the Powers would recognize as king and, hence, as Samoa's signatory to the Act. With similar inconsistency, the Powers also professed to recognize 'the independence of the Samoan government'.

## Provisions of the Berlin Act

In contemplating how Samoa should be governed, the Berlin conference took for its orientation the political and economic problems and interests of Europeans, leaving the Samoans' affairs largely out of account, except in so far as they impinged on foreign concerns. The principal changes proposed were directed towards the following objectives: to make the government less dependent on agreement among local representatives of the three Powers:[1] to strengthen the judiciary; to reorganize public finance; to re-establish the municipality of Apia; to ensure the maintenance of peace among the Samoans; and to see that the Samoan Government had responsible and reliable European advisers. Faced, however, with a great complexity of divergent and conflicting interests and having to think more about accommodating or protecting them than resolving or overriding them, the conference, a somewhat perfunctory affair anyway, did not contribute much to the solution of Samoa's problems of government. Taking as its starting point the existing system of extra-territoriality, which it altered and supplemented, the conference actually aggravated the jurisdictional tangle, creating institutions and laying down procedures so cumbersome and often so ill defined, that the result almost defies description.

As to the permanent apparatus of government, the major innovation for which the Berlin Act provided was the establishment of a Supreme Court *with a single judge*—the 'Chief Justice of Samoa'—who was to be nominated by the three Powers or, failing agreement among them, by the monarch of Sweden and Norway. The appointment of the Chief Justice was to be made by the Samoan Government, which was allowed no option of rejecting a nominee, and his salary of $6,000 per annum was, after the first year of the court's existence, to be paid from local revenue. The Chief Justice's decisions were to be final and were to be binding on all the residents of Samoa and all four governments party to the Berlin Act. Provision was made, however, for any of the four governments to complain of his 'misconduct in office', and given 'sufficient cause', he might be removed at the request of any two of the treaty Powers, which term by definition excluded Samoa. Despite its name, the Supreme Court had, according to the stipulations and implications of the Berlin Act, only sectional and specialized jurisdictions. Most classes of cases between or pertaining only to Samoans[2] were entirely outside

1 The past necessity of this, especially in the absence of telegraphic links with Samoa, had invited excessive controversy and misunderstanding.

2 Provisions of the Act applying to Samoans generally applied also to other Pacific islanders who were in Samoa as free immigrants or visitors and who were not the subjects of a foreign Power. Most of these others were from Niue, Tonga and the Cook Islands.

its prescribed competence, the principal exceptions being two types of civil suits, namely, disputes over the royal succession and those over rights in real property, in which the court had exclusive jurisdiction. It was left to the Samoan Government to provide facilities for the hearing of other civil suits between Samoans, including residents of the municipality of Apia, whose local tribunal could not adjudicate civil issues.[3] The Samoan authorities also had criminal jurisdiction over Samoans, except when they offended against foreigners. This power, too, extended to the municipal area, but only in regard to acts not covered by the town regulations, under which any offender was to be tried in the first instance by the local magistrate. Allowed to hear appeals from the municipal court,[4] a function which the consular board had exercised under the 1879 convention, the Chief Justice did therefore have limited criminal jurisdiction in cases to which the private parties were Samoans, though the public authority concerned was of course, European. With respect to the Samoan judiciary, then, the Supreme Court as established by the Berlin Act was not at all supreme, but by later arrangement with the Samoan Government, this gap left by the Act was filled, the Chief Justice being permitted to take appeals from decisions of Samoan magistrates.

The position was even more complex when it came to cases between or involving Samoans and foreigners. As noted, the Chief Justice alone was empowered to hear disputes over real property. All other civil suits between Samoans and foreigners were also within his exclusive jurisdiction. So too were cases arising from criminal acts committed by Samoans against foreigners, with the exception that the Chief Justice had only appellate jurisdiction relative to breaches of the municipal regulations. As to the criminal acts of foreigners against Samoans, however, the Supreme Court's jurisdiction was limited to its appellate rights within the substantive and territorial scope of the Apia regulations *unless* it happened that the defendant was not a subject of one of the treaty Powers. In the latter event, the Supreme Court had exclusive jurisdiction apart from cases brought under the municipal regulations. If a foreign defendant charged with a criminal act against a Samoan (or a Samoan authority) could be tried by neither the Apia magistrate nor the Chief Justice, he came under the jurisdiction of his consul—or, if he was British, the Deputy Commissioner and other judges in the hierarchy of the Western Pacific High Commission. This power of the consular

---

[3] Not even challenges to decisions of the municipality were to be heard by the municipal tribunal. These were to go to the Supreme Court in the form of appeals.

[4] A case where the penalty imposed by the magistrate had exceeded a fine of twenty dollars or a prison term of ten days could be appealed to the Supreme Court.

and commissioner's courts, originating in various treaties and foreign legislative acts, was of residual character. In similar fashion, and within the same limits of nationality, the Berlin Act allowed metropolitan law to take precedence over all but municipal statutes, laws of the Samoan government approved by the three Powers and, of course, the Berlin Act itself and those carried over from Samoa's earlier treaties with the Powers.

The criminal jurisdiction to which a foreigner was subject coincided with the above pattern when the private complainant, if any, was a foreigner too. If, for example, an American committed an assault upon another foreigner, whether an American or not, the case would come before the United States consular court, provided the offence had occurred outside the municipal area. As to civil suits, however, those between persons of different nationalities were within the Chief Justice's sole jurisdiction. Only if the parties to a civil case were of the same nationality and were not disputing rights in real property would they go before a consular court, assuming they were subjects of a treaty Power. As to what should be done if they were French, say, the Berlin Act was silent, leaving open the slight possibility of their both claiming the protection of one of the consuls and submitting their case to him, or the more likely chance of the Chief Justice's assuming jurisdiction on the basis of his right to interpret the Act.

Aside from the appellate and special civil jurisdiction of the Supreme Court, then, the principal judicial reform undertaken by the Berlin conference was the provision of surer means of settling civil disputes between foreigners of different nationalities—means not dependent on consular co-operation and reciprocity. That the consuls should, within the limits of their respective national 'communities', retain much of their former jurisdiction was not unreasonable. But it was an unwarranted complication to leave them with what was, after all, virtually the same criminal jurisdiction they had had over foreigners since the revocation of the municipal convention of 1879. As many as five different courts were now eligible in the first instance to try foreigners charged with criminal offences, jurisdiction being determined in each case by national status and/or the locale of the crime; and among these courts there were considerable variations as to appeal rights and maximum penalties. Why, for example, should a Dane who committed an assault at Leulumoega be tried first and finally in the Supreme Court when a British subject, in the same circumstances, would go before a commissioner's court from which he might appeal? If charged within the municipality, then of course both would be tried by the same judge, and both would have the right of appealing to the Chief Justice. As one result of such inequities, which could be further elaborated but need not be, the consuls experienced difficulty in co-ordinating their efforts to enforce the Samoan

BB

laws endorsed for observance by nationals of the three Powers, while
Europeans naturally came to resent the fact that the principle of equality
before the law, though applicable to the jurisdictions of the Chief
Justice and municipal magistrate, had not been as widely adopted as
conditions in Samoa seemed to require. Indeed, legal discrepancy and
discrimination had become more prominent features of the judicial
'system' than ever before.

Returning more specifically to the Supreme Court, it should be noted
that the Chief Justice, as well as having civil and criminal jurisdiction,
was also to act as adviser, arbiter and even administrator in certain affairs
of government and state. The effect of these additional powers, justified
in part by the complexity of Samoa's burden of law, was to make the
Chief Justice the most important official in the condominium. As suggested already, it was his responsibility to settle questions concerning
the meaning or application of the Berlin Act, and further, he was to
decide any issue between the Samoan Government and a treaty Power
which proved incapable of adjustment by 'mutual accord'. Moreover,
the Chief Justice was to share with the king the control over leasing
of Samoan land and he was to advise the Samoan Government regarding
the passage of laws for the maintenance of order, punishment of crime
and collection of taxes outside the municipality. Although the government was not obliged to take his advice, it did, as will be shown, rely
heavily upon him not only for information but also for the ostensible
source of measures unpopular among the Samoans. Finally, the Chief
Justice was the authority upon which the municipal administration of
Apia ultimately depended for its stability and continuity.

For while the Berlin conference, in restoring the municipality, did not
revive the consuls' power to act together as a court of appeal, it did give
them a collective responsibility for legislation. The consuls were not,
however, to be members of the municipal council, which was now to
consist only of six taxpayers' representatives elected by territorial rather
than national constituencies, plus a voting chairman selected by the
three Powers or on their behalf by the executive head of another foreign
government. Having made this concession to democracy, the Berlin
conference proceeded to set up the consuls as a restraining influence,
assuring the Powers an equal voice at a vital stage in the legislative
process. Thus, regulations approved by a majority of the councillors
would require the unanimous consent of the consuls in order to pass
directly into law, but, on the other hand, amendments unanimously
proposed by the consuls would have to be approved by a majority of
councillors. It was in the event of a deadlock that the Chief Justice was
to take charge, having the final authority to modify and approve regulations over which the consular board and municipal council were unable

to agree. The remaining functions of the Chief Justice in the administration of the town were the establishment of the electoral machinery and the supervision of elections, the swearing in of councillors and other officials and the regulation of the sale and lease of land.

The powers allotted the municipal government by the Berlin Act were much the same as had been laid down by the 1879 convention, with a few additions such as the right to provide a postal service and to collect the proceeds of certain levies previously forbidden by foreign treaties. Again, the council was to appoint the magistrate and other local officers, excluding its own chairman or (as he was entitled) president, who was also to serve as the chief executive of the municipality, the treasurer of Samoa and, at the king's pleasure, a general adviser to the Samoan Government. Unlike the Chief Justice, the President was permitted to receive instructions from the Powers, but only from the three of them jointly. Lastly, the Berlin Act introduced a limit upon the municipal magistrate's jurisdiction, in terms of the penalties he might impose, the maximum being a fine of two hundred dollars or a prison term of one hundred and eighty days; but no specific limit was set upon the penalties for which local regulations might provide, the implication being that the consuls, the Chief Justice and Samoan judges might share any residue of original court jurisdiction required to be exercised under municipal law.

Public finance was another sphere in which 'the independence of the Samoan government' was encroached upon by the Berlin Act, a large number of specific fund-raising measures being laid down and provision being made for the sharing of public revenue by the central government and the municipality. The entrenchment of these measures in the Act was not to 'prejudice . . . the right of the native Government to levy and collect other taxes in its discretion upon the natives of the islands and their property, and with the consent of the consuls . . . upon all property outside the Municipal District'; but since most of the likely sources of revenue had already occurred to and been pounced upon by the conferees at Berlin, there was little effective authority left to the Samoan Government except that of levying higher taxes within the limited range of its jurisdiction, a dubious course when the Samoans were, if anything, already in line for being over-taxed. For example, it was stipulated in the Act that there should be paid by or on behalf of *all* Samoans and other Pacific islanders settled in Samoa a head tax of one dollar per annum, which would be hard enough to collect as it was without increasing the rate. In one significant instance the Powers made a concession to local requirements, cancelling the free trade sections of their treaties and imposing import and export duties. The rates established, however, were quite low: two per cent *ad valorem* on imports other than liquor, tobacco and arms, on which various excises were to be payable; and 1.5, 2 and 2.5 per cent *ad valorem* on exports of cotton, coffee and copra, respectively. At the same time—and this was to apply generally to public revenues—it was provided that the Samoan Government might draw only upon the proceeds of taxes collected *outside* the municipality, which, because Apia was made the sole port of foreign entry, reserved the whole of the customs revenue from imports for expenditure by the municipal administration, while five-sixths of the returns on export duties, that part actually paid at Apia, was similarly apportioned. Among the remaining sections of the Berlin Act were the most successful and constructive of all, those pertaining to the settlement of land claims and related matters, which will be considered separately in due course. Another provision aimed at, but not to be achieved, was the close regulation of the arms trade, that long-standing problem which had been so intimately linked with the land question. A more workable control, because of the slighter consumer demand, was the prohibition of intoxicants to Samoans and other islanders, which, like the armaments measure, was a carry-over from earlier legislation. Lastly, and in a different vein, the Berlin Act was to be subject to amendment by the same process originally bringing it into force—'by the consent of the three Powers with the adherence of Samoa'.

## From Berlin to the Beach

A necessary accompaniment to the Berlin Act was the Powers' agreement to recognize the same set of chiefs as comprising the Samoan central government and jointly to support and maintain them in that position. This understanding, which was given practical force by the almost constant presence in Samoa of a warship of one nationality or another, gradually made of Samoan factionalism, as of inter-Power relations, a less attractive arena for the working out of local European rivalries. Not that Samoan politics entirely lost their savour for foreigners—there were always some, the gun-runners, the office-seekers, the title-gatherers, who took a keen interest in it—but political forces on the Beach became more independent of the Samoans, tending to act rather through the apparatus of the condominium. That the Berlin Act offered considerable scope for such manoeuvring will be apparent from what has been said of its provisions. Concentrating the greatest authority at two points, the Supreme Court and the office of President, but still leaving the consuls and municipal magistrate substantial responsibilities, the Act set up among the appointed officials an intricate struggle for power and jurisdiction which was beyond the influence, though not the constitutional right, of the Chief Justice wholly to resolve, while the elected municipal councillors and other foreign residents, reacting with a consciousness of belonging to the place, put up strenuous resistance to the top-heavy government by outsiders with which they felt they had been improperly saddled. But by suppressing various Samoan attempts to overthrow the official régime at Mulinu'u and by revising a few of the more troublesome provisions of the Berlin Act—for example, to allow the Samoan Government to have up to one-third of the customs revenue[5]—the Powers managed to keep the condominium going for what was by previous standards a very long time—unconscionably long, in the opinion of many Europeans.

A most striking feature of the condominium was the engagement of many distinguished, often very competent, Europeans in its politics and administration: for example, the first Chief Justice, Otto Cedercrantz, 'a Swedish Judge of high repute'; his American successor, Henry Ide, a well-known lawyer and company director; the British Land Commissioner, Bazett Haggard, a brother of the novelist; Graf Senfft von Pilsach, the first of a series of Germans to occupy the office of President; and, of course, Robert Louis Stevenson of Vailima, who dabbled in both Samoan affairs and the politics of the Beach. Apart from the disposition of foreign land claims, however, this access of talent, marked, too, by consular appointments of a higher standard, contributed little to the progress of Samoa. From the large accumulation of correspondence and reports one gains, rather, the impression of ability and energy being frittered away in petty controversy and bureaucracy, mainly in the running of European affairs at Apia. As was observed of the municipality in the 1880s, so now was it true that the trouble taken to set up and operate the administration was far out of proportion to the magnitude of the local problems and interests which occasioned it. By 1895, for example, the foreign immigrant population of Samoa had risen to only four hundred, of whom some two hundred and sixty lived at or near Apia.[6] The entire resident population of the municipal district was less than one thousand, the electors numbered but two hundred, and Apia's annual revenue, customs duties excluded, was a mere eight thousand dollars. Despite favourable predictions made upon the signing of the Berlin Act, Samoa's subsequent economic growth had been slight, an increase in the annual output of copra to between five and six

5 To a maximum amount of $8,000 per annum. This revision followed a controversy in Samoa during the course of which the Chief Justice had decided that, regardless of the wording of the Berlin Act, all export duties and two-thirds of the import duties should be collected for the benefit of the Samoan government (BCP 6973, 134-6; FOCP 6251, 129-30, Memo by C. B. Robertson, 24 June 1892; USCD Apia/21, Blacklock to Wharton, 27 March 1893).

6 FOCP 6663, 96-101, Census of foreign population, March 1895. The four hundred included about twenty Chinese from Hong Kong and twenty American Mormon missionaries.

thousand tons being offset by the D.H.P.G.'s abandonment of cotton and coffee production. Moreover, the D.H.P.G., through the effects of improvident management and the extension of British control into areas of the Pacific from which cheap labour had once been readily available, had, in the late 1880s, stopped enlarging its plantations. Thus, while there had been a steady increase in shipping tonnages, chiefly because of the establishment of new steamship services through Samoa, the actual volume of trade had not greatly appreciated. In 1894, a 'good' year, the net proceeds of customs duties totalled only about $27,500, the Samoan Government's share of which was little more than the amount of the Chief Justice's salary.[7] Obviously, then, the Berlin Act imposed upon Samoa a government it could not afford[8]—a government whose actual running costs alone could not be met without foreign assistance. For the projects essential to the development of the territory there was but a pittance left, and most of that went into improvements at Apia. Even then, noted one critic in 1895, Apia had no regular wharf, no public school, no fire-control equipment, no proper footpath. But there were five different courts there in which a case of common assault might be heard.

## The settlement of European land claims

Not an economical venture in itself, not a direct contributor to economic development, the condominium none the less had to its credit two reforms of economic significance. The first of these was a measure of immediate import only: the local devaluation of the South American dollar to an equivalent of three shillings sterling or seventy-five American cents. At this fixed rate the freer circulation and exchange of mixed currencies was possible, and on the strength of it, a British partnership opened a banking house at Apia, breaking the D.H.P.G.'s hold on foreign exchange transactions. The second reform was more momentous, destined to be the one durable monument to the Berlin Act: the settlement of foreign land claims, complemented by the establishment of a land titles registry.

The idea of setting up a special land tribunal or commission, for which the Berlin Act provided, was by no means a new one. With the advice of J. C. Williams, various chiefs meeting at Apia in 1873 had proposed such a body, hoping it would ameliorate the effects upon the Samoans of the first great wave of land speculation; and soon after-

---

[7] FO, Report for the year 1894 on the trade of Samoa, No. 1587, 7-8.

[8] In June 1892 the consuls, on temporarily assuming the duties of the President, discovered that the Samoan Government had a credit balance of about $75 and owed more than $9,500 for salaries, not including the Chief Justice's (SGP 11/3, Consuls to Malietoa, 20 June 1892).

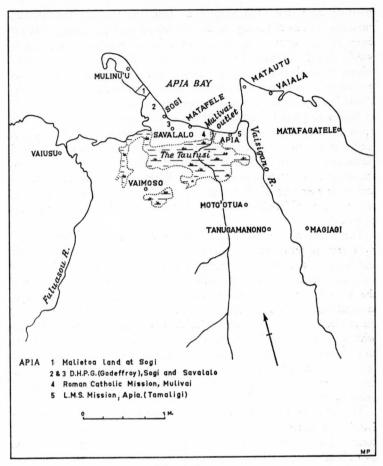

The Apia area

wards, Steinberger had, though for rather different reasons, made a
similar proposal which had been widely accepted in Samoa but never
acted upon. Later, as the application of foreign treaty rights had been
explored, interest in a land commission had picked up. In the first
place, what constituted a 'regular' and 'customary' manner of selling
land? The terms were so vague, the nature of Samoan land rights
apparently so involved, the evidence of the misappropriation of land so
great, and the Samoans so eager to contest most of the recent sales to
foreigners that the existing court facilities and procedures were, on those
grounds alone, obviously unequal to the task of deciding claims and

granting land titles. But more than that, the problem was also an international one requiring, in the conditions then pertaining, that the three Powers agree to uniform standards of 'regularity', a necessity which would not have been removed even had there been no land subject to conflicting European claims. Thus, the establishment of an international land commission had often been suggested during the 1880s, but not until Germany's attempts to gain political ascendancy in Samoa had failed did the need for a joint approach impinge equally upon all three Powers. Meanwhile, with the exception of inquiry into land transactions between Europeans, local proceedings relating to land claims continued to run largely to political intrigue, pressure and bribery, the object of which was to secure from Samoan chiefs, including judges and other members of diverse governments, written acknowledgements of the validity of foreign claims that might be represented as instruments of 'title'.[9]

The article of the Berlin Act dealing with land titles was headed by a section providing for control over future transactions. The sale and lease of land within the municipal district were permitted; but no such undertaking, whoever the parties concerned, could proceed without the written approval of the Chief Justice. To ensure 'that the agricultural lands and natural fruit lands of Samoans' should not be 'unduly diminished', the sale of land by Samoans outside the municipality was wholly prohibited; and, whereas the Samoans there were to be allowed to lease out their land, no leasehold contract could be finalized for a period of more than forty years in the first instance, and then only with the written approval of 'the Chief Executive Authority of Samoa' (namely, the king) and the Chief Justice.

The subsequent sections of the article were taken up mainly with the Land Commission and its proceedings. The Commission was to be composed of 'three impartial and competent persons', one to be named by each of the treaty Powers, with provision being made for a 'Natives' Advocate', an officer to be appointed by the king, on the Chief Justice's approval, to represent Samoan interests and advise the Land Commissioners on questions concerning the Samoans' customary land rights and usages. Apart from the salary of the Natives' Advocate, which was to be

[9] e.g. a document signed by Malietoa Laupepa and various members of his government certifying that the land claims of the C.P.L.C.C. and Cornwall were based upon sales properly executed by the Samoan owners and guaranteeing that W. McArthur & Co. would be protected when conducting surveys of the land and completing payment for it (SLC 2815, statement by Samoan officials, 23 October 1884). The McArthur firm had acquired interests in both the C.P.L.C.C. and Cornwall speculations and represented a syndicate which, partly on the strength of land-holdings in Samoa, was trying to get the islands annexed by Britain and placed under New Zealand control.

fixed and paid by the Samoan Government, the other expenses of the Commission were to be met by the treaty Powers, each paying a one-third share. Over a period of no more than two years—the time had to be extended to more than three and a half—'the Commission [was] to investigate all claims of foreigners to land in Samoa, whether acquired from natives or from aliens, and to report to the [Supreme] Court in every case the character and description of the claim, the consideration paid, the kind of title alleged to be conveyed and all the circumstances affecting its validity'. With each report the Commission was to state 'whether the alleged title should be recognized and registered or rejected, in whole or in part', incorporating within its recommendation the terms of any 'just and equitable' compromise settlement of which the litigants, if the case required and its nature permitted, might have expressed their mutual approval. All undisputed claims which the Commission might unanimously report as valid were to be confirmed without question by the Supreme Court, but the Chief Justice was to have the final decision in every other case—that is, of a disputed claim, of an undisputed claim declared invalid, or of any claim on which the Commission was unable to make a unanimous recommendation. Claims finally declared wholly or partly valid were to be subject to registration and the issuance of title deeds by means left to be determined by the Chief Justice who, when the time came, adopted the Torrens system.

The Act then proceeded to lay down certain criteria of validity. All land bought by foreigners from Samoans before 28 August 1879, the date of the Anglo-Samoan treaty, were to be 'held as validly acquired— but without prejudice to rights of third parties—if purchased from Samoans in good faith, for a valuable consideration, in a regular and customary manner'. It was further stipulated that 'the undisputed possession and continuous cultivation of lands by aliens for ten years or more, [should] constitute a valid title by prescription to the lands so cultivated'. Otherwise, land acquired in good faith and subsequently improved upon the basis of a title found to be defective might be 'confirmed in whole or in part upon the payment by the occupant to the person or persons entitled thereto of an additional sum to be ascertained by the Commission and approved by the [Supreme] Court as equitable and just'. Next, the Act provided for the summary rejection of all claims to or interests in land arising from 'mere promises to sell, or options to buy', from conveyances containing, when signed, 'no descrip-tion of the land conveyed sufficiently accurate to enable the Commission to define the boundaries thereof', from conveyances expressing either no consideration or consideration 'manifestly inadequate and unreasonable', from consideration not fully paid, or from conveyances of any type based upon consideration given in arms or liquor in violation of Samoan and

municipal laws of 1880. Finally, the Berlin Act, by omitting to recognize
the previous existence of any authority competent to rule on the legality
of foreign land claims in Samoa, denied claimants before the Commission any prejudicial benefit, from the acknowledgements of title and
certificates of negotiated settlement which Samoans had been variously
prevailed upon to give in the past, except that such documents might be
entered as evidence regarding the particulars of land transactions.

These standards of validity greatly simplified the work of the Land
Commission, enabling it to evaluate and dispose of many of its nearly
four thousand cases without critical and time-consuming reference to
'the recondite customs of Samoans'.[10] For a start, a high proportion of
claims to very large blocks of land were found to stem from glaringly
defective conveyances and were accordingly rejected in their entirety,
the Commission even being spared the trouble of arranging recovery of
the consideration given the vendors, for which action the Berlin Conference had not allowed. Among the easy victims was the C.P.L.C.C.'s
'414 square mile contract', a composite 'option to buy', from which there
proceeded rival sets of claims, one raised by a group of San Francisco
businessmen whom Clay and others had gulled into purchasing the
Collie and Stewart deeds, and two more brought by British investors
who, through Clay, had succeeded to marginal rights in the C.P.L.C.C.
interests.[11] The rejection of this contract thrice over accounted for about
forty per cent of the crude total area of 1.7 million acres represented by
the claims the Commission examined.[12] Also thrown out on *prima facie*
evidence were several claims made by W. McArthur & Co. on the
strength of unredeemed mortgages dating from the time of the
Tamasese-Brandeis affair. Against a sum of $352 still owed it by
'Safotulafai', for example, the firm sought an equitable title to a block
of seven thousand acres originally accepted as security from various
chiefs of that village. Ruling that the amount of consideration was
immaterial with regard to the mortgage deeds, the Commission none
the less avoided the question of the Samoans' contracting rights in these
cases by finding the land itself to have been inadequately described,[13] a
defect apparent in many other instances as well. Alternatively, it might
have been shown that some of the mortgages held by W. McArthur &
Co. had been given against payment in arms, another intrinsic though

10 FOCP 6663, 14, Report by B. M. Haggard, 31 December 1894.
11 SLC 2815 and 2901; *Samoa Weekly Herald*, 31 December 1892. The British
claims, which were complementary, derived from different versions of the same
contract.
12 SLC 1287.
13 See the accompanying table (FOCP 6663, 3, Review of Land Claims examined
by the Samoan Land Commission; MS., Gurr, 10, E. W. Gurr's summary of land
claims).

not so readily established defect of numerous conveyances. Also hard to prove conclusively, but allegedly a common practice, was the purchasers' alteration or completion of deeds after their original execution, of which the Commission discovered clear enough evidence in a few cases to warrant discountenancing the claims for that reason.[14] As for insufficiency of consideration, it does not appear that this criterion, by itself, figured very largely in the overthrow of claims, the more obvious cases of underpayment having also brought forth evidence of other defects less subject to differences of opinion.

Working more in the favour of claimants, and at the same time saving the Commission much detailed investigation, was the provision for recognition of prescriptive rights, which pertained in a very large number of cases where small blocks of land had been bought with some knowledge of and respect for the Samoans' customary usage, a common characteristic of land transactions prior to the *faitasiga* war. Without this provision, reported Bazett Haggard, 'the labours of the Commissioners would have seemed . . . interminable',[15] for otherwise, the Berlin Act conservatively required that every claim demonstrably based upon a conveyance which was internally sound must then be examined further for evidence of the Samoan signatories' authority to enter into the contract, even if no Samoan objection to the claim was raised before the Land Commission. No doubt prescriptive rights were necessarily recognized in some cases of substantial misappropriation. Perhaps, too, they were incorrectly found in some other cases, though the Commission, not least because its local assistants had reason to spin out the hearings and with them their jobs, clearly took considerable pains to explore the history of long-established land improvements and cultivations and to encourage Samoan objectors to come forward. Partly to facilitate the appearance of Samoan witnesses, the Commission held some of its sessions in the outer districts, while Samoan suspicion of its purpose and proceedings, especially strong in parts of Atua, was carefully explained away rather than being allowed to prejudice the people's defence against foreign land claims.

The final *prima facie* test of a land claim will be obvious: had the same property, or any part of it, been previously alienated or encumbered by the same people? If it had—as was the case, for example, with some of the outstanding D.H.P.G. mortgages, which conflicted with earlier transactions by Cornwall—the claim was, of course, rejected to the extent of the duplication without the Commission's having to consider any question of the customary rights of the Samoans. In some instances,

[14] FOCP 6663, 14, Report by B. M. Haggard, 31 December 1894.
[15] *loc. cit.*

noted Haggard, the same land had been paid for three times over, a source of grievance which the unsuccessful claimants were precluded by the Berlin Act from pursuing at law.

There still remained to be conducted, however, a formidable amount of investigation into the nature of the original negotiations from which claims derived and into the rights of the parties thereto. In many cases, claims had to be evaluated solely in terms of whether they had been acquired from Samoans who had had authority to dispose of the land concerned. Had the Samoan signatories to a contract had such authority *in their own right*? If not, had they been delegated the authority, for example, on the strength of an agreement reached by people who shared the right to dispose of the land? If neither of these conditions applied, had payment for the land been so distributed as to imply the later approval or endorsement of the alienation by those who would have had the authority to transact it in the first place? If, thus tested, an alleged title was shown to be defective, the claim was rejected, *provided the land had never been developed*. Given, however, any measure of improvement or cultivation—without, of course, the establishment of prescriptive rights—the land was then, in accordance with the Berlin Act, held to be encumbered by a foreign interest *if it had been acquired and occupied in good faith*. Needless to say, 'good faith' abounded and could be plausibly argued in the context of such an arcane subject as Samoan customs, which had never been codified; but the qualification was not an unreasonable one considering the guarantees which the Samoans, by no means innocent of improper dealing in land, had already been given by the Act. Assuming that an element of good faith was acknowledged, it only remained for a compromise settlement to be arranged: for the claimant to release part of the land to the 'Samoan owners' or to give them a further sum as final payment for part or all of it, the terms depending mainly on the extent and value of the development he had carried out.

Among the problems encountered in the foregoing process of sociological investigation and historical reconstruction was the necessity of relying heavily upon verbal evidence. Even if some or all of the parties to a land conveyance were still alive, the character of their original negotiations and subsequent relations was still largely the subject of allegation and hearsay. Since Europeans had developed so little of the land they claimed, the burden they bore of proving their past observance of the Samoans' customary rights and usages was consequently very great. An additional advantage to the Samoans was the conservative approach taken by the Commission towards determining the limits of their authority to alienate land. One general rule adopted was that no chief would be regarded as having personally had the sole right to dis-

# A SUMMARY OF CLAIMS INVESTIGATED BY THE SAMOAN LAND COMMISSION, 1891-4

| Nationality of Claimants | Number and approximate area represented by Claims examined | | | | | | How the Claims were disposed of | | | | | | | | | |
| --- | --- | --- | --- | --- | --- | --- | --- | --- | --- | --- | --- | --- | --- | --- | --- | --- |
| | Uncontested | | Contested | | Total | | Wholly confirmed | | Confirmed in part | | Not unanimously decided | | Withdrawn | | Rejected | |
| | No. | Acreage | No. | Acreage | No. | Acreage | No. | Acreage | No. | Acreage | No. | Acreage | No. | Acreage | No. | Acreage |
| German .. | 378 | 7,170 | 1,044 | 127,249 | 1,422 | 134,419 | 1,023 | 53,045 | 104 | 42,978 | 18 | 5,004 | 186 | 6,546 | 91 | 26,846 |
| English .. | 553 | 4,700 | 1,204 | 1,245,570 | 1,757 | 1,250,270 | 686 | 13,011 | 179 | 105,939 | 1 | 1 | 86 | 6,842 | 805 | 1,124,477 |
| American .. | 148 | 9,262 | 159 | 293,484 | 307 | 302,746 | 207 | 18,127 | 8 | 2,498 | .. | .. | 30 | 1,291 | 62 | 280,830 |
| French .. | 259 | 589 | 67 | 1,718 | 326 | 2,307 | 296 | 1,028 | 13 | 417 | .. | .. | 7 | 280 | 10 | 582 |
| Others .. | 86 | 360 | 44 | 1,791 | 130 | 2,151 | 99 | 466 | 7 | 1,628 | .. | .. | 15 | 32 | 9 | 25 |
| Total .. | 1,424 | 22,081 | 2,518 | 1,669,872 | 3,942 | 1,691,893 | 2,311 | 85,677 | 311 | 153,460 | 19 | 5,005 | 324 | 14,991 | 977 | 1,432,760 |

## Synopsis

| Nationality | | | | | | Area claimed (acres) | Area confirmed |
| --- | --- | --- | --- | --- | --- | --- | --- |
| German .. | .. | .. | .. | .. | .. | 134,419 | 75,000 = 56 per cent |
| English .. | .. | .. | .. | .. | .. | 1,250,270 | 36,000 = 3 per cent |
| American .. | .. | .. | .. | .. | .. | 302,746 | 21,000 = 7 per cent |
| French .. | .. | .. | .. | .. | .. | 2,307 | 1,300 = 57 per cent |
| Others .. | .. | .. | .. | .. | .. | 2,151 | 2,000 = 95 per cent |
| | | | | | | 1,691,893 | 135,300 = 8 per cent |

pose of any land except what he might have been acknowledged without
substantial objection to have acquired or had set aside for his specific
use and control, for example, Malietoa Laupepa's house site at Sogi.
That is not to say that a conveyance signed by one chief alone was,
barring the class of exception just noted, necessarily held to be invalid.
It had to be shown, however, that others had consented to his signing
or had shared the proceeds of the sale—that he had acted, in a sense,
as trustee or representative of a group of 'owners'. With regard to
cultivated areas, the usual requirement, broadly interpreted, was as
follows: that all the people who would have shared the right to nominate
a successor to the *matai* that managed the land in question should have
agreed to or accepted the fact of its sale. There were, of course, many
intricate variations of this theme—affecting, for example, the relative
rights of *tama tāne* and *tama fafine*, of *matai* having joint *pule,* and of
junior and senior *matai*—but the general principle was, quite clearly,
that the sharing of tenure rights made the disposal of land a group
responsibility. Thus, to refer to a case already described, the sale of
Vaitele's planted lands by two outsiders, one of whom had been
Tamasese, was ruled unsound by the Commission, despite the attempts
of Samoans as well as European witnesses to impute to high chiefs a
sovereign power of overlordship. Because the Vaitele sale had been
frequently disputed, the D.H.P.G. had no prescriptive right in the land
it had developed, but 'good faith' pertained and secured the firm by way
of compensation for its investment, a large portion of the block that
Weber had originally purchased.[16]

There was more uncertainty shown regarding undivided bush or 'back'
land, appropriative and controlling rights in which are, for that matter,
still in the process of being worked out by the Samoans. In the nineteenth century, much of the hinterland was unexploited, while in Savai'i
there were large areas which the people had scarcely any knowledge of,
let alone occasion to use. In what detail, then, should the principle of
joint or group control be applied? It would appear that the Land
Commission, though continuing to reject claims resting upon the contention that single chiefs had had absolute right of disposal, was otherwise more content to accept the absence of objections as evidence that
bush land had been properly sold—or, conversely, to regard those
Samoans who asserted likely claims to controlling interests as having
the delegated, if not the sole, authority to alienate the land. In practice,
the Samoans' interests were still adequately protected, for of the amount
of hinterland allegedly purchased only a small part had been developed,
while if many Samoans placed relatively little value upon their land

16 SLC 3267.

reserves, numerous objectors none the less appeared when the Commission called for them.

Some of the more outstanding examples of bush-land claims were those made by Frank Cornwall—and duplicated by his New Zealand creditors—against enormous tracts in Savai'i, most of which island he had ostensibly bought. Cornwall had usually set about purchasing land, in the first instance, from one or more high-ranking chiefs, with whom he would enter into a contract agreeing to pay a set amount, expressed in cash, for an area whose limits would be described in terms of natural landmarks and/or political boundaries. Several of the people with whom he had thus dealt had not even been residents of Savai'i at the time, though they had had kinship and political connections there. The *aloali'i* Tualau Siale,[17] for example, had removed from Palauli to Leulumoega many years before but presumed, in 1877, to sell thirty-five thousand acres at and around Lata, the site of Cornwall's only plantation development in Savai'i. The payment of two thousand dollars for this land had been given in trade goods, including imported timber for the building of Tualau's European-style house at Leulumoega.[18] Other chiefs among Cornwall's original vendors had been residents of Savai'i but had in almost every instance given him undertakings in excess of their authority, as when one of the several holders of the Masoe title and one of the nine Tufuga titleholders, both of Asau, had joined with a chief of Manono to sell *eighty-six thousand acres* in and adjacent to the sub-district of Vaisigano for the sum of one thousand dollars. Commenting on this land, Cornwall said ingenuously:

This was sold on account of friendship. I was looked upon as one of the family. Masoe's daughter is Nelson's wife [August Nelson having been Cornwall's agent for northern Savai'i]. I could have had the land for $100.[19]

On other occasions Cornwall had clearly dealt with the leaders of one war party or another, who to secure supplies had appropriated land in which they may have had an interest but, if so, one shared with some of their enemies, as instanced by the sale of Fa'asaleleaga bush reserves by two chiefs of the local Puletua faction, Pa'ū and Lauaki.[20]

Cornwall's original Savai'i contracts, which he had had 'approved'

[17] Son of the Tualau Popotunu mentioned in chapter 6, above. Tualau Siale's son later held the Alipia title at Leulumoega.

[18] SLC 3267, deed of 14 March 1877. The house was built at Vaialua, where the *fale pule* of A'ana was situated (SLC 3255, testimony of H. J. Moors, who observed that 'Tualau and Cornwall were great friends').

[19] SLC 3255, Cornwall's testimony of 15 June 1893.

[20] ibid., testimony of August Nelson.

and 'validated' by various Samoan government officials,[21] were patently
defective by virtue of the vendors' insufficient authority and often of the
inadequacy of the purchase prices. More than that, there were some
cases in which even the small payments due had never been made in
full, it having been Cornwall's practice to take land deeds in consideration of trade goods to be given out on request, several of which accounts
had remained unsettled.[22] Had his transactions proceeded no farther,
his claims would have been ready casualties, but they had been fortified
by supplementary contracts. In effect—and probably by design too, for
Cornwall had surely more than a passing acquaintance with Samoan
land rights—his initial contracts had put him in a position from which
he could endeavour to buy up whatever other interests might, in his
opinion, be rightfully argued against his pretence of ownership. It was
the ensuing host of quit claim deeds executed over a period of several
years, that made Cornwall's speculations the subject of a protracted
investigation, for the Land Commission had to determine whether he
had eventually contracted for all the controlling rights in any of the
Savai'i blocks he claimed, and, if so, whether he had given, altogether,
a sufficient consideration. In most cases, however, there were strenuous
Samoan objections raised, not least because Cornwall's boundaries en-
compassed coastal as well as back land; and finally, only the Lata claim
was upheld by the Commission, and that merely to the extent of an
equitable share of about one-third the estimated acreage of the block.[23]

Admittedly, Cornwall's Savai'i speculations represent a rather extreme
case, but that being so, the fate of his claims before the Commission
points up all the more clearly the great importance of the factors of
occupation and development in the establishment of foreign land titles
in Samoa. After all, many of the Godeffroy and D.H.P.G. purchases
had been defective, too, while Weber, if challenged by Samoans on
account of them, had been much less amiable and flexible in his response
than Cornwall, much less willing to put off objectors with extra outlays
of cash and goods. Yet the German firm had invested far more than
other claimants in the improvement of its land, with the consequence
that German interests fared much better over all than those of either
British or American nationality. Even after 'deducting the area of . . .
impossible claims from the total . . . claimed by British subjects', noted

---

[21] e.g. SLC 3267, statement of M. K. LeMamea, 'Secretary to the General Government of Samoa', 13 December 1879, certifying that Tualau Siale had the sole
right to sell certain lands which were claimed by people of Sala'ilua. The
'General Government' was that set up at Leulumoega under the supervision of
Bartlett.

[22] e.g. vendors had died and the accounts had not been transferred to other chiefs.

[23] SLC 3255, Group report of 30 November 1894. But the Supreme Court later
granted Cornwall—or rather his estate, for he had died—small equities in other
Savai'i land.

Haggard, only eleven per cent of the remaining acreage was recommended by the Commission for retention by the purchasers,[24] whereas the corresponding ratio for German claims was fifty-six per cent. In all, the Commission proposed confirmation of the foreign ownership of about 135,000 acres, or nearly one-fifth the total area of Samoa, which figure was only slightly altered by the final decisions of the Chief Justice.

One effect of the Commission's investigations was to remove the land issue from the milieu of foreign political intrigue in Samoa, though to be sure, the courts still had some contention to resolve, for example, among the various parties that had succeeded to interests in the relatively small areas granted under C.P.L.C.C. deeds of purchase. As for the Samoans, they had come off extremely well, especially considering the reckless abandon with which many of their leaders had undertaken to divest them of their land. In a few places, notably around Apia where several villages had actually been displaced by German plantation development, land was still in short supply, but generally there were ample reserves, now freed of foreign claims and placed under strict control as regards future alienation. The Samoans could well ask themselves if any colonial government by a single Power would have considered their land interests as favourably as the condominium had.

## Samoan 'independence'

Helpful and constructive as the Land Commission was, the Berlin Act none the less represented, for many Samoans, a very mixed blessing whose worst features emerged before its best ones. Put in general terms, the principal occasion of grievance was the fact that the Mulinu'u government was made a sort of loose appendage to the condominium—a state somewhat reminiscent of developments immediately following the negotiation of Samoa's foreign treaties. In matters affecting the Samoans alone, and not the subject of specific provisions of the Berlin Act, the government was actually free to do much as it pleased, always allowing for the readiness of the President and Chief Justice to recommend what *should* be done. Moreover, the Samoans were left to determine the form of the government, exclusive of the institutions established or recognized by the Act and of the articulation required between the Samoan administration and that of the condominium. It was thus on the responsibility of Samoans that the new Mulinu'u régime, though otherwise similar to previous ones, had no Ta'imua. But if the Powers' proclaimed recognition of the government's autonomy was not a complete fiction, the Berlin Act still incorporated certain provocative measures affecting the make-up and proceedings of the government. And since these were measures to which Samoans unaided could not give full

[24] FOCP 6663, 16-17, Memo by Haggard, 1894 [?].

CC

effect and which the Powers, though prepared to intervene in the interests of peace, were not set up to enforce either, the Mulinu'u government may be said to have exhibited to the Samoan people, the objectionable influence of colonialism without having for itself the larger measure of alien support and the smaller share of responsibility that would normally have gone with colonial rule.

One decision of the Berlin conference which met a hostile response in Samoa was that requiring the annual levy of a head tax. There was, among other things, still too much hard feeling over the exactions of the Tamasese-Brandeis régime for any new tax, however or by whomever imposed, to be generally acceptable to the Samoans. Besides, the present tax, fixed at a rate of one dollar per year *per person*, threatened to be almost as burdensome as the one Brandeis had contrived, in that the latter, though requiring payment of two dollars a year, had been levied only on the able-bodied. With the object of facilitating the enforcement of the new revenue measure, the Mulinu'u government, acting on advice from the Chief Justice, resorted in 1891 to a system of tax-farming, four prominent chiefs being appointed collectors in each of the eight districts and promised, in lieu of salaries, a ten per cent share of the money they were able to account for.[25] This innovation proved, however, a dismal failure; for after two years the Samoans, scheduled to pay in a gross annual sum of about thirty thousand dollars, were more than forty thousand dollars behind in their tax payments, and all attempts to collect from them had, for the time being, ceased.[26] It was the ensuing financial crisis, a matter of particular concern to the Chief Justice who depended on the Samoan Government for his salary, that led to the amendment of the Berlin Act to allow the Mulinu'u treasury a share of the customs revenue. As for the head tax, it continued to be levied annually, but it was never collected in full.

The main question raised by the Berlin Act, however, pertained to the kingship, conflict over which eventually wrecked the condominium. The Berlin conference had started, somewhat imaginatively, with the assumption that Samoa must have a monarch and had then proceeded to usurp the right to choose him, the provision for his election by the Samoans being a pious declaration whose observance was forthwith excluded, ostensibly because of the 'present disordered condition' of the government in Samoa. In fact, the government—that is, the successor to the Tamasese-Brandeis régime at Apia Bay—had been no more 'disordered' than its predecessors, though in being conducted merely by the consuls and a provisional council of chiefs, including Mata'afa, it

[25] MS., Gurr, 9, 'E fa'atonuina atu ai o le lafoga a tupe . . .', 20 March 1891. The eighth district was Tutuila.
[26] BCP 6973, 128, Cusack-Smith to Salisbury, 2 March 1892.

had had a less elaborate form. But that was beside the point, for the state of the government had never had any serious bearing on the kingship question at Berlin. The position had been, rather, that Germany would not accept at any price the candidacy of Mata'afa, the nominal leader of the forces that had engaged and inflicted heavy losses on German marines. Since the defeated Tamasese had obviously been out of the running, only one likely contender remained, Malietoa Laupepa, whom the three Powers agreed to recognize as king and whom Germany returned to Samoa soon after the Berlin conference had ended.

To put a legal face on this intervention in Samoan affairs, the Powers had ignored the events of the late 1880s and resurrected a relic of the past, the *Lackawanna* settlement, according to which Laupepa was still deemed to be king, despite the limit of seven years that had been placed on his term of office.[27] As for Tamasese's vice-kingship, a provision of the same settlement, it was also conveniently forgotten. Before details of the Berlin negotiations became known in Samoa, however, the kingship issue had arisen there as a matter of course, following the formal declaration of peace and the return of Laupepa; and representatives of the victorious party, confronted by what was in effect Laupepa's abdication, had in October 1889 agreed unanimously to have Mata'afa as king (Tupu o Samoa) and Laupepa as alternate or vice-king (Sui Tupu o Samoa). This decision, which was estimated to have the approval of about three-quarters of the Samoans, had thereafter been supported by statements from Laupepa insisting that the Malietoa-Mata'afa alliance be kept united and intact. Wearied and dispirited by his two years in exile, Laupepa had indeed appeared more than content to stand down in favour of Mata'afa.[28]

Only when it was learned, about a month later, that Mata'afa was unacceptable to the Powers did the 'disordered condition' envisaged at Berlin actually start to develop in Samoa. The consuls, who had feared all along that the Samoans might be acting too hastily, made the first move, that of issuing a joint proclamation presuming to annul the selection of Mata'afa. In other words, the Samoans were to have another chance to make a 'free' choice that coincided with the wishes of the Powers. This, in the opinion of the editor of the *Samoa Times*, would be achieved with no difficulty at all.

We have made careful enquiries, and are glad to find that no jealousy or illfeeling had been created by the Consuls' proclamation. . . . and

27 USCP, 61 C., 2 S., Senate Doc., Berlin Act, article 1,1576. It may be recalled that the three Powers had acquired, by means of a local convention, the right to have the Samoans' choice of king referred to them for approval. No right of nomination had been formally conceded them.

28 *Samoa Times*, 3 October and 12 October 1889.

SAMOA 1830 TO 1900

that both Malietoa and Mataafa feel perfectly agreeable. The choice of either would be satisfactory to both. The re-establishment of the name of Malietoa to the Kingship, whether held by Mataafa or Malietoa Laupepa, is of no material difference to the Malietoa party.[29]

It would appear that, by some arrangement between them, the two high chiefs were in fact prepared to adjust to the dictates of the Berlin Act, for at a second meeting, called by them, Mata'afa 'resigned' and Laupepa 'accepted' the kingship in his place. This time, however, the measure of agreement among their combined supporters was not as great.[30] Weighty decisions were not so easily reversed nor the fact of a great military success, in which Laupepa had played no part, so readily swept aside. Tending to drive the wedge deeper was a circumstance which the editor of the *Samoa Times*, thinking in terms of democratic representation, had naively cited as a point in Laupepa's favour: that Tamasese and his people would rather have him as king than 'their late conqueror' Mata'afa.[31] They would indeed, and as soon as the consuls had happily recognized the newly 'elected' Laupepa as Samoa's monarch, representatives of the Vaivai came to pay him their respects and acknowledge him as their king.[32] Thus, the Powers, having ignored the lessons of the past and adhered to a concept of central government for which Samoa was not well-suited, had managed, by putting extraneous issues before political expediency and by ill-timing Laupepa's return, to compromise the Mālō-Vaivai relationship, probably their best guarantee of a stable monarchy. What did it matter that 'real friendship' seemed to exist between Laupepa and Mata'afa, that either seemed 'willing to give place to the other for the peace and good of [the] country', when even supposing such observations to have been correct, each chief's political pretensions were still substantially determined by Samoans who were not so 'enlightened'?

During the discussion of the Berlin Act which now followed among the Samoans, widespread criticism was expressed, particularly of the head-tax measure and the apparent fact of Laupepa's being set up as king for life. Even on Laupepa's side there were misgivings about the tax, but in as much as the Act, together with the consuls' joint proclamation of recognition, implied foreign support of the king and his government, he had no trouble securing his partisans' permission to sign the Act and thereby enter into a new phase of Samoa's treaty relations with

[29] *Samoa Times*, 16 November 1889.

[30] USCD Apia/18, proclamation by *ali'i* and *faipule* of Samoa, 5 December 1889. The list of names appended to this proclamation indicated the existence of several divisions already, the most notable of which pertained to Manono.

[31] *Samoa Times*, 16 November 1889.

[32] USCD Apia/18, Blacklock to Wharton, 30 December 1889 (enclosing report of meeting of Tamasese chiefs with Laupepa, 16 December 1889).

the Powers.[33] While the Mulinu'u government and the apparatus of the condominium were being established, the political front was at least outwardly calm, a state which Laupepa tried to preserve by requiring that most of the officials, including the Faipule, stay away from Mulinu'u except when attending formal meetings, such as those held to enact laws. This was, however, a period of watchful waiting, during which Mata'afa ominously remained in residence at Apia Bay and continued to use the name of Malietoa, though failing to secure from Laupepa's side an acknowledgement of his claim to share equally in the title.[34] The first break came in 1891, when several events occurred to provoke the hardening of political commitments. In March, soon after the Chief Justice had been installed and had taken up his position of 'adviser' to the Mulinu'u government, a retrospective levy of head tax was announced, with provision being made for the previously-mentioned system of tax-farming. Allowing the poor return to have been due in part to the almost universal opinion that only the work force should ever be taxed anyway,[35] this measure was still a test of the government's political support which exposed its weakness in a number of areas. Another significant event, occurring in April, was the death of Tamasese,[36] which, rather like Laupepa's deportation in 1887, had the effect of simplifying the struggle for power. Soon afterwards, both Laupepa and Mata'afa, the first of whom had the larger backing in A'ana, laid claim to the *pāpā* of that district.[37] In turn, Laupepa called a fine-mat distribution to declare and set the seal upon his accession to the position of Tupu, that is, to consolidate his own support and challenge his rival; while Mata'afa, for his part, removed to Malie, taking that Malietoa village as the centre of an opposition movement or 'government'.[38] The 'real friendship' between the two chiefs had clearly come to naught.

In the past, the political fortunes of Mata'afa and Laupepa had, in each case, run to a pattern. The former, according to the opportunities open to him, had chopped and changed between the Tupua and Malietoa sides, for one reason or another always failing to gain top honours and slipping back into relative obscurity. Laupepa, on the other hand, had

[33] ibid., Malietoa Laupepa to consuls, 17 April 1890 (with Blacklock to Wharton, 19 April 1890).

[34] MS., Gurr, 7/2, Malietoa Talanivalu (Laupepa) to Malietoa Mata'afa, 29 July 1890.

[35] e.g. MS., Gurr, 7/2, Proceedings of A'ana District meeting, 26 May 1892; USCD Apia/20, Blacklock to Wharton, 9 November 1892.

[36] *Samoa Times*, 18 April 1891.

[37] MS., Gurr, 7/2, *ali'i* and *faipule* of Leulumoega to Malietoa Mata'afa, 28 December 1891.

[38] MP I, 'Tusi uiga i Malie. T.A. 1891-92', containing letters to and from Malietoa Laupepa, and to and from Mata'afa, relative to their intrigues and counterintrigues.

usually got off to a bad start, but he had been consistent in his basic
political alignments and from every contest had emerged occupying a
leading position. In the early 1890s the two chiefs remained true to
established form. Again, Laupepa made a poor showing at first—not by
losing a battle, but by failing to engage in one. For a period of two
years there were always 'good reasons' why his party should not meet
with force the challenge made against it. The fundamental problem, no
doubt, was the reluctance of the Malietoa people, who were divided
between the two contenders, to fight among themselves, lest in the process they lose their pre-eminence to the Tupua side.[39] The resemblance to
conditions in the 1860s, when Laupepa and Talavou had been rivals,
will be apparent.[40] On the present occasion, Malie and about half the
rest of Tuamasaga were teamed with most of Manono, forming the
nucleus of the Mata'afa party, which also had by way of alliances substantial backing in Atua and Itu-o-Fafine and also some elsewhere. The
core of Laupepa's support consisted of Afega and the balance of the
remaining half of Tuamasaga, together with most of Fa'asaleleaga, with
which faction were loosely allied the majority of the people of the A'ana
and Itu-o-Tane and at least half of Atua.[41] On paper, then, Laupepa had
the larger party, but on both sides the prevailing spirit of the moment was
not that of war but of political intrigue and negotiation, one of the first
objects of which was to secure general recognition of a single Malietoa.[42]

The second problem, aggravated by the first, concerned the position of
the Powers. It was surely due in part to their choice of Laupepa that he
now had more Samoan support than Mata'afa, but when it came to the
immediate and practical question of crushing a 'rebellion', what would
they do? Until it was known what action, if any, the Powers would
take, the local European officials, and also some of the leading chiefs of
the Mulinu'u régime, were against the government's launching an attack
or provoking hostilities. Laupepa was accordingly persuaded to give up
his plan for gathering and distributing fine mats.[43] A short time later,

[39] e.g. MP I, Telea to chiefs of Vaimauga and Si'umu, 5 July 1891.
[40] cf. chapter 11, above.
[41] MP I, *passim*.
[42] e.g. MP I, *Faipule* of the *mālō* of Malietoa at Mulinu'u to Mata'afa, 8 July 1891
and 'I.T.M. Mata'afa, Le Tupu o Samoa' to 'Tuisimau ma lou Tuamasaga', 3
June 1892. Each letter was headed 'Mālō o Samoa'.
[43] MP I, Lauaki to Malietoa Laupepa, 27 October 1891. The ceremony that Laupepa
wanted held would have involved the accumulation of mats from the *aiga* which
acknowledged him as their *tama* (willingly or otherwise) and, by way of contracting for services, the redistribution of them to all the principal orator groups
which would accept them. On the largest scale, this process could run to a series
of distributions resulting in confirmation of the *tama'āiga* as Tafa'ifā. Mata'afa
had had the same plan as Laupepa, but had been prevented from carrying it out.
It had been Tamasese's attempt to accumulate mats in respect of the Tafa'ifā

however, he began using the Tui A'ana title and, perhaps with the hope of getting around his foreign advisers, made appeals to his connections in various districts for a series of 'independent' actions against his enemies.[44] These appeals, however, failed and an impasse was reached. So many of the government's supporters and sympathizers were then unwilling to fight that some direct encouragement, even active assistance, was wanted from the Powers if the Malie opposition were to be broken up immediately. But because war seemed unlikely, the political situation had not taken on a sufficiently critical appearance to convince the Powers that intervention was really necessary.

As long as it was uncertain to which party the distinction of Mālō would pertain—it was claimed by the leaders of both—the task of enforcing the laws of Mulinu'u proved almost impossible to discharge, except among the Malietoa people loyal to Laupepa. The 'rebels', of course, flatly refused to recognize the laws at all, and to have tried subjecting them to Mulinu'u's alleged authority would have meant war. The situation was not much different, however, on the fringes of Laupepa's own party, among the people who 'looked towards' him rather than Mata'afa but were not going to be among the first to enter the barricades for him. In the Savai'i sub-district of Vaisigano, for example, Laupepa's local judge, Tonumaipe'a Tulei, was told by former adherents of Tamasese that they acknowledged no laws of the Mulinu'u régime because they saw no evidence that a Mālō had been 'established'. To that end, they argued, the treaty Powers had contributed nothing, having only protected Laupepa, not actively advanced his cause. Let it be shown that the king really had a Mālō and then the people would respect and observe the decisions taken at Mulinu'u.[45] But here was the germ of another paradox, for while the Powers were being criticized for not backing up the party they recognized and, in a sense, had created, Laupepa would have been much more highly regarded if he had not depended upon or waited for them to assist him. As Tulei protested in his report to Mulinu'u, the Mālō was certainly in existence already and he believed it would never fall, yet 'the will of God [was] not known'.[46]

As the Powers dallied, considering various objections to the initiation

which had finally precipitated the war of 1887-8. After that the next general 'call for the mats' was in 1901, when one large distribution was conducted for Mata'afa under German supervision (GCA 176/1, Gosche to Salt, 29 November 1900; *Samoanische Zeitung*, 22 June 1901).

[44] MP I, King Malietoa to *faipule* at Mulinu'u, 23 December 1891 (and accompanying letters to chiefs of various districts, 21 December 1891).

[45] MS., Gurr, 14, Tonumaipe'a Tulei to Malietoa Laupepa, 1 July 1891.

[46] *loc. cit.* Tulei had seen how chiefly authority had been enhanced by the British administration of Fiji and he expressed to Laupepa the wish that the Mulinu'u régime should have similar support from one or more of the treaty Powers.

of hostilities, the Malie party grew increasingly provocative in word and gesture until, by mid-1893, the balance of opinion within the Mulinu'u régime had shifted in favour of mounting an early attack, regardless of whether it had foreign support. That opinion, Laupepa told the consuls, was unalterable. If the Powers helped, that would please him; but they must do nothing to prevent or frustrate the assault, lest his party break up as a consequence.[47] Succumbing to this argument, which no doubt had some validity, Germany and Britain quickly detailed three warships to Samoa under instructions to act as required on behalf of Laupepa's government. By the time the vessels arrived, however, the conflict had already started and the aggressors, greatly outnumbering the Mata'afa forces,[48] were clearly headed for victory. None the less, the naval commanders intervened, with the object of punishing the 'rebels' and restoring peace and, as a result, the war ended on an unprecedentedly harsh and false note that was to reverberate throughout Samoa for a long while thereafter. Holed up at Manono, whence they had fled from Malie, the Mata'afa warriors were required by the commanders, under guarantee of safe conduct, to surrender their leaders and their arms and subsequently to return to their homes, which demand, once complied with, was followed by the government party's sacking of a defenceless Manono, a contravention of terms previously accepted by Laupepa and his chiefs. Despite the 'perfidy' of the government, the commanders proceeded to make an 'example' of its enemies: Mata'afa and ten other prominent chiefs were exiled to the Marshall Islands for an indefinite period; twenty-four of the 'worst characters' among the remaining leaders were sentenced to three years' imprisonment with hard labour, with provision being made for the government's confiscation of their lands if they tried to escape;[49] eighty-seven other 'chiefs and heads of families' were fined two hundred dollars each, to be paid within a year, during which time their lands would be held as security; and fines totalling nearly seventeen thousand dollars were levied upon sixteen villages.[50] In Tutuila, where an offshoot of Mata'afa's revolt had developed, similar action was taken.[51]

For several months after the fighting had stopped, warships remained in Samoa, and though a proposed plan of general disarmament was

[47] USCD Apia/21, Malietoa to Blacklock, 20 May 1893 (with Blacklock to Wharton, 23 May 1893).

[48] Though most of Laupepa's warriors came only from Tuamasaga, Fa'asaleleaga and Falealili (in Atua).

[49] Some of these prisoners were soon pardoned and released (USCD, Apia/21, Schmidt to consuls, 18 June 1894).

[50] USCD Apia/21, Blacklock to Quincy, 15 August 1893; *Samoa Times*, 'The Samoan Civil War of 1893'.

[51] USCD Apia/21, Blacklock to Quincy, 7 September 1893 (with enclosures), and Blacklock to Uhl, 1 January 1894 (with enclosures).

abandoned as impracticable, the government was given naval assistance towards collecting head tax, most of the levy for 1892 being paid by the end of 1893! Then, as the stormy season began, the naval commanders, mindful of the Apia 'hurricane' disaster of 1889, departed, leaving Laupepa and his chiefs to carry on alone. Unaided, the government soon proved, however, pathetically infirm and quite incapable of enforcing its edicts. Foreigners, not Samoans, had 'established' the Mālō, and if it were to persist with any effect under its present leadership, foreigners would have to maintain it. More than that, Mata'afa's removal had opened the way to other contenders for the *pāpā*, one of these being the second Tamasese, the son of the first, who drew away much of Mulinu'u's A'ana and Atua support and with it Laupepa's hold on the Tui A'ana title. Indeed, as soon as Mata'afa's movement had been crushed and the German and British warships had left, a new 'rebellion' was hatched at Leulumoega and Lufilufi which, for the next five years, kept re-emerging during the seasons when there were no warships in Samoa. Whatever control the government seemed to have outside its own body of partisans was achieved largely by means of periodic naval intervention on its behalf. Needless to say, the small increment of revenue thereby gained from the head tax, a measure taken by Laupepa and the European officials as one of the principal criteria of the government's success and by its opponents as a major object of resistance, was never equal to the cost of collecting it.[52]

Long before the government ceased to exist it was breaking up from within, a process which was both cause and effect of its heavy reliance upon foreign support. Apart from the objections raised by some members of the government to the pursuit of financial and other policies that seemed to favour alien interests at the expense of the Samoans, there was the question of Laupepa's ill health to consider. By the end of 1896 he was an invalid, reported to be suffering from some form of paralysis, and it was assumed that he had only a short while to live. Who, then, would succeed him? His own son, Tanumafili, was very young at that time, hence not a likely contender by Samoan standards. Fa'alata, the son of Talavou, was more acceptable, and already moves were afoot in Fa'asaleleaga, where he lived, to advance his claim to the Malietoa title. Relative to broader issues than that of the Malietoa title alone, however, Fa'alata was also a parvenu compared with Mata'afa, who, owing to the untimely intervention of the Powers, had not been greatly discredited by his defeat in 1893. What is more, Mata'afa had equal superiority on the Tupua side. Accordingly, there developed a movement, cutting across the Mulinu'u government and the long-smouldering 'Tūmua rebellion',

[52] FOCP 6437, 6511, 6663, 6818, 6855, 6901, 6946, 7025, and USCD, Apia/21-24, *passim*.

to secure his return to Samoa, in order that the strongest possible contender might be ready to lay claim to Laupepa's place as Tupu.[53] Laupepa was furious at first, obviously because he had other ideas on the matter, but once the chiefs who controlled the Mata'afa title had pledged their allegiance to Mulinu'u, he agreed to ask the Powers for Mata'afa's release,[54] which request was granted on the proviso that the exiled chiefs should take a similar oath of loyalty.[55] By coincidence, this decision became known in Samoa just as Laupepa died—it was late in August 1898—and Mata'afa returned home a month later, at a most propitious time for the launching of a new political adventure.[56]

[53] USCD, Apia/23, Churchill to Rockhill, 11 January 1897.

[54] USCD, Apia/24, Churchill to Day, 4 October 1897.

[55] In the interests of peace, the consuls argued that Mata'afa, if loyal to the government, might be able to suppress the main opposition party, Tamasese's (FOCP 7141, Maxse to Salisbury, 19 April 1898).

[56] USCD, Apia/24, Osborn to Moore, 30 August 1898, 31 August 1898 (with draft of Mata'afa's oath of allegiance to 'the Government heretofore existing under King Malietoa Laupepa and to the successor of the said Malietoa Laupepa when chosen'), and 26 September 1898.

# CONCLUSION: THE END OF THE CONDOMINIUM[1]

UNDER the Berlin Act, Malietoa Laupepa's successor was to 'be duly elected according to the laws and customs of Samoa'. When news of Laupepa's death was received in Berlin, the German foreign minister, Count von Bülow, made a suggestion for the partition of the islands that would, instead, have terminated both the Act and the kingship.[2] The British and American Governments considered, however, that events should be allowed to develop in the way the Act envisaged.

In Samoa the situation was a complex one. No law had been made regarding the election of a king. Indeed, any attempt to establish a formal electoral procedure would have encountered the opposition of a large part of the country. Contention for the kingship was too closely related to the traditional quest for titular supremacy. Yet the office of king was not, in its nineteenth-century form, a traditional one. The manner in which custom was applicable to the conduct of an election was therefore open to dispute. Moreover, there were at least five possible contenders, of whom Mata'afa Iosefo, Tupua Tamasese Lealofi and Laupepa's schoolboy son, Tanumafili, were the strongest. For these reasons, early meetings at Mulinu'u attended by the Faipule, government officers and other leading Samoans produced no agreement.

Tūmua and Pule claimed that the right to choose a king resided with them. They favoured Mata'afa. He alone possessed the requisite experience and standing; and his succession to Malietoa Laupepa would best preserve the delicate balance between the different sections of Samoan society. His reception on his return from Jaluit also showed that a large proportion of Samoans expected him to become king. Spokesmen for Tūmua and Pule therefore addressed letters to the consuls asserting their rights and stating their conclusions. On 12 November they announced that Mata'afa had been elected king at a meeting at Leulumoega.[3]

The right of Tūmua and Pule to decide the issue was rejected by many Faipule and government officers, including those who favoured Tanumafili, and by the supporters of Tamasese. Three days after the purported election, a meeting was held at Mulinu'u of those who had held office

[1] Written by J. W. Davidson.
[2] Lepsius et al., Die Grosse Politik, XIV, 567-8.
[3] FOCP 7142, 140, Tūmua chiefs to consuls, 12 November 1898.

under Laupepa. On that occasion a proposal was made by Lauaki Namu-
lau'ulu Mamoe—probably the most influential participant in the proceedings at Leulumoega—that the consuls should be informed that the
Samoan people wished Mata'afa to be king, since a majority of those
present, in fact, favoured him. A letter was drafted to that effect, but it
was signed only by Mata'afa's supporters.[4]

None of the three consuls expressed a firm preference, at that stage,
for any of the contenders. They were all worried, however, by the differences of opinion among the Samoans and anxious that they should be
quickly resolved. The Berlin Act provided that any dispute relating to
the 'election or appointment' of a king should be referred to the Chief
Justice. But the latter was already in a position of some delicacy. Just as
the controversy over the kingship was developing, he had declared, in a
judicial decision, that the President of the municipality had acted improperly.[5] Since the Chief Justice, William Lea Chambers, was an
American and the President, Dr Raffel, a German, the decision had both
exacerbated personal antipathies and caused the Germans to raise doubts
as to the jurisdiction of the Supreme Court. The German consul thus
had misgivings about referring the matter of the kingship to Chambers
for decision. He suggested that adult males (who were to be identified
by their having been tattooed) should be asked to vote; but, as this procedure was of doubtful legality under the Act, he accepted a proposal
favoured by his two consular colleagues and the Chief Justice. This latter
was for a meeting between Chambers and representatives of the rival
contenders, at which the Samoans would be asked to sign an agreement
regarding procedure.[6]

After the meeting at Leulumoega on 12 November, Tamasese had
abandoned his candidature for the kingship and proposed, instead, that
he should become vice-king under Tanumafili. There were thus two
active groups, those supporting Mata'afa and the Tanumafili-Tamasese
combination, respectively; and each of these was invited to nominate thirteen representatives. The twenty-six Samoans met the Chief Justice on 26
November. The draft agreement presented by the latter proposed that
all parties should accept the relevant provisions of the Berlin Act as
binding. The decision at Leulumoega should be regarded as Mata'afa's
nomination, and other contenders should have till 19 December to

---

[4] MS., Te'o Tuvale.

[5] In his decision in the case of Gurr v. Raffel. Gurr, acting on behalf of a client,
had directly approached the Samoan Government in a matter which Raffel considered should have been presented through him, since, as President of the
municipality, he was the government's adviser. In retaliation, Raffel had inter-
cepted and retained a letter from Malietoa to Gurr (FOCP 7142, 22-4, 42-3,
93-9).

[6] ibid., 137-40, Maxse to Salisbury, 28 November 1898.

nominate. If further nominations were received, the Chief Justice would announce his decision within ten days.[7]

At this meeting, as at the earlier one on 15 November, Lauaki pleaded for unanimous support of Mata'afa. He explained how it had been solemnly resolved at the signing of the *Lackawanna* agreement in 1881 that Malietoa Laupepa's successor should be a representative of Sa Tupua. This promise, he declared, could not be broken. Lauaki's speech greatly impressed its hearers; and the meeting adjourned to consider its implications. After consideration, however, Tanumafili's supporters decided to persist with his candidature. The Mata'afa party, as a consequence, declined to sign the proposed agreement. By this refusal, its leaders seem to have hoped to prevent the issue coming before the Supreme Court and to leave the way open for its solution by other means. During the following weeks, they installed themselves at Mulinu'u and treated Mata'afa as though he were already king. They disseminated rumours that the consuls had decided to recognize Mata'afa and sought to intimidate their opponents in all parts of the country. Moreover, they were aware that the Germans—probably not uninfluenced by the ethnologist, Augustin Krämer—now favoured their candidate.[8]

On 19 December, however, following the formal nomination of Tanumafili, Chambers began to hear the case for the two contenders. On behalf of Tanumafili, it was claimed that he held the titles of Tuia'ana, Tuiatua, Gatoaitele and Tamasoāli'i, as well as that of Malietoa. Lauaki, speaking for Mata'afa, denied that Tanumafili held any of these titles. Not even that of Malietoa had been conferred in accordance with custom. In this contention Lauaki was supported by spokesmen for Malie and Manono. Since Lauaki himself was the most important orator of Safotulafai, Tanumafili lacked the support of at least three of the centres involved in the bestowal of the title. In addition, at the age of eighteen, he was far too young, in Samoan eyes, for the assumption of high office. Even if the promise of 1881 were held to be irrelevant, Tanumafili's case was thus a fatally weak one. But these considerations did not influence the Chief Justice's decision. Towards the end of the hearing, the two counsel appearing for Tanumafili raised the question of Mata'afa's eligibility. They argued that the Act must be read in conjunction with the protocols of the Berlin conference. That of the fifth session included an agreement that Mata'afa should be ineligible for the king-

[7] ibid., 149-50, Chambers to consuls, 29 November 1898.

[8] Krämer, who published the very important work *Die Samoa-Inseln* several years later, was in Samoa at this time and in touch with both the German consul and Mata'afa (e.g. see FOCP 7233, Sturdee to Pearson, 14 December 1898). On the general position at this time see: FOCP 7233, 52-3, Memoranda by Chief Justice, 29 November, 1, 2, 7 December 1898; and USCD 25, Osborn to Hill, 27 December 1898.

ship. Since this had never been revoked, it was, they contended, still binding. Chambers accepted this argument; and on 31 December he declared that Malietoa Tanumafili—as he referred to him—was the only eligible candidate and therefore King of Samoa.[9]

During the preceding weeks, large numbers of Samoans from the outer villages had gathered in and around Apia. Many of them carried arms. The Mata'afa party, which believed that Europeans had sought to influence the Chief Justice against it, was not unprepared for the actual decision. On 1 January 1899 its forces advanced on the town and overwhelmed their opponents. Tanumafili, Tamasese Lealofi and several of their leading supporters took refuge on board H.M.S. *Porpoise*, which was anchored in the harbour. On 4 January the consuls recognized a provisional government composed of Mata'afa and the thirteen chiefs and orators who had been representing his interests, with Dr Raffel as its principal executive officer.[10]

The provisional government's main concern was the issue of the kingship. It attempted to close the Supreme Court. It threatened Tanumafili and Tamasese with a permanent loss of all their rights unless they accepted Mata'afa. It imprisoned or banished many leading supporters of Tanumafili and disarmed his fighting men, who were compelled to acknowledge Mata'afa as king. Its individual members sought to harass groups favouring Tanumafili in their own districts; and, in some places, villages were looted and burned. But, since the government recognized that the issue would not be resolved by the Samoans alone, it also prepared a statement to the Powers explaining why, in its opinion, Mata'afa was the only acceptable candidate and therefore the only man who could unite the country.[11]

Gradually, as January and February passed, the situation became more strained. The Germans firmly supported the provisional government, while the British and Americans became increasingly antagonistic to it. Formally, the German attitude derived from the joint consular decision of 4 January and from the proposition that a government of some kind must be kept in being till the crisis was finally ended. But, practically, it was intended to advance German interests by confirming Mata'afa's leadership. The attitude of the British and Americans had an equally complex basis. They were anxious to uphold the decision of the Supreme

[9] On the Supreme Court hearing see: MS., Gurr, 6, 18; FOCP 7233, 54-8, extract from *Samoan Weekly Herald*, 24 December 1898; ibid., 149-52, decision of Chief Justice.

[10] FOCP 7233, 140-9, Report of events in Samoa from 31 December 1898 to 15 January 1899; and MS., Te'o Tuvale.

[11] FOCP 7233, 132-69, Maxse to Salisbury, 23 January 1899 (and enclosures); FOCP 7234, 50-61, Maxse to Salisbury, 22 March 1899 (and enclosures); MS., Gurr, 6, 17.

Court and to show disapproval of many of the actions of the provisional government; but they were also motivated by a belief that many of Mata'afa's supporters would abandon him once Tanumafili was firmly established as king.

Early in March the Anglo-American position was strengthened by the arrival of Admiral Kautz, in u.s.s. *Philadelphia*, with instructions from Washington 'to act in concert with the majority of the Consular Representatives of the Treaty Powers'.[12] Kautz convened a meeting of the consuls and naval officers of the three Powers and, since the British and Americans were of the same opinion, issued a proclamation declaring that 'it was agreed' that the provisional government was illegal. This action provoked a counter proclamation by the Germans and led to the resumption of civil war. The provisional government retired from Mulinu'u, but its armed forces re-formed on the outskirts of Apia. British and American warships shelled the positions where these forces were congregated. And, on 23 March, Tanumafili was installed as king, at Mulinu'u, by his foreign protectors. During the ensuing month, the forces of the new government were armed and organized by the British; and they were supported in action against the forces of Mata'afa by men from the British and American warships. In the environs of Apia law and order were restored, though largely by the British. But the country as a whole was even farther from possessing a stable and effective administration than it had been at the beginning of January.[13]

The governments of the three Powers had all been greatly distressed by the news that civil war had again broken out. There was a widespread conviction that many of their officials in Samoa—both consular and naval —had acted rashly. Admiral Kautz was sent amended instructions; and President McKinley telegraphed his regrets to the German Emperor for what had occurred. The Germans proposed that all three governments should withdraw the officials who had been involved in recent events. This suggestion was declined by Britain and ignored by the United States. But another German proposal gained the support of the other Powers. This was for the immediate despatch of a tripartite commission. It was agreed that the commission should exercise full political authority while it was in the islands, that it should report on the causes of the recent troubles, and that it should make recommendations for the future. On one matter, however, there was an initial difference of opinion. The

---

12 FOCP 7234, 68-9, Kautz to consuls, 11 March 1899.

13 On the events of this period see: FOCP 7234, 64-73, Maxse to Salisbury, 22 March 1899 (and enclosures); ibid., 108-9, Maxse to Salisbury, 8 April 1899 (and enclosures); ibid., 109-16, Maxse to Salisbury, 14 April 1899 (and enclosures); USCD 25, Osborn to Hill, 28 April 1899 (and enclosures); and MS., Te'o Tuvale.

Germans, for obvious reasons, insisted that the commission's decisions should be unanimous, while the British held that, in respect of most subjects, a majority opinion should suffice. Eventually, however, Count von Bülow remarked to the British ambassador that the impasse threatened 'to very seriously impair the good relations' between the two countries; and, shortly afterwards, the British Government accepted the requirement of unanimity.[14]

The commissioners appointed were Baron Speck von Sternberg, Mr Charles Eliot and Mr Bartlett Tripp. The two former were diplomatic officers serving in Washington, the latter a former American minister to Vienna. They arrived in Apia on 13 May, in u.s.s. *Badger*.

Fighting had ceased when news of the commission's appointment was received in Samoa. But the situation was that of an armed truce, and both parties were anxious for a genuine peace. The commission decided that its first task should be to seek the surrender of all Samoan firearms. Since Tanumafili's forces were effectively controlled by the British, it saw its main problem as that of persuading Mata'afa and his followers of the advantages of the proposal. European residents assured the commissioners that their chances were slim and that, if promises were given, they would not be kept. They were somewhat surprised therefore that, at their first meeting with Mata'afa, he solemnly declared: 'Mataafa . . . will surrender his guns'.[15] They were greatly relieved when, at the time agreed on, most of the Mata'afa party's guns were handed over and arrangements were made for the surrender of those that it had not, by then, been possible to bring in. This success removed the one difficulty that might have stood in the way of the disarming of Tanumafili's forces.[16]

When the two armies had been, in effect, disbanded, and their members had begun to trickle back to their villages, the commissioners were able to turn to the other aspects of their work. They believed that the existence of the kingship had been the major cause of trouble. Since contention for it was so closely related to the traditional rivalry between the leading chiefs and their followers, unsuccessful candidates and their supporters were bound to oppose the elevation of a chief chosen from their opponents. All the commissioners had private doubts about the Chief Justice's decision; but they agreed that it should not be challenged. Instead, they proposed to Tanumafili that he should abdicate. This proposal seems not to have been unwelcome to him. He had become a

---

[14] Langer, *The diplomacy of imperialism 1890-1902*, 622; Ryden, 562-4; FOCP 7234, 6-17, 12-23 *passim*.

[15] Tripp, *My trip to Samoa*, 64.

[16] On the proceedings of the commission, see: FOCP 7235, *passim*; USCD 25, Osborn to Hill, 12 June 1899; Tripp, *passim*.

candidate through family pressure, not personal ambition; and he had experienced little but humiliation, danger and discomfort since his candidature had been successful. For months he had been suggesting that he should go overseas to continue his education. On 10 June he resigned his office. On the same day the commission issued a proclamation. After referring to the abdication, it stated that the kingship was abolished and ordered that the functions formerly vested in the king and his councillors should be performed by the consuls during the period that the commission itself remained in Samoa.

The commissioners then turned to the problem of formulating recommendations for the future government of the country. In principle, they all favoured some form of partition of the islands; but, in case this should not commend itself to the Powers, they drafted a series of radical amendments to the Act of 1889. These provided for the vesting of executive power in an Administrator, appointed by the three metropolitan governments, and of legislative power in a Legislative Council, composed of the Administrator and three nominated members. The Samoans would be associated with public affairs through the introduction of a system 'analogous to that which works successfully in Fiji'. Samoa would be divided into districts based, so far as possible, on the traditional district organization. In each district, a chief would be appointed and given limited powers. The district chiefs (or 'Governors') would jointly constitute a 'Native Assembly' that would meet annually to discuss 'native' problems and make recommendations to the Administrator and Legislative Council.[17]

With this work of constitution-making completed, the commissioners set out on a tour of the country, in order to explain their proposals. On their return to Apia, they held a meeting of some 400 chiefs for the same purpose. Despite their bizarre disregard for Samoan custom, and for many of the factors that had produced thirty years of intermittent civil war, they encountered little open opposition. Indeed, the proposals were formally endorsed by representatives of both Mata'afa's and Tanumafili's parties. The two groups of representatives also went through a ceremony of reconciliation in the presence of the commissioners. The compliancy of the Samoan leaders owed something, no doubt, to their weariness with fratricidal strife and as much to their wish to show respect to visiting strangers of high rank; but, in all probability, it owed most of all to the unreality to them of the proposals and to the novelty of the situation in which they were placed. It had little relevance to their future attitudes or political behaviour.

Before they left Samoa in the second half of July, the commissioners

17 FOCP 7235, 52-63, High Commission to Salisbury, 18 July 1899 (and enclosures).

**DD**

had to establish a provisional government to hold office till effect could be given to their recommendations, or till some alternative solution should be agreed to. They decided that this should be composed of the consuls of the three Powers, with the recently installed President of the municipality, Dr Wilhelm Solf, as its adviser.

Meanwhile, further consideration had been given in German official circles to the question of partition—both as an isolated problem and as part of a broader redefinition of spheres of influence in the extra-European world.[18] When the commissioners had completed their work, the subject was taken up more openly. In August and early September the German Government ascertained that the Americans were favourably disposed and would be satisfied if the United States obtained Tutuila and Manu'a. For the Germans, the problem thus became one of reaching an agreement with Great Britain. The British Government, initially, was reluctant to negotiate, in part because of the strong feeling in New Zealand and Australia that Samoa should be annexed by Britain. But British involvement in the Boer War made it important to maintain friendly relations with Germany. When the German Emperor accepted an invitation to visit England in November, his government insisted that an Anglo-German agreement on Samoa should be reached before his arrival.

The negotiations between the two governments were complicated but low-keyed. German interest in Samoa was based on sentiment, rather than economic or strategic considerations. Indeed, the German colonial council resolved that Samoa should be abandoned in return for concessions elsewhere. On the British side, it was not believed that a German colony in Samoa would be a serious danger to Australia and New Zealand. None the less, many alternative solutions were advanced and rejected before a settlement was reached and embodied in an agreement signed on 14 November. Under this agreement, all of Samoa west of 171° west longitude would become German. In return, Germany transferred to Britain her treaty rights in Tonga, agreed to a shifting of the boundary between the British and German spheres in the Solomons, and made a number of other concessions.[19]

Although certain lesser problems still remained to be settled, the Anglo-German agreement really determined the future status of Samoa. A tripartite convention was signed on behalf of all three Powers on 2 December; and in the early months of 1901 Germany and the United States established administrative control in their respective parts of the

18 e.g. see GFO South Seas no. 5: Samoa Islands, I, Hatzfeldt to Hohenlohe, 9 March 1899.

19 There is a considerable literature on the partition of Samoa. See especially: Langer, 619-24, 626-28A; Ryden, 558-74; FOCP 7314, *passim*.

archipelago. Samoan leaders were resentful that their country had been partitioned. Many in the western islands were angry, too, that it should be the Germans who were their new rulers. But, as the problem of governing a multi-cultural community had proved beyond their capacity, it had been inevitable that their future should be decided in the light of Western diplomatic interests, rather than their own. They had lost an independence that had become largely nominal; but, as the future was to show, they had lost none of their will to retain their own culture or to struggle for control of their own affairs.

# Bibliography

[This Bibliography includes all manuscript sources and printed official records that were included in the card bibliography compiled by the author. Published books and articles, newspapers and unpublished theses have been included only if they are cited in the footnotes.]

## I MANUSCRIPT SOURCES

**A OFFICIAL**

### Germany

Consulate, Apia. Fragmentary records, 1879-99. Held at the National Archives of New Zealand, Wellington

Foreign Office, Berlin. Documents relating to three-power negotiations in 1899. South Seas Series No. 5: Samoa Islands. Vols 1-4, 7-9. Held at the Hauptarchiv, Berlin

Reichstag Papers, Nos 110, 138, 210 and 214, 1889. Held at the National Archives of New Zealand, Wellington

### Great Britain

Admiralty, London. Adm. 1-: Cruise reports. Held at the Public Record Office, London

Colonial Office, London. C.O. 225: Western Pacific High Commission, Original Correspondence. Held at the Public Record Office, London

Commander-in-chief, Australian Station. In-letters and out-letters. 41 vols. Held at the National Archives of New Zealand, Wellington

Consulate, Apia. Records. Series 1—Foreign Office to Consul; 2—General Inwards Correspondence; 3—Consul to Foreign Office; 4—Letters to Samoan Government and Chiefs; 5—General Outwards Correspondence. Also miscellaneous, uncatalogued fragments. Held at the National Archives of New Zealand, Wellington

Consulate, Tahiti. Records. Miscellaneous Vol. 1, 1827-42. Held at the Mitchell Library, Sydney

Deputy Commissioner, Western Pacific, Apia. Letterbooks, Vols 1 (1878-84) and 2 (1893-6). Also miscellaneous fragments 1878-83. Held at the National Archives of New Zealand, Wellington

Foreign Office, London. F.O. 58: Pacific Islands, 1822-1905. 345 vols. Complete series consulted for 1839-60, incidental references thereafter. Held at the Public Record Office, London

Secretary of State for Foreign Affairs. Despatches, 1840. A1282. Report concerning the conduct of C. H. Hart of the cutter *Lambton* at Ascension and Nuttic in 1836 and 1837: and concerning Capt. Dendoit. Held at the Mitchell Library, Sydney

## Hawaii

Government Archives, Honolulu. Foreign Office and executive records, 1853-9 and 1887

## Samoa

Brandeis, Eugen. Tamasese-Brandeis Papers, 1887-8; official records kept by Brandeis. Held at the National Archives of New Zealand, Wellington

Government, Apia. Papers relating to the Administration under the Berlin Act during the 1890s. Held at the National Archives of New Zealand, Wellington

Government, Apia. Miscellaneous land cases and legal records, 1874, 1895 and 1899. Held at the National Archives of New Zealand, Wellington

Land Commission and Supreme Court, Apia. Records of disposition of land claims. Held at the Public Record Office, Apia

Malietoa Government, Apia. Papers, 1891-9. Held at the National Archives of New Zealand, Wellington

Steinberger, Albert S. Papers, 1873-5. Held at the Marist Archives, Mulivai

Taimua-Faipule Government, Apia. A324: records, in-letters and out-letters 1876-7. Held at the Mitchell Library, Sydney

Western Samoa Land and Titles Court. Genealogical records, n.d. Held at the office of the Court

*American Administration*

Government, Pago Pago. Records. Few references only to 19th century. Held at Pago Pago

*British Military Administration*

Native Department. Records. Series 1—Inward letters, 1914-18; 2—Miscellaneous official papers. Held at the National Archives of New Zealand, Wellington

*German Administration*

Administration, Apia. Various records, including District Administration. Various dates. Held at the National Archives of New Zealand, Wellington

## United States

Consular Despatches. 1843-1901. 26 vols. Held at the U.S. National Archives, Washington, D.C.

Consular Instructions. U.S.C.I./9-19, 1864-74. Held at the U.S. National Archives, Washington, D.C.

Navy. Letters from Commanders to Secretary of Navy. Microcopy 147, Rolls 21 (2 Jan. 1836 to 29 Dec. 1837), 97 (1 Jan. to 30 April 1872), 103 (1 Jan. to 30 June 1875) and 106 (1 May to 30 June 1876). Held at the U.S. National Archives, Washington, D.C.

Navy. Letters from Commanding Officers of Squadrons to Secretary of Navy. Microcopy 89, Roll 37; Pacific Squadron, 4 Aug. 1854 to 30 June 1856. Held at the U.S. National Archives, Washington, D.C.

Navy. Records relating to exploring expedition under the command of Lt Charles Wilkes, 1836-42. Microcopy 75. Held at the U.S. National Archives, Washington, D.C.

B MISSION

London Missionary Society, London. South Seas Journals. Various dates. Held at the L.M.S., Livingstone House, London

London Missionary Society, London. South Seas Letters, 1836-79. Held at the L.M.S., Livingstone House, London

Methodist Church of Australasia, Department of Overseas Missions. Official records, Vols 13-26, 102, 115, 115a and 171. Held at the Mitchell Library, Sydney

C PRIVATE

Bates, George Handy. Samoan papers. Relate to Commissioner's investigation of 1886 and Berlin negotiations of 1889. Described in William D. Lewis, *Calendar* (*q.v.*). Held at the University of Delaware

Brown, George. Correspondence and papers, 1870-1917. Vols 1 (A1686-18), 4(A1686-21) and 5 (A1686-22). Held at the Mitchell Library, Sydney

——, Letterbooks, 1865-75. 2 Vols (A1686-1 and A1686-2). Held at the Mitchell Library, Sydney

——, Journal, 1860-74. 3 vols (A1686-8 to A1686-10). Held at the Mitchell Library, Sydney

——, Proverbs of Samoa, 1913. A1686-27. Held at the Mitchell Library, Sydney

——, 'Some nature myths from Samoa', 1910. With A1686-25. Held at the Mitchell Library, Sydney

Buzacott, Aaron. Journal, 1842. A381. Held at the Mitchell Library, Sydney

——, Journal of visit to Samoa, 1836. A381. Held at the Mitchell Library, Sydney

Churchill, William. 'Samoa o le Vavau', c. 1902. Typescript, English and Samoan. Held at the Auckland Institute and Museum

Darnand, J. 'Un premier siècle d'Apostolat à Samoa', 1945. Typescript. Held at the Marist Archives, Mulivai

Deihl, Joseph R. Papers, various dates. Held at the Marist Archives, Mulivai

Dumont d'Urville, J. S. C. 'Voyage of the "Coquille", 1822-25, and of the "Astrolabe", 1826-29'. A1827. Held at the Mitchell Library, Sydney

Dyson, Martin. Journals. 4 vols, 1858-65 (A2579), 1867-72 (A2580), 1881-83 (A2581) and 1890 (A2582). Held at the Mitchell Library, Sydney

——, 'Life of a Meltham Methodist', 1830-94. A2584. Held at the Mitchell Library, Sydney

——, 'Light and shade in Samoan Missionary life', n.d. With other papers on Samoa, A2583. Held at the Mitchell Library, Sydney

Ella, Samuel. Correspondence and papers, 1836-98. 15 vols (A202 to A216). Held at the Mitchell Library, Sydney

——, Diary, 1847-51. B248. Held at the Mitchell Library, Sydney

——, Letterbooks, 1849-75. 2 vols (A200). Held at the Mitchell Library, Sydney

Ella, Samuel and J. B. Stair. Miscellaneous Samoan manuscripts. A229. Held at the Mitchell Library, Sydney

Elyard, W. Papers. Vol. IV (A2884), 1823. Held at the Mitchell Library, Sydney

Gipps, Sir George, Governor of N.S.W. Despatches, 1840. Also contains material by Thomas Heath. Held at the Mitchell Library, Sydney

Graf, Max. Papers. Held at the Department of Pacific History, Australian National University, Canberra

Grey, Sir George. Manuscript Collections. File 58: Samoa, Politics and Government. Held at the Auckland Public Library

Gunson, W. Niel. 'Evangelical missionaries in the South Seas, 1797-1860', 1959. Ph.D. thesis, Australian National University, Canberra

Gurr, Edwin W. Papers, personal and official, chiefly 1885-1900. Held at the Alexander Turnbull Library, Wellington

Hale, Horatio. Notebook, n.d. A321. Held at the Mitchell Library, Sydney

Hardie, Charles. Diary, 1835-37. Containing cuttings, etc. of later dates. A368. Held at the Mitchell Library, Sydney

Henry, Brother Fred. 'A history of Samoa'. Apia, Education Dept. of Western Samoa, n.d. 127 pp. cyclostyled. A copy held at the Department of Pacific History, Australian National University, Canberra

Hope, Charles W. Journals, 1865-68. Covering cruise of H.M.S. 'Brisk'. 2 vols. Held at the Alexander Turnbull Library, Wellington

Horn, Jason. 'Primacy of the Pacific under the Hawaiian Kingdom', 1951. M.A. thesis, University of Hawaii, Honolulu

Lapérouse, Jean F. G. de and J. S. C. Dumont d'Urville, et al. Letters and documents concerning the expedition in 'la Boussole' and 'l'Astrolabe', 1781-93. A304. Held at the Mitchell Library, Sydney

Marsden, Samuel. Papers. Vol. 5. Held at the Mitchell Library, Sydney

Parkes, Sir Henry. Correspondence. A885, A895, A925 and A929. Held at the Mitchell Library, Sydney

Pirie, Peter N. D. 'The geography of population in Western Samoa', 1963. Ph.D. thesis, Australian National University, Canberra

Rees, W. L. 'German activities in Samoa', 1886. A2615. Held at the Mitchell Library, Sydney

Roberts, Quincy F. 'A history of the Samoan Islands', c. 1928. Typescript. Held at the Marist Archives, Mulivai
——, 'Raising Old Glory over Uncle Sam's newest possession, Swain's Island', 1929. Typescript. Held at the Marist Archives, Mulivai
Slatyer, Thomas. Journal, 1840-45. 1 vol. (A1770). Held at the Mitchell Library, Sydney
Stevenson, Robert L. and R. T. Chatfield. Assorted Letters. As25. Held at the Mitchell Library, Sydney
Stout, Sir Robert. Papers. Files 1A, 1B, 2 and 24. Held at the Alexander Turnbull Library, Wellington
Te'o Tuvale. Account of Samoan history up to 1918. Included with papers of E. Riddell. Held at the Mitchell Library, Sydney
Turner, Peter. Journals. 3 vols, up to 1835 (B302), 1836 (B303), 1837 to June 1839 (B304). Held at the Mitchell Library, Sydney
Westbrook, George E. L. Papers, chiefly pre-1900. Held at the Alexander Turnbull Library, Wellington
Whittle, John S. Private Journal, 1838-41. Related to voyages of U.S.S. 'Vincennes', 'Sea Gull' and 'Peacock'. Vol. 1. Held at the Alderman Library of University of Virginia, Charlottesville
Williams, John. Journal of voyage with Charles Barff, 1830. A403 and A1636 (copy by Barff). Held at the Mitchell Library, Sydney
——, Journal, 1832. Held at the L.M.S., Livingstone House, London
Wilson, Samuel. Papers, 1833-40. A383. Held at the Mitchell Library, Sydney

## II  PRINTED SOURCES

A  OFFICIAL

### Australasia

Federal Council of Australasia. Official record of debates, 1886-99. Hobart, 'The Mercury' Office

### Australia

Historical Records of Australia. Series I: Governors' despatches to and from England, 1788-1848. Parliamentary Library. Vols. 1 and 3

### Germany

Auswärtiges Amt. Weissbücher, 1st session, 6 Teil 1-2, 1885: German Interests in the South Seas. German Foreign Ministry

### Great Britain

Foreign Office. Confidential Prints, Nos 2849 (1876); 3372 and 3375 (1877); 3535 and 3846 (1878); 4127 (1880); 4467 (1881); 5065, 5105 and 5150 (1885); 5159, 5199, 5258 and 5310 (1886); 5532 (1887); 5570 (1888); 5725, 5779 and 5827 (1889); 5921 (1890); 6075 (1891); 6155 and 6251 (1892); 6299 and 6391 (1893); 6437

and 6511 (1894); 6553 and 6663 (1895); 6818 (1896); 6855, 6901
and 6946 (1897); 7025 (1898); 7141-2, 7233 and 7235 (1899); 7134
and 7234 (1900); 7471 (1901). London, H.M.S.O.
Foreign Office. Diplomatic and consular reports on trade and finance
No. 1598 *Western Pacific, Report for the year 1894 on the trade of
Samoa*. London, H.M.S.O., 1895
Foreign Office, Historical Section. *German colonization*. Handbook No.
42, 1920
Parliament. Command papers, Nos 3863 and 3905 (1884); 4273 and
4584 (1883-5); 5629 (1889); 6973 (1893); 9506 (1889). London,
H.M.S.O.
Parliament. Parliamentary paper No. 425, 1837. Vol. VII, pp 1-304.
Report of the Select Committee on aborigines, Feb. to June, 1837

## New Zealand

Census and Statistics Office of the Dominion of New Zealand. *Official
Year Book*, 1883-. Wellington, Govt Printer
General Assembly. Parliamentary Papers Nos E-4 (1870); E-4 (1871);
E-2 (1872); F-3 3a, 3b, 3c (1873); A-3, 3a, 3b (1874); A-6 (1879);
A-4 (1884); A-3 (1884); A-1 (1885); A-4d (1885); A-9 (1885); A-3
(1887); A-6 (1894); A-4b (1928). Wellington, Govt Printer

## Samoa

Government. *O Tulafono i le Faasalaina o Solitulafono*. Apia, 1892
Government. *Samoa Royal Gazette*. Apia, 1892-99
Municipality of Apia. *Municipal Regulations, 1879-80*. Apia, Griffiths,
n.d.
Municipality of Apia. *Revised ordinances and regulations of the Munici-
pality of Apia, 1891-94*. Apia, 1894

## United States

Congress. House Documents No. 105 (23rd Congress, 1835); Vol. 1,
Nos. 1 and 2 (54th Congress, 1895 and 1896). Washington, Govt
Printing Office
Congress. House Executive Documents Vol. 14, No. 161 (44th Congress,
1876); Vol. 9, No. 44 (44th Congress, 1877); Vol. 28, No. 238 (50th
Congress, 1888). Washington, Govt Printing Office
Congress. House Report No. 212 (35th Congress), 1858. Washington,
Govt Printing Office
Congress. Senate Documents Vol. 2, No. 48 (61st Congress, 1910).
General Act providing for the neutrality and autonomous govern-
ment of the Samoan Islands, 1889. Washington, Govt Printing Office
Congress. Senate Executive Documents Vol. 2, No. 45 (43rd Congress,
1874); Vol. 1, No. 2 (46th Congress, 1879); Vol. 6, No. 97 (53rd
Congress, 1895). Washington, Govt Printing Office

Crose, W. M. *American Samoa. A general report by the Governor.* 1913. Washington, Govt Printing Office

B  NEWSPAPERS AND PERIODICALS

*Les Annales de La Propagation de La Foi.* 1846-75, Lyon. Vols XIX-XLIV
*Des Annales de La Société de Marie.* 1858-1900, Lyon and Roanne. Series I, Vols I-X
*Chronicle.* 1837-1866, London Missionary Society, London
*The Colonist.* 1835-1841, Sydney
*Daily Atlas.* 1832-61, Boston, Massachusetts
*Frank Leslie's Illustrated Newspaper.* New York
*New Bedford Mercury.* 1807-95(?), New Bedford, Massachusetts
*Plattsburg Republican.* 1811-1914, New York
*Samoa Times and South Seas Gazette.* 1877-81, Apia
*Samoan Reporter.* 1845-70, London Missionary Society, Leulumoega
*Samoanische Zeitung.* 1901-15, Apia
*Samoa Weekly Herald.* 1888-, Apia
*San Francisco Evening Post.* 1871-1913, San Francisco, California
*Sydney Morning Herald.* 1831-, Sydney


C  BOOKS AND ARTICLES

Aube, Théophile. *Entre deux campagnes: notes d'un marin.* Paris, Berger-Levrault, 1881. 315 pp.
Barnes, William H. ed. *The story of Laulii, a daughter of Samoa.* San Francisco, Winterburn, 1889. 255 pp.
Behrens, Karl F. *Histoire de l'expedition de trois vaisseaux envoyés par la compagnie des Indes Occidentales des Provinces-Vries, aux Terres Australes en 1721.* Vol. 1. The Hague, Compagnie des Indes Occidentales, 1739. 224 pp.
Bérard, M. *Campagne de la corvette 'l'Alcmène' en Océanie, pendant les années 1850 et 1851.* Paris, Paul Dupont, 1854. 184 pp.
Bougainville, Louis A. de. *A voyage round the world performed by order of His Most Christian Majesty in the years 1766-9.* London, Nourse, 1772. 476 pp.
Bowden, Keith Macrae. *George Bass, 1771-1803: his discoveries, romantic life and tragic disappearance.* Melbourne, O.U.P., 1952. 171 pp.
Brenchley, Julius L. *Jottings during the cruise of H.M.S. 'Curaçoa' among the South Sea islands in 1865.* London, Longmans Green, 1873. 487 pp.
Brookes, Jean Ingram. *International rivalry in the Pacific Islands, 1800-1875.* Berkeley, University of California Press, 1941. 454 pp.
Buck, Peter H. *Vikings of the Sunrise.* New York, Stokes, 1938. 335 pp.
Bull, W. K. *A trip to Tahiti and other islands in the South Seas.* Melbourne, Edgar Ray, 1858. 36 pp.

Cazalis, E. *Rapport du Capitaine E. Cazalis, commandant 'l'Arche-d'Alliance': campagne dans l'Océanie et autour du monde pendant les années 1850, 1851, et 1852.* Paris, Bureaux de l'Union-Maritime, 1853. 64 pp.

Cooper, H. Stonehewer. *Coral Lands.* Vol. 2. London, Richard Bentley, 1880. 370 pp.

Derrick, R. A. *A history of Fiji.* Vol. 1 (to 1874). Suva, Printing and Stationery Department, 1946. 250 pp.

D'Ewes, J. *China, Australia, and the Pacific islands in the years 1853-56.* London, Richard Bentley, 1857. 340 pp.

Dumont d'Urville, J. S. C. *Voyage au Pole Sud et dans l'Océanie sur les corvettes 'l'Astrolabe' et la 'Zelée' exécuté par ordre du roi pendant les années 1837-40, sous le commandement de M. J. Dumont d'Urville.* Vol. 4. Paris, Gide, 1842. 411 pp.

Dyson, Martin. *My Story of Samoan Methodism, or a brief history of the Wesleyan Methodist Mission in Samoa.* Melbourne, Fergusson and Moore, 1875. 100 pp.

Edwards, Edward and George Hamilton. *Voyage of H.M.S. 'Pandora' despatched to arrest the mutineers of the 'Bounty' in the South Seas, 1790-91.* London, Francis Edwards, 1915. 177 pp.

Ellison, Joseph W. *Opening and penetration of foreign influence in Samoa to 1880.* Oregon, Oregon State College monograph, Studies in History, No. 1, 1938. 108 pp.

Erskine, John E. *Journal of a cruise among the islands of the Western Pacific including the Feejees and others inhabited by the Polynesian negro races, in H.M.S. 'Havannah'.* London, Murray, 1853. 488 pp.

Freeman, J. D. 'The Joe Gimlet or Siovili cult: an episode in the religious history of early Samoa.' In J. D. Freeman and W. R. Geddes *eds, Anthropology in the South Seas. Essays presented to H. D. Skinner.* New Plymouth, Avery and Sons. 1959. pp. 185-200

——, 'The tradition of Sanalala.' Wellington, *J. Polynesian Soc.* 56(3), 1947. pp. 295-317

Goodenough, J. G. *ed. Journal of Commodore Goodenough during his last command as senior officer on the Australian Station, 1873-1875.* London, King, 1876. 369 pp.

Halligon, J. *Six mois à travers l'Océanie: souvenirs d'un officier de la corvette 'l'Ariane'.* Brest, Dumont, 1889. 336 pp.

Hood, T. H. *Notes on a cruise in H.M.S. 'Fawn' in the Western Pacific in the year 1862.* Edinburgh, Edmonston and Douglas, 1863. 268 pp.

Hübner, *Baron* J. A. de. *Through the British Empire.* London, Murray, 1886. 2 vols, 462 and 515 pp.

Jore, L. *George Pritchard, l'adversaire de la France à Tahiti (1796-1883).* Paris, Libraire Larose, 1939. 115 pp.

Koskinen, Aarne A. *Missionary influence as a political factor in the Pacific Islands.* Helsinki, Finnish Academy of Science, 1953. 263 pp.

Kotzebue, Otto von. *A new voyage round the world in the years 1823-26.* Vol. 1. London, Colburn and Bentley, 1830. 341 pp.

Krämer, Augustin F. *Salamasina. Bilder aus altsamoanischer Kultur und Geschichte.* Stuttgart, Strecker and Schroder, 1923. 245 pp.
————, *The Samoan Islands.* Translated from the German. Rarotonga, 1941. 2 vols in 9
Note: this is a mimeographed English translation of Krämer's book *Die Samoa-Inseln: Entwurf einer Monographie mit besonderer Berücksichtigung Deutsch-Samoas.* Stuttgart, Schweizerbartsche Verlag, 1902. 2 vols
Lafond de Lurcy, Gabriel. 'Quelques Semaines dans l'Archipel de Samoa'. Extract from the *Bulletin de la Société de Géographie*, January, 1845. Paris, Bourgogne et Martinet. 28 pp.
Langer, William L. *The diplomacy of imperialism, 1890-1902.* New York, Alfred A. Knopf, 1951. 797 pp.
Lapérouse, Jean F. G. de. *A voyage round the world, in the years 1785, 1786, 1787, and 1788.* Vol. 3. London, Johnson, 1798. 448 pp.
Lepsius, Johannes, *et al. Die Grosse Politik der Europäischen Kabinette 1871-1914: Sammlung der Diplomatischen Akten des Auswärtigen Amtes.* Berlin, Deutsche Verlagsgesellschaft für Politik und Geschichte, 1922-4. Vols 4, 8 and 14
London Missionary Society. *O le Tusi faalupega o Samoa.* Malua, L.M.S. Press, 1930
Lovett, Richard. *The history of the London Missionary Society, 1795-1895.* Vol. 1. London, Henry Frowde, 1899. 832 pp.
[Lucett, E.] *Rovings in the Pacific from 1837 to 1849; with a glance at California.* Vol. 2. London, Longmans, 1851. 371 pp.
Lundie, G. A. *Missionary life in Samoa, as exhibited in the journals of the late G. A. Lundie, during the revival in Tutuila, in 1840-41.* Edited by his mother. Edinburgh, Oliphant, 1846. 294 pp.
McArthur, Norma. *Island populations of the Pacific.* Canberra, A.N.U. Press, 1967. 381 pp.
Masterman, Sylvia. *The origins of international rivalry in Samoa, 1845-1884.* London, Allen and Unwin, 1934. 233 pp.
Monfat, *Father* A. *Les Samoa, ou Archipel des Navigateurs. Etude historique et religieuse.* Lyon, E. Vitte, 1890. 414 pp.
Monk, W. *ed. Dr Livingstone's Cambridge Lectures.* Cambridge, Deighton, Bell, 1858
Morrell, W. P. *Britain in the Pacific Islands.* Oxford, Clarendon Press, 1960. 454 pp.
Murray, A. W. *Forty years' mission work in Polynesia and New Guinea from 1835 to 1875.* London, Nisbet, 1876. 509 pp.
————, *Missions in Western Polynesia, being historical sketches of these missions, from their commencement in 1839 to the present time.* London, John Snow, 1863. 489 pp.
Newbury, C. W. 'Aspects of French policy in the Pacific, 1853-1906'. California, *Pacific Historical Review* 27, Feb., 1958. pp. 45-56
Nightingale, Thomas. *Oceanic sketches.* London, Cochrane, 1853. 132 pp.

EE

Oceanus *pseud*. Letter to Editor. *Nautical Magazine*, 19 March 1814. pp. 380-2

Pembroke, George R. and G. H. Kingsley. *South Sea bubbles*. London, Richard Bentley, 1873. 323 pp.

Pratt, George. 'The genealogy of the Kings and Princes of Samoa.' Melbourne, *Australian Association for the Advancement of Science, Report 2*, 1890. pp. 655-63

Pritchard, William T. *Polynesian reminiscences; or life in the South Pacific Islands*. London, Chapman and Hall, 1866. 428 pp.

Prout, Ebenezer. *Memoirs of the life of the Rev. John Williams, missionary to Polynesia*. London, John Snow, 1843. 618 pp.

Rieman, George B. *Papalangee, or, Uncle Sam in Samoa: a narrative of the cruise of the U.S. steamer 'Narragansett' among the Samoan, or Navigator Islands, Polynesia*. Oakland, Butler and Stilwell, 1874. 43 pp.

Rowe, N. A. *Samoa under the sailing gods*. London and New York, Putnam, 1930. 339 pp.

Ryden, G. H. *The foreign policy of the United States in relation to Samoa*. New Haven, Yale University Press, 1933. 634 pp.

St Julian, Charles. *Note on the latent resources of Polynesia*. Sydney, Kemp and Fairfax, 1851. 129 pp.

——, *Official report on Central Polynesia*. With *Gazetteer of Central Polynesia* by Edward Reeve. Sydney, John Fairfax, 1857. 75 pp.

Samoa Times. *The Samoan Civil War of 1893*. Apia, 1893. 16 pp. Material reprinted from the *Samoa Times*

Seward, F. W. *Reminiscences of a war-time statesman and diplomat, 1830-1915*. New York, Putnam, 1916. 489 pp.

Shipley, Conway. *Sketches in the Pacific: the South Sea Islands drawn from nature and on stone*. London, 1851. 27 pp.

Simmons, J. *Livingstone and Africa*. London, English Universities Press, 1958. 180 pp.

Stackpole, Edouard A. *The Sea-hunters: the New England whalemen during two centuries 1635-1835*. New York, Lippincott, 1953. 510 pp.

Stair, John B. *Old Samoa, or flotsam and jetsam from the Pacific Ocean*. London, Religious Tract Society, 1897. 296 pp.

Tripp, Bartlett. *My trip to Samoa*. Cedar Rapids, Iowa, The Torch Press, 1911

Trood, Thomas. *Island reminiscences*. Sydney, McCarron, Stewart, 1912. 159 pp.

Wakeman, E. *Report of Captain E. Wakeman to W. H. Webb on the islands of the Samoa group, latitude 13° 30' south, longitude 168° to 173° west, Pacific Ocean, Sept. 20th, 1871*. New York, Slote and Jones, 1872. 18 pp.

Walpole, Frederick. *Four years in the Pacific, in Her Majesty's ship 'Collingwood' from 1844 to 1848*. London, Richard Bentley, 1849. 415 pp.

Ward, John M. *British policy in the south Pacific 1786-1893: a study in British policy towards the South Pacific Islands prior to the establishment of governments by the great powers.* Sydney, Australasian Publishing Co., 1948. 364 pp.

Ward, R. Gerard *ed. American Activities in the Central Pacific, 1790-1870.* Vols 1-4. Ridgewood, N.J., The Gregg Press, 1966-7.

Wilkes, Charles. *Narrative of the United States Exploring Expedition during the years 1838, 1839, 1840, 1841, 1842.* London, Wiley and Putnam, 1845. 5 vols, 434, 476, 438, 539 and 558 pages plus atlas

Williams, John. *A narrative of missionary enterprises in the South Sea Islands.* London, John Snow, 1838. 590 pp.

Williamson, Robert Wood. *Religious and cosmic beliefs of Central Polynesia.* Vol. 1: *Religious and Social organization in Central Polynesia.* Vol. 2: *Essays in Polynesian Ethnology.* Cambridge, C.U.P., 1933. 2 vols

Zimmerman, Alfred. *Geschichte der Deutschen Kolonialpolitik.* Berlin, Mittler, 1914. 336 pp.

# Index

# 450

INDEX

456    INDEX

Tui Manu'a, 260n

Tui Manu'a, lineage, 57; title, 58

Tuiā, Ta'imua, 315n

Tuiatafu, 354, 356n

Tuilaepa Matetau, 90

Tuimaleali'ifano, lineage, 54; title, 288, 383n

Tuimaleali'ifano Sualauvī, 117 and n

Tuisalega, Faipule, 316n

Tuitele, 260n, 317n

Tulāfale, 23, 43, 46, 54, 56, 57, 101; functions, 24-6; represented on Ta'-imua, 315

Tumua, 56; 'Tumua rebellion', 423-4; see also Tumua and Pule

Tumua and Pule, 56, 292; members become Ta'imua, 304-5; claim right to choose king, 425

Tunumafono lineage, 54

Tupa'i, Faipule, 316n

Tupapau, 119

Tupou, Joel, 93-4

Tupou, Matekitoga, 212n

Tupo o Samoa, 58n, 363; office to Talavou, 363; to Laupepa, 419

Tupu o Salafai title, 117, 118

Tupua, lineage, 46n, 47n, 54, 57, 59n, 71, 393; unites Tui A'ana and Tui Atua, 58n, 60 and n; member to head Ta'imua, 305; member to be king, 311, 314, 427; relations with Tamasese and Mata'afa, 362, 364, 382-4, 419, 420; 'Tupua party', 374 and n; title, 287n; contention for, 118, 312, 382-4, 423

Tupua Tamasese Lealofi, 423, 426, 428; contender for kingship, 425

Tupua Tamasese Titimaea, 287, 372, 412, 421, 423; founder of 'Aiga o Mavaega, 46 and n; kinship tie with Galumalemana, 287n; becomes Tui A'ana, 362; increased Tupua support for, 364; declared king, 374n, 382; becomes vice-king, 375; loses vice-kingship, 417; agreement with Germany, 380; withdraws from Malietoa Laupepa government, 381; forms government with German support, 382-95 passim; requests German pension, 383n; claims Tui Atua title, 384, 394; claims pāpā of Tuamasaga, 394; pāpā of Tamasoāli'i irregularly bestowed on, 394n; aims at status of Tafa'ifā, 393-4; defeated by Mata'afa Iosefo, 395; prefers Malietoa Laupepa to Mata'afa as king, 418; death, 419

Turnbull, W. C., 178

Turner, G. A., Jr, 306, 330 and n, 337

Turner, Peter, 83-6 passim, 92, 93,

125n, 138n

Tuscarora, U.S.S., 310, 312, 313, 318, 335 and n

Tutuila, 61, 67, 70n, 85n, 88, 89, 94n, 115, 120, 123, 126n, 133, 141, 165n, 257n, 304, 316n, 342, 394, 416n; lineage structure, 52 and n; religious 'revival' at, 109-14; revolt of L.M.S. teachers at, 128-30; port code, 148 and n, 149, 279; chiefs appeal to Britain, 159 and n, 160, 167 and n; 'Tutuila flag', 279; opposition to Steinberger, 319, 320 and n, 321; support for Tamasese, 384; sacked by Malietoa Laupepa, 422

United States, consular representation, 157-8, 324; naval activity, 152-6, 200, 211-12, 336, 429; policy towards Samoa, 277, 293-4, 297, 301, 306, 307, 325n, 327, 329, 344, 366, 383; treaties, 349 and n, 350, 351, 359, 392-3; three-Power conference, 382, 385; Berlin Act, 396; attitude towards German ambitions, 381, 425, 432

United States Exploring Expedition, 151

Unshelm, August, 240, 250-2

Upolu, 46, 57, 61, 70, 77, 87n, 90n, 117, 119, 125, 126, 133, 144n, 148 and n, 178n, 194, 207, 257 and n, 261, 271, 281, 292, 306, 319, 374; description, 1-2; lineage structure, 52, 53, 58; petition for protectorate, 170-1

Va'a lotu, 69, 70

Va'aalo, 14

Vaiala, 247, 361 and n

Vaialua, 413n

Vai'inupō, see Malietoa Vai'inupō

Vailele, 15n, 247, 363n

Vailima, 403

Vailoa, 162n

Vaimauga sub-district, 115, 162n, 164-8 passim, 176, 211, 212, 214, 300, 308, 315n, 320n, 376; lineage structure, 53-4; political neutrality, 120, 227, 228; law codes, 246, 247, 248, 261, 311; support for Puletua, 345

Vaimoso, 53, 162n, 361n

Vaipouli, 363n

Vaisigano sub-district, see Itu Vaisigano

Vaisigano River, 162, 167n, 178, 230

Vaitele, 15n, 280, 287-8, 363n, 412

Vaivai, 62-3

Vaivase, 363n

Van Camp, Aaron, 178, 185n, 240, 241, 327, 348; U.S. commercial agent, 234, 236; 'Van Camp affair', 222n, 233-9

S A V A I ' I

FALEALUPO

*Tufutafoe*

*Papa* *Sataua* *Vaisala* *Asau*

GAGAIFOMAUGA *Matautu* *Fagamalo* *Saleaula*

*Safune* *Safotu*

**VAISIGANO**

*lava flow* •*Aopo*

*lava flow*

**GAGA'EMAUG**

*Neiafu* ALATAUA WEST

*Falelima* SALEGA

*Samata*

SATUPA'ITEA

**FA'ASALELE**

*Pu*

*L*

*Sa* *Iv* *Sa*

*Sala'ilua*

**PALAULI**

**SATUPA'ITEA**

**PALAULI**

*Tufu Gautavai* *Papa* *Satupa'itea* *Vailoa*

*Tafua*

APOLI
MA

— 14°00'S —

WESTERN SAMOA

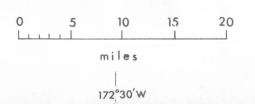

0        5        10        15        20

miles

172°30'W